CPU Design and Practice

Wenxiang Wang • Jinzhang Xing

CPU Design and Practice

机械工业出版社
CHINA MACHINE PRESS

Springer

Wenxiang Wang
Chip R&D Department
Loongson Technology Corporation Ltd
Beijing, China

Jinzhang Xing
Chip R&D Department
Loongson Technology Corporation Ltd
Beijing, China

Translated by
Rongmin Lu
Institute of Computing Technology, Beijing, China

Miao Hao
Institute of Computing Technology, Beijing, China

Tianhao Xu
Institute of Computing Technology, Beijing, China

ISBN 978-981-96-6572-3   ISBN 978-981-96-6573-0   (eBook)
https://doi.org/10.1007/978-981-96-6573-0

Jointly published with China Machine Press, Beijing, China.
The print edition is not for sale in Mainland China. Customers from Mainland China please order the print book from: China Machine Press, Beijing, China.

This Springer imprint is published by the registered company Springer Nature Singapore Pte Ltd.
The registered company address is: 152 Beach Road, #21-01/04 Gateway East, Singapore 189721, Singapore

If disposing of this product, please recycle the paper.

Preface

CPU, which stands for Central Processing Unit, is also known as the processor. It is the core component of modern electronic computers. If you want to understand how a computer is built and operates, delving into the design of the CPU is very useful. However, will this beautiful wish encounter the harsh reality? After all, when it comes to CPUs, people immediately think of products made by internationally renowned companies such as Intel, AMD, Apple, ARM, and Qualcomm, and then consider CPU design to be an unattainable thing. It seems like a fantasy for ordinary learners to master it.

So, is CPU design really difficult? To be honest, it is indeed not easy to create a product that meets world-class standards. Despite its small size, the CPU is an extremely complex system. The challenge of designing a CPU tests the ability of a team to develop complex systems engineering. However, since the introduction of the first CPU in the 1960s, the basic technologies involved in CPU design have become very mature. At the same time, the level of automation in design tools has greatly improved. It is no longer an unattainable dream for ordinary learners to gain an initial understanding of the field of CPU design.

During the process of training new engineers and teaching university students, we have received feedback that is not very optimistic. For most newcomers, designing an entry-level CPU is still quite challenging. Based on our growth experiences in research and development, as well as the feedback obtained from training and teaching, we believe that the biggest challenge lies in the fact that designing a CPU requires a comprehensive grasp of various kinds of knowledge, and beginners often encounter difficulties at the "integration" stage. It is no exaggeration to say that for every aspect of knowledge required to design an entry-level CPU, we can find many excellent textbooks, lecture notes, papers, and code. If we simply hand these materials over to a beginner and let them design a CPU through self-study, only a minority of very intelligent people would be able to succeed. To cultivate a large number of high-quality talents urgently needed by the industry in a short period of time, relying solely on the intelligence of learners is not feasible. Effective learning and training methods need to be found.

The team at Loongson, where the author of this book is part of, has been independently developing CPU products for over 20 years, accumulating a wealth of practical experience in CPU design. In this book, we will combine our own research and development practices to introduce, as clearly and accessibly as possible, how to design an entry-level CPU from scratch step by step, as well as what knowledge to master, what design principles to follow, what design risks to avoid, and what development techniques can be used in the process. We hope that these experiences summarized from engineering practice can serve as a valuable supplement to the knowledge delivery part of university courses, helping more beginners to master the knowledge of CPU design more quickly and solidly, and to possess the capability to design CPUs.

Content Arrangement of This Book

This book is logically divided into three parts. Chapters 1 to 3 constitute the first part, which introduces the process of CPU development in the industry, as well as essential foundational knowledge in CPU design, such as local and remote FPGA experimental platforms, FPGA on-board implementation, and Verilog application examples. Chapters 4 to 10 form the second part. In this section, we start with the design of a single-cycle CPU that implements only five instructions, and gradually introduce pipeline design, add instructions, increase support for exceptions and interrupts, and complete the design and implementation of the AXI bus interface, TLB MMU, and high-speed cache (Cache), ultimately completing the design of an entry-level CPU. Such a CPU is no longer just a course assignment design, but a real design that can meet the needs of most practical embedded application scenarios and can run a teaching operating system. Chapters 11 and 12 make up the third part, in which we provide guidance and suggestions for readers preparing for advanced design, including advanced experimental development environments and commonly used design optimization solutions.

A brief introduction to the content of each chapter in the book is as follows.

Chapter 1 provides a brief introduction to the research and development process of CPU chip products, giving readers an initial understanding of the entire process of CPU product development and laying the foundation for the study of subsequent chapters.

Chapter 2 introduces the hardware experimental platform and FPGA design process. It includes an introduction to the Loongson architecture teaching hardware experimental platform, as well as the general FPGA design process and the FPGA design process based on the Vivado tool.

Chapter 3 reviews the content related to digital logic circuit design. By combining the actual design and development needs of CPUs, it provides suggestions on how to use Verilog code for digital logic circuit design and offers examples of synthesizable Verilog descriptions of digital logic circuits commonly used in CPU design. Additionally, this chapter will discuss common errors in digital logic circuit functional simulation and their debugging methods. For beginners lacking experience in circuit simulation and debugging, this section is highly instructive.

Chapter 4 introduces the design of a single-cycle CPU. The chapter will start with the design of a single-cycle CPU that supports five instructions and then gradually expand the design to support 20 instructions. During the presentation of the design, it will also interweave the introduction of the experimental environment required for verifying the design and the simulation debugging method based on trace comparison.

Chapter 5 introduces the design of a simple pipelined CPU. This chapter will improve the single-cycle CPU design completed in the previous chapter by introducing pipelining, starting with the transformation into a pipeline without considering hazards, then discussing how to resolve hazards with stalling, and finally introducing data forwarding. While presenting the design methods, this chapter will also share some simulation debugging techniques for CPU design.

Chapter 6 introduces how to continue implementing support for more general user-mode instructions in the pipelined CPU, including arithmetic and logical operations, multiplication and division operations, branch instructions, and memory access instructions.

Chapter 7 introduces the implementation of exceptions and interrupts. This chapter first briefly reviews the basic concepts of exceptions and interrupts, as well as the specific definitions of exceptions and interrupts in the LoongArch instruction set. It then describes how to implement support for exceptions and interrupts on the basis of the CPU completed in the previous chapter. With these two features, the CPU can run some simple embedded operating systems.

Chapter 8 introduces the design of the AXI bus interface. This chapter begins with a brief review of the relevant content of the AXI bus protocol required to complete the CPU design, and then completes the addition of the AXI bus interface in the CPU through three phased tasks: implementing an SRAM-like bus interface, implementing an SRAM-to-AXI bridge, and integrating an SRAM-to-AXI bridge.

Chapter 9 introduces the design of the Memory Management Unit (MMU). This chapter first reviews the knowledge related to the MMU, and then completes the entire MMU design through several phased tasks: the design and implementation of the TLB module, the implementation of MMU-related control status registers and instructions, and the integration of the TLB module into the pipeline to support MMU-related exceptions.

Chapter 10 introduces the design of Cache. This chapter focuses only on the simplest cache design, and its design tasks are also broken down into three progressive phased tasks: cache module design, cache module integration, and support for cache maintenance instructions.

Chapter 11 introduces the advanced experimental development environment. This section of the experimental environment is primarily built on the Loongson Education Open Source Chip Development Platform, Chiplab, and specifically covers the organization and composition of the entire development environment, as well as the introduction of software simulation verification and FPGA board-level functional validation.

Chapter 12 provides our suggestions on some advanced design optimization schemes, mainly involving how to further increase the clock frequency, how to perform superscalar design, how to design a dynamic scheduling mechanism, how to design a branch predictor, how to optimize memory access performance, and how to support multi-core.

The appendices of this book provide supplementary introductions to the local experimental environment used in this book, as well as the installation and use of the Vivado software.

Acknowledgments The writing of this book has been greatly supported by Loongson Technology Corporation, where the author is employed. It is with the help of many colleagues from various departments that we have been able to write this book from scratch and complete the development of all the experimental tasks. Here, we express our gratitude for their selfless support! Special thanks go to the colleagues and students from the Loongson company's chip research and development department, education business division, and Loongson laboratory. Without their hard work, this book would not have been published.

We are also very grateful to the Computer Science and Technology Teaching Guidance Committee of the Ministry of Education, the System Capacity Training Teaching Research Expert Group, and the experts and teachers from the Huazhang Branch of China Machine Press. We thank all the teachers who are committed to cultivating computer system capabilities among college students in our country. It is their passion and unremitting efforts that have inspired us to write this book. We sincerely hope that this book can contribute to the cause of cultivating computer system capabilities among college students in our country.

We would also like to express our special thanks to the students who participated in the computer architecture seminar course at the University of Chinese Academy of Sciences, as well as the participants of the past "Loongson Cup" National Student Computer System Capability Challenge. Their feedback has enriched and completed the content of this book.

Given the vast and complex nature of CPU design and development, despite our best efforts to present the core content, there may still be omissions. We sincerely welcome any criticism and corrections from teachers and readers.

Beijing, China

Wenxiang Wang
Jinzhang Xing

Contents

About the Authors

Wenxiang Wang Ph.D., senior engineer, is Chief Architect of the processor core at Loongson Technology Co., Ltd., and an Adjunct Professor at the University of Science and Technology of China. His main research interests include processor architecture design, processor verification, and performance analysis and optimization of computer systems. He has participated in several national "Core Electronics Devices, High-End General-Purpose Chips, and Basic Software Products" (National Major Science and Technology Project), 863, and 973 projects. He has published more than ten papers in domestic and international journals and conferences, applied for dozens of patents, and been granted more than ten patents. Since 2012, he has served as the leader of the IP group in the Chip R & D Department of Loongson Technology, responsible for the development, research, and maintenance of the Loongson series CPU IP cores, and participated in formulating the LoongArch instruction set architecture specifications. He is the author of *CPU Design and Practice, Computer Architecture, Fundamentals of Computer Architecture* and other works.

Jinzhang Xing He graduated with a master's degree from the Institute of Computing Technology, Chinese Academy of Sciences. In 2015, he joined Loongson Technology Co., Ltd. He has long been engaged in the research and development of processor core structures and is one of the main structural designers of the Loongson series processor cores. In recent years, he has actively participated in providing technical support and training for the CPU Design Competition (Loongson Cup) of the National Computer System Development Capability Competition.

List of Figures

List of Tables

Chapter 1
Overview of the CPU Chip Development Process

As a practical book, before we start talking about CPU design, we would like to give you a general overview of the process of developing CPU chips in the industry. This part of the book will help you to build up an understanding of CPU development and then understand which part of the development process in the real world corresponds to the technologies taught in each chapter of the book. After all, a good engineer cannot "see the wood for the trees."

1.1 CPUs and CPU Cores

First of all, we need to distinguish the concepts of central processing unit (CPU) and CPU core. In the 1970s and 1980s, transistor integration density was not as high as it is now, and the main part of a CPU chip was a CPU core. With the rapid evolution of the IC technology, the integration density of transistors on a single silicon chip has become higher and higher. Nowadays, the common CPU chip is no longer the traditional "arithmetic logic unit + control unit," but a system on chip (SoC), and the CPU core is only a core IP of the SoC.

Taking the Loongson 3A5000 general-purpose processor chip as an example, the chip you usually see is shown in Fig. 1.1a. At the bottom of the chip is a circuit board with many pins, and on top of it is a plastic or metal case, in which the core silicon part of the chip is encapsulated. The circuit layout shown in Fig. 1.1b corresponds to the silicon part of the chip.

Four LA464 CPU cores are integrated in the Loongson 3A5000. For convenience, the locations and shapes of the four LA464 CPU cores are identified in Fig. 1.1b by rectangular boxes. As you can clearly see, the CPU core is an important part of a processor chip, but a processor chip contains more than CPU cores. For Loongson 3A5000, in addition to the processor cores, it contains a shared L3

W. Wang, J. Xing, *CPU Design and Practice*,
https://doi.org/10.1007/978-981-96-6573-0_1

cache, Hyper-Transport high-speed bus interface controller and PHY, DDR3/DDR4 memory controller and PHY, and a series of other functional modules.

It would be difficult to cover all the design processes of a modern processor chip in a single book. For example, the design of the DDR3/DDR4 memory controller and the Hyper Transport high-speed bus interface controller integrated in the Loongson 3A5000 could be written in books separately. In this book, we focus only on the CPU core, which is the actual core of the processor chip that executes instructions, performs calculations, and controls. Therefore, for the rest of the book, we will not strictly distinguish between the terms "CPU" and "CPU core."

1.2   Development Process of Chip Products

The development process of processor chips is roughly the same as that of general chips and usually goes through the following five stages:

1. Chip definition: In this stage, it is necessary to carry out market researches, formulate the definition of chip specifications for customer needs, and conduct feasibility analysis and demonstration.
2. Chip design: The chip design stage can be further divided into silicon design and encapsulation design. (The chips that you usually see are the ones that have been encapsulated into a tube case.)
3. Chip manufacturing: After the wafer design and encapsulation design are completed, they will be delivered to the factory and enter the chip manufacturing stage. Chip manufacturing includes mask manufacturing, wafer production, and encapsulation production.
4. Chip sealing: When the wafer and encapsulation tube case are produced, it enters the chip sealing stage. Usually mid-test needs to be carried out on the wafer (some low-cost chips do not have this step), and then scribing and encapsulating are performed, and encapsulated chips are tested finally. After passing both the mid-test and the final test, we can basically ensure that these chips do not have any errors introduced in the production process, and we can carry out the final validation of the chips.

5. Chip verification: In the final verification process, it is not enough to have a chip, but it is necessary to solder the chip to a predesigned and produced circuit board, assemble the machine, and load the software before the verification process. During the verification stage, the chip's technical indicators are evaluated, and when anomalies are found, the cause of the error should be identified. If the problem is with the design of the chip, the design error needs to be corrected, and the manufacturing, sealing, and verification process will be carried out again.

At present, the separation of chip design and manufacturing has become a mainstream trend in the industry. Chip design (Fabless) companies focus on chip definition and design, and manufacturing and sealing are mostly outsourced, such as Apple, Qualcomm, AMD, Arm, etc. Foundry companies, on the other hand, focus on chip manufacturing and do not do design themselves, such as TSMC, Global Foundries, SMIC, and Shanghai Huahong, which focus on chip manufacturing and do not design their own chips. Under this system of industrial division of labor, the value of a chip is mainly given by the design of the chip.

1.3   Work Stages of Chip Design

For a CPU, the silicon design work can be further divided into nine stages as follows:

1. Clarify design specifications.
2. Develop design scheme.
3. Perform design description (write RTL code).
4. Functional and performance verification.
5. Logical synthesis.
6. Layout planning.
7. Place and route.
8. Netlist logic verification, timing check, layout verification.
9. Delivered to tape out.

Whether it is a hardware product or a software product, the design specification must be clearly defined at the beginning of the design to determine the boundary constraints of the design. For CPU design and development, typical design specifications include supported instruction sets, main frequency, performance, area, power consumption targets, and interface signal definitions.

Once the design specifications have been defined, a design scheme is given. The design scheme is usually a behavioral description of the CPU micro-architecture in natural language or high-level modeling language from a more abstract point of view. For example, how many stages the CPU is divided into, how many instructions can be processed in each stage of the pipeline, how many computational components there are, what is the scheduling mechanism of instruction execution, and so on, all of these should be given in detail in the design scheme.

Once the design scheme is in place, the behavioral level description needs to be further converted into a hardware description language (HDL) description that can be handled by the EDA synthesis tool. This process is usually done by humans. In recent years, there have been many positive attempts in academia and industry to automate the conversion of high-level descriptions to low-level descriptions, where a high-level modeling language description can be converted to an HDL description or even synthesized directly into gate-level circuits. However, with the current state of the art, the quality of circuits designed by experienced engineers is still much higher for CPU designs than for high-level synthesis tools or HDL language generators. Due to the "winner-takes-all" nature of CPU products, simply shortening the time-to-market does not provide a lasting commercial advantage, so the circuit quality requirements for CPUs are much higher than those for domain-specific accelerators. Therefore, in the short term, CPU products will still rely mainly on manual labor from design scheme to design description.

The register-transfer level (RTL) description allows us to perform functional and performance verification at this level. Functional and performance verification is the process of proving that the functionality and performance of a design are correct as defined in the design specification, and it identifies and corrects logic implementation errors introduced during the design description phase. If functional or performance errors are found, it is necessary to go back to the design description phase to make changes, or even back to the design scheme phase to make changes to the unreasonable areas, and then conduct functional and performance verification again. Throughout the design process, we iterate through these phases until all the functional and performance verifications have been passed. The concept of "verifications" is mentioned repeatedly here, and it is very similar to the concept of "test" in software development. The reason why we do not use the word "test" is that the concept of "test" in the field of chip design and manufacturing has a different meaning. Although testing in the field of chip design and manufacturing is also to check whether the function and performance of the circuit meet the design specifications, what it finds and corrects is the circuit faults introduced during the production of the chip.

After verification that the functionality and performance metrics are as expected, the RTL level description is converted to a gate level netlist by the EDA synthesis tool. The synthesis tool will try to ensure that the synthesized gate-level netlist meets the timing, area, and power requirements based on the constraints given by the designer.

The next step is to plan the layout of the final realized circuit, i.e., to plan the layout of the interface pins and the relative position of the main data paths. At present, the quality of this work by experienced engineers is still higher than that of the automated tools. However, in recent years, the gap between the two is gradually decreasing as AI technology has been deeply applied in this field. Once the layout has been planned, the automated place and routing tool reads in the previously synthesized netlist and generates a layout of the circuit.

After the circuit layout is generated, in addition to design rule checking of the layout itself and circuit/layout consistency checking, static timing analysis and power analysis are also required for the final design to ensure that the frequency and power targets are met, and at the same time, the extracted delay information is backnoted into a netlist for functional simulation verification with SDFs for delay and timing checking. After the various verification checks, the layout can be delivered to the factory for production.

In general, the design and development process for CPUs is essentially the same as for other types of very large-scale digital integrated circuits. After all, from a circuit perspective, a CPU is a digital logic circuit. However, CPU is a special kind of digital logic circuit, which has its own characteristics in design, implementation, and function verification. For the beginners of CPU design, the difficulties in learning often focus on these three aspects. The following chapters of this book will focus on these three aspects.

Chapter 2
Hardware Experiment Platform and FPGA Design Flow

Through the study of the previous chapter, we have already gained an understanding of the typical stages in chip design. However, the tape-out verification phase is difficult to implement in practical scenarios such as daily teaching, so we turn to using FPGAs as the verification platform for design. In this chapter, we will introduce the FPGA experimental platform recommended in this book and its general design process. Readers who are familiar with this content may skip this chapter.

Learning Goals for this Chapter
- Understand the hardware experiment platform used for practical objects in this book.
- Proficient in the Xilinx Vivado integrated design environment, using the project method operated under the graphical interface to complete the FPGA design process from RTL to bitstream files.

Practical Tasks of this Chapter
There is only one practice task in this chapter. Readers are requested to refer to the description in this chapter to complete the task after studying the contents of this chapter.

2.1 Hardware Experiment Platform

In this book, we use "Loongson CPU Design and Architecture Teaching Experiment System" or "Loongson Remote Experiment Platform for System Capability Training" as the designed FPGA verification platform, the former for local verification and the latter for remote verification.

W. Wang, J. Xing, *CPU Design and Practice*,
https://doi.org/10.1007/978-981-96-6573-0_2

2.1.1   *Loongson CPU Design and Architecture Teaching Experiment System*

"Loongson CPU Design and Architecture Teaching Experiment System (hereinafter referred to as the"Experiment Box") adopts the local use method, i.e., users can directly download the synthesized design files to the FPGA of the Experiment Box through the JTAG cable and operate the peripherals on the FPGA development board in the Experiment Box on the spot.

2.1.1.1   Introduction

When you open the experiment box, you can see that there is an FPGA development board (A in Fig. 2.1) and a series of accessories and cables, including a power adapter (B in Fig. 2.1), a USB cable (C in Fig. 2.1) connected to the FPGA download adapter, a serial cable (D in Fig. 2.1), a USB-to-serial connector (E in Fig. 2.1), a USB extension cable (F in Fig. 2.1), and a network cable (G in Fig. 2.1). **Only** the power adapter (B in Fig. 2.1) and the FPGA download adapter USB cable (C in Fig. 2.1) **are required** to complete the tasks in Part II of this book. It is recommended that you leave the rest of the cables in their originally stowed state to prevent damage or loss.

When you want to download the synthesized bitstream file to the experiment box for debugging, please insert the DC port of the power adapter into the power socket on the FPGA development board (A in Fig. 2.2), and insert the square port of the USB cable into the port of the download adapter on the bottom left side of the board (refer to connection of the C cable in Fig. 2.1), and then connect the USB port of the cable to the debugging host. After that, toggle the power switch (B in Fig. 2.2) on the board. Under normal circumstances, the power indicator (C in Fig. 2.2) on

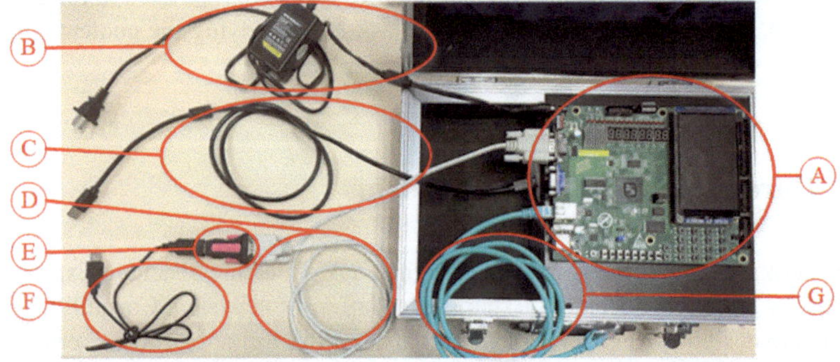

Fig. 2.1 General view of the experiment box

Fig. 2.2 Top view of the Experiment Box FPGA Development Board

the board will light up, indicating that the board has been powered up and can be operated subsequently.

The core device on the FPGA development board is the left-of-center FPGA chip (D in Fig. 2.2). The experiment box uses a Xilinx Airtx-7 series FPGA chip, specifically modeled as XC7A200T-FBG676, which has a large number of internal logic units and a large number of pins, and belongs to the high-end products in the Airtx-7 series.

Compared with most of the Xilinx FPGA development boards used for embedded system development, the FPGA development board integrated in the experiment box has a rich set of peripherals for the experiment teaching needed for digital circuits, computer organization, computer architecture, operating system, and other courses, and these peripherals take up a large part of the board's area. Here we only introduce the peripheral interfaces related to the practical tasks in this book, including dual-color LEDs (E in Fig. 2.2), single-color LEDs (F in Fig. 2.2), digital tubes (G in Fig. 2.2), FPGA reset button, and so on. (H in Fig. 2.2), dip switches (I in Fig. 2.2), pulse switches (J in Fig. 2.2), and a 4 × 4 keypad (K in Fig. 2.2). Readers who are interested in other interfaces can refer to the description in Appendix A.

2.1.1.2 Attentions for the Use of the Experiment Box

According to the past use, we summarize some of the recommendations for the use of the experiment box as follows:

1. After utilizing the experiment box, ensure that all accessories and cables are meticulously arranged and stowed away, and then slowly close the lid of the experiment box. If you feel a lot of resistance to close the lid, please open the lid to straighten out the accessories and cables, and then try to close the lid again, forcing the lid to close may damage the experiment equipment.
2. The experiment box is only required for on-board debugging after the functional simulation has been verified and the bitstream file has been successfully generated. Before that, it is not necessary to power up the experiment box and connect it to the computer.
3. When using the kit, place it on a flat, stable surface with sufficient contact area. Do not place the chamber on your lap, on a book bag, in the corner of a desk, etc.
4. Before downloading the bitstream file, please connect the power cable and download cable, and make sure that the FPGA board is **powered on**!
5. Never connect any exposed pins on the board with a conductor (wire, wet hands, tea or coffee, etc.).

2.1.2 Loongson Remote Experiment Platform for System Capability Training

The "Loongson Remote Experiment Platform for System Capability Training" (hereinafter referred to as the "Remote Experiment Platform") adopts the method of remote use. In this experiment platform, the development board array (shown in Fig. 2.3) composed of several FPGA development boards is placed in the form of a server in the cloud, and the user logs in to the FPGA server locally through the network to indirectly complete the operation of the FPGA.

The user can see a virtual FPGA board interface on the interactive mode web page (as shown in Fig. 2.4). The icons in this interface correspond to some simple peripherals on the FPGA board, including 2 digital tubes and 16 single-color LEDs from left to right in the upper part of the interface, and 32 dip switches, reset switches, single-step clock switches, and 4 pulse switches from left to right in the bottom of the interface. When the user clicks on the switches in the interface on the web page, the operation will be sent to the FPGA server in the cloud through the network, and the server will convert it into the actual operation of the hardware FPGA board. At the same time, all kinds of information output from the FPGA board will be received by the server and fed back to the interactive interface of the webpage through the network. For more information about "Loongson Remote Experiment Platform for System Capability Training," you can refer to the online help document provided by the experiment platform.

Fig. 2.3 Remote FPGA experiment platform

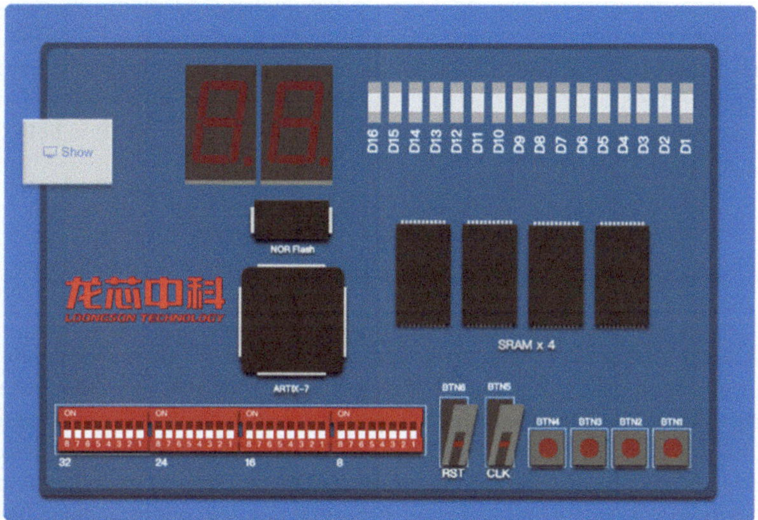

Fig. 2.4 Interactive website interface of remote FPGA experiment Platform

Because there are no significant differences in the specific operational content
of the two types of experiment platforms, the practical tasks related to the later
part of this book will be mainly explained for the local experiment platform.
The practical task materials accompanying this book will be released in different
versions according to the different experiment platforms, and readers can choose
the corresponding version according to the actual situation.

2.2 FPGA Design Flow

Field-programmable gate array (FPGA) is a special type of integrated circuit. This special feature is reflected in its circuit function after the chip is manufactured and can be adjusted through the programming configuration, while the traditional special-purpose integrated circuits (application-specific integrated circuit, referred to as ASIC) does not have this characteristic. To make an analogy, the traditional ASIC chip design is like drawing on a piece of paper; after the drawing is done, there is no way to modify it, while FPGA chip design is like drawing on the blackboard; after the drawing is done, you can erase and redraw if you think it's not suitable. This programmable feature of FPGA provides an excellent hardware platform for us to carry out the experimental courses of digital circuits, principle of composition, architecture, and so on. First of all, it is a real integrated circuit chip, not a simulation of the behavior of the circuit under the simulation software, which can make the hardware experimental courses really "hard," so that the practical experience of the learners is closer to the actual workflow in the industry. Secondly, adjusting the design on FPGAs does not require reflow or redesign of soldered PCBs but only requires adjusting the design code and rerunning the synthesis and implementation process of FPGAs once again, which is as short as a few minutes and as long as a few days to get a functionally adjusted chip for debugging, which is both time-saving and money-saving.

2.2.1 General Design Flow for FPGAs

FPGA is a special kind of integrated circuit, which means it is first and foremost an integrated circuit. Most of today's integrated circuits are transistorized integrated circuits, with CMOS transistorized integrated circuits being the most common. What is a transistorized integrated circuit? In layman's terms, it is a circuit consisting of many transistorized logic gates and memory cells connected by metal wires to provide a certain logic function. However, this does not mean that you need to connect the transistors by hand with wires when designing digital logic circuits. Instead, we generally write the code in an HDL language (e.g., Verilog) and run synthesis software (e.g., Vivado), and the circuit is designed. This process is actually very similar to the ASIC design process that is common in industry today. There are generally five steps in the FPGA design process:

1. Circuit design.
2. Code writing.
3. Functional simulation.
4. Synthesis and implementation.
5. On-board debugging.

2.2.1.1   Circuit Design

First, we need to formulate a circuit design plan based on the requirement specifications. For example, if the requirement is to design a LoongArch CPU, we need to decompose and refine the requirement step by step to get a circuit design solution that can meet the requirement. We have to decide how many pipeline stages, how many flip-flops here, how many operators there, how they are connected, how the state transition behavior of the whole circuit is, and so on. Usually, it is sufficient to refine the circuit design down to the RTL level, not down to the logic gate level or the transistor level.

2.2.1.2   Coding

The work of the coding phase is to take the circuit design solution completed in step 1 and express it in HDL as a form that EDA tools can understand. In this book, we use Verilog HDL.

2.2.1.3   Functional Simulation

The functional simulation phase is to verify the functional simulation of the design described in HDL in step 2. Functional simulation is a software simulation to see if the logic and functional behavior of the circuit meets the original design requirements. Typically, we assign a specified excitation to the circuit and see if the output of the circuit meets the expectations. If it does not, then there is an error in the logic function of the circuit. This error is either due to a mistake in the design of the circuit in step 1, or the code written in step 2 does not conform to the design of the circuit. If a functional error is found, you need to go back to the previous step and correct it and then follow the process step by step. This iteration continues until no more errors are found, and you can move on to the next stage.

It should be noted that since we are modeling the circuit at the RTL level, the delay of the circuit is not considered in the functional simulation phase.

2.2.1.4   Synthesis and Implementation

The synthesis and implementation phase completes the conversion from HDL code to real circuit. This process is similar to a compiler converting a high-level programming language into binary code for the target machine. This phase is divided into two subphases: synthesis and implementation. The synthesis phase compiles the HDL description of the design into a logic netlist of basic logic cells, although this netlist is not yet the final gate-level circuit netlist. The implementation phase maps the synthesized logic netlist to specific circuits in the FPGA, i.e., mapping the basic logic units in the netlist to the hardware logic modules inside the FPGA chip (called "place"). Subsequently, based on the topology of the layout, the mapped logic modules are connected (called "route") using the wiring resources inside the FPGA chip.

If no exception occurs throughout synthesis and implementation, the EDA tool will generate a bitstream file. In layman's terms, this bitstream file describes the final circuit implementation, except that only the FPGA chip can understand it.

2.2.1.5 On-Board Debugging

As the old saying goes, "It's a mule or a horse that comes out for a walk." No matter how correct the functional simulation is, it is still necessary to see whether the actual circuit can work normally. In the debugging stage on the board, the first step is to download the bitstream file generated in the synthesis and implementation stage to the FPGA chip and then run the circuit to observe whether it works properly, and if problems occur, we have to debug and locate the cause of the error.

To summarize, the general FPGA design flow introduced above gives a general overview, so that readers can first establish a correct overall concept, and there are many more details in the FPGA design flow, which will be introduced in subsequent chapters so that readers will not find it difficult to digest and absorb them all at once. In fact, there are some other steps in the FPGA design flow that are not listed in this book, because they are not involved in the practical tasks, so readers can study them again according to their actual needs in their future study and work.

2.2.2 *Vivado-Based FPGA Implementation Flow*

In the general design flow of FPGA mentioned above, EDA tools are used in the three steps of "functional simulation," "synthesis and implementation," and "board debugging." Our hardware experimental platform is a Xilinx FPGA chip, so it is natural to use the Vivado integrated design and development environment provided by Xilinx. Although Vivado is not particularly rich in functional simulation and waveform debugging, the CPU of our design is relatively small, so Vivado can meet the requirements. If you do not have Vivado software in your environment, you can install Vivado by referring to the instructions in Appendix B.

Vivado provides two ways to work with FPGA designs: Project mode and Non-project mode. In Project mode, designers can operate in Vivado's graphical interface or run a Tcl script in Vivado Tcl Shell, while in Non-Project mode, designers can only run a Tcl script, and the commands used in the scripts of the Non-project mode and the Project mode are different. Considering that GUI operation is more suitable for beginners than Tcl script, which is a more advanced development method for large-scale projects, the examples and experiments in this book are all described in using the GUI operation mode of the Project mode.

If you have not used Vivado for FPGA development and implementation before, you can refer to the examples in Appendix C to familiarize yourself with its basic use.

2.2.3 Tips for Using Vivado

Based on past usage, we have summarized some recommendations for Vivado usage below:

1. Try not to install and use Vivado on a system running under a system-level virtual machine, such as VMWare, VirtualBox, etc. Vivado requires a large amount of memory during the synthesis process, so the time it takes to run Vivado under a virtual machine increases nonlinearly, especially if the memory allocated to the virtual machine is only 1 or 2 GB. If you are not running Vivado in a system-level virtual machine, the wait time can be unbearably long. If you are not running Vivado in a system-level virtual machine, have enough memory (e.g., no less than 4 GB) and a processor that is not too weak (e.g., no less than Intel's tenth generation Core performance), but Vivado is still running slowly; it is advisable to check whether your computer's disk access performance is too low.
2. If Vivado is already installed on your computer, you do not need to reinstall it. If the version is too low, you can simply upgrade to the latest version.
3. If you have Linux installed on the bare metal, you can install Vivado for Linux directly, which is a little faster than Vivado for Windows. However, you are likely to have problems installing the FPGA download cable driver. There are a variety of reasons for this problem, so please check the Internet for a solution. However, since you have already installed Linux on bare metal, I'm sure you are prepared for this.
4. Do not allow Chinese characters to appear in the path where the project is located, and do not allow the project to be located in a directory that is too deep, resulting in an excessively long path.
5. Don't set your computer's username with Chinese characters, or you'll have all sorts of weird problems. Although you can find some solutions on the Internet, they are not guaranteed to work for all problems.
6. If you find that Vivado does not recognize the board properly during the on-board debugging phase, follow the steps below to troubleshoot:

   1. Check if the FPGA board is powered on. If it is powered on, but you are not sure, you can power off and power on again.
   2. Check that the FPGA download adapter's USB cable is properly connected to the computer and to the adapter.
   3. Check that the cable driver is properly installed.

      - Under Windows system, if the driver is installed properly, you can see the entry "Programming cables →Xilinx USB Cable" in the interface of Device Manager. If you can't find this entry in the Device Manager interface, it means that the USB Cable driver of the downloaded adapter has not been installed properly; please refer to Step 4 to install it.

- If the system is installed on a virtual machine (although we already strongly discourage running Vivado under a virtual machine), you will also need to check the USB-related configuration in the virtual machine software to ensure that USB is fully forwarded to the virtual machine. For Virtualbox, select "Assign VM → Settings → USB Devices → Add Filter." (By default, add a USB filter with empty values for all fields, which will match all USB devices connected to the computer.)

4. If you find that the driver for the USB Cable of the downloaded adapter is not installed properly under Windows or Linux, please refer to https://china. xilinx.com/support/answers/59128.html to install the driver. If this does not work, it is recommended to look for a solution to the problem on the Xilinx website.
5. Enter the disconnect_hw_server command under the Vivado Tcl Console panel and select "Open target → Auto Connect."
6. Restart Vivado and repeat step 5.
7. Reboot your computer, and repeat Steps 3–5.
8. If available, try the box on another computer, or try the current computer with another box, to confirm whether the box or the computer have problems.

2.3 Tasks and Practices

2.3.1 Experimental Environment That Accompanies This Book

Beginning in this chapter, a series of practical tasks will be conducted. There are two ways to access the experimental environments that accompany these practical tasks:

- **Option 1**: You can clone the entire repository for the local experimant box[1] or remote experiment platform[2] to a local path **without Chinese character**. The master branch of the repository contains all the files for the lab development environment.
- **Option 2**: The reader can download the corresponding zip file directly from the page of local experiment box[3] or remote experimant platform[4] according to the

---

[1] https://gitee.com/loongson-edu/cdp_ede_local
[2] https://gitee.com/loongson-edu/cdp_ede_remote
[3] https://gitee.com/loongson-edu/cdp_ede_local/releases
[4] https://gitee.com/loongson-edu/cdp_ede_remote/releases

expXX of the practical task to be carried out, and unzip it to a local path **without Chinese character**. The unzipped directory will include only the relevant files required for the practical task, and also some generated files required for the practical task.

We recommend the first option and strongly suggest that readers use the git tool to manage the code version of their development process. In most cases, however, the first option requires the reader to configure the functional test points of the func test program, compile the func program, and reconfigure the RAM for storing instructions in the FPGA verification environment according to the task to be accomplished, which will be described in detail as the experiment progresses.

The compilation of the func program in option 1 requires that the reader has a Linux environment on his/her computer, so if the reader finds this difficult, he/she may consider using method 2 for the experimental tasks. In the case of approach 2, even though most (even all) of the environments for many of the tasks are the same, we recommend that you extract a separate directory for each task. Although it is primitive and inefficient, it is still a feasible method of version management.

2.3.2 Practical Task 1: Running Lights

After completing this chapter, readers are expected to complete the following practical tasks:

1. Using the three files provided in the experimental environment: scroller.v (design file), scroller.xdc (constraints file) and testbench.v (test file), build the Vivado project, and complete the simulation and boarding of the running light design.

Documents to be referenced in order to complete the above practical tasks include, but are not limited to:

1. The contents of this chapter (if you don't have a local lab box or remote lab platform or don't perform on-board experiments, you can skip the relevant sections).
2. Appendices B and C in this book.

Please refer to the method described in Sect. 2.3.1 to obtain the experimental development environment required for this practical task. The specific experimental environment is located at dc_env/exp1/ directory with the following directory structure:

```
|--scroller.v     design file
|--scroller.xdc   constraints file
|--testbench.v    test file
```

Chapter 3
Fundamentals of Digital Logic Circuit Design

The ability to design digital logic circuits is the foundation for completing the CPU design in this book. However, beginners do not need to have a comprehensive grasp of digital logic circuit design before starting CPU design. This chapter will briefly review relevant knowledge of digital logic circuit design and methods for circuit simulation and debugging, based on the needs of CPU design and illustrated through examples.

Learning Goals for this Chapter
- Review the digital logic circuits and their corresponding Verilog description forms that must be mastered to design a CPU.
- Understand the difference between synchronous and asynchronous RAM and their timing behavior.
- Understand the common errors in the functional simulation of digital logic circuits, and acquire a preliminary knowledge of their debugging methods.

Practical Tasks of this Chapter
Three practical tasks are organized in this chapter (see Sect. 3.3 of this chapter). The reader can complete these tasks on the basis of the contents of this chapter, and the correspondence between them is as follows:

- Section 3.1 corresponds to Task 2 (Sect. 3.3.1) and Task 3 (Sect. 3.3.2).
- Section 3.2 corresponds to Task 4 Sect. 3.3.3.

3.1 Digital Logic Circuit Design and Verilog Code Development

Mastering the knowledge of digital logic circuits and having the ability to program in Verilog language are the foundation for completing the CPU design in this

© The Author(s), under exclusive license to Springer Nature Singapore Pte Ltd. 2025 19
W. Wang, J. Xing, *CPU Design and Practice*,
https://doi.org/10.1007/978-981-96-6573-0_3

book. In previous teaching and training, we found that most beginners have a good grasp of the knowledge of digital logic circuits; after all, digital logic circuits are a compulsory course for most engineering students in their undergraduate stage. However, their Verilog programming ability varies greatly. Many students spend too much time in experiments, because their Verilog programming ability is not up to par. For this phenomenon, we were once confused, because the syntax of Verilog language is very simple, and only a subset of it (called "synthesizable Verilog subset") is used when designing CPUs. Why is it difficult to master? Later, we realized that language is just a means, and the degree of mastery of a programming language is not related to the language itself. For example, the syntax of C language is very simple and can be learned in a short time, but can someone who learns the syntax in a short time become a C language programming expert? Of course not. High-level C language programmers often have a good foundation in data structures and algorithms and have a thorough understanding of compilation, assembly, linking, and other aspects. If the software they write is relatively large, they also need to have certain experience in software engineering development. The same is true for Verilog language. To achieve a high level of Verilog programming, first of all, we must have the awareness of circuit design; secondly, we must know how to describe different circuits in Verilog language; and thirdly, we must know how EDA tools handle the Verilog code written during simulation, synthesis, and implementation. From this perspective, it is indeed not easy to learn Verilog language well.

If you have only a preliminary understanding of Verilog, we do not expect you to have an epiphany after completing this chapter. You still need a lot of hands-on practice to understand the various details of Verilog programming. Therefore, this section will be mainly explained through examples, providing a foundation for imitation first, and then through multiple practices, allowing everyone to constantly experience the process of hands-on and ultimately learn to write a synthesizable digital logic circuit using Verilog language. Even if you think your Verilog programming skills are already very good, we recommend you to refer to the code style in this section. From our engineering practice experience, this code style is reasonable and efficient. If you already have good Verilog programming skills and want to continue to improve, we recommend you to read *Verilog and System Verilog Gotchas: 101 Common Coding Errors and How to Avoid Them*, written by Stuart Sutherland and Don Mills. The content of this book cannot be written without rich practical experience, and you can learn a wealth of engineering practice knowledge from this book.

3.1.1 Hardware Circuit Oriented Design Mindset

If you want to write a real physically realizable circuit in Verilog, you must first design it. Circuit design requires a hardware circuit-oriented design mindset. So, what kind of thinking is this?

The core of the hardware circuit oriented design way of thinking is actually **"Datapath + Control Logic."**

Let's start with datapath. We won't go into the precise conceptual definition of a datapath here but just want to remind the reader that a datapath is intuitively a spatial thing. A circuit is an object that you can see and touch. For example, if you look at a circuit board, there are electronic devices on it and wires connecting them, and these devices and wires make up a circuit. The inside of a chip is similar in that it has both devices and wires, only smaller in physical size. What is transmitted between these devices in a circuit? Electromagnetic signals. When we discretize these electromagnetic signals, we can further assume that what is being passed between these devices is data. Data comes in at the input of a circuit system, is processed through various pathways, and is then transmitted out at the output of the circuit system. The path through which this data flows in the circuit system is the datapath. Obviously, the datapath is an important part of the circuit system. In digital logic circuits textbooks, circuit design schemes are often described in diagrams that are not flowcharts but circuit structure diagrams. Circuit structure diagrams are used to depict the design of the datapath in a circuit.

One of the salient features of the datapath is that if it is realized, it is always there and does not disappear; if it is not realized, it does not exist and does not appear out of nowhere. For example, if you have both a bedroom and a kitchen in your house, the kitchen will always be there when you are sleeping in the bedroom, and it will not appear temporarily when you want to cook. Back to circuit design, when you design a CPU's ALU, you don't just call an adder to handle addition instructions and a shifter to handle shift instructions. The ALU needs to support both addition and shift instructions, so it needs both an adder and a shifter. When performing addition instructions, the input data flowing into the ALU will flow to the adder, and the output result processed by the adder will flow to the output of the ALU. When performing shift instructions, the input data flowing into the ALU will flow to the shifter, and the output result processed by the shifter will flow to the output of the ALU. At this point, two paths appear in your design: "ALU inlet →adder inlet →adder outlet →ALU outlet" and "ALU inlet →shifter inlet →shifter outlet →ALU outlet." The question then arises: How to make sure that the data only goes through the adder path for addition instructions and only through the shifter path for shift instructions? You must be thinking of adding switches to the paths, right? That's the right idea. However, it is often difficult to physically switch circuits on CMOS circuits. What can we do? Let's try to solve this problem by using logical switches. We can add a selector that functions as an "either/or" switch at the location of "adder outlet → ALU outlet" and "shifter outlet → ALU outlet." Which output it selects depends on the type of instruction: For an add instruction, the selector output selects the value coming from the adder exit; for a shift instruction, the selector output selects the value coming from the shifter exit.

When designing a circuit, the datapath is the foundation, and the control logic is based on the datapath. The datapath is like the human body's bones, muscles, respiratory system, blood circulation system, and digestive system, while the control logic is like the human body's nervous system, which is connected to all parts of the body by a center (brain). When designing a circuit system, only after determining the datapath can you consider how to control the selection signals of each multiplexer and the write enable signals of each memory device in the control logic design.

Again, always think through the circuit design before you start writing code.

3.1.2 Top-Down Design Segmentation Process

When considering the design of a complex circuit system, beginners often do not know where to start. We recommend a "**top-down, module-by-module, level-by-level**" design approach. The following is a brief example.

Suppose we are designing a CPU, first draw a box on a piece of paper to indicate that it is a CPU, and then think about what inputs and outputs the CPU has. First, the CPU is actually a synchronized finite state machine (FSM) circuit, so it needs clock and reset inputs. Second, the CPU has to access memory and I/O, so we need to draw the interfaces for memory access and I/O access. After some in-depth analysis and thinking, we know that there are several functional modules inside the CPU, such as instruction fetching, decoding, executing, memory accessing, and writing back, so we can draw five small boxes in the big box, corresponding to each of these modules. These modules can be connected by lines with arrows. These modules can also be subdivided. For example, the decoding module can be divided into a part that generates control signals based on the instruction code and a part that reads the register file. How far should the modules be subdivided? The author's personal preference is that the subdivision is finished when the contents of the corresponding box of the module can be expressed in HDL in one go. As you can see, the granularity of the subdivision has a lot to do with the experience of the designer. If you are not yet experienced, we recommend that you use a finer granularity.

It is usually not possible to get the best design by considering the above circuit structure only once, and it is necessary to iterate and adjust the design many times before writing the code, which is called "planning before moving." **We strongly recommend that readers consider the circuit structure design thoroughly before writing the HDL code.** In practice, some people like the incremental code development method of "add a little, debug a little, add a little, debug a little," which may be suitable for the development of all kinds of software, but not suitable for the design of a circuit system, or at least not suitable for the design of a CPU. Because the relationship between each part of the CPU is very close, and often the whole body will be affected by a single change, so a change in one place often involves changes in many related places. More changes will result in a higher probability of errors, which in turn leads to more changes, and ultimately to a vicious circle. Such a code development process is prone to divergence and cannot be converged to a stable state in a controlled time. The CPU design in this book is relatively simple and can be implemented in a few thousand lines of Verilog code, and the test program set is very small, so the reader may be able to complete it within the specified time by using the trial-and-error code development methodology. However, we still hope that the reader will develop the habit of "making decisions before making moves" and put as much iteration as possible in the designing phase rather than in the code writing phase. A student once shared with me his process of designing a CPU. He thought about each design process over and over again, and "agonized" over it for several days, and then when the design ideas were straightened out and the solution matured, it only took him several hours to actually write the code. The debugging process went smoothly, and the errors found were mainly syntax errors, and only a few logic errors really occurred, because we hadn't thought about this situation before. This student's code design and development process is what we recommend, and we hope that all readers will work in this direction as well.

3.1.3   Verilog Programming Style for Behavioral Descriptions

After designing the circuit, the next task is how to describe it in Verilog HDL. In general, there are two programming styles that can be used when describing a circuit using Verilog, one is called behavioral description and the other is called circuit description. As the name implies, behavioral description style focuses on the behavior of a module, while circuit description style directly describes the logic of a circuit. A description that instantiates a series of logic gates and connects them together is the circuit description style. We recommend the behavioral description style, because it is intuitive, efficient, and easy to maintain.

When adopting the behavioral description style, there is one issue that needs to be taken into account: Whether the behavior of the circuit deduced by the EDA tool from the Verilog code in the synthesis phase is consistent with the designer's expectations. Instead of analyzing and discussing this issue, we take a more hands-on approach: We give examples of Verilog behavioral descriptions of common circuits in CPU design, so that readers can learn by imitation. According to our many years of practical experience, the description style given in the example is safe for the current mainstream EDA tools. Readers can quickly master Verilog programming through imitation.

3.1.4   Verilog Description of Common Digital Logic Circuits

According to the hardware circuit oriented design thinking introduced above, a CPU can be seen as a series of digital logic circuits built up from a series of "small blocks" by adopting the top-down, level-by-level decomposition design methodology. In this section, we will list the Verilog code implementations of the various "building blocks" required in CPU design for your imitation and reference. **It is important** that you have a good understanding of how these circuits are described. If you do not understand some elements of Verilog syntax at the beginning of your study, please consult your own textbook on Verilog. By imitating, practicing, learning, and thinking, you can gradually master Verilog programming for designing digital logic circuits.

3.1.4.1 Some Hard Rules

There are some hard rules that must be followed in the CPU designs covered in this book, including:

1. The `initial` statement **is prohibited** in the code.
2. `casex`, `casez` **are prohibited** in the code.
3. The use of "#" to express circuit delays **is prohibited** in the code.
4. The clock signal `clock` **is only allowed** in the `always @(posedge clock)` statement.
5. All triggers with resets in the code are either all synchronous resets or all asynchronous resets.

3.1.4.2 Module Declaration and Instantiation

Because Verilog is used to describe circuits, "modules" are defined. The syntax associated with modules includes module declarations and module instantiations, which are similar to function declarations and calls in C. The following is a code example of module declaration and instantiation.

```verilog
module bottom #(
    parameter A_WIDTH = 8,
    parameter B_WIDTH = 4,
    parameter Y_WIDTH = 2
)(
    input  wire [A_WIDTH-1:0] a,
    input  wire [B_WIDTH-1:0] b,
    input  wire [      3:0] c,
    output wire [Y_WIDTH-1:0] y,
    output reg               z
);


    ......


endmodule

module top;
```

```
wire [15:0] btm_a;
wire [ 7:0] btm_b;
wire [ 3:0] btm_c;
wire [ 3:0] btm_y;
wire        btm_z;

bottom #(
    .A_WIDTH (23),
    .B_WIDTH ( 9),
    .Y_WIDTH ( 7)
)
inst_btm(
.a (btm_a), // I
.b (btm_b), // I
.c (btm_c), // I
.y (btm_y), // O
.z (btm_z)  // O
);

endmodule
```

The code above requires attention to the following three points:

1. The port declaration coding style in the example is strongly recommended.
2. It is strongly recommended to use the name-related port assignment in the example when instantiating the module.
3. If there are ports that interface with two modules, it is recommended that the ports on both sides be defined with the same name or a name that has a high degree of similarity.

As for the above example of the port width parameterization example do not require you to master, many Verilog textbooks do not have this example, written here just to facilitate access.

Let's go further and discuss an issue that beginners have a hard time grasping—when to encapsulate some logic into a module and when to use it? In fact, there is no standard answer to this question, and it has a lot to do with the designer's personal experience. Based on our own experience, we would like to make the following suggestions:

1. If a piece of logic will be used at least twice, and the readability (number of lines of code, code meaning) of the code is better than writing the logic directly when it is instantiated as a module, then it should be encapsulated as a module, such as a decoder or a multiplexer.
2. If the functional specification of a logic is very clear and the number of signals interacting with the outside world is not very large, then it should be encapsulated into modules, such as ALU, regfile, etc.

3. An existing module has reached the size of thousands of lines of code and can be considered to be split into several small modules, such as a CPU divided into several modules according to the pipelines.
4. It is recommended that a file contains only one module and the file and the module with the same name, to facilitate the maintenance of the code later.

3.1.4.3   Basic Logic Gates

Verilog descriptions of some common basic logic gates are listed below:

```verilog
wire [7:0] a;
wire [7:0] b;

assign y1 = ~a;         // not
assign y2 = a & b;      // and
assign y3 = a | b;      // or
assign y4 = a ^ b;      // xor
assign y5 = ~(a & b);   // nand
assign y6 = ~(a | b);   // nor
```

These are bitwise operations; note that it's "&" not "&&" and "|" not "||."

If the signals on either side of the operator are single bits, should you use "&" and "|" or "&&" and "||"? We suggest the code style is: When the code wants to express a logical relationship, such as "Condition A1 is satisfied and Condition A2 is satisfied, or Condition B is satisfied," then use "&&" and "||"; when the code wants to express logic gates, such as the precedence generation logic in a precedence adder, or the Wallace tree in a multiplier, then use "&" and "|."

3.1.4.4   Priority of Operators

It is important to emphasize the priority of Verilog operators here; see Fig. 3.1. One should note that the binary operations "+" and "-" have very high priority, e.g., `assign res[31:0]=a[31:0]+b[0]&&c[0];`; the operation on the right side of the expression is a 1 bit result, not a 32 bit result as we thought, and the statement is equivalent to `assign res[31:0]=(a[31:0]+b[0])&&c[0];`.

Using the priority of Verilog operators can make expressions concise and easy to read, since sometimes too many parentheses can make it difficult to read. However, if you don't remember the operator precedence well, check the precedence rules, or be honest and add parentheses to differentiate between them; after all, correctness comes first.

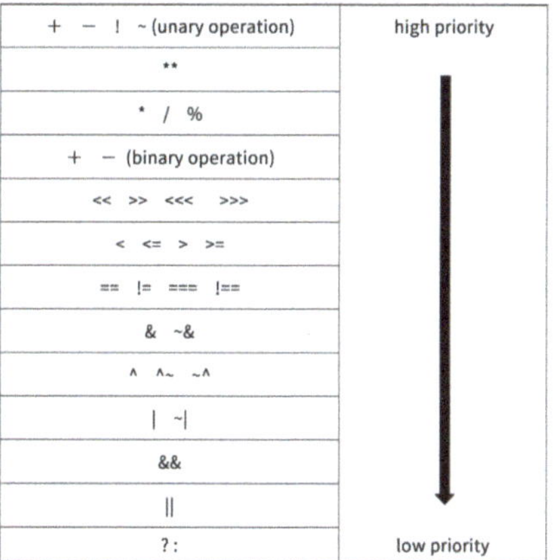

Fig. 3.1 Verilog operator prioritization

3.1.4.5   Decoder

A Verilog description of a 3-8 decoder is given below.

```verilog
module decoder_3_8(
    input  wire [2:0] in,
    output wire [7:0] out
);

assign out[0] = (in == 3'd0);
assign out[1] = (in == 3'd1);
assign out[2] = (in == 3'd2);
assign out[3] = (in == 3'd3);
assign out[4] = (in == 3'd4);
assign out[5] = (in == 3'd5);
assign out[6] = (in == 3'd6);
assign out[7] = (in == 3'd7);

endmodule
```

With the above examples, you should be able to easily imitate the 2–4 decoder and 4–16 decoder. Of course, if you encounter 6–64, 7–128, etc. decoders, it will be more difficult to write them in the above way. If you are interested, you can refer to the information to learn how to use `generate for` statement to improve the coding efficiency.

We hope that with the above example, the reader can visualize what it is like to describe a circuit at the behavioral level. In this example of a 3–8 decoder, what is the behavior of the output out to generate bit 0? It sets 1 when the input equals 0, and 0 otherwise, so the Verilog code written in the behavioral style is `assign out[0] = (in == 3'd0);`.

As an example, in the process of designing a CPU, how to write the signal `inst_is_add_w` that generates the current instruction as add.w from 32-bit
instruction code? By checking the instruction code definition of add.w in the
instruction manual, we know that bits 31 to 15 of the instruction code must
be 17'b00000000000100000, and the rest of the bits are used to express the
register number of the register operand, which is a variable. Therefore the signal
`inst_is_add_w` can be described as follows:

```verilog
assign inst_is_add_w = inst[31:15]==17'b00000000000100000;
```

Isn't this method of description quite intuitive?

3.1.4.6 Encoder

Let's take the Verilog description of the 8-3 encoder as an example, which can be
written in the following way:

```verilog
module encoder_8_3(
    input  wire [7:0] in,
    output wire [2:0] out
);

assign out = in[0] ? 3'd0 :
             in[1] ? 3'd1 :
             in[2] ? 3'd2 :
             in[3] ? 3'd3 :
             in[4] ? 3'd4 :
             in[5] ? 3'd5 :
             in[6] ? 3'd6 :
                     3'd7;

endmodule
```

With this approach, the functionality is fine, but the implementation is a bit
redundant. This is in fact a priority encoder, and if it is guaranteed that the design
input in will always have at most one 1, the so-called at-most-one-hot vector, then
the following can be used:

```verilog
module encoder_8_3(
    input  wire [7:0] in,
    output wire [2:0] out
);

assign out = ({3{in[0]}} & 3'd0)
           | ({3{in[1]}} & 3'd1)
```

```
          | ({3{in[2]}} & 3'd2)
          | ({3{in[3]}} & 3'd3)
          | ({3{in[4]}} & 3'd4)
          | ({3{in[5]}} & 3'd5)
          | ({3{in[6]}} & 3'd6)
          | ({3{in[7]}} & 3'd7);

endmodule
```

The above two ways of describing the code are equivalent when the input has one or only one 1, but the output is not the same when the input is all zeros. This should be noted when using them.

A typical application of the encoder logic in CPU design is to generate the opcode `alu_op` for the ALU module from the result of the instruction decoding. `alu_op` can be encoded in the latter way, since the decoder part of the processor processes only one instruction at any given time.

3.1.4.7 Multiplexer

Multiplexer is a common type of logic used in CPU design, and it is recommended that you have a good understanding of them. Usually, the textbooks of digital logic circuits describe a multiplexer with logic gates such as nand, or nor. If you write the Verilog code of a multiplexer in this way, it will be very troublesome, especially when you need to write a dozens-to-one multiplexer. So how to solve this kind of problem?

Let's look at the case where the select signal select has not been decoded yet. It is deliberately assumed that the number of inputs selected is not a power of 2 and that the output is all zeros when the select input exceeds the selectable range. The Verilog description is as follows:

```
module mux5_8b(
    input  wire [7:0] in0, in1, in2, in3, in4,
    input  wire [2:0] sel,
    output wire [7:0] out
);

assign out = (sel==3'd0) ? in0 :
             (sel==3'd1) ? in1 :
             (sel==3'd2) ? in2 :
             (sel==3'd3) ? in3 :
             (sel==3'd4) ? in4 :
                           8'b0;

endmodule
```

Compared to the case statement, the above expression is simple and intuitive. Moreover, the case statement has a major disadvantage, which is that the output variable is declared as reg type even though it is a combinational logic. Therefore, there is no need to use the case statement to write a multiplexer.

However, the above example introduces unnecessary priority relationships, such that sel is naturally not 0 when it is 1. So, this multiplexer could be written as follows:

```verilog
module mux5_8b(
    input  wire [7:0] in0, in1, in2, in3, in4,
    input  wire [2:0] sel,
    output wire [7:0] out
);

assign out = ({8{sel==3'd0}} & in0)
           | ({8{sel==3'd1}} & in1)
           | ({8{sel==3'd2}} & in2)
           | ({8{sel==3'd3}} & in3)
           | ({8{sel==3'd4}} & in4);

endmodule
```

Reviewing the above code, you will see that it is actually a combination of the decoder and the multiple selector based on the decoded vectors.

If you write it this way, don't forget to write the 8 in "{8{}}"; otherwise, the result out will only have the 0th bit correct, and bits [7:1] will all go to 0. Be especially careful with this type of clerical error, as it is not a syntax error and debugging tools do not report such errors.

If the select signal is already in the form of a decoded bit vector, it is also easy to write it as follows:

```verilog
module mux5_8b(
    input  wire [7:0] in0, in1, in2, in3, in4,
    input  wire [4:0] sel,
    output wire [7:0] out
);

assign out = ({8{sel[0]}} & in0)
           | ({8{sel[1]}} & in1)
           | ({8{sel[2]}} & in2)
           | ({8{sel[3]}} & in3)
           | ({8{sel[4]}} & in4);

endmodule
```

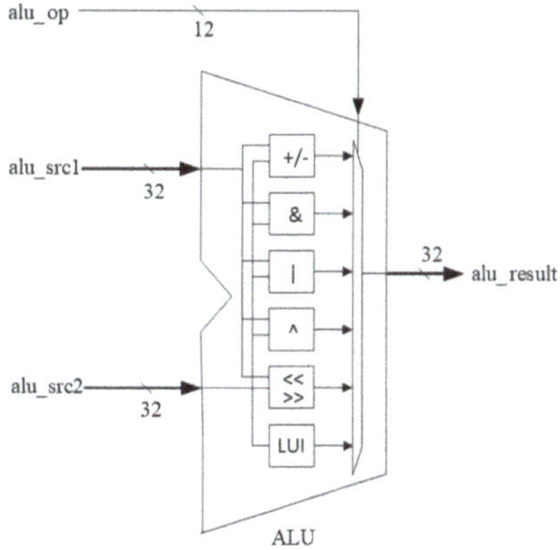

Fig. 3.2 Circuit structure of the ALU in a simple LoongArch CPU

3.1.4.8   ALU in a Simple LoongArch CPU

We use the ALU in a simple LoongArch CPU as an example of a more complex combinational logic design. In addition to addition, subtraction, and comparison operations, this ALU also performs shift operations and logic operations. How should its circuit be designed?

From the design analysis (see Chap. 4, Sect. 4.3.1 for details), it can be seen that the ALU contains logic that performs addition, subtraction, comparison, shift, and logic operations, and the inputs of the ALU are transmitted to these logics at the same time, and each of these logics performs operations simultaneously, and then a multiplexing circuit is used to select the desired result as the output of the ALU. The structure of the circuit is shown in Fig. 3.2.

The control signal `alu_op` for the entire ALU is in the form of a 12-bit at-most-one-hot code. The Verilog description is shown below:

```verilog
module simple_alu(
    input  wire [11:0] alu_op,
    input  wire [31:0] alu_src1,
    input  wire [31:0] alu_src2,
    output wire [31:0] alu_result
);

wire op_add;    // add
wire op_sub;    // sub
wire op_slt;    // signed set on less than
wire op_sltu;   // unsigned set on less than
wire op_and;    // bit-wise and
wire op_nor;    // bit-wise nor
wire op_or;     // bit-wise or
wire op_xor;    // bit-wise xor
```

```verilog
wire op_sll;    // logic shift left
wire op_srl;    // logic shift right
wire op_sra;    // arithmetic shift right
wire op_lui;    // load top bits

assign op_add  = alu_op[ 0];
assign op_sub  = alu_op[ 1];
assign op_slt  = alu_op[ 2];
assign op_sltu = alu_op[ 3];
assign op_and  = alu_op[ 4];
assign op_nor  = alu_op[ 5];
assign op_or   = alu_op[ 6];
assign op_xor  = alu_op[ 7];
assign op_sll  = alu_op[ 8];
assign op_srl  = alu_op[ 9];
assign op_sra  = alu_op[10];
assign op_lui  = alu_op[11];

wire [31:0] add_sub_result;
wire [31:0] slt_result;
wire [31:0] sltu_result;
wire [31:0] and_result;
wire [31:0] nor_result;
wire [31:0] or_result;
wire [31:0] xor_result;
wire [31:0] sll_result;
wire [31:0] srl_result;
wire [31:0] sra_result;
wire [31:0] lui_result;


assign and_result = alu_src1 & alu_src2;
assign or_result  = alu_src1 | alu_src2;
assign nor_result = ~or_result;
assign xor_result = alu_src1 ^ alu_src2;
assign lui_result = alu_src2;


wire [31:0] adder_a;
wire [31:0] adder_b;
wire        adder_cin;
wire [31:0] adder_result;
wire        adder_cout;
```

```verilog
assign adder_a   = alu_src1;
assign adder_b   = (op_sub | op_slt | op_sltu) ? ~alu_src2 :
↪   alu_src2;
assign adder_cin = (op_sub | op_slt | op_sltu) ?      1'b1 :
↪   1'b0;
assign {adder_cout, adder_result} = adder_a + adder_b +
↪   adder_cin;

assign add_sub_result = adder_result;


assign slt_result[31:1] = 31'b0;
assign slt_result[0]    = (alu_src1[31] & ~alu_src2[31])
                        | ((alu_src1[31] ~^ alu_src2[31]) &
↪   adder_result[31]);

assign sltu_result[31:1] = 31'b0;
assign sltu_result[0]    = ~adder_cout;

assign sll_result = alu_src1 << alu_src2[4:0];

assign srl_result = alu_src1 >> alu_src2[4:0];

assign sra_result = ($signed(alu_src1)) >>> alu_src2[4:0];

assign alu_result = ({32{op_add|op_sub }} & add_sub_result)
                  | ({32{op_slt        }} & slt_result)
                  | ({32{op_sltu       }} & sltu_result)
                  | ({32{op_and        }} & and_result)
                  | ({32{op_nor        }} & nor_result)
                  | ({32{op_or         }} & or_result)
                  | ({32{op_xor        }} & xor_result)
                  | ({32{op_lui        }} & lui_result)
                  | ({32{op_sll        }} & sll_result)
                  | ({32{op_srl        }} & srl_result)
                  | ({32{op_sra        }} & sra_result);

endmodule
```

According to the above sample code, I hope the reader to focus on the following
four points:

1. When writing code, it is important to give variables good names, neither too
   long nor too short, and to express their semantics as aptly as possible. One of
   the characteristics of good code is that it is "code as comment." Sometimes,

    seemingly useless code, such as the bit-by-bit assignment of `alu_op` to the `op_XXX` variable in the above example, can make the code much more readable.

2. Spaces, alignment, and blank lines in code, like punctuation and paragraphs in an article, can also significantly improve the readability of code.

3. The adder can be described directly by the "+" operator, and the shifter by the "<<", ">>" and ">>>" operators to describe shifters. This is because today's EDA synthesis tools are smart enough to deduce from these operators that the designer needs more complex circuits such as adders and shifters and then pick the appropriate circuits from their own IP libraries to embed in your design based on the implementation constraints.

4. In Verilog, ">>" is only treated as a logical right shift, so arithmetic right shifts require special consideration. The above example uses the "$signed" built-in function and the ">>>" operator directly to accomplish the arithmetic right shift.

3.1.4.9 Flip-Flop

Flip-flops are the most frequently used sequential logic in our CPU designs, and it is important that you know the Verilog descriptions of the flip-flops well.

(1) For an ordinary positive edge triggered D flip-flop, the Verilog description is as follows:

```verilog
module dff(
    input  wire clk,
    input  wire din,
    output reg  q
);
    always @(posedge clk) begin
        q <= din;
    end
endmodule
```

The timing characteristics of a D flip-flop are shown in Fig. 3.3.

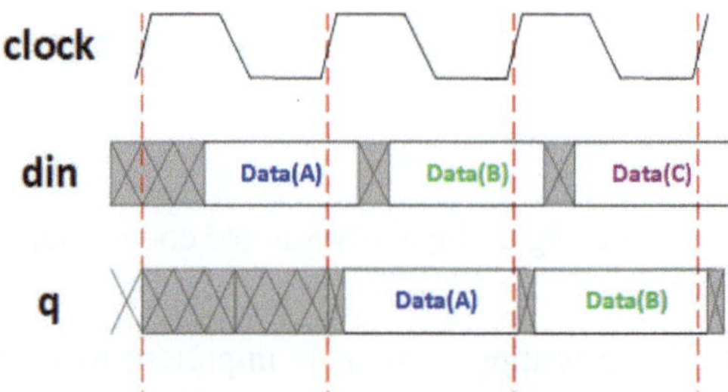

Fig. 3.3 D Flip-flop timing characteristics

(2) The Verilog description of a D flip-flop with synchronized reset is written in two ways.

Way one:

```verilog
module dff_r(
    input  wire clk,
    input  wire rst,
    input  wire din,
    output reg  q
);
always @(posedge clk) begin
    if (rst) q <= 1'b0;
    else     q <= din;
end
endmodule
```

Way two:

```verilog
module dff_r(
    input  wire clk,
    input  wire rst,
    input  wire din,
    output reg  q
);
always @(posedge clk) begin
    q <= ~rst & din;
end
endmodule
```

The functionality of the circuit is the same in both ways, but we recommend the more behavioral style of way one. Because the reset operation usually has the highest priority, the if...else... style makes it easier to read the code at a glance and less likely to make a mistake.

(3) The Verilog description of a D flip-flop with a write enable input is also written in two ways.

Way one:

```verilog
module dff_en(
    input  wire clk,
    input  wire en,
    input  wire din,
    output reg  q
);
```

```
always @(posedge clk) begin
    if (en) q <= din;
end
endmodule
```

Way two:

```
module dff_en(
    input  wire clk,
    input  wire en,
    input  wire din,
    output reg  q
);
always @(posedge clk) begin
    q <= en ? din : q;
end
endmodule
```

The functionality of the circuit is the same in both styles. We also recommend the way one for the same reasons as before, it looks more intuitive and has some additional benefits—most EDA tools automatically insert gated clocks or introduce gated flip-flops only for codes using the first style.

The examples here are all single-bit flip-flop, and the reader is free to generalize them to the multi-bit case.

3.1.4.10   Register File in a LoongArch32 CPU

In layman's terms, a register file is a "pile of registers" using a two-dimensional organization. In a simple LoongArch32 CPU with a single-issue five-stage pipeline, GR corresponds to a 32-item, 32-bit register file. In order to support the pipeline, the register file must be able to read two 32-bit numbers and write one 32-bit number per cycle. This register file also has a special feature that register 0 is always 0. The corresponding Verilog code is as follows:

```
module regfile(
    input  wire        clk,
    input  wire [ 4:0] raddr1,
    output wire [31:0] rdata1,
    input  wire [ 4:0] raddr2,
    output wire [31:0] rdata2,
    input  wire        we,
    input  wire [ 4:0] waddr,
    input  wire [31:0] wdata
```

```verilog
);
reg [31:0] reg_array[31:0];
// WRITE
always @(posedge clk) begin
    if (we) reg_array[waddr]<= wdata;
end
// READ OUT 1
assign rdata1 = (raddr1==5'b0) ? 32'b0 : reg_array[raddr1];
// READ OUT 2
assign rdata2 = (raddr2==5'b0) ? 32'b0 : reg_array[raddr2];
endmodule
```

In the above example, rf[waddr], rf[raddr1], rf[raddr2] means that the decoder circuits for write and read addresses need to be derived by the synthesis tool. In fact, a more specific description is shown below. Here we assume that decoder_5_32 is a 5-32 decoder module.

```verilog
module regfile(
    input  wire          clk,
    input  wire [ 4:0] raddr1,
    output wire [31:0] rdata1,
    input  wire [ 4:0] raddr2,
    output wire [31:0] rdata2,
    input  wire          we,
    input  wire [ 4:0] waddr,
    input  wire [31:0] wdata
);
reg  [31:0] reg_array[31:0];
wire [31:0] waddr_dec, raddr1_dec, raddr2_dec;

decoder_5_32 U0(.in(waddr ), .out(waddr_dec));
decoder_5_32 U1(.in(raddr1), .out(raddr1_dec));
decoder_5_32 U2(.in(raddr2), .out(raddr2_dec));

//WRITE
always @(posedge clk) begin
    if (we & waddr_dec[ 0]) reg_array[ 0]<= wdata;
    if (we & waddr_dec[ 1]) reg_array[ 1]<= wdata;
    ......
    if (we & waddr_dec[31]) reg_array[31]<= wdata;
end
//READ OUT 1
assign rdata1 = ({32{raddr1_dec[ 1]}} & reg_array[ 1])
              | ({32{raddr1_dec[ 2]}} & reg_array[ 2])
```

```
              . . . . . .
           | ({32{raddr1_dec[31]}} & reg_array[31]);
//READ OUT 2
 assign rdata2 = ({32{raddr2_dec[ 1]}} & reg_array[ 1])
              | ({32{raddr2_dec[ 2]}} & reg_array[ 2])
              . . . . . .
           | ({32{raddr2_dec[31]}} & reg_array[31]);
 endmodule
```

The second approach is just to deepen the reader's understanding of rf[addr], which is short but has a lot of logic in it. We recommend that you use the first style in your normal design.

Please consider the question, when the write enable is valid (we=1) and the write address is the same as the read address, is the result of the read the old value in the register or the newly written value?

3.1.4.11   RAM

By RAM we mean SRAM, which is usually used to implement instruction memory and data memory in the CPU. It is similar in logical behavior to the aforementioned register file, but there are differences in the underlying implementation. When writing Verilog code, it is usually not possible to describe RAM by behavioral derivation but by instantiating RAM IP. The reader will learn this through the practical tasks in this chapter, so we won't discuss it here.

3.1.4.12   Pipeline

First of all, it should be noted that pipelined circuits are purely a concept of digital circuits, and we should not think of pipelines in processors when we talk about pipelines.

Let's look at how to design a non-blocking three-stage pipeline circuit. The circuit structure of this pipeline is shown in Fig. 3.4, where `pipe1_data`, `pipe2_data`, and `pipe3_data` are all triggers that store the data of each level of the pipeline.

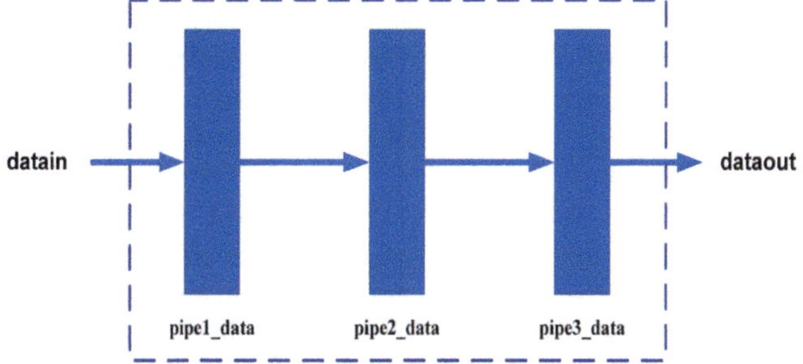

Fig. 3.4 Non-blocking pipeline circuit architecture

Below is an example of the Verilog code for this pipelined circuit. As you can see, the non-blocking pipeline is actually multiple flip-flops connected in sequence.

```verilog
module non_stall_pipeline #
(
    parameter WIDTH = 100
)
(
    input  wire              clk,
    input  wire [WIDTH-1:0] datain,
    output wire [WIDTH-1:0] dataout
);
reg [WIDTH-1:0] pipe1_data;
reg [WIDTH-1:0] pipe2_data;
reg [WIDTH-1:0] pipe3_data;

always @(posedge clk) begin
    pipe1_data <= datain;
end

always @(posedge clk) begin
    pipe2_data <= pipe1_data;
end

always @(posedge clk) begin
    pipe3_data <= pipe2_data;
end

assign dataout = pipe3_data;

endmodule
```

A non-blocking pipeline usually corresponds to the ideal case, but in many cases, the pipeline will be blocked. This means that as soon as the back of the pipeline is blocked, the front of the pipeline is also blocked. Since the back pipeline is not working, there is no way for the system to receive new data, so the front pipeline must keep its data in the current pipeline (i.e., it is blocked). If the previous pipeline still sends data to the next pipeline, the data will be lost. Unless the entire system has a data loss detection and retransmission mechanism in the upper layer, the underlying pipeline circuitry needs to have a mechanism to avoid data loss in the event of blocking.

From the above analysis, it appears that in order for the pipeline to cope with blocking, we need to try to keep the data at one pipeline stage. Recall the timing behavior characteristics of the flip-flop with enable that we described earlier. As long as the write enable of the flip-flop is invalid, even if the value on the D input of the flip-flop changes, the contents stored in the flip-flop remain unchanged. The register file and RAM also have similar characteristics, i.e., as long as its write enable signal remains invalid, the data stored in it remains unchanged. As you can see, the core to make the pipeline cope with blocking is to control the write enable signals of the pipeline caches at all stages.

So how to control these write enable signals? Two design strategies are given here. Let's take a manual production pipeline as an example.

- Strategy 1: Have a production pipeline supervisor who can see the status of all stages of the pipeline at the same time and give orders to all the pipelines. Once the supervisor realizes that one stage is blocked at a given time, he or she sends an order to all stages before that one to stop forwarding at the next time.
- Strategy 2: Assign a supervisor to each stage of the pipeline who communicates with the supervisors at the front and back stages to decide whether to send something forward at the next moment. In the case of one stage of the assembly pipeline, it sends a "I have something to deliver to you next" request to the stage after it, and a "I can receive something from you next" feedback to the stage before it. Because the pipelines are connected in a chain, a pipeline receives both feedback from the latter stage about whether it can receive something at the next moment and a request from the former stage about whether it has something to deliver at the next moment. If a pipeline has something at the current moment and wants to pass it to the following pipeline at the next moment, but the following pipeline says that it can't receive it at the next moment, then that pipeline will continue to hold the current moment at the next moment, which is blocking.

Clearly, both strategies can accomplish the task. The circuit design we present next uses the second design strategy.

The circuit structure of the pipeline we designed is shown in Fig. 3.5. The arrows in the figure indicate, respectively, that the pipelined stages interact with each other and determine the current stage Logic and signals for streamline cache write enable control.

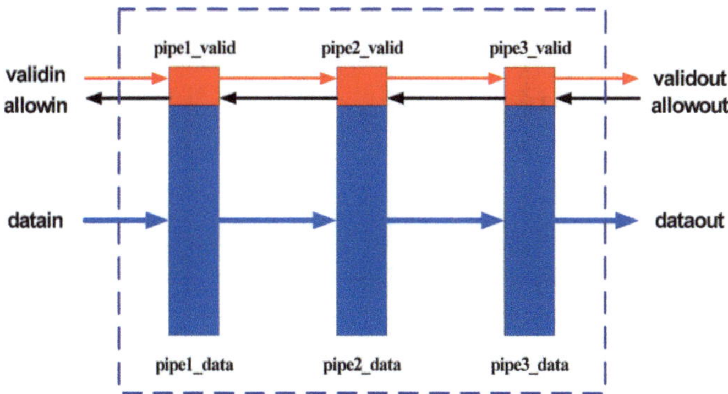

Fig. 3.5 Blocking pipeline circuit architecture

The following is a sample Verilog code for this pipeline circuit.

```verilog
module stallable_pipeline #
(
    parameter WIDTH = 100
)
(
    input  wire                 clk,
    input  wire                 rst,
    input  wire                 validin,
    input  wire [WIDTH-1:0] datain,
    input  wire                 out_allow,
    output wire                 validout,
    output wire [WIDTH-1:0] dataout
);
reg                pipe1_valid;
reg [WIDTH-1:0] pipe1_data;
reg                pipe2_valid;
reg [WIDTH-1:0] pipe2_data;
reg                pipe3_valid;
reg [WIDTH-1:0] pipe3_data;

// pipeline stage1
wire                pipe1_allowin;
wire                pipe1_ready_go;
wire                pipe1_to_pipe2_valid;
assign pipe1_ready_go = ......
assign pipe1_allowin = !pipe1_valid || pipe1_ready_go &&
↪   pipe2_allowin;
assign pipe1_to_pipe2_valid = pipe1_valid && pipe1_ready_go;
```

```verilog
always @(posedge clk) begin
    if (rst) begin
        pipe1_valid <= 1'b0;
    end
    else if (pipe1_allowin) begin
        pipe1_valid <= validin;
    end
    if (validin && pipe1_allowin) begin
        pipe1_data <= datain;
    end
end

// pipeline stage2
wire            pipe2_allowin;
wire            pipe2_ready_go;
wire            pipe2_to_pipe3_valid;
assign pipe2_ready_go = ......
assign pipe2_allowin = !pipe2_valid || pipe2_ready_go &&
↪   pipe3_allowin;
assign pipe2_to_pipe3_valid = pipe2_valid && pipe2_ready_go;
always @(posedge clk) begin
    if (rst) begin
        pipe2_valid <= 1'b0;
    end
    else if (pipe2_allowin) begin
        pipe2_valid <= pipe1_to_pipe2_valid;
    end

    if (pipe1_to_pipe2_valid && pipe2_allowin) begin
        pipe2_data <= pipe1_data;
    end
end

// pipeline stage3
wire            pipe3_allowin;
wire            pipe3_ready_go;
assign pipe3_ready_go = ......
assign pipe3_allowin = !pipe3_valid || pipe3_ready_go &&
↪   out_allow;
always @(posedge clk) begin
    if (rst) begin
        pipe3_valid <= 1'b0;
    end
    else if (pipe3_allowin) begin
```

```verilog
            pipe3_valid <= pipe2_to_pipe3_valid;
      end

      if (pipe2_to_pipe3_valid && pipe3_allowin) begin
          pipe3_data <= pipe2_data;
      end
  end

  assign validout = pipe3_valid && pipe3_ready_go;
  assign dataout  = pipe3_data;

endmodule
```

The `pipeX_valid` bit in the above code is called the valid bit of the Xth pipeline stage, which is realized by using a flip-flop. A value of 1 indicates that there is valid data at current clock cycle of pipeline stage X. A value of 0 indicates that there is no valid data at current clock cycle of pipeline stage X. The advantage of defining the valid bit is that when clearing the pipeline, you don't need to set all the values in the data field of each stage of pipeline to invalid values but only need to set the valid bit of the pipeline stage to 0, thus saving logic resources. However, it should be noted that when generating control signals based on the data field information of each pipeline stage, do not forget to check whether the valid signal of this stage is valid or not.

The `pipeX_allowin` signal is passed from stage X to stage X-1. A value of 1 indicates that the next clock cycle stage X pipeline stage can be updated with data from the current clock cycle stage X-1 pipeline stage, while a value of 0 indicates that the next clock cycle the X pipeline stage cannot receive new data.

The `pipeX_ready_go` signal describes the completion status of the processing task at stage X at current clock cycle. A value of 1 indicates that the data processing task at stage X has been completed and can be passed to the X+1 pipeline stage. For example, if the CPU execution pipeline stage uses iterative operation to calculate division, which takes several clock cycles to complete, then the ready_go signal of the execution pipeline stage will be 0 until the execution pipeline stage's division is completed.

The `pipeX_to_pipeY_valid` signal is passed from stage X to stage X+1. A value of 1 indicates that data from stage X pipeline stage is expected to enter stage X+1 pipeline stage in the next clock cycle.

After understanding the meaning of the above signals, the reader is free to deduce how the whole circuit realizes the control of pipeline blocking in conjunction with the pipeline time diagram.

3.2   Common Errors in Functional Simulation of Digital Logic Circuits and Their Debugging Methods

When designing a CPU, the most time-consuming part of the process is to formulate the design and to debug. No one is perfect, and even the best designers cannot guarantee that their code is bug-free, so debugging is one of the necessary skills for programmers. During the hardware design process, the work of finding bugs and debugging can be carried out in the functional simulation stage or in the actual circuit testing stage. Because of the short cycle time between code writing and functional simulation, and the wealth of information observed during functional simulation, it is common to find as many bugs as possible during the functional simulation phase. In this book, we recommend that every practical task must pass the functional simulation phase before proceeding to the on-board debugging phase.

For beginners, there is less experience in circuit programming and debugging with Verilog, and Verilog describes circuits, which are different from the objects described by C, C++, Java, Python, etc. Therefore, the debugging techniques of Verilog are different from those of general programming languages, and it is difficult for readers to borrow the debugging techniques of C and C++ programs into Verilog. As a simple example, many students will use the "print method" to debug C programs (although the method is a bit rustic, but most of the time it can solve the problem), but this method is not applicable when debugging a Verilog program. In view of this, we will introduce some common debugging methods used in digital logic circuit design.

3.2.1   Functional Simulation Waveform Analysis

In the video materials introducing IC designers, we often see IC designers carrying out debugging work with multimeters, oscilloscopes, logic analyzers, and other testing tools at hand. These tools are indeed IC designers for the actual circuit debugging "tool," because the information obtained by these instruments can provide an objective basis for us to locate and analyze errors. In the real world, it is through a variety of instruments to observe the debugging process and results, so we are in the simulation through a variety of means of observation to "emulate" the results of the instrument this "real," embodied in the simulation waveform. You can imagine that we have an extremely powerful logic analyzer that can capture every signal in your designed circuit at every moment during operation and display it for you to see. Therefore, when debugging a digital logic circuit design, it is always necessary to observe the simulation waveforms to determine the location of circuit errors. Some people may have different opinions: No, I debugged the circuit by printing out the information from the simulation, by adding monitoring code to the testbench, checking certain signals in the design, and printing out the error message when I found an outlier. I can't say that this way is wrong, but if you think about it, you will find that the essence of the two ways of observation is the same: The object of observation are the signals in the circuit design, but one way is to display the signals as images for the eyes to see, and the other way is to represent the signals as data files and then analyze them with the program. Each of the two methods has its own application scenario and can be used in combination. However, direct observation of simulated waveforms is a more convenient method that everyone should master.

In the previous chapter, when introducing the Vivado-based FPGA design flow, we have demonstrated how to perform functional simulation and introduced the simulation debugging interface. These are the basic tools for analyzing waveforms in functional simulation, and it is important that you master them. There is no other way to achieve this goal than practicing through practical tasks. Next, we will introduce some advanced knowledge related to functional simulation waveform analysis.

3.2.1.1 Ideas for Observing Simulated Waveforms

When analyzing a problem, the approach is most crucial; otherwise, it's just brute force. Why is there a huge difference in efficiency between different people when they are watching waveforms to locate errors? Our experience is that people who know how to watch waveforms have their own "rules." Next, we will talk about some of the "rules" that we have found out in practice.

Step 1: Familiarize Yourself with the Design to be Debugged
Debugging without understanding the design is like searching for treasure without a map, and its low efficiency is imaginable. People may think that such a simple reason still need to emphasize? But in fact, beginners are most likely to ignore this point. Unless the entire design code is written by yourself, you will always be involved in debugging other people's code, and some people even can't explain their own design. We often come across the following scenario, which is both funny and frustrating:

Student: Teacher, I can't get it to work, can you help me?

Teacher: Okay, let me take a look. (The teacher looks at the waveform and finds an abnormality, but when he looks at the code, he doesn't understand it.) What is the meaning of the code in this place? What is your design intention?

Student: This is . . . . . . and this is . . . . (After stammering for a while, there is nothing more.)

Teacher: (The teacher reads the code and understands it) Oh, did you originally intend to design it as . . . . . .

Student: Yes, yes, yes, that's what it means. Oh, I know where I made a mistake.

Dear readers, we sincerely hope that such a scenario will not happen to you. So, before you start debugging, ask yourself if you fully understand the design. If there is something you don't know or understand, make sure you understand the design first, so that you can sharpen your knife before you cut your wood.

Step 2: Find a Point of Error That You Can Pinpoint

Once a design function simulates an error, it must mean that at some point the value of some signal is not correct, and these points are error points (but they are not always the source of the problem). When you start debugging, you must find an error point. For a simple circuit design, this is easy to find, because a robust functional verification platform will monitor the design's outputs and other signals during simulation and report an error if the outputs are not as expected. From the error messages, you can find out what signals are at fault and discover the simulation moment at which the error occurs.[1] However, for complex designs such as CPUs, the output messages of functional simulation errors usually do not directly tell you which signals are at fault. In this case, how can you locate the error signal from the output message? We will explain this in more detail later when we start practicing CPU design.

Step 3: Look at the Signals Along the Logic Chain of the Design in Reverse, Level by Level, Until the Source of the Error is Found

The point of error we find may not be the source of the error, but we must start at the source of the error when correcting it. The state changes of signals in digital logic circuits are interlocked and follow a strict logical cause and effect relationship, so if we start from an error point and trace forward along this logical chain, we will surely be able to find the source of the error. In the process of reverse tracing, most people are more skillful in the reverse analysis of simple combinational logic, but they are a bit "scared" of circuits containing sequential logic. Therefore, we will focus on how to look at the waveforms in this case.

When observing the waveform of a circuit containing sequential logic, the first step is to capture the clock signal. The key here is not to catch the wrong clock signal. At the beginning of learning, the designs that you are exposed to often only have one global clock, but in real designs, there are often multiple clocks, such as a CPU using one clock and a peripheral using another clock. Due to the fact that clock signals are generally referred to as clk or clock within each module, it is difficult to identify the problem in the waveform window if the clock signal is captured incorrectly. Incorrect clock signals can cause unnecessary trouble to your analysis work.

Once we have the clock signals, we need to determine whether the sequential logic we are looking at (e.g., flip-flop, synchronous RAM) is triggered by the positive or negative edge of the clock. If we trace from the combinational logic all the way back to the Q side of a flip-flop or RAM, then we need to capture the non-clock input signals of this flip-flop or RAM and then follow the time axis backward on the waveform (in the waveform is to look to the left) to find the positive or

---

[1]This is limited to verifying that the error information on the platform has been developed in a relatively standardized manner. If readers develop their own verification platform, they should include information such as error time, error signal, expected value, observation value, etc. in the error message, and the error signal should reflect the level of the module.

negative edge of the clock when the error value was written and then continue to trace back to the combinational logic that generates the inputs of this flip-flop or RAM and repeat this process until we find the bug. While searching along the time axis, be sure to find the real moment when the error value was written. Here are some typical examples.

Example 1 (Flip-flops Without Write Enable) If the current cycle is the first cycle in which an error occurs in the Q value of the flip-flop, analyze the combinational logic that generates the D input of the flip-flop in the previous cycle.

Example 2 (Flip-Flops with Write Enable) If the current cycle is the first cycle in which the Q value of the flip-flop is in error, we need to move forward along the time axis from this cycle to the latest cycle in which the write enable signal is active. We then determine whether the write enable signal should be enabled for this cycle according to the design intent. If it should be enabled, then the problem is with the write data, and we continue to trace the combinational logic that generates the write data input to the flip-flop. If it should not be enabled, then the problem is with the write enable signal, and we will continue to trace the logic that generates the write enable signal of the flip-flop. However, sometimes you will find that the write enable signal should be asserted at this point in time and the data written is correct, so this is another case of error, where there is a write enable signal after this point in time that is not asserted when it should be. Based on the design intent, we need to start from the earliest wrong beat of flip-flop Q and observe whether the match between write enable and D input is as expected one cycle at a time, until we find the cycle where the write enable is not set properly.

Example 3 (Single-port Synchronized RAM) The first step is to find the nearest valid read command along the time axis, starting from the first cycle when the Q value was wrong. Again, a valid read command means that the chip select (and read enable) signals of the RAM are active, but the write enable is not active.[2] During the clock cycle in which the valid read command is initiated, the address inputs to the RAM should be checked to see if they are correct at this point in time. If it is not correct, the combinational logic that generated the address input should be traced. If the address inputs are correct at the moment, then there are several cases to consider.

- **Case 1:** We suspect that the last write to the RAM address was wrong.
- **Case 2:** We suspect that a write command that should have been issued between the last write to RAM and this read was not issued.

---

[2]Although some RAMs also have an explicit output on the Q-side on the next cycle of a write command, we do not recommend that the reader take advantage of the RAM's Q-side output in this case in his design. In other words, we recommend that whenever a value needs to be read from the RAM, a read command should be issued first rather than utilizing the side effects of a write command for this purpose.

- **Case 3:** We suspect that a read command that should have been issued at a later point in time was not issued, or that it was issued at the wrong time.

  Case 1 has two sub-scenarios.

- **Case 1-1:** At the time of the last write command to this address, a write to this address in RAM was indeed required, but the data written was wrong. At this point, we stop at the write error and continue to trace the combinatorial logic that generated the write data.
- **Case 1-2:** The last time a write command was issued to this address, there was no need to write to this address in RAM, and there are two error possibilities.

  - **Case 1-2-1:** If we need to write another address at this point in time, but the address is incorrectly changed to the current address, then we need to trace the combinatorial logic that generated the address.
  - **Case 1-2-2:** If the RAM should not be written at all at this point in time, but the chip select and write enable signals are set incorrectly and the address happens to be this address, then the combination of the chip select and write enable logic needs to be generated retrospectively.

For case 2, start from the last time a write command was issued to the address, and check the logic that generates the RAM chip select and write enable, cycle by cycle, in accordance with the design intent, to find the moment when you expected a write command to be issued, and find out why it was not activated.

For case 3, check the logic that generates the RAM chip-select and write-enable combinations from the most recent read command backward, cycle by cycle, according to the design intent, and find the moment when you would expect the chip-select to be active and the write-enable to be inactive (i.e., the moment of the read), and find out why it is not enabled.

The register file is traced in a similar way to synchronous RAM, so we won't go into detail here.

3.2.1.2 Practical Tips for Improving Waveform Analysis Efficiency

(1) Record Data of All Signals in One Simulation

Using the waveform viewing and analysis method described in the previous section, "looking at signals in reverse stepwise along the logic chain of the design," we often add new signals to the waveform window as we analyze them. However, if you create a Vivado project and then do not do anything with it, then the newly added signals will only appear in the simulation time after they have been added and the simulation continues to run. This results in having to rerun the simulation when it is necessary to view the waveform from the current moment forward (which is quite common). If the error occurs at a later point in time, then waiting for the simulation to re-execute to a point near the error can be very time-consuming. Is there a way to record all the signals in one simulation? Yes, there is! But it requires special settings.

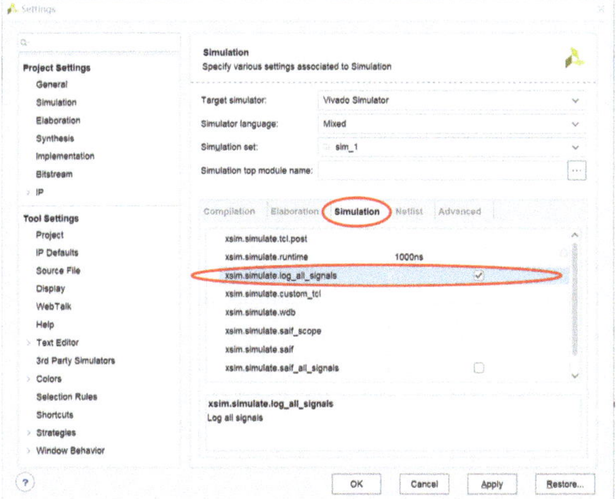

Fig. 3.6 XSim setup screen for recording all signals at once

In the project view of Vivado, click on the left side of the "PROJECT MANAGER" →"Settings," in the pop-up settings interface, select "Project Settings" →"Simulation," the pop-up settings interface shown in Fig. 3.6. In the right part of the "Simulation" label, and then find the following "xsim.simulate.log_all_signals" option and check, click OK to save the configuration. When you run the simulation again after this operation (if you have already started the simulation, please close the simulation interface and run it again), all signals will be logged at once. If you add any new signals during the waveform viewing process, all the waveforms from simulation time 0 will be displayed immediately.

This is a very necessary setting. When the author first started using Vivado, he didn't know that it could be configured this way, so he debugged it without Vivado XSim. This configuration has a significant impact on debugging efficiency and is recommended as a default.

(2) Marking Important Moments

From the previous description, we know that when looking at the simulated waveforms of a circuit with timing logic, it is inevitable to look forward/backward along the time axis. When we analyze an error moment, we find that there may be several paths leading to the error point. Usually, we can only trace along one path first, and if we find that this path is not problematic, we will go back to the error moment we just found and trace from another path. Many beginners spend a lot of time on the "go back to the point of error we just found" action, because they don't remember which point in time they were at when they were faced with a blank signal. Therefore, we strongly suggest: During waveform analysis, promptly mark (Marker) the moments you consider important.

Fig. 3.7 Waveform control toolbar marking and scaling functions

The way to make a marker is very simple: Click the left mouse button on the waveform at the moment you are interested in, then the cursor will appear at the moment you are interested in, and click the button in the toolbar above the waveform as shown in Fig. 3.7-1, and you have made a marker. Afterward, whether you move the waveform directly to the Marker or use the Quick Move Cursor button in the toolbar above the waveform to locate the Marker(shown as 2 and 3 in Fig. 3.7), you will be able to move the cursor to the Marker. This will substantially improve positioning efficiency.

(3) Proficiency in the Use of Waveform Reduction and Amplification Functions
In addition to using the marking function, skillful use of the zoom-in and zoom-out functions can also speed up the back-and-forth movement along the time axis. Basically, when you are ready to move backward and forward in a wide range, first click the Zoom Out button in the toolbar on top of the waveform (shown in Fig. 3.7-5) to reduce the waveform to a suitable level, then drag the scroll bar below the waveform to the vicinity of the moment you want to observe, and then click the waveform to zoom out. With the cursor at this point, click on the zoom button in the toolbar above the waveform (shown in Fig. 3.7-4) to zoom in on the waveform to a point where you can see the signal clearly.

(4) Segmentation and Grouping of Correlated Signals
When debugging complex designs, many signals are usually added to the waveform, which can cause confusion when looking up and down at the signals. It is recommended to separate the related signals by Divider or Group. For example, when analyzing the waveforms of the CPU of a pipeline, you can put the signals belonging to the same stage of pipeline in the same group. To create a divider, right click on the signal name at the previous signal where you want to add a blank line, open the menu bar, and select "New Divider." To delete a division, click on the division and press the Del key. To create a group, select the signal you want to put into a group, and then right click to open the menu bar and select "New Group." Users can name the group; when there are more than one group, it is recommended to name the group in order to distinguish it. The signals in a group can be stowed or expanded as needed for debugging.

(5) Quickly Locate Multi-bit Wide Signals with Value Lookups
Sometimes it is necessary to look forward or backward from a certain point in time to find a point in time when a multi-bit wide signal is equal to a certain value. Unless you are sure that the result you are looking for will occur within a few clock

cycles before or after that moment, it is highly recommended to use the Find Value method instead of dragging the scroll bar under the signal with the mouse to find it manually. To find value, click on the signal name of the signal you want to find, right click on it, open the menu bar and select "Find Value," then a toolbar related to the search will appear on top of the waveform, and you can enter the data according to its prompts. Unfortunately, Vivado's XSim does not support wildcard characters for value search, so users can only partially realize the fuzzy search function by adjusting the Matching method in the search toolbar.

3.2.2 Debugging Waveform Exception Class Errors

Waveform anomaly errors are errors that can be detected by directly observing the waveform without analyzing the function of the circuit design; for example, an "X" appears in the waveform. Waveform errors are shallow errors, and it is easy to find the cause of the error, but beginners are often at a loss when faced with these types of errors because of their lack of experience.

We have subdivided the waveform exception class of errors into the following categories:

- The signal is "Z."
- The signal is "X."
- Waveform stops.
- Cross-edge sampling, where the positive edge samples the value of the data being sampled after the positive edge.
- Waveform oddities, i.e., the simulated waveform graphs show oddities, are errors that are unrelated to the function of the designed circuit.

3.2.2.1 The Signal Is "Z"

"Z" denotes high resistance; for example, an open circuit will be displayed as high resistance; this error is often caused by the following two reasons:

1. A variable declared as wire type in RTL is never assigned a value.
2. The signal called by the module is not connected resulting in a signal dangling.

Figure 3.8 shows an example of the second case.

In the above example, the following points should be noted:

(1) Signals unconnected during module instantiation. Unconnections consist of two types: explicit unconnections, such as c() in Fig. 3.8a; implicit unconnections, for example, when the module adder is called in Fig. 3.8a, the unconnected port a is implicitly unconnected. Explicit unconnections are usually set by human intentionally, only for output class interface; implicit unconnections are mostly

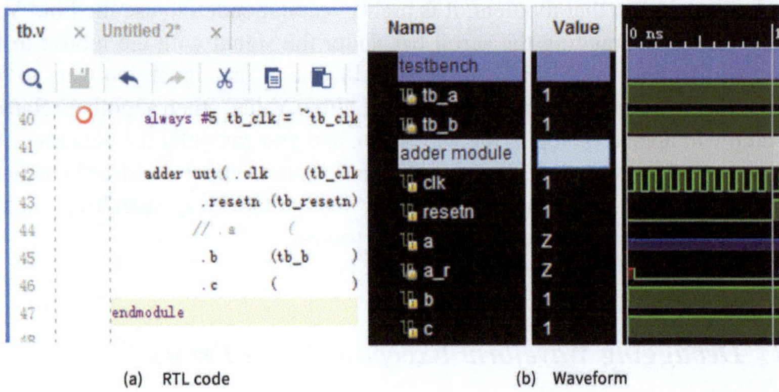

(a)   RTL code   (b)   Waveform

Fig. 3.8 Example of error with "Z" signal. (**a**) RTL code (**b**) Waveform

caused by negligence, which is an error caused by code irregularity, and it is often the main reason to cause the signal to be "Z."

(2) In the adder module, port a is not connected so that a is "Z," and port c is also not connected, but c is a fixed value. This is because port a is an input and port c is an output. The output class interface is not connected because the signal is not used in the main module and may have been intentionally set up by a human, and all input class interfaces are not allowed to be left dangling when they are called.

(3) In the adder module, the a signal is "Z" from the time of 0, but the a_r signal becomes "Z" only at about 100 ns. This is because the a signal is a port and is not connected when it is called, so it is "Z" from the time of 0, but the a_r signal is an internal register, and the a signal is used in the assignment from the time of 100 ns, so it becomes "Z."

In response to the above, we have the following recommendations:

- When writing RTL, pay attention to the code specification, especially when the modules are called; they should correspond one by one in the order of the interfaces.
- All input class interfaces are not allowed to be floating when called.
- Once a signal is found to be "Z," the factor signal that generated the signal should be traced forward to see which signal is "Z," all the way to the input connector in the module, and then correct it.
- It is possible that the "Z" is only present in certain bits of the vector signal, and the same traceability is applied. A width mismatch in one of the interfaces at the time of the call can also cause some bits of the interface to be "Z."

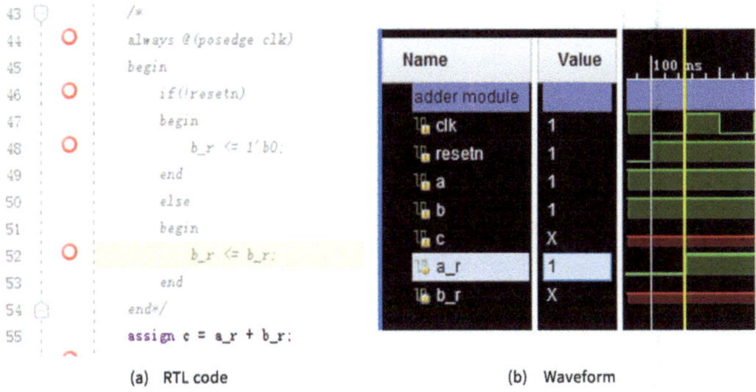

(a) RTL code   (b) Waveform

Fig. 3.9 Example of error with "X" signal. (**a**) RTL code (**b**) Waveform

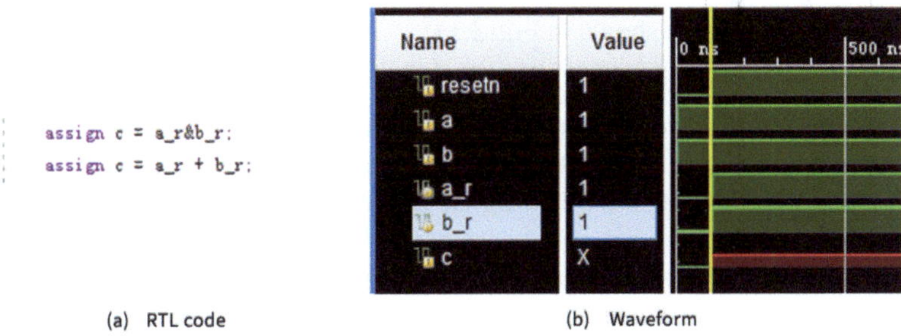

(a) RTL code   (b) Waveform

Fig. 3.10 Example of a multi-driver triggering an "X". (**a**) RTL code (**b**) Waveform

3.2.2.2   The Signal Is "X"

"X" indicates an indeterminate value, and this error is often the result of one of two things:

1. Variables declared as reg type in RTL have never been assigned a value.
2. Multi-driven code in RTL can sometimes cause this type of error. Some multi-driven code will not result in an "X," because some multi-driver code may be handled automatically by Vivado, but this is actually a risky situation; some multi-driven code will result in a synthesis failure and will explicitly report a multi-driven error.

The first scenario is shown in Fig. 3.9.

In Fig. 3.9, the b_r signal is never assigned a value after it is declared, resulting in a value of "X," and the subsequent c signal, due to the use of the b_r signal, resulting in a value of "X" as well.

Vivado also produces an "X" during simulation for multiple drivers (two or more circuit units driving the same signal), as shown in Fig. 3.10.

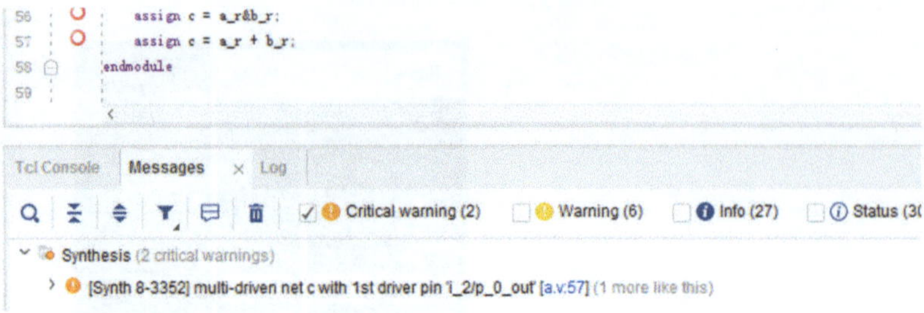

Fig. 3.11 Critical warning reported by multiple drivers in Vivado warning

Tracing the cause of the signal as an "X" in this case may be difficult, so you can try to synthesize first and observe the Critical warning prompt, which will report a multi-driven warning, as shown in Fig. 3.11.

We have the following suggestions for signal "X" cases:

- Once a simulation error is found to come from a signal that appears to be an "X," the simulation is corrected by tracing back forward through the factor signals that generated the signal to see which signal was an "X," all the way back to a signal that was not assigned a value and correct it.
- If none of the factor signals are "X," then it may be caused by multiple drivers. At this point, synthesize first, and then troubleshoot Error and Critical warning.
- The register signal may also have a value of "X" during the reset phase if it does not have a reset value, but this situation may not introduce an error.
- The result of an or operation with "X" and 1 is 1, and the result of an and operation with "X" and 0 is 0.

3.2.2.3 Waveform Stop

Waveform stop means that the simulation stops at a certain point and can no longer move forward, but the simulation still shows that it is still running; this kind of error is often caused by the existence of combinational loops in the RTL. An example of a waveform stop is shown in Fig. 3.12.

Some of the waveform stopping errors are manifested by clicking "run all," but the waveform stops immediately and a fatal is detected, as shown in Fig. 3.13; you can see that the simulation has reached the limit of 10000 iterations, which is caused by the fact that the simulation of combinational loops automatically stops after reaching the upper limit of the number of iterations. The reason for this is that the simulation of the combined loop has reached the limit of 10000 iterations, and the simulation stops automatically.

Not all combinational loops result in waveform stops. Some complex combinational loops (such as those formed across multiple modules) may be handled

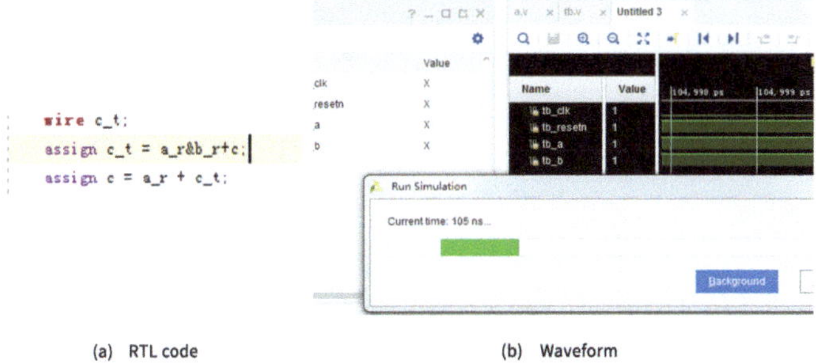

(a)   RTL code   (b)   Waveform

Fig. 3.12   Waveform stop example. (**a**) RTL code (**b**) Waveform

Fig. 3.13   Another manifestation of waveform stopping

automatically by the tool, but such handling is risky and may result in "simulation passes, board fails."

The so-called combinational loop means that a certain generating factor in the combinational logic expression of signal A is B, and the combinational logic expression of B uses signal A. For example, in the source code of Fig. 3.12, c_t is used in c, and c is used in c_t. The simulator will calculate all the expressions for this cycle with nested combinational logic loops, which will cause the simulator to loop through the calculations, and then cause it to be unable to exit, eventually leading to a phenomenon that causes the waveform to stop.

It is not easy to troubleshoot which part of the code has a combinational loop when a waveform stop occurs, and we recommend the following steps:

1. Synthesize the design first as soon as the waveform is found to have stopped.
2. Review the Error and Critical warning prompts generated by the synthesis and try to correct them. For example, the combined loop in the example in Fig. 3.12 was synthesized by Vivado into a multi-driven critical warning prompt, as shown in Fig. 3.14.

In addition, the Tcl command `report_timing_summary` in the Vivado project checks for combinational loops and reports the results. Unfortunately, for the example in Fig. 3.14, the command does not check for combinational loops, most likely due to the fact that the logics are automatically changed to multi-driven during synthesis.

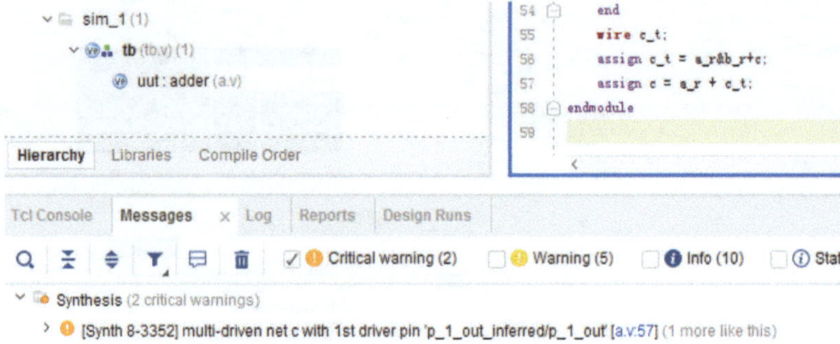

Fig. 3.14 Combinatorial logic reports critical warning for multiple drivers

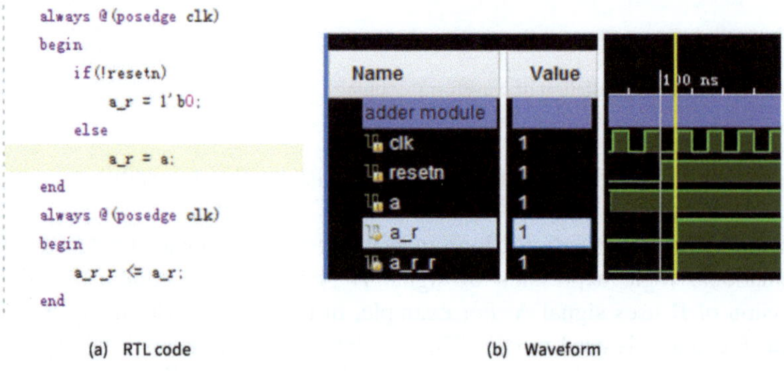

(a) RTL code   (b) Waveform

Fig. 3.15 Example of cross-edge sampling. (**a**) RTL code (**b**) Waveform

3.2.2.4 Over-Edge Sampling

Over-edge sampling is when a sampled signal is sampled at the positive edge to
its value after the positive edge and is generally considered to be an error caused
by improper use of the blocking assignment "=" and the non-blocking assignment
"<=" in the RTL.

An over-edge sampling is a well-hidden error that can often be confused with a
logic error. At first glance, the waveform looks normal, and it takes a long time for
the error to occur after the over-edge sampling. Therefore, you can start debugging
according to the logic error first, and if you find that the data sampling is abnormal,
then you need to check whether the over-edge sampling error occurs or not.

An example of over-edge sampling is given in Fig. 3.15.

As shown in Fig. 3.15, at 105 ns, when the positive edge of clk arrives, both a_r
and a_r_r change to 1 (i.e., the value of a). a_r is 0 before 105 ns and is 1 after
105 ns. a_r is 0 before 105 ns, and 1 after 105 ns. From the source code, a_r_r
samples the value of a_r at the positive edge and then samples the value of a_r as
1 at 105 ns, which means it samples the value of a_r after the same positive edge.
That is, the value of a_r is sampled after the same positive edge.

A deeper reason for this is the mixing of blocking assignment "=" and non-blocking assignment "<=" in Verilog. In the source code of Fig. 3.15, a_r uses blocking assignments and a_r_r uses non-blocking assignments. Each assignment is divided into two steps: The first step is to compute the expression on the right side of the equation; the second step is to assign the signal on the left side. These two steps are abbreviated as calculation and assignment. On a positive edge, all signals driven by the positive edge are processed in the following order:

1. Blocking assignment is processed first, i.e., the calculation and assignment are completed, and the assignment is completed immediately after the calculation of the same signal. Blocking assignments in the same always block are executed serially in order from top to bottom, and blocking assignments in different always blocks are executed serially in order according to the implementation of the tool used to complete the calculation and assignment one by one.
2. Perform the computation of non-blocking assignments. For all non-blocking assignments, the values on the right-hand side of the equation are computed simultaneously.
3. At the end of the positive edge, all non-blocking assignments simultaneously complete the final assignment action.

From the above description, we can see that the non-blocking assignment is processed in the last time step of the positive edge, which is later than the blocking assignment. Therefore, in the example in Fig. 3.15, the assignment of a_r_r is later than the assignment of a_r, resulting in an over-edge sampling.

Unless specifically designed, over-edge sampling is generally considered to be a design error. We have the following suggestions for dealing with over-edge sampling errors:

- Pay attention to the code specification when writing RTL, all always written timing logic is only allowed to use non-blocking assignments.
- Once an over-edge sampling is detected, the sampled signal is traced back until it reaches a signal that blocks the assignment and is subsequently corrected.

3.2.2.5 Waveform Oddities

We have categorized all types of waveform errors that we have not been able to think of so far as waveform oddities. When waveform oddities occur, it is important to distinguish whether the error is in the simulation tool or in the RTL code.

(1) Observe the error signals and analyze the cause. If you are sure that there is no error in the RTL, and the waveform display is too strange (e.g., always 32'hxx?x0x?), it is most likely that the simulation tool is wrong. In this case, you can restart Vivado or your computer or even rebuild the project to see if you can solve the problem.
(2) If you really can't distinguish the type of error from the waveform, you can try to synthesize it first and look at the Error, Critical warning and warning prompts

after synthesizing. Among them, Error is the one that must be corrected, Critical warning is the one that is strongly recommended to be corrected, and warning is the one that is recommended to be corrected as much as possible.

(3) Vivado will not report warnings for code that does not meet the specifications, which requires a careful review of the code.

3.3 Tasks and Practices

After completing this chapter, readers are expected to complete the following three practical tasks:

1. Register file simulation (see Sect. 3.3.1 for details).
2. Synchronous, asynchronous RAM simulation, synthesis, and implementation (see Sect. 3.3.2 for details).
3. Design and debugging of digital logic circuits (see Sect. 3.3.3 for details).

3.3.1 Practical Task 2: Register File Simulation

This practical task requires:

1. Functional simulation of a register file design is performed to understand the behavioral characteristics by observing its simulation waveforms.

The register file source code provided in the experimental environment is a "two reads and one write" structure; that is, there are two read ports (the read port has no enable bit control, indicating always enable) and a write port. The interface signals are shown in Table 3.1.

Table 3.1 Register file interface signals

Name	Width	I/O direction	Description
clk	1	input	clock
raddr1	5	input	read address 1 for reg.file
rdata1	32	output	read data 1 for reg.file
raddr2	5	input	read address 2 for reg.file
rdata2	32	output	read data 1 for reg.file
we	1	input	write enable for reg.file
waddr	5	input	write address for reg.file
wdata	32	input	write data for reg.file

Please refer to the method described in Sect. 2.3.1 to obtain the experimental development environment required for this practical task. The specific experimental environment is located at **dc_env/exp2/**, which has the following directory structure:

```
|--regfile.v              Register file source file
|--rf_tb.v                Register file test bench file
```

It is recommended to refer to the following steps to complete this practical task:

1. Create a new project using Vivado.
2. Click "Add Sources," and select "Add Design Sources" to add `regfile.v`.
3. Click "Add Sources," and select "Add Simulation Sources" to add `rf_tb.v`.
4. Perform a simulation test on the project, and observe the read and write behavior of the register file in conjunction with the waveforms.

3.3.2 Practical Task 3: Synchronous, Asynchronous RAM Simulation, Synthesis, and Implementation

This practical task requires:

1. Using Xilinx library IP to instantiate a synchronous RAM, simulate to observe behavior, synthesize, and implement to see timing results and resource utilization.
2. Using Xilinx library IP to instantiate a synchronous RAM, simulate to observe behavior, synthesize, and implement to see timing results and resource utilization.
3. Comparative analysis of observed phenomena.

Please refer to the method described in Sect. 2.3.1 to obtain the experimental development environment required for this practical task. The specific experimental environment is located at **dc_env/exp3/**, which has the following directory structure:

```
|--block_ram_top.v        top file of synchronous RAM
(Block RAM) source code
|--distributed_ram_top.v  top file of asynchronous RAM
(Distributed RAM)
|--ram.xdc                 constraint file for synthesis and
implementation
|--ram_tb.v                test bench for simulation
```

The design top-level file provided by the experimental environment is used to encapsulate both types of RAMs into the same module name and interface. The RAM top-level interface signals of the encapsulated are shown in Table 3.2

```
## Warning: One or more parsing issues, see `problems()`
## for details
```

Table 3.2 Top-level interface signals after wrapped RAM

Name	Width	I/O direction	Description
clk	1	Input	clock
ram_wen	1	Input	write enable of RAM: 1 for write..0 for read
ram_addr	16	Input	address of RAM, both for write and read
ram_wdata	32	Input	write data of RAM
ram_rdata	32	Output	read data of RAM

Note: The wrapped RAM interface has no chip select signal; i.e., the chip select enable is always active.

The reference steps for creating a synchronized RAM project are as follows:

1. Create a new project using Vivado.
2. Click "Add Sources," and select "Add Design Sources" to add `block_ram_top.v`.
3. Click "Add Sources," and select "Add Constraints" to add `ram.xdc`.
4. Click on "Add Sources," select "Add Simulation Sources," and add `ram_tb.v`.
5. Refer to Sect. 3.1 to call the Xilinx library IP to generate a synchronous RAM (Block RAM, depth 65536, width 32, chip select enable signal set to always active).

The reference steps for creating a asynchronous RAM project are as follows:

1. Create a new project using Vivado.
2. Click "Add Sources," and select "Add Design Sources" to add `distributed_ram_top.v`.
3. Click "Add Sources," and select "Add Constraints" to add `ram.xdc`.
4. Click on "Add Sources," select "Add Simulation Sources," and add `ram_tb.v`.
5. Refer to Appendix D, Sect. D.1 to call the Xilinx library IP to generate a asynchronous RAM (Distributed RAM, depth 65536, width 32).

After completing the creation of the projects, simulate them and compare the similarities and differences in read and write behaviors. After completing the simulation of the projects, synthesize and implement them, refer to the method introduced in Appendix D, Sect. D.1 to check the timing results and resource utilization, and analyze them in conjunction with the read/write timing.

In the course of practice, special attention should be paid to the following points:

- When generating IPs, please name the corresponding IPs as `block_ram` and `distributed_ram`, if you name the IPs wrongly, the IPs will report errors. If the generated IP cannot be renamed, you can delete the IP and regenerate it again.
- When generating an IP, you can click on the diagram on the left side of the window to view the interface information. When the parameters are correct, the port name and width should correspond to the call in the specified top-level file.

- Interested readers are encouraged to do their own research, refer to the information on synchronous/asynchronous RAM customization, and compare the effects of the parameters based on the simulated waveforms.
- Make sure that the constraint file (ram.xdc) is properly loaded before synthesizing the program.
- Please be careful to select add simulation source when adding testbench; otherwise, it will lead to wrong top-level files and incorrect synthesis results.
- When synthesizing a program, the synthesis time will vary somewhat depending on the computer used and may take a lot of time, so plan ahead and schedule your time.
- The generation of timing reports and resource reports requires viewing the results after the synthesis, and realization is complete.

3.3.3 Practical Task 4: Design and Debugging of Digital Logic Circuits

This practical task requires:

1. debug and correct functional errors in a given digital logic circuit design.
2. The correct function can be realized after boarding.

Please refer to the method described in Sect. 2.3.1 to obtain the experimental development environment required for this practical task. The specific experimental environment is located at **dc_env/exp4/**, which has the following directory structure:

```
|--show_sw.v            source file of digital circuit design
|--show_sw.xdc          constraint file for synthesis and
implementation
|--tb.v                 test bench for simulation
```

The design in show_sw.v has a total of five functional errors. The correct function of the design is the following:

1. Get the status of the four dip switches on the rightmost side of the development board (noted as "toggle up is 1, toggle down is 0," the actual level of the dip switches on the development board is "toggle up is low, toggle down is high"), a total of 16 statuses (the numbers are numbered 0-15). There are 16 states (the numbers are 0~15).
2. The leftmost digital tube shows the status of four dip switches in real time. The leftmost digital pipe only supports displaying 0~9, if the status of the dip switches is 10~15, then the display status of the digital tube is not changed (the previous display value is displayed).
3. The four monochrome LEDs on the rightmost side will show the status of the last dipswitch, supporting the display of 0~15 (the corresponding LEDs will be on when the dipswitch is turned on).

Table 3.3 Signals for the example design

Name	Width	I/O direction	Description
clk	1	input	clock
resetn	1	input	reset
switch	4	input	corresponding to the four right most dial switches on the development board
num_csn	8	output	digital tube chip selection signal
num_a_g	7	output	7-segment signal of digital tube

For example, in the initial state, if the four dip switches are set down and the reset button is pressed, the digital tube will display 0, and the LEDs will not light up; if the dip switches are set to 1, the digital tube will display 1 and the LEDs will not light up; if the dip switches are set to 3 again, the digital tube will display 3 and the LEDs will display 1.

The provided design source code contains five bugs, four of which are the first four cases of waveform anomalies mentioned in Sect. 3.2.2: Signal is "Z," Signal is "X," Waveform Stop, and Cross-edge Sampling, and the other bug is a functional bug.

The top-level interfaces for the example designs provided in this task are shown in Table 3.3.

Please refer to the following steps to complete this practice task:

1. Study Sect. 3.2 of this chapter and Sect. D.1 of Appendix D.
2. Create a new project using Vivado.
3. Click "Add Sources," and select "Add Design Sources" to add show_sw.v.
4. Click "Add Sources," and select "Add Constraints" to add the show_sw.xdc.
5. Click "Add Sources," select "Add Simulation Sources," and add tb.v.
6. Understand the functionality of the example design, analyze the simulation top-level tb.v, and understand the behavior of the simulation. Note that the level of the dip switches on the development board is "toggle up for low, toggle down for high," and the level behavior of the monochrome LEDs is "high level not on, low level on." The top level of the simulation, tb.v, is also designed according to this level.
7. Perform simulation and debugging with simulation-assisted tricks (splitting, grouping, color changes, flags, etc.) to find all bugs.
8. Once the simulation is complete, synthesize, implement, and generate the bitstream file.
9. After generating the bitstream file, connect to the development board, and verify the board. (This step can be skipped if you do not have a local or remote FPGA lab platform, or if you are not conducting on-board experiments.)

Chapter 4
Design A Single-Cycle CPU

In the previous chapters, we have introduced the relevant experimental platforms and reviewed digital logic circuits and Verilog programming which is foundational for CPU design. From this chapter, we will enter the main part of the book, basic CPU design. We will start from designing and realizing a "mini" single-cycle CPU with only five instructions and add instructions and other functions step by step. Finally, we will design a pipelined CPU that supports TLB MMU and Cache and can run an operating system.

In this chapter, we will focus on the design of a single-cycle CPU. The work is divided into two phases: first, design a single-cycle CPU with 5 instructions; second, add instructions to 20. This chapter is organized with a slower pace to cater for beginners. The design scheme and experimental environment are intertwined to follow the learning habits of beginners. But for readers who already have foundation in CPU design, it is recommended to go through this chapter and its practical tasks quickly, mainly to be familiar with the terminology, design style, and experimental development environment of this book, so that you can move on to the practical tasks in the following chapters more smoothly.

Learning Goals for this Chapter
- Establish the cognitive link between design and Verilog implementation.
- Develop good Verilog coding habits.
- Master some methods for debugging in CPU functional simulation, and acquire basic debugging capability.

Practical Tasks of this Chapter
There are two practical tasks in this chapter (see Sect. 4.6). Readers can complete these tasks after learning this chapter. The correspondence between sections and tasks is as follows:

- Sections 4.1 and 4.2 are corresponding to Task 5 (Sect. 4.6.1).
- Sections 4.3 and 4.4 are corresponding to Task 6 (Sect. 4.6.2).

© The Author(s), under exclusive license to Springer Nature Singapore Pte Ltd. 2025
W. Wang, J. Xing, *CPU Design and Practice*,
https://doi.org/10.1007/978-981-96-6573-0_4

4.1   Five-Instruction Single-Cycle CPU

Everything is difficult at the beginning. We manage the complexity of the designed CPU by reducing the number of instructions implemented. We choose 5 instructions from LoongArch32-Reduced Instruction Set: add.w, addi.w, ld.w, st.w, and bne. Though there are merely five instructions, they can be implemented to build the basic framework of a single-cycle CPU, and can be used to run a useful small program.

4.1.1   General Idea of CPU Design

Before we start designing a five-instruction, single-cycle CPU, let's ask ourselves a question: What are the design inputs and design outputs when designing a CPU?

The answer is that the input to the design is the instruction set architecture (ISA), and the output of the design is a digital logic circuit that implements the functions defined by the ISA. The next step is to first understand the ISA and then to design the circuit structure of the CPU based on the general design methodology of digital logic circuits.

4.1.1.1   Instruction Set Architecture

The ISA is the language system of the computer hardware, also called machine language, which is the interface between the computer software and hardware and reflects the basic functions of the computer. ISA is a document that defines each element of the instruction system. The CPU experiments in this book are based on the LoongArch32 Reduced (LA32R) instruction set architecture. This ISA is streamlined from the LoongArch32 ISA. The functions of LA32R are complete and can support the mainstream UNIX-like operating systems. For details, please refer to the *LoongArch32 Reduced Instruction Set Architecture Reference Manual* (hereinafter referred as *Instruction Manual*). Considering that many of the readers of this book are students in university who seldom read this kind of documents, here are some tips for reading.

The *Instruction Manual*, as a specification document, mainly describes the details of the instruction set but rarely discusses why it is designed in such way and even more rarely has examples. There is a significant difference between this style of writing and that of textbooks, theses, and technical reports. As a result, many students and readers spend a lot of time reading it but do not know what it is all about. It is not easy for them to memorize it after reading it. We should use *Instruction Manual* as tools rather than textbooks. In order to "use" *Instruction Manual* well, we need to acquire the ability from systematic theoretical study. For example, we can study the second part of *Fundamentals of Computer Architecture*

(3rd edition) to understand the meanings and uses of the basic components of the instruction set, the design concepts and main features of the RISC instruction set, and the similarities and differences between various typical RISC instruction set. Based on these general understanding, we can go through the *Instruction Manual* and then read the relevant chapters word by word when you are designing a specific program clarifying the specific details. In this book, we will also refer to the relevant chapters of the *Instruction Manual* in relation to the specific design requirements and introduce their relationship with the basic concepts in the textbook when necessary, so as to help readers in their study and practice.

The *LoongArch32 Reduced Instruction Set Architecture Reference Manual* can be roughly divided into four parts: Overview (Chapter 1), User Mode (Chapters 2–3), Privileged Mode (Chapters 4–7), and Instruction Coding (Appendix B). The practical tasks in this book will follow the steps of implementing the user-mode instructions first and then the privileged-mode functions. When implementing user-mode instructions, we will mainly refer to Section 1.2~1.4 in Chapter 1 of the *Instruction Manual*, Chapter 2, and Appendix B. (Chapter 3 involves Floating-Point instructions, which is not involved in the practical tasks of this book.) In this part, the functional introduction of instructions will be divided into chapters according to the functional characteristics instead of the dictionary order of instruction mnemonics, which is more convenient for software developers to find; the instruction codes are unified in Appendix B, which will save readers the work of collecting instruction code information from different places in the *Instruction Manual*. When implementing the functions related to the privileged mode, the definitions of privilege levels, exceptions, and interrupts and memory management are defined in Section 4.1, Chapter 6, and Chapter 5 of the *Instruction Manual*, respectively. The use of privileged-mode functions by the software requires the use of privileged instructions and control status registers, which are defined in Section 4.2 and Chapter 7 of the *Instruction Manual*, respectively. The entire privileged-mode section is described with minimal redundancy, so that when implementing a specific function, readers need to combine the information in Section 4.1, Chapter 5 and Chapter 6, and in Section 4.2 and Chapter 7 to fully understand.

4.1.1.2   General Methodology for CPU Design

Returning to the question posed at the beginning of this section, since we are designing a CPU as a digital logic circuit, its design should follow the general method of digital logic circuit design. Not only does the CPU have to perform operations, but it also has to maintain its own state, so the digital logic circuit of the CPU must have both combinational logic circuits and sequential logic circuits. The data input, operation, storage, and output of the CPU flow on the combinational logic circuits and sequential logic circuits, which are often called as datapath. Therefore, in order to design the CPU as a digital logic circuit, the first thing to do is to design the datapath. Meanwhile, the datapath will have a multiplexer and sequential logic components, so that there are also corresponding control signals.

The logic that generates these control signals is called control logic. Therefore, from a macro point of view, the design of a CPU is to design its **datapath and control logic**.

So, how to design the "datapath and control logic" according to the specification in ISA? The basic method is to functionally decompose the instructions defined in the *Instruction Manual* one by one to obtain a series of operations and objects of operations. Obviously, these operations and objects must correspond to their respective datapaths. Since there are some identical or similar operations and objects between instructions, we can design only one set of datapath for multiple instructions to share. In the case where there is a difference that makes it impossible to share the datapath, we can design a set of datapaths for each of the instructions and then use a multiplexer to select the desired result from them.

4.1.2   Datapath of Five-Instruction Single-Cycle CPU

We will follow the general design methodology mentioned before, analyze add.w, addi.w, ld.w, st.w, and bne instructions, and build CPU datapaths.

4.1.2.1   Instruction add.w

Let's analyze what datapath components are needed for instruction add.w.

First, the instruction is fetched from memory. How? CPU treats the PC of this instruction as a virtual address, using the address translation unit to get the physical address, and then accesses the memory. Therefore, datapath components include PC, address translation unit, and memory.

1. PC

Since this CPU is a 32-bit processor, PC width is 32 bits. A set of 32-bit flip-flops will be used to store the PC. (Later, for the sake of brevity, we will use PC to represent the set of 32-bit flip-flops used to store the PC, if this does not lead to confusion.) The output of the PC will be sent to the address translation unit to get physical address. Up to present, there are two inputs to PC, one is the reset value 0x1C000000, and the other is the value obtained by updating PC + 4 for every instruction executed after the reset is reversed. The 4 here means addressing 4 bytes, i.e., the width of one instruction, so PC + 4 is the PC value of the instruction after the current instruction. The reset value 0x1C000000 of PC refers to Section 6.3 in *Instruction Manual*.

2. Address Translation Unit

As mentioned above, PC will be input to the virtual-to-physical address translation unit for address conversion. This component is seldom mentioned in most textbooks. However, we emphasize that the address that appears in the program running on the

CPU at any given time is virtual address, while the addresses used by the CPU itself to access memory and I/O are physical address. Even if a ISA specifies that the value of a physical address always equal to the virtual address value, it does not mean that the two concepts are equivalent and interchangeable. We emphasize the virtual-physical address translation unit at the outset, so that the reader will know where to start when implementing the TLB MMU later.

How does the virtual address translate into physical address? Before implementing TLB MMU, the CPU will merely support Direct Address Translation mode (see Section 5.2 of *Instruction Manual*). In this address translation mode, when the physical address of the CPU is also implemented as 32-bit wide, the value of the physical address is directly equal to the value of the virtual address.

3. Instruction RAM

After obtaining the physical address required for fetching the instruction, the next step is to send the address to the memory. We follow the classic model from textbooks and use on-chip RAM as the memory and split the RAM into two physically independent RAMs, the instruction RAM and the data RAM, to simplify the design.

(1) Asynchronous Read Instruction RAM

After practical tasks in Chap. 3, readers can have a clear understanding of the timing characteristics of RAM. The RAMs commonly used in current engineering are **Synchronous Read RAM**;[1] i.e., the read request and address are sent in the first cycle, and the read data is output in the second cycle. However, it is impossible to implement a single-cycle CPU with this kind of RAM, unless it does not implement any load instruction. So Synchronous Read RAM can merely be used into a multi-cycle CPU. Therefore, we temporarily use an **Asynchronous Read RAM**[2] to implement the instruction RAM and data RAM in the single-cycle CPU design. The read timing behavior of Asynchronous Read RAM is similar to that of a register-file read, where the data is tapped when the read enable and read address are given, and the write timing behavior is the same as that of a Synchronous Read RAM.

Due to the implemented CPU's instruction width being 32 bits, the width of the instruction RAM must be at least 32 bits to ensure the ideal requirement of executing one instruction per cycle. Since the instruction RAM is essentially memory, its addressing unit is a byte, so the address input port of the instruction RAM cannot be directly connected to the physical address after virtual-to-physical address translation. In the given design, we have determined the width of the instruction RAM to be 32 bits, at which point the address input for the instruction RAM is the result of rounding down the instruction address after dividing by 4.

Although the instruction RAM is temporarily implemented with asynchronous read behavior, we still need to reserve a read enable input port for it. This is to

---

[1] Corresponding to block RAM in Xilinx FPGA.
[2] Corresponding to distributed RAM in Xilinx FPGA.

ensure the unity of the interface when the RAM is replaced with a synchronous read RAM during the implementation of the pipelined CPU later on. The read enable of the instruction RAM as a control signal will be introduced later.

(2) Fetched Instructions
The 32-bit data output from the instruction RAM is the instruction code, and the LoongArch instruction system uses little-endian addressing, so the 32-bit data output from the instruction RAM is in the same byte order as defined in the *Instruction Manual*, requiring no adjustment of byte order.

4. Analysis of Instruction Definition
After datapath has been established in the fetch part and the instruction has been fetched, the rest datapath of the instruction must be designed according to the instruction definition. The definition of this instruction is in the *Instruction Manual*, Section 2.2.1.1, while the coding format is in Appendix B.

Let's first look at the definition of the encoding format of the instruction. It adopts the 3R-type instruction encoding format, in which the instruction code of the bits 31..15 (opcode field) must be `0b0000000000000100000` (the leading character `0b` indicates a subsequent binary format). Once this field of the fetched instruction code satisfies this value, the instruction is an `add.w` instruction. In this case, the value of bits 9...5 of the code indicates the `rj` register number, the value of bits 14...10 indicates the `rk` register number, and the value of bits 4...0 indicates the `rd` register number.

Further, the definition of an instruction consists of two main parts: the instruction format definition and the instruction function description.

The instruction format is the format of the instruction in assembly language. Here, pay attention that the register number of the destination operand is placed at first, followed by the register numbers of the source operands, `rj` and `rk`, in that order. When you debug the CPU later on, you will certainly look at the source code of test program, most of which is written in assembly language, and the disassembled code of compiled executable files. Therefore, reading the meaning of each instruction is an essential skill.

Instruction descriptions contain both natural language and pseudo-code forms. These two forms are not simple duplications. Generally, pseudo-code descriptions are less prone to ambiguity, while natural language can emphasize more technical details, such as the determination of exceptions and the handling of special cases. The two complement each other to form a precise definition of the instruction. The pseudo-code descriptions used here are more intuitive, and most of the operations are self-explanatory. If you want to know the exact definitions of the operators and functions, you can refer to Appendix A of the *Instruction Manual*.

Back to the specific analysis of the instruction `add.w`. We understand that the `add.w` instruction reads the value of general-purpose register `rj` and general-purpose register `rk`, adds the two numbers together, and writes the result to general-purpose register `rd`. This means that a general-purpose register file and an adder need to be added to the datapath.

5. General-Purpose Register File

We have introduced the concept of register file in Chap. 3 when we reviewed digital logic circuits. According to the definition in *Instruction Manual* (see Section 2.1.2.1 for details), the CPU we design should have a 32-item, 32-bit wide register file. According to the definition of the instruction add.w, the register file should have at least two read ports and one write port in order to complete the instruction add.w in one cycle. When we design at the top level of the CPU, we consider the general-purpose register file as a submodule. In other words, at this level of design, we do not consider the internal implementation of the general-purpose register file module but only focus on its interface and the functional characteristics it exhibits externally. Here we focus on the connection of the input/output ports of the general-purpose register file.

We connect the address input of the read port 1 of the register file to the rj field of the instruction code, the address input of the read port 2 to the rk field of the instruction code, and the address input of the write port to the rd field of the instruction code. The enable signals of the read and write ports are treated as control signals, which will be described later.

6. Adder

The operation of the instruction add.w requires an adder that takes two 32-bit inputs, src1 and src2, and outputs a 32-bit result. Similar to the general-purpose register file mentioned above, at this stage, we also treat the adder as a submodule, focusing only on the connections of its input/output ports.

We connect rdata1, the output of general-purpose register file read port 1 (i.e., the value of register rj), to src1 of the adder, rdata2, the output of general-purpose register file read port 2 (that is, the value of register rk), to src2 of the adder, and result, the output of the adder, to the general-purpose register file write data port, wdata.

At this point in the introduction, all the datapaths required by the instruction add.w have been constructed, as shown in Fig. 4.1.

4.1.2.2 Revisiting Module Division

Before delving into the analysis of new instructions, let's revisit the issue of how to divide modules. In the previous Chap. 3, this was briefly mentioned, but the examples were too simplistic to form an effective understanding.

From the datapath design process of the add.w instruction, readers should be able to appreciate the benefits of encapsulating RAM, register files, and adders into modules. This approach allows us to design the top level of the CPU without involving in too many low-level circuit details. So, how should modules be divided? Based on personal experience, we offer the following suggestions:

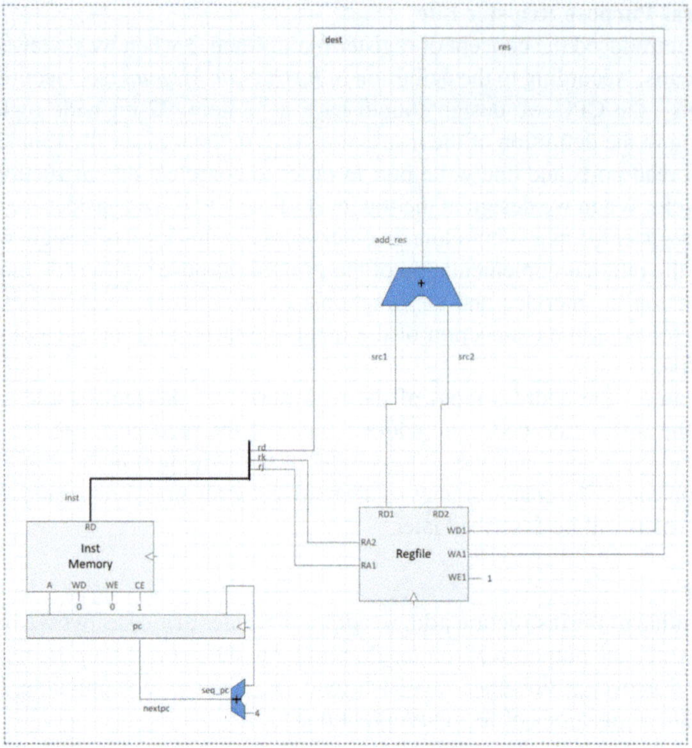

Fig. 4.1 Single-cycle CPU datapath for add.w

1. If there are many design details at a certain level, and it is difficult to draw a clear structural diagram, then it is possible to consider encapsulating a part of the logic into a module, thereby replacing this part of the content with a box in the structural diagram.

2. The interface of the module should not be too complex. Obviously, the encapsulated module should not have too many interfaces; otherwise, the diagram will still be difficult to draw clearly. If the divided module still has nearly a hundred or even hundreds of interface signals, then the division may not be very good. Here, the focus is mainly on lower-level modules, while higher-level modules tend to have many ports.

3. Logic that can be used in multiple places in a design, or has a standard and universal function, and can be reused in multiple designs, is also suitable for encapsulation into modules, for example, decoders, multiplexers, register files, RAM, FIFO, etc. If possible, these modules should also be developed into parameterized configurations, so that they can be reused in new designs, and some module-level verification work can also be saved.

4. For combinational logic distributed in two modules, the data on it should try to present a single-direction flow, at most one way and then back. If the data

between the combinational logic of the two modules goes back and forth multiple times, then it is necessary to examine whether the module division is reasonable.

4.1.2.3 Instruction `addi.w`

Upon reviewing the definition of the addi.w instruction in the instruction manual and comparing it with the previously discussed add.w instruction, it can be observed that the addi.w instruction and the add.w instruction perform highly similar functions. The only difference lies in the fact that the second source operand in the addi.w instruction is not derived from a register but is directly obtained from the immediate field in the instruction code. The similarity in function between these two instructions implies that for the instruction fetching, execution, and result writing-back phases, the majority of the datapaths can be reused. However, since there are differences between addi.w and add.w, the main task in designing the addi.w instruction is to consider how to accommodate these differences while maximizing the reuse of the datapaths. Let's analyze starting with the differences.

Firstly, it should be self-evident that the adder can be fully reused. When processing the add.w instruction, the second source operand is the output data rdata2 from the read port 2 of the general register file. In contrast, when processing the addi.w instruction, the second source operand is the data formed by sign-extending the bits 21..10 of the instruction code to 32 bits. The second input data source for the adder needs to be handled differently, which is reflected in the circuit design by introducing a 32-bit "two-to-one" component. Specifically, we connect the data input port in0 of this "two-to-one" component to the output data rdata2 of the read port 2 of the general register file, the data input port in1 to the data formed by sign-extending the bits 21..10 of the instruction code to 32 bits, and the data output port out to the second data input of the adder. It is clear that there is still an input for the selection signal of this "two-to-one" component that has not been connected. We treat the selection signal inputs of these multiplexers as control signals, which will be introduced uniformly later. Here, it is only hinted that the instruction encoding definitions of addi.w and add.w are distinguishable, and this information can be used to generate the control signals for the multiplexers.

With further consideration for the addi.w instruction, the design adjustments to the CPU datapath are complete, as shown in Fig. 4.2.

4.1.2.4 Instruction ld.w

According to the definition of ld.w instruction in the instruction system specification document, if not considering the content related to exceptions, the function of the ld.w instruction in the instruction fetching phase is the same as that of computational instructions such as add.w. Further analysis of its execution phase yields the following three key points:

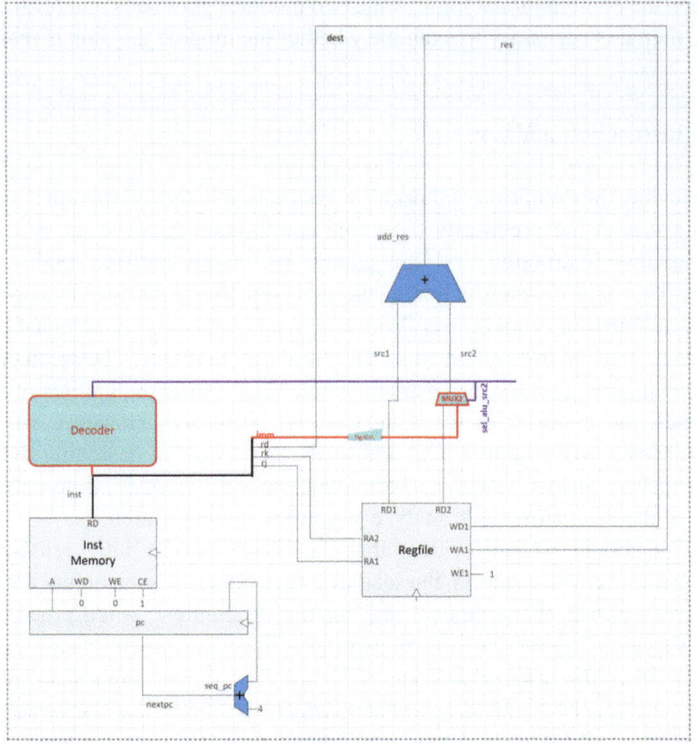

Fig. 4.2 Single-cycle CPU datapath after adding addi.w

1. The value of the base register rj is added to the immediate number si12 in the instruction code to obtain the virtual address vaddr.
2. Translate the virtual address vaddr to the physical address paddr through virtual-to-physical address mapping.
3. Based on paddr, data is read from memory.

1. Memory Address Generation

Carefully comparing the calculation required in the first point above with the calculation of the addi.w instruction, it will be found that the functions of the two are completely identical. This means that the ld.w instruction can fully reuse the datapath of addi.w during the execution phase, and the control signal values at the "two-way selection" end of the path are also the same as those of the addi.w instruction.

The translation process of virtual and physical addresses in the second point above follows the same specification as the process of translating the PC to a physical address during the instruction fetching phase. However, since the translated physical address will be used for data accessing rather than instructions fetching, a separate virtual-to-physical address translation unit is required. Its input is connected to the output of the adder's result, and its output is connected to memory—specifically, the data RAM in the design.

2. Data RAM

To achieve the goal of executing one ld.w instruction per cycle, the data RAM employs the same "asynchronous read RAM" as the instruction RAM. As for the specific specifications of the RAM, since the ld.w instruction accesses a 32-bit wide word each time, the width of the RAM should not be less than 32 bits. In the given design, the width of the data RAM is set to 32 bits. At this time, the address input of the data RAM is the value obtained by dividing the physical memory address by 4 and rounding down, and the data output of the data RAM is the result of the ld.w instruction execution.[3]

Although the data RAM is temporarily implemented with asynchronous read behavior, we still need to reserve a read enable input port for it. This is to ensure the uniformity of the interface when the RAM is replaced with a synchronous read RAM in the later stages of implementing a pipelined CPU. The read enable of the data RAM, as a control signal, will be introduced uniformly later.

3. Register File Write-Back Result Selection

With the introduction of the ld.w instruction, there are two sources for writing back to the general-purpose register file: One is the result of the adder (corresponding to the add.w and addi.w instructions), and the other is the output of the data RAM. Clearly, we can introduce a "two-out-of-one" component, with its data input in0 connected to the result of the adder, and in1 connected to the output of the data RAM. The selected result is connected to the data input wdata of the general-purpose register file write port. As for which item of the general-purpose register file the ld.w instruction writes to, it is determined by the rd field in the instruction code, which is the same as the addi.w instruction, so the generation logic of the address input for the general-purpose register file write port can reuse existing logic.

Thus, after further considering the ld.w instruction, the design adjustments to the CPU datapath are completed, as shown in Figure@ref[4] (Fig. 4.3).

4.1.2.5   Instruction st.w

Upon reviewing the definitions of the st.w in the instruction manual and compare it with ld.w instructions, it is evident that both instructions share identical stages for instruction fetching, address calculation, and virtual to physical address translation.

---

[3]The correct description here requires an implicit premise, that is, the memory address accessed by ld.w is a multiple of 4. When the address is not a multiple of 4, executing ld.w will trigger a misaligned address exception.

[4]mailto:Figure@ref

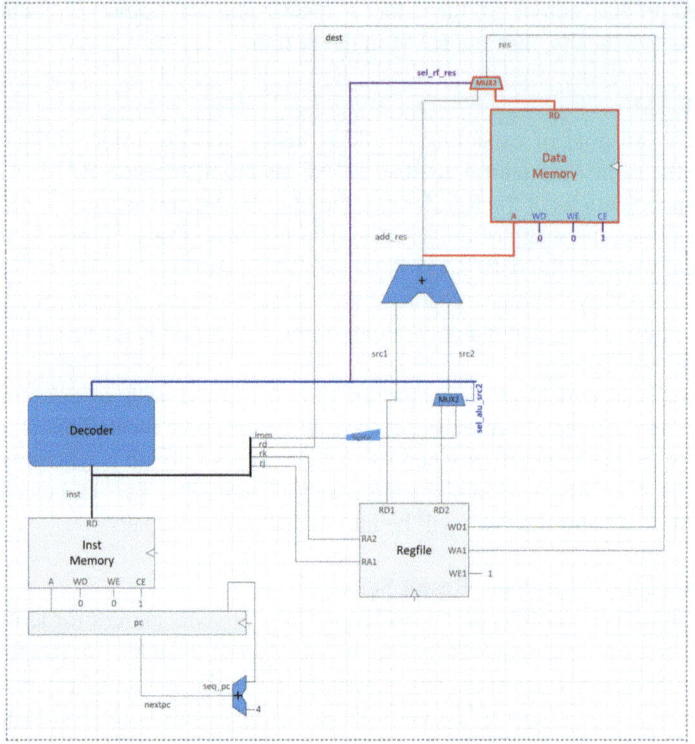

Fig. 4.3 Single-cycle CPU datapath after adding ld.w

The primary difference lies in the fact that the ld.w instruction reads from the data RAM and writes to the general-purpose register, whereas the st.w instruction reads from the general-purpose register and writes to the data RAM. Consequently, the existing datapaths can largely be reused, with the need to add new datapaths specifically for writing to the data RAM.

We will introduce the write enable for the data RAM as a control signal later on. For now, the main focus is on the design of the datapath for the data input of the data RAM write port. According to the instruction definition, the value written to memory is the content of the rd register, which means that rd also serves as a source operand. A straightforward design approach would be to add another read port to the register file, but this solution has too large an area overhead. The design solution proposed here is to maintain the two existing read ports of the register file and introduce a "two-out-of-one" component. Its data input in0 is connected to the rk field of the instruction code, and data input in1 is connected to the rd field of the instruction code. The selected result is input to the address input raddr2 of the register file read port 2. Finally, the output rdata2 from the general-purpose register file read port 2 is connected to the write data input port wdata of the data RAM.

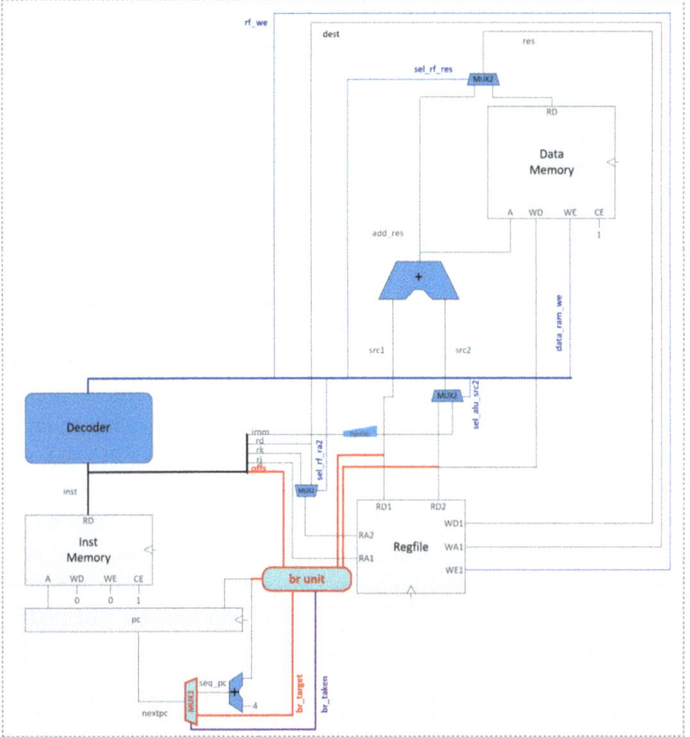

Fig. 4.4 Single-cycle CPU datapath after adding st.w

Thus, after further consideration of the st.w instruction, the design adjustments to the CPU datapath are completed, as shown in Fig. 4.4.

4.1.2.6   Instruction bne

By examining the definition of the bne instruction in the instruction manual, we can summarize the three key functions of branch instructions:

1. Evaluate the Branch Condition, and determine whether to perform a jump.
2. Calculate the Jump Targets.
3. If a jump is to be taken, change the PC to the target address; otherwise, increment the PC by 4.

1. Evaluate the Branch Condition
The bne instruction determines whether to jump based on a numerical comparison between two source operands from registers. How should the branch comparison logic be designed? One approach is to reuse the adder in the ALU to subtract the two

source operands and see if the result is all zeros; another approach is to implement a separate branch comparison logic. If we only look at these two instructions and the CPU is implemented as a single-cycle, the first approach is actually feasible. However, considering the implementation of more transfer instructions in the future, and the more efficient handling of control hazards in pipelined CPUs, the second approach will be more reasonable. Here, we directly choose the second design approach.

Let me digress for a moment. In real engineering, the process of CPU structure design is a process of repeated iteration and gradual refinement, not as smooth and seamless as described in textbooks. For beginners, this iterative process is even more necessary. When readers are engaged in practical tasks such as AXI, TLB, etc., they often have the urge to overturn their previous designs. This situation usually arises, because they are stuck in the implementation of a functional point, and it is difficult to get the correct code with a "fixing the symptom rather than the cause" approach, which only makes the situation more chaotic, and in the end, they would rather redo the entire design. In fact, this phenomenon is normal, and it should not be considered as a lack of ability. What we want to remind everyone is that the reason for wanting to start over is that the previous top-level design did not consider the situation comprehensively enough, so the redesign must be a reconstruction based on a more comprehensive consideration. If you haven't had that feeling of suddenly seeing the bigger picture from a higher perspective, don't rush to overturn the design.

Back to the branch comparison logic of the bne instruction. The main body of this logic is a 32-bit full comparator, which uses the result of whether the two numbers are equal to produce the final result of whether the branch jump condition is established.

Another thing to note is that the second source operand used for comparison in the bne instruction comes from the rd field register, not the rk field register. In the implementation of the st.w instruction datapath, a datapath has been designed to read data from the register file's read port 2 based on the register number in the rd field, which can be reused here.

2. Calculate the Jump Targets

The bne instruction is a PC-relative branch transfer instruction, meaning that their jump targets are obtained by adding a fixed offset to their own PC. This offset is a constant value, placed as an immediate number within the instruction code, and according to the instruction manual, it is located in the 25..10 bits of the instruction code. This immediate field starts at the same position as the immediate field analyzed in the addi.w, ld.w, and st.w instructions, with the difference being that its width is 16 bits. Here, we need to consider the design of the datapath for this "PC+offs" addition operation. The most straightforward design plan is to reuse the implemented adder. If we only consider the design of a single-cycle CPU, this design idea is quite good. However, considering the subsequent pipeline CPU design to reduce the blocking overhead caused by control hazards as much as possible, the processing of transfer instructions will be moved as early as possible in the pipeline.

Therefore, if a separate adder is used to complete the calculation of the jump target, it will be more convenient to optimize the structure later. We adopt the second design idea here.

Additionally, there is a small detail to note: The immediate offset offs of the branch instruction is shifted two bits to the left before being added to its own PC. This is because all instructions in the LoongArch instruction set are 32 bits wide and require PC to be aligned to a 4-byte boundary, so the offset value encoded in the branch instruction does not need to retain the lowest two bits, thus achieving a larger jump range.

3. Update PC

After considering the branch instructions, the update of the PC in the processor is no longer just the case of "current PC plus 4" but also includes the situation where it is updated to the jump target when a branch instruction is taken. In the design, we introduce a 2-to-1 multiplexer component that selects the next instruction's PC corresponding to either situation to become the nextPC used for updating the PC. The result of PC plus 4 is connected to the in0 of the "multiplexer," and the jump target address of the branch instruction is connected to the in1 of the "multiplexer." There are two conditions for selecting in0: First, the current instruction is not a branch instruction; second, the current instruction is a branch instruction, but this branch instruction does not branch. There is only one condition for selecting in1: The current instruction is a branch instruction and it branches.

However, there is another design approach for the PC update logic, where nextPC always comes from the result of a single "PC plus offset" adder. When there is no branch instruction or there is a branch instruction that does not jump, the offset input to the adder is 4; otherwise, it is the relative offset of the branch instruction. For a single-cycle CPU, this design approach is actually quite good. However, when we consider the subsequent pipeline CPU design, it is more appropriate to divide the PC update into two major categories: sequential instruction fetching and nonsequential instruction fetching, because the former's update source is limited to the location of the PC, while the latter will have various situations, and the update source is located in several other positions within the CPU. Then, calculating the update values from each position first and then passing them to the PC for a simple multiplexer operation is more reasonable in terms of circuit delay and code readability.

Thus, the further consideration of the design adjustment of the CPU datapath after the bne instruction is completed, as shown in Fig. 4.5.

4.1.3   *Five-Instruction Single-Cycle CPU Control Signal Generation*

In this section, we trace all control signals starting from the PC along the datapath.

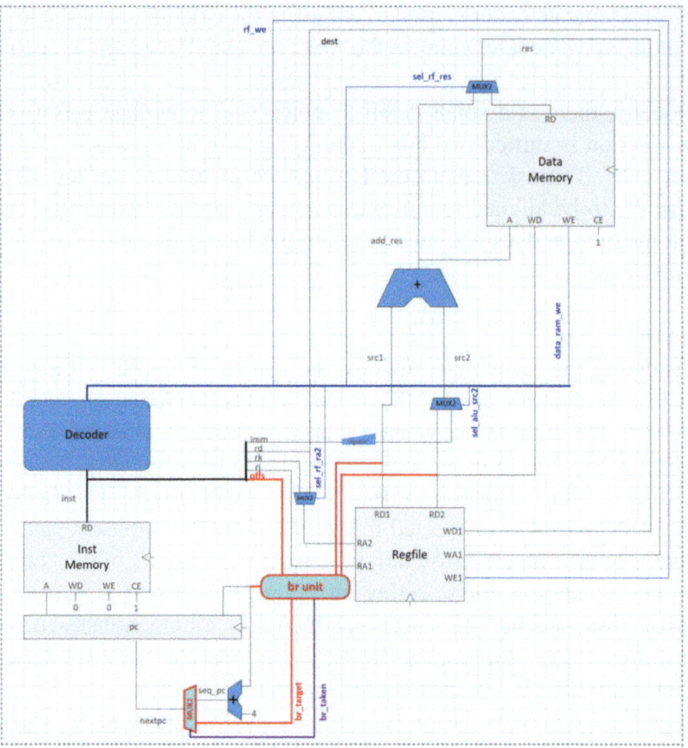

Fig. 4.5 Single-cycle CPU datapath after adding bne

1. The input generation logic of the PC, GenNextPC, contains a "multiplexer" component. Its two inputs are in0 corresponds to the sequential instruction fetch PC (i.e., PC+4) and in1 corresponds to the jump target of the bne instruction. We use the signal br_taken, which indicates the branch instruction jump, as the selection signal for this "multiplexer," selecting in1 when it is 1, otherwise selecting in0.

2. The write enable signal of the instruction RAM, inst_ram_we, is active high. Our current design does not consider operations such as self-modifying code, so the instruction RAM will not have write requests from the CPU. At the same time, the initialization of the instruction RAM content is loaded by the internal circuitry of the FPGA itself, not written through external devices (such as DMA), so the inst_ram_we signal is always 0.

3. The read address generation logic of the general register file read port 2, GenRFRdAddr2, contains a "multiplexer" component, with two inputs: in0 corresponds to the rk field of the instruction code, and in1 corresponds to the rd field of the instruction code. The selection signal of this "multiplexer" component, sel_rf_ra2, is a 1-bit signal, selecting in1 when it is 1, otherwise selecting in0.

4. The source operand input src2 generation logic of the adder, GenAdderSrc2, contains a "multiplexer" component, with two inputs: in0 corresponds to the data read out from the general register file read port 2, and in1 corresponds to the si12 field of the instruction code sign-extended to 32 bits. The selection signal of this "multiplexer" component, sel_adder_src2, selects in1 when it is 1, otherwise selecting in0.
5. The write enable signal of the data RAM, data_ram_we, is active high.
6. The write enable signal of the general register file is rf_we, active high.
7. The write data generation logic of the general register file, GenRFRes, contains a "multiplexer" component. Its two inputs are: in0 corresponds to the ALU computation result alu_res, and in1 corresponds to the load operation return value ld_res read from RAM. The selection signal of this "multiplexer" component, sel_rf_res, is a 1-bit signal, selecting in1 when it is 1, otherwise selecting in0.

After sorting out the control signals required in the datapath of five-instruction single-cycle CPU, the resulting design is shown in the Fig. 4.6.

We analyze each instruction one by one and get the correspondence between each instruction and all the control signals, as shown in Table 4.1.

The table above, which illustrates the relationship between instructions and control signals, is crucial for designing the logic for generating control signals. As you continue to add instructions in future practices, both dimensions of the table will expand, but the fundamental principle remains consistent. It is essential for all readers to understand the content of this table.

With the table above, what is the specific control signal generation logic? A readable coding style is to first generate 1-bit identifier signals for each instruction based on the instruction code and then use these instruction identifier signals to produce the final control signals. The logic of instruction identifier signals in VerilogHDL is described as follows:

```
assign op_31_26 = inst[31:26];
assign op_25_22 = inst[25:22];
assign op_21_20 = inst[21:20];
assign op_19_15 = inst[19:15];

decoder_6_64 u_dec0(.in(op_31_26), .out(op_31_26_d));
decoder_4_16 u_dec1(.in(op_25_22), .out(op_25_22_d));
decoder_2_4  u_dec2(.in(op_21_20), .out(op_21_20_d));
decoder_5_32 u_dec3(.in(op_19_15), .out(op_19_15_d));

assign inst_add_w  = op_31_26_d[6'h00] & op_25_22_d[4'h0] &
 ↪  op_21_20_d[2'h1]
                    & op_19_15_d[5'h00];
assign inst_addi_w = op_31_26_d[6'h00] & op_25_22_d[4'ha];
......
```

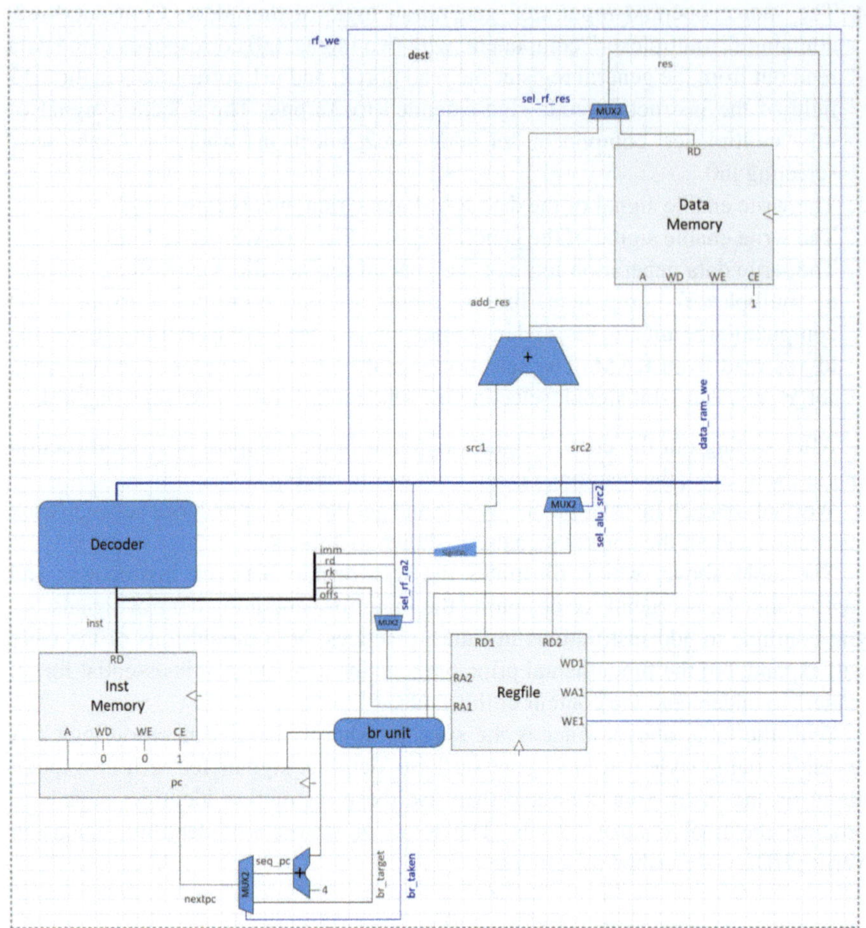

Fig. 4.6 Single-cycle CPU microarchitecture design

Table 4.1 Five-instruction single-cycle CPU control signals generation list

...1	br_taken	sel_rf_ra2	sel_adder_src2	data_ram_we	rf_we	sel_rf_res
add.w	0	0	0	0	1	0
addi.w	0	0	1	0	1	0
ld.w	0	0	1	0	1	1
st.w	0	1	1	1	0	0
bne	?	1	0	0	0	0

An example VerilogHDL code for generating the `data_ram_we` signal is given below:

```
assign data_ram_we = inst_st_w;
```

From the example above, it can be seen that as long as the correspondence between instructions and control signals is clearly organized, the logic for generating control signals becomes quite straightforward. Even without using case statements, the logic is still clear and easy to understand.

4.2   Verification of Five-Instruction Single-Cycle CPU

Up to this point, we have developed a design plan for a five-instruction single-cycle CPU. Following the stages of chip design work introduced in Chap. 1, we now need to describe this design plan using the Verilog language and then carry out functional and performance verification. How to describe the circuit presented in the design plan with Verilog has been introduced in Chap. 3. Here, we will provide a more specific introduction on how to verify the functional correctness of the CPU.

4.2.1   Quick Start Guide for Five-Instruction Single-Cycle CPU Experimental Development Environment

As the saying goes, "a good horse with a good saddle." In order to successfully complete the CPU design experiments, we need a suitable experimental development environment. This book is equipped with a series of CPU experimental development environments. These environments will integrate more new features as the functions of the CPU increase. They are built along the same lines, so that readers can spend less effort on learning the experimental environments as long as they follow the experimental schedule we have organized. Then, we will access the simplest five-instruction single-cycle CPU experimental development environment and learn the quick steps to get started with it.

4.2.1.1   Obtain the Experimental Development Environment

The five-instruction single-cycle CPU experimental development environment is obtained in the same way as in the previous practical tasks. If you are unfamiliar with it, please review the introduction in Sect. 2.3.1. Again, make sure that the development environment is located in a location without non-ASCII character in the path.

The development environment for the five-instruction single-cycle CPU is located in the first-level subdirectory minicpu_env of the project.

4.2.1.2 Develop CPU Code

Write the Verilog code of CPU in your customary text editor.[5] Note that the module names and interface signals of the top-level modules must be defined according to the specifications.

4.2.1.3 Integrate CPU

In the normal experiment procedure, you need to copy the written Verilog code of the CPU to the specified directory of the experiment development environment. However, in order to minimize the difficulty of the beginner's phase, we have already prepared a set of Verilog code for the first five-instruction single-cycle CPU experiment. Readers need to fill in the blanks. The code is located in the `minicpu_env/miniCPU/` directory.

4.2.1.4 Open Vivado Project

Create the Vivado project in the `minicpu_env/soc_verify/run_vivado/` directory. If no project has been created in this directory, please refer to the steps described in Appendix D.2 to create a project using the `create_project.tcl` file in the `minicpu_env/soc_verify/run_vivado/` directory. If a project has already been created in that directory as described above, you can directly run `loongson.xpr` in the `minicpu_env/soc_verify/run_vivado/project/` directory.

4.2.1.5 Simulate to Verify CPU

Perform a Simulation in the opened Vivado project. Observe the simulation output log to determine if there are any errors.

---

[5]The text editor integrated in Vivado is relatively simple in its functionality. We highly recommend you to use a text editor dedicated to code development.

4.2.1.6 Verify CPU on FPGA

If the Simulation process is errorless, we can start Synthesis and Implementation. If successful, we can test our CPU on the FPGA board. If the FPGA test match with the experimental requirements, the experiment is successful. Otherwise, we need to debug and troubleshoot the issues.

4.2.2 Introduction to the Organizational Structure of the `minicpu_env` Experimental Development Environment

The directory structure of the entire `minicpu_env` experimental development environment and a brief description of the functions of each part are shown below:

```
|--miniCPU/              The RTL code of implemented CPU
|  |--minicpu_top.v     Top-level module of the single-cycle CPU
↪  with 5 instructions
|  |--regfile.v         Register file module within the CPU
|  |--tools.v           Basic functional modules within the CPU
|
|--func/                Function verification test programs
|  |--inst_ram.coe      Binary data file for the test program
↪  used on the FPGA board
|  |--inst_ram.mif      Binary data file for the test program
↪  used in functional simulation
|  |--inst_ram.txt      Assembly code explanation for the test
↪  program
|
|--soc_verify/          Verification environment for the
↪  implemented CPU
   |--rtl/              Directory for SoC design code used for
   ↪  verification
   |  |--soc_mini_top.v  Top-level file of the SoC
   |  |--CONFREG/        confreg module, used to access
   ↪  peripherals such as LEDs and dip switches on the
   ↪  experimental board
   |  |--xilinx_ip/      Customized Xilinx IP, including
   ↪  clk_pll, inst_ram
   |
   |--testbench/        Simulation environment
   |
   |--run_vivado/       Vivado project's running directory
      |--constraints/   Constraints for Vivado project design
```

4.2.2.1   Functional Simulation

Functional verification of digital circuits is to check whether the designed digital circuit functionally meets the design goals. Readers who have developed a C program before would know that the finished program should be tested for correctness. The intent of functional verification is the same as functional testing in software development. The so-called functional simulation is the verification by means of simulation (software emulation) rather than by means of actual circuit testing. Figure 4.7 shows a basic framework for functional simulation verification of digital circuits.

In this basic framework, we give some specific input stimulus to the design under test (DUT) and then observe whether the output result of the DUT is as we expect.

When verifying the functional simulation of a CPU design, we follow the same idea as above. But the specific method of input stimulus and output result checking is different from that of a simple digital circuit design. Functional simulation of simple circuits usually involves generating a series of varying stimulus signals, inputting them to the input ports of the circuit being verified, and observing the signals at the output ports of the circuit to determine whether the results are as expected. However, since the only inputs and outputs of a CPU are `clock`, `reset`, and `I/O`, it is inefficient to directly drive and observe the inputs and outputs.

We use a test program as the stimulus for CPU functional verification. The input stimulus is a sequence of test instructions, usually machine code written in assembly or C language and compiled by a compiler. By observing whether the execution result of the test program meets the expectation, we can judge whether the CPU function is correct or not. The efficiency of verification is greatly improved in this

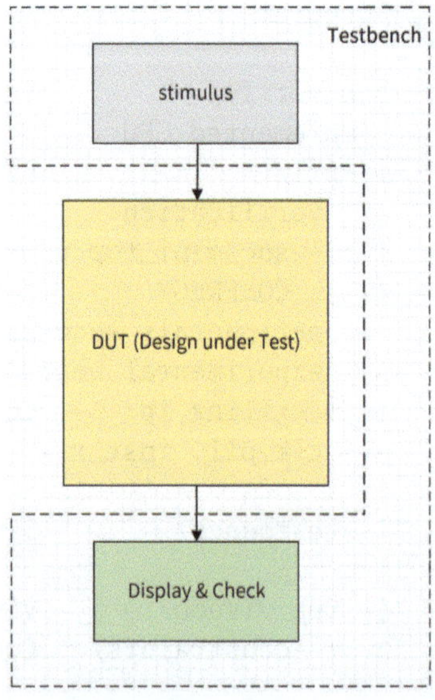

Fig. 4.7 Basic framework for functional simulation verification

way. But the debugging difficulty of locating the error point after the verification process is also increased accordingly. Fortunately, the debugging difficulty of the first five-instruction single-cycle CPU experiment is relatively low. The debugging techniques introduced in Chap. 3, Sect. 3.2 can basically complete the practical tasks. Later, as the difficulty of the experiment increases, our experimental environment will also provide a set of debugging tools based on trace comparison, which can help to locate the error points more quickly in the debugging process.

4.2.2.1.1 Computer Hardware Systems Simulated by Verification Environment

Simply realizing a CPU does not have much practical use. Usually we need to build a computer hardware system based on the CPU. We follow the same idea in verifying the functionality of the CPU; i.e., we build a computer hardware system based on the implemented CPU and then run the test program on this computer hardware system to verify the functionality of the CPU. This computer hardware system will be implemented by FPGA development board. The core is a system on chip (SoC) implemented on the FPGA. This SoC is connected to the clock crystal, reset circuitry, and peripheral interfaces such as LEDs, digital tubes, and pushbuttons on the board through the pins. Inside, the SoC is also a small system. In verifying a five-instruction single-cycle CPU, we use the simplest SoC, SoC_Mini, whose internal structure is shown in Fig. 4.8, and the corresponding RTL code is located in `minicpu_verify/rtl/`. The core of SoC_Mini is the miniCPU, which is the core of the CPU that we will implement, which interacts with the instruction RAM (`inst ram`) to fetch instructions and interacts with the `confreg` to access peripherals. In addition, the mini-system contains a PLL module.

The relationship between instruction RAM and CPU is clear now. The functions of PLL and `confreg` are briefly explained here.

The clock (from the clock crystal) provided to the FPGA chip on the development board is 100 MHz. If we use this clock directly as the clock for each module in SoC_Mini, it means that the miniCPU should be able to reach at least 100 MHz. This may be a strict requirement for beginners, so we added a PLL IP to use the

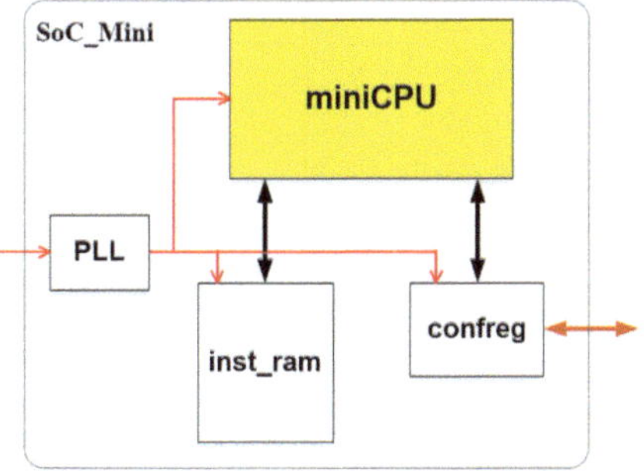

Fig. 4.8 Simple hardware system for verifying miniCPU

100 MHz input clock as the reference clock and output a lower frequency clock as the clock input to the miniCPU.

confreg are configuration registers inside the SoC. In the SoC system built in the experimental development environment, CPU accesses the confreg to drive the LEDs and digital tubes on the board and receives inputs from the external pushbuttons. Briefly explain the mechanism of this control: the external LEDs, digital tubes, and pushbuttons are directly connected to the FPGA pins, and the LEDs and digital tubes can be controlled by controlling the high and low levels on the output pins of the FPGA. Similarly whether a pushbutton is pressed or not can be judged by observing the electrical level changes on the input pins of the FPGA. These FPGA pins are further connected to certain bits of the confreg. Therefore, CPU can write the confreg to control the electrical level of the output pins to control the LEDs and digital tubes and also read the confreg to know whether the pins connected to the pushbuttons are high or low.

A special reminder to readers is that since the entire SoC_Mini design is implemented into the FPGA chip, the top module chosen for synthesis and implementation should be soc_mini_top, not the minicpu_top that written by ourselves.

4.2.2.1.2   Top-Level Interface of the miniCPU

In order to fast integrate CPU into the above experimental development environment for verification, we clearly define the top module interface of CPU. Top-level interface of the miniCPU is defined in detail as shown in Table 4.2.

Table 4.2 Top module interface signals of miniCPU

Name	Width	I/O direction	Description
clk	1	Input	Clock signal from the output of clk_pll
resetn	1	Input	Reset signal for low level synchronous reset
inst_sram_we	1	Output	RAM write enable signal which is active high
inst_sram_addr	32	Output	RAM read/write address of byte addressing
inst_sram_wdata	32	Output	RAM write data
inst_sram_rdata	32	Input	RAM read data
data_sram_we	1	Output	RAM write enable signal which is active high
data_sram_addr	32	Output	RAM read/write address of byte addressing
data_sram_wdata	32	Output	RAM write data
data_sram_rdata	32	Input	RAM read data

4.3   20-Instruction Single-Cycle CPU

We have completed a five-instruction single-cycle CPU. Although it can already run some small, simple programs, it is still a bit weak. Starting from this section, we try to add instructions to CPU, so that it can eventually support 20 instructions: add.w, addi.w, sub.w, ld.w, st.w, bne, beq, b, bl, jirl, slt, sltu, slli.w, srli.w, srai.w, lu12i.w, and, or, nor, xor. With these 20 instructions, we can develop richer test programs. The 15 new instructions among these 20 instructions can be categorized into ALU and Branch according to their functions. We continue to use the method of analyzing each instruction to first improve the datapath and then adjust the control signals.

4.3.1   Datapath for Newly Added ALU Class Instructions

4.3.1.1   Instruction sub.w

Checking the definition of sub.w in *Instruction Manual*, we can basically get the point that sub.w and add.w have generally the same function. The difference is that the latter does addition while the former does subtraction. This means that, except for the arithmetic parts, all other datapaths required to implement sub.w can reuse that of add.w.

The most straightforward way to implement the different components is to add a subtractor and then choose between its result and the result of the adder to get the desired result. This implementation is correct, but we can optimize it further. Consider the following properties of the complementary addition and subtraction operations:[6]

$$[A]_{\text{comp}} - [B]_{\text{comp}} = [A - B]_{\text{comp}} = [A]_{\text{comp}} + [-B]_{\text{comp}} = [A]_{\text{comp}} + (\overline{[B]_{\text{comp}}}) + 1$$

This means that with a few simple changes to the inputs of the two's complement adder, it can be made to do both addition and subtraction. This is done by adding multiplexer circuits to the source operand 2 input and the carry-in input of the adder, respectively. The second source operand input is src2 when processing addition, and it is the bitwise negation of src2 when processing subtraction, and the carry-in input is 0 for addition and 1 for subtraction. The selection signals of these new multiplexers will be described as control signals later on. The control signals can be implemented by the difference of the instruction codes.

Thus the datapath required by sub.w is designed.

---

[6][A]$_{\text{comp}}$ indicates the complement representation of the value A.

4.3.1.2 Instruction `slt` and `sltu`

Checking definitions of `slt` and `sltu` in the *Instruction Manual,* we find that these two instructions are also arithmetic instructions. If we compare them with the `add.w` and `sub.w`, the difference is only from the arithmetic process. All other datapaths are the same. It is natural to reuse the existing datapaths for the same functions. The main consideration here is how to adjust the datapath to support the function required by the new instruction.

First, let's look at one of the most intuitive implementations, which is to add a comparator that handles signed and unsigned comparisons of two 32-bit data. The two inputs of the comparator are the same as those connected to the adder, and a control signal input is used to identify whether the comparison is signed or unsigned. The output of the comparison is either 0 or 1. Then, a 32-bit multiplexer component is added to the output port of the adder, with `in0` connected to the output of the original adder and `in1` connected to the result of the comparator.

Continue to consider how to implement the comparator. We can see that if we use the < operator, the < can only produce a comparison of unsigned numbers, so how can we describe a comparison of signed numbers? There must be a way. But it requires additional circuit logic. There is also the problem that after writing a < in Verilog to describe an unsigned comparison of two numbers, the actual circuit is selected from the built-in library of EDA synthesis tools based on timing and area constraints. Typically, the comparator circuit is simpler than the adder circuit but still consumes some logic resources.

Can we utilize existing resources of arithmetic logic? Think about how human compare two numbers. Generally, we subtract two numbers and check whether it is a positive or negative value. Does this mean that we can reuse the circuit of an adder to substract two numbers and then generating the results of `slt` and `sltu` based on the result of the subtraction? The answer is yes. Thus, we can save the resources of a comparator, and the final circuit delays are not that significant between the two designs.[7] Next, let's see how we can reuse the adder to implement the logic for `slt` and `sltu`.

Since we have already analyzed the implementation of `sub.w`, we will not repeat how to subtract with an adder by reusing the existing datapath. Let's first look at how to handle the comparison of signed numbers. According to human thinking, the first case is that one is the positive and the other is the negative. Here, the negative number is definitely smaller than the positive number. Only when the two numbers have the same sign do we need to look at the result of the subtraction. When the subtraction result is negative, the number being subtracted is smaller than the subtracting number. The treatment of unsigned numbers is slightly more complicated. Since both numbers are nonnegative, the only way to tell is to look

---

at the result of the subtraction. But we can't tell if the result is positive or negative by looking at bit 31 of the result, because the sign digit of the result is in bit 32. But where is the value of bit 32? One way to deal with this is to change the 32-bit adder to a 33-bit one. When processing a non-sltu instruction, the 32-bit input data is sign-extended to 33 bits. When processing a sltu instruction, the 32-bit input data is zero-extended to 33 bits. In this way, bit 33 of the result directly reflects the positive or negative case of the result. Another way to make judgment is to use the 32-bit adder's carry-out result, Cout. When Cout is 1, the result is positive, and when Cout is 0, the result is negative. These two ways of processing are logically equivalent, readers can deduce for it.

To summarize, by reusing the operation of GR[rj]-GR[rk], the results of slt and sltu are obtained based on the positive or negative of the source operand, the positive or negative of the sum, and the positive or negative of the carry-out (Cout). These results, along with the original adder results, are then passed through a 2-to-1 multiplexer to get the result of the execution of the arithmetic class instruction, which is then fed to the multiplexer input that produces the final write register value. In this way, the required datapaths for slt and sltu are designed.

4.3.1.3   Instruction slli.w, srli.w and srai.w

Checking the *Instruction Manual*, we can see that slli.w, srli.w, and srai.w are three shift instructions, which represent logical left, logical right, and arithmetic right shifts, respectively. All three instructions have two source operands, one from the rj entry of the general-purpose register file and the other is the value in the ui5 field of the instruction code. The results of all three instructions are written to rd of the general-purpose register file. The datapaths for reading the rj entry and writing the rd entry of the general-purpose register file already exist and can be reused. The rest of the shift operation can obviously not be realized by an adder, so we need to add a **shifter** datapath.

1. Input and Output of the Shifter

The shifter has two data inputs, the 32-bit shifted value shft_src and the 5-bit shifted amount shft_amt, as well as a control input that determines the type of shifting operation, shft_op, and the final 32-bit shifted result, shft_res. shft_src is derived from the output rdata1 of general-purpose register file, so the shft_src follows the same datapath as instructions such as add.w and sub.w. The shft_amt comes from the ui5 field of the instruction code, which at first glance does not appear to have such a datapath for the source operand so far. But we can see that the value of the ui5 field is the same as the lowest five bits of the si12 field of addi.w, ld.w, st.w, and so on. Our shift logic only uses bits 4...0 of the shft_amt (meaning that it doesn't matter when bits 31...5 of the source operand 2 are used at this point), so we can in fact reuse the instruction code si12 that we have already implemented as a datapath to the source operand 2. Finally, the final selection circuit for the result of the arithmetic instruction is extended from

2-to-1 multiplexer to three-to-one multiplexer because of the output of the shifter, `shft_res`, as the new data input, `in2`.

2. Implementation of the Shifter

The most straightforward way to implement the shifter is to use `shft_src <<` `shft_amt`, `shft_src >> shft_amt` and `$signed(shft_src) >>> shft_amt` to describe the logic of logical left, logical right, and arithmetic right shifts, respectively. Then pass the three results through a 3-to-1 multiplexer to select the final result `shft_res` based on `shft_op`.

Since shift logic is essentially decode and multiplexing logic, a 32-bit shifter is 32 sets of 32-to-1 multiplexers, which has a large area and long latency. Implementing this with three separate shift operators usually means[8] that there are three 32-bit 32-to-one multiplexers, and then a 32-bit three-to-one multiplexer, which has a large area overhead.

In the CPU reference design for the practical tasks of this chapter, another code design is adopted, unifying logical right shift and arithmetic right shift to be implemented by a single barrel shifter circuit, which readers can appreciate on their own. Here, we introduce another design which is for the optimization of circuit area. The basic idea is to reverse the order of the shifted data, so that the left-shift operation is converted to a right-shift operation. The implementation is illustrated below:

```
assign shft_src = op_srl ? {src[ 0], src[ 1], src[ 2], src[
   ↪   3],
                           src[ 4], src[ 5], src[ 6], src[
↪   7],
                           src[ 8], src[ 9], src[10],
↪   src[11],
                           src[12], src[13], src[14],
↪   src[15],
                           src[16], src[17], src[18],
↪   src[19],
                           src[20], src[21], src[22],
↪   src[23],
                           src[24], src[25], src[26],
↪   src[27],
                           src[28], src[29], src[30],
↪   src[31]}
```

---

[8]Some EDA tools already have strong optimization capabilities. When the three expressions are written in a prescribed code style, the tool can find that their function can be achieved by sharing a common barrel shifter, and then it will only derive a set of barrel shifter circuit. Since this circuit-level optimization is closely related to the characteristics of the EDA tool itself, we do not present it here as the main content. If interested, readers can further read the manuals of the tools they use in their actual work.

```
                                : src[31:0];
  assign shft_res = shft_src[31:0] >> shft_amt[4:0];
  assign sra_mask = ~(32'hffffffff >> shft_amt[4:0]);
  assign srl_res = shft_res;
  assign sra_res = ({32{src[31]}} & sra_mask) | shft_res;
  assign sll_res = {shft_res[ 0], shft_res[ 1], shft_res[ 2],
  ↪   shft_res[ 3],
                    shft_res[ 4], shft_res[ 5], shft_res[ 6],
  ↪   shft_res[ 7],
                    shft_res[ 8], shft_res[ 9], shft_res[10],
  ↪   shft_res[11],
                    shft_res[12], shft_res[13], shft_res[14],
  ↪   shft_res[15],
                    shft_res[16], shft_res[17], shft_res[18],
  ↪   shft_res[19],
                    shft_res[20], shft_res[21], shft_res[22],
  ↪   shft_res[23],
                    shft_res[24], shft_res[25], shft_res[26],
  ↪   shft_res[27],
                    shft_res[28], shft_res[29], shft_res[30],
  ↪   shft_res[31]};
```

In the above description, only the logic for generating `shft_res` is a full 32-bit shifter. Although the logic for generating `sra_mask` also uses the >> operator, the synthesis tool optimizes the generated circuits for constant-value passing, because the shifted data is constant-valued, and the actual logic resources consumed are much less than a full 32-bit shifter. Although `shft_src` and `sll_res` generating logic in the circuit has a 32-bit data reverse operation, these logics are all represented as simple wiring when synthesized into circuits. The second description reduces the logic resource overhead, while the delay of the circuit is slightly increased, which is a gain and a loss. The choice of the description is based on the specific design requirements. If the main frequency requirement is not high or the shifter logic is not located in the critical path of the entire CPU, then the second description is obviously better.

At this point, the datapath design is adjusted to further consider `slli.w`, `srli.w`, and `srai.w`.

4.3.1.4   Instruction `lu12i.w`, `and`, `or`, `nor` and `xor`

Except `lu12i.w`, `and`, `or`, `nor`, and `xor` are bitwise logic instructions. The operation of all the logic operation instructions is to write the value of `rj` and of `rk` of the register file to `rd` of the register file after performing the corresponding logic operation bit by bit. It can be seen that the functions of reading and writing general-purpose register file of these instructions can reuse the existing datapaths. The only thing that needs to be added is the datapath for accomplishing the specific logic operation.

For `lu12i.w`, we only need to write the source operand's the immediate number `si20` in bits 24...5 of the instruction code to `rd` of the general-purpose register file. These two write operations can reuse the existing datapaths. The datapath of the source operand to the arithmetic logic can be expanded from a 2-to-1 multiplexer to a three-to-one multiplexer to generate the source operand 2. The specific operation of `lu12i.w` is actually a 12-bit trailing zero shift of the immediate number `si20`.

4.3.1.5 ALU

Up to now, we can concentrate the logic of `add.w`, `addi.w`, `sub.w`, `slt`, `sltu`, `slli.w`, `srli.w`, `srai.w`, `lu12i.w`, `and`, `or`, `nor`, `xor` into one module. This module is used to process these arithmetic and logical operations, so it is called ALU (arithmetic logic unit). The main purpose of introducing this level of division into the ALU module is to reduce the design complexity and optimize the circuit timing by decoding the control signals required in datapaths at two levels. The details of the two-level decoding will be described in detail later.

The ALU module has two 32-bit inputs, `alu_src1` and `alu_src2`, a 32-bit result output, `alu_res`, and a control signal input, `alu_op`. In addition, there is a 32-bit output, `mem_addr`, which comes directly from the calculations of the ALU's internal adder, used to access the RAM address by the `ld.w` and `st.w` instructions. Some readers may ask, when executing `ld.w` and `st.w`, isn't the value of this `mem_addr` output the same as the `alu_res` output? Why don't we just use `alu_res` instead of `mem_addr`? The answer is to optimize the timing. The delay of the `alu_res` output of the ALU module is a few more gates of selection logic than the delay of the `mem_addr` output. Since the address to access the RAM can't come from a shifter or any other logic, using the `mem_addr` directly for the RAM address reduces the unnecessary latency overhead on that path.

At this point, the design of the single-cycle CPU with the addition of 11 new ALU-type instructions is complete, and its structure is shown in Fig. 4.9.

4.3.2 Datapath for New Branch Class Instructions

4.3.2.1 Instruction beq

Checking the *Instruction Manual*, we can see that the only difference between beq and bne lies in the condition of judging whether to jump or not, so it is only necessary to extend the branch decision comparison logic, so that it can choose different ways of judging according to the different types of instructions.

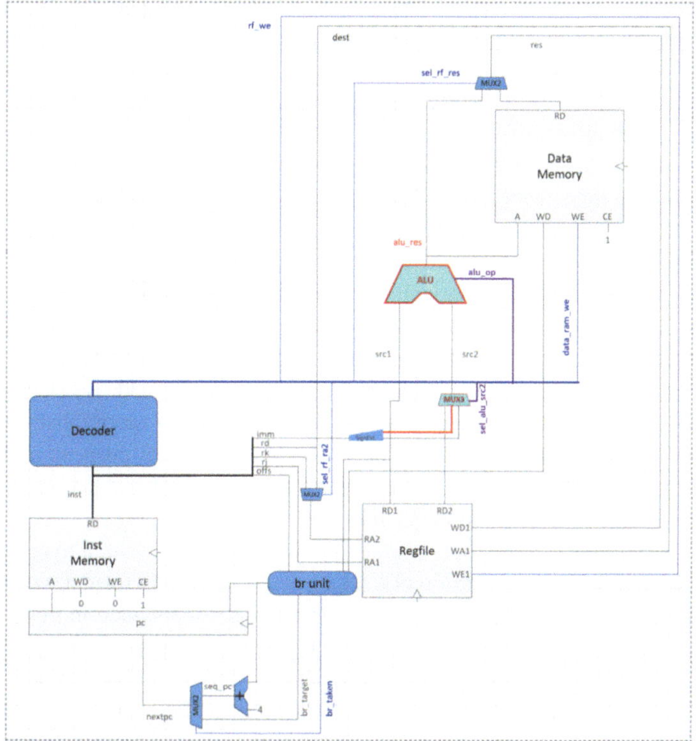

Fig. 4.9 Single-cycle CPU datapath after adding 11 ALU class instructions

4.3.2.2   Instruction b and bl

Let's take a closer look at the b and bl branch instructions. By comparing their definitions to beq and bne, the following three differences can be observed:

1. These two instructions always jump without the need for conditional judgment;
2. The PC-relative offset has been increased to 26 bits;
3. The bl instruction also writes the general-purpose register while performing the jump.

The design change resulting from the first difference is as simple as adding two new always jump cases to the branch instruction jump conditional judgment logic.

The second difference can be addressed by introducing a multiplexer into the input of the adder that calculates the jump target, choosing between 16-bit offsets and 26-bit offsets, depending on whether it is beq, bne, or b, bl. Readers must be familiar with the introduction of 2-to-1 multiplexer. Pay attention to the sign extension of the offs. If the circuit designs to first go through multiplexer and then sign extended, remember that the multiplexer cannot simply be written as assign sel_offs_res = sel_br_offs ? {inst[9:0], inst[25:10]} :

`inst[25:10];`, with `sel_offs_res` sign extended followed. In the previous `assign` statement, the data widths on either side of the operator ":" are different. Verilog syntax will do zero-extend on `inst[25:10]` to 26 bits, which obviously results in the final offset to the PC being the zero-extended value of `inst[25:10]`, rather than the sign-extended value required by the definition of the instruction.

The third difference corresponds to the concept of **link operations**. As we know, function calls in high-level languages introduce two jumps: call jumps to the entry point of the called function and return jumps back to the instruction after the call point. Since a function may be called in more than one place, the destination of the return cannot be determined statically. It can only be determined during dynamic execution. The LoongArch ISA accomplishes this by using a jump instruction with a link operation that writes the PC of the jump instruction plus 4 to a general-purpose register (usually general-purpose register 1[9]), i.e., the return address corresponding to the call point is written to a general-purpose register. To accomplish the return jump, we only need to take out the value stored in this general-purpose register and use it as the jump target address to complete the jump. This is accomplished by using an indirect jump instruction, such as the `jirl`.

When `bl` completes a link operation, the return address is written to register 1 by default. If you look at the definition of the instruction encoding format, you will find that the register number of this destination operand is not encoded in fields like `rd`, `rj`. It is implicit. This requires us to adjust the generation logic of the address input `waddr` of the general-purpose register file write port in the existing datapath and add a multiplexer, whose input `in0` is `rd` in the instruction code, and whose input `in1` is the fixed value 1.

When `bl` completes a link operation, the return address written to register 1 is the value of PC plus 4. In current single-cycle CPU designs, there seems to be an existing computational datapath (the one that generates the sequential fetch in `nextPC`). However, we do not recommend this design, because this datapath does not naturally continue in a pipelined CPU, and forcing it to continue would introduce an objective additional overhead. Instead, we use an adder that calculates the result of `add.w` and `sub.w` to do this calculation. However, we need to have the two source operands for this addition ready. The source operand 1 of the former adder comes only from the output `rdata1` of the read port 1 of the general-purpose register file. We need to add a 32-bit 2-to-1 multiplexer here, `in0` to access the output `rdata1`, and `in1` to access the PC of the current instruction. The source operand 2 input logic of the adder is adjusted to a three-to-one multiplexer by adding a constant value 4 as the new input `in2`.

At this point, the design of the CPU datapath has been adjusted after further consideration of `b` and `bl`.

---

[9]In LoongArch ABI, general purpose register 1 serves as the return address register.

4.3.2.3 Instruction `jirl`

`jirl` is an indirect jump instruction. Checking its definition in the *Instruction Manual*, the following features can be summarized:

1. Conditional judgment is not required. This instruction will definitely make a jump;
2. It contains a link operation, and the return address is written to the `rd` general-purpose register;
3. The destination address of the jump is obtained by adding the value of `rj` of the general-purpose register file to the immediate offset value in the instruction code.

To address the first characteristic, simply add a new case for always jumping in the branch instruction's jump condition logic.

For the second feature, it is basically possible to reuse the datapath established in the previous `bl` for calculating the return address, except that the write address to the general-purpose register file comes from the `rd` field of the instruction instead of a fixed constant value of 1. It is clear that the datapath for generating the write address to the register file is also reusable.

The third feature requires a further adjustment to the `nextPC` generation logic. We propose to add an adder to add the output `rdata1` from general-purpose register file read port 1 and the sign extension of bits 25...10 in the instruction code shifted two bits to the left. At the same time, change the `nextPC` generation logic from 2-to-1 multiplexer to a three-to-one multiplexer, whose data inputs `in0`, `in1` are the same as those of the original 2-to-1 multiplexer. The new third data input `in2` comes from the result of the new calculation of the indirect jump target.

At this point, the design of the CPU datapath has been adjusted after further consideration of `jirl`.

The structure of the single-cycle CPU with the addition of four branch instructions is shown in Fig. 4.10.

4.3.3 Control Signals Adjustment After Adding New Instructions

In this section, we comb through all the control signals along the datapath, starting with the PC.

1. PC input generation logic `GenNextPC` contains a three-to-one multiplexer. Its three inputs are: `in0` corresponds to the sequential PC, i.e., PC+4, `in1` corresponds to the jump target of relative PC branch instructions such as b and beq, and `in2` corresponds to the jump target of indirect branch instructions such as `jirl`. The selection signal `sel_nextpc` for this three-to-one multiplexer is designed as an at-most-one-hot code, i.e., the signal is 3 bits wide, each bit

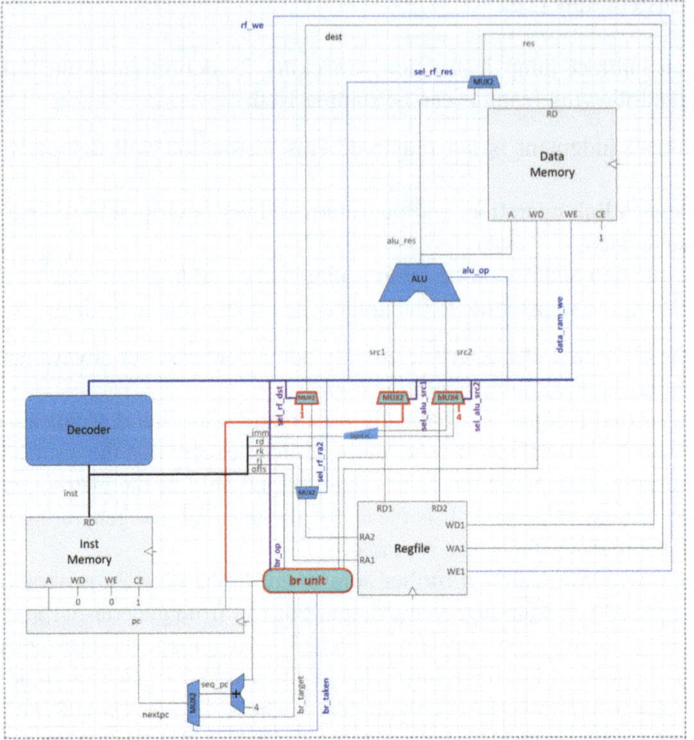

Fig. 4.10 Single-cycle CPU design after adding four branch class instructions

corresponds to a data input, and at most one bit is set to 1 in any legal selection signal.

2. Instruction RAM write enable signal `inst_ram_we`, active high. Our current design does not consider self-modifying code, so the instruction RAM will not receive any write request from the CPU. Meanwhile, the initialization of the instruction RAM content is loaded by the internal circuit of FPGA and is not written by external devices (e.g., DMA), so the `inst_ram_we` signal is constant at zero.

3. Read address generation logic of general-purpose register file read port 2 `GenRFRdAddr2` contains a multiplexer circuit with two inputs: `in0` corresponds to the `rk` field of the instruction code, and `in1` corresponds to the `rd` field of the instruction code. The select signal for this multiplexer, `sel_rf_ra2`, is a 1-bit signal, 1 for selecting `in1`, otherwise `in0`.

4. Offset generation logic for PC-relative branch instructions `GenBROffs` contains a multiplexer whose two inputs are: `in0` corresponds to the sign extension value after the 16-bit offsets shifting two bits to the left, and `in1` corresponds to the sign extension value after the 26-bit offsets shifting two bits to the left. The

selection signal `sel_br_offs` for this multiplexer is a 1-bit signal, 1 for `in1`, otherwise `in0`.

5. ALU `alu_src1` generation logic `GenALUSrc1` contains a multiplexer whose two inputs are: `in0` corresponds to the output of the general-purpose register file read port 1, and `in1` corresponds to the PC. The selection signal of this multiplexer, `sel_alu_src1`, is a 1-bit signal, 1 for `in1`, otherwise `in0`.

6. ALU `alu_src2` generation logic `GenALUSrc2` contains a four-to-one multiplexer whose four inputs are: `in0` corresponds to the output of the general-purpose register file read port 2, `in1` corresponds to the signed extension of the `si12` in the instruction code to 32 bits, `in2` corresponds to the constant value 4, and `in3` corresponds to the zero extension of the `si20` in the instruction code to 32 bits. The selection signal `sel_alu_src2` for this four-to-one multiplexer is designed as a one-hot code with four bits.

7. The selection signals for the multiplexers inside the ALU are generated through re-decoding of `alu_op`. `alu_op` is designed as a one-hot code; each bit corresponds to one kind of operation supported by the ALU, with a total of 12 bits. The correspondence between each bit and instruction is shown in Table 4.3. Columns 2 and 3 of Table 4.3 show that one operation supported by ALU may correspond to multiple instructions. By extracting the same operation between different instructions, the same `alu_op` can be generated. This reduces the complexity of the design by focusing only on the operations realized by the ALU instead of the instructions when designing the control signals for the datapaths inside the ALU. This will become more obvious as the number of instructions increases in practice.

8. Data RAM write enable signal `data_ram_we`, active high.

9. The write enable signal for the general-purpose register file is `rf_we`.

10. The general-purpose register file write address generation logic `GenRFDst` contains a multiplexer whose two inputs are `in0` for the `rd` field of the instruction and `in1` for the constant 1. The select signal, `sel_rf_dst`, is 1

Table 4.3 The correspondence between aluop and instruction in ALU

Bit	alu_op	Instruction
0	op_add	add.w, addi.w, ld.w, st.w, bl, jirl
1	op_sub	sub.w
2	op_slt	slt
3	op_sltu	sltu
4	op_and	and
5	op_nor	nor
6	op_or	or
7	op_xor	xor
8	op_sll	slli.w
9	op_srl	srli.w
10	op_sra	srai.w
11	op_lui	lu12i.w

	sel_nexpc	inst_ram_ce	inst_ram_we	sel_rf_ra1	sel_br_offs	sel_alu_src1	sel_alu_src2	alu_op	data_ram_ce	data_ram_we	rf_we	sel_rf_dst	sel_rf_res
add.w	001	1	0	0	0	0	0001	000000000001	0	0	1	0	0
addi.w	001	1	0	0	0	0	0010	000000000001	0	0	1	0	0
sub.w	001	1	0	0	0	0	0001	000000000010	0	0	1	0	0
ld.w	001	1	0	0	0	0	0010	000000000001	1	0	1	0	1
st.w	001	1	0	1	0	0	0010	000000000001	1	1	0	0	0
beq	010	1	0	1	0	0	0001	000000000000	0	0	0	0	0
bne	010	1	0	1	0	0	0001	000000000000	0	0	0	0	0
b	010	1	0	0	1	0	0001	000000000000	0	0	0	0	0
bl	010	1	0	0	1	1	0100	000000000001	0	0	1	1	0
jirl	100	1	0	0	0	1	0100	000000000001	0	0	1	0	0
slt	001	1	0	0	0	0	0001	000000000100	0	0	1	0	0
sltu	001	1	0	0	0	0	0001	000000001000	0	0	1	0	0
slli.w	001	1	0	0	0	0	0010	000100000000	0	0	1	0	0
srli.w	001	1	0	0	0	0	0010	001000000000	0	0	1	0	0
srai.w	001	1	0	0	0	0	0010	010000000000	0	0	1	0	0
lu12i.w	001	1	0	0	0	0	1000	100000000000	0	0	1	0	0
and	001	1	0	0	0	0	0001	000000010000	0	0	1	0	0
nor	001	1	0	0	0	0	0001	000000100000	0	0	1	0	0
or	001	1	0	0	0	0	0001	000001000000	0	0	1	0	0
xor	001	1	0	0	0	0	0001	000010000000	0	0	1	0	0

Fig. 4.11 Generation list for control signals in single-cycle CPU

bit. The selection signal of this "choose one" section, `sel_rf_dst`, is 1 bit, 1 for in1, otherwise in0.

11. The general-purpose register file write data generation logic, `GenRFRes`, contains a multiplexer curcuit whose two inputs are: in0 for the ALU calculation result `alu_res`, in1 for the load operation return value `ld_res` read from RAM. The select signal of the multiplexer, `sel_rf_res`, is 1 bit, 1 for selecting in1, and in0 otherwise.

After sorting out the 13 groups of control signals required in the single-cycle CPU datapath, we can analyze each instruction one by one and get the correspondence between each instruction and all the control signals, as shown in Fig. 4.11.

After completing the design of the datapaths and control signals as described above, we have a 20-instruction single-cycle CPU architecture as shown in Fig. 4.12.

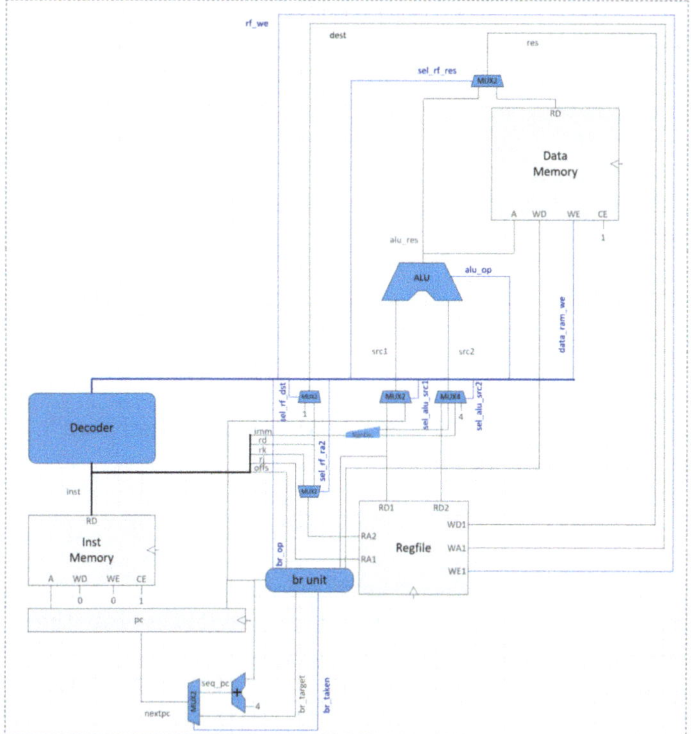

Fig. 4.12 20-instruction single-cycle CPU microarchitecture design

4.4 Verification of 20-Instruction Single-Cycle CPU

As mentioned earlier, with 20 instructions, we can develop much richer test programs. From the verification of 20-instruction single-cycle CPU, we will upgrade the experimental development environment. This environment can be obtained as described in Sect. 2.3.1.

4.4.1 `mycpu_env` Experimental Development Environment Organization Description

The upgraded experimental development environment is located under the first-level subdirectory `mycpu_env`. Its directory structure and the functions of each part are described below:

```
|--gettrace/               Generate the reference trace
|   |--src/                Design code directory
```

```
|   |   |--tb_top.v              Top module of the simulation,
↪  grabing the debug info
                                 into golden_trace.txt
|   |   |--soc_lite_top.v        SoC_Lite top module
|   |   |--refCPU/               Reference processor design that
↪  generates trace
|   |   |--CONFREG/              Confreg module for peripheral
↪  devices such as LEDs,
                                 dial switches, etc. on the board
|   |   |--BRIDGE/               With a 1×2 bridge module, CPU's
↪  data sram interface
                                 accesses both confreg and data_ram
|   |--gettrace.xpr              Vivado project
|   |--golden_trace.txt          Reference trace generated by
↪  running the func test
                                 programs. We need to generate it by
                                 ↪  ourselves
|
|--func/                         Function verification test programs
|   |--include/                  Shared header files for the
↪  functional verification test programs
|   |   |--sysdep.h              GCC macro definitions commonly used
|   |   |--asm.h                 Macro definitions for LoongArch
↪  compilers, such as LEAF(x)
|   |   |--regdef.h              Mnemonics for 32 registers in
↪  LoongArch32 ABI
|   |   |--cpu_cde.h             Macro definitions for SoC_Lite
↪  parameters, such as base
                                 address of digital tubes in confreg
|   |   |--inst_test.h           Macro definition header files used
↪  for each function test point
|   |--inst/                     Assembly programs for each function
↪  test
|   |   |--Makefile              Makefile called by Makefile in the
↪  upper directory
|   |   |--n*.S                  Function test points written in
↪  assembly language
|   |--obj/                      Function tests compiling results
↪  directory
|   |   |--*                     Described in the following
↪  subsection for details
|   |--start.S                   The bootstrap code and main
↪  function
```

```
|   |--Makefile              Makefile for compiling function
↳  tests
|   |--bin.lds               The result of compiling
↳  "bin.lds.S", which can be
                             removed by the command "make reset"
|   |--convert.c             C source code for generating coe
↳  and mif files.
|
|--myCPU/                    CPU RTL code written by readers
|
|--soc_verify/              SoC system verification environment
↳  for CPU designed by readers
    |--soc_dram/             Verification environment
    ↳  corresponding to CPU external
                             connection to distributed RAM
|   |--rtl/               SoC_Lite RTL code
|   |   |--soc_lite_top.v  SoC_Lite top module
|   |   |--CONFREG/        Confreg module for peripheral
↳  devices such as LEDs,
                             dial switches, etc. on the board
|   |   |--BRIDGE/         With a 1×2 bridge module, CPU's
↳  data sram interface
                             accesses both confreg and data_ram
|   |   |--xilinx_ip/       Customized Xilinx IP, including
↳  clk_pll, inst_ram and data_ram
|   |--testbench/           Functional simulation verification
↳  environment
|   |   |--mycpu_tb.v       Simulation top module which catch
↳  debug info and
                             compare it with golden_trace.txt
|   |--run_vivado/          Vivado project running directory
|       |--constraints/     Vivado project design constraints
|       |--mycpu_dram_prj/ Vivado project files directory
```

Incidentally, from Practical Task 6, all the practical tasks in Part 2 of this book will use mycpu_env experimental development environment. So, this experimental environment contains more contents. You don't need to master all of them at once but just need to gradually master the new contents according to the progress of the experiment. You may notice that there are some parts of this directory that are not listed and described above. These unlisted parts are not related to the practical tasks at this stage and will be introduced later in the related experimental tasks.

Fig. 4.13 The SoC used to verify myCPU

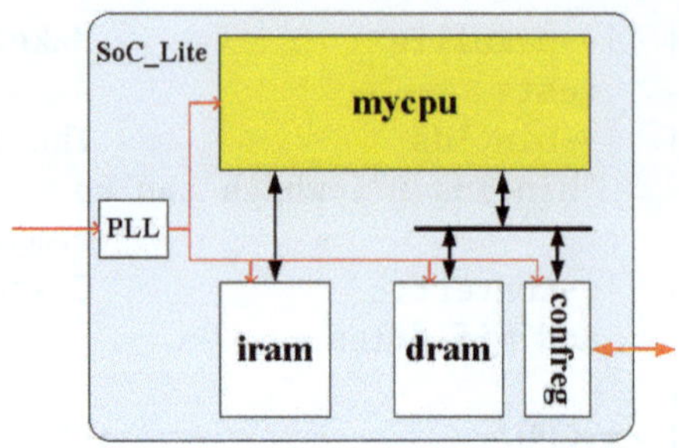

4.4.1.1   Introduction to SoC_Lite Architecture

The system on chip used in `mycpu_env` experimental development environment has also been upgraded to `SoC_Lite`. Its internal structure is schematically shown in Fig. 4.13.

As you can see, `SoC_Lite` has an extra data RAM and a one-part-two component between myCPU and data RAM, confreg than the previous `SoC_Mini`. The relationship between the data RAM and CPU has been explained before. Here is a brief explanation of the one-part-two component between myCPU and data RAM, confreg.

There is a one-part-two component between mycpu and dram, confreg. This is because in the LoongArch ISA, all I/O device registers are memory-mapped. The confreg we implement here is no exception. Memory-mapped access means that the registers in an I/O device each have a unique memory address, which can be accessed by the CPU through load and store instructions. However, dram as memory is also accessed by load and store instructions. So how do you know whether a load or store instruction is accessing a confreg or a dram? When we design a SoC, we use the address to differentiate between them. Therefore, when designing the datapath of the SoC, it is necessary to introduce a one-part-two component, which generates the selection control signal by judging the address range of the accessed memory.

4.4.2   Debugging Framework Based on Trace Comparison

In Practical Task 5, we used a more primitive debugging approach. With the increasing complexity of the implemented CPU, this debugging method is a disaster for beginners. For this reason, we have provided a set of debugging tools based on trace comparison, which help to locate things more quickly during the debugging process.

4.4.2.1 Debugging Tools Based on Trace Comparison

Readers may have used single-step debugging when debugging C programs. In the case of running each line of code in "slow motion," it is possible to see in time whether the running behavior of each line of code meets the expectation, thus locating the error point in time. The set of debugging tools based on trace comparison that we provide to readers in our experimental development environment draws on this "single-step debugging" strategy.

The way to realize this is: We first run the test instruction sequence on a known functionally correct CPU, record the PC, and write register information of each instruction as golden_trace; then run the same instruction sequence when verifying myCPU; and compare the PC and write register information of myCPU with the previous golden_trace when myCPU writes the registers of each instruction. If it is different, then immediately report an error and stop the simulation.

Readers who are familiar with LoongArch instructions may ask: Some branch and store instructions don't write registers, so there's no way to judge them in the way described above. These questions are quite right. However, if the branch jump is wrong, then the PC of the first instruction in the wrong path which writes register will be different from the one in golden_trace, and it will report an error and stop. If the store instruction is executed wrongly, then the value written to a register by the load instruction that reads from this location will be different from the one in golden_trace, so it will also report an error and stop. Although the position of the error report is a little bit backward, there is still a pattern in general. It is possible to realize timely error reporting for branch and store instructions, but it will further increase the complexity of the debugging interface on myCPU and also limit the flexibility of myCPU to implement branch and store instructions to a certain extent. After weighing the advantages, we adopt the design idea of solving most of the problems with a small amount of input.

Above, we have introduced the basic idea of using trace to locate errors in functional simulation verification. Below we will introduce how to generate golden_trace and how to use golden_trace for comparison during myCPU verification.

4.4.2.2 Generating golden_trace with the Reference Model

Once the functional verification program func has been compiled, you can use the gettrace project to run the simulation to generate the reference trace. gettrace uses the same SoC_Lite architecture as the one used to verify the myCPU, with the main difference being that it integrates a verified and fully functional reference processor core.

The top module of the simulation is `gettrace/src/tb_top.v`. The important code related to catching `golden_trace` is as follows:

```verilog
......
// trace directory
`define TRACE_REF_FILE "../../../../golden_trace.txt"
// after func finishs, CPU will loop at 32'h1c000100
`define END_PC 32'h1c000100
......
assign debug_wb_pc        = soc_lite.debug_wb_pc;
assign debug_wb_rf_we     = soc_lite.debug_wb_rf_we;
assign debug_wb_rf_wnum   = soc_lite.debug_wb_rf_wnum;
assign debug_wb_rf_wdata  = soc_lite.debug_wb_rf_wdata;
......
// open the trace file
integer trace_ref;
initial begin
    trace_ref = $fopen(`TRACE_REF_FILE, "w");
end


// generate trace
always @(posedge soc_clk)
begin
    // trace sampling time
    if(|debug_wb_rf_we && debug_wb_rf_wnum!=5'd0)
    begin
        // sampled signals
        $fdisplay(trace_ref, "%h %h %h %h" ,
            `CONFREG_OPEN_TRACE ,
            debug_wb_pc, debug_wb_rf_wnum,
    debug_wb_rf_wdata_v);
    end
end
......
```

Signals sampled by trace include the following:

1. PC for the Write Back (WB) instruction.
2. Write enable signal for the WB instruction.
3. The destination register number of the WB instruction.
4. The write-back value of the WB instruction.

Obviously, the CPU does not write back every time, so the trace sampling needs to be timed in a certain way. The write enable of a write-back instruction means that the instruction is valid for the write enable signal of the general-purpose register file and the write-back destination register number is not 0. Can you understand why the instruction samples only when the write-back destination register is not 0?

4.4.2.3   Monitoring myCPU with `golden_trace`

The `SoC_Lite` used for myCPU functional verification is the same architecture as in the `gettrace` project, but the testbench is different. See `mycpu_verify/soc_verify/soc_XXX/testbench/mycpu_tb.v`, with highlights of the code as follows:

```verilog
......
// trace directory
`define TRACE_REF_FILE "../../../../../../gettrace/golden_trace.txt"
// data in digital tubes register in confreg
`define CONFREG_NUM_REG soc_lite.confreg.num_data
// after func finishs, CPU will loop at 32'h1c000100
`define END_PC 32'h1c000100

......
assign debug_wb_pc          = soc_lite.debug_wb_pc;
assign debug_wb_rf_we       = soc_lite.debug_wb_rf_we;
assign debug_wb_rf_wnum     = soc_lite.debug_wb_rf_wnum;
assign debug_wb_rf_wdata    = soc_lite.debug_wb_rf_wdata;

......
//get reference result at falling edge
reg [31:0] ref_wb_pc;
reg [4 :0] ref_wb_rf_wnum;
reg [31:0] ref_wb_rf_wdata_v;
always @(negedge soc_clk)
begin
    // trace reading time is the same as trace sampling time
    if(|debug_wb_rf_we && debug_wb_rf_wnum!=5'd0 && !debug_end
        && `CONFREG_OPEN_TRACE)
    begin
        // sampled signals
        $fscanf(trace_ref, "%h %h %h %h" , trace_cmp_flag ,
                ref_wb_pc, ref_wb_rf_wnum, ref_wb_rf_wdata);
    end
end


// compare result with trace signals at rising edge
always @(posedge soc_clk)
begin
    if(!resetn)
    begin
        debug_wb_err <= 1'b0;
    end
    // result comparing time is the same as trace sampling time
    else if(|debug_wb_rf_we && debug_wb_rf_wnum!=5'd0 && !debug_end
            && `CONFREG_OPEN_TRACE)
    begin
```

```verilog
        if (  (debug_wb_pc!==ref_wb_pc) || (debug_wb_rf_wnum!==ref_wb_rf_wnum)
            ||(debug_wb_rf_wdata_v!==ref_wb_rf_wdata_v) )
        begin
            $display( ⌋
            ↪  "--------------------------------------------------------------"⌋
            ↪  );
            $display("[%t] Error!!!",$time);
            $display("    reference: PC = 0x%8h, wb_rf_wnum = 0x%2h, wb_rf_wdata
            ↪  = 0x%8h",
                      ref_wb_pc, ref_wb_rf_wnum, ref_wb_rf_wdata_v);
            $display("    mycpu    : PC = 0x%8h, wb_rf_wnum = 0x%2h, wb_rf_wdata
            ↪  = 0x%8h",
                      debug_wb_pc, debug_wb_rf_wnum, debug_wb_rf_wdata_v);
            $display( ⌋
            ↪  "--------------------------------------------------------------"⌋
            ↪  );
            // mark the error
            debug_wb_err <= 1'b1;
            #40;
            // find error and then finish simulation
            $finish;
        end
    end
end
......
//monitor test
initial
begin
    $timeformat(-9,0," ns",10);
    while(!resetn) #5;
  $display("===============================================================");
    $display("Test begin!");
    while(`CONFREG_NUM_MONITOR)
    begin
        // for every 10000ns, print the PC of the WB instruction,
        // helping judge whether CPU is crashed
        #10000;
        $display ("        [%t] Test is running, debug_wb_pc = 0x%8h",
        ↪  debug_wb_pc);
    end
end

//test end
wire global_err = debug_wb_err || (err_count!=8'd0);
always @(posedge soc_clk)
begin
    if (!resetn)
    begin
        debug_end <= 1'b0;
    end
    else if(debug_wb_pc==`END_PC && !debug_end)
    begin
        debug_end <= 1'b1;
```

```verilog
        $display("=================================================================");
        $display("Test end!");
        $fclose(trace_ref);
        #40;
          if (global_err)
          begin
              // find error and then print "Fail"
              $display("Fail!!!Total %d errors!",err_count);
          end
          else
          begin
              // no error and then print "PASS"
              $display("----PASS!!!");
          end
        $finish;
    end
  end
  ......
```

4.4.3   *Functional Test Programs* func

In addition to the new `gettrace`, readers can notice that `mycpu_env/func/` content increases a lot than the `minicpu_env/func/` before. Here are some brief descriptions of the new func programs.

4.4.3.1   Description of func

The `func` programs are divided into `func/start.S` and `func/inst/*.S`, both LoongArch32 assembly programs:

1. `func/start.S` : The main function, which performs the necessary startup initialization, and then calls each assembly program under `func/inst/`.
2. `func/inst/*.S` : The assembly program for each instruction or function point.
3. `func/include/*.h` : Test program configuration information and macro definitions.

The body of the `func/start.S` is divided into three main parts. See the comments for details.

```
   ......
  # The following is the setup of LEDs and digital tubes at the
  ↪   beginning of the program.
  # The single-color LEDs are off, and the dual-color LEDs are
  ↪   one red and one green.
      LI (a0, LED_RG1_ADDR)
```

```
    LI (a1, LED_RG0_ADDR)
    LI (a2, LED_ADDR)
    LI (s1, NUM_ADDR)

    LI (t1, 0x0002)
    LI (t2, 0x0001)
    LI (t3, 0x0000ffff)
    lu12i.w s3, 0
    NOP4

    st.w t1, a0, 0
    st.w t2, a1, 0
    st.w t3, a2, 0
    st.w s3, s1, 0
# The following is to run each function test point,
# wait for a period of time after executing idle_1s for each
↪   test.
# The digital tube will plus 1 and show.
inst_test:
    bl n1_lu12i_w_test      #lu12i.w
    bl idle_1s

    bl n2_add_w_test    #add.w
    bl idle_1s
......
# The following is to show the test result.
# If PASS, the dual-color LEDs will light up two green
↪   colors,
# and the single-color LEDs will not light up.
# If Fail, the dual-color LEDs will light up two read colors,
# and all single-color LEDs are on.
test_end:
    LI  (s0, TEST_NUM)
    NOP4
    beq s0, s3, 1f

    LI (a0, LED_ADDR)
    LI (a1, LED_RG1_ADDR)
    LI (a2, LED_RG0_ADDR)

    LI (t1, 0x0002)
    NOP4

    st.w zero, a0, 0
```

```
    st.w t1, a1, 0
    st.w t1, a2, 0
......
```

The test program for each function test point in the `inst/` directory is named `n#_*_test.S`, where # is the number. If there are 15 function points to test, they are numbered from `n1` to `n15`. The test code is roughly as follows. Please pay special attention to the sections of the code that maintain the function point number (the high 8 bits of the s0 register) and the number of function points (the low 8 bits of the s3 register).

```
......
LEAF(n1_lu12i_w_test)
    addi.w    s0, s0 ,1              # load test number s0++
    addi.w    s2, zero, 0x0
    lu12i.w   t2, 0x1
    ###test inst
    addi.w    t1, zero, 0x0
    TEST_LU12I_W(0x00000, 0x00000)
    ......                           # test program, omitted
    TEST_LU12I_W(0xff0af, 0xff0a0)
    ###detect exception
    bne       s2, zero, inst_error
    ###score ++                      # s3 store pass number of the
    ↪  tests, plus 1 each case
    addi.w    s3, s3, 1
    ###output (s0<<24)|s3
inst_error:
    slli.w    t1, s0, 24
    NOP4
    or        t0, t1, s3             # upper 8-bit of s0 is number
    ↪  of the tests

                                     # lower 8-bit of s3 is pass
                                     ↪  number of the tests
                                     # show the "or" result of s0
                                     ↪  and s3 on tubes

    NOP4
    st.w      t0, s1, 0              # s1 store the address of the
    ↪  digital tubes
    jirl      zero, ra, 0
END(n1_lu12i_w_test)
```

From the above, we can see that the behavior of the test program is: When passing the first function test, the digital tubes will display `0x0100_0001` and then execute `idle_1s`; passing the second function point test, the digital tubes will display `0x0200_0002` and then execute `idle_1s`..., and so on. Therefore, digital tubes should always be the same for the upper 8-bit and lower 8-bit when passing all function test point. If the digital tubes change from **0x0500_0005** to **0x0600_0005** in the middle of the test, it means there is an error in running the sixth function test point.

Finally, the code for the `idle_1s` function in `start.S` uses a loop to pause the execution of the test program. The main code is as follows:

```
idle_1s:
        ......
    # initialize t3        // read switch_interleave in
    ↪   confreg
    # switch_interleave: {switch[7], 1'b0, switch[6], 1'b0,
    ↪   ..., switch[0], 1'b0}
    ld.w    t2, t0, 0
    NOP4
    xor     t2, t2, t1     // 0 for switch on, so need "xor"
    ↪   to get negative
    NOP4
    slli.w  t3, t2, 9      # t3 = switch interleave << 9
    NOP4

sub1:
    addi.w  t3, t3, -1     // t3 sub 1

    # get min{t3, switch_interleave}
    # switch_interleave: {switch[7], 1'b0, switch[6], 1'b0,
    ↪   ..., switch[0], 1'b0}
    ld.w    t2, t0, 0
    NOP4
    xor     t2, t2, t1
    NOP4
    slli.w  t2, t2, 9      # switch interleave << 9
    NOP4                   // above ld.w, xor and slli.w get
    ↪   switch_interleave again
    sltu    t4, t3, t2     // unsigned number comparison:
                           // if t3 < switch_interleave, then
                           ↪   t4 = 1
    NOP4
    bne     t4, zero, 1f   //if t4 != 0, i.e. t3 >=
    ↪   switch_interleave, then jump to 1f
    nop
    addi.w  t3, t2, 0      //otherwise, let t3 =
    ↪   switch_interleave
    NOP4
1:
```

```
bne       t3, zero, sub1 // if t3 != 0, then jump to start
↪  of loop
jirl      zero, ra, 0    // finish idle_1s
```

From the above code, we can see that `idle_1s` will set the loop count based on the state of the switch. In the simulation environment, we will simulate the state of the switch to be all dialed down to minimize the number of `idle_1s` cycles. The reason for this setting is that the FPGA operation is much faster than the simulation speed. Assuming that it takes 10^6 CPU cycles to run a program, and assuming that the CPU runs at 10 MHz on the FPGA, it takes only 0.1 s to run a program on the FPGA. Similarly, if we simulate this program, assuming that the CPU running frequency is also set to 10 MHz, does it take only 0.1 s to run the program? Obviously this is not possible. The simulation is a software to simulate the CPU operation; that is, it has to simulate the internal changes of the CPU for each cycle. To run this program, we need to simulate ten^6 CPU cycles. We tested on a mainstream X86 desktop in 2016 and found that the Xsim simulator that comes with Vivado to run the simulation of `SoC_Lite` takes about 600us for each simulation cycle, which means that the actual time spent on Xsim to simulate 10^6 cycles is about 10 minutes.

For the same program, it takes about 10 minutes to run the simulation test, while it takes only 0.1 seconds to run it on the FPGA (or even less. If CPU is running at 50 MHz, it takes only 0.02 s to run the program). So if we don't control the `idle_1s` function when running the simulation, we may fall into long time waiting. Similarly, if we set the `idle_1s` function to be very short when we put on the board (e.g., the switches are all dialed down), then the `idle_1s` time is too short to see the accumulation of the digital tubes.

If you find that the digital tubes accumulate too slowly during the operation on the board, please decrease the value set by the DIP switch. If you find that the digital tubes accumulate too fast, please dial up the switches.

4.4.3.2   func Test Point Configuration

`mycpu_env/func/inst/` contains all the function test points. Readers need to configure `mycpu_env/func/include/test_config.h` according to the task number of the practice when carrying out the specific experiments. The contents of this file are as follows:

```
// ========================================================================
// exp6          : n1~n20   SHORT_TEST1 1 NOP_INSERT 0 TEST1 1 TEST2 0 TEST3 0
//                          TEST4 0 TEST5 0 TEST6 0 TEST7 0 TEST8 0 TEST9 0
// exp7          : n1~n20   SHORT_TEST1 0 NOP_INSERT 1 TEST1 1 TEST2 0 TEST3 0
//                          TEST4 0 TEST5 0 TEST6 0 TEST7 0 TEST8 0 TEST9 0
// exp8~9        : n1~n20   SHORT_TEST1 0 NOP_INSERT 0 TEST1 1 TEST2 0 TEST3 0
//                          TEST4 0 TEST5 0 TEST6 0 TEST7 0 TEST8 0 TEST9 0
// exp10         : n1~n36   SHORT_TEST1 0 NOP_INSERT 0 TEST1 1 TEST2 1 TEST3 0
```

```
//                           TEST4 0 TEST5 0 TEST6 0 TEST7 0 TEST8 0 TEST9 0
// exp11           : n1~n46  SHORT_TEST1 0 NOP_INSERT 0 TEST1 1 TEST2 1 TEST3 1
//                           TEST4 0 TEST5 0 TEST6 0 TEST7 0 TEST8 0 TEST9 0
// exp12           : n1~n47  SHORT_TEST1 0 NOP_INSERT 0 TEST1 1 TEST2 1 TEST3 1
//                           TEST4 1 TEST5 0 TEST6 0 TEST7 0 TEST8 0 TEST9 0
// exp13~16        : n1~n58  SHORT_TEST1 0 NOP_INSERT 0 TEST1 1 TEST2 1 TEST3 1
//                           TEST4 1 TEST5 1 TEST6 0 TEST7 0 TEST8 0 TEST9 0
// exp18           : n1~n70  SHORT_TEST1 0 NOP_INSERT 0 TEST1 1 TEST2 1 TEST3 1
//                           TEST4 1 TEST5 1 TEST6 1 TEST7 0 TEST8 0 TEST9 0
// exp19, 21~22 : n1~n72  SHORT_TEST1 0 NOP_INSERT 0 TEST1 1 TEST2 1 TEST3 1
//                           TEST4 1 TEST5 1 TEST6 1 TEST7 1 TEST8 0 TEST9 0
// exp23           : n1~n79  SHORT_TEST1 0 NOP_INSERT 0 TEST1 1 TEST2 1 TEST3 1
//                           TEST4 1 TEST5 1 TEST6 1 TEST7 1 TEST8 1 TEST9 0
// ===============================================================================

//===============================================================================
//SHORT_TEST1: less test case for n1~n20.
//             Only set for exp6.
//===============================================================================
#define SHORT_TEST1 0

//===============================================================================
//NOP_INSERT: Insert 4 nop insts between every alu operation.
//             Only set for exp7.
//===============================================================================
#define NOP_INSERT 0

#define TEST1 0
#define TEST2 0
#define TEST3 0
#define TEST4 0
#define TEST5 0
#define TEST6 0
#define TEST7 0
#define TEST8 0
#define TEST9 0
```

Before starting a new practical task, please check the values of the 12 configuration macros SHORT_TEST1, NOP_INSERT, TEST1~TEST9 corresponding to the experiment according to the header comment information in test_config.h, and modify the definitions of these macro variables in the lower part of the file.

4.4.3.3   Installation of LoongArch GCC Cross Compile Tool Chain

To compile the func program on our own, we need to use the LoongArch32R GCC cross compile tool chain. The toolchain can be installed either by downloading the source code from https://gitee.com/loongson-edu/la32r-toolchains or by installing the package directly from https://gitee.com/loongson-edu/la32r-toolchains/releases. We will focus on the latter method here.

When downloading the installation package, please choose the version according to machine X86 or LoongArch. Download the package `loongarch32r-linux-gnusf-*.tar.gz` to Linux file system. It is important to note that the current X86 version of the LoongArch32R GCC cross compiler only supports 64-bit systems (running `uname -a` under the system and showing the architecture as `x86_64`). Next:

(1) Open a terminal, go into the directory where the tar file is located, and unzip it:

```
$ sudo tar zxvf loongarch32r-linux-gnusf-*.tar.gz -C /opt/
```

(2) Ensure that `/opt/loongarch32r-linux-gnusf-*/bin/` exists, and execute the follow:

```
$ echo "export
↪  PATH=/opt/loongarch32r-linux-gnusf-*/bin/:$PATH" >>
↪  ~/.bashrc
```

(3) Reopen a terminal, type `loongarch32`, and hit tab. If you get `-linux-gnusf-` or something like that, the toolchain has been installed successfully. At this point, you can write a `hello.c` and compile it with the toolchain to see if it works.

```
$ loongarch32r-linux-gnusf-gcc hello.c
```

4.4.3.4   func Test Program Compile Script Description

The compile script for func is `func/Makefile` in the verification directory, for those who are interested in Makefile. The script supports the following commands:

- `make help` : View help information.
- `make` : Compile to get the result used in simulation.
- `make clean` : Remove `*.o`, `*.a` and `./obj/` directories.

4.4.3.5   func Test Program Compile Result Description

`func` test program compile results are located under `func/obj/`. The practical tasks in second part of the book related to a total of three files. Each file is specifically explained in Table 4.4.

Table 4.4 func test program compile result files

File	Explanation
inst_ram.coe	Coe file for re-customizing inst ram
inst_ram.mif	Mif file read by inst ram when simulation
test.s	Disassmebly file from main.elf

4.4.3.6   func Test Program Loading

The test program we have developed is compiled with the GCC tool to form an ELF-formatted executable file, `main.elf`. So are we going to run this ELF-formatted executable file directly on our own CPU design? Obviously not. Our test environment is called "bare metal." It is a hardware system without any operating system or monitoring environment. So there is no file system, executable loader, or any other software.

What we really want is the code and initial data of `main.elf`.[10] We just need to extract the code and initial data, put the code into instruction RAM, and put the initial data into data RAM, and then we can run the CPU up. So we use the `objcopy` utility in the tool chain to extract the `.text` section of the `main.elf` to generate the binary data file `main.bin` and extract the `.data` section of the `main.elf` to generate the binary data file `main.data`.

The next step is to "load" this information into RAM. We utilize the initial content loading feature of the block RAM IP of the Xilinx FPGA. This feature requires the loaded content to be generated as a text file in a specified format. We further converted the `main.bin` and `main.data` into the required text files. Each binary data file generates a `coe` file and a `mif` file. The data content of these two files is actually identical, except for the other formatting information of the documents. `coe` files are used to generate the on-board configuration files, while `mif` files are used for functional simulation. We recommend that you do not directly modify the coe file or the mif file to change the stimulus during debugging unless you know exactly which part of the verification is affected by your modifications.

4.4.3.7   Function (func) Test Simulation Verification Result Assessment

There are two ways to determine the simulation results.

The first method, and the easiest, is to see if the Vivado console prints `Error` or `PASS`. The correct console message is shown in Fig. 4.14.

---

[10]In later experiments, test program needs a certain amount of input data, which would take more CPU execution time if it is generated by immediate number loading. We will pass the input data to the test program in the form of global static variables with initial values. The initial values of these global variables will be recorded in a read-only segment of the ELF file.

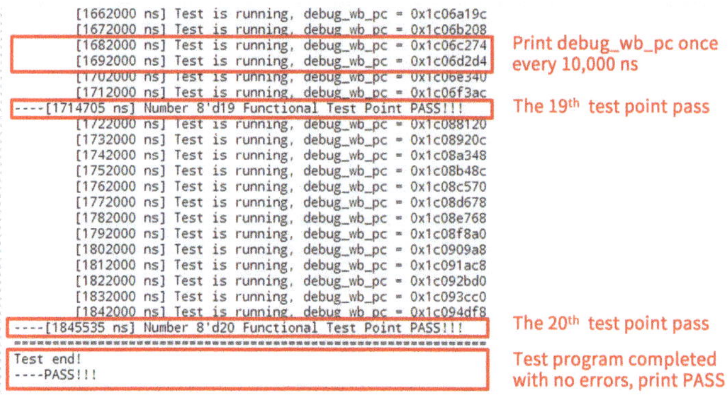

```
        [1662000 ns] Test is running, debug_wb_pc = 0x1c06a19c
        [1672000 ns] Test is running, debug_wb_pc = 0x1c06b208
        [1682000 ns] Test is running, debug_wb_pc = 0x1c06c274
        [1692000 ns] Test is running, debug_wb_pc = 0x1c06d2d4
        [1702000 ns] Test is running, debug_wb_pc = 0x1c06e340
        [1712000 ns] Test is running, debug_wb_pc = 0x1c06f3ac
----[1714705 ns] Number 8'd19 Functional Test Point PASS!!!
        [1722000 ns] Test is running, debug_wb_pc = 0x1c088120
        [1732000 ns] Test is running, debug_wb_pc = 0x1c08920c
        [1742000 ns] Test is running, debug_wb_pc = 0x1c08a348
        [1752000 ns] Test is running, debug_wb_pc = 0x1c08b48c
        [1762000 ns] Test is running, debug_wb_pc = 0x1c08c570
        [1772000 ns] Test is running, debug_wb_pc = 0x1c08d678
        [1782000 ns] Test is running, debug_wb_pc = 0x1c08e768
        [1792000 ns] Test is running, debug_wb_pc = 0x1c08f8a0
        [1802000 ns] Test is running, debug_wb_pc = 0x1c0909a8
        [1812000 ns] Test is running, debug_wb_pc = 0x1c091ac8
        [1822000 ns] Test is running, debug_wb_pc = 0x1c092bd0
        [1832000 ns] Test is running, debug_wb_pc = 0x1c093cc0
        [1842000 ns] Test is running, debug_wb_pc = 0x1c094df8
----[1845535 ns] Number 8'd20 Functional Test Point PASS!!!
========================================================
Test end!
----PASS!!!
```


Fig. 4.14 Console message of passing simulation verification

The second method is to observe the correct execution behavior of the func through the waveform window and grab the confreg module's signals `led_data`, `led_rg0_data`, `led_rg1_data`, `num_data` (as shown in Fig. 4.15):

1. At the beginning, single-color LEDs are written all 1 to indicate total turned-off, dual-color LEDs are written **0x1** and **0x2** to indicate one red and one green, and the digital tubes are written all 0;
2. During execution, single-color LEDs extinct all the time, dual-color LEDs are one red and one green, and the upper 8 bits and lower 8 bits of the digital tubes are accumulated synchronously;
3. At the end, single-color LEDs are written all 1 to indicate total extinction, dual-color LEDs are both written **0x1** to indicate two greens, and the digital tubes synchronize with the upper 8 bits and the lower 8 bits, corresponding to the number of test function points.

4.4.3.8   func Test FPGA Verification Result Judgment

There is only one way to determine the correctness of the result when verifying on FPGA. The correct execution behavior of func is:

1. At the beginning, single-color LEDs are all off, the dual-color LEDs are one red and one green, and the digital tubes display all zeros;
2. During execution, single-color LEDs are all off, the dual-color LEDs are one red and one green, and the upper 8 bits and lower 8 bits of the digital tubes are accumulated synchronously;
3. At the end, single-color LEDs are all off, the dual-color LEDs are two greens, and the digital tubes synchronize with the upper 8 bits and the lower 8 bits, corresponding to the number of test function points.

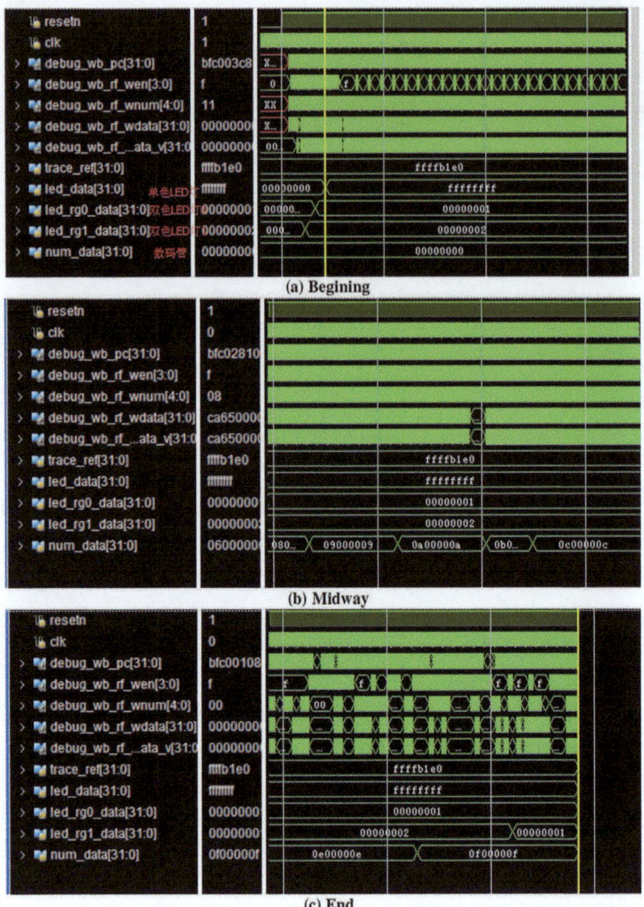

(a) Begining

(b) Midway

(c) End

Fig. 4.15 The correct simulation waveform

If there is an error during the execution of the func, the first difference between the upper 8 bits and lower 8 bits of the digital tubes is the function point number of the test error. The final result is that single-color LEDs light up all the time, dual-color LEDs light up two reds, and the values of the upper 8 bits and the lower 8 bits of the digital tubes are not the same.

The final FPGA verification pass is similar to Fig. 4.16, with the upper and lower 8 bits of the digital tubes showing the number of function points running.

Fig. 4.16 The correct FPGA verification

4.4.4   Experimental Flow Based on `mycpu_env` Experimental Development Environment

`mycpu_env` experimental development environment enriches the func test programs and introduces the trace comparison debugging mechanism. The whole experimental procedure also adds two steps of compiling the test programs and generating comparison traces compared to that based on the `minicpu_env` experimental development environment. Let's summarize them.

4.4.4.1   Obtain the Experimental Development Environment

`mycpu_env` experimental development environment is obtained in the same way as in the previous practical tasks. If you are unfamiliar with it, please review the introduction in Sect. 2.3.1. The development environment is located in the first-level subdirectory `mycpu_env` of the project.

4.4.4.2   Develop CPU Code

The operation of this step is consistent with that of the `mini_cpu` experimental development environment.

4.4.4.3   Integrate CPU

The operation of this step is consistent with that of the `mini_cpu` experimental development environment. Codes should be updated to `mycpu_env/myCPU/`.

4.4.4.4   Compile Test Programs

This is a new step. If you have downloaded and extracted the `expXX.zip` package for your experiment, and you do not want to change the test programs during the experiment, you can skip this step, for the package already contains the compiled results. Otherwise, go to the func directory and modify the test configuration file `test_config.h` in the include directory according to the experiments to be performed, and then run `make clean` before running `make`.

If you are running Vivado under Windows: Make sure that your virtual machine is running a Linux operating system with the LoongArch-GCC cross compile tool installed, and set the func directory to be a shared directory of the virtual machine.[11] Perform the above compilation on the virtual machine's Linux operating system, and go back to Windows operating system to confirm that the contents of the `func/obj/` directory are the latest compilation.

See Sect. 4.4.3.3 for information on installing the LoongArch-GCC cross compile tool.

4.4.4.5   Generate Comparison Trace

Go to `gettrace/` directory, open the Vivado project `gettrace.xpr`, perform simulation, and generate the reference result `golden_trace.txt`. Make sure that at this time inst_ram loaded is actually the result compiled in the previous step. The `golden_trace.txt` will not be complete until the simulation run is finished.

---

[11] For compiling the programs involved in the experiments in this book, the Windows Subsystem for Linux 2 (WSL2) that comes with the Windows operating system is perfectly adequate. WSL2 does not need to set share directory. It can access the XXX directory on a Windows system by accessing `/mnt/XXX`.

4.4.4.6   Simulate to Verify CPU

The operation of this step is consistent with that of the `mini_cpu` experimental development environment.

4.4.4.7   Verify CPU on FPGA Board

The operation of this step is generally consistent with that of the `mini_cpu` experimental development environment. If the simulation result is correct, we can enter FPGA verification procedure. Go back to the project of mycpu, perform synthesis and implementation. After the success, test on FPGA, and observe whether the digital tubes on the experimental box displays the results consistent with the requirements. If the result is consistent, the experiment is successful; otherwise, we will go to the following debugging stage to investigate the problem.

4.4.4.8   Debug on CPU

This procedure should also be available in the `mini_cpu` based experimental development environment but is not emphasized due to the low difficulty of the initial experiments. When debugging, please follow the steps below to position bugs, and then repeat the three processes of simulation verification, FPGA verification, and debugging until it is correct.

1. Review the generated, downloaded bit file for accuracy.

   - If the generated bit file is judged to be incorrect, then regenerate it.
   - If the generated bit file is judged to be correct, then go to Step 2.

2. Review the simulation results for correctness.

   - If the simulation verification results are incorrect,[12] then return to the previous simulation verification step.
   - If the simulation verification results are correct, then go to Step 3.

3. Check the timing report after Implementation (at the left of the Vivado GUI: "IMPLEMENTATION" →"Open Implemented Design" →"Report Timing Summary").

   - If the timing is found to be unsatisfied, then optimize the unsatisfied path in the Verilog design, and go back to the previous simulation verification sequentially; or reduce the running frequency of `SoC_Lite`, i.e., reduce the

---

[12]If you test on FPGA before simulation verification passes, all we can do is to praise for your courage.

output frequency of the `clk_pll` module, and then go back to the previous FPGA verification procedure to perform the operations sequentially.

- If the timing is satisfied, then go to Step 4.

4. Carefully troubleshoot `Warning` at Synthesis and Implementation.

   - Critical warnings are strongly recommended to be corrected, and warnings are recommended to be corrected as much as possible. Then go back to the previous FPGA verification procedure to perform each operation in order.
   - If there are no more correctable Warning, then go to Step 5.

5. Manually check the RTL code to avoid multi-drivers, misused blocking assignments, misconnected module ports, misconnected clock reset signals, and wrong-direction inputs and outputs when module instantiated. Check the "cool" style code imitated from elsewhere. Find out if there are any values that have been forced during simulation, resulting in inconsistencies between the simulation and the FPGA.... If you can't find the problem by just looking at the code, then go to Step 6.
6. Refer to Appendix D.5, "Online Debugging with Chipscope" for FPGA online debugging. If the problem cannot be solved after hours of debugging, then go to Step 7.
7. Reflect. Actually, what else can we do but reflect?

Based on our teaching and training experience, we would like to remind readers that many "simulation passes, but FPGA fails" are caused by one of the following problems:

1. Multi-drivers.
2. The signal direction of the module's input/output ports is incorrect.
3. Clock reset signal is connected incorrectly.
4. Code is not standardized, blocking assignment is used in wrong way, or `always` statement is used arbitrarily.
5. There is an `X` for control signal during simulation. During simulation, remove `X` when `X` exists and remove `Z` when `Z` exists. In particular, `X` and `Z` should not appear on the top module interface of the design.
6. Timing violations.
7. Signals on the control path in the module are not reset.

4.4.5 *`mycpu_env` Experimental Development Environment Advanced Usage*

4.4.5.1 Regenerate `golden_trace.txt`

Whenever we update the func program and recompile it, remember to regenerate `golden_trace.txt` in `gettrace` as follows:

1. Open the gettrace project, and make sure that the macro definition INST_COE in
   soc_lite_top.v points to the mif file generated by the updated func.
2. Run the simulation. golden_trace.txt in the gettrace directory will be
   updated after the simulation is finished.

4.4.5.2   Re-customize inst_ram

Whenever we update the func program and recompile it, we need to recustomize
inst_ram to apply the latest contents under func/obj/.

Note that only the soc_verify project needs to re-customize inst_ram, while
the gettrace project does not since it has the macro INST_COE in soc_lite_top.v
pointing directly to the mif file in the func/obj/ directory. The process of re-
customizing inst_ram is as follows:

1. Find inst_ram IP in the Sources window, double-click or right-click on it, and
   click Re-customize IP... to enter the customization interface.
2. In the re-customize IP interface (as shown in Fig. 4.17), select the Other
   Options tab, check Load Init File, and select the newly generated
   inst_ram.coe in Coe File by clicking Browse, click OK.
3. Click Generate in the Generate Output Product pop-up window (select
   global or ooc mode as needed) to complete the recustomization of inst_ram.

4.4.5.3   Replace mif File for Fast Simulation

The content of this subsection is for reference only. If you do not master the content
of this section, it does not affect the practical tasks at all.

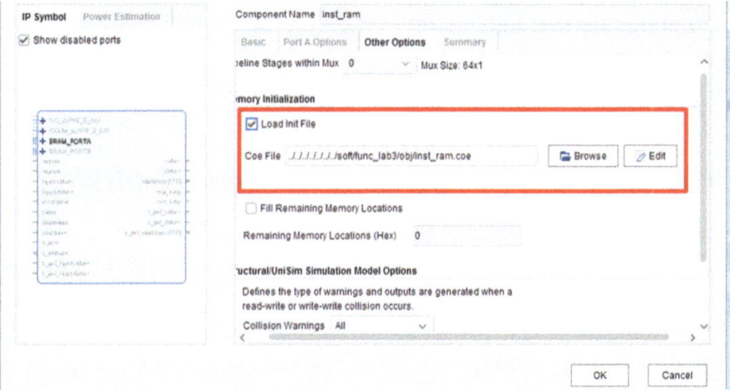

Fig. 4.17 Interface of recusomizing inst ram IP

The re-customization of the `inst_ram` described in the previous section is time-consuming, so you can choose to directly replace the mif file in the Vivado project if you only want to simulate with updated `inst_ram` initial values. Taking single-cycle CPU development environment as an example, after starting the simulation interface, you will find the following directory `soc_verify/soc_dram/run_vivado/mycpu_prj1/mycpu.sim/sim_1/behave/xsim/`. Replace `inst_ram.mif` in this directory with the `inst_ram.mif` in the `CPU_CDE/func/obj/`. Click `Restart` (**Note: Not "Relaunch Simulation"**) and go back to the 0 cycle. Click `run all` to start the simulation, so the initial value of `inst_ram` will be changed to the updated `inst_ram.mif`.

Note: Whenever you open a new simulation or click `Relaunch Simulation`, the `inst_ram.mif` file will be regenerated based on the previously customized `inst_ram`.

4.5   CPU Design Experiment Functional Simulation Debugging Skills

In the previous chapter, we have introduced some common debugging methods and techniques for functional simulation of digital logic circuit design. In this section, we will introduce more debugging skills in the context of CPU digital logic circuits and the experimental development environment provided by us.

Here we still use the observation of simulation waveforms as the main method of CPU functional simulation verification. In the previous chapter, we gave the basic idea of observing the functional simulation waveforms of digital logic circuits, and the core of the idea is to "Find a point of error that you can pinpoint, and then Look at the signals along the logic chain of the design in reverse, level by level, until the source of the error is found." CPU is also a digital logic circuit, so its function simulation verification debugging also follows this idea. Therefore, we summarize the specific debugging methods mainly based on the special characteristics of CPU function simulation verification.

4.5.1   Why Use Trace Comparison Debugging Tools?

Through the introduction of the CPU design experiment environment in the previous section, readers already know that when verifying the function of a CPU, a sequence of test instructions (or a test program) is used as the stimulus for CPU function verification. Whether the verification passes or fails is based on whether or not the execution result of the test program meets the expectation. The advantage of this verification method is that it can be used for both simulation and machine testing. But the disadvantage is that the error we can inspect is often far away from the source of the error. Readers may not have an intuitive idea of what the disadvantage means. Let's take an example to illustrate.

For example, if we want to verify that the CPU has correctly implemented the `add.w` instruction by means of a test program, it is natural to develop the test program with this flow: First, store operands into two registers; then execute an `add.w` using these two registers as the source registers, and, at the same time, store the correct result into another register different from the destination of `add.w`; finally, compare the registers with the desired result and the destination of `add.w`. If they are not equal, call the print function to output an error message to the terminal. Otherwise, continue with other subsequent tests. According to this flow, assuming that there is an error in the CPU design that causes an error in `add.w`, by the time the verifier sees the error message in the terminal, the CPU has actually executed all the instructions of the compare instruction and the function that prints the error message. If the output function of the whole system has its own internal software cache, then the error message will be written to the output device even later. In other words, the CPU could have executed hundreds of instructions between the time `add.w` went wrong and the time you saw the error message. What's the problem with this? The problem is that after you open the simulation waveform, the CPU behaves normally for hundreds or even thousands of cycles forward from the last moment, which means that it's futile to look for any signals during those hundreds or even thousands of cycles. If you don't have a way to quickly locate the moment of execution of the erroneous `add.w`, you'll spend a lot of useless debugging time.

Some readers may say that it can be easily solved. We can print out in the error message that this is the x test case of the y test program and then follow this information to locate the instruction being tested. That's a good idea, but it doesn't solve all the problems, because you have to realize that it's not the software that's wrong, it's the CPU design that's wrong, and there are all sorts of reasons why things can go wrong. As in the previous example, the test to check that `add.w` is executed correctly does not only include `add.w` but also other instructions. If these instructions are executed incorrectly, you will still see a message saying that `add.w` test is wrong, but it may not be the fact. Some readers may think that if we use other instructions in the test that have already been tested in previous test cases, then we shouldn't get errors with other instructions. We can only say that this is a good wish. Regardless of how we write the test for the first instruction (which means writing a test program with only one instruction), the assumption that an instruction that has already been tested can be used later without making a mistake is not valid. What makes debugging a CPU design difficult is that the same instruction may be correct for one sequence of instructions but incorrect for a different sequence of instructions. Therefore, an instruction that passes a previous test may not be error-free in a later test sequence.

To summarize what I have said above: **The source of a CPU execution error can travel a long way through the logical path of the test program before it is discovered by the verifier.** In the verification method of using test programs to test the CPU design, the biggest workload in the debugging process is to find the instruction that corresponds to the source of the error.

At this point, readers may understand why we provide a set of debugging tools based on trace comparison in the experimental development environment. Because through this means, **in most cases**, the simulation and verification platform can immediately report the error when the instruction at the source of the error has just been executed. Specifically, you can capture the `debug_wb_err` signal in the `mycpu_tb` module in the waveform. The moment it changes from 0 to 1 is the moment when the instruction that fails the trace comparison is writing back to the write register. Isn't it very simple? You can instantly locate the instruction that went wrong.

4.5.2   *"Blind Zone" in Trace Comparison Debugging Tools and Their Countermeasures*

However, the trace comparison mechanism is not infallible, which means that there are still errors that cannot be detected in time by trace comparison. We have summarized the following three cases:

1. The CPU under test is dead. The waveform shows that the clock signal is still increasing with time, but the CPU is not writing back instructions.
2. The CPU under test is executing a dead loop, and there are no instructions to write registers in this dead loop. For example, a program fragment such as `1: b 1b; nop`.
3. The CPU under test executed the store instruction incorrectly.

For the first two cases, we introduced another monitoring mechanism in the experimental development environment: by using the verilog `$display` system call to directly output the write-back PCs to the terminal every 10000 ns in the testbench `mycpu_tb`. If the terminal no longer outputs the PCs of the write-back stage, or if the outputs are the same PCs, it means that the CPU is dead. If the PCs output from the terminal have a clear pattern and keep repeating within a small range, it means that it is stuck in a dead loop. At this time, you need to find the first string of abnormal outputs and find the simulation time at the beginning of the prompt. We should check the waveform backward from this simulation time (no need to look forward) to find the first moment when there is a write register signal at the write-back stage. Then the error must have occurred sometime after that time.

In the third case, the store instruction with the execution error will be reported by the load instruction that accesses the relavant address later,[13] so you will see the trace comparison mechanism report an error and stop at a load instruction.

---

[13] The reason for using "relavant address" instead of "same address" is that as long as there is an overlap between the address area written by store and the address area read by load, it will be reflected, and at this time the two address-related load and store instructions may not be strictly the same.

When you check the execution process of this load instruction and find that the load instruction itself is executed without any problem, then the problem is highly likely the store instruction that accesses the relevant address in front of it. Either the store instruction that should write to this address has written the wrong value, or the store instruction that should write the value to this address has not written the value, or the store instruction that should not access this address has mistaken the address and changed the value of this location by mistake. Which one is the cause, you need to combine the program behavior and waveform feedback to debug. It should be said that this kind of store instruction execution error is the most difficult to debug. In order to debug this kind of error, you need to master the skill of looking at the disassembly instructions as described in the next section.

4.5.3   *Learn to Read Assembly and Disassembly Code*

In order to verify the function of the CPU that we have written, we need to run a verification program on CPU. Such a verification program is usually written in C or Assembly language. C language is easier and faster to write and suitable for complex programs, while Assembly language is a bit more complicated but can clearly control the order of instructions and compilation results. For example, sometimes we need to verify that the CPU handles the specific instruction sequence stream correctly, so it is suitable to write in Assembly language. In addition, C language can also be embedded Assembly programming. This mixed programming method of Assembly and C language is suitable for improving the performance of the program or to achieve specific functions.

In the following, we will briefly introduce the LoongArch32 assembly and disassembly code to help readers with their initial reading of the LoongArch32 assembly and disassembly code. To learn more about the specific toolchain compilation process and the low-level principles of elf files, you can refer to the book *Programmer's Self-Cultivation*. The book is an introduction to the x86 instruction set, so the examples are different from LoongArch32. But the principles are the same and can be applied to the LoongArch32 instruction set with some modifications. Similarly, the book *See MIPS Run*, although aimed at the MIPS instruction set, is still a classic introduction to the low-level programming model and how the software stack on it operates and is well worth a read.

Generally, programmers write assembly programs with the suffix `.S`. For example, we often see the file name `start.S` in a compiled directory, which is a human-written assembly program. For the assembly/disassembly files automatically generated by the compilation toolchain, the suffix is `.s`.

4.5.3.1 Common Assembly Code

The common assembly code format is as follows:

```
    ##s4, exception pc
        .globl  _start
        .globl  start
        .globl  __main
    _start:
    start:
        li.w       $t0, 0xffffffff
        addi.w     $t0, $zero, -1
        b          locate

    ##avoid "j locate" not taken
        lu12i.w  $t0, -0x80000
        addi.w   $t1, $t1, 1
        or       $t2, $t0, $zero
        add.w    $t3, $t5, $t6
        ld.w     $t4, $t0, 0

    ##avoid cpu run error
        .org   0x0ec
        lu12i.w  $t0, -0x80000
```

There are four types of functional statements in this code:

1. Annotation: e.g., `##...`, see Sect. 4.5.3.2 for detail.
2. Label: e.g., `_start:` and `start:`, see Sect. 4.5.3.3 for detail.
3. Pseudo instruction: e.g., `.globl` and `.org`, see Sect. 4.5.3.4 for detail.
4. Assembly instruction: e.g., `b locate` (`locate` is a label), `li.w`, `addi.w`, etc., see Sect. 4.5.3.5 for detail.

4.5.3.2 Annotation Code

In LoongArch32 assembly, there are usually two types of annotation code supported by the assembler:

1. `#`: Indicates an annotation from the current character to the end of the line;
2. `/*...*/`: The same as the C language syntax. Annotation is inside the block.

It's worth stating that `#` has other uses for preprocessing directive characters. For example, `#define`, `#if` and `#include` are not annotations but preprocessing directives, similar to C.

`#if` together with `#elif`, `#else` and `#endif` can realize conditional compilation as follows:

```
run_test:
#if CMP_FUNC==1
    bl   shell1
#elif CMP_FUNC==2
    bl   shell2
#elif CMP_FUNC==3
    bl   shell3
#elif CMP_FUNC==4
    bl   shell4
#else
    b    go_finish
#endif
go_finish:
```

4.5.3.3 Label

The label is used to replace the start address of this assembly instruction, which is actually equivalent to defining a variable that points to the start address of the assembly instruction. The definition format is `<label>:`.

The naming of label follows the format of variable naming in assembly and can be any legal characters in C (case characters, numbers, and underline) and can also contain the character . For example, `.t0` can be a legal label.

There is a special class of labels that are numeric markers, such as `1:` and `2:` in the example below, which are numeric labels. Thay are definitions. 2b is a reference of numeric label 2.

```
      slli.w    $t0, $t0, 16
  1:
      addi.w    $t0, $t0, 1
  2:
      addi.w    $t0, $t0, -1
      bne       $t0, $zero, 2b
      jr        $ra
```

Numeric labels have the effect of local labels: The reference format `<numeric label>f` means to look for the nearest number in the forward program; the reference format `<numeric label>b` means to look for the nearest number in the backward program. For example: `1f` means to look for the nearest 1 in the forward program, i.e., to look downward to find the nearest 1 in the code; 2b means to find the nearest 2 in the backward program. In the above code, 2b is the reference to the label 2 defined at the instruction `addi.w t0, -1`. As the reference to the numeric label follows the principle of proximity, so the numeric label can be redefined and re-referenced without causing confusion, greatly facilitating the writing of assembly programs (programmers do not need to rack their brains to name some temporary or simple jump labels).

4.5.3.4 Pesudo Instruction

It is also common to see pseudo instructions in LoongArch32 assembly programs, such as `.globl`, `.text`, `.org` and `.align`, etc. The function of pseudo instructions is to direct the assembler.

- `.globl` declares that the variable is global and can be referenced by other files.
- `.text` tells the assembler to place subsequent code in `.text` sections unless otherwise specified. Similar functions to `.text` are `.section .rodata` (read-only data section), `.data` (data section), `.section .sdata`, `"aw"` (small data section, used to optimize the generated code, the `s` prefix means small), and so on.
- `.org` and `.align` indicate the alignment format: `.org <n>` is an offset of n from the start address, `.align <n>` is an alignment of 2^n bytes. For example, `.org 0x100` requires the low address to be 0x100 (i.e., the start address is offset by n); `.align 2` requires alignment by 2^2 bytes (i.e., the last two digits of the address are zero).

4.5.3.5 Assembly and Machine Instructions

An assembly instruction is a superset of a machine instruction, which means that a machine instruction must also be an assembly instruction. An assembly instruction is an instruction that can be written directly in an assembly file as the input of the assembler. By contrast, a machine instruction is the output of an assembler, and each machine instruction corresponds to a unique instruction code for the machine to recognize and execute. Different assemblers may support different assembly instructions, but the machine instructions they support for the same architectural version must be the same.

Machine instructions are also directly supported by the CPU we are implementing. The instructions we see in the instruction list in the *Instruction Manual* are machine instructions. For example, the `add.w` instruction is directly a machine instruction. Usually, an assembly instruction corresponds to a machine instruction.

However, there are some assembly instructions that correspond to multiple machine instructions in one. Why do we need such assembly instructions? The answer is to make the assembly code more readable and easier to write. For example, there is a very common programming need to load an immediate number or the address of a variable. If the address of an immediate number or variable is an "irregular" 32-bit number, there is obviously no way to encode it in a machine instruction; e.g., the assembly instruction `li.w t0, 0x12345678` aims to load the

Table 4.5 An 'li.w' assembly instruction corresponding to one or more machine instructions

Assembly instruction	Corresponding machine instructions
li.w t0, 0x12340000	lu12i.w $t0, 0x12340
li.w t0, 0xfffff865	addi.w $t0, $zero, 0x865-0x1000
li.w t0, 0x12348765	lu12i.w $t0, 0x12348; ori $t0, $t0, 0x765

Table 4.6 Conventional naming and usage of general-purpose registers in ilp32 ABI

Register number	Mnemonic	Usage	Saved by callee in function call
$r0	$zero	Constant zero	Unused
$r1	$ra	Return address	No
$r2	$tp	TLS	Unused
$r3	$sp	Stack pointer	Yes
$r4-$r11	$a0-a7	Argument register	No
$r12-$r20	$t0-$t8	Temporary register	No
$r21	$x	Reserved	Unused
$r22	$fp	Frame pointer	Yes
$r23-$r31	$s0-$s8	Subroutine register variables	Yes

32-bit number 0x12345678 into $t0 register, which corresponds to two machine instructions, seeing the third case in Table 4.5. Even though some cases (such as the first two cases in Table 4.5) can correspond to a single instruction, we still prefer to use a non-machine assembly instruction such as li.w, because the behavior of the program is more obvious.

One point to note in Table 4.5 is that the addi.w instruction cannot be written as addi.w $t0, $zero, 0x865. This is because addi.w treats 0x865 as a signed number, but this is beyond the range of the addi.w immediate number field. If you want to represent 0x865 as a binary number, you have to convert it to a signed number by subtracting 0x1000. Generally, we call li.w, which does not exist in the *Instruction Manual* but can be recognized by the assembler and converted into a specific machine instruction sequence (one or more), a macro instruction. Once you come across new macros, we can summarize them and not get confused when they are not in the *Instruction Manual*. (Thinking: In the previous example, there was an instruction jr $ra. Is it a macro instruction? If so, what specific machine instruction does it correspond to?)

4.5.3.6   Conventional Naming and Usage of General-Purpose Registers

The ABI used in our experiments is the ilp32, whose naming and usage conventions for general-purpose registers are shown in Table 4.6:

4.5.3.7 Disassembly Commands and Code Reading

After compiling the program written in Assembly or C language, the executable file obtained is an elf format file. The elf file can be disassembled by using the `objdump` command. The file after disassembling is usually suffixed as `.s`.

For example, assuming that the elf file is `main.elf`, to disassemble this file, we can execute the following command at the linux command line:

```
$ loongarch32r-linux-gnusf-objdump  -ald  main.elf  >
↪  test.s
```

Or

```
$ loongarch32r-linux-gnusf-objdump  -alD  main.elf  >
↪  test.s
```

In the above command, `loongarch32r-linux-gnusf-objdump` is the command of the cross compile tool `objdump`, `-ald` or `-alD` is the command arguments, `main.elf` is the name of the elf file, > is the redirection command (which redirects the terminal output to the subsequent file `test.s`), and `test.s` is the name of the redirected file.

The specific meanings of the command arguments are described below:

1. `-a`: To display the header information of the elf file.
2. `-l`: To display line numbers in the source code, usually used in conjunction with `-d` or `-D`. It requires a parameter `-g` when compiling to generate the elf file (which can retain debugging information in the compilation result).
3. `-d`: To disassemble only the `.text` section, other sections such as `.data` section will not be disassembled.
4. `-D`: To disassemble all sections.

The format of the disassembly file is shown in Fig. 4.18. Each instruction occupies one line and contains three parts of information: instruction address, instruction code, and instruction assembly format.

In addition to disassembling the elf file, we can also use `readelf` (The cross compile tool is `loongarch32r-linux-gnusf-readelf`.) to read the elf file and display the structure of the elf file, such as the starting address and size of the `.text` section.

4.6 Tasks and Practices

After completing this chapter, readers are expected to complete the following two practical tasks:

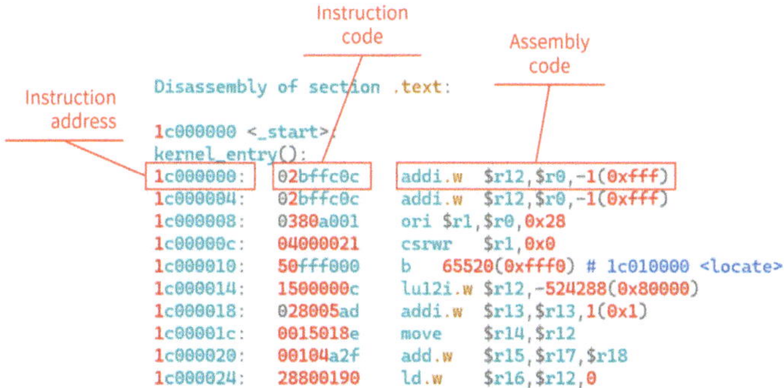

Fig. 4.18 Example of format of disassembly file

1. Complete the design code, and verify the five-instruction single-cycle CPU. See Sect. 4.6.1.
2. Fix bugs in existing implementations, and complete the design and verification of a 20-instruction single-cycle CPU. See Sect. 4.6.2.

4.6.1 Practical Task 5: Five-Instruction Single-Cycle CPU

This practical task requires the following:

1. Read and understand the code provided in the lab environment and add the missing code, so that the design can be verified through simulation and on FPGA.

Please refer to the method described in Sect. 2.3.1 to obtain the experimental development environment required for this practical task. The specific experimental environment is located at **mini_env/**, whose organization and usage have been described in Sect. 4.2 of this chapter and will not be repeated here.

Once the lab environment is ready, please refer to the following steps to complete this practical task:

1. Open the miniCPU project in the **minicpu_env/soc_verify/run_vivado/** directory. If necessary, please refer to Appendix D.4 for upgrading the project and IP.
2. Re-customize the **inst_ram** in the miniCPU project, and select the coe file corresponding to the func (**minicpu_env/func/inst_ram.coe**).
3. Run the simulation of the miniCPU project (click **run all** directly after entering the simulation interface) to start debugging. You can modify the switch value in the **minicpu_env/soc_verify/testbench/minicpu_tb.v** and observe whether the output value of the led meets the expectation (each time the switch value is modified, the simulation has to be resimulated). (Because the test program of this experiment is Fibonacci program. The Fibonacci series is: 0,

1, 1, 2, 3, 5, … Starting from the third term, each term is equal to the sum of the previous two terms. The third term of the series is specified as f(1), i.e., f(1)=1, f(2)=2,f(3)=3,f(4)=5, … To dial the switch is to modify n. The output value of LEDs is corresponded to f(n).)
4. After passing Simulation, Synthesis, and Implementation, generate the bitstream file and test it on FPGA. (Please skip this step if you don't have a hardware experiment platform.)

4.6.2   Practical Task 6: 20-Instruction Single-Cycle CPU

This practical task requires:

1. Read and understand the code provided in `mycpu_env/myCPU/` with the design scheme described in this chapter.
2. Complete the code and debug. There are some bugs in the provided code; please fix them by checking the simulation waveforms, so that the design can be verified by simulation and on FPGA.

Please refer to the method described in Sect. 2.3.1 to obtain the experimental development environment required for this practical task. The specific experimental environment is located at `mycpu_env/`, whose organization and usage have been described in Sect. 4.4 of this chapter and will not be repeated here.

Once the lab environment is ready, please refer to the following steps to complete this practical task:

1. Modify the func configuration file, `mycpu_env/func/include/test_config.h`, select the configuration of `exp6`, and compile. (If you obtained the experimental development environment from the package `exp6.zip`, please skip this step.)
2. Open the gettrace project, `mycpu_env/gettrace/gettrace.xpr` (The IP core in this Vivado project was created using Vivado2019.2. If you open it with a higher version of Vivado, refer to Appendix D.4 for the IP core upgrade). Run the simulation of the gettrace project (After entering the simulation interface, click `run all`, and wait for the simulation to finish), and generate a new reference trace file `golden_trace.txt` (`mycpu_env/gettrace/golden_trace.txt`). The `golden_trace.txt` will not be complete until the simulation has finished running. (If you obtained the experimental development environment from the package `exp6.zip`, please skip this step.)
3. Start the project in `mycpu_env/soc_verify/soc_dram/run_vivado/` to verify myCPU. If you have not created a project in this directory, please refer to the steps described in Appendix D.2 to create a project using the `create_project.tcl` file in this directory. If necessary, please refer to Appendix D.4 to upgrade the IP core.

4. Refer to Sect. 4.4.5.2 of this chapter to re-customize `inst_ram` in the project. (If you obtained the experimental development environment from the package `exp6.zip`, please skip this step.)
5. Run the simulation in the project (click `run all` directly after entering the simulation interface), and carry out the function verification until the simulation test is passed.
6. Generate a bit stream file after Synthesis and Implementation in the project, and verify it on FPGA. (Please skip this step if you don't have a hardware experiment platform.)

Chapter 5
Design a Simple Pipelined CPU

In the previous chapter, we have designed and implemented a 20-instruction single-cycle CPU. In this chapter, we will learn how to transform a single-cycle CPU into a single-issue, five-stage pipelined CPU. It is a little difficult for beginners. In order to reduce the difficulty of learning, we have further broken down the design of a simple pipelined CPU into three small, step-by-step phases:

- Phase 1: We will try to introduce pipelining based on a single-cycle CPU but not consider dealing with the hazards caused by the various types of correlations.
- Phase 2: We introduce the hazards caused by the various types of correlations in the pipeline and give a design solution for resolving the hazards by blocking. In the practical tasks in this chapter, readers can improve the CPU implementation based on the design we have given in Phase 1.
- Phase 3: We introduce the pipeline forwarding technique and give a design. In the practical tasks in this chapter, readers will be able to design and adjust the design based on the CPU implementation in Phase 2.

Learning Goals for this Chapter
- Continue to establish the cognitive link between design and Verilog implementation.
- Develop good Verilog coding habits.
- Further improve the ability to debug errors in CPU functional simulation verification.

Practical Tasks of this Chapter
There are three practical tasks in this chapter (see Sect. 5.5). Readers can complete these tasks after learning this chapter. The correspondence between sections and tasks is as follows:

- Section 5.1 corresponds to Task 7 (Sect. 5.5.1).
- Section 5.2 corresponds to Task 8 (Sect. 5.5.2).
- Section 5.3 corresponds to Task 9 (Sect. 5.5.3).

© The Author(s), under exclusive license to Springer Nature Singapore Pte Ltd. 2025   135
W. Wang, J. Xing, *CPU Design and Practice*,
https://doi.org/10.1007/978-981-96-6573-0_5

5.1   Design Pipelined CPU Without Considering Hazards

We move on to pipelined CPU design. In this section, we address only two design problems: One is to slice the datapath of a single-cycle CPU into multiple stages, and the other is to make the multiple stages "flow down." By "flow down," we mean that, ideally, each stage of the pipeline has one instruction and can process this instruction in one clock cycle.

5.1.1   Add Interstage Buffers

Recalling the general design of pipelined circuits mentioned in Chap. 3, we know that the original purpose of pipelining circuits is to shorten the delay of the combinational logic's critical paths between sequential logics and to increase the circuit's clock frequency without decreasing the circuit's processing throughput. In terms of the final realization of the circuit design, a piece of combinational logic is divided into several phases according to the function, and timing devices (usually flip-flops) are inserted between the combinational logic of each functional phase. The output of the combinational logic of the previous phase is connected to the input of the timing devices, and the input of the combinational logic of the subsequent phase comes from the output of these timing devices.

5.1.1.1   Divide Pipeline Stages

Since the CPU we are designing is a digital logic circuit, the pipelining of the CPU circuits follows the same design methodology as above. The most difficult part of a real CPU design is deciding how many stages of combinational logic in a single-cycle CPU to divide into and what functions to include in each stage. This design decision needs to be made in the context of the CPU product's performance (including clock frequency), power consumption, area, and the specific process characteristics used. For beginners, this part of the design is too much, too detailed, and too deep, so we will directly use the classic single-issue five-stage pipeline. The five-stage pipeline is divided into the following order from the front to the back: the instruction fetch stage (IF), the instruction decode stage (ID), the execute stage (EXE), the memory access stage (MEM), and the write back stage (WB). The main function of the fetch stage is to fetch the instruction. The main function of the decode stage is to parse the instruction to generate control signals and read the general-purpose register file to generate the source operand. The main function of the execute stage is to perform arithmetic-logic operations on the source operand or to calculate the address of the memory access instruction. The main function of the memory access stage is to access memory. The main function of the write back stage is to write the result to the general-purpose register file. In accord with this pipeline stage division scheme, we split the datapath of the previously designed single-issue CPU into five segments and add flip-flops as pipeline buffers between each segment.

It is necessary to explain how to name the flip-flops between pipeline stages. Many textbooks identify these flip-flops by the names of the two pipeline stages; e.g., the flip-flop between the fetch stage and the decode stage is labeled "IF/IDreg." For the sake of simple coding, the reference designs given in this book do not use this identification. We assign the flip-flops to the flow stage to which its output corresponds. Therefore, a flip-flop located between the fetch stage and the decode stage is labeled as "IDreg." This naming style comes from our observing habits when debugging in simulation waveforms; that is, except for the hold time around the sampling edge of the flip-flop clock (which can be regarded as instantaneous and infinitesimal when zero-latency simulation is used), the data stored in the flip-flop is all related to the combinational logic of its outputs. What is mentioned here is just a naming convention. There is no right or wrong, good or bad. Later in this book, we will adopt this single-stage pipeline identification method.

5.1.1.2   Contents in Stage Buffers

The contents in stage buffers can be categorized into control contents and data contents.

The current pipelined CPU design only needs to consider the validity of each pipelined stage buffer, so the control contents in the buffers only need one bit of validity. A value of 0 indicates that the data stored in the pipeline buffers at this stage is invalid, while a value of 1 indicates that data is valid.

The next major design task is to consider what data content is in each buffer. Obviously, if signal (**both data and control signals**) from the original single-cycle CPU are inserted into the pipeline buffers, then the data content of **these** pipeline buffers must include the signals that will be separated. We bolded the word "these" to remind you that a single signal line may be separated multiple times by multiple stages of pipeline buffers. The data contents of each of these buffers should contain information about the data carried by the signal. Here are three examples to illustrate this.

Example 1 An instruction gets its write enable signal and write address signal of the general-purpose register in the decode stage. But these signals are not used until the instruction is located in the WB stage; i.e., these signals are separated by the three pipeline stages buffers (EXE, MEM, and WB), so these signals have to be stored in the buffers of these three pipeline stages.

Example 2 The instruction generates the control signal alu_op of ALU in the decode stage, and uses it in the EXE stage, which is separated by the EXE-stage pipeline buffer, so alu_op needs to be stored in the EXE-stage pipeline buffer.

Example 3 The ALU result `alu_res` is generated in the EXE stage, and the load access result read from the data RAM is generated in the MEM stage. So the logic of selecting the general-purpose register file write value from the ALU result and the load access result can only be completed in the MEM stage at the earliest time, and so the `alu_res` is required to be stored in the MEM-stage pipeline buffer.

To summarize, after inserting into the pipeline buffer, the signal is stored in the pipeline buffer at all stages that it passes through, from the pipeline stage in which it was generated to the pipeline stage in which it is used.

5.1.2 *Introduction of Synchronous Read RAM*

As mentioned in the previous section on single-cycle CPU datapath design, to ensure that an instruction can be completed in a single cycle, "Asynchronous Read RAM" is temporarily used to realize instruction RAM and data RAM and then adjusted back to "Synchronous Read RAM" when designing a pipelined CPU. We will now discuss this design adjustment.

First, let's review the difference in timing characteristics between synchronous and asynchronous read RAM. A synchronous read RAM requires two clock cycles for a single read operation, the first of which sends the read enable and address to the RAM, and the second of which returns the read result to the RAM.

When using asynchronous read RAM, the CPU sends the read enable and read address to the instruction RAM during the fetch stage, and the result (instruction code) of the instruction RAM is obtained within the same clock cycle, so the instruction code can be written into the pipeline buffer of the decode stage when the rising edge of the clock arrives. Obviously, when we change the instruction RAM from asynchronous read RAM to synchronous read RAM, the instruction code cannot be obtained at the time of the rising edge of the clock, so it is necessary to adjust the datapath design of the CPU.

One design consideration is to design the fetch stage to take up two clock cycles, the first cycle to send the read enable and read address and the second cycle to get the data returned from the RAM before proceeding to the decode stage. This is a clumsy solution. In the best case, the CPU can only process one instruction every two cycles. The performance loss is very serious.

Another design consideration is to use rising edge triggering for all pipeline buffers and falling edge triggering for the instruction RAM. This design is a "sounds good" solution. If you are interested in implementing it on an FPGA, you will find that the frequency of the final circuit will be significantly reduced. The reason for this is related to the low-level circuit implementation mechanism of FPGA, which I will not explain here. In fact, not only FPGA but also ASIC, we should try to avoid using the same rising and falling edges of the clock in the same design to reduce the burden on the physical design.

After rejecting the above two designs, we consider distributing the instruction RAM accesses to two consecutive stages in the pipeline, which satisfies the timing characteristics of synchronous RAM reads and also achieves the theoretical peak throughput rate of one instruction per cycle. Without increasing the number of pipeline stages, there are only two design options:

- **Option 1**: Make the read request of the instruction RAM in the fetch stage, so that the output of the instruction RAM is completed while the instruction is in the decode stage.
- **Option 2**: A read request to instruction RAM is initiated at the "update PC stage" (i.e., `nextPC` is the read address of instruction RAM instead of PC), so that the output of instruction RAM is done, while the instruction is in the fetch stage.

In Option 2, the so-called "update PC stage" is not a real pipelined stage but can be said to be a "pseudo-pipelined stage." This stage does not have its own pipelined buffer. Its combinational logic takes its inputs from the pipelined buffers of the IF, ID, etc. stages, and the output is the nextPC. This stage is labeled as the pre-IF stage. This design can be understood as splitting the fetch stage into two stages, pre-IF and IF, and the pre-IF stage is only responsible for generating nextPC, which is sent to the IF stage to update the PC register. By convention, we still call pre-IF and IF stages together as the fetch stage.

So how to choose between these two options? For an ASIC implementation, the second option is better. For AISC implementation, the clk-to-Q delay of synchronous read RAM is larger than the Setup delay of its input port and will be much larger than the clk-to-Q delay of the trigger. If the first scheme is adopted, the decode stage will have two paths: "RAM Read $\longrightarrow$ General Purpose Register File Read" and "RAM Read $\longrightarrow$ Instruction Decode $\longrightarrow$ ALU Source Operand Select." Latency of the general-purpose register readout and instruction decode in these two paths is already not short. When added the clk-to-Q latency of the RAM readout, the latency of the whole path will become very large. However, this is not the case with the FPGA implementation. Since the RAM for synchronous timing behavior on FPGA is implemented as so-called "block RAM," the low-level circuitry is the same as the RAM in the ASIC designs mentioned above. For Xilinx 7 series and more advanced FPGA, the maximum frequency of these RAMs is usually over several hundred MHz. When we use FPGA to implement a slightly more complex circuit such as a CPU, the logic circuits outside of the RAM can reach up to 100–200MHz, so the clk-to-Q latency of the block RAM itself is no longer a major obstacle. If the RAM capacity used is not particularly large, the number of block RAMs used in the FPGA is not very large, and the wire distance is not very long, then the total delay of the RAM readout process is not very large. Considering this particular situation on the FPGA, the first option has some validity.

In our reference design, the second design scheme is still adopted. Although the first design scheme is easier to realize under the current design requirements, it will bring some trouble in the subsequent practice. Because the instructions in the decode stage come directly from the readout port of the RAM, when the instruction in the decode stage is blocked for many cycles, how to maintain the instructions read out from the RAM unchanged is a headache problem. If readers are willing to try the first design option in practice, we have no objection, but only if the timing behavior of synchronous RAM reading is well understood. We would also like to remind that if the first design scheme is adopted, remember not to save the instruction RAM readout to the pipeline buffer in the decode stage before decoding and reading the register file, but directly use the instruction RAM readout to decode and read the register file.

After discussing the synchronous read RAM design adjustment for the instruction RAM, the design adjustment for the data RAM can be done in the same way. Please refer to the reference design here for your own experience. As a reminder, in the reference design, the read request or write request of the data RAM is issued when the instruction is in the EXE stage, and the read data of the data RAM is returned when the instruction is in the MEM stage.

Synchronous Read RAM Read Hold Functionality
The "Synchronous Read RAM Read Hold" functionality discussed here means that for some RAMs, from the clock edge of the last valid read command, the Q side of the RAM will hold the data corresponding to the read operation until the next valid command is sampled. Please note that the command must be valid; for example, the read command can only be valid if the chip enable signal of the RAM is valid. So when the chip enable signal of the RAM is invalid, even if the address of the RAM keeps changing, the RAM does not receive any new read command.

The RAM read hold functionality described here may vary in detail for RAMs from different IP vendors. For example, in some cases, the Q output of RAM is held between two consecutive read commands, i.e., if a read command is sent first, and then a write command is sent later, the Q output of the RAM still holds the result of the previous read. For another example, in order to hold the Q output of the RAM, the clock of the RAM must be supplied after sending a read command and must not be turned off. Although most of the RAMs provided by IP vendors have read hold functionality, if you want to use this feature, you should consult the RAM's technical documentation to clarify the behavior before using it.

Although the RAM read hold functionality will not be used in the scope of this section, in subsequent practice, the pipelined CPU can be blocked and stalled. This means that an instruction may issue a RAM read request in one cycle but not be able to proceed to a later pipeline stage in the next cycle. It is necessary to ensure that the instruction will still be able to get the correct content from the RAM output port when it finally reaches the later pipeline stage. If the read hold functionality of the RAM is utilized, the generation logic of the RAM address input can be moderately simplified, only that the chip select enable signal of the RAM needs to be controlled more finely.

5.1.3 Adjust Datapath for Updating PC

5.1.3.1 Adjust Datapath for Updating PC of Branch Instruction

Since the information for calculating the jump target address comes from the instruction code and the general-purpose register file, the branch instruction can calculate the correct jump direction and target as early as in the decode stage. In order to minimize the control-hazard pipeline blocking, we arrange the timing of updating PC by the jumping branch instruction when it is in the decode stage. At this point, we should note that for the nextpc generation logic in the pre-IF stage, the PC used for calculating the jump target of PC-relative branch is the PC of the branch instruction in the decode stage, not the PC of the fetch stage at this time.

5.1.3.2 Adjust Datapath for Updating PC When Resetting

The reference design given in this chapter resets the PC register to `0x1BFFFFFC` when the reset signal is active, instead of `0x1C000000` as specified in the instruction manual, which is just a logic-saving trick. Since the request to the instruction RAM comes from the `next_pc` in the pre-IF stage instead of the PC in the fetch stage, this allows the first fetch request after the reset is reversed to be at `0x1C000000` without adding any new multiplexer logic.

5.1.4 Control Signals in Pipelined CPU Without Considering Hazards

In the previous section, we gave a general approach to the design of pipelined circuits. Here we adapt the pipeline control signals in the circuit to the actual situation without considering hazards, which mainly involves how to set `ready_go` signal at each stage.

For the IF stage, since the instruction is only fetched from the instruction RAM, the instruction RAM must be able to return the instruction code when the instruction is in the fetch stage, so the `ready_go` signal of the fetch stage is always 1.

For the ID stage, the `ready_go` signal is always 1 as well, since the decode and read register file are all completed in one cycle.

For the EXE stage, the `ready_go` signal of the EXE stage is always 1, because all the instructions currently being processed only take one cycle to complete in this stage.

For the MEM stage, since data is currently accessed from the data RAM, when the load class instructions is located at MEM stage, the data RAM must be able to return data, so the `ready_go` signal in the MEM stage is always 1.

For the WB stage, since the write back to the register file must be completed within one cycle, the WB stage of the `ready_go` signal is always 1.

In summary, the `ready_go` signals of the five stages are all 1. The purpose of explaining each of them here is twofold: firstly, to remind you to know why these signals are always set to 1 and secondly, to remind you not to rush to simplify these constant 1s by bringing them into the logic of generating other control signals. These `ready_go` signals will become more and more complex as the complexity of the design increases.

At this point, a pipelined CPU with 20 LoongArch instructions has been designed, regardless of hazards. Although this CPU has the characteristics of pipeline, it can only run specially processed LoongArch executable programs.

5.1.5 *Handle the Reset*

Here is a discussion of a topic that is less often covered in textbooks, reset. Since it is a reset signal, it should initialize all software-perceivable states of the CPU to a uniquely determined state for as long as it is in effect. This may sound a bit convoluted. What a reset actually accomplishes is that no matter how many times a CPU is rebooted, it will behave the same way every time it runs the same program. For example, the state of where the CPU takes its first instruction after a power-on reset must be determined, which is specified in the *Instruction Manual* in Section 6.3. What about the state of the general-purpose register file? What about the state of memory? We find that these questions are not specified in the *Instruction Manual*. It means that the CPU's circuits do not have to set the values in these registers or memories to a defined value, while the reset signal is active. Their reset (initialization) is done by software.

The reference design we gave only considers the case where the reset signal is a synchronous reset. There is no need to argue for whether the reset signal is synchronous or asynchronous for digital logic circuits like CPU, just like whether it is better to have a big endian or a small endian. Readers can choose according to their own preferences. But remember, once you decide, you can only[1] use the chosen method in one design.

Finally, we would like to clarify one of the most common mistakes that beginners may make. It is initiating the first instruction fetch request externally, while the reset signal is active. In the design scenarios we have encountered so far, this is feasible, since reading the instruction RAM more or less often will have no side effects. However, in most real systems, the first instruction after a processor core reset is not fetched from the internal instruction RAM, but from the on-chip ROM external

---

[1]In fact, a more rigorous wording would be "as far as possible." But this leads to a question of degree, and for beginners, or within the scope of the practical tasks covered in this book, we give stricter limits to reduce the difficulty of mastery.

to the processor core, or even Flash external to the CPU chip. The processor core accesses this ROM or Flash, usually by initiating an (on-chip) bus access request. The processor core is usually the later part of the CPU chip to be reset. At the later stage of the processor core hardware reset, most of the external buses and device modules have already been reset and are in an operational state. If the processor core has started to continuously initiate access requests to the external buses at this point in time, the buses and peripherals will respond to the access requests. But at this point, the processor core is still in the process of being reset. When the reset is revoked, the state of the external bus as perceived by the processor core and the actual state of the bus will be inconsistent, resulting in errors.

5.2   Instruction-Level Dependency and Pipeline Hazards

We now move on to the second phase of our simple pipelined CPU design. We will analyze the effect of instruction dependency on the pipelined CPU design based on the design of the first phase and then make adjustments to our CPU design. Please refer to Section 9.3 of *Fundamentals of Computer Architecture (3rd edition)* or other related literature for instruction dependency and pipelining hazards. The process of analysis is omitted here with a few key points summarized as follows:

(1) The data hazards that need to be resolved on a single-issue static pipelined CPU are those related to read-after-write (RAW) dependency on registers. Write-after-write (WAW) and write-after-read (WAR) dependency on registers do not cause pipeline hazards, and all types of dependency on memory do not cause pipeline hazards.

(2) For single-issue static pipelined CPU, if the implemented instruction set does not have a branch delay slot, the pipeline hazards caused by control hazard must be considered in the absence of an implementation such as a branch target buffer (BTB), since branch instructions can only be processed (executed) at the earliest possible time in the decode stage.

(3) The handling of structural hazards on a single-issue static pipelined CPU can be simplified as: If an instruction in a forward pipeline cannot run, then an instruction in a backward pipeline cannot run either.

To address the third point, the stage-by-stage interlocking control mechanism used in the pipelined CPU design given above ensures that if any stage fails to move forward, all the backward stages can be stopped in time without losing data, so structure hazards have been resolved.

Next, we will focus on pipeline hazards related to RAW data hazards and control hazards.

5.2.1   Handle Pipeline Hazards Caused by RAW Data Dependency

The case that causes pipeline hazard related to register RAW is that the instruction that produces the result (the "writer") has not yet written the result back to the general-purpose register file, and the instruction that needs the result (the "reader") is already in the decode stage. The value it reads from the general-purpose register file is the old value, not the new value.

How can this error be avoided? One intuitive solution is to let the instruction that needs a result wait in the decode stage until the resulting instruction writes the result to the general-purpose register file before moving to the execute stage. In this section, we use this idea to adapt the design.

The key point in this set of design ideas is how to generate the conditions that control whether an instruction in the decode stage moves on or blocks, which centers on determining whether there is RAW dependency between instructions in different stages of the pipeline that can cause hazards. Combined with our design of five-stage pipelined CPU, this judgment can be described as follows: If an instruction in the decode stage has a source operand from a **non-zero** register and then if the register number of any of these source operands is the same with the register number (**non-zero**) of the destination operand of an instruction that is currently in the execute, memory access, or write back stage, then the instruction in the decode stage has a RAW dependency that can cause hazard with the instruction in the execute, memory access, or write back stage.

In the specific description given above, some readers may not understand why the source register number of a decode-stage instruction should also be compared with the destination register number of a write-back-stage instruction. The reason is that the behavior of the readout data when the register file is read and written at the same time is not properly understood. Thinking back to the behavior of the register stack analyzed in Chap. 3, Practical Task 1, if the address of the read port is the same as the write address in the clock cycle in which the write enable is active (the write enable will be sampled by the rising edge of the clock cycle between this clock cycle and the next clock cycle), the old value of the item will only appear on the port where the data is read out and not the data that is written on the write port at this time. As long as you understand this timing feature, you will naturally know that the instructions of the decode stage and the instructions of the write back stage are needed to compare the register numbers.

In translating the description given in the previous section into a concrete code implementation, there is an implicit detail that is easily overlooked by beginners, that is, to make sure that the two registers being compared are both valid. There are three aspects to this. First, whether the commands being compared have a source or destination register operand. For example, the addi.w instruction only has the source operand of the rj register, but no source operand for the rk register. Another example, the bl instruction does not have a source operand for a register, and the beq and bne branch instructions do not have a destination operand for a register.

Second, if the definition of an instruction does have a register source or destination operand, but the register number is 0, then there is no need to compare. Because the value of register 0 is always 0 in the LoongArch architecture, there is no special handling of the dependency that exists for this register. Third, whether or not there is an instruction in the pipeline stage used for comparison, as long as there is no instruction, the register number, instruction type, and other information in the pipeline buffer for that stage are invalid. If these special cases are not taken into account when writing the comparison logic, the processor will not be faulty, but it will be blocked unnecessarily in some cases, resulting in a loss of performance.

After determining the RAW dependency that will cause a hazard, the last step is to block the instruction at the decode stage when the condition is valid. Remember the `ready_go` signal at each stage of the flow? Here, we just need to adjust the `ready_go` signal of the decode stage. Obviously, it is not always 1 anymore. If there is a RAW dependency between the instruction in the decode stage and the instructions in the next three stages, namely, execute, memory access, and write back, that could cause a hazard, then you have to set the `ready_go` signal to 0.

5.2.2 Handle Pipeline Hazards Caused by Control Dependency

In the previous CPU pipeline slicing, the processing logic related to nextpc in the branch instruction operation (determining whether to jump or not, and the jump target) has been placed in the decode stage, so the key design point related to control dependency is to cancel the instruction that may be in the fetch stage and on the wrong execution path and not to allow this wrongly fetched instruction to enter into the CPU pipeline for execution.

In order to understand why the control dependency can be resolved by performing the above processing, we suggest that readers: (1) review the timing characteristics of the synchronous read RAM, so as to make it clear that the read request and address of the instruction RAM are issued in the pre-IF stage and that the instruction is waiting for the instruction RAM to return the read data when the instruction is in the fetch stage; and (2) draw a pipeline timing diagram to help understand the situation. With these preparations, we will then "deduce" the execution of the branch instruction in the existing five-stage pipelined CPU. Suppose there is a branch instruction whose PC is 0x1000, in the first clock cycle, it is in the fetch stage, and at this time, the pre-IF stage is calculating nextpc at the same time. At this point, it is not possible for nextpc to be calculated based on the branch instruction in the fetch stage. The instruction code of the branch instruction has just been read out from the instruction RAM, and the CPU doesn't know whether this instruction is a branch instruction or not, and it doesn't know whether it jumps or not, and where it jumps, and both of these two aspects of information can only be obtained after it moves to the decode stage. Therefore, in the first clock cycle, nextpc can only be set to 0x1004 according to the default situation of sequential fetch. In the second clock cycle, the branch instruction with PC=0x1000 comes to the decode stage, and **the instruction with PC=0x1004 comes to the fetch stage**. If the branch instruction finds out that it doesn't jump after the decode stage, then the pre-IF stage continues to send out the fetch instruction PC=0x1008 in sequence, and the instruction with PC=0x1004 in the fetch stage is also the instruction in the program's expected execution path, which will stay in the pipeline to continue to be executed. If the branch instruction finds that it needs to jump after processing in the decode stage (assuming that the target address of the jump is 0x2000), then even if it immediately sets nextpc generated in the pre-IF stage to 0x2000, it will not be able to change the status that the instruction with PC=0x1004 is in the fetch stage. Obviously, the instruction with PC=0x1004 is not an instruction that is on the expected execution path of the program, and it cannot be executed (otherwise, it will incorrectly change the processor state). One way to deal with this "unwanted guest" is to keep it out of trouble (i.e., some textbooks give the solution of treating this instruction as a nop instruction), and the other way is to get it out of the program (i.e., the option we are suggesting here to get rid of that instruction).

We do not recommend the option of treating a fetch error as a nop instruction. The disadvantages are twofold: First, this nop instruction cannot be marked with any exception; otherwise, it will violate the requirement of precise exception.[2] To deal with this, it is necessary to distinguish this hardware-automatically converted nop instruction from the normal nop in the program, which is a futile burden; second, the conversion of the instruction into a nop instruction requires the modification of 32 wires, which makes the fan out of the control signals larger and the latency worse than the recommended scheme. In addition, it should be reminded that all-zero code in the LoongArch instruction set are not nop instructions, so don't use the way of erasing all-zero code to set nop instructions.

Why do we recommend the option of canceling instructions? Recall from our pipeline design reference how we indicate the presence or absence of instructions in the pipeline. We do this by using the 1-bit valid at each stage of the pipeline. So, to cancel an instruction, we simply erase **the valid that accompanies the instruction** to 0. Note that we emphasize "the valid that accompanies the instruction," not the valid of the fetch stage. Let's look at the following common beginner's mistake. Suppose the code for the valid of the fetch stage is as follows, without taking into account the cancelation of the jump branch instruction:

```verilog
always @(posedge clock) begin
    if (reset)
        fs_valid <= 1'b0;
    else if (fs_allowin)
        fs_valid <= to_fs_valid;
end
```

---

[2]Some readers may not yet understand the exception content. We can come back here and think about it later in the experiment on exception support.

Assume that the branch instruction jump cancel signal inputting to the fetch stage is `br_taken_cancel`. This is how some beginners cancel the mistaken instruction:

```verilog
always @(posedge clock) begin
    if (reset)
        fs_valid <= 1'b0;
    else if (br_taken_cancel)
        fs_valid <= 1'b0;
    else if (fs_allowin)
        fs_valid <= to_fs_valid;
end
```

We guess that the above code was written with the idea that the instruction to be canceled is in the fetch stage, so it needs to be cleared to 0 when `br_taken` takes effect. The above code is wrong. Readers can try to deduce the behavior of the above code. When the instruction is not blocked at the fetch stage, this code not only fails to cancel the instruction that was fetched by mistake but also causes the instruction at the jump target of the branch instruction not to be fetched into the pipeline. If we compare this to the design scheme we emphasized above, which is to "set valid to 0 for the instruction that accompanies the fetched instruction," we can be able to see what the problem is. If the fetched instruction is not blocked in the fetch stage, it will come to the decode stage in the next clock cycle, so we need to set the valid from the fetch stage to the decode stage to 0 instead of setting the valid into the fetch stage to 0. Therefore, the logic for writing the valid into the decode stage should be adjusted:

```verilog
always @(posedge clock) begin
    if (reset)
        ds_valid <= 1'b0;
    else if (br_taken_cancel)
        ds_valid <= 1'b0;
    else if (ds_allowin)
        ds_valid <= fs_to_ds_valid;
end
```

However, is the code like the above complete? In the current scenario, it is a correct change. Since the instruction RAM always returns the read data in the next clock cycle after the read request, the instruction in the fetch stage will not wait for the instruction to be fetched. So `br_taken_cancel` must be valid when the fetched instruction in the fetch stage is going to the decode stage. (This derivation is left to readers.) However, once the taken instruction will not return immediately, that is, the instruction in the fetch instruction stage may wait for the instruction to be fetched, the only adjust of the write logic of `ds_valid` is not enough. It is also necessary to adjust the write logic of `fs_valid` at the same time, as follows:

```verilog
always @(posedge clock) begin
    if (reset)
        fs_valid <= 1'b0;
    else if (fs_allowin)
        fs_valid <= to_fs_valid;
    else if (br_taken_cancel)
        fs_valid <= 1'b0;
end
```

It looks a lot like the wrong change, except that the `if` branch for `br_taken_cancel` clearing 0 has been moved to the bottom. However, the meaning of this seemingly simple repositioning has changed dramatically. Expanding the last line of the `fs_valid` clear 0 condition, we have `!reset && !fs_allowin && br_taken_cancel`, whereas `!reset && !fs_allowin` implies `fs_valid && ( !fs_ready_go || !ds_allowin)`, which means that, to paraphrase in natural language, "when the fetch stage has an instruction and cannot proceed to the next stage in the next clock cycle." In this case, if a branch instruction jumps, then the instruction in the fetch stage needs to be canceled.

Finally, I would like to add a note about the valid timing of the `br_taken_cancel` signal. Since the branch instruction may need to process the source operand to get the jump or not and the target of the jump, this kind of instruction, even if it reaches the decode stage, may be blocked due to the RAW dependency of the registers. So before it gets the correct source operand (i.e., before the RAW dependency blocking is lifted), it is important **not to** make the `br_taken_cancel` signal valid.

At this point, we have a CPU that can correctly handle the various types of pipeline hazards. Although it may be a bit low performance at times, it will at least be able to correctly execute a normal LoongArch executable program.

5.3   Design Pipeline Data Forwarding

We are now entering the final phase of our simple pipelined CPU design. We will continue to explore a higher performance solution, the Forwarding technique, for handling hazards caused by RAW dependency in pipelined CPU.

We introduced the use of blocking instructions at the decode stage to solve the pipeline hazard caused by the RAW dependency of registers. Readers should have observed a phenomenon in Practical Task 8, that is, while the instruction that needs the result is waiting at the decode stage, the instruction that provide the result before it has already generated the result which has not yet been written to the register file. Is it possible for the forward-stage instruction to directly transfer the generated result to the backward-stage instruction, so that the backward-stage instruction does not need to wait? The answer is yes. The design based on this idea is the forwarding of pipelined CPU, also called bypass. The basic principle is not difficult to understand. You can refer to Section 9.3.1 of *Fundamentals of Computer Architecture (3rd edition)* or other related literature. The next step is to analyze and discuss how to design the bypass. We will continue to design the datapath before processing the control signals.

5.3.1 Design Forwarding Datapath

5.3.1.1 The Forwarding Path of the Operation Result

Let's first look at how to handle the instruction that produces the result if it is add.w. The result of the add.w instruction in the execute stage can only go to the buffer in the memory access stage, so we need to add a special path to pass the result directly to the backward-stage instructions. Is it enough to add only this one forward path? Obviously not. When the add.w instruction is in the memory access stage, its result can only go to the buffer in the write back stage. So it needs to add another path for passing the result. Otherwise, the backward-stage instructions will still be stuck, because they can't get the result in time. If we continue to analyze, we will also find that when the add.w instruction is located in the write back stage, it also needs to add another independent forwarding path.

When we consider the forwarding path design, the add.w instruction represents those instructions that produce results at the execute stage. However, the ld.w does not belong to this category. It does not produce results until the memory access stage. Nevertheless, when analyzed, we see that the ld.w instruction is perfectly fine to reuse the forwarding paths that were added at the memory access and write back stages to prepass the results of add.w-like instructions. Because the forward path merely passes the results through, having the register number and the value is sufficient and has nothing to do with what the instruction that produces the result does.

The abovementioned forwarding path is realized in the diagram of the CPU structure as three lines with arrows. Where do the lines start and end? Let's first look at how the results of the execute stage are forwarded. Let's start with two common errors among beginners.

The First Wrong Scheme The starting point is located at the result output of the execute stage ALU, and the end point is located at the input data generation logic of the execute stage ALU.

The Second Wrong Scheme The starting point is located at the Q-port output of the flip-flops that hold the execute stage ALU result in the memory access stage pipeline buffer, and the end point is located at the logic for generating read outputs from the register file at decode stage.

If you draw the forwarding path of these two schemes on the structure diagram, you will immediately notice that it is incorrect. In the first case, there is a combinational loop from the output of the ALU to the input of the ALU. In the second case, the instruction at the execute stage doesn't get the result of its previous instruction at all. Why do some people make such intuitive mistakes? Often it is because they do not follow the "design before coding" procedure and rush to change the code before thinking clearly about the design, resulting in a logically confusing design. So here again, do not take the design process lightly, and do not try to save time by not drawing structural design diagrams when designing.

Two possible design options are given here.

Option 1, the starting point is located at the result output of the execute stage ALU, and the end point is located at the decode stage register file readout result generation logic.

Option 2, the starting point is located at the Q-port output of the flip-flops that hold the execute stage ALU result in the memory access stage pipeline buffer, and the end point is located at the input data generation logic of the execute stage ALU.

Both programs are functionally correct. Readers can use the sequence add.w r2, r1, r1; sub.w r3, r2, r2 to deduce two instructions in the pipeline. You will find that when the sub.w instruction follows the add.w instruction in the pipeline, the value of the source operand, r2, must be the value of the result of the calculation by the add.w instruction when it is in the ALU. We summarize the characteristics of option 1 as "the result of the combinational logic is forwarded to the decode stage register readout," and the characteristics of option 2 as "the previous result stored in the pipeline buffer is forwarded to the ALU input of the execute stage." An important difference between the two options is whether the end point is at the end of the combinational logic at the decode stage or at the beginning of the combinational logic at the execute stage.

Which is better? It is not clear yet, we need to continue to consider the starting and end points of the remaining forwarding paths along the lines of the two options. For option 1, the starting point of the forwarding path for the memory access stage result is the output of the multiplexer of the output of the data RAM and the ALU result stored in the memory access stage buffer. The starting point of the forwarding path for the write back stage result is the result of the write back stage that will be written to the register file. Everything is in harmony. For option 2, the starting point of the forwarding path for the memory access stage result is the output of the Q-port of the flip-flops that stores the result of the memory access stage in the pipeline buffer of the write back stage. The forwarding path of the result of the write-back stage is …. It seems that there is no more path to forward the result of the write back stage. If the write back stage is the add.w r2, r1, r1 instruction, and the decode stage is the sub.w r3, r2, r2 instruction, there are no instructions to write the r2 register on the execute or access stage. Unless you change the forward path, forwarding the result of the write back stage to the Q-side output of the decode stage register readout, the next sub.w r3, r2, r1 instruction will not move to the execute stage. In order to eliminate as much blocking as possible by forwarding, we find that either option requires the forwarding path ending at the decode stage register readout. Therefore, we prefer option 1, where all the forwarding paths end up at the same place, so that the logic for generating the correct register source operand from the forwarding result can be centralized in one place.

If option 1 above is still more or less subjective, let's look at another scenario. Remember that in order to solve control hazards in pipeline, we process all branch instructions at the decode stage. The currently implemented branch instructions, beq, bne, and jirl, all have register source operands. If there is a RAW dependency between them and their predecessor instructions, then they must block themselves until the result is written to the register file, unless the forwarding paths end at the decode stage. Now, it makes more sense to choose option 1. In our experience, option 1 has fewer traps for beginners, so the rest of the presentation will be based on option 1 only.

5.3.1.2   Multiplexer Selection for Forwarding Results

Once the forwarding path is constructed, the entire pipelined CPU forwarding datapath still has a tail to design, that is, how to adjust the logic of the decode stage to generate the register read result. From a spatial point of view, the value of register source operand 1 of the decode stage instruction can be the output from general-purpose register file read port 1 and can also come from the results forwarded from the execute, memory access, and write back stages. Similarly, the value of register source operand 2 of the decode stage instruction can come from the output of general-purpose register file read port 2 and can come from the results forwarded from the execute, memory access, and write back stages. So we need to add two four-to-one multiplexers, with selection priority. Why do we need to priority four-to-one multiplexers here? Let's look at an extreme example. For example, the instruction sequence add.w r4, r1, r1; add.w r4, r2, r2; add.w r4, r3, r3; sub.w r6, r5, r4. When add.w r4, r1, r1 is at the write back stage, add.w r4, r2, r2 is at the memory access stage, and add.w r4, r3, r3 is at the execute stage, then which value should sub.w r6, r5, r4 at the decode stage choose for the source operand 2? Obviously, we should choose the result that was forwarded from the execute stage. So you can see that the choice of which result to forward depends not only on whether the register number of the source operand is the same as the register number of the result to be forwarded but also on the priority relationship between the different pipeline stages.

Here's a digression. In our previous analysis, readers can see that we often assume an instruction sequence and then deduce their execution in the designed pipelined CPU, so as to compare and evaluate different design scenarios, and then get a more concise and reasonable design scheme. Please master this methodology step by step. Remember that we have repeatedly emphasized the need to "plan before you act" in circuit design, so how do you "plan" when designing a CPU? It is to use the hypothetical instructions sequence introduced here to deduce the execution. Why do we use the hypothetical scenario of "thinking and acting" instead of the scenario embodied in the verification? The reason is that the biggest risk in any verification approach based on test cases is the completeness of the scenarios covered by the stimulus. Although validators have a range of technical and engineering tools to minimize this risk, as designers, and especially as structural designers, we cannot rely on the completeness of the verification cases for the correctness of the design. The structural designer's rigorous deduction of various possible scenarios during design is the "first lock" to ensure the correctness and reliability of the final design, while the verification work of the validator is the "second lock" to ensure the correctness and reliability of the design. We need to put on "double insurance"!

5.3.2   *Control Signals of Forwarding Pipeline*

So far, we have designed the new datapath and the control signals for the four-to-one multiplexers in the path that are added by forwarding. If you were to follow this design for a blocking CPU and run all the test cases, you would be happy to see that the tests pass. Unfortunately, however, your design of a pipelined CPU with forwarding is not correct at this point. You will find that the same program, running on this pipelined CPU with forwarding in the same amount of time as the CPU with only blocking capabilities. Isn't the purpose of introducing forwarding to improve performance? After all this effort, the performance has not improved at all. What is the problem? The problem is that the blocking control signal of the decode stage has not been modified. It is still blocking in the strictest way. So, should we just change the `ready_go` of the decode stage to a constant 1 with a stroke of a pen? Calm down. Look at this sequence: `ld.w r2, r1, 0x0; add.w r4, r3, r2.` If the `ld.w` instruction is at the execute stage and the `add.w` instruction is at the decode stage, can the `add.w` instruction go to the execute stage on the next cycle? Obviously not, because at this moment, the `ld.w` instruction located in the execute stage does not generate the final result. So even if you have the forwarding path, there is no correct data. The `add.w` instruction must be stopped in the decode stage, until the `ld.w` instruction reaches the memory access stage, then it can get the correct value through the forwarding path from the memory access stage to the decode stage, entering into the execute stage in the next cycle. Therefore, when the instruction at the decode stage has a RAW dependency with the current ld.w instruction at the execution stage, the `ready_go` signal of the decode stage should be set to 0. With only 20 instructions implemented in the CPU, this is the only blocking condition of the decode stage after the introduction of the forwarding. As more instructions are implemented later, readers must pay attention to whether the condition of `ready_go` needs to be adjusted or not.

5.3.3   *Clock Frequency Degradation Due to Forwarding*

The forwarding pipelined CPU design presented in this section is relatively easy to implement and minimizes pipeline blocking due to RAW dependency. But there is no such thing as a free lunch. One drawback of this design is that it increases the latency of the CPU's critical path, resulting in a decrease in CPU frequency. We are going to show you how to analyze the critical path latency in your design.

The design changes in the forwarding CPU are the modification of the `ready_go` signal generation logic in the decode stage, the addition of a few more wires, and the addition of two four-to-one multiplexers. For the first change, the `ready_go` signal generation logic is simpler rather than more complex, so the modification should not cause the frequency to drop. As for the second change, the addition of bypasses of the three stages of execution, memory access, and write back will indeed increase the output loads of the last one or two levels of these logic devices, thus leading to an increase in the latency of these logic devices. However, the current design is very small in scale, and the added wire distance is not that far away, so the increase in the latency should not be a major contradiction in the decrease in the main frequency. Therefore, the addition of the two four-to-one multiplexers at the decode stage becomes the main suspect. When we read the final timing report, we find that the increase in critical path delay is not just the delay of one four-to-one multiplexer. So at this point, we can basically conclude that the two four-to-one multiplexers must have been involved in introducing a new combinational logic path with unusually long latency.

So we go back to the design and comb through all the combinatorial logic paths passing through these two four-to-one multiplexers, and the answer gradually emerges. "Execute stage pipeline buffer flip-flops Q-port" →ALU →Forwarding path →"Decode stage four-to-one multiplexer" →"Determination logic of branch instruction jump direction" →"GenNextPC's four-to-one multiplexer" →"Instruction address translation for fetch request" →"Address input port of instruction RAM."

We hope that readers can master the above approach to identifying the critical path in a design based on combing through the design rather than just looking at the timing reports provided by the EDA tool. Timing reports are important to look at, but they only give you hints and feedback. The proper way to analyze the design is to start with the design. We do not make the timing optimization of these critical paths as the guiding goal of this book. Therefore, we will simply provide some ideas for those who would like to learn more.

If you completely discard forwarding, you will have the highest clock frequency and low pipeline efficiency. If you maximize forwarding, you will have the highest pipeline efficiency but low clock frequency. The performance optimization here is to find a balance between the clock frequency and the pipeline efficiency. Through analysis, we will find that the conflict focuses on the forwarding of branch instructions. If we analyze further, we will find that if we don't directly forward the ALU combinational output to the decode stage branch instruction, instead, forward the stored ALU result (in the memory access stage pipeline buffers), the critical path can also be eliminated. In this way, we only block the branch instruction for a cycle in some cases. If this happens infrequently in the running program, the overall execution efficiency of the program in the pipeline will not be reduced by much, and at the same time, due to the increase of the CPU frequency, the overall performance will be improved.

5.4 CPU Design Experiment Function Simulation Advanced Debugging Skills

5.4.1 Which Signals to Capture for CPU Debugging and How to Look at Them

5.4.1.1 Valid and PC signals Are Essential

From the previous section, it is clear that debugging the CPU must be done in conjunction with the instruction sequence of the test program. We read the source code of test program and its disassembly code to understand the instruction sequence executed by the CPU. How can we quickly connect them to the captured signals? The central link is the PC of the instruction. That is the reason why our reference design passes the PC from the fetch stage all the way down the pipeline even if current CPU design does not support exceptions. Each stage of the pipeline has the PC of the instruction currently being processed in its buffer. By capturing the PC signals of each stage in the waveform window, we can see at a glance how an instruction progresses through the pipeline.

In addition to the PC signal of each stage, the `valid` signal of each stage should also be captured in this style of code in our reference design. For any given stage, do not analyze the other signals of the stage during the cycle when its valid is 0, unless your design intent is to have the cycle valid at 1 and you are analyzing why it is not set to 1.

The rest of the signals that are more commonly captured are the write enable, address, and data of instruction writing to the general-purpose register file at the write back stage, the signals on the instruction RAM and data RAM access interfaces, and the instruction code at the fetch or decode stage. However, these signals do not have to be captured every time, depending on your debugging needs.

5.4.1.2 Group Signals for Each Pipeline in an Orderly Manner

For pipelined CPU, it is highly recommended that you place signals from the same stage in the same group and then place the groups in top-down or bottom-up order according to the order of the pipeline stages.

As the design matures and solidifies, and as you accumulate debugging experience, we recommend that you capture the basic, commonly used signals for each stage, and group and place them according to the above suggestions. Then save these basic signals into a signal file. In this way, when you restart the simulation, you can display these basic signals as soon as the simulation is finished, which saves the time of adding them again.

5.4.1.3 Traverse Instructions Before Traverse Pipeline

Assuming the signal waveforms are all laid out as suggested above. Then what should we do to see such a colorful waveform? As we said in the introduction of debugging method, we have to find the instruction that corresponds to the source error and then analyze which part of the circuit is wrong with this instruction.

As a first step of locating instructions, it is recommended that you focus only on one stage of the pipeline, usually the write back stage. Based on the valid and PC signals at the write back stage, combined with the instruction sequence identified in the disassembly code, you can move back and forth in the waveform to locate the faulty instruction. As a reminder, if you are moving beyond your field of view, consider looking up the signal value in the waveform to speed up the movement and accuracy.

After finding the suspicious instruction, look at the disassembly code according to its PC, and find out whether it is a write to general-purpose register file, a write to memory, or a branch-and-jump instruction. If it is a write to general-purpose register file, start from the signals that access the register file at the write back stage. If it is a write to memory, start from the signals that access the data RAM at the execute stage. If it is a branch, start from the `br_taken` and `target` signals that affect the `nextPC` generated by this instruction at the decode stage. Then you can follow the datapath of the CPU design in reverse.

Once the execution of a suspect instruction in the CPU has been reversed, either the error in the CPU design has been clarified, or the instruction is not the source of the error. Then locating the instruction returns to locating the instruction either forward or backward along the timeline.

5.5 Tasks and Practices

After completing this chapter, readers are expected to complete the following three practical tasks:

1. Simple pipelined CPU without considering hazards. See Sect. 5.5.1.
2. Blocking techniques to resolve hazards. See Sect. 5.5.2.
3. Forwarding techniques to resolve hazards. See Sect. 5.5.3.

5.5.1   Practical Task 7: Simple Pipelined CPU Without Considering Hazards

This practical task requires the following work based on the single-cycle CPU implemented in Practical Task 6:

1. Adjust the CPU top module interface by adding the instruction RAM chip select signal `inst_sram_en` and the data RAM chip select signal `data_sram_en`.
2. Adjust the CPU top module interface signal `inst_sram_we` and `data_sram_we` from a 1-bit write enable to a 4-bit byte write enable.
3. Design a single-issue, five-stage pipelined CPU that does not consider hazards.
4. Run the func corresponding to exp7, and pass simulation and FPGA verification.

Please refer to the method described in Sect. 2.3.1 to obtain the experimental development environment required for this practical task. The specific experimental environment is located at `mycpu_env/`. **Instead of using the `soc_dram/`, the `soc_bram/` subdirectory should be used for verification.**

Changing CPU-accessed instruction RAM and data RAM from distributed RAM to block RAM, we adjust the experimental development environment as well: It is still the `mycpu_env` experimental environment, and the location and usage of the `gettrace/`, `func/`, and `myCPU/` remain unchanged, except that the `soc_bram/` is used instead of the `soc_dram/` in the `soc_verify/`. The organization and usage of files in the `soc_bram/` are similar to those in the `soc_dram/`. The directory structure and functions of the experimental development environment are shown below:

```
|--gettrace/                 Generate the reference trace
|--func/                     Function verification test programs
|--myCPU/                    CPU rtl code written by readers
|--soc_verify/               SoC system verification environment
↪   for CPU
  |--soc_bram/               Verification environment
    ↪   corresponding to CPU external
                             connection to block RAM
  |   |--rtl/                SoC_Lite rtl code
  |   |   |--soc_lite_top.v  SoC_Lite top module
  |   |   |--CONFREG/        Confreg module for peripheral
    ↪   devices such as LEDs,
                             dial switches, etc. on the board
  |   |   |--BRIDGE/         With a 1×2 bridge module, CPU's
    ↪   data sram interface
                             accesses both confreg and data_ram
  |   |   |--xilinx_ip/      Customized Xilinx IP, including
    ↪   clk_pll, inst_ram and data_ram
  |   |--testbench/          Simulation environment
```

```
|  |   |--mycpu_tb.v         Simulation top module which catch
↪   debug info and
                            compare it with golden_trace.txt
|   |--run_vivado/           Vivado project running directory
|       |--constraints/      Vivado project design constraints
|       |--mycpu_bram_prj/   Vivado project files directory
```

The instruction RAM and the data RAM from Practical Task 7 are implemented as block RAM, which need to be accessed with a chip select signal. For this reason, the myCPU top module interface adds the chip select signals `inst_sram_en` for the instruction RAM and `data_sram_en` for the data RAM, both of which are 1-bit and active high.

Although only `st.w` has been implemented in Practical Task 7, considering the requirements of the following tasks, both `inst_sram_we` and `data_sram_we` in the top module interface of myCPU have been changed from 1 bit to 4 bits, and their meanings have been changed from RAM write-enable to RAM byte-write-enable.

Once the lab environment is ready, please refer to the following steps to complete this practical task:

1. Update CPU code at `mycpu_env/myCPU/`.
2. Modify the func configuration file, `mycpu_env/func/include/test_config.h`, select the configuration of `exp7`, and compile. (If you obtained the experimental development environment from the package `exp7.zip`, please skip this step.)
3. Open the gettrace project, `mycpu_env/gettrace/gettrace.xpr` (The IP core in this Vivado project was created using Vivado2019.2. If you open it with a higher version of Vivado, refer to Appendix D.4 for the IP core upgrade). Run the simulation of the gettrace project (After entering the simulation interface, click `run all` and wait for the simulation to finish), and generate a new reference trace file `golden_trace.txt` (`mycpu_env/gettrace/golden_trace.txt`). The `golden_trace.txt` will not be complete until the simulation has finished running. (If you obtained the experimental development environment from the package `exp7.zip`, please skip this step.)
4. Start the project in `mycpu_env/soc_verify/soc_bram/run_vivado/` to verify myCPU. If you have not created a project in this directory, please refer to the steps described in Appendix D.2 to create a project using the `create_project.tcl` file in this directory. If necessary, please refer to Appendix D.4 to upgrade the IP core.
5. Refer to Chap. 4 Sect. 4.4.5.2 to re-customize `inst_ram` in the project. (If you obtained the experimental development environment from the package `exp7.zip`, please skip this step.)
6. Run the simulation in the project (click `run all` directly after entering the simulation interface), and carry out the function verification until the simulation test is passed.

7. Generate a bit stream file after Synthesis and Implementation in the project, and verify it on FPGA. (Please skip this step if you don't have a hardware experiment platform.)

5.5.2 Practical Task 8: Blocking Technique to Resolve Hazards

This practical task requires the following work based on the CPU implemented in Practical Task 7:

1. Add appropriate logic to handle pipeline hazards associated with register RAW data dependency (only blocking techniques are required for this task).
2. Run the func corresponding to exp8, and pass simulation and FPGA verification.

Please refer to the method described in Sect. 2.3.1 to obtain the experimental development environment required for this practical task. The specific experimental environment is located at `mycpu_env/`, and continue to use the `soc_bram/` subdirectory.

Once the lab environment is ready, please refer to the following steps to complete this practical task:

1. Update CPU code at `mycpu_env/myCPU/`.
2. Modify the func configuration file, `mycpu_env/func/include/test_config.h`, select the configuration of `exp8`, and compile. (If you obtained the experimental development environment from the package `exp8.zip`, please skip this step.)
3. Open the gettrace project, `mycpu_env/gettrace/gettrace.xpr` (The IP core in this Vivado project was created using Vivado2019.2. If you open it with a higher version of Vivado, refer to Appendix D.4 for the IP core upgrade). Run the simulation of the gettrace project (After entering the simulation interface, click `run all` and wait for the simulation to finish), and generate a new reference trace file `golden_trace.txt` (`mycpu_env/gettrace/golden_trace.txt`). The `golden_trace.txt` will not be complete until the simulation has finished running. (If you obtained the experimental development environment from the package `exp8.zip`, please skip this step.)
4. Start the project in `mycpu_env/soc_verify/soc_bram/run_vivado/` to verify myCPU. If you have not created a project in this directory, please refer to the steps described in Appendix D.2 to create a project using the `create_project.tcl` file in this directory. If necessary, please refer to Appendix D.4 to upgrade the IP core. If there is a project in this directory that has been created by a previous practice task, you can update the file list of CPU implementations in the project by referring to the steps described in Appendix D.3 after opening the project.

5. Refer to Chap. 4 Sect. 4.4.5.2 to re-customize `inst_ram` in the project. (If you obtained the experimental development environment from the package `exp8.zip`, please skip this step.)
6. Run the simulation in the project (click `run all` directly after entering the simulation interface), and carry out the function verification until the simulation test is passed.
7. Generate a bit stream file after Synthesis and Implementation in the project, and verify it on FPGA. (Please skip this step if you don't have a hardware experiment platform.)

5.5.3 *Practical Task 9: Forwarding Technique to Resolve Hazards*

This practical task requires the following work based on the CPU implemented in Practical Task 8:

1. Add appropriate data forwarding paths to minimize blocking.
2. Run the func corresponding to exp9, and pass simulation and FPGA verification. Further, the func running time in simulation is reduced compared with that of exp8.

Please refer to the method described in Sect. 2.3.1 to obtain the experimental development environment required for this practical task. The specific experimental environment is located at `mycpu_env/`, and continue to use the `soc_bram/` subdirectory.

Once the lab environment is ready, please refer to the following steps to complete this practical task:

1. Update CPU code at `mycpu_env/myCPU/`.
2. Modify the func configuration file, `mycpu_env/func/include/test_config.h`, select the configuration of `exp9`, and compile. (If you obtained the experimental development environment from the package `exp9.zip`, please skip this step.)
3. Open the gettrace project, `mycpu_env/gettrace/gettrace.xpr` (The IP core in this Vivado project was created using Vivado2019.2. If you open it with a higher version of Vivado, refer to Appendix D.4 for the IP core upgrade). Run the simulation of the gettrace project (After entering the simulation interface, click `run all` and wait for the simulation to finish), and generate a new reference trace file `golden_trace.txt` (`mycpu_env/gettrace/golden_trace.txt`). The `golden_trace.txt` will not be complete until the simulation has finished running. (If you obtained the experimental development environment from the package `exp9.zip`, please skip this step.)
4. Start the project in `mycpu_env/soc_verify/soc_bram/run_vivado/` to verify myCPU. If you have not created a project in this directory, please

refer to the steps described in Appendix D.2 to create a project using the `create_project.tcl` file in this directory. If necessary, please refer to Appendix D.4 to upgrade the IP core. If there is a project in this directory that has been created by a previous practice task, you can update the file list of CPU implementations in the project by referring to the steps described in Appendix D.3 after opening the project.

5. Refer to Chap. 4 Sect. 4.4.5.2 to re-customize `inst_ram` in the project. (If you obtained the experimental development environment from the package `exp9.zip`, please skip this step.)

6. Run the simulation in the project (click `run all` directly after entering the simulation interface), and carry out the function verification until the simulation test is passed.

7. Generate a bit stream file after Synthesis and Implementation in the project, and verify it on FPGA. (Please skip this step if you don't have a hardware experiment platform.)

Chapter 6
Add More User-Mode Instructions into Pipeline

In this chapter, we describe how to add more user-mode instructions into an existing simple pipelined CPU. Specifically:

- Arithmetic logic instructions: `slti`, `sltui`, `andi`, `ori`, `xori`, `sll`, `srl`, `sra`, `pcaddu12i`; Sect. 6.1.
- Multiplication and division instructions: `mul.w`, `mulh.w`, `mulh.wu`, `div.w`, `mod.w`, `div.wu`, `mod.wu`; Sect. 6.2.
- Branch instructions: `blt`, `bge`, `bltu`, `bgeu`; Sect. 6.3.
- Load and store instructions: `ld.b`, `ld.h`, `ld.bu`, `ld.hu`, `st.b`, `st.h`; Sect. 6.4.

Learning Goals for This Chapter
- Deepen the understanding of pipeline structure and design.
- Learn how to add user-mode instructions into CPU

Practical Tasks of This Chapter
There are two practical tasks in this chapter (see Sect. 6.5). Readers can complete these tasks after learning this chapter. The correspondence between sections and tasks is as follows:

- Sections 6.1 and 6.2 are corresponding to Task 10 (Sect. 6.5.1).
- Sections 6.3 and 6.4 are corresponding to Task 11 (Sect. 6.5.2).

6.1 Add Arithmetic Logic Instructions

The design process for adding instructions generally consists of three steps:

1. Carefully read the instruction manual to clarify the functional definition of the instruction to be implemented.

© The Author(s), under exclusive license to Springer Nature Singapore Pte Ltd. 2025   161
W. Wang, J. Xing, *CPU Design and Practice*,
https://doi.org/10.1007/978-981-96-6573-0_6

2. Consider the design adjustment of the datapath according to the function of the instruction, reuse what can be reused as much as possible, and add what should be added.
3. According to the adjusted datapath, sort out the control signals corresponding to all instructions (including the original and new instructions).

For the definitions of `slti`, `sltui`, and other arithmetic logic instructions to be added in this chapter, please read the *Instruction Manual* first. The following analysis assumes that readers are already familiar with the contents of this part.

6.1.1   Add Instruction `slti` and `sltui`

If we compare the `slti` and `slt` instructions, we will find that the comparison operation between the two source operands and the destination registers written back are exactly the same. The difference only lies in the source of the operands. However, if you compare the `slti` instruction with the `addi.w` instruction, you will see that the sources of the operands are the same. This means that the processing of `slti` instruction can reuse the datapaths of `slt` instruction in execute, memory access, and write-back stages on one hand, and reuse the datapaths of `addi.w` instruction in decode stage on the other hand. Accordingly, the control signals required by the `slti` instruction at each of the above stages are consistent with the control signals of the corresponding instructions of the reused datapaths.

Comparing and analyzing `sltui` with `sltu` and `addi.w` instructions in the same way, we can get the design idea that the processing of `sltui` instruction. It can reuse the datapaths of `sltu` instruction in execution, memory access, and write-back stages on one hand, and reuse the datapaths of `addi.w` instruction in decode stage on the other hand. Accordingly, the control signals required by the `sltui` instruction at the above stages are the same as the control signals of the corresponding instructions of the reused datapaths.

6.1.2   Add Instruction `andi`, `ori`, and `xori`

Comparing `andi`, `ori`, and `xori` instructions with `and`, `or`, and `xor` instructions, we can see that they perform the same logical operations and write back to the same target register number source. Therefore, these instructions reuse the datapaths of the former instructions in execute, memory access, and write-back stages. Accordingly, the control signals required by these instructions at the above stages are the same as the control signals of the corresponding instructions of the reused datapaths.

However, the second source operand of `andi`, `ori`, and `xori` is a zero extension of the 12-bit immediate number `ui12`. There is no existing datapath that can be reused, so it is necessary to adjust the datapath in the decode stage. We can add an input of "zero-extension of the instruction code immediate number field ui12 to 32 bits" to the multiplexer that generates the second source operand. Since the specification of the multiplexer has changed, it is not only andi, ori, and xori but also the previously implemented instructions that need to generate the correct control signals for this newer multiplexer.

6.1.3 Add Instruction sll.w, srl.w, and sra.w

We still adopt the above idea of comparing and analyzing with instructions with similar operations to add sll.w, srl.w, and sra.w instructions. After analyzing, we can see that the datapaths of these instructions in execute, memory access, and write-back stages can be reused with those of slli.w, srli.w, and srai.w instructions respectively, and the datapaths of these three instructions in the decode stage can be reused with those of add.w instruction. The rest of the work is to set the control signals of these instructions at each stage to match the instructions of the datapaths they multiplex.

6.1.4 Add Instruction pcaddu12i

By analyzing the definition of the pcaddu12i instruction, it is found that the instruction completes an addition operation and the result is written to the rd general-purpose register, which is consistent with the add.w instruction; the processing of the source operand 1 PC of the instruction is consistent with that of the bl instruction in calculating PC+4, and the processing of the source operand 2 {si20, 12'b0} is consistent with that of the lu12i.w instruction. Therefore, the pcaddu12i instruction, on the one hand, can reuse the datapath of the add.w instruction in the execute (excluding the preparation of source operands), memory access, and write-back stages, and on the other hand, it is possible to multiplex the datapaths of the bl and lu12i.w instructions in the decode and execute (where the source operands are prepared) stages, respectively. Accordingly, the control signals required for the pcaddu12i instruction correspond to the control signals of the instruction result multiplexer.

6.2 Add Multiplication and Division Instructions

For integer complement multiplication, the multiplication of two 32-bit binary numbers produces a 64-bit binary result. This result cannot fit into one item of the general-purpose register file because the width of each item is 32 bits. Therefore, the

LA32R ISA defines three instructions, `mul.w`, `mulh.w`, and `mulh.wu`, to perform the integer multiplication operation. The `mulh.w` and `mul.w` instructions both multiply two 32-bit signed integers and write the high 32 bits and low 32 bits of the product to the destination general-purpose register rd respectively; the `mulh.wu` and `mul.w` instructions both multiply two 32-bit unsigned integers and write the high 32 bits and low 32 bits of the product to the destination general-purpose register rd respectively. The reason why the lower 32 bits of the product of signed number multiplication and unsigned number multiplication are used by `mul.w` instruction is that when the binary values of the input data are the same, the binary values of the lower half of the result of signed and unsigned number multiplication are the same.

For integer complement division, dividing two 32-bit binary numbers produces a 32-bit quotient and a 32-bit remainder. The LA32R ISA defines the `div.w` and `mod.w` instructions to compute the quotient and remainder of dividing two signed numbers, and the `div.wu` and `mod.wu` instructions to compute the quotient and remainder of dividing two unsigned numbers.

In the above multiplication and division instructions, the two source operands of these instructions all come from `rj` and `rk` registers respectively, and the result is written to the `rd` register, which is the same as the `add.w` instruction. Therefore, the datapath of `add.w` can be reused in the decode and write-back stage of the pipeline, and the same control signals can be generated. The main design adjustment in the datapath is to add multiplier and divider components. We will show two ways of designing the multiplier and divider components with different levels of difficulty. The first approach is to use the Xilinx IP (see Sect. 6.2.1), and the second approach is to implement the multiplier unit (see Sect. 6.2.2) and the divider unit (see Sect. 6.2.3) at the logic gate level. Obviously, the latter approach requires much more design and debugging time than the former; however, there is much more can be learned. So readers can decide whether to use the second approach or not, depending on personal preference and learning progress.

6.2.1   Use Xilinx IP to Implement Multiplier and Divider Components

6.2.1.1   Use Xilinx IP to Implement Multiplier Component

The simplest way to use the Xilinx IP to implement a multiplier component is to use code of the following form:

```
wire [31:0] src1, src2;
wire [63:0] unsigned_prod, signed_prod;

assign unsigned_prod = src1 * src2;
assign signed_prod   = $signed(src1) * $signed(src2);
```

The synthesis tool in Vivado encounters the * operator as it does the + and >> operators in the code above, and finds a suitable multiplier circuit from its own IP library to implement into the design based on the timing and other constraints given in the design. Based on our experiments, for the Artix-7 family of FPGA, Vivado now implements the * operator by default using the DSP48 device (which contains a solid 16-bit multiplier circuit), so the final circuit is usually well timed and consumes almost no LUT resources. The multiplier circuits derived in this way have two 32-bit inputs and one 64-bit output, and have one-cycle latency, which means that the result can be output within the same clock cycle as the input data.

However, as you will also notice from the reference code given, the Xilinx multiplier IP can only do signed or unsigned multiplication. So in order to implement the `mulh.w` and `mulh.wu` instructions, we have to instantiate two multiplier IPs. This approach looks not that advanced. In fact, 32-bit signed/unsigned multiplication can be uniformly converted to 33-bit signed multiplication by converting a 32-bit signed/unsigned number to a 33-bit signed number: for a 32-bit signed number, the highest bit is expanded by the sign bit; for 32-bit unsigned numbers, the highest bit is expanded by 0. The highest 2 bits of the 66-bit product result can be left alone after this process. Bits [63:32] and [31:0] of the result are selected according to the definition of the instruction.

6.2.1.2   Use Xilinx IP to Implement Divider Component

The main reason we do not use operators such as / and % to allow the synthesis tool to derive the implementation of the divider component is that the Vivado synthesis tool would implement a single-cycle divider using a LUT, which would have very long timing delay. Next, we describe how to customize the divider IP based on the interactive interface.

Click on `IP Catalog` in the project navigation bar, and then search for `div` in the window that appears on the right, as shown in Fig. 6.1.

Double-click the `Divider Generator` item in the search result. Open the IP setting interface, and set the parameters in order, as shown in Fig. 6.2.

Fig. 6.1 In the "IP Catalog" interface, select "Divider Generator"

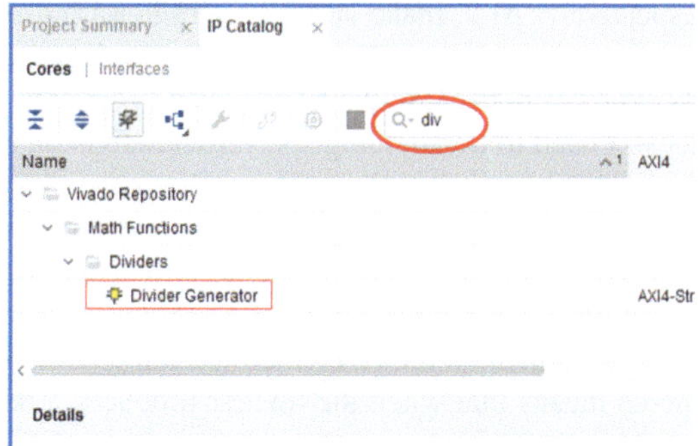

Fig. 6.2 Set parameters of
the divider IP core

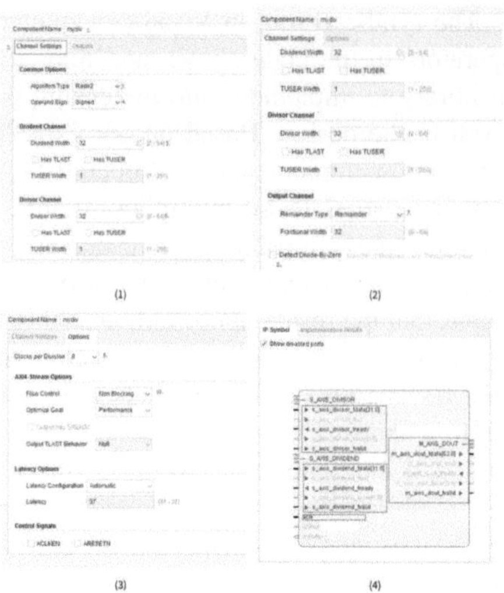

The important IP setting options for the divider are labeled and described in the
figure. The name of the divider can be adjusted according to your own preferences,
and does not necessarily have to be the name of the example in the figure. In the
`Channel Settings` tab, the first step is to select the algorithm for the IP of the
divider, and here we suggest the Radix2 algorithm. The advantage of the Radix2
algorithm is that it consumes fewer resources, but the disadvantage is it consumes
more iteration cycles to complete the operation. Usually, the proportion of fixed-
point division operations in an application is very low, and the compiler usually
implements a division operation with add, subtract, and shift instructions as much
as possible. So the number of cycles required to implement the division instruction is
slightly higher, but it does not affect the average performance of the application too
much. The `Channel Settings` tab also allows you to select whether the division
operation is signed or unsigned. Similar to the multiplier IP described in the previous
section, two divider IPs, signed and unsigned, need to be generated to implement
the `div.w/mod.w` and `div.wu/mod.wu` instructions, respectively. The next two
places, 5 and 6, define the bit width of the dividend and divisor to be 32 bits,
respectively. At 7, make sure to select `Remainder Type` as `Remainder` to ensure
that the remainder type is integer. We don't need to check the `Divide-By-Zero`
checkbox at 8, because the LoongArch ISA states that the division instruction itself
doesn't need to do anything special with division by 0, leaving that to the software.
In the `Options` tab, select the number of cycles to process a division at 9. This
number is the cycles between successive division operations, not the number of
cycles to complete a division operation. The number of cycles to complete a division
operation is determined by the `Latency Options` parameter in Fig. 6.2c. At 10,
the flow control on the AXI interface can be `Non Blocking` as we suggested. This
choice means that when the divider produces a result, the result must be available

externally and will not be blocked. In our single-issue static pipelined CPU, this condition always holds. (Readers are invited to think about the reasons for this.)

Although we have chosen the `Non Blocking` flow control strategy, since the divisor IP currently available in Vivado must be AXI interfaced, we are going to go over some of the signals associated with the module's interface. Looking at Fig. 6.2d, we see in general the dividend and divisor channels, as well as the quotient and remainder channels. The 32-bit input signal `s_axis_dividend_tdata` in the dividend channel corresponds to the dividend data; the 32-bit input signal `s_axis_divisor_tdata` in the divisor channel corresponds to the divisor data; and the result of the quotient and remainder are unified from the 64-bit signal `m_axis_dout_tdata` in the quotient and remainder channel, where bits [63:32] store the quotient and bits [31:0] store the remainder.

For two input channels and one output channel, in addition to the data signals described above, each channel has a pair of `tvalid` and `tready` signals. This is a pair of "handshake" control signals, which works similarly to the `valid` and `allowin` signals we use in the CPU pipeline. tvalid is a request signal and tready is an answer signal. If the sampled value of tvalid and tready are both equal to 1 on the rising edge of the clock, a successful handshake is completed between the sender and receiver of the request. If we assume that the receiver has a set of flip-flops, so the so-called successful handshake means that the sender's data is written to the receiver's buffers, that is, after this rising edge of the successful handshake, the trigger buffers will change to the sender's data.

Let's assume that the generated divider IP is called during the execute stage. `s_axis_dividend_tvalid` and `s_axis_divisor_tvalid` should be set to 1 at the same time, while the division instruction is in the execute stage and no data has been successfully entered into the divider. When finding `s_axis_dividend_tready` and `s_axis_divisor_tready` feedback is 1 (at this point, seeing both tvalid and tready are 1 at a rising edge of a clock indicates a successful handshake), it is necessary to clear `s_axis_dividend_tvalid` and `s_axis_divisor_tvalid` to 0. Ensure `s_axis_dividend_tvalid` and `s_axis_divisor_tvalid` set to 1 at the same time, so that `s_axis_dividend_tready` and `s_axis_divisor_tready` of the divisor IP feedback generated here can be set to 1 at the same time. We emphasize again that after the tready of the dividend and divisor inputs are set (i.e., after the handshake is successful), the tvalid must be undone. Otherwise, the divider will think there is a new division operation coming up.

After completing the handshake of the input data, the division instruction needs to wait for the final output result of the divider IP in the execute stage. When `m_axis_dout_tvalid` is set to 1, it means the division calculation is completed. At this point, the division instruction can take out the result from `m_axis_dout_tdata` and enter the forward stages of the pipeline. Since we set the flow control policy to `Non Blocking`, there is no need for external feedback of tready signals on the output channel; in other words, no matter how many results are generated and when they are generated, the external world should be able to process them in time.

With the implementation scheme described in this section, even though the execution of division starts and produces the result in the execute stage of the CPU, the pipeline control has to be adjusted in a targeted way because the operation will take multiple clock cycles. Specifically, when a division instruction is executed in the execute stage, the `ready_go` of this pipeline stage is valid only after the completion signal (`m_axis_dout_tvalid` signal of the Xilinx divider IP is 1) is returned by the divider component.

If you don't want to spend more time on the design and implementation of multiplier and divider circuits in your CPU design, then just follow the methodology described in this section and skip the rest Sects. 6.2.2 and 6.2.3.

6.2.2   Circuit-Level Multiplier Implementation

The shift multiplier works in the same way as normally used long multiplication, i.e., it converts a 32-bit multiplication into 32 groups of 64-bit additions. It is important to note that the product of the complements of two numbers is not equal to the complement of the product. If $[Y]_{comp} = y_{31}y_{30}\ldots y_1y_0$, then

$$[X \times Y]_{comp} = [X]_{comp} \times (-y_{31} \times 2^{31} + y_{30} \times 2^{30} + \ldots + y_1 \times 2^1 + y_0 \times 2^0)$$

That is, $[X \times Y]_{comp}$ is not equal to $[X]_{comp} \times [Y]_{comp}$. Instead, it is the result of multiplying $[X]_{comp}$ by a number that inverts the highest bit of $[Y]_{comp}$ and leaves the other bits unchanged. See Section 8.3 of *Fundamentals of Computer Architecture (3rd edition)* for detailed derivation. Taking a 4-bit multiplier as an example: $0101(5) \times 1001(-7) = 1011101(-35)$, the multiplication of the simple complement is computed as follows (each partial product is sign-extended) (Fig. 6.3):

In the complement multiplication operation, it is sufficient to subtract the highest partial product term of Y and add the other partial product terms. However, when doing addition and subtraction, be sure to extend the sign bits so that the product terms are aligned.

Complement multiplication can be performed using the Booth Radix-2 Algorithm to unify the partial products into the same form.

Fig. 6.3 Example of simple complement multiplication process

				0	1	0	1
			×	1	0	0	1
+	0	0	0	0	1	0	1
+	0	0	0	0	0	0	
+	0	0	0	0	0		
−	0	1	0	1			
	1	0	1	1	1	0	1

6.2.2.1 Booth Radix-4 Encoding

For 32-bit multiplication, both the simple complement multiplier described above and the Booth Radix-2 Algorithm implementation require 32 partial products to be added to get the result, with significant latency and hardware overhead. The introduction of Booth Radix-4 Encoding largely reduces the number of additions.

For

$$(-y_{31} \times 2^{31} + y_{30} \times 2^{30} + \ldots + y_1 \times 2^1 + y_0 \times 2^0)$$

make following transformations:

$$(-y_{31} \times 2^{31} + y_{30} \times 2^{30} + \ldots + y_1 \times 2^1 + y_0 \times 2^0)$$

$$= (y_{29} + y_{30} - 2 \times y_{31}) \times 2^{30} + (y_{27} + y_{28} - 2 \times y_{29}) \times 2^{28} + \ldots$$

$$+ (y_1 + y_2 - 2 \times y_3) \times 2^2 + (y_0 - 2 \times y_1) \times 2^0$$

$$= (y_{29} + y_{30} - 2 \times y_{31}) \times 2^{30} + (y_{27} + y_{28} - 2 \times y_{29}) \times 2^{28} + \ldots$$

$$+ (y_1 + y_2 - 2 \times y_3) \times 2^2 + (y_{-1} + y_0 - 2 \times y_1) \times 2^0$$

where y_{-1} takes the value 0.

According to the above equation, the -1 bit of Y can be complemented with 0 first, and then the 3 bits of Y are scanned each time to determine the partial product term, so that the number of product terms is reduced to half, and 32-bit multiplication requires only 15 additions. The rules for Booth Radix-4 Encoding are shown in Table 6.1.

For example, 0101(5) × 1001(-7), where $[X]_{comp}$= +0101, $2[X]_{comp}$= +01010, $-[X]_{comp}$= -0101 = +1011, $-2[X]_{comp}$= -01010 = +10110. Calculation shows as follows (Fig. 6.4):

It can be seen that after using the Booth Radix-4 Encoding for the 4-bit multiplication, the partial product's number is reduced from 4 to 2, and it takes one addition instead of 3, which greatly improves efficiency.

Table 6.1 Booth Radix-4 encoding rules

y_{i+1}	y_i	y_{i-1}	Operation
0	0	0	no add(+0)
0	0	1	complement add $X(+[X])_{comp}$
0	1	0	11 add $X(+[X])_{comp}$
0	1	1	11 add $2X(+[X]$ shifting left$)_{comp}$
1	0	0	complement sub $2X(-[X]$ shifting left$)_{comp}$
1	0	1	complement sub $X(-[X])_{comp}$
1	1	0	complement sub $X(-[X])_{comp}$
1	1	1	no add (+0)

Fig. 6.4 Example of Booth Radix-4 encoding complement multiplication

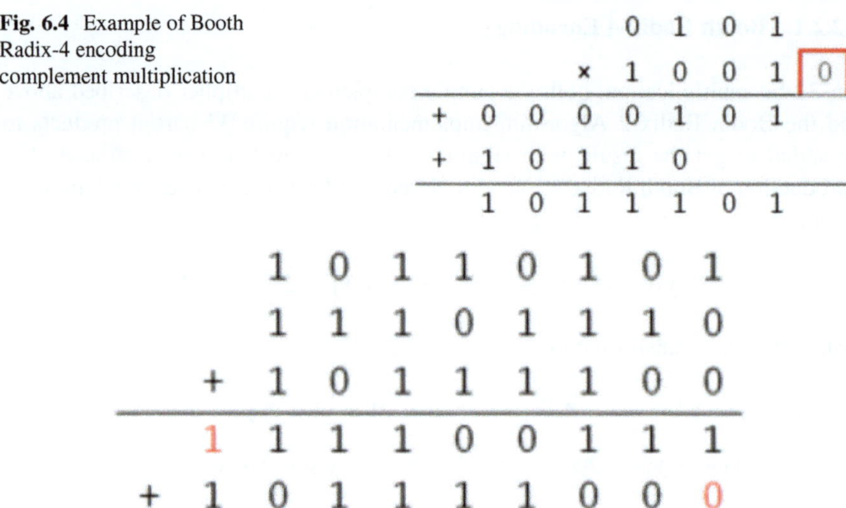

Fig. 6.5 Example of complement multiplication operation carry-save addition

6.2.2.2 Carry-Save Adder

For 32-bit multiplication, even with Booth Radix-4 Encoding, the 16 partial products need to be performed 15 times close to 64 bits addition. Normally doing one 65-bit addition is already very delayed. If you do 15 accumulating additions, it will be even less efficient. For adding multiple numbers, consider using a carry-save adder that does not wait for a carry-in signal.

A carry-save adder uses a full adder to convert three additions into two additions, one of which is composed of all the local sums and the other is composed of all the carry-out signals to the higher place. The following example shows the operation of a carry-save adder.

$$10110101 \ (-75) + 11101110 \ (-18) + 10111100 \ (-68) = 111100111 \ (-25)$$
$$+ \ 101111000 \ (-136)$$

Each bit of the carry-save adder is calculated independently of the other bits, so there is no carry-in delay. In the example, the three lowest bits are 1, 0, and 0, resulting in 1, carry-out to 0. The three highest bits are 1, 1, and 1, resulting in 1, carry-out to 1. The same is true for the other bits, with the result shifted one place to the left at the end (Fig. 6.5).

6.2.2.3 The Wallace Tree

For operations where many addends are to be added to get a single result, a layer of carry-save adders (i.e., a set of full adders) can be used to convert to about 2/3 addends, then a layer of carry-save adders can be used to convert to about 4/9

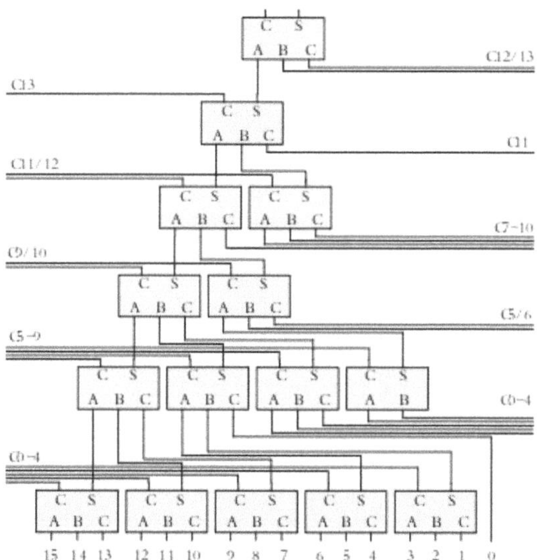

Fig. 6.6 One-bit Wallace tree with 16 numbers summed

addends, and so on until the final conversion to 2 addends. This construction is called a Wallace tree.

With the Booth Radix-4 Encoding, a 32-bit multiplication is converted to a sum of 16 64-bit partial products. The number of addends can be reduced to two by using a six-layer Wallace tree. Figure 6.6 shows a Wallace tree constructed for 1 bit of the 16 partial products.

6.2.2.4   32-bit Complement Multiplier Using Booth Radix-4 Encoding + Wallace Tree

It is not difficult to design a 32-bit fixed-point complement multiplier based on Booth encoding and Wallace tree. The structure of which is shown in Fig. 6.7.

Part (1) of the above figure uses the Booth Radix-4 Algorithm to obtain 16 partial products, where P is 64-bit partial product and c is 1-bit to indicate the inverse of the multiplied number.

Part (2) is similar to a matrix transpose, where 16 64-bit partial products are transposed into 64 16-bit numbers to be used as inputs at each bit of the Wallace tree. This part only has wires without any extra circuit units.

Part (3) is the Wallace tree, a collection of 64 1-bit Wallace trees. Note that every 1-bit Wallace tree has a carry-in signal from the lower bits, while the carry-out of the highest bit Wallace tree to the higher bit is ignored. This is because the largest number that can be obtained by multiplying a 32-bit signed number by a 32-bit signed number is $-2^{31} \times -2^{31} = 2^{62}$, which can be accommodated by using a 64-bit signed number. Even if the highest bit of the Wallace tree is brought into the

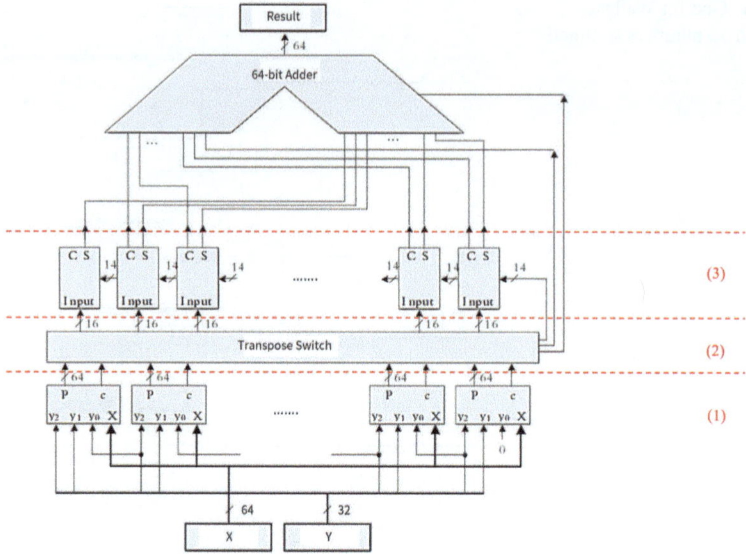

Fig. 6.7 32-bit complement multiplier structure

operation, what is obtained is an extension of the sign bit, so it can be omitted directly.

6.2.2.5 Further Optimization of Multiplier

(1) Implementation of Unsigned Multiplication with Fixed-Point Complement Multiplier

The above sections describe complement multipliers, which are obviously for signed multiplication. In the instruction set, besides signed multiplication, there is also unsigned multiplication, so the multiplier we implement needs to support unsigned multiplication as well.

Signed and unsigned multiplication refers to whether the source operands of the multiplication are treated as signed or unsigned numbers, e.g., a number stored in a 32-bit register as 0x80000000 is -2^{31} if it is treated as a signed number (all signed numbers stored in the computer are in complement form), or 2^{31} if it is treated as an unsigned number.

Although an unsigned number looks very different from a signed number, an unsigned number can be regarded as a signed number with a sign bit of 0 by adding a 0 in front of the highest bit of the unsigned number. Meanwhile, for a signed number, extending one sign bit before the highest bit, the value of the representation remains unchanged. By this method of adding one more place before the highest place, it is possible to unify signed and unsigned numbers, and accordingly, a 32-bit number extends to a 33-bit number.

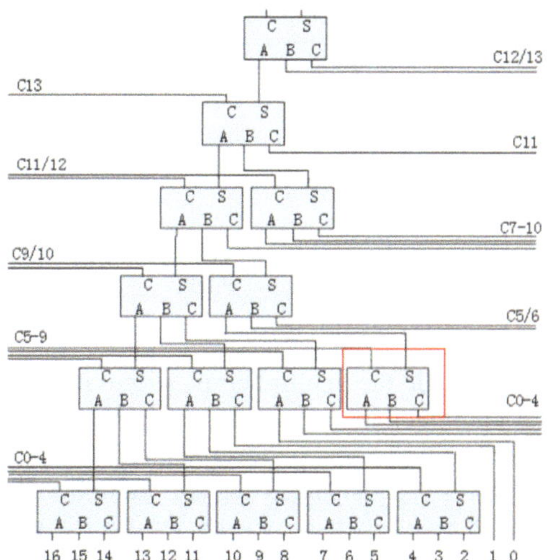

Fig. 6.8 One-bit Wallace tree with 17 numbers summed

Therefore, a 33-bit signed multiplier can be implemented, making it possible to do both signed and unsigned multiplication operations. Before each operation, the source operand needs to be extended to 33 bits by adding the sign bit before the highest bit for signed numbers and 0 before the highest bit for unsigned numbers. For a 32-bit number `0x8000_0000`, it needs to be extended to 33-bit `0x0_8000_0000` as an unsigned number, and to `0x1_8000_0000` as a signed number. Note that a 33-bit number encoded with Booth Radix-4 results in a 17-bit partial product and the structure of the Wallace tree must be adjusted accordingly, as shown in Fig. 6.8.

(2) Pipeline Improvement

The single-cycle 32-bit complement multiplier designed according to the above description has a maximum delay time of about 36 ns obtained by the synthesis tool, which is too long, so the multiplier can be improved by pipelining, i.e., it can be divided into a number of pipeline stages. After the pipeline improvement, the operation frequency of the whole multiplier can be improved while it still generally supports the execution of one multiplication every cycle.[1]

The pipeline should be sliced as balanced as possible, i.e., the delay time of each stage should not differ too much. For example, if the multiplier is split into two stages, the longest delay time after slicing should be as close as possible to half of the delay time of a single cycle. The position of the pipeline can be determined based on the structure of the multiplier, and then evaluated using the synthesis tool after the slicing is complete. A two-stage pipelined multiplier can occupy both execute and memory access stages in the CPU without delaying the overall CPU.

---

[1] Exceptional cases may exist given the fact that it is not possible to start a new execution every clock cycle if there is a RAW dependency between neighboring multiplication operations.

Table 6.2 Recommended main interfaces of multiplier module

signal	width	I/O direction	function
mul_clk	1	input	clock signal for multiplier module
resetn	1	input	reset signal and active low
mul_signed	1	input	control of signed and unsigned multiplication
x	32	input	multiplicand
y	32	input	multiplier
result	64	output	multiplication result

Although the multiplier is sliced into two stages, it is recommended that the multiplier be written as a separate module so that it is easy to replace the entire multiplier and perform module-level verification of the multiplier. The main interfaces recommended for the multiplier module implementation are shown in Table 6.2.

The sliced pipeline stage is also included in the multiplier module. The input signals of the module come from the execute stage, and the output signals are fetched at the memory access stage and forwarded back or entered into the write-back stage, so there is only one set of inter-pipeline registers inside the multiplier module.

6.2.2.6   Multiplier Module-Level Verification

After implementing a multiplier module, it is a good idea to perform a module-level random verification to ensure correct functionality.

For multiplier module that are sliced into a two-stage, this can be done using the module-level verification environment in `mycpu_env/module_verify/mul_verify/`, whose testbench top module `mul_tb` is as follows:

```verilog
`timescale 1ns / 1ps

module mul_tb;

    // Inputs
    reg mul_clk;
    reg resetn;
    reg mul_signed;
    reg [31:0] x;
    reg [31:0] y;

    // Outputs
    wire signed [63:0] result;
```

```verilog
// Instantiate the Unit Under Test (UUT)
mul uut (
    .mul_clk(mul_clk),
    .resetn(resetn),
    .mul_signed(mul_signed),
    .x(x),
    .y(y),
    .result(result)
);

initial begin
    // Initialize Inputs
    mul_clk = 0;
    resetn = 0;
    mul_signed = 0;
    x = 0;
    y = 0;
    #100;
    resetn = 1;
end
always #5 mul_clk = ~mul_clk;

// Generate random multipliers and sign control signal
always @(posedge mul_clk)
begin
    // $random is system call, which can generate 32-bit
    ↪   random signed number
    x            <= $random;
    y            <= $random;
    // Add a joint. {$random} can generate a
    ↪   non-negative number. %2 can get 0 or 1.
    mul_signed <= {$random}%2;
end

// Store multipliers and sign control signal because of
↪   the two-stage pipeline
reg [31:0] x_r;
reg [31:0] y_r;
reg        mul_signed_r;

always @(posedge mul_clk)
begin
    if (!resetn)
    begin
```

```verilog
            x_r           <= 32'd0;
            y_r           <= 32'd0;
            mul_signed_r <= 1'b0;
        end
        else
        begin
            x_r           <= x;
            y_r           <= y;
            mul_signed_r <= mul_signed;
        end
    end

// Reference result
wire signed [63:0] result_ref;
wire signed [32:0] x_e;
wire signed [32:0] y_e;
assign x_e        = {mul_signed_r & x_r[31],x_r};
assign y_e        = {mul_signed_r & y_r[31],y_r};
assign result_ref = x_e * y_e;
assign ok         = (result_ref == result);

// Print result
initial begin
    $monitor("x = %d, y = %d, signed = %d, result =
    ↪  %d,OK=%b",
              x_e,y_e,mul_signed_r,result,ok);
end

// Judge the result
always @(posedge mul_clk)
begin
    if (!ok)
    begin
        $display("Error: x = %d, y = %d,result = %d,
        ↪  result_ref = %d, OK=%b",
              x_e,y_e,result,result_ref,ok);
        $finish;
    end
end

endmodule
```

Note that variables related to calculations must be declared with `signed` to indicate a signed number. If testbench shows that OK=1, the result is correct. Otherwise, there is an error in the operation and the simulation will stop.

6.2.3 Circuit-Level Divider Implementation

Dividers are categorized into absolute value and complement divider based on whether or not the source operand is converted to an absolute value. Usually, the result of absolute value divider is the absolute value of quotient and remainder, so the complement of quotient and remainder should be calculated at the end. By contrast, the result of complement divider is the complement, but the calculation process may subtract unexpected divisor, so the remainder needs to be adjusted.

6.2.3.1 Iterative Divider

The divider is usually iterative, and a simple iterative division is the trial quotient method. The quotient of a 32-bit division is at most 32 bits, so you can try 0 or 1 from the 31st to the 0th bit of the quotient in order, which is similar to the manual division calculation.

Depending on whether or not the remainder is restored when there is insufficient subtraction (quotient is 0) during the iteration process, there are two types of methods: the method that restores the remainder (circular subtraction) and the method that does not restore the remainder (alternating addition and subtraction). Alternate addition and subtraction means that an insufficient subtraction is considered to be an over-subtraction, and instead of restoring the remainder, the next iteration will add the remainder to make up for the over-subtraction. This is possible because, assuming that the second addition is r_2+x, where r_2 is the remainder of the previous subtraction, that is, r_1-2x, which is equivalent to r_1-x, the same as restoring the remainder. As to why the previous subtraction subtracts 2x (twice as much as the latter), let's suppose the dividend is abcd (four digits) and the divisor is yz (two digits), iterating from the higher to the lower digits results in first ab-yz, which is equivalent to ab00-yz00, and then second bc-yz, which is equivalent to bc0-yz0. In other words, the first time it's 2x, and the second time it's x. That's the reason why using shifters in the division implementation.

In fact, all the iterative dividers, absolute value or complement dividers, circular subtraction or alternate addition and subtraction, etc. are based on the same principle: determine the size of the remaining dividend and divisor, derive the quotient, and update the remaining dividend. In practice, the above divisors are categorized according to different processing methods.

For example, for a complement divider, in the case of signed division, suppose the dividend is `0xffff_ffff` and the divisor is `0x1111_1111`, that is, the dividend is negative and the divisor is positive. Obviously, comparing the size of the dividend

Table 6.3 Rules of sign bit
of division results

dividend	divisor	quotient	reminder
positive	positive	positive	positive
positive	negative	negative	positive
negative	positive	negative	negative
negative	negative	positive	negative

and the divisor requires the use of addition. At this time, if using the restoration of the remainder method, it is a circular addition complement divider. If using the non-restoration of the remainder method, and in the iterative process, if the remainder is added to a positive number, it means that the result is added unexpectedly (absolute value is subtracted unexpectedly). Then, addition needs to be changed to subtraction, which is the alternate addition and subtraction complement divider.

In the case of the 1-bit restoring division of the absolute value iterative divider, the operation is divided into three steps.

Step 1. Determine the Sign of the Quotient and Remainder from the Dividend and Divisor, and Calculate the Absolute Values of the Dividend and Divisor

According to the definition of the instruction in the *Instruction Manual*, the sign of the remainder is to be the same as the sign of the dividend, so that the sign of the quotient and remainder can be determined from Table 6.3.

In the case of unsigned number, the number stored in the computer is its original code, i.e., the absolute value is the number. For signed number, if the number is positive, then the number saved in the computer is its two's complement representation, which is also its original code, i.e., the absolute value is the number; if the number is negative, the computer stores its two's complement representation; to obtain its absolute value, simply invert all bits (including the sign bit) of the complement and add 1.

Step 2. Iterate to Obtain the Absolute Value of the Quotient and Remainder

The iterative operation is performed as follows:

1. Complement 32 zeros to the 32-bit dividend, denoted A[63:0], and record the divisor as B[31:0], the resulting quotient as S[31:0], and the remainder as R[31:0].
2. In the first iteration, take the higher 33 bits of A, i.e., A[63:31], and subtract them from the result {1'b0, B[31:0]}, which is the result of adding 0 to the higher bits of B. If the result is negative, then the corresponding bit of the quotient (S[31]) is 0, and the dividend stays unchanged. If the result is positive, then the corresponding bit of the quotient is recorded as 1, and the corresponding bit of the divisor (A[63:31]) is updated to the result of the subtraction.
3. The second iteration is to take A[62:30] and subtract it from {1'b0, B[31:0]}, updating S[30] and A[62:30].
4. Do as 3 until the 0th of S is counted.

Step 3. Adjusting the Final Quotient and Remainder
The quotient and remainder obtained in step 2 are the corresponding absolute value. Convert the quotient and remainder to signed numbers according to the sign of the quotient and remainder determined in step 1, and submit the result.

The following is an example of iterative division using 8-bit complement division: $10010101(-107) \div 00011101(29)$.

First, since the dividend is negative and the divisor is positive, determine the quotient to be negative and the remainder to be negative, and compute to get the absolute dividend 01101011 and the absolute divisor 00011101. Then, the operation of iterative subtraction is performed.

The first iteration gets the highest position of the quotient (Fig. 6.9):

In the above figure, row 1 shows the absolute value of the quotient, row 2 shows the absolute value of the dividend before the first cycle, and row 3 shows the absolute value of the divisor, row 4 shows the result of the subtraction, and the last row is the absolute value of the dividend after the execution of the first cycle.

In the first six iterations, the absolute value of the dividend does not change, so these iterations are omitted. Looking directly at the seventh iteration, the result is as follows (Fig. 6.10):

8th iteration to get the absolute values of the final quotient and remainder (Fig. 6.11):

So, we can get the absolute value of the quotient is 00000011 and the absolute value of the remainder is 00010100 (truncate to the lower 8 bits).

Finally, the quotient and remainder are converted to complements. Since it was determined earlier that the quotient is negative and the remainder is also negative, we get the quotient 11111101 (-3) and the remainder 11101100 (-20).

Here to remind readers: To find the absolute value of a negative signed number, you "invert and add 1" to get the result. For a positive signed number, the absolute value is the number itself. To find the negative signed number from an absolute

Fig. 6.9 Division example of first iteration

									0							
	0	0	0	0	0	0	0	0	0	1	1	0	1	0	1	1
−	0	0	0	0	1	1	1	0	1							
	1	1	1	1	0	0	0	1	1							
	0	0	0	0	0	0	0	0	0	1	1	0	1	0	1	1

Fig. 6.10 Division example of seventh iteration

										0	0	0	0	0	0	1
	0	0	0	0	0	0	0	0	0	1	1	0	1	0	1	1
−								0	0	0	0	1	1	1	0	1
								0	0	0	0	1	1	0	0	0
	0	0	0	0	0	0	0	0	0	0	1	1	0	0	0	1

Fig. 6.11 Division example of eighth iteration

									0	0	0	0	0	0	1	1
	0	0	0	0	0	0	0	0	0	0	1	1	0	0	0	1
−								0	0	0	0	1	1	1	0	1
								0	0	0	0	1	0	1	0	0
	0	0	0	0	0	0	0	0	0	0	0	1	0	1	0	0

value, you "invert and add 1." To find the positive signed number from an absolute value, the result is the absolute value itself.

As you can see from the above calculation, the register for the quotient of the division is obtained sequentially from high to low, which is the same as a 32-bit left-shifted register. The quotient obtained in each iteration is placed in bit 0. The dividend is subtracted from the divisor by taking upper 33 bits, and update these 33 bits. It is equivalent to a 64-bit left-shifted register, where the upper 33 bits are subtracted from the divisor and the 33 bits are updated.

A schema of iterative division result can be drawn from the above description.

6.2.3.2   Use Iterative Divider to Make Unsigned Division

If you just let the iterative divider perform the operation in step 2, it is an unsigned divider. So, a control signal is needed in the iterative divider, so that the division does not adjust the value in steps 1 and 3, which derives the unsigned division result. This allows the divider to perform unsigned operations.

6.2.3.3   Control Signals in Iterative Divider

The first step of the iterative divider operation is to obtain the dividend, divisor, and control signals, and the third step is to output the result to the next stage, which takes one cycle each. The second step is the iterative operation, which takes 32 cycles. Thus, a division requires 34 cycles in total. It is possible to build a counter in divider that starts counting from 0 at the beginning of division. When the count reaches 33, set the division completion signal to 1 and stop counting until the next division starts.

Like multiplier, it is recommended to package the divider as a separate module. The main interfaces recommended for implementation are shown in Table 6.4.

6.2.3.4   Further Optimization of Divider

In the above examples, the division is done for trying one bit, but it is possible to do it in two bits, at the cost of worse timing and more resources.

The following division can be observed:

1. `0x7777_7777/0x7777_7776`: you will find that the upper 31 bits of quotient are all 0.
2. `0x2000_0001/0x2`, you will find that the lower 30 bits of quotient are all 0.
3. `0x2000_0003/0x2`, you will see that the middle 29 bits of quotient are all 0.

We have seen that iterative division often has a bunch of zeros in the middle. It is very common for software programs to have a bunch of zeros at the beginning of the quotient. It is possible to consider division with an early start or early end. The

Table 6.4 Recommended main interfaces of divider module

signal	width	I/O direction	function
div_clk	1	input	clock signal for divider module
resetn	1	input	reset signal and active low
div	1	input	division operation signal which is set 0 when no new division enters after finishing current division
div_signed	1	input	control of signed and unsigned division
x	32	input	dividend
y	32	input	divisor
s	32	output	quotient of division result
r	32	output	reminder of division result
complete	1	output	division complete signal which is set when inner count reaches 33

presence of a series of zeros in between can potentially accelerate iteration, but it requires certain design skills.

Note that the main consideration for all division is to implement with ease in hardware. Many operations that we consider simple may be complex to implement in hardware. For example, determining the number of consecutive zeros at the beginning of a 32-bit number, i.e., finding the leading zeros of a 32-bit number, seems easy, but its hardware implementation requires intensive resource.

6.2.3.5   Divider Module-Level Verification

After implementing a division module, it is a good idea to perform a module-level random verification to ensure correct functionality. This can be done using the module-level verification environment in `mycpu_env/module_verify/div_verify/`, whose testbench top module `div_tb` is as follows:

```verilog
`timescale 1ns / 1ps

module div_tb;

    // Inputs
    reg div_clk;
    reg resetn;
    wire div;
    reg div_signed;
    reg [31:0] x;
    reg [31:0] y;

    // Outputs
    wire [31:0] s;
    wire [31:0] r;
    wire complete;
```

```verilog
    // Instantiate the Unit Under Test (UUT)
    div uut (
        .div_clk(div_clk),
        .resetn(resetn),
        .div(div),
        .div_signed(div_signed),
        .x(x),
        .y(y),
        .s(s),
        .r(r),
        .complete(complete)
    );

    initial begin
        // Initialize Inputs
        resetn = 0;
      #100;
        resetn = 1;
    end
    initial
    begin
        div_clk = 1'b0;
        forever
        begin
            #5 div_clk = 1'b1;
            #5 div_clk = 1'b0;
        end
    end


    // Generate division signal. Division is running.
    reg div_is_run;
    integer wait_clk;
    initial
    begin
        div_is_run <= 1'b0;
        forever
        begin
            @(posedge div_clk);
            if (!resetn || complete)
            begin
                div_is_run <= 1'b0;
                wait_clk <= {$random}%4;
            end
            else
            begin
                repeat (wait_clk)@(posedge div_clk);
                div_is_run <= 1'b1;
                wait_clk <= 0;
            end
        end
    end
    // Generate random sign control signal, divisor and dividend
```

```verilog
assign div = div_is_run;
always @(posedge div_clk)
begin
    if (!resetn || complete)
    begin
        div_signed <= 1'b0;
        x            <= 32'd0;
        y            <= 32'd1;
    end
    else if (!div_is_run)
    begin
        div_signed <= {$random}%2;
        x            <= $random;
        y            <= $random;
        // The posibility of 0 generated for divisor is too small
        ↪   to be catched.
    end
end


//------{Compute reference result} begin
// Step 1, get absolute value of x and y and the sign of quotient
↪   and reminder
wire x_signed = x[31] & div_signed; // sign of x, 0 for unsigned
wire y_signed = y[31] & div_signed; // sign of y, 0 for unsigned
wire [31:0] x_abs;
wire [31:0] y_abs;
// Here the ^ operation must use brackets, because + is prior to ^
↪   in verilog.
assign x_abs = ({32{x_signed}}^x) + x_signed;
assign y_abs = ({32{y_signed}}^y) + y_signed;
// sign of quotient, 0 for unsigned
wire s_ref_signed = (x[31]^y[31]) & div_signed;
// sign of reminder, 0 for unsigned
wire r_ref_signed = x[31] & div_signed;

// Step 2, get absolute value of quotient and reminder
reg [31:0] s_ref_abs;
reg [31:0] r_ref_abs;
always @(div_clk)
begin
    s_ref_abs <= x_abs/y_abs;
    r_ref_abs <= x_abs-s_ref_abs*y_abs;
end

// Step 3, get final result of quotient and reminder
wire [31:0] s_ref;
wire [31:0] r_ref;
// Here the ^ operation must use brackets, because + is prior to ^
↪   in verilog.
assign s_ref = ({32{s_ref_signed}}^s_ref_abs) +
↪   {30'd0,s_ref_signed};
assign r_ref = ({32{r_ref_signed}}^r_ref_abs) + r_ref_signed;
//------{Compute reference result} end
```

```verilog
// Compare the result with the reference
wire s_ok;
wire r_ok;
assign s_ok = s_ref==s;
assign r_ok = r_ref==r;
reg [5:0] time_out;

// Print result in form of 33-bit signed number whether it is
↪  32-bit signed or unsigned
// So that we can easily print the result in radix 10
wire signed [32:0] x_d     = {div_signed&x[31],x};
wire signed [32:0] y_d     = {div_signed&y[31],y};
wire signed [32:0] s_d     = {div_signed&s[31],s};
wire signed [32:0] r_d     = {div_signed&r[31],r};
wire signed [32:0] s_ref_d = {div_signed&s_ref[31],s_ref};
wire signed [32:0] r_ref_d = {div_signed&r_ref[31],r_ref};
always @(posedge div_clk)
begin
    if (complete && div) // Division finished
    begin
      if (s_ok && r_ok)
      begin
          $display("[time@%t]: x=%d, y=%d, signed=%d, "
                   "s=%d, r=%d, s_OK=%b, r_OK=%b",
                   $time,x_d,y_d,div_signed,s_d,r_d,s_ok,r_ok);
      end
      else
      begin
          $display("[time@%t]Error: x=%d, y=%d, signed=%d, s=%d, "
                   "r=%d, s_ref=%d, r_ref=%d, s_OK=%b, r_OK=%b",
                   $time,x_d,y_d,div_signed,s_d,
                   r_d,s_ref_d,r_ref_d,s_ok,r_ok);
          $finish;
      end
    end
end
always @(posedge div_clk)
begin
    if (!resetn || !div_is_run || complete)
    begin
        time_out <= 6'd0;
    end
    else
    begin
        time_out <= time_out + 1'b1;
    end
end
always @(posedge div_clk)
begin
    if (time_out == 6'd34)
    begin
        $display("Error: div no end in 34 clk!");
```

```
            $finish;
        end
    end

endmodule
```

At this point, all the user-mode arithmetic logic instructions in LA32R have been implemented.

6.3 Add Branch Instructions

Before adding branch instructions, we briefly review the design points associated with branch instructions in a simple pipeline:

1. There are two elements of a branch instruction: whether to jump or not and the jump target when jumping.
2. The branch instructions in LoongArch ISA include branch instructions and jump instructions. The former requires judgment whether to jump, and the latter must jump.
3. There are two ways to calculate the jump target of the branch instructions in LoongArch ISA: one is the PC of the branch instruction plus the offset in the branch instruction code, and the other is the value in the general-purpose register plus the offset immediate in the branch instruction code.
4. Branch instructions in LoongArch ISA does not generate register writes except for link-type branch instructions, which write their own PC plus 4 (i.e., the return address) to a general-purpose register.
5. In a single-issue five-stage pipelined CPU, the processing of branch instructions is carried out at the decode stage. When a jump occurs, the nextPC is updated as the jump target while canceling the instructions on the wrong execution path that may be retrieved by the fetch stage. Therefore, we can resolve the pipeline control hazards.

Point 5 above tells us that for the new branch instruction, generating nextPC should be put into the decode stage. As for how to generate the control signal of whether to jump or not, how to generate the jump target, and whether to write the return address to the general-purpose register, there is already a framework in the existing CPU. Next, we will sort out the instructions to be implemented and analyze how they are processed under the existing processing framework.

6.3.1 Add Instruction blt, bge, bltu, and bgeu

By analyzing the definitions of blt, bge, bltu, and bgeu instructions, it can be seen that their functions are very similar to those of beq and bne. The difference only lies in the condition of whether to jump or not. Therefore, to add these instructions, it is only necessary to extend the logic of judging whether a branch instruction jumps or not, that is, on the basis of GR[rj] = GR[rd], GR[rj] $\neq$ GR[rd], adding GR[rj] $<_{\text{signed}}$ GR[rd], GR[rj] $\geq_{\text{signed}}$ GR[rd], GR[rj] $<_{\text{unsigned}}$ GR[rd], and GR[rj] $\geq_{\text{unsigned}}$ GR[rd]. The rest of the logic can be directly reused the datapath of beq and bne, and the generation of the related control signals can also refer to the control signals of them.

At this point, all the user-mode branch instructions in LA32R have been implemented.

6.4 Add Memory Access Instructions

6.4.1 Add Instruction ld.b, ld.h, ld.bu, and ld.hu

By analyzing the definitions of ld.b, ld.h, ld.bu, and ld.hu and comparing them with the definition of ld.w, we can get:

1. The source of operands for calculating virtual addresses, the method of address calculation, and the rules for mapping virtual and real addresses are identical.
2. The result of their access is all written back to the rd register.
3. They differ from the ld.w instruction only in the bit width of the data retrieved from memory.

Consider the microarchitecture design. Since the data RAM is 32-bit wide, the data RAM access address is removing the lowest two bits of the computed address.

To summarize, the datapath and control logic of these four instructions at the decode, execute, and write-back stages can be fully reused in the design of the ld.w instruction. The following is a discussion of how to deal with the differences between the instructions.

6.4.1.1 Select Desired Content from Data RAM Output Results

Since the data RAM is four bytes wide, ld.b and ld.bu can access any of these four bytes, and ld.h and ld.hu can access either the lower or upper two bytes. That is, the data needed for these instructions does not always appear in the lowest position of the data RAM output. Therefore, we need to introduce a multiplexer. Readers may ask: this is supposed to be a byte right-shifted operation. But think about it: isn't a shifter essentially a multiplexer in its implementation?

The selection signals of this multiplexer are generated from the lowest two bits of the access address and the type of access operation. The design principle is straightforward. Readers can try to deduce it.

6.4.1.2 Extend Selected Content to 32-bit

The `ld.b`, `ld.bu`, `ld.h`, and `ld.hu` instructions get data from the data RAM that is smaller than the width of the general-purpose registers, so the data needs to be extended to 32 bits for the final write to the registers. The sign or zero extension is determined by the instruction. `ld.b` and `ld.h` are sign extension, and `ld.bu` and `ld.hu` are zero extension. So why are they categorized as sign-extended load and zero-extended load? Because C language has `signed char`, `unsigned char`, and `signed short`, `unsigned short`, and arithmetic operations such as addition and subtraction are only available for 32-bit source operands, the data must be loaded from memory into registers by extending the sign/zero to 32-bit according to the signed/unsigned attributes of the data before subsequent arithmetic operations can be performed. Although it is theoretically possible to define byte and half-word sign-extension and zero-extension instructions to accomplish the extension operations required here, many ISAs define sign-extension and zero-extension loading instructions, respectively, because such extension operations may occur frequently in real applications, and the resource overhead of extending after memory accessing internally is not too great.

The above datapath for selecting the desired content from the data RAM return value and extending the content to 32 bits are new for our CPU. It is recommended to implement this datapath in the memory access stage. Because these instructions, like `ld.w`, cannot forward to the decode stage until they stay at the memory access stage, the blocking control signals in the decode stage need little adjustment. From timing point of view, the additional multiplexer logic triggers certain circuit delay, but won't cause a significant drop in frequency, even if it is on the critical path. We will not future explore the design adjustment for such frequency loss considering the targeted level of design proficiency of the book aims to provide and try to keep the design as simple as possible..

Finally, in the current design, the lowest two bits of the access address and the type of access operation have not been transferred from the decode or execute stage to the memory access stage, and need to be added to the datapath now.

6.4.2 Add Instruction `st.b` and `st.h`

By analyzing the definitions of `st.b` and `st.h` and comparing them with the definition of `st.w`, we can get:

1. The source of operands for calculating virtual addresses, the method of address calculation and the rules for mapping virtual and real addresses are identical.
2. The data to be stored in the data RAM are from the `rd` register.
3. `st.b` instruction only writes 1 byte to the data RAM and `st.h` instruction only writes 2 bytes to the data RAM.

According to the above summary, the key to implement the `st.b` and `st.h` instructions lies in how to write bytes or half-words on a 4-byte-wide RAM, which can be realized by the byte write enable of the RAM. The so-called byte write-enable is that each byte of each item (or line) has its own individual write-enable. It can be seen that, when implementing the `st.b` instruction to write data RAM, if the lowest two bits of the address are equal to `0b00`, then the byte write-enable is `0b0001`; if the lowest two bits of the address are equal to `0b01`, then the byte write-enable is `0b0010` ... When implementing the `st.h` instruction, if the lowest two bits of the address are equal to `0b00`, then the byte write-enable is `0b0011`. For `st.w`, the byte write-enable is constant at `0b1111`.

Once the byte write-enable is determined, the next step is to generate the write data. The `st.b` instruction, for example, always writes the lowest byte of the `rd` register to memory, but it does not necessarily write the lowest byte in the data RAM. Some readers immediately think of the data could be byte shifted, and write the following code:

```verilog
assign st_data = op_st_b ? (vaddr[1:0]==2'b00 ? {24'b0,
  ↪  rd_value[7:0]} :
                              vaddr[1:0]==2'b01 ? {16'b0,
  ↪  rd_value[7:0], 8'b0} :
                              vaddr[1:0]==2'b10 ? {8'b0,
  ↪  rd_value[7:0], 16'b0} :

  ↪  {rd_value[7:0], 24'b0}
                                        ) :
                    op_st_h ? (vaddr[1:0]==2'b00 ? {16'b0,
  ↪  rd_value[15:0]} :

  ↪  {rd_value[15:0], 16'b0}
                                        ) :
                              rd_value;
```

Is the code above correct? Yes, it is. Does the above code work well? So-so.

In fact, the following code is also correct. Readers can try to deduce it. As a hint, consider it with the byte write-enable:

```verilog
assign st_data = op_st_b ? {4{rd_value[ 7:0]}} :
                 op_st_h ? {2{rd_value[15:0]}} :
                           rd_value[31:0];
```

Isn't this latter code much more concise? And this code has less logic and better timing. So, writing code is the same as writing an essay. Good writing requires a lot of thought and refinement.

At this point, all the user-mode instructions showed in this chapter have been implemented.

6.5 Tasks and Practices

After completing this chapter, readers are expected to complete the following two practical tasks:

1. Add arithmetic logic, and multiplication and division instructions. See Sect. 6.5.1.
2. Add branch instructions and memory access instructions. See Sect. 6.5.2.

6.5.1 Practical Task 10: Add Arithmetic Logic, and Multiplication and Division Instructions

This practical task requires the following work based on the CPU implemented in Practical Task 9:

1. Add arithmetic logic instructions: `slti`, `sltui`, `andi`, `ori`, `xori`, `sll`, `srl`, `sra`, `pcaddu12i`.
2. Add multiplication and division instructions: `mul.w`, `mulh.w`, `mulh.wu`, `div.w`, `mod.w`, `div.wu`, `mod.wu`.
3. Run the func corresponding to exp10, and pass simulation and FPGA verification.

Please refer to the method described in Sect. 2.3.1 to obtain the experimental development environment required for this practical task. The specific experimental environment is located at `mycpu_env/`, and continue to use the `soc_bram/` subdirectory.

Once the lab environment is ready, please refer to the following steps to complete this practical task:

1. Update CPU code at `mycpu_env/myCPU/`.
2. Modify the func configuration file, `mycpu_env/func/include/test_config.h`, select the configuration of `exp10`, and compile. (If you obtained the experimental development environment from the package `exp10.zip`, please skip this step.)
3. Open the gettrace project, `mycpu_env/gettrace/gettrace.xpr` (The IP core in this Vivado project was created using Vivado2019.2. If you open it with a higher version of Vivado, refer to Appendix D.4 for the IP core upgrade). Run the simulation of the gettrace project (after entering the simulation interface, click `run all` and wait for the simulation to finish), and generate a new reference trace file `golden_trace.txt` (`mycpu_env/gettrace/golden_trace.txt`). The `golden_trace.txt` will not be complete until the simulation has finished running. (If you obtained the experimental development environment from the package `exp10.zip`, please skip this step.)

4. Start the project in `mycpu_env/soc_verify/soc_bram/run_vivado/` to verify myCPU. If you have not created a project in this directory, please refer to the steps described in Appendix D.2 to create a project using the `create_project.tcl` file in this directory. If necessary, please refer to Appendix D.4 to upgrade the IP core. If there is a project in this directory that has been created by a previous practice task, you can update the file list of CPU implementations in the project by referring to the steps described in Appendix D.3 after opening the project.
5. Refer to Chap. 4 Sect. 4.4.5.2 to re-customize `inst_ram` in the project. (If you obtained the experimental development environment from the package `exp10.zip`, please skip this step.)
6. Run the simulation in the project (click `run all` directly after entering the simulation interface), and carry out the function verification until the simulation test is passed.
7. Generate a bit stream file after Synthesis and Implementation in the project, and verify it on FPGA. (Please skip this step if you don't have a hardware experiment platform.)

6.5.2   Practical Task 11: Add Branch and Memory Access Instructions

This practical task requires the following work based on the CPU implemented in Practical Task 10:

1. Add branch instructions: `blt, bge, bltu, bgeu`.
2. Add memory access instructions: `ld.b, ld.h, ld.bu, ld.hu, st.b, st.h`.
3. Run the func corresponding to exp11, and pass simulation and FPGA verification.

Please refer to the method described in Sect. 2.3.1 to obtain the experimental development environment required for this practical task. The specific experimental environment is located at `mycpu_env/`, and continue to use the `soc_bram/` subdirectory.

Once the lab environment is ready, please refer to the following steps to complete this practical task:

1. Update CPU code at `mycpu_env/myCPU/`.
2. Modify the func configuration file, `mycpu_env/func/include/test_config.h`, select the configuration of `exp11`, and compile. (If you obtained the experimental development environment from the package `exp11.zip`, please skip this step.)
3. Open the gettrace project, `mycpu_env/gettrace/gettrace.xpr` (the IP core in this Vivado project was created using Vivado2019.2; if you open it with a

higher version of Vivado, refer to Appendix D.4 for the IP core upgrade). Run the simulation of the gettrace project (after entering the simulation interface, click `run all` and wait for the simulation to finish), and generate a new reference trace file `golden_trace.txt` (`mycpu_env/gettrace/golden_trace.txt`). The `golden_trace.txt` will not be complete until the simulation has finished running. (If you obtained the experimental development environment from the package `exp11.zip`, please skip this step.)

4. Start the project in `mycpu_env/soc_verify/soc_bram/run_vivado/` to verify myCPU. If you have not created a project in this directory, please refer to the steps described in Appendix D.2 to create a project using the `create_project.tcl` file in this directory. If necessary, please refer to Appendix D.4 to upgrade the IP core. If there is a project in this directory that has been created by a previous practice task, you can update the file list of CPU implementations in the project by referring to the steps described in Appendix D.3 after opening the project.

5. Refer to Chap. 4 Sect. 4.4.5.2 to re-customize `inst_ram` in the project. (If you obtained the experimental development environment from the package `exp11.zip`, please skip this step.)

6. Run the simulation in the project (click `run all` directly after entering the simulation interface), and carry out the function verification until the simulation test is passed.

7. Generate a bit stream file after Synthesis and Implementation in the project, and verify it on FPGA. (Please skip this step if you don't have a hardware experiment platform.)

Chapter 7
Support Exception and Interrupt

In the previous chapters, we have implemented a pipelined CPU with 46 LoongArch instructions. But so far we have only implemented the user mode of instruction set. In order to build a small computer system based on this CPU, we have to add the privileged mode of the instruction set step by step. This chapter describes how to support the exception and interrupt in the CPU.

Learning Goals for this Chapter
- Understand the software-hardware coordinated mechanism for exception and interrupt.
- Understand the concept of precise exception and how to handle them.
- Learn how to support exception and interrupt in pipelined CPU.

Practical Tasks of this Chapter
There are two practical tasks in this chapter (see Sect. 7.5). Readers can complete these tasks after learning this chapter.

7.1 Basic Concepts of Exception and Interrupt

Readers can refer to Section 3.2 of *Fundamentals of Computer Architecture (3rd edition)* or other sources to learn the basic concepts of exception and interrupt. Here we will summarize the key concepts according to the needs of CPU design. From the perspective of CPU implementation, interrupt is also a special kind of exception, so in the following expressions, unless it refers to interrupt exclusively, we will use the word "exception" to refer to "exception" and "interrupt."

© The Author(s), under exclusive license to Springer Nature Singapore Pte Ltd. 2025   193
W. Wang, J. Xing, *CPU Design and Practice*,
https://doi.org/10.1007/978-981-96-6573-0_7

7.1.1   Exception Handling Is a Software-Hardware Coordinated Process

First of all, it is important to understand that exception handling is a software-hardware coordinated process. "Exceptions" are not the norm, and the frequency of their occurrence is not high, but they are relatively complex to handle. Based on the design principle of "use material where it is needed most," we want to use software program rather than hardware logic to handle these complex exceptions to the extent possible. This ensures that the complexity of the hardware design is kept under control and that there is no significant loss in performance.

Most of the exception handling is done by the exception handler (software), but the beginning and ending stages of exception handling must be done by hardware.

Exception Handling Start-Up Phase

The exception-triggering conditions are judged by hardware, and the information for the exception handler such as the type of the exception and the PC of the instruction that triggers the exception is automatically saved by the hardware. In addition, the hardware needs to jump to the entry point of the exception handler and ensure that the processor is at a privileged state after jumping to the exception handler entry point. The exception handler then takes over the subsequent processing.

Exception Handling Closure Phase

After the exception handler has completed all processing, it needs to return to the instruction (or a pre-specified program entry) where the exception occurred to restart execution. In addition to performing a jump, we need to change the privilege level back to the level before the exception occurred.

7.1.2   Precision Exception

In order to correctly implement exception in the CPU, we need to emphasize the concept of "precise exception." What does "precise exception" mean? The effect is that when the system software returns from handling an exception, the instruction that caused the exception and the instructions that follow it are treated as if the exception never occurred. The "before and after" is determined by the order defined in the program.

In the above statement, who is being to feel "as if no exceptions had occurred"? It is the instruction. The content has not changed from the perspective of the instruction. Here, we have used the anthropomorphism "perspective," which is vivid, but not precise enough from a conceptual point of view. We need to say a few more words.

What can the instruction "see"? It can only see what is defined in ISA, not the microarchitectural aspects that are not defined in ISA. For example, PC, general-purpose registers, memory, and the privilege level of the processor are visible to the instruction, while each pipeline stage of the processor is invisible to the instruction.

How do instructions "see"? A rigorous and comprehensive formulation of this process is abstract and lengthy, so we will express it here in a slightly more engineering way, using a few typical examples to illustrate.

Example 1 If an instruction has a source operand for a register, it does not "see" the register in the CPU pipeline until the source operand is generated at the decode stage.

Example 2 If it is a load instruction, it does not "see" the value in memory in the CPU pipeline until memory access stage.[1]

Example 3 If it is a privileged instruction, i.e., it can only be executed when the CPU is in a privileged state, and assuming that the checking of the legality of the privileged instruction is carried out at the decode stage, the instruction cannot "see" the privilege level of the CPU until the decode stage.

Example 4 Assuming that certain address spaces are accessible only to programs in the privileged state, any instruction must "see" the privilege level of the CPU at the time it issues a fetch request during the fetch stage.

From these four examples, readers can more or less understand how instruction "see" in a CPU. The reason for focusing on this process is that, from a pure programmer's perspective, each update of the instruction to the processor's state should be atomic and instantaneous, but when the program is actually running in the processor, the update to the processor's state involved in a single instruction is distributed and delayed. As processor designers, we need to use this distributed, delayed real processor to construct an atomic, instantaneous abstract processor for the software engineers.

7.2 Exception-Related Definitions in LoongArch ISA

With the general concept of exception in mind, let's analyze the exception-related functionality of the LoongArch ISA to form our final design.

---

[1]Readers might argue that the earliest "see" at a memory value at this address is when the execute stage issues a data RAM read request. This would be true if the load instruction's access results at the memory access stage came only from the Q-port output of the data RAM. If it is also possible for the load instruction to get a value directly forwarded by the store instruction at the memory access stage, then the statement in the text would be more appropriate. The text gives a statement that is correct in most cases.

7.2.1 Control Status Register

As mentioned earlier, exception handling is a software-hardware coordinated process. In this process, the hardware logic circuits and the exception handling software need to interact with each other as necessary. In order to achieve precise exception, these interactions cannot affect the software context seen by the user program. (Readers can consider why.) The LoongArch ISA defines a separate set of registers for this type of interaction, collectively known as the control status register (CSR).

For the exception and interrupt handling in this chapter, the related CSRs are CRMD, PRMD, ECFG, ESTAT, ERA, BADV, EENTRY, SAVE0~3, TID, TCFG, TVAL, and TICLR. For the detailed definitions of these registers, please refer to Chapter 7 of the *Instruction Manual*. For readers who are new to LoongArch ISA, it is recommended that they go through the contents of related registers in Chapter 7 first to get a preliminary impression of a few registers without going into details. Then read Chapter 6 of the *Instruction Manual* to understand the general handling of exception and interrupt by the processor hardware. Finally, when finalizing the design and encountering CSR-related contents, carefully review the contents of Chapter 7 of the *Instruction Manual* focusing on the specific details.

It should also be noted that the "read/write" attributes in the CSR register definition descriptions in the *Instruction Manual* are described from the perspective of software programs. They are related to the read and write attributes of these registers in specific hardware implementations, but they do not correspond directly. The read/write attributes seen in the hardware implementation are described later in this chapter when the design details are explained.

7.2.2 Exception Detection

The exceptions that need to be realized in this chapter include interrupt INT, fetch address error ADEF, address unaligned ALE, system call SYS, breakpoint BRK, and instruction nonexistence INE, totaling six kinds. Considering that except for interrupt, other exception conditions in the *Instruction Manual* are scattered in the definition of each instruction that may be related to them, the determination of each exception triggering condition is summarized here for the convenience of readers' understanding.

7.2.2.1 CPU Core Receives Interrupt

Note that this subsection should be read in conjunction with Sections 6.1, 7.4.4, and 7.4.5 of the *Instruction Manual*.

As defined by the LoongArch ISA, 12 wire interrupts can be recorded within each processor core. Except for the inter-core interrupt, which are for multicore scenarios not considered here. There are eight hardware interrupts, two software interrupts, and one timer interrupt.

The source of hardware interrupt is external to the processor core. Readers can think of each LoongArch processor core as having eight interrupt input pins. The device or interrupt controller connects a valid interrupt signal that is active at high level, which is directly sampled by the eight bits 9...2 (corresponding to 8 flip-flops on the RTL) of the IS (Interrupt State) field of the internal ESTAT CSR. The software interrupts are set by the software as the name suggests. Two software interrupt can be set and deactivated by writing 1 or 0 to the bits 1...0 of the IS field of the ESTAT CSR with the CSR write instruction. The status of the timer interrupt is recorded in bit 11 of the IS field of the ESTAT CSR. (More information on timer interrupt can be found later in Sect. 7.2.2.2.)

Bits 11, 9...0 of the IS field of the ESTAT CSR record the status of the 11 interrupt mentioned above, and all of them are active high. However, the processor core determines whether an interrupt is received not only by the presence of a valid value in these bits but also by the interrupt enable status. There are two levels of interrupt enable: the low level is the local interrupt enable corresponding to each interrupt, which is controlled by bits 11, 9...0 of the LIE (local interrupt enable) field of the ECFG CSR; the high level is the global interrupt enable, which is controlled by the IE (interrupt enable) field of the CRMD CSR.

Taking the above into account, the internal flag signal has_int of the processor core that determines that an interrupt has been received can be implemented as

```
assign has_int = ((csr_estat_is[12:0] & csr_ecfg_lie[12:0]) !=
↪    13'b0)
              && (csr_crmd_ie == 1'b1);
```

Obviously, the has_int signal can be raised regardless of whether one or more external interrupts are received, i.e., the CPU hardware does not take into account the details of the difference.[2] When more than one interrupt is received at the same time, the subsequent processing is left to the software interrupt handler.

7.2.2.2   Inner-Core Timer Interrupt Detection

Timer interrupt is often used in operating system scheduling and timing implementations. This interrupt is derived from a timer and is usually implemented either inter-core or inner-core. LoongArch ISA uses an inner-core implementation of the timer interrupt source. Simply put, a 32-bit counter is implemented inside each LoongArch32 processor core, which decrements by 1 every clock cycle when the timer function is enabled, and a timer interrupt is triggered when it reaches the value of 0. The details of the definition are described below: (1) The software configuration of the timer is focused on the TCFG (Timer Config) CSR, including its

---

[2]This is the way it is handled only in LA32R. The hardware in the commercial version of LoongArch can handle multiple interrupt received at the same time at a fixed priority.

start-up enable, initial countdown value, and countdown mode. There are two types of countdown modes, one is to stop counting after decreasing to 0, and the other is to load the initial countdown value automatically after decreasing to 0 to start a new round of countdown again. (2) The clock of the timer is the same clock as the timer accessed by the `rdcntv{l/h}.w` instruction, and requires a fixed frequency. Within the scope of this book's practical tasks, we do not yet consider the processor core's frequency to be changed variably, so we can use the clock of the processor core's pipeline. (3) The current count value of the timer can **only** be obtained by reading the TVAL CSR for approximation,[3] which comes from a different timer with the value read by the `rdcntv{l/h}.w` instruction. (4) When the timer counts down to 0, the hardware sets bit 11 of the IS field of the ESTAT CSR to 1. The software clears bit 11 of the IS field of the ESTAT CSR to 0 by writing an 1 to the CLR bit of the TICLR CSR. **Please pay special attention to the wording of this description. It does not say "bit 11 of the IS field of the ESTAT CSR is always sampled as the result of a decision on whether the timer value is equal to 0," nor does it say "setting the timer value to a non-zero value clears bit 11 of the IS field of the ESTAT to 0." These two descriptions in quotation marks are incorrect. Some beginners tend to misunderstand the *Instruction Manual* like these.** If the bolded text is still not clear to readers, then look at the following code for comparison:

```verilog
always @(posedge clock) begin
    csr_estat_is[11] <= (timer_cnt[31:0]==32'b0);
end
```

The way it is written above is based on misperception, while the code below is the correct one:

```verilog
always @(posedge clock) begin
    if (csr_tcfg_en && timer_cnt[31:0]==32'b0)
        csr_estat_is[11] <= 1'b1;
    else if (csr_we && csr_num==`CSR_TICLR
                    && csr_wmask[`CSR_TICLR_CLR]
                    && csr_wvalue[`CSR_TICLR_CLR])
        csr_estat_is[11] <= 1'b0;
end
```

Compare the two pieces of code above and carefully consider the difference, and then think again why the setting and clearing of the timer interrupt status bit is defined in such a "roundabout" way (hint: pulse signal, level interrupt).

---

[3] The reason for the approximation is that the timer decrements by 1 every clock cycle. The execution of the CSR read instruction to read the TVAL register takes multiple clock cycles. So it can only reflect the value of the timer in one certain clock cycle during this CSR instruction is executed.

In addition, experienced readers may see a small problem in the second correct code above: what if the `if` and `else if` conditions are both valid? Yes, theoretically, such case exists. The code we've given you already took this case into account and adjusted setting 1 to a higher priority, with the intention of not missing interrupt where possible. However, the hardware has its limitation, and I'm sure readers can easily come up with other scenarios where timer interrupt is missed. In fact, only when the software is not well-designed can there be a scenario where the processing of a timer interrupt is "slow" enough that the next (or even later) timer interrupt occurs before the software has cleared the current timer interrupt status bit.

7.2.2.3   Fetch Address Error Exception ADEF Detection

The LoongArch ISA requires that the PCs of all instructions be word-aligned (the lowest two bits of the address are all zeros). When this requirement is violated, a fetch address error exception is detected. The incorrect PC value is recorded in hardware in the BADV CSR. The ERA CSR, which records the return address of the exception, should record the PC in error. However, since a fetch address error exception does not normally return to the PC in error after processing, the information recorded in the ERA CSR is meaningless. Software normally reads the information in the BADV CSR during diagnostic procedures.

7.2.2.4   Address-Unaligned Exception ALE Detection

The address-unaligned exception is only for the load and store instructions. It is triggered when the lowest bit of the address of the `ld.h`, `ld.hu`, and `st.h` instructions is not 0, or when the lowest two bits of the address of the `ld.w`, `st.w`, `ll.w`,[4] and `sc.w` instructions are not all zeros. In this case, the "virtual" address is recorded by hardware in the BADV CSR, and the rest is handled according to the general procedure of the exception.

7.2.2.5   Instruction Nonexistence Exception INE Detection

When the retrieved instruction code does not belong to any of the instructions that have been realized,[5] the instruction nonexistence exception will be triggered, and the rest will be handled according to the general procedure of the exception.

---

[4]The `ll.w` and `sc.w` instructions have not been implemented yet. We list here so that readers can get the right impression.

[5]Strictly, defined in the instruction set. This description is used here to match the progression of advanced practice in this book. Otherwise the decoding unit needs to make decoding judgments for all instructions defined in LA32R ISA.

7.2.2.6 System Call SYS and Breakpoint Exception BRK Detection

System call exception is triggered when executing SYSCALL instruction. Breakpoint exception is triggered when executing BREAK instruction. The rest are handled according to the general procedure of the exception.

7.2.3 Hardware General Process After Responding to an Exception

In addition to the special handling operations specified above, the general process of the hardware after responding to an exception is defined in Section 6.2.3 of the *Instruction Manual* for readers' reference. Moreover, the exception entry is defined in Section 6.2.1 of the *Instruction Manual*.

7.2.4 Exception Return Instruction

Section 7.1 mentioned that at the end of the exception handling phase, the exception handler completes two operations: one is to return to the location where the exception occurred, and the other is to restore the privilege level at which the exception occurred. These two operations need to be synchronized, i.e., they are best accomplished with a single instruction. In LoongArch ISA, the ERTN instruction is defined to accomplish these two operations atomically.[6] The ERTN instruction jumps to the pointer value stored in the ERA CSR as the target address, and at the same time writes the values in the PPLV and PIE fields of the PRMD CSR to the PLV and IE fields of the CRMD CSR respectively.

7.2.5 CSR Read and Write Instructions

LoongArch ISA does not define arithmetic logic instructions that directly manipulate the CSR registers. Instead, it defines three CSR read/write instructions that are used to interact between the general-purpose registers and the CSR registers. Please refer to Section 4.2.1 of the *Instruction Manual* for the definition of these three instructions. As a reminder for beginners, the csrwr instruction writes the old value written to the CSR register into the rd general-purpose register. In fact, the csrwr instruction can be treated as a csrxchg instruction with the write mask fixed to all

---

[6]Atomicity in this context means that it is no longer divisible from the software perspective. For a software program, a machine instruction is already an indivisible minimum unit of execution.

ones. Readers can refer to Chapter 3 of *Fundamentals of Computer Architecture (3rd edition)* for a detailed example of why this CSR read/write instruction is defined and how it is used.

7.3   Design Points for Exception and Interrupt Implementation in Pipelined CPU

After understanding the specifics of the LoongArch ISA with respect to exception and interrupt, we will analyze the design points from the perspective of processor microarchitecture design.

7.3.1   Exception Detection Implementation

From the previous basic concepts, we already know that the detection of exception is done by hardware. Therefore, let's first consider how to generate the detection logic for each exception one by one.

7.3.1.1   Fetch Address Error Exception Detection Logic

According to Sect. 7.2.2.3, the lowest two bits of the PC should be judged. If it is not 2'b00, then fetch address error exception is raised. We recommend that this judgment be performed at the pre-IF stage. Strictly speaking, an abnormal fetch address should not be used to issue a fetch request. PC is already completely incorrect, so its access behavior is no longer expected by the software programmer, and in the worst case, it may lead to crashes and other errors. As of the current practical tasks, we only fetch instructions from the instruction RAM (meaning that any fetch request is only responded by the instruction RAM), and the fetch address has already erased the lowest two bits of the PC to all zeros. So even if a PC with a fetch address error issues a fetch request, it will not have an unrecoverable negative effect. What we discuss here can be considered as setting the stage; later in this book, when we talk about the implementation of the AXI bus interface, we will revisit this design point that beginners often overlook.

7.3.1.2   Address Unaligned Exception Detection Logic

According to Sect. 7.2.2.4, it is necessary to judge the address of the load and store instructions. When the access address is unaligned, this exception flag will be raised. In line with the design idea in the previous section, we recommend that the above judgment be performed at the execute stage when issuing a memory access request, so that the memory access request can be stopped at the wrong address when an abnormality is detected.

7.3.1.3 Instruction Nonexistence Exception Detection Logic

According to Sect. 7.2.2.5, it is known that the instruction nonexistence exception requires decoding of the instruction to get the detection result. Since we need to decode each realized instruction in the decode stage to generate control signals, it is natural to get the condition of "not any realized instruction."

7.3.1.4 System Call and Breakpoint Exception Detection Logic

According to Sect. 7.2.2.6, the detection of system call and breakpoint exception is straightforward, i.e., if it is decoded as a `syscall` instruction, it sets the system call exception flag, and if it is decoded as a `break` instruction, it sets the breakpoint exception flag.

7.3.1.5 Interrupt Detection Logic

The first step in detecting an interrupt is to generate an "interrupt received" flag in the processor core, the detection of which is described in Sect. 7.2.2.1. Timer interrupt generation in the processor core can be referred to Sect. 7.2.2.2. This section focuses on how received interrupt signals are flagged onto instructions.

We find that all the previous exceptions are generated by the attributes of the instruction (or program) itself, while interrupts are triggered by external events, and there is no direct correspondence between them and the instruction. Since we consider interrupt as a special kind of exception, it means that we would like to handle both non-interrupt and interrupt exceptions through a set of exception handling framework. Our design approach is to dynamically tag an asynchronous interrupt event on an instruction, which is then assigned an interrupt exception, and then handled very similarly to other exception. In a five-stage pipeline CPU, there may be multiple instructions at the same time, so which instruction is the right one to mark the interrupt on? Theoretically, any instruction at any level of the pipeline can be selected to be marked with an interrupt exception. As a compromise between the overhead of precise exception implementation and the latency of interrupt response, we usually mark interrupt on instructions at the decode stage. However, please realize that this is not the only design option.

The observant readers may ask, since LoongArch can only receive level interrupt inputs, the signal generated internally by the CPU to indicate whether there is an interrupt or not will be maintained for many cycles. So will it mark many instructions with interrupt, and will this cause any problems? The answer is no. First of all, for a program segment interrupted, even if multiple instructions are marked with interrupt, according to the need for precise exception implementation that will be discussed later, only the instruction at the top of the program sequence will be reported with an interrupt, and the instructions following it will be canceled, so that a single interrupt will not be reported more than once. As for the hardware reporting of interrupt, after entering the interrupt exception handling program, the IE bit of the CRMD CSR has been set to 0 by the hardware (see Section 7.4.1 in *Instruction Manual*), and the "interrupt received" signal inside the processor core will not be valid any more.

7.3.2   Implement Precision Exception

We know that after an exception occurs, the processor hardware needs to set some CSRs, enter the highest privileged state, and jump to the corresponding exception handler entry. Meanwhile, from the analysis in Sect. 7.3.1, we know that different types of exception detection logic can be found in different pipelines of the processor core. Is it true that once an exception occurs, the processor should immediately generate actions such as modifying the CSRs and jumping to the exception handler entry? If we do this, then there will be multiple sources of updates to the CSRs and the fetch PCs due to the exception, and we can only choose one source to update at the same time, so we will encounter the problem of how to choose... In fact, in order to realize a precise exception, we find that we do not need to modify the CSRs or jump to the exception handler entry as soon as an exception occurs.

The analysis of precise exception in Sect. 7.1.2 clearly shows that only the instructions in the pipeline need to be considered when an exception occurs. Apparently, for those instructions whose program sequence precedes the exception instruction, if they have already executed and exited the pipeline, then they must have produced the execution effect; and for those instructions whose program sequence follows the exception instruction and has not yet been executed, by the time they are actually fetched into the pipeline, it must be the time after the exception handler has returned. These instructions naturally follow the precise exception semantics.

When an exception occurs, what should be done with the instructions that are already in the pipeline? There are many ways to do this. Here is a common design idea: **the logic for detecting the exception is distributed in each pipeline stage, close to the datapath associated with it. After the exception is detected, the exception information will be attached to the instruction and carried all the way along the pipeline, and the exception will not be reported until the write-back stage, at which time the CSRs will be updated according to the exception information carried. At the same time when the write-back instruction reports an exception, the status of all pipeline-stage buffers will be cleared, and nextPC will be set as the exception handler entry address.** Of course, the pipeline stage for reporting exception does not necessarily have to be the last stage (write-back stage), but can be the execute stage or memory access stage, which will also reduce the design burden. **However, it should be noted that the principle of choosing the pipeline stage for reporting exception is that no new exception can be generated at the pipeline stage after this stage (e.g., if the pipeline stage for reporting exception is the execute stage, it is required that no new exception can be generated or tagged on the memory access stage or write-back stage), or else it violates the requirement of precise exception.**

Briefly analyze the reasonableness of the above approach. By the time an exception instruction reaches the write-back stage, the instructions preceding it in the program sequence have already exited the pipeline, so the execution effects of those instructions have already been generated. The fact that all pipelines are cleared when a write-back instruction reports an exception means that the instructions that have already entered the CPU pipeline after the exception instruction (including the exception instruction) will **totally not** produce execution effects. The exception handler entry address enters the CPU pipeline as early as the next cycle after the exception is reported, so the processor state it "sees" is that of a completed update.

In the above description, the word "totally not" is bolded and emphasized because the feature is not that obvious. Although all writes to general-purpose registers are done at the write-back stage, store-type instructions write to data RAM at the execute stage. Therefore, if there is an instruction to report an exception at the write-back stage in the current cycle and a store instruction at the memory access stage, then if nothing was done at the execute stage for those instructions in the last cycle, memory will have been modified by the instruction following the exception by the time the exception is reported, which violates the precise exception. So what can be done? At this stage, a simple and effective way is that if the store instruction wants to issue a write request at the execute stage, then it should check whether there are instructions at the current memory access and write-back stages that have been flagged as exception or may be flagged as exception, and it also needs to check that it has not generated an exception or flagged an exception. Fortunately, for the currently implemented instructions and exception types, no more exceptions are detected at the memory access and write-back stages. In other words, the store instruction at the execute stage only needs to check if there are any instructions that have been flagged as exception currently at the memory access and write-back stages, and of course, it also checks to see if it has been flagged as an exception at the execute stage. In this case, the exception information is stored in the pipeline buffer, so there is no significant impact on the timing of the write-enable signals in the data RAM. In a real processor, the store instruction does not actually modify memory at the execute stage, but only after the store instruction has finished executing at the write-back stage. This functionality is usually supported by a structure such as a store buffer or store queue.

7.3.3   *Implement Control Status Registers*

In the previous contents, the control status register operation has appeared continuously. Considering that the implementation of this part is seldom covered in general textbooks, and many beginners have a feeling of not being able to start, therefore, some issues that need to be paid attention to are specially introduced here.

One of the major differences between the CSRs and the general-purpose registers and floating-point registers that you generally learn about is that CSRscan not only be read and written directly by software with instructions but also can be updated directly by the hardware or can directly control the behavior of the hardware. Chapter 7 of the *Instruction Manual* describes the various CSRs. It is important to understand each field of each CSR, especially how they interact with the processor hardware for control and status information. You should clarify how the hardware and software work together in the processing from the principles of privileged mode including privilege levels, exception, and memory management.

7.3.3.1   Code Organization of Control Status Register

CSRs are accessed by CSR instructions such as `csrrd`, `csrwr`, and `csrxchg`, and interact with pipelines and interfaces at various stages in the processor core. The first requirement tends to be implemented centrally, while the latter seems to be implemented decentrally. So how should the code be organized for the implementation? The most reasonable answer is centralize and decentralize when needed, depending on the situation, but I'm sure it is disturbing for beginners. So we'll give you the clear advice:

1. Centralize all CSRs into one module;
2. Module interfaces are divided into two categories: interfaces for instruction access and interfaces for control and status signals that directly interact with the logics inside processor;
3. The instruction access interface contains a read enable (`csr_re`),[7] a register number (`csr_num`), a register read return value (`csr_rvalue`), a write enable (`csr_we`), a write mask (`csr_wmask`), and write data (`csr_wvalue`);
4. Interface signals that directly interact with the processor inner hardware are defined independently as necessary and do not need to be coded uniformly, e.g., the exception handler entry address `ex_entry` for the pre-IF stage, the interrupt valid signal `has_int` for the decode stage, the `ertn` instruction execution valid signal `ertn_flush` from the write-back stage, the exception trigger signal `wb_ex` from the write-back stage, and the exception types and subtypes `wb_ecode`, `wb_esubcode`, and so on.

---

[7] Implementations suggested later in this book use asynchronous reads similar to register file reads, so the read enable can actually be omitted.

The above suggestion may not be the most elegant implementation, but it does provide a clear interface and facilitates code maintenance and error location during incremental development. There is no strict limit to whether the CSR module is instantiated within a pipeline module or in parallel with the pipeline modules, although we prefer the latter option.

7.3.3.2　Control Status Register Read and Write Source Sorting

According to the previous introduction, each CSR will be implemented in the CSR module. By analyzing the definitions of CSRs in the *Instruction Manual*, we find that a single CSR may contain multiple fields, and the maintenance rules of different fields in the same CSR may not be the same. Based on this finding, we suggest readers to take a field in a CSR as the basic unit of code implementation, instead of taking a CSR as a whole. In the following, we will analyze the different fields of a CSR one by one and give an example of implementation.

(1)　PLV field in CRMD

Stated in *Instruction Manual*, the PLV field of the CRMD can be updated by the CSR instruction, and be updated when triggering exception or when `ertn` instruction is executing. Its Verilog code can be realized as follows:

```verilog
always @(posedge clock) begin
    if (reset)
        csr_crmd_plv <= 2'b0;
    else if (wb_ex)
        csr_crmd_plv <= 2'b0;
    else if (ertn_flush)
        csr_crmd_plv <= csr_prmd_pplv;
    else if (csr_we && csr_num==`CSR_CRMD)
        csr_crmd_plv <=
↪    csr_wmask[`CSR_CRMD_PLV]&csr_wvalue[`CSR_CRMD_PLV]
                        | ~csr_wmask[`CSR_CRMD_PLV]&csr_crmd_plv;
end
```

The above implementation indicates that the PLV field of the CRMD needs to be set to all zeros (highest priority) during reset, as defined in Section 6.3 of the *Instruction Manual*. In addition, when updated by CSR write operations (corresponding to the `csrwr` and `csrxchg` instructions), it is necessary to take into account the write mask. This code is easy to understand, as each write condition and value can be matched with the definition in the *Instruction Manual*. When realizing this code, just focus on the input signals of the CSR module and make sure that they are not connected incorrectly.

However, while the above style of code is intuitive, it has one of the most risky points for introducing errors, that is, `if ... else` and `if ... else if` has a form of priority. This means that you can't just look at the conditions after a single `if` to see whether it is executed correctly. For example, if the code is `if (cond_A) do_A else if (cond_B) do_B else if (cond_C) do_C`, then the condition for the `do_C` action to occur is actually `!cond_A && !cond_B && cond_C`, not simply `cond_C`.

(2) IE field in CRMD

Stated in *Instruction Manual*, the maintenance of the `IE` field of CRMD is very similar to that of the PLV. Its Verilog code can be realized as follows:

```verilog
always @(posedge clock) begin
    if (reset)
        csr_crmd_ie <= 1'b0;
    else if (wb_ex)
        csr_crmd_ie <= 1'b0;
    else if (ertn_flush)
        csr_crmd_ie <= csr_prmd_pie;
    else if (csr_we && csr_num==`CSR_CRMD)
        csr_crmd_ie <=
    csr_wmask[`CSR_CRMD_PIE]&csr_wvalue[`CSR_CRMD_PIE]
                        | ~csr_wmask[`CSR_CRMD_PIE]&csr_crmd_ie;
end
```

Comparing the code of `IE` and `PLV` of CRMD, we can find that the conditions of each `if` branch are the same, and the processing code under each branch is also very similar, so in this case, we feel that it is better to centralize the assignments of multiple fields of a CSR into one `always` block.

(3) DA, PG, DATF, and DATM fields in CRMD

At present, the processor we designed has not realized all the functions of MMU and only supports direct address translation mode. So the DA, PG, DATF, and DATM fields of the CRMD can be set to constant values temporarily. The functions of the DA and PG fields can be improved in the practical tasks in Chap. 9, and the functions of the DATF and DATM domains can be further improved in the practical tasks in Chap. 10:

```verilog
assign csr_crmd_da   = 1'b1;
assign csr_crmd_pg   = 1'b0;
assign csr_crmd_datf = 2'b00;
assign csr_crmd_datm = 2'b00;
```

(4) PPLV and PIE fields in PRMD

Stated in *Instruction Manual*, the maintenance of the PPLV and PIE fields of PRMD is very similar. The code is implemented as follows:

```verilog
always @(posedge clock) begin
    if (wb_ex) begin
        csr_prmd_pplv <= csr_crmd_plv;
        csr_prmd_pie  <= csr_crmd_ie;
    end
    else if (csr_we && csr_num==`CSR_PRMD) begin
        csr_prmd_pplv <=
↪   csr_wmask[`CSR_PRMD_PPLV]&csr_wvalue[`CSR_PRMD_PPLV]
                            |
↪   ~csr_wmask[`CSR_PRMD_PPLV]&csr_prmd_pplv;
        csr_prmd_pie  <=
↪   csr_wmask[`CSR_PRMD_PIE]&csr_wvalue[`CSR_PRMD_PIE]
                            |
↪   ~csr_wmask[`CSR_PRMD_PIE]&csr_prmd_pie;
    end
end
```

Some readers may be confused with the above code about why there is no logic to set the initial value when the reset is active. Since the *Instruction Manual* does not define that the above CSR fields need to be reset, it is still satisfied the ISA to write the code as above. In other words, it is up to the software engineers to make sure that an update to these CSR fields occurs before the values are read. For example, the `ertn` instruction cannot be executed after a processor core reset if no exceptions have occurred or if the PPLV and PIE fields for PRMD have not been set by software.

(5) LIE field in ECFG

Stated in *Instruction Manual*, the LIE field of the ECFG will only be updated by the CSR instruction. The Verilog code implementation is as follows:

```verilog
always @(posedge clock) begin
    if (reset)
        csr_ecfg_lie <= 13'b0;
    else if (csr_we && csr_num==`CSR_ECFG)
        csr_ecfg_lie <= csr_wmask[`CSR_ECFG_LIE]&13'h1bff
↪   &csr_wvalue[`CSR_ECFG_LIE]
↪

                            |
↪   ~csr_wmask[`CSR_ECFG_LIE]&13'h1bff&csr_ecfg_lie;
end
```

(6) IS field in ESTAT

The updated information for bits $1\ldots0, 9\ldots2, 11$, and 12 of the IS field in ESTAT come from different sources, which is updated respectively by the CSR instruction, by sampling the hardware interrupt input pins of the processor core, by writing to the timer counter and the TICLR.CLR field, and by sampling the inter-core interrupt input pin of the processor core. Bit 10 is undefined and is held constant at 0 to be on the safe side. Its Verilog code can be realized as follows:

```verilog
always @(posedge clock) begin
    if (reset)
        csr_estat_is[1:0] <= 2'b0;
    else if (csr_we && csr_num==`CSR_ESTAT)
        csr_estat_is[1:0] <=
↪   csr_wmask[`CSR_ESTAT_IS10]&csr_wvalue[`CSR_ESTAT_IS10]
                            |
↪   ~csr_wmask[`CSR_ESTAT_IS10]&csr_estat_is[1:0];

    csr_estat_is[9:2] <= hw_int_in[7:0];

    csr_estat_is[10] <= 1'b0;

    if (timer_cnt[31:0]==32'b0)
        csr_estat_is[11] <= 1'b1;
    else if (csr_we && csr_num==`CSR_TICLR &&
↪   csr_wmask[`CSR_TICLR_CLR]
            && csr_wvalue[`CSR_TICLR_CLR])
        csr_estat_is[11] <= 1'b0;

    csr_estat_is[12] <= ipi_int_in;
end
```

The design of bit 11 of the IS field has been discussed in the previous Sect. 7.2.2.2, so we will not repeat it. Here, please compare the update logic of bits $1\ldots0$ and $9\ldots2$ of the IS field, and analyze them with the definition of the read/write attributes in the *Instruction Manual*, so as to deepen the understanding of the read/write attributes "RW" and "R" of the CSR register field.

(7) Ecode and EsubCode fields in ESTAT

The Ecode and EsubCode fields of ESTAT need to be filled with the exception-type encoding when the exception is triggered. In the previous section on the implementation of precise exception, it was mentioned that an exception is detected at each relevant point in the pipeline, and an exception flag is generated to signal the exception, which is then passed along the pipeline until the write-back stage. Is it better to pass a separate flag signal for each exception along the pipeline, or the

Ecode and EsubCode values that have been encoded according to the *Instruction Manual*? For beginners, it is recommended to pass one flag per exception and encode the Ecode and EsubCode values at the write-back stage to the CSR module. This is the easiest way to ensure readability of the code. In this way, the Verilog code is realized as follows:

```verilog
always @(posedge clock) begin
    if (wb_ex) begin
        csr_estat_ecode    <= wb_ecode;
        csr_estat_esubcode <= wb_esubcode;
    end
end
```

(8) PC field in ERA

When an exception is triggered by an instruction at the write-back stage, the PC to be recorded in the ERA register is the PC of the current write-back stage. The Verilog code implementation is as follows:

```verilog
always @(posedge clock) begin
    if (wb_ex)
        csr_era_pc <= wb_pc;
    else if (csr_we && csr_num==`CSR_ERA)
        csr_era_pc <=
    ↪  csr_wmask[`CSR_ERA_PC]&csr_wvalue[`CSR_ERA_PC]
                     | ~csr_wmask[`CSR_ERA_PC]&csr_era_pc;
end
```

(9) VAddr field in BADV

The VAddr field of BADV is similar to the PC field of ERA. It records information about the write-back instruction when it triggers an exception. It is important to note that before exception handling is implemented, the processor pipeline does not need to store the full virtual address of the load and store instructions at the memory access and write-back stages. In order to maintain the VAddr field of BADV correctly, we need to add the corresponding datapaths at the execute, memory access, and write-back stages. Whether to add a new vaddr field or to reuse other field in the pipeline buffer of the memory access and write-back stages is not critical in implementation. Readers can choose the implementation scheme according to their preference. The Verilog code implementation is given below:

```verilog
assign wb_ex_addr_err = wb_ecode==`ECODE_ADE ||
    ↪  wb_ecode==`ECODE_ALE;

always @(posedge clock) begin
```

```verilog
    if (wb_ex && wb_ex_addr_err)
        csr_badv_vaddr <= (wb_ecode==`ECODE_ADE &&
                              wb_esubcode==`ESUBCODE_ADEF) ?
↪   wb_pc : wb_vaddr;
end
```

(10) VA field in EENTRY

The `VA` field of `EENTRY` can only be updated by the CSR instruction, and its implementation is relatively simple. The Verilog code is as follows:

```verilog
always @(posedge clock) begin
    if (csr_we && csr_num==`CSR_EENTRY)
        csr_eentry_va <=
↪   csr_wmask[`CSR_EENTRY_VA]&csr_wvalue[`CSR_EENTRY_VA]
                          |
↪   ~csr_wmask[`CSR_EENTRY_VA]&csr_eentry_va;
end
```

(11) SAVE0~3

SAVE0~3 are provided to the privileged software for temporary storage of values. Its implementation is relatively simple. The Verilog code is as follows:

```verilog
always @(posedge clock) begin
    if (csr_we && csr_num==`CSR_SAVE0)
        csr_save0_data <=
↪   csr_wmask[`CSR_SAVE_DATA]&csr_wvalue[`CSR_SAVE_DATA]
                          |
↪   ~csr_wmask[`CSR_SAVE_DATA]&csr_save0_data;
    if (csr_we && csr_num==`CSR_SAVE1)
        csr_save1_data <=
↪   csr_wmask[`CSR_SAVE_DATA]&csr_wvalue[`CSR_SAVE_DATA]
                          |
↪   ~csr_wmask[`CSR_SAVE_DATA]&csr_save1_data;
    if (csr_we && csr_num==`CSR_SAVE2)
        csr_save2_data <=
↪   csr_wmask[`CSR_SAVE_DATA]&csr_wvalue[`CSR_SAVE_DATA]
                          |
↪   ~csr_wmask[`CSR_SAVE_DATA]&csr_save2_data;
    if (csr_we && csr_num==`CSR_SAVE3)
        csr_save3_data <=
↪   csr_wmask[`CSR_SAVE_DATA]&csr_wvalue[`CSR_SAVE_DATA]
```

```
                                |
  ↪   ~csr_wmask[`CSR_SAVE_DATA]&csr_save3_data;
end
```

(12) TID

The TID register is also relatively simple to maintain, with the following Verilog
code:

```
always @(posedge clock) begin
    if (reset)
        csr_tid_tid <= coreid_in;
    else if (csr_we && csr_num==`CSR_TID)
        csr_tid_tid <=
  ↪   csr_wmask[`CSR_TID_TID]&csr_wvalue[`CSR_TID_TID]
                        | ~csr_wmask[`CSR_TID_TID]&csr_tid_tid;
end
```

(13) En, Periodic, and InitVal fields in TCFG

Maintaining the update of each field in TCFG is relatively simple. The complexity
lies in the control of `timer_cnt` by each field, which will be explained in the
following section on **TVAL**. A sample Verilog of TCFG is given below:

```
always @(posedge clock) begin
    if (reset)
        csr_tcfg_en <= 1'b0;
    else if (csr_we && csr_num==`CSR_TCFG)
        csr_tcfg_en <=
  ↪   csr_wmask[`CSR_TCFG_EN]&csr_wvalue[`CSR_TCFG_EN]
                        | ~csr_wmask[`CSR_TCFG_EN]&csr_tcfg_en;

    if (csr_we && csr_num==`CSR_TCFG) begin
        csr_tcfg_periodic <=
  ↪   csr_wmask[`CSR_TCFG_PERIOD]&csr_wvalue[`CSR_TCFG_PERIOD]
                                |
  ↪   ~csr_wmask[`CSR_TCFG_PERIOD]&csr_tcfg_periodic;
        csr_tcfg_initval  <=
  ↪   csr_wmask[`CSR_TCFG_INITV]&csr_wvalue[`CSR_TCFG_INITV]
                                |
  ↪   ~csr_wmask[`CSR_TCFG_INITV]&csr_tcfg_initval;
    end
end
```

(14) TimeVal field in TVAL

The `TimeVal` field of the TVAL is a software read-only field that returns the value of the timer counter, so it can be implemented as a wire instead of a reg. The key point of the design here is the implementation of `timer_cnt`, which is used as the timer counter. The Verilog code implementation is given below:

```verilog
reg           csr_tcfg_en;
reg           csr_tcfg_periodic;
reg  [29:0] csr_tcfg_initval;
wire [31:0] tcfg_next_value;
wire [31:0] csr_tval;
reg  [31:0] timer_cnt;


assign tcfg_next_value =  csr_wmask[31:0]&csr_wvalue[31:0]
                        | ~csr_wmask[31:0]&{csr_tcfg_initval,
                                          csr_tcfg_periodic,
↪   csr_tcfg_en};

always @(posedge clock) begin
    if (reset)
        timer_cnt <= 32'hffffffff;
    else if (csr_we && csr_num==`CSR_TCFG &&
    ↪   tcfg_next_value[`CSR_TCFG_EN])
        timer_cnt <= {tcfg_next_value[`CSR_TCFG_INITVAL],
↪   2'b0};
    else if (csr_tcfg_en && timer_cnt!=32'hffffffff) begin
        if (timer_cnt[31:0]==32'b0 && csr_tcfg_periodic)
            timer_cnt <= {csr_tcfg_initval, 2'b0};
        else
            timer_cnt <= timer_cnt - 1'b1;
    end
end

assign csr_tval = timer_cnt[31:0];
```

Two points in the abovementioned code may be slightly difficult to be understood. Explanations are as follows:

1. We update the `timer_cnt` at the same time the software configures the timer (i.e., when updating the TCFG CSR). Specifically, when the software enables the timer (i.e., the En field of the TCFG is set to 1), the initial value of the timer written to the timer configuration register at this time is updated to `timer_cnt`; when the software disables the timer, `timer_cnt` will not be updated. Since the timer is updated when the software writes the TCFG, the value to be written in TCFG (`tcfg_next_value`) is used instead of the existing value in TCFG.

2. When `timer_cnt` decrements to all 0's and the timer is not in periodic mode, there is no logic in the code to deal with this, so `timer_cnt` will continue to decrement by 1 to `32'hffffffffff`. However, since the timer is nonperiodic at this point, it should stop counting, which is why the `timer_cnt` self-decrease enable condition looks at the `tmer_cnt!=32'hffffffffff` condition in addition to `csr_tcfg_en`.

(15) CLR field in TICLR

The `CLR` field of TICLR is very special, its read/write attribute is "W1," which means that the software can only write 1 to it to produce the execution effect (i.e., the hardware only captures the action of writing 1 to the CLR of TICLR), and write 0 is invalid. Meanwhile, the value read out by the **software** will always be 0. Therefore, the CLR field of TICLR doesn't need to define a reg to correspond to it. We only need to define a wire which is always 0 for the CSR to read out later:

```
assign csr_ticlr_clr = 1'b0;
```

(16) CSR Readout Logic

In the previous contents, for the sake of code readability and maintainability, each field of CSR is split to realize the logic of updating and maintaining; however, when the CSR instruction reads the value, each CSR needs to be reassembled to return a 32-bit value. The Verilog code is shown below:

```
wire [31:0] csr_crmd_rvalue = {23'b0, csr_crmd_datm,
  ↪  csr_crmd_datf, csr_crmd_pg, csr_crmd_da, csr_crmd_ie,
  ↪  csr_crmd_plv};
wire [31:0] csr_prmd_rvalue = {29'b0, csr_prmd_pie,
  ↪  csr_prmd_pplv};
wire [31:0] csr_ecfg_rvalue = {19'b0, csr_ecfg_lie};
......
assign csr_rvalue = {32{csr_num==`CSR_CRMD}} & csr_crmd_rvalue
                  | {32{csr_num==`CSR_PRMD}} & csr_prmd_rvalue
                  | {32{csr_num==`CSR_ECFG}} & csr_ecfg_rvalue
                  ......
```

7.3.4 Handle Control Status Registers Hazards

Section 7.3 of the *Instruction Manual* refers to the concept of "control status register-related hazards" and says that hardware is responsible for maintaining them in the LoongArch ISA. Since this concept is rarely covered in textbooks, we will explain it here.

In the previous introduction on pipelined CPU design, we have analyzed the data dependency around general-purpose registers resulting in data hazard. The hazard caused by the CSR is similar to that hazard. It is caused by the RAW dependency around CSR, which is revealed by the multistage pipelined CPU design.

The most typical CSR RAW dependency is when a `csrwr` or `csrxchg` instruction modifies a CSR and then a `csrrd`, `csrwr`, or `csrxchg` instruction reads the same CSR. In order to solve the hazard caused by this dependency, the simplest and most effective way is to put all the CSR read/write instructions to be handled in the same stage of pipeline. This solution is effective and simple to implement but has the disadvantage of causing some performance loss. The reason for the performance loss is that if we put the CSR instruction to write CSR to the write-back stage, then there is a two-cycle execution delay between the CSR instruction and the subsequent instructions that use the return value of the CSR instruction as the source operand, i.e., the second instruction that reads the return value of the CSR instruction has to block itself at the decode stage until the previous CSR instruction reaches the write-back stage. So why don't we use forwarding to solve the hazard caused by RAW? The main reason is that the CSR instruction is a privileged instruction, only being used by the kernel and other privileged software. Even if it can be used, it is not very common to write a CSR and then read it out immediately. Optimizing the performance of such a rare scenario would have little effect on the overall performance. The input-output ratio is too low, so we do not consider it.

In addition to the above RAW dependency between CSR instructions, there are other types of CSR RAW dependency. Through the analysis in the previous Sect. 7.3.3, we know that there are different readers and writers in each field of CSR. These writers and readers with RAW dependency will cause hazards if they are not at the same stage. There are mainly four cases as shown in Table 7.1.

The idea of resolving hazards caused by dependency is simply "blocking + forwarding." Here, we focus on blocking to solve the problem. The implementation of blocking for cases 1, 2, and 3 mentioned here is straightforward. Determine whether there is a writer of the write-related object in these cases at the execute, memory access, and write-back stages. If there is, block reader at the decode stage **and do nothing** (doing nothing means neither marking interrupt nor modifying the fetch PC). The biggest implementation difficulty seems to be the case 4, since the earliest time that the writer and the associated object can be known is at the decode

Table 7.1 Other situations that may cause control status registers hazards

Writer	Dependent target	Reader
csrwr or csrxchg	CRMD.IE, ECFG.LIE, ECFG.IS[1:0], TCFG.En, TICLR.CLR	the instruction at decode stage (mark interrupt)
csrwr or csrxchg	ERA, PRMD.PPLV, PRMD.PIE	ertn
ertn	CRMD.IE	the instruction at decode stage (mark interrupt)
ertn	CRMD.PLV	the fetch PC

stage, but by that time the fetch stage is likely to have an instruction already in it, and the pre-IF stage is likely to have sent out an inappropriate PC fetch request,[8] which means that blocking alone will not solve the problem completely. For this reason, a special solution is introduced: the `ertn` instruction does not modify the CRMD until the write-back stage, and at the same time **clears the pipeline and updates the fetch PC**, which is the origin of the `ertn_flush` signal mentioned above. For the pipelined buffers, this signal has the same effect as the exception signal `wb_ex`, except that it is not a software-visible exception. Why does this solution solve the problem in case 4? Readers can try to think about it.

7.4 Implement Other Instructions

After supporting the timer interrupt, we implement three more timer-related instructions in this section: `rdcntvl.w`, `rdcntvh.w`, and `rdcntid`. `rdcntvl.w` and `rdcntvh.w` read the low 32-bit and high 32-bit values of the timer and write them into the `rd` register, respectively. The timer here is realized by a 64-bit counter, reset to 0 and incremented by 1 every clock cycle after reset. The counter cannot be modified by software, but can only be read by the `rdcntvl.w` and `rdcntvh.w` instructions. **It is a separate counter, not the countdown counter used to generate the timer interrupt.** However, both counters are clocked at the same constant frequency. Within the scope of the practical tasks in this book, it is possible to use the pipeline clock without considering how this constant frequency clock is implemented. `rdcntid` instruction reads the contents of the TID CSR.

Since 64-bit timers cannot be modified by software, the `rdcntvl.w` and `rdcntvh.w` instructions can read their values at the execute, memory access, and write-back stages. It is recommended that they be read at the execute stage to minimize unexpected blocking. `rdcntid` instruction reads the TID CSR, which can be modified by the CSR instruction. So it is simple to postpone its read of the CSR to the write-back stage.

It should also be noted that the encoding of the `rdcntvl.w rd`, `rdcntvh.w rd`, and `rdcntid rj` in the LA32R ISA corresponds to `rdtimel.w rd, zero`, `rdtimeh.w rd, zero`, and `rdtimel.w zero, rj` in the LoongArch ISA. In the disassembly you will see the assembly mnemonic form corresponding to the LoongArch ISA.

---

[8]Beginners may have a hard time understanding this sentence, so please wait until you have completed the AXI bus interface practical tasks to understand.

7.5 Tasks and Practices

After completing this chapter, readers are expected to complete the following two
practical tasks:

1. Support system call exception. See Sect. 7.5.1.
2. Support additional exceptions and interrupts. See Sect. 7.5.2.

7.5.1 Practical Task 12: Support System Call Exception

This practical task requires the following work based on the CPU implemented in
Practical Task 11:

1. Add instructions: `csrrd`, `csrwr`, `csrxchg`, `ertn`.
2. Add control status registers: `CRMD`, `PRMD`, `ESTAT`, `ERA`, `EENTRY`, `SAVE0~3`.
3. Add `syscall` instruction and support system call exception.
4. Run the func corresponding to exp12, and pass simulation and FPGA verification.

Please refer to the method described in Sect. 2.3.1 to obtain the experimental
development environment required for this practical task. The specific experimental
environment is located at `mycpu_env/`, and continue to use the `soc_bram/`
subdirectory.

Once the lab environment is ready, please refer to the following steps to complete
this practical task:

1. Update CPU code at `mycpu_env/myCPU/`.
2. Modify the func configuration file, `mycpu_env/func/include/test_config.h`, select the configuration of `exp12`, and compile. (If you obtained the
   experimental development environment from the package `exp12.zip`, please
   skip this step.)
3. Open the gettrace project, `mycpu_env/gettrace/gettrace.xpr` (the IP core
   in this Vivado project was created using Vivado2019.2; if you open it with a
   higher version of Vivado, refer to Appendix D.4 for the IP core upgrade). Run the
   simulation of the gettrace project (after entering the simulation interface, click
   `run all` and wait for the simulation to finish), and generate a new reference
   trace file `golden_trace.txt` (`mycpu_env/gettrace/golden_trace.txt`).
   The `golden_trace.txt` will not be complete until the simulation has finished
   running. (If you obtained the experimental development environment from the
   package `exp12.zip`, please skip this step.)
4. Start the project in `mycpu_env/soc_verify/soc_bram/run_vivado/` to
   verify myCPU. If you have not created a project in this directory, please
   refer to the steps described in Appendix D.2 to create a project using the
   `create_project.tcl` file in this directory. If necessary, please refer to

Appendix D.4 to upgrade the IP core. If there is a project in this directory that has been created by a previous practice task, you can update the file list of CPU implementations in the project by referring to the steps described in Appendix D.3 after opening the project.

5. Refer to Chap. 4 Sect. 4.4.5.2 to re-customize `inst_ram` in the project. (If you obtained the experimental development environment from the package `exp12.zip`, please skip this step.)

6. Run the simulation in the project (click `run all` directly after entering the simulation interface), and carry out the function verification until the simulation test is passed.

7. Generate a bit stream file after Synthesis and Implementation in the project, and verify it on FPGA. (Please skip this step if you don't have a hardware experiment platform.)

7.5.2 Practical Task 13: Support Additional Exceptions

This practical task requires the following work based on the CPU implemented in Practical Task 12:

1. Support exceptions: `ADEF`, `ALE`, `BRK`, `INE`.
2. Support interrupt, including two software interrupts, eight hardware interrupts, and timer interrupt.
3. Add control status registers: `ECFG`, `BADV`, `TID`, `TCFG`, `TVAL`, `TICLR`.
4. Add instructions: `rdcntvl.w`, `rdcntvh.w`, `rdcntid`.
5. Run the func corresponding to exp13, and pass simulation and FPGA verification.

Please refer to the method described in Sect. 2.3.1 to obtain the experimental development environment required for this practical task. The specific experimental environment is located at `mycpu_env/`, and continue to use the `soc_bram/` subdirectory.

Once the lab environment is ready, please refer to the following steps to complete this practical task:

1. Update CPU code at `mycpu_env/myCPU/`.
2. Modify the func configuration file, `mycpu_env/func/include/test_config.h`, select the configuration of `exp13`, and compile. (If you obtained the experimental development environment from the package `exp13.zip`, please skip this step.)
3. Open the gettrace project, `mycpu_env/gettrace/gettrace.xpr` (the IP core in this Vivado project was created using Vivado2019.2; if you open it with a higher version of Vivado, refer to Appendix D.4 for the IP core upgrade). Run the simulation of the gettrace project (after entering the simulation interface, click `run all` and wait for the simulation to finish), and generate a new reference

trace file `golden_trace.txt` (`mycpu_env/gettrace/golden_trace.txt`). The `golden_trace.txt` will not be complete until the simulation has finished running. (If you obtained the experimental development environment from the package `exp13.zip`, please skip this step.)

4. Start the project in `mycpu_env/soc_verify/soc_bram/run_vivado/` to verify myCPU. If you have not created a project in this directory, please refer to the steps described in Appendix D.2 to create a project using the `create_project.tcl` file in this directory. If necessary, please refer to Appendix D.4 to upgrade the IP core. If there is a project in this directory that has been created by a previous practice task, you can update the file list of CPU implementations in the project by referring to the steps described in Appendix D.3 after opening the project.

5. Refer to Chap. 4 Sect. 4.4.5.2 to re-customize `inst_ram` in the project. (If you obtained the experimental development environment from the package `exp13.zip`, please skip this step.)

6. Run the simulation in the project (click `run all` directly after entering the simulation interface), and carry out the function verification until the simulation test is passed.

7. Generate a bit stream file after Synthesis and Implementation in the project, and verify it on FPGA. (Please skip this step if you don't have a hardware experiment platform.)

Chapter 8
AXI Bus Interface Design

Starting in this chapter, we will enter a new phase—adding the AXI bus interface to the designed CPU. In most real computer systems, the CPU interacts with the system's memory and peripherals through the bus. Without the bus, the CPU is a "lightweight" and can't do anything. The bus interface can be self-defined or follow industry standards. Obviously, adherence to industry standards facilitates integration with a large number of third-party IPs. Therefore, the AMBA AXI bus protocol has been chosen as the protocol specification for the CPU bus interface.

The design task in this chapter has two difficulties: first, how to adjust the CPU internally to adapt to the memory access behavior under the bus interface and, second, how to design an interface that follows the AXI bus protocol. In order to minimize the difficulty of the design, we divide this part of the design work into three phases according to the experience of engineering practice:

- Phase 1: Adjust the original CPU SRAM interface to SRAM-like bus interface. The SRAM-like bus only adds handshaking signals on the basis of the SRAM interface, which can reduce the design complexity of directly realizing the AXI bus.
- Phase 2: Design and implement an "SRAM-like-to-AXI" adapter bridge, and connect it with the CPU completed in Phase 1, and run AXI fixed Latency Verification. The reader will begin this phase by learning and implementing the AXI bus protocol.
- Phase 3: Refine the CPU for Phase 2 and complete the AXI random delay verification.

Learning Goals for This Chapter
- Understand the general principles of on-chip buses.
- Master the design of the interaction between the bus interface and the CPU internal pipeline.

W. Wang, J. Xing, *CPU Design and Practice*,
https://doi.org/10.1007/978-981-96-6573-0_8

Practical Tasks of This Chapter

There are three practical tasks in this chapter (see Sect. 8.5 of this chapter). The reader can complete these tasks as part of his or her study of this chapter, and the correspondence between the two is as follows:

- Sections 8.1 and 8.2 of this chapter correspond to Practical Task 14 (Sect. 8.5.1).
- Sections 8.3 and 8.4 of this chapter correspond to Practical Task 15 (Sect. 8.5.2) and Practical Task 16 (Sect. 8.5.3).

8.1   SRAM-Like Bus

Why do we need to define an SRAM-like bus protocol? The starting point is twofold:

1. Some beginners have no idea how to change the AXI interface from the existing SRAM interface for instruction fetch and memory access.
2. Some beginners use the features of the AXI protocol too aggressively, making the design too complex and causing many errors.

If we introduce our SRAM-like bus protocol in one sentence, it would be "An SRAM interface enhanced with a handshake mechanism."

8.1.1   Master and Subordinate

First of all, the bus is the channel through which the processor interacts with memory and peripherals, and the interaction behavior is specified as two types of operations, read and write. Since it is an interaction, there must be at least two participating subjects, and we refer to the initiating party as the "master" and the responding party as the "subordinate." For a read operation, the master makes a read request; the subordinate receives the request and returns the data; for a write operation, the master makes a write request and sends the data; the subordinate receives the request and the data.

8.1.2   Definition of SRAM-Like Bus Interface Signals

A description of the SRAM-like bus interface signals is listed in Table 8.1.

All the signals in the above table correspond to the original SRAM interface signals except for the signals size, addr_ok, and data_ok. Among them, req corresponds to en, wr corresponds to (!wen), and wstrb corresponds to wen. The meanings of the signals that correspond to each other have not been changed, so we will not explain them again. We focus on the new signals size, addr_ok, and data_ok.

Table 8.1 SRAM-like bus interface signals

signal	bit width	orientation	description
clk	1	input	clocks
req	1	master->slave	Request signal, 1 for read/write request, 0 for no read/write request.
wr	1	master->slave	1 indicates that this is a write request, and 0 indicates that this is a read request.
size	2	master->slave	The number of bytes transferred for this request, 0: 1 byte; 1: 2 bytes; 2: 4 bytes.
addr	32	master->slave	Address of the request
wstrb	4	master->slave	Byte write enable for this write request.
wdata	32	master->slave	Write data for this write request
addr_ok	1	slave->master	Address transmission for this request done, read: address received; write: address and data received
data_ok	1	slave->master	Data transfer done for this request, Read: data returned; Write: data write completed.
rdata	32	slave->master	The read data returned by this request.

Table 8.2 Relationship between SRAM-like size and memory access

Instructions in pipeline	calculated address	Address send to SRAM-like interface	size	meaning
fetch instruction	addr[1:0]==0	addr[1:0]==0	2	Access 4 Bytes
ld.w, st.w	addr[1:0]==0	addr[1:0]==0	2	Access 4 Bytes
ld.h, ld.hu, st.h	addr[1:0]==0	addr[1:0]==0	1	Access 2 Bytes
ld.h, ld.hu, st.h	addr[1:0]==2	addr[1:0]==2	1	Access 2 Bytes
ld.b, ld.bu, st.b	addr[1:0]==0	addr[1:0]==0	0	Access 1 Bytes
ld.b, ld.bu, st.b	addr[1:0]==1	addr[1:0]==1	0	Access 1 Bytes
ld.b, ld.bu, st.b	addr[1:0]==2	addr[1:0]==2	0	Access 1 Bytes
ld.b, ld.bu, st.b	addr[1:0]==3	addr[1:0]==3	0	Access 1 Bytes

For the size signal, since there are arsize and awsize signals on the AXI bus protocol, it is necessary to transmit this signal to the AXI interface via the SRAM-like interface. The relationship between the size signal and the different access operations in the SRAM-like interface is shown in Table 8.2.

Also, for write transactions, the correspondence between size and addr[1:0] and wstrb is shown in Table 8.3.

The `addr_ok` signal is used in conjunction with the req signal to complete the handshake for read and write requests. It is considered to be a successful request handshake only when seeing the req and `addr_ok` are 1 at the same time on the rising edge of `clk`.

The `data_ok` signal has dual meanings. For a read transaction, it is a valid signal for data return; for a write transaction, it is a valid signal for write completion. Regardless of whether `data_ok` expresses a response to a read transaction or a write transaction, it is collectively referred to as a data response. In the SRAM-

Table 8.3 Relationship among SRAM-like size, addr and wstrb

	data[31:24]	data[23:16]	data[15:8]	data[7:0]	wstrb
size=0,addr=0	–	–	–	valid	0b0001
size=0,addr=1	–	–	valid	–	0b0010
size=0,addr=2	–	valid	–	–	0b0100
size=0,addr=3	valid	–	–	–	0b1000
size=1,addr=0	–	–	valid	valid	0b0011
size=1,addr=2	valid	valid	–	–	0b1100
size=2,addr=0	valid	valid	valid	valid	0b1111

like interface, the master can always receive the data response, so the master is no longer configured to receive the handshake signal of `data_ok`. In other words, if there is a request that does not return a data response, a `data_ok` of 1 on the rising edge of clk is considered a successful data response handshake.

8.1.3   Read and Write Timing for SRAM-Like Buses

Figures 8.1 and 8.2 show the timing relationships for one read transaction and one write transaction on the SRAM-like bus, respectively.

Figure 8.3 gives the timing relationship for sequential writes and reads on the SRAM-like bus. In the case of sequential write and read, the `data_ok` returned from a party is returned strictly in the order in which the requests were sent. In this figure, the `data_ok` of the write transaction is returned first because the write request is issued before the read request, but it is possible to complete the handshake for other read and write transactions several times after the successful handshake for one read or write transaction and before the response is returned. That is, on the interface's signal, it is possible that(req1&addr_ok) → (req2&addr_ok) → (req3&addr_ok) → (req4&addr_ok) →... →data_ok1 sequence of handshake signals. When considering the design, the more such transactions that have been requested but not yet responded to, the more complex the design becomes. To control the number of such transactions to simplify the design, you can pause sending requests for new transactions by pulling down the req signal on the master side, and you can pause receiving requests for new transactions by pulling down the `addr_ok` signal on the subordinate side.

Figure 8.4 gives an illustration of the timing relationship between successive reads and writes on the SRAM-like bus. Note that when both `addr_ok` and `data_ok` are valid, they correspond to different bus transactions: `addr_ok` indicates a successful request handshake for the current transfer transaction, and `data_ok` indicates a successful data response handshake for the previous transfer transaction. In addition, it is possible for the successful read data response handshake to precede the successful write request handshake.

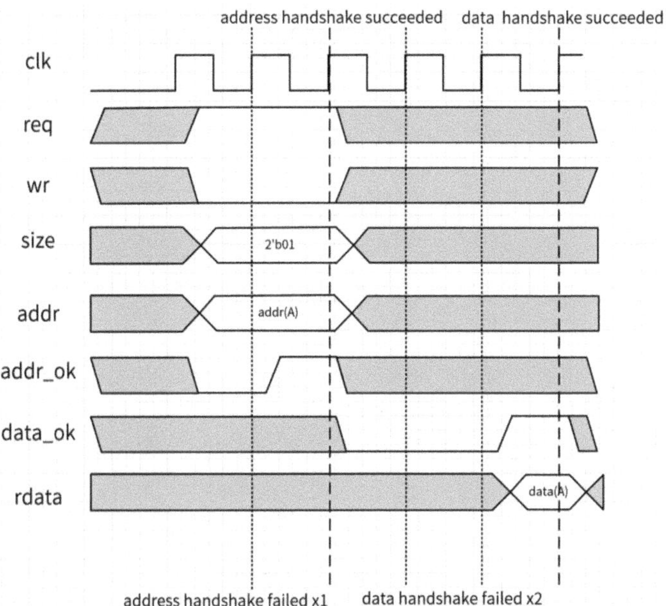

Fig. 8.1 Time diagram of one SRAM-like read transaction

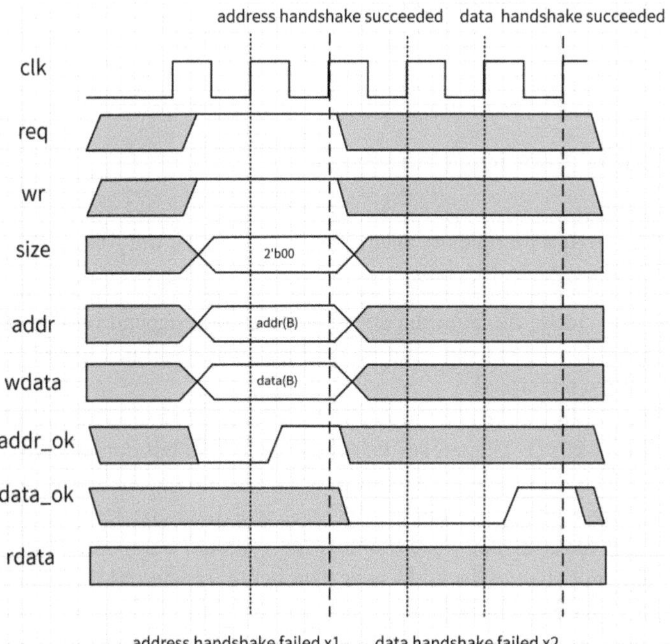

Fig. 8.2 Time diagram of one SRAM-like write transaction

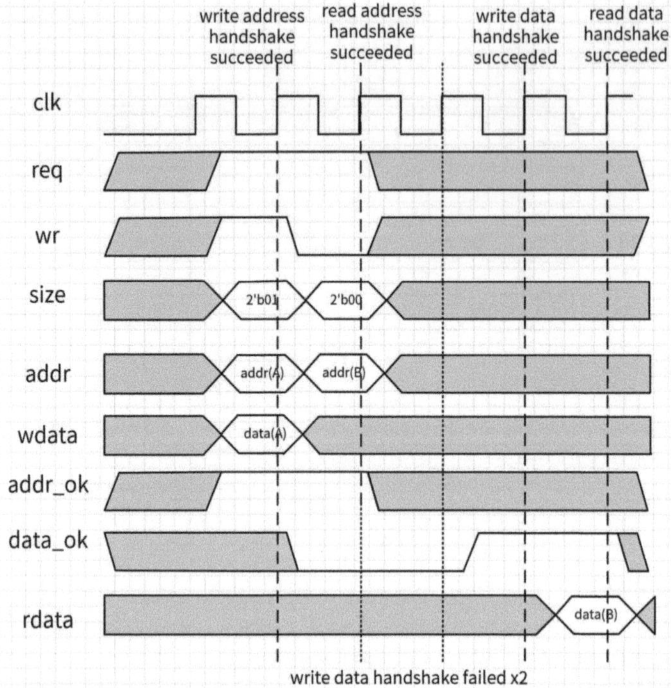

Fig. 8.3 Sequential write-read transactions on SRAM-like bus

8.1.4 SRAM-Like Bus Constraints

To reduce the design complexity of the SRAM-like bus, the following constraints are placed on the SRAM-like bus:

1. The value of `addr_ok` from the subordinate cannot depend on the value of the `req` initiated by the master. That is, the logic that generates the `addr_ok` must not look at the req signal.
2. The master is allowed to change `wr`, `size`, `addr`, `wstrb`, and `wdata` when `req` is 1 and `addr_ok` is 0. This means that the SRAM-like bus can change the type of request and the address when a request for an operational address is raised but not received. This is different from the AXI bus, which will be described later, in that the AXI bus requires that once the host has initiated a transfer of an address or data, it may not change the address or data being transferred until the handshake for that transfer is successful.

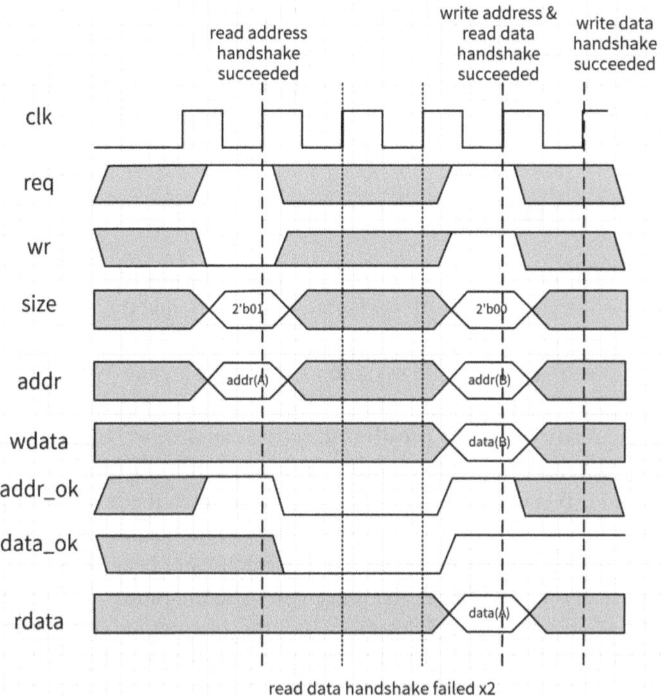

Fig. 8.4 Sequential read-write transactions on SRAM-like bus

8.2 SRAM-Like Bus Design

In the existing CPU, the instruction fetch and memory access parts use the standard
SRAM interface, which needs to be modified into a SRAM-like bus interface. From
the analysis in Sect. 8.1, we know that to change the standard SRAM interface
to a SRAM-like interface, we only need to add three signals: size, addr_ok, and
data_ok.

Among the three signals to be added, the signal size is very simple to generate,
it can be generated directly according to the attributes of the request, and we need
to focus on the addr_ok and data_ok signals.

In the existing CPUs, the access to SRAM in the instruction fetch and memory
access stage is accomplished in two adjacent pipeline stages. The first pipeline stage
sends out the request and the second pipeline stage receives the response. This
pipelining pattern does not need to be adjusted; what needs to be adjusted is the
control logic of the state of each pipeline stage.

8.2.1 Considerations for the Design of Indexing

Let's start by looking at what adjustments should be made during the instruction fetch stage.

8.2.1.1 Consider `ready_go`

Based on our reference design, the address request of instruction fetch is issued in the pseudo-pipeline stage of pre-IF (generating nextPC), and the data return is done in the IF pipeline stage.

First of all, pre-IF also needs to maintain a ready_go signal. When fetching from the instruction RAM, the request sent at the pre-IF pseudo-pipeline stage is always received, so the ready_go of the pre-IF instruction can always be set to 1. However, the situation is different now, as the `addr_ok` from the SRAM-like bus may not be 1 all the time, and if it is 0, it means that the request to fetch the instruction address is not received by the external part of the CPU. Since all the instruction has to do at the pre-IF stage is to send the request, and the request has not been received, ready_go is naturally 0. ready_go can be set to 1 only when req and `addr_ok` are set to 1.

For the IF stage, in previous design, when the instruction is fetched from the instruction RAM, the instruction code from the next cycle of the request will be returned, so the only task of the instruction in the IF flow stage—to get the instruction code—can be completed successfully, so ready_go is always set to 1. When we introduce the SRAM-like bus, the situation becomes more complicated. Only when `data_ok` returns 1 does the instruction code appear on the interface, and only in this case can the ready_go signal at the IF stage be set to 1.

In summary, both the instruction address request and the instruction code return require handshaking, and their impact on the two stages of the instruction fetch phase is reflected in the `ready_go` signals of the pre-IF and IF stages. Can you once again appreciate the magical effect of the pipeline control signal `ready_go` that seems to cure all ills?

8.2.1.2 Consider `allowin`

In the previous subsection, only the `ready_go` signals at the pre-IF and IF stages were considered, but for the pipeline stage-by-stage interlocking control mechanism, the allowin signals at the IF and ID stages need to be considered as well.

We first consider the pre-IF stage. pre-IF stage generates the nextPC and sends the address request for instruction fetch, and waits for `addr_ok` to set ready_go When ready_go is 1 and IF-allowin is 1, the instruction of pre-IF stage flows to IF stage, and pre-IF stage maintains the address request for instruction fetch for the next instruction. According to the combination of pre-IF-ready_go and IF-allowin, there are four possibilities:

1. pre-IF-ready_go=0, IF-allowin=0: Obviously, the pre-IF stage just continues to send address requests.
2. pre-IF-ready_go=0, IF-allowin=1: Obviously, as in the first case, the pre-IF stage continues to send address requests.
3. pre-IF-ready_go=1, IF-allowin=1: indicates that the fetch request sent at the pre-IF stage has been received and the IF stage allowin is 1; the current instruction flows into the IF stage. This case is also very simple.
4. pre-IF-ready_go=1, IF-allowin=0: indicates that the request to fetch the instruction issued by the pre-IF stage has been received but the IF stage al- lowin is 0. This case is the most complicated and it faces two problems, which are discussed in detail here:

   - **Question 1:** When "pre-IF-ready_go=1, IF-allowin=0," can the instruction blocked at pre-IF stage continue to enable the req signal in the next cycle (i.e., continue to send a request for the PC to fetch the instruction address)? Apparently not, because at this cycle, both req and `addr_ok` on the SRAM-like interface are 1, and the request has already been received by the external CPU. So if req is turned on in the next cycle, the SRAM-like bus will treat it as a new request, and will return as many read requests as it has received from the external CPU. Unless you know this very well, and then design a rigorous filter of the excess return data, you are bound to mess up the instruction-to-PC correspondence at the IF stage. Typically, you will see several instructions in a row that have the correct PC trace, but the instructions are the same. Therefore, **it is important to note that if an instruction fetch request is received by the SRAM-like interface at the pre-IF stage, but the instruction does not make it to the next stage of the flow on the next cycle, then no more instruction fetch requests can be sent to the PC from the next cycle onward**.
   - **Question 2:** When "pre-IF-ready_go=1, IF-allowin=0," the pre-IF address request has been received by the external party, and then the external party may return the instruction corresponding to this request at any time. If the instruction to be fetched by pre-IF stage is received before IF-allowin=1, what should be done? Obviously, the instruction fetched at the pre-IF stage is not yet available at the IF stage (since IF-allowin=0), but the fetched instruction will only remain on the rdata side of the SRAM-like bus interface for one cycle. If we choose to discard the instruction returned in the current cycle, we have to let the pre-IF stage resend the address request, and the outside world will only return the data once for each request. If we don't resend the request, the outside world will not return the instruction of the pre-IF stage, and the CPU will enter the dead state. If we don't want to discard the instruction returned in the current cycle, then we need to set up an instruction buffer to save the instruction which has already been retrieved but cannot enter the IF stage, and the pre-IF stage should also suspend sending the fetch request

(otherwise, the new received request will return a new instruction code, which will overwrite the instruction saved in the cache). When the instruction cache is active, instructions entering the IF stage from the pre-IF stage do not have to wait for `data_ok` from the instruction RAM but are taken directly from the instruction cache.

- The solutions given in the analysis can solve the aforementioned two problems but are slightly more complex in design. For beginners, we would like to introduce a simpler solution—**only when the allowin of IF stage is 1 the pre-IF stage can send out address request to the outside world**. After this process, when pre-IF stage `ready_go` is 1, the `allowin` from IF stage must be 1, and there will be no "pre-IF-ready_go=1, IF-allowin=0," so you won't run into problems one and two analyzed above. However, there is no free lunch in this world; this simple solution has relatively poor circuit delay. If the reader tries to give up this solution to increase the main frequency during the realization process, then he or she should consider how to solve the problems I and II analyzed above. In this case, it is important to note that the ready_go at the pre-IF stage does not depend only on the `addr_ok` signal but also on the fact that the request has already been received.

After considering the pre-IF stage, let's consider the case of IF stage, IF stage waits for `data_ok` to set ready_go, when ready_go is 1 and ID-allowin is 1, the instruction of IF stage will flow to ID stage, and IF stage will maintain the next instruction to return to ID stage, or enter into invalid state (IF-valid is 0). According to the combination of IF-ready_go and ID-allowin, there are four possibilities as follows (the following cases default IF-valid to 1, which means there is a valid instruction at IF stage, if there is no valid instruction at IF stage, it will not flow to ID stage):

1. IF-ready_go=0, ID-allowin=0: Obviously the IF stage just continues to wait for the instruction to return.
2. IF-ready_go=0, ID-allowin=1: This is the same as the first case, and the IF stage continues to wait for the instruction to return.
3. IF-ready_go=1, ID-allowin=1: indicates that the IF stage has received an instruction and the ID stage is also allowed to enter, then the current instruction enters the ID stage in the next cycle, which is a straightforward case.
4. IF-ready_go=1, ID-allowin=0: indicates that the IF stage has received the instruction but the ID stage is not allowed to enter; this is the most complicated case and needs to be considered.

Unlike the previous discussion of pre-IF cases, the fourth case at the IF stage is unavoidable. There are only two ways to deal with it, namely, discarding and refetching or temporary caching. Considering that the state machine design of the refetching idea is more complicated and beginners are prone to make mistakes, we recommend the temporary caching scheme, i.e., a group of register is set up to save the instruction retrieved at IF stage, and when the group of triggers has valid data, the data saved by the group of triggers will be selected as the instruction retrieved at IF stage to be sent to ID stage, and the instruction will be immediately entered into ID stage when the allowin at ID stage is 1. At this time, the ready_go signal of IF stage should be further adjusted, it can't only look at the data_ok returned by the instruction RAM interface, but also look at whether there is a valid instruction in the cache of the temporary instruction; if there is, the ready_go of IF stage should be set to 1.

8.2.1.3 Consider Exception Clearing Pipeline

If we design a CPU that supports exceptions and interrupts, then there are cases where exceptions and interrupts have to clear the pipeline, which are labeled as Cancel. With the introduction of the SRAM-like bus interface, the case of Cancel also requires special consideration.

Let's first look at Cancel at the pre-IF stage, which is discussed in two scenarios depending on whether or not the pre-IF has completed the address request:

1. to_fs_valid=0: indicates that the address request sent by the pre-IF stage has not been received by the external part of the CPU (addr_ok has not been received). According to Sect. 8.1.4, the SRAM-like bus allows requests to be changed in the middle of a request, so adjusting the address request sent by the pre-IF stage directly according to the Cancel message will not have any effect.
2. to_fs_valid=1: indicates that the address request sent by the pre-IF stage is exactly (or has already been[1]) received by the external part of the CPU; at this time, if there is a Cancel, although it is possible to send a new instruction fetch request immediately according to the Cancel content, it is important to be aware that the first instruction data received by the IF stage in the subsequent return is the return to the current Canceled instruction request. The first instruction data received by the IF stage is the return of the currently canceled fetch request.

Let's look at Cancel at the IF stage, which can be discussed in two ways depending on the value of allowin at the IF stage:

1. IF-to-pre-IF-allowin=1: indicates that there is no valid instruction in IF stage, or there is valid instruction but it is going to flow to ID stage; then IF-valid will be set to 0 or 1 according to to_fs_valid. At this time, if IF stage receives Cancel, then IF-valid trigger will be set to 0 in the next cycle.
2. IF-to-pre-IF-allowin=0: Indicates that there is a valid instruction at the IF stage and the instruction cannot flow to the ID stage, which can be divided into two cases:

---

[1] If the design scheme of sending request only when the IF stage allowin is valid as described earlier in this chapter is not adopted for pre-IF stage request, then there may be a situation that the request of pre-IF stage to fetch the instruction has already been received by the instruction RAM, but the instruction is not able to enter into the IF stage, and in this case the to_fs_valid of the pre-IF stage will also be set to 1.

- IF-ready_go=1: It indicates that IF stage has received `data_ok` exactly or already; at this time, there is no pending SRAM-like bus transaction at IF stage, so direct Cancel (set IF-valid to 0) will not have any effect. Note that the IF stage has a group of triggers that save the returned instruction; when Canceling, the valid signal that indicates the instruction data which is saved in this group of triggers should also be cleared to zero.
- IF-ready_go=0: indicates that the IF stage is still waiting for `data_ok`; at this time, the IF stage is waiting for the completion of the SRAM bus transaction; you can directly Cancel (set IF-valid to 0). Note that the first return instruction data received by IF stage afterward is the response to the current instruction fetch request that has been canceled due to an exception.

Scenario 2 at the pre-IF stage above has one thing in common with Scenario 2-2 at the IF stage: after a Cancel, the first returned instruction data subsequently received at the IF stage is a return to the currently Canceled fetch request. Obviously, the first instruction data received subsequently should be discarded, and should not be allowed to flow to the ID stage. This situation should be taken into account when designing the IF stage state machine. If this problem is not solved, the CPU may get the error that the PC and the instruction code of the first instruction returned by the IF stage after the exception Cancel pipeline do not correspond to each other. There are two ways to solve this problem:

1. Introduce a new state in the IF stage state machine (which indicates that it is waiting for a `data_ok` and discarding the current returned instruction data).
2. A new trigger is added to the IF stage with a reset value of 0. This trigger is set to 1 when the aforementioned case 2 of the pre-IF stage and case 2-2 of the IF stage are encountered, and it is set to 0 when `data_ok` is received. When this trigger is 1, the combinational logic erases the ready_go of the IF stage to zero, thus achieving the design of discarding the first returned instruction data.

Both of these implementations are essentially the same. In addition, they both default to the premise that after Cancel, the IF stage needs to discard at most one of the instructions returned. If your design requires that the IF stage discard up to two instructions after Cancel, then you need to improve the above implementation.

8.2.1.4   Consideration of Transfer Calculations Not Completed

There is one case of "write-after-read" correlation, Load-to-Branch, where the i-th instruction is a Load and the $i + 1$-th instruction is a transfer (jump or branch) instruction, and the transfer instruction has at least one source register that is the same as the destination register of the Load instruction, i.e., the Branch has a "write-after-read correlation" with the Load. In this case, when the transfer instruction is at the ID stage, the Load instruction cannot get the Load result at the EX stage, so the transfer instruction cannot calculate the correct jump direction or jump target, which is called "transfer calculation not completed." At this time, the nextPC generated by the transfer information (br_bus) sent from the ID stage to the IF stage is incorrect, and the nextPC is maintained by the pre-IF. If the pre-IF stage initiates the fetch pointing address request with the wrong nextPC, there is a good chance that the request will be received externally by the CPU and eventually returned. If left unattended, the pipeline will treat this incorrectly fetched instruction as a jump target for subsequent processing, resulting in an error.

Some readers may think: if it is already clear whether the allowin of the IF stage is 1 when the pre-IF stage sends a request to fetch the instruction, then if the transfer instruction calculation of the ID stage is not finished, the pipeline will be blocked. Consequently the IF stage is also blocked, and the allowin of the IF stage to the pre-IF stage will be 0, and the pre-IF stage will not send the request. As a result, the error analyzed above won't occur, so no additional processing is needed. At first glance, this analysis seems to make sense, but it introduces an implied condition, i.e., "it blocks the pipeline, and then the IF stage is also blocked," which is incorrect. **When the instruction RAM no longer returns data for a fixed number of cycles, but may return data for a random number of cycles, there may not be an instruction at the IF stage when there is an instruction at the ID stage. The randomization of the number of clock cycles of memory access latency introduced by the bus interface is one of the most common design difficulties that beginners tend to overlook, so it must always be a focus of attention.**

Since an incomplete transfer calculation can still lead to an error, it needs to be handled specifically. There are two ways to solve the problem: blocking and discarding. Usually, for beginners, the blocking fetch design is more intuitive to understand and implement, so this book will only analyze this idea, and those who are interested in the other idea can try it by themselves. Under the blocking fetch design, one specific design scheme is add a new control signal br_stall on the br_bus from the ID stage to the instruction fetching stage, and set br_stall to 1 when there is a transfer instruction on the ID stage and it is in the unfinished state of computation; when the pre-IF stage sees that br_stall is 1, it will pause to send out the fetch request until br_stall is 0 again.

8.2.2   *Memory Access Design Considerations*

In this section, let's consider the design adjustments to the memory access part after introducing the SRAM-like bus interface. We divide the access memory into load and store; the two categories were analyzed in turn.

The logical changes of the load instruction design can be largely drawn on the adjustments of the fetch instruction design introduced in the previous subsection. The EX stage of the load memory access request corresponds to the pre-IF stage of the fetch request, and the MEM stage of the receive data return corresponds to the IF stage of the fetch return. The design adjustments are centered on the following points:

1. At the stage where the accessing request is send, the instruction must complete the address request handshake (`addr_ok` is or has been 1) before moving to the next stage.
2. At the satge where the instruction receives data, it waits for the data return handshake to complete (`data_ok` is or has been set to 1) before moving to the next stage.
3. In the case where the access request of an instruction is received and data is returned, but the instruction cannot proceed to the next stage because the allowin returned from the next stage is invalid, it is recommended that the access request be issued only when the allowin returned from the next stage is valid to simplify the design.
4. For memory access requests that have already been received, if their corresponding instructions are canceled due to an abnormal clearing of the pipeline, make a note of these access requests and discard them when their data is returned.[2]

In addition to the above design points, another reminder of a design detail that beginners tend to make mistakes: if in the original design, the valid signal of the MEM stage participating in the generation of the forward pass is the valid signal of the MEM stage, it is important to adjust it to the ms_to_ws_valid of the MEM stage into the WB stage.

Let's look at the design adjustments to the store instruction. First of all, the store instruction makes the same changes at the EX stage as the load operation by sending all the contents of the write request at once. The reason for this simplicity is the definition of the `addr_ok` signal in the SRAM-like bus interface: "When the operation is a write operation, an `addr_ok` of 1 indicates that both the write address and the write data have been received." Second, the store instruction also sees the `data_ok` signal at the MEM stage before it can proceed to the next stage. Most of the readers may find this design requirement strange—the store instruction does not need to wait for data return, so why does it need to see the `data_ok` signal? The reason is that the SRAM-like bus returns `data_ok` for both read and write. If the store instruction enters the WB stage without seeing the `data_ok` signal at the MEM stage, the `data_ok` signal seen by the subsequent load instruction at the MEM stage may be the `data_ok` signal corresponding to the previous store instruction, which will cause the load instruction to think that the data has been returned and then fetch a wrong data. As to why the `data_ok` return signal is defined in the SRAM-like bus interface for write requests, the reader will understand the design intent after learning about the read-after-write processing of the AXI bus later in this chapter.

---

[2]The store instruction has already guaranteed that it will not be canceled by an exception when it sends a store request in order to achieve a precise exception. If the conditions for the load instruction to issue a store request are set to the same strictness, this situation will not occur, and there is no need for additional processing.

8.3   AXI Bus Protocol

For the AXI bus protocol, the reader is referred to Section 6.2, Part 1 of *Fundamentals of Computer Architecture (3rd Edition)* for an introduction to the key elements of the AXI specification. On this basis, it is recommended that the reader study the AXI v1.0 specification, "AMBA AXI Protocol Specification v1.0," which is a short and easy-to-understand specification.

In the following section, we will point out the key points of the AXI bus protocol that are closely related to this experiment, taking into account the practical engineering experience. Again, please familiarize yourself with the AXI bus protocol in conjunction with the Fundamentals of Computer Architecture or the AXI specification before studying this section alone to complete the design.

8.3.1   AXI Bus Signal List

The AXI bus signals that are relevant to the practical tasks in this chapter are listed in Table 8.4, and the signals marked with "*" are the ones that you must master. In the comments column, we give some design suggestions for the practical tasks in this chapter. For example, the signal arlen has a comment "fixed to 0," which suggests that the reader can set the output of this signal to 0. Since we have not implemented Cache, any read request can be completed with only one bus transfer, and the corresponding arlen is 0. The comment for rresp is "Ignorable," which means that the signal rresp can be left out of your interface design, since currently it does not take into account the special handling of Bus Error cases, and does not utilize the bus for atomic accesses.

```
## Warning: One or more parsing issues, see `problems()`
## for details
```

8.3.2   Preliminary Interpretation of the AXI Bus Protocol

Fundamentals of Computer Architecture (3rd edition) and the AXI specification have already introduced what the AXI protocol is in rigorous, correct, and comprehensive language, and we are not going to repeat these concepts and definitions in this section. Instead, we will explain the design intent of the various signals and provisions of the AXI protocol based on our understanding of actual engineering practices. Since we are not the designers of the AXI protocol specification, the following explanations are not necessarily narrow, and they are just a reference to help you deepen your understanding.

Table 8.4 AXI32 interface signals

signal	bit width	orientation	functionality	comments
			AXI Clock and Reset Signals	
aclk*	1	input	AXI Clock	
aresetn*	1	input	AXI reset, active low	
			Read request channel, (starts with ar)	
arid*	4	master—>slave	ID number of the read request	Instruction fetch for 0; memory access for 1.
araddr*	32	master—>slave	Address of the read request	
arlen	8	master—>slave	Read request control signal, length of requested transfer (number of data transmission cycles)	Fixed to 0
arsize*	3	master—>slave	Read request control signal, the size of the transfer (number of bytes per beat of the data transfer)	
arburst	2	master—>slave	Read request control signal, transmission type	Fixed to 0b01
arlock	2	master—>slave	Read request control signal, atomic lock	Fixed to 0
arcache	4	master—>slave	Read request control signal, CACHE Attribute	Fixed to 0
arprot	3	master—>slave	Read request control signal, Protection Attributes	Fixed to 0
arvalid*	1	master—>slave	Read request address handshake signal, read request address is valid	
arready*	1	slave—>master	Read request address handshake signal, slave ready to receive address transmission	
			Read response channel, (starts with r)	
rid*	4	slave—>master	ID number of the read request, the rid of the same request should be the same as the arid	0 corresponds to instrction fetch; 1 corresponds to memory access.
rdata*	32	slave->master	Readback data for read requests	
rresp	32	slave->master	Read request control signal, whether this read request is successfully completed or not	negligible
rlast	31	slave->master	Read request control signal, indication signal of the last beat of data for this read request	negligible

(continued)

Table 8.4 (continued)

signal	bit width	orientation	functionality	comments
rvalid*	31	slave->master	Read request data handshake signal, read request data is valid	
rready*	31	master->slave	Read request data handshake signal, master ready to receive data transfer	
			Write request channel, (starts with aw)	
awid*	34	master->slave	ID number of the write request	Fixed at 1
awaddr*	32	master—>slave	Address of the write request	
awlen	38	master->slave	Write request control signal, length of the requested transfer (number of data transfer beats)	Fixed to 0
awsize*	33	master->slave	Write request control signal requesting the size of the transfer (number of bytes per beat of data transfer)	
awburst	32	master->slave	Write request control signal, transmission type	Fixed to 0b01
awlock	32	master->slave	Write Request Control Signal, Atomic Lock	Fixed to 0
awcache	4	master->slave	Write request control signal, CACHE attribute	Fixed to 0
awprot	3	master->slave	Write request control signal, protection attribute	Fixed to 0
awvalid*	1	master->slave	Write request address handshake signal, write request address is valid	
awready*	1	slave->master	Write request address handshake signal, slave ready to receive address transfer	
			Write data channel, (starts with w)	
wid*	4	master->slave	ID number of the write request	Fixed at 1
wdata*	32	master->slav	Write data for write requests	
wstrb*	4	master->slave	Write request control signal, byte select bit	
wlast	1	master->slave	Write request control signal, indication signal for the last beat of data for this write request	Fixed at 1

(continued)

Table 8.4 (continued)

signal	bit width	orientation	functionality	comments
wvalid*	1	master->slave	Write request data handshake signal, write request data is valid	
wready*	1	slave->master	Write request data handshake signal, slave side ready to receive data transfer	
			Write response channel, (starts with b)	
bid*	4	slave->master	Write the ID number of the request, bid, wid and awid should be the same for the same request	negligible
bresp	2	slave->master	Write request control signal, whether this write request is completed successfully or not	negligible
bvalid*	1	slave->master	Write request response handshake signal, write request response is valid	

1. Handshakes

As mentioned earlier, the bus is the channel through which the processor interacts with memory and peripherals. In order to interact, both sides must be in sync with each other. The AXI bus protocol uses a handshake mechanism to achieve synchronization, either by agreeing on a time in advance or by handshaking.

The CPU pipeline we designed earlier also uses handshaking, so you should know that completing a handshake requires a pair of signals—a request and an answer—is used to implement the handshake, the valid, and ready signals, which are present on each channel of the AXI protocol. Given the AXI protocol is defined for a synchronous digital logic circuit design, the valid and ready signals are not asynchronous interlocks. Both the master and the subordinate look at this pair of signals on the rising edge of the clock. Figure 8.5 is a timing diagram that we have taken from the AXI specification to express the relationship between valid and ready. The rising edge indicated by the arrow in the figure is the point at which the transfer occurs.

The handshaking mechanism between the initiator and the receiver on each channel is exactly the same as the handshaking mechanism between the pipelines inside our CPU. You can imagine that there are two stages of pipelined buffers on each channel, one on the initiator (the side whose valid signal is the output) and one on the receiver (the side whose ready signal is the output). The handshake interaction for a bus request is to write information from the initiator's pipelined cache to the receiver's pipelined cache. valid on the AXI bus is p1_to_p2_valid on our CPU, and ready on the AXI bus is p2_allowin on our CPU.

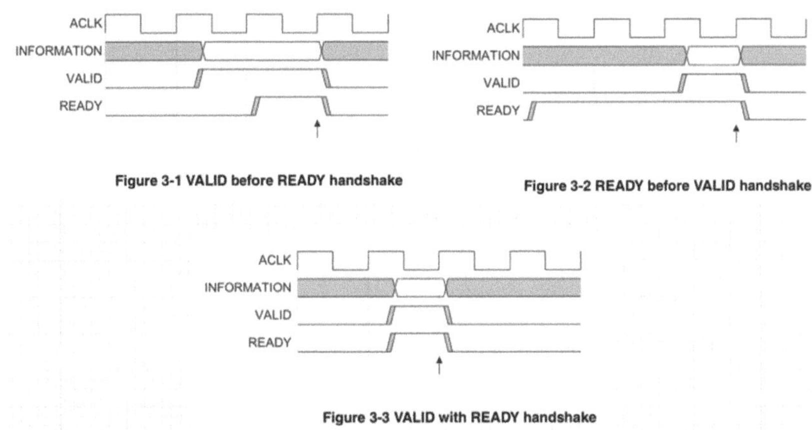

Fig. 8.5 Relationship between valid and ready in the AXI bus protocol

Figure 8.5 also contains an important piece of information: in the AXI bus protocol, there is no order of precedence between the valid and ready handshake signals when they are made valid. In fact, the AXI specification specifies the dependency of valid and ready on a per-channel basis:

- The validity of valid must not depend on whether ready is valid.
- The validity of ready can depend on the validity of valid.

The above restriction is to avoid deadlocks. Therefore, it is important that you do not base your decision about setting valid on whether ready is 1 or not.

2. Bus Transactions and Bus Transfers

Read and write operations between the master and subordinate over the bus are interactive processes that may involve many signals and last for multiple cycles on the bus. For a high-performance on-chip bus, such as the AXI bus, there may be several different read and write operations on the bus at the same time. Therefore, it is not easy to describe the behavior of the bus only from the perspective of signals, and thus the term bus transaction is used. A bus transaction corresponds to a complete read or write. It is a higher level of abstraction that describes the behavior of the bus, and is the main point of interest when designing bus interfaces.

A bus transaction consists of multiple bus transfers. A bus transfer is only active for the clock cycle in which both valid and ready are active (i.e., the handshake is successful). Figure 8.6 shows an AXI read bus transaction with one transfer on the read request channel (dashed box) and four transfers on the read response channel (solid boxes).

The Fundamentals of Computer Architecture, 3rd Edition, Section 6.2, Part 1, and the AXI specification give timing diagrams for bus transactions for single reads, overlapping reads, and single writes on the AXI bus, which the reader may refer to get a better understanding of the AXI bus.

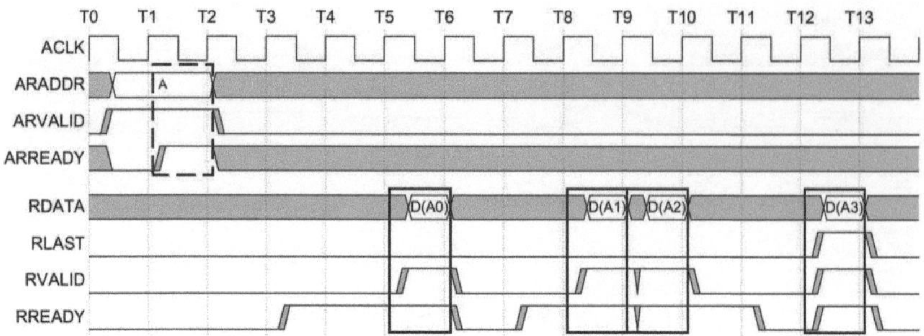

Fig. 8.6 AXI bus transactions and bus transfers

3. Address, Size, and Data

When a master and a subordinate interact, they exchange the data. This involves the following set of issues:

- How do you differentiate these data? Distinguished by address.
- What is the smallest granularity of addressing? The addressing granularity of the AXI bus is at the byte level.
- The amount of data in each interaction may vary. How to know? The master will inform the slave of the amount of data to be transferred.

As you can see, for any bus protocol, address, data, and size (sometimes further divided into two elements: number of transmissions and width of transmission) are essential.[3] For the AXI bus protocol, the signals are araddr, arsize, arlen, rdata, awaddr, awsize, awlen, wdata, and wstrb. These signals are the main signals and should be mastered.

4. Multiple Channels

The channels correspond to the underlying signal lines. A channel is a road, and the address and data information described earlier are the cars traveling on the road. Five channels are defined in the AXI protocol to achieve very high bus transfer performance.

Let's first talk about the separation of read and write. Because both read and write operations interact with addresses and data, if the read and write use the same channel, you can't write when you read, and you can't read when you write. If you assign separate channels to read and write, the two operations can be carried out independently without interfering with each other. Whether they are combined or separated is essentially a trade-off between resources and performance, depending on the designer's focus. AXI is concerned with performance, so it has adopted a

---

[3] Some buses transmit in both directions, so there is also an element of direction. However, the AXI bus is unidirectional, so this element does not exist.

design that separates the read and write channels. For those interested, the AHB bus protocol is a combination of read and write channels.

Next, let's talk about the channels that are divided into read or write channels. We can use an analogy to illustrate the roles of the read request channel and the read response channel. The read request channel is the equivalent of a buyer placing an order on a shopping site (note that there is a handshake in this process), and the read data channel is the equivalent of a courier company delivering goods from the seller to the buyer (obviously there is a handshake in this process as well). The write request channel and write response channel are similar to the read channel, except that they can be compared to a buyer returning an item to a seller, where the buyer and seller negotiate the need to return the item (the write request channel), and the courier company transports the item from the buyer to the seller (the write data channel). The seller receives the returned goods and sends a confirmation message back to the buyer, which is the write response channel.

5. Transactional Handshake Dependencies Between Channels

Since a read transaction and a write transaction have to be completed through multiple transfers over multiple channels, and each channel has its own handshaking mechanism, what dependencies around the same transaction should be followed for handshaking between different channels? This also needs to be defined. Figure 8.7 shows a diagram of the handshake dependencies that we have extracted from the AXI specification.[4] The double arrows in the diagram indicate that a dependency must exist, and the single arrows indicate that a dependency can exist. We will focus on the must-have dependencies indicated by the double arrows.

In Fig. 8.7, the upper half represents a read transaction, and only when arvalid and arready are both valid can the subordinate set the corresponding rvalid of the returned data as valid. This is intuitive. What everyone must remember is that if a read request of a read transaction has not been received by the subordinate, then at this time rvalid has nothing to do with the current read transaction. Ensure that the state machine you design does not act incorrectly.

In the lower part of Fig. 8.7, the subordinate will only send back a write response if both the write request and the last transfer of write data have been received by the subordinate. This is also intuitive. As with the processing of the read transaction above, there is no need to look at the bvalid until after both the write request and the write data have been sent. One interesting aspect of this section is that there is no dependency between the write request and the write data, so it is theoretically possible to send the write data before the write request. However, this is counterintuitive and not beneficial to the CPU bus interface design. It is recommended that you make awvalid valid along with the wvalid of the first transfer.

---

[4]The dependency diagram for write transactions was extracted from the AXI3 specification because we felt that it made more sense to represent it.

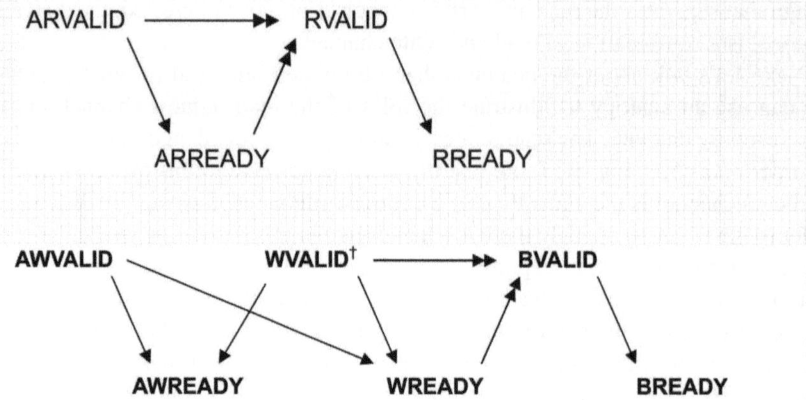

† Dependencies on the assertion of **WVALID** also require the assertion of **WLAST**

Fig. 8.7   AXI bus transaction handshake dependency

6. Concurrent Visits

For buyers, you can place an order for one item and then purchase the next item after receiving it, or you can place multiple orders at the same time and wait to receive them. For sellers, you can process one order at a time, or you can process multiple orders at the same time. The latter corresponds to concurrent access on the AXI bus. For a master, it can make multiple requests in a row, even if the data needed for the previous request has not been transferred. For a subordinate, it can receive new requests from one or more masters without having transmitted the data required by the previous requests. This concurrent access is objectively guaranteed by the separation of the request channel from the data channel. Therefore, in the AXI bus protocol, the read channel is divided into read request and read response channels, and the write channel is divided into write request, write data, and write response channels.

7. Out-of-Order Response

In layman's terms, a transaction's out-of-order response means that a later request may return data first. Allowing transactions to respond in an out-of-order fashion is intended to improve bus transfer performance. When multiple masters are integrated into a system, or when the masters support out-of-order mechanisms, then bus out-of-order responses can significantly improve performance. The practical task in this book is to design a single-core static pipelined CPU with minimal performance gains from bus out-of-order response.

When designing the CPU bus interface, we have to pay attention to the possible effects of disorder to make sure the design is correct. For beginners, issues are most likely to arise in the design of the read channel. Note that unless you are making a series of read requests that all use the same ID, you should consider the case where the data from the later request is returned first. If you want the first request to always return first, then you must set the IDs of these requests to the same value.

8. ID

Because the AXI bus protocol supports concurrent accesses and promiscuous responses, the correspondence between requests and responses requires additional information to maintain. Specifically, this is accomplished through the ID signaling on each channel. Remember what we said before "bus transaction" perspective; AXI on the ID is the ID of the transaction, for example, the master sends a read request, arid is set to 0, after a period of time, the master receives a read response, how to determine that the data returned is corresponding to the request they sent before? The answer is to look at whether rid is equal to 0. Write processing is similar, write address is sent from the write request channel, write data is sent from the write data channel, how does the subordinate know which write address corresponds to a write data? The answer is whether the awid of the write address and the wid of the write data are equal.

However, it should be noted that the AXI protocol specification only mandates that different transactions can be assigned different IDs. In other words, different transactions can be assigned the same ID.

9. Role of the Write Response Channel

Many beginners do not understand why the AXI protocol defines a write-response channel and feel that it is not useful. To explore this question, we must stand in the perspective of the system-on-chip to observe and analyze the behavior of the AXI bus when it handles "write-after-read-related" accesses. For example, suppose there is only one master device in the system, the CPU, and the original value at address A is 0. Now the CPU writes 1 to address A via the AXI bus, and after the last data is written (wvalid && wlast && wready == 1), the CPU reads the address A via the AXI bus again, and what is the value returned? Wouldn't you think that it would apparently be a 1. However, with the AXI bus, a return value of 0 is also compliant, meaning that the bus meets the AXI protocol specification in all places, and there are no implementation errors, and it is possible to return 0.

How does this counterintuitive phenomenon occur? It is the result of a combination of two causes. One is that the read and write channels are separated. Separation means that the two channels do not interact with each other; they each do their own thing. The second reason is that the AXI bus can have as many levels of cache as you want between the master and the final accessed subordinate. For these two reasons, it is entirely possible that the write address and write data sent by master are blocked on the write channel, while the read request sent out later is transmitted unimpeded on the read channel, and eventually the accessing subordinate sees the read request first and then the write request, so the subordinate returns an old value of zero.

This situation seems very special, but it is plausible, which means that the probability of it occurring is not 0. When designing a computer, we must guard against these special situations that can lead to errors.

How can this be handled? It seems that even if a write request is sent, a read request may not be sent immediately. How long do we have to wait? Is 10,000 years enough? No, because it is possible that a write request could be blocked for 20,000 years. Note that it is possible, as long as the probability of this happening is not sure to be zero; then, it is possible. The final solution was to introduce a write response channel in the AXI protocol. This message is sent from the subordinate indicating that it has received the write data, and when the master receives this message and then sends a read request, it shall be safe. Since electrical signals do not travel faster than the speed of light, the read request must arrive at the subordinate after the write data arrives at the subordinate.

10. Burst Transmission Mode

Why design a burst transmission model? Let's illustrate with an example. Assuming that the width of the data read on the bus is 32 bits, how do you send a bus request when you want to read 512 bits of contiguous data? One way is to send 16 4-byte read address request; this means 16 handshakes on the read address channel. If, for timing reasons, the master and subordinate are not able to communicate with each other one cycle at a time, so the 16 handshakes will take a lot of time. Thus, we considered whether it might be possible to design a mechanism that would allow the master to interact with the subordinate just once to complete the transmission of 512 bits of continuous address data. This is called a burst transmission pattern. In order to describe a burst transfer mode, three pieces of information are needed: the starting address, the pattern of address changes, and the number of address changes. Taking the read channel as an example, this corresponds to araddr, arburst, and arlen, respectively. Currently, cache has not been implemented in our design, and there will be no need for burst transmission on the 32-bit data width AXI bus interface. Therefore, we can wait until cache is realized before adjusting the design of the bus interface.

8.3.3 *Relationship of SRAM-Like Bus Interface Signals to AXI Bus Interface Signals*

If you compare the SRAM-like bus interface signals with the AXI bus interface signals, you can see that the SRAM-like bus combines reads and writes, but still separates requests and responses, so that requests and responses for different bus transactions can be overlapped, thus improving bus transfer efficiency. Furthermore, the SRAM-like bus does not support out-of-order responses, thus simplifying the design. Overall, the behavior of the SRAM-like bus interface is simpler than the AXI bus interface, so converting the SRAM-like bus to an AXI bus is simple because most signals can be found with their counterparts.

For the req signal, when req=1 and wr=0, it corresponds to the arvalid signal of the AXI bus; when req=1 and wr=1, it corresponds to the awvalid signal and wvalid signal of the AXI bus.

For the `addr_ok` signal, when it corresponds to a read transaction, it corresponds to aready on the AXI bus, and when it corresponds to a write transaction, there is no simple corresponding signal, but it means that both awready and wready on the AXI bus have been or are at 1. The correspondence is a bit complicated, and the reader needs to pay attention to it when designing the "SRAM-like-AXI" adapter bridge. This is a somewhat complex correspondence that the reader should be aware of when designing a "SRAM-like-AXI" adapter bridge.

The `data_ok` signal corresponds to rvalid on the AXI bus for read transactions and bvalid on the AXI bus for write transactions.

The addr signal corresponds to araddr on the AXI bus for read transactions and awaddr on the AXI bus for write transactions.

The size signal corresponds to arsize on the AXI bus for read transactions and awsize on the AXI bus for write transactions.

In addition, rdata corresponds to rdata of the AXI bus, wdata corresponds to wdata of the AXI bus, and wstrb corresponds to wstrb of the AXI bus.

8.4 SRAM-AXI-Like Adapter Bridge Design

Having understood the AXI bus protocol and the SRAM-like bus protocol, we begin to consider how to design an SRAM-like-AXI adapter bridge.

8.4.1 Top-Level Interface of the Adapter Bridge

Currently, our designed CPU has an SRAM-like interface for the instruction fetch section and an SRAM-like interface for the memory access section. The adapter bridge we are designing needs to connect to the CPU, so it should have two SRAM-like interfaces. As a simple CPU, there is usually a bus interface to the outside world, so the adapter bridge we are designing should have an AXI interface. The relationship of the entire adapter bridge to the rest of the CPU and to the rest of the SoC is shown in Fig. 8.8.

It should be reminded that the SRAM class in the SRAM-like-AXI adapter bridge is a subordinate and not a master, so don't reverse the signal direction of these two interfaces. After writing the code, it is better to double-check the direction of the port definition manually, so as to avoid getting into the predicament of "pass in simulation, but fail in board."

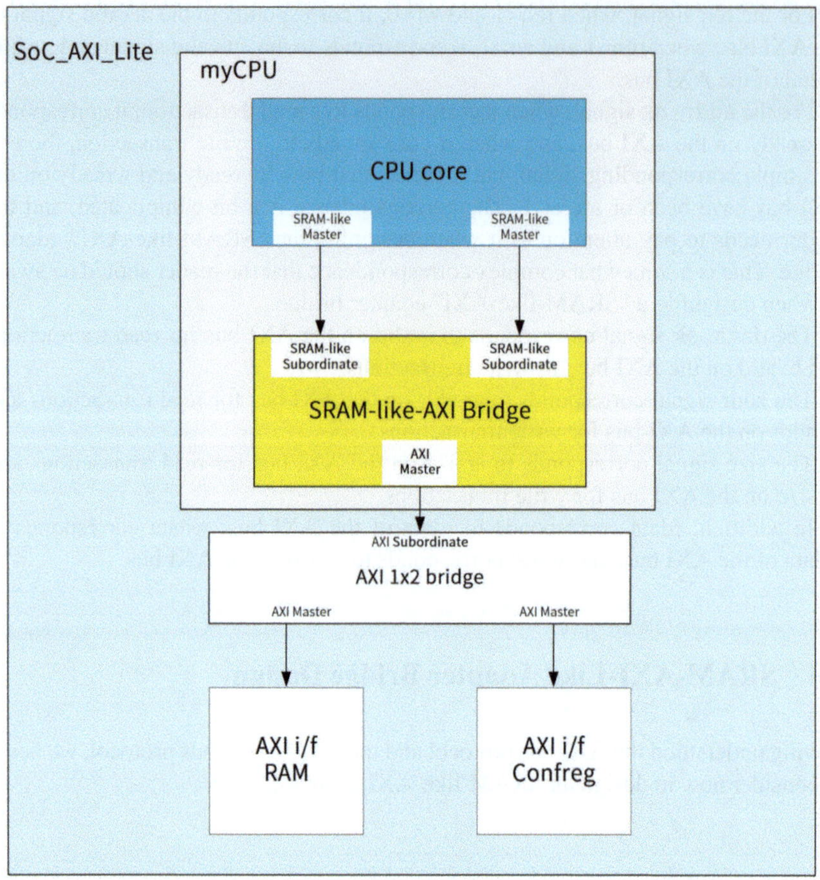

Fig. 8.8 SRAM-like-AXI adapter bridge in SoC AXI lite

8.4.2 Design Requirements for Adapter Bridges

This section gives the design requirements for the adapter bridge. Some of these requirements are to ensure correct functionality, and some are to match the design and verification environment we have in place. These requirements must be implemented in the design:

1. While aresetn is in effect, all valid outputs on the AXI Master side must be 0, and all ready class outputs cannot be X-value.
2. All valid output signals of AXI Master must not allow the combinational logic to come from the ready input signal of the same channel (it is OK for the timing logic to come from ready).

3. For all ready output signals on the AXI Master side, the combinational logic must not be allowed to use valid input signal (timing logic from valid is possible) from the same channel.
4. Regardless of the read or write request, the transaction on the SRAM-like interface should strictly correspond to the transaction on the AXI interface. In particular, be careful not to send a transaction on the SRAM-like interface multiple times on the AXI bus, nor to combine multiple read or write transactions from the SRAM-like interface with consecutive addresses into a single AXI bus transaction.
5. On the read request, write request, and write data channels on the AXI master side, if the ready of the master's output is 0 when the valid is set to 1, the master is not allowed to change all output signals of the channel until the ready signal is 1. This is different from the SRAM-like bus, which allows midway change requests.
6. When the AXI Master initiates a read request, it must first ensure that the request is not address-dependent on a "write request that has been sent but for which no write response has been received." The simplest and most straightforward solution is to stop initiating read requests as long as there is a write request until the master receives a write response. A more refined and efficient solution is to record the address, bit-width, and byte-write-enablement information of write requests that have been sent but have not yet received a write response, and then query and compare this information with subsequent read requests before deciding whether to send them.
7. Write-to-read data forwarding is not allowed within the adapter bridge; if there is a write-after-read correlation, it must be handled by blocking reads.

8.4.3 Design Recommendations for Adapter Bridges

This section gives recommendations for the design of the adapter bridge, all of which are based on sacrificing some performance and area for simplicity in the control logic. You may take them or leave them. The advantage of not adopting them is that you can gain a deeper understanding of why they were made through more agonizing in the design phase and bug fixing in the debugging phase:

1. All outputs of the AXI Master terminal come directly from the flip-flop Q terminal, except for signals that can be set to a constant value.
2. A cache is reserved for read data, and data received from the rdata port is first stored in this reserved cache.
3. The same number of rdata caches is reserved for up to several "read transactions that have completed the read request handshake but have not yet returned data" supported on AXI.
4. The arid corresponding to fetch is always 0 and the arid corresponding to load is always 1.

5. The state machines controlling AXI reads and writes are divided into four independent state machines: one for the read request channel, one for the read response channel, one for the write request and write data, and one for the write response.
6. Input signals connected to SRAM-like subordinate do not need to be latched before use.
7. A read request on the SRAM-like bus from the data side has a fixed higher priority than a read request on the SRAM-like bus from the pointer side.
8. If the addr_ok and data_ok signals output from the SRAM class subordinate side are from the combinational logic, do not introduce the valid and ready signals from the AXI interface into this combinational logic.

8.5   Tasks and Practices

After completing this chapter, readers are expected to complete the following three practical tasks:

1. Add SRAM-like bus support. See Sect. 8.5.1.
2. Add AXI bus support. See Sect. 8.5.2.
3. Complete the AXI Random Delay Verification. See Sect. 8.5.3.

8.5.1   Practical Task 14: Add SRAM-Like Bus Support

This practical task requires the following work based on the CPU implemented in Practical Task 13:

1. Modify the CPU external interface to a SRAM-like bus interface.
2. Complete the random delay function verification of exp14 corresponding func in the SoC verification environment of block RAM with handshaking mechanism.

Please refer to the method described in Sect. 2.3.1 to obtain the experimental development environment required for this practical task. The specific experimental environment is located at `mycpu_env/`. **Instead of using the `soc_bram/`, the `soc_hs_bram/` subdirectory should be used for verification.**

Along with the replacement of the CPU-accessed instruction RAM and data RAM implementations from normal block RAM to block RAM with handshaking mechanism, the experimental development environment needs to be further adjusted: it is still the mycpu_env experimental environment, and the location and usage of the get-trace/, func/, and myCPU/subdirectories remain unchanged, except that the soc_verify/ subdirectory no longer uses the soc_bram/ subdirectory but uses the soc_hs_bram/subdirectory instead. The soc_verify/ subdirectory no longer uses the soc_bram/ subdirectory, but instead uses the soc_hs_bram/subdirectory, and the files in the soc_hs_bram/ subdirectory are organized and used in a similar way as in the soc_bram/ subdirectory. The directory structure of the experimental development environment and the functions of each section are shown below:

```
|--gettrace/                      Generate the reference trace
|--func/                          Function verification test programs
|--myCPU/                         CPU rtl code written by readers
|--soc_verify/                    SoC system verification environment for CPU
   |--soc_hs_bram/                Verification environment corresponding to
    ↪  CPU external
                                  connection to handshaking block RAM
   |   |--rtl/                    SoC_Lite rtl code
   |   |   |--soc_lite_top.v      SoC_Lite top module
   |   |   |--CONFREG/            Confreg module for peripheral devices such
    ↪  as LEDs,
                                  dial switches, etc. on the board
   |   |   |--BRIDGE/             With a $1\times 2$ bridge module, CPU's
    ↪  data sram interface
                                  accesses both confreg and data_ram
   |   |   |--ram_wrap/           RAM module packaged in SRAM-like interface
   |   |   |--xilinx_ip/          Customized Xilinx IP, including clk_pll,
    ↪  inst_ram and data_ram
   |   |--testbench/              Simulation environment
   |   |   |--mycpu_tb.v          Simulation top module which catch debug
    ↪  info and
                                  compare it with golden_trace.txt
   |   |--run_vivado/             Vivado project running directory
   |       |--constraints/        Vivado project design constraints
   |       |--mycpu_hs_bram_prj/  Vivado project files directory
```

Once the lab environment is ready, please refer to the following steps to complete this practical task:

1. Update CPU code at `mycpu_env/myCPU/`.
2. Modify the func configuration file, `mycpu_env/func/include/test_config.h`, select the configuration of **exp14**, and compile. (If you obtained the experimental development environment from the package `exp14.zip`, please skip this step.)
3. Open the gettrace project, `mycpu_env/gettrace/gettrace.xpr` (the IP core in this Vivado project was created using Vivado2019.2; if you open it with a higher version of Vivado, refer to Appendix D.4 for the IP core upgrade). Run the simulation of the gettrace project (after entering the simulation interface, click `run all` and wait for the simulation to finish), and generate a new reference trace file `golden_trace.txt` (`mycpu_env/gettrace/golden_trace.txt`). The `golden_trace.txt` will not be complete until the simulation has finished running. (If you obtained the experimental development environment from the package `exp14.zip`, please skip this step.)
4. Start the project in `mycpu_env/soc_verify/soc_hs_bram/run_vivado/` to verify myCPU. If you have not created a project in this directory, please refer to the steps described in Appendix D.2 to create a project using the `create_project.tcl` file in this directory. If necessary, please refer to Appendix D.4 to upgrade the IP core.

5. Refer to Chap. 4 Sect. 4.4.5.2 to re-customize `inst_ram` in the project. (If you obtained the experimental development environment from the package `exp14.zip`, please skip this step.)
6. Run the simulation in the project (click `run all` directly after entering the simulation interface), and carry out the function verification until the simulation test is passed.
7. Generate a bit stream file after Synthesis and Implementation in the project, and verify it on FPGA. (Please skip this step if you don't have a hardware experiment platform.)

1. Board Certification Requirements

When verifying on the board, it is required to "press the reset key after switching the dip switches at random," and the CPU can pass the 58 verifications of the individual function points corresponding to exp14.

"Pressing the reset button after switching the dipswitch at random" sets the initial random seed (the random seed is used to generate random number of delay cycles for the inst/data ram access) and starts the function verification program. Since there are many instructions in the verification program, different random seeds will lead to different sequence of random number of delay cycles for fetching or data accessing, and the CPU execution state will be very different, so it is very common to have an error after switching the initial random seed.

Please pay attention to the specific operation of the upper board verification: switch the eight dip switches to random state; press the reset key; after releasing the reset key, the digital tube starts to accumulate, and at this time, you can switch the switch to control the acceleration of wait_1s accumulation.

2. Function of Dip Switches

As you can see from the above, the dip switches have two functions when verifying on the board:

- Function 1: During reset, the dip switches control the initial random seed, which in turn controls the generation sequence of random number of delay cycles that the CPU fetches instruction or accesses data.
- Function 2: After reset, the dip switches control the number of cycles of wait_1s, that is, they control the speed of digital tube accumulation.

For Function 2, in the 58 function points test, a `wait_1s` function will be interspersed between every two function points, and `wait_1s` completes the function of timing through a cycle: the cycle number of `wait_1s` is controlled by a dip switch, and the cycle number can be set to be $(0\sim0xaaaa) \times 2^9$. When verifying the board, it is recommended to select a reasonable `wait_1s` delay time after reset through the dip switch. When verifying on the board, it is recommended to select a reasonable `wait_1s` delay time through the dipswitch after reset.

For function 1, in order to verify the function of myCPU as much as possible, a randomization mechanism is set in CPU_CDE_SRAM for the access delay: the access delay taps are generated by a 32-bit pseudo-random number generator

switch	led	seed_init
led[15:0]= {{2{switch[7]}}, {2{switch[6]}}, {2{switch[5]}}, {2{switch[4]}}, {2{switch[3]}}, {2{switch[2]}}, {2{switch[1]}}, {2{switch[0]}}}		
3 types of random delay: (1) long delay: seed_init[7:0]!=8'hff (2) short delay: seed_init[7:0]==8'hff, (3) no delay: seed_init[15:0]==16'h00ff		
8'h00	16'h0000	{7'b1010101, 16'h0000}
8'h01	16'h0003	{7'b1010101, 16'h0003}
8'h02	16'h000c	{7'b1010101, 16'h000c}
8'h03	16'h000f	{7'b1010101, 16'h000f}
...	...	...
8' hff	16'hffff	{7'b1010101, 16'hffff}

Fig. 8.9 FPGA board random seed setting rule

(implemented in the confreg.v file). The initial random seed of the pseudo-random number generator is specified by the macro RANDOM_SEED in confreg.v for simulation verification, and by the dipswitch state sampled during reset for onboard verification.

There are eight dip switches on the lab box, and the actual levels are 0 on and 1 off, but for the sake of the following description, we will write it down as 1 on and 0 off. The actual levels of the 16 monochrome LEDs are drive 0 on, drive 1 off. The actual level of the 16 monochrome LEDs is drive 0 is on, drive 1 is off, and similarly, we write: drive 1 is on, drive 0 is off.

During board verification, pressing the reset button will automatically sample the values of the eight dip switches as the initial random seed and display the initial random seed with the lower 16 bits on the monochrome LEDs. The correspondence between the random seed and the dip switches during board verification is shown in Fig. 8.9. It should be noted that the delay types are divided into three categories according to the dip switch values: long delay, short delay, and no delay type. These three types of delays should be overridden during board verification.

3. "Simulation Passes, But the Board Does Not" Debugging Methods
[Scenario 1] When verifying on the board, I found that the digital tube did not have any accumulation.

This can be due to one of the following issues:

1. Multiple drivers.
2. The input/output ports of the module are connected to the wrong signal direction.
3. Clock reset signal is connected incorrectly.
4. Code is not standardized, blocking assignment is used indiscriminately, and always statement is used arbitrarily.
5. There is "X" for control signal during emulation. During simulation, there is "X" to emphasize "X" and "Z" to emphasize "Z." It is important to note that "X" and "Z" do not appear on the top-level interface of the design.
6. Timing violations.
7. Signals on the control path in the module are not reset.

[Scenario 2] When verifying on the board, it is found that the test passes under some random seeds and errors under some other random seeds.

Please follow the steps below for debugging:

1. Confirm the initial random seed of the error during board verification, modify the definition value of macro RANDOM_SEED in `mycpu_env/soc_verify/soc_hs_bram/rtl/CONFREG/confreg` file, change it to the initial random seed of the error, and then conduct simulation. If there is an error, debugging will be performed; if no error is found in the simulation, the next initial random seed with error will be found in the verification on the board. If no error occurs in the simulation after trying several initial random seeds, go to step 2.
2. In the case of "simulation does not reproduce the onboard error with the same initial random seed," take the following steps: investigate the possible causes listed, review the code and reflect on the design, or use Vivado's logic analyzer for in-circuit debugging (refer to Appendix D, Sect. D.5).

[Scenario 3] When verifying the board, only some of the function points pass the test under any random seed.

This may be the reason for both of the above situations, please check in turn.

8.5.2   Practical Task 15: Adding AXI Bus Support

This practical task requires the following work based on the CPU implemented in Practical Task 14:

1. Modify the top-level interface of the CPU to an AXI bus interface. The CPU has only one external AXI interface, and needs to arbitrate instruction fetching and data access internally. It is recommended to implement a SRAM-AXI-like 2x1 adapter bridge in this task, and then splice in the SRAM-like interface of the CPU completed in practice task 1 to encapsulate the myCPU as an AXI interface.

2. Complete the fixed-delay functional verification of the exp15 func counterpart in a SoC verification environment using the AXI bus, requiring successful simulation and board verification.

Please refer to the method described in Sect. 2.3.1 to obtain the experimental development environment required for this practical task. The specific experimental environment is located at `mycpu_env/`. **Instead of using the soc_hs_bram/, the soc_axi/ subdirectory should be used for verification.**

Along with the change of the CPU external access interface from block RAM with handshaking mechanism to AXI bus interface, the experiment development environment needs to be further adjusted: it is still the mycpu_env experiment environment, and the location and usage of the gettrace/, func/, and myCPU/ subdirectories remain unchanged except that the soc_verify/ subdirectory is no longer used, but instead of the soc_axi/ subdirectory. The soc_axi/ subdirectory is used instead of the soc_hs_bram/ subdirectory. The directory structure of the experimental development environment and the functions of each section are shown below:

```
|--gettrace/                  Generate the reference trace
|--func/                      Function verification test programs
|--myCPU/                     CPU rtl code written by readers
|--soc_verify/                SoC system verification environment for CPU
   |--soc_axi/                Verification environment corresponding to CPU
   ↪   external
                              connection to AXI
   |   |--rtl/                SoC_Lite rtl code
   |   |   |--soc_lite_top.v  SoC_Lite top module
   |   |   |--CONFREG/        Confreg module for peripheral devices such as
   ↪   LEDs,
                              dial switches, etc. on the board
   |   |   |--ram_wrap/       Support random delay access to the packaged
   ↪   AXI RAM module
   |   |   |--axi_wrap/       AXI's 1x1 adapter, which connects the CPU to
   ↪   the Crossbar,
                              is used to smooth out the differences between
                              ↪   the
                              emulation and the upper board.
   |   |   |--xilinx_ip/      Customized Xilinx IP, including clk_pll,
   ↪   axi_ram and axi_crossbar_1x2,
   |   |--testbench/          Simulation environment
   |   |   |--mycpu_tb.v      Simulation top module which catch debug info
   ↪   and
                              compare it with golden_trace.txt
   |   |--run_vivado/         Vivado project running directory
   |       |--constraints/    Vivado project design constraints
   |       |--mycpu_axi_prj/  Vivado project files directory
```

Once the lab environment is ready, please refer to the following steps to complete this practical task:

1. Update CPU code at `mycpu_env/myCPU/`.

2. Modify the func configuration file, `mycpu_env/func/include/test_config.h`, select the configuration of `exp15`, and compile. (If you obtained the experimental development environment from the package `exp15.zip`, please skip this step.)

3. Open the gettrace project, `mycpu_env/gettrace/gettrace.xpr` (the IP core in this Vivado project was created using Vivado2019.2; if you open it with a higher version of Vivado, refer to Appendix D.4 for the IP core upgrade). Run the simulation of the gettrace project (after entering the simulation interface, click `run all` and wait for the simulation to finish), and generate a new reference trace file `golden_trace.txt` (`mycpu_env/gettrace/golden_trace.txt`). The `golden_trace.txt` will not be complete until the simulation has finished running. (If you obtained the experimental development environment from the package `exp15.zip`, please skip this step.)

4. Start the project in `mycpu_env/soc_verify/soc_axi/run_vivado/` to verify myCPU. If you have not created a project in this directory, please refer to the steps described in Appendix D.2 to create a project using the `create_project.tcl` file in this directory. If necessary, please refer to Appendix D.4 to upgrade the IP core.

5. Refer to Chap. 4 Sect. 4.4.5.2 to re-customize `inst_ram` in the project. (If you obtained the experimental development environment from the package `exp15.zip`, please skip this step.)

6. Run the simulation in the project (click `run all` directly after entering the simulation interface), and carry out the function verification until the simulation test is passed.

7. Generate a bit stream file after Synthesis and Implementation in the project, and verify it on FPGA. During board verification, it is required that the eight dip switches are in the state of "high 4 down, low 4 up" (corresponding to the random latency type of the access is no latency), and the func can be run correctly. (Please skip this step if you don't have a hardware experiment platform.)

8.5.3   Practical Task 16: Complete AXI Random Delay Verification

This practical task requires the following work based on the CPU implemented in Practical Task 15:

1. Improve the AXI bus interface design so that it can be verified in a SoC verification environment using the AXI bus for the random delay function of the exp16 corresponding func, which is required to be successfully verified by simulation and onboard verification.

Please refer to the method described in Sect. 2.3.1 to obtain the experimental development environment required for this practical task. The specific experimental environment is located at `mycpu_env/`, and continue to use the `soc_axi/` subdirectory.

Once the lab environment is ready, please refer to the following steps to complete this practical task:

1. Update CPU code at `mycpu_env/myCPU/`.
2. Modify the func configuration file, `mycpu_env/func/include/test_config.h`, select the configuration of `exp16`, and compile. (If you obtained the experimental development environment from the package `exp16.zip`, please skip this step.)
3. Open the gettrace project, `mycpu_env/gettrace/gettrace.xpr` (the IP core in this Vivado project was created using Vivado2019.2; if you open it with a higher version of Vivado, refer to Appendix D.4 for the IP core upgrade). Run the simulation of the gettrace project (after entering the simulation interface, click `run all` and wait for the simulation to finish), and generate a new reference trace file `golden_trace.txt` (`mycpu_env/gettrace/golden_trace.txt`). The `golden_trace.txt` will not be complete until the simulation has finished running. (If you obtained the experimental development environment from the package `exp16.zip`, please skip this step.)
4. Start the project in `mycpu_env/soc_verify/soc_axi/run_vivado/` to verify myCPU. If you have not created a project in this directory, please refer to the steps described in Appendix D.2 to create a project using the `create_project.tcl` file in this directory. If necessary, please refer to Appendix D.4 to upgrade the IP core. If there is a project in this directory that has been created by a previous practice task, you can update the file list of CPU implementations in the project by referring to the steps described in Appendix D.3 after opening the project.
5. Refer to Chap. 4 Sect. 4.4.5.2 to re-customize `inst_ram` in the project. (If you obtained the experimental development environment from the package `exp16.zip`, please skip this step.)
6. Run the simulation in the project (click `run all` directly after entering the simulation interface), and carry out the function verification until the simulation test is passed.
7. Repeat the previous step several times, requiring the macro `RANDOM_SEED` to be modified to cover the three random delay types described earlier in this chapter.
8. Generate a bit stream file after synthesizing in the project of verifying myCPU, and verify it on the board. When verifying on the board, please make sure that the func can be run correctly by pressing the reset button after switching the dip switches randomly, and if there is the phenomenon of "simulation passes, but not on the board," please debug it according to the method described in Sect. 8.5.1. (Please skip this step if you don't have a hardware experiment platform.)

Chapter 9
Storage Management Unit Design

Storage management is one of the most important functions of a modern operating system, and it requires some support from the CPU hardware to accomplish it in a hardware-software cooperative manner. The logic in the CPU hardware that participates in this process is usually called the memory management unit (MMU). Up to now, the CPUs designed for the practical tasks in this book have only implemented the simplest direct address translation mode. Starting from this chapter, we will complete the design of the rest of the MMU. The difficulty of this part of the design is that it involves a lot of technical details, and it is not easy for beginners to prioritize. Therefore, we have divided the whole design into three phases for you to complete in a modular and step-by-step manner.

- Phase 1: We will focus on the design of the TLB module itself.
- Phase 2: We integrated the TLB module into an existing CPU and implemented MMU-related instruction and control state registers.
- Phase 3: We added support for MMU-related exceptions and performed joint verification of all features.

Before starting this phase of the design, please study Section 3.3 of *Fundamentals of Computer Architecture (3rd edition)* or other relevant documents. The focus of this study is to understand the hardware-software interaction process around the MMU in a computer system. Based on the principle of this interaction process, it will be easier to connect the MMU definitions in the instruction system specification into an organic whole, and then design the related functions in the CPU.

Learning Goals for This Chapter
- Knowledge of TLB MMUs.
- Understand the MMU-related control state registers and instructions in the LoongArch architecture.
- Understand the address translation mechanism in the CPU and understand the LoongArch architecture TLB-related exceptions and their handling.

© The Author(s), under exclusive license to Springer Nature Singapore Pte Ltd. 2025   257
W. Wang, J. Xing, *CPU Design and Practice*,
https://doi.org/10.1007/978-981-96-6573-0_9

- Learn how to add TLB support to a pipelined CPU.

Practical Tasks of This Chapter

There are three practical tasks in this chapter (See Sect. 9.5 of this chapter). Readers can complete these tasks on the basis of learning the contents of this chapter; the correspondence between them is as follows:

- The content of Sects. 9.1 and 9.2 corresponds to Practice Task 17 (Sect. 9.5.1).
- The content of Sects. 9.1 and 9.3 corresponds to Practice Task 18 (Sect. 9.5.2).
- The content of Sects. 9.1 and 9.4 corresponds to Practice Task 19 (Sect. 9.5.3).

9.1 Storage Management Unit-Related Specification Definition Sorting

The MMU-related contents of the LoongArch instruction system definition are mainly introduced in Chapter 5 of the instruction manual, and the definition of the control status registers involved in the introduction of Chapter 5 is mainly concentrated in Section 7.5 of the instruction manual. Please read these two sections first. In this section, we will briefly summarize the contents of this part to give beginners an idea of how to understand and master the contents of this part.

First of all, we need to understand the basic process of the CPU hardware when it comes to accessing the virtual and physical address translation. If it is direct address translation mode, the physical address is directly equal to the virtual address, and there is almost no additional privilege compliance checking; if it is mapped address translation mode, the first step is to look up the CSR.DMW0 and CSR.DMW1 registers to see if it is **legal** to fall into a direct mapping window, and if it is, the physical address is translated from the configuration information of the hit window; if there is no hit in the direct mapping window, then it is necessary to look up the TLB; if a **legal** page table entry can be found in the TLB, then it will be translated into a physical address based on the information of the page table entry, or else it will trigger the corresponding exception to be processed by the system software. The rules for finding the direct mapping window and generating the physical address are described in detail in Section 5.2.1 of the instruction manual. If you are not sure about the definition of CSR.DMW0/1, please refer to Section 7.5.9 of the instruction manual for details of TLB search and physical address generation rules in Section 5.4.4 of the instruction manual through pseudo-code. If you are not sure about the organization of TLBs and the definition of each field in the table entries, please refer to Sections 5.4.1 and 5.4.2 of the instruction manual. The concept of storage access type is involved in many places in the study of the above physical-virtual conversion process. Since we haven't implemented Cache yet, we can't go into the details of its function for now.

Second, it is necessary to know how to configure the software for the information required in the above process of physical-virtual address translation. For the PG and

DA bits of CSR.CRMD, which are used to distinguish the direct address translation mode from the mapped address translation mode, the kernel software can modify them with the CSR instruction. The information of the direct mapping window is stored in the two CSRs of DMW0 and DMW1, which can be modified by the core software with the CSR instruction as well. The reading and writing of the TLB is a little bit more complicated, which requires a set of CSR registers to be used as the interface for reading and writing of the TLB, so that the system software needs to use the CSR instruction to fill the information to be written to these CSRs first, and then use the TLBWR or TLLBWR instruction to modify the information. When the system software writes TLB, it needs to use the CSR instruction to fill the information to be written into these CSRs first, and then utilize the TLBWR or TLBFILL instruction to write the information into the TLB, and the process of reading the TLB table entries is the same as the opposite, i.e., it uses the TLBRD instruction to read out the content of the TLB table entries into the CSRs which act as the interfaces first, and then the information is taken out from the CSRs through the CSR instruction. This set of CSRs for TLB read/write interaction is listed in the first category of Subsection 5.4.3.3 of the instruction manual.

Finally, we need to understand the new exceptions that need to be added in the implementation to introduce the mapped address translation mode, including TLB refill exception, page invalid exception, page modification exception, and page privilege level noncompliance exception. The TLB refill exception is used to notify the system software to fill the required TLB table entries into the TLB, and the rest of the page invalid exception, page modification exception, and page privilege level noncompliance exception are used to notify the system software to allocate and manage the page table. The conditions for triggering these exceptions are specified in Section 5.4.4 of the instruction manual. When these exceptions are triggered, the hardware needs to store the virtual address that triggered the exception into CSR.BADV and the [31:12] bits of the virtual address into the VPPN field of CSR.TLBEHI, in addition to the operations that the hardware needs to perform when a normal exception is triggered. It is also important to note that the entry for the TLB refill exception is configured separately through CSR.TLBRENTRY, not through CSR.EENTRY. An additional note on the relationship between the mapped address translation mode and the address error exceptions (including the Fetch instruction Address Error Exception ADEF and the Access Instruction Address Error Exception ADEM) is that there are some differences between the 32-bit and 64-bit LA architectures in this regard. In the 64-bit LoongArch64 architecture, the mapped address translation mode is accompanied by the notion of a legal virtual address[1] and the resulting increase in the decision condition of ADEF and ADEM exceptions—an illegal virtual address that cannot hit the direct mapping window

---

[1]See Section 5.2 of the Dragoncore Architecture Reference Manual Volume 1: Infrastructure for details: "The rule for determining the legitimacy of the virtual address space when using page table mapping mode in the LA64 architecture: the [63:VALEN] bits of a legitimate virtual address must be the same as the [VALEN-1] bits, i.e., all the bits above the [VALEN-1] are its symbols."

triggers an address error exception. However, for the 32-bit LoongArch32 Reduced architecture, there are no inaccessible address voids in the virtual address, and the entire virtual address space can be considered legitimate, so the introduction of the mapped address translation mode does not add an address error exception condition.

After clarifying the above specification definition of MMU in the instruction set, we will start from the TLB module to add MMU functions in the processing step by step.

9.2 TLB Module Design Analysis

By combing the knowledge about TLB module and the structural characteristics of CPU pipeline, we analyze the design of TLB module as follows:

(1) The main body of the TLB module shall be a lookup table with a two-dimensional organizational structure. Each item of the lookup table is divided into two parts; the first part stores information that participates in both read/write and lookup/comparison, including E, VPPN, PS, ASID, and G. The second part participates in read/write only, including PPN0, PLV0, MAT0, D0, V0, PPN1, PLV1, MAT1, D1, and V1. The number of items in the lookup table is defined by the implementer.

(2) The TLB module should support the virtual and physical address conversion requirements of the two parts, i.e., both parts need to perform lookups on the TLB module, and the corresponding lookup functions of the two parts are consistent. When searching, it is necessary to input s_vppn, s_va_bit12, and s_asid information to the TLB module, and the information outputted by the TLB module includes s_found, s_ppn, s_ps, s_plv, s_mat, s_d, and s_v. Among them, the input s_vppn comes from the 31...13 bits of the virtual address of the access memory, and the input s_va_bit12 comes from the 12 bits of the virtual address of the access memory. The input s_vppn comes from bits 31..13 of the visited virtual address, s_va_bit12 comes from bit 12 of the visited virtual address, and s_asid comes from the ASID field of the CSR. s_found and s_plv are used to determine if a page privilege level noncompliance exception is generated, and the results of s_found, s_v, and s_d are used to determine if a page modification exception is generated.

(3) In order for the pipeline to operate at full capacity without streaming, the TLB module should be able to support simultaneous lookups on both instruction fetch and memory access, which means that there should be two sets of lookup ports.

(4) The TLB module needs to support the lookup operation of the TLBSRCH instruction. We propose to reuse the lookup instructions to find the TLB ports, i.e., reuse s_vppn and s_asid for inputs, and reuse the existing s_found for outputs; in addition to this, an extra s_index output is needed to record the number of hits, which is used to populate CSR.TLBIDX with the information.

(5) The TLB module needs to support the write operations of the TLBWR and TLBFILL instructions. It is recommended to design a separate port for this purpose. In this case, we need to input the write address w_index to the TLB module, and write the TLB table entries w_e, w_vppn, w_ps, w_asid, w_g, w_ppn0, w_plv0, w_mat0, w_d0, w_v0, w_ppn1, w_mat1, w_mat1, w_d1, w_v1. Because it is a write operation, there must be a write enable input signal we.

(6) The TLB module needs to support the read operation of the TLBRD instruction. We prefer to design a separate port for this purpose. In this case, we need to input the read address r_index to the TLB module, and the TLB module needs to output the results of reading, such as r_e, r_vppn, r_ps, r_asid, r_g, r_ppn0, r_plv0, r_mat0, r_d0, r_v0, r_ppn1, r_plv1, r_mat1, r_d1, and r_v1.

(7) The TLB module needs to support the lookup and invalidation operations of the INVTLB instruction. The information used in the lookup for different ops can reuse the lookup port of TLB which memory access uses, but an additional invtlb_op input is needed to identify the port of invtlb. invtlb's invalidation operations all directly set the E position of eligible TLB table entries to 0 based on lookup results within the TLB module.

From the above analysis, we get the following definition of the interface and the main internal signals of the TLB module:

```verilog
module tlb
#(
    parameter TLBNUM = 16
)
(
    input  wire                     clk,

    // search port 0 (for fetch)
    input  wire [              18:0] s0_vppn,
    input  wire                      s0_va_bit12,
    input  wire [               9:0] s0_asid,
    output wire                      s0_found,
    output wire [$clog2(TLBNUM)-1:0] s0_index,
    output wire [              19:0] s0_ppn,
    output wire [               5:0] s0_ps,
    output wire [               1:0] s0_plv,
    output wire [               1:0] s0_mat,
    output wire                      s0_d,
    output wire                      s0_v,

    // search port 1 (for load/store)
    input  wire [              18:0] s1_vppn,
    input  wire                      s1_va_bit12,
```

```verilog
input  wire [                   9:0] s1_asid,
output wire                          s1_found,
output wire [$clog2(TLBNUM)-1:0] s1_index,
output wire [                  19:0] s1_ppn,
output wire [                   5:0] s1_ps,
output wire [                   1:0] s1_plv,
output wire [                   1:0] s1_mat,
output wire                          s1_d,
output wire                          s1_v,

// invtlb opcode
input  wire                          invtlb_valid,
input  wire [                   4:0] invtlb_op,

// write port
input  wire                          we,     //w(rite) e(nable)
input  wire [$clog2(TLBNUM)-1:0] w_index,
input  wire                          w_e,
input  wire [                  18:0] w_vppn,
input  wire [                   5:0] w_ps,
input  wire [                   9:0] w_asid,
input  wire                          w_g,
input  wire [                  19:0] w_ppn0,
input  wire [                   1:0] w_plv0,
input  wire [                   1:0] w_mat0,
input  wire                          w_d0,
input  wire                          w_v0,
input  wire [                  19:0] w_ppn1,
input  wire [                   1:0] w_plv1,
input  wire [                   1:0] w_mat1,
input  wire                          w_d1,
input  wire                          w_v1,

// read port
input  wire [$clog2(TLBNUM)-1:0] r_index,
output wire                          r_e,
output wire [                  18:0] r_vppn,
output wire [                   5:0] r_ps,
output wire [                   9:0] r_asid,
output wire                          r_g,
output wire [                  19:0] r_ppn0,
output wire [                   1:0] r_plv0,
output wire [                   1:0] r_mat0,
output wire                          r_d0,
```

```verilog
    output wire                          r_v0,
    output wire [            19:0] r_ppn1,
    output wire [             1:0] r_plv1,
    output wire [             1:0] r_mat1,
    output wire                          r_d1,
    output wire                          r_v1
);

reg   [TLBNUM-1:0] tlb_e;
reg   [TLBNUM-1:0] tlb_ps4MB; //pagesize 1:4MB, 0:4KB
reg   [        18:0] tlb_vppn     [TLBNUM-1:0];
reg   [         9:0] tlb_asid     [TLBNUM-1:0];
reg                 tlb_g         [TLBNUM-1:0];
reg   [        19:0] tlb_ppn0     [TLBNUM-1:0];
reg   [         1:0] tlb_plv0     [TLBNUM-1:0];
reg   [         1:0] tlb_mat0     [TLBNUM-1:0];
reg                 tlb_d0        [TLBNUM-1:0];
reg                 tlb_v0        [TLBNUM-1:0];
reg   [        19:0] tlb_ppn1     [TLBNUM-1:0];
reg   [         1:0] tlb_plv1     [TLBNUM-1:0];
reg   [         1:0] tlb_mat1     [TLBNUM-1:0];
reg                 tlb_d1        [TLBNUM-1:0];
reg                 tlb_v1        [TLBNUM-1:0];

......

endmodule
```

The next step is to consider the internal design of the TLB module, which is actually the design and implementation of the three sets of lookup, read, and write operations. There is no need to introduce the implementation of the read and write operations; you can refer to the logic design of the regfile in the CPU and the Verilog code implementation. The only thing we need to pay attention to is that the PS field of the read/write interface of the TLB module is 6 bits, but since the LoongArch Lite version only supports 4 KB and 4 MB page sizes, the TLB module only uses 1 bit for storing the information of these two page sizes, and a simple conversion is needed.

For the lookup implementation, the pseudo-algorithmic description of the TLB lookup process given in the instruction manual is described in serialized terms. Instead of comparing item 0 and then item 1 in the implementation of the circuit ......, we compare all items at the same time. Assuming that our TLB has 16 items, we need to generate a 16-bit-wide lookup result `match[15:0]` using combinational logic. Bit 0 of this result corresponds to the comparison result of item 0, and bit 1 corresponds to the comparison result of item 1 …… The Verilog code is shown below:

```verilog
assign match0[ 0] = (s0_vppn[18:10]==tlb_vppn[ 0][18:10])
                 && (tlb_ps4MB[ 0] || s0_vppn[9:0]==tlb_vppn
    [0][9:0])
                 && ((s0_asid==tlb_asid[ 0]) || tlb_g[ 0]);
assign match0[ 1] = (s0_vppn[18:10]==tlb_vppn[ 1][18:10])
                 && (tlb_ps4MB[ 1] || s0_vppn[9:0]==tlb_vppn
 ↪  [1][9:0])
                 && ((s0_asid==tlb_asid[ 1]) || tlb_g[ 1]);
 ……
assign match0[15] = (s0_vppn[18:10]==tlb_vppn[15][18:10])
                 && (tlb_ps4MB[15] ||
 ↪  s0_vppn[9:0]==tlb_vppn[15][9:0])
                 && ((s0_asid==tlb_asid[15]) || tlb_g[15]);

assign match1[ 0] = (s1_vppn[18:10]==tlb_vppn[ 0][18:10])
                 && (tlb_ps4MB[ 0] || s1_vppn[9:0]==tlb_vppn
    [0][9:0])
                 && ((s1_asid==tlb_asid[ 0]) || tlb_g[ 0]);
assign match1[ 1] = (s1_vppn[18:10]==tlb_vppn[ 1][18:10])
                 && (tlb_ps4MB[ 1] || s1_vppn[9:0]==tlb_vppn
    [1][9:0])
                 && ((s1_asid==tlb_asid[ 1]) || tlb_g[ 1]);
 ……
assign match1[15] = (s1_vppn[18:10]==tlb_vppn[15][18:10])
                 && (tlb_ps4MB[15] ||
 ↪  s1_vppn[9:0]==tlb_vppn[15][9:0])
                 && ((s1_asid==tlb_asid[15]) || tlb_g[15]);
```

As long as this query comparison result is generated, then whether or not to look for a hit found is to see if match is not equal to all 0. The logic to read out information such as the PFN of the hit item is also easy to implement; please refer to Sect. 3.1 for a description of a multiplexer where the select signal is the decoded bit-vector information.

Let's analyze how the various lookup operations required by the INVTLB instruction are supported. Since the current TLB physical-virtual address translation process adopts the parallel lookup mechanism, the lookup of INVTLB instruction also adopts the parallel lookup mechanism, i.e., the matching judgment of each item of TLB is performed at the same time. The main point of design is how to deal with the matching of each item. By analyzing the definition of each operation of INVTLB instruction, it is found that the matching of each operation can be decomposed into a number of "sub-matching" logical combinations; specifically, four "sub-matching" judgment conditions can be obtained: (1) cond1, whether the

G domain is equal to 0; (2) cond2, whether the G domain is equal to 1; (3) cond3, whether s1_asid is equal to the ASID domain; and (4) cond4, whether s1_vppn matches the VPPN and PS domains. Then, the matching condition of invtlb op=0, 1 can be expressed as cond1||cond2, op=4 can be expressed as cond1&&cond3, op=5 can be expressed as cond1&&cond3&&&cond4, op=6 can be expressed as (cond1&&cond3&&cond4), op=6 can be expressed as (cond1&cond3&&cond4), and op=4 can be expressed as (cond1&cond3&cond3&cond4). The match condition for op=5 can be expressed as cond1&&cond3&&cond4, and the match condition for op=6 can be expressed as (cond2||cond3)&&cond4. At the same time, it is easy to know that the match condition for op=6 is the lookup match condition for physical-virtual address translation between fetch and access, and thus the lookup match function required by the two types of operations can be unified into one set of logic. The difference between the two types of operations is only the further operation based on the search result. For INVTLB instruction, the operation of invalidating the corresponding TLB table entry is to set tlb_e[i] equal to inv_match[i] equal to 1 to zero.

9.3 MMU-Related Control Status Registers and Instructions Implementation

In order to add MMU functionality to the CPU, in addition to integrating the TLB module designed in the previous section, it is necessary to implement a series of MMU-related control status registers and instructions. These control status registers include the DA and PG fields of the CRMD used to distinguish address translation modes, the DMW0 and DMW1 used to directly map address translation modes, and the TLB read/write lookups related to ASID, TLBEHI, TLBELO0, TLBELO1, and TLBIDX, which are preferred to be placed in the same module as the CSRs that have already been implemented, allowing the data paths for CSR instructions to access these CSRs can be reused in the existing design. As for the MMU logic that needs to use the information from these CSRs for fetching and accessing, it is directly derived from the CSR module and sent to the required place. The implementation of the CSRs themselves can be easily derived from the instruction manual definitions and will not be repeated here. This section discusses the handling of CSR-related conflicts and the implementation of the TLB instruction.

9.3.1 Conflict Handling for MMU-Related Control Status Register-Related Triggers

Among the MMU-related CSRs, the DA and PG of CRMD, DMW0, DMW1, and ASID will directly affect the fetch request at the pre-IF stage. Similar to the analyzing process described in Sect. 7.3.4 on the processing of the ertn instruction, the conflict caused by the modification of the control registers (domains) by the CSR instruction cannot be avoided by blocking the subsequent instructions. It is because the earliest time to know whether a CSR instruction modifies the above control registers is at the ID stage, but at this time, there may already be an instruction at the IF stage that has been retrieved by performing the physical-virtual address translation according to the old MMU information, so it is obvious that this instruction has to be canceled and then refetched. Since unfetching is unavoidable, it is better to solve this kind of conflict by using only the mechanism of unfetching. A feasible solution is that whenever a CSR instruction is found in the pipeline that may cause a conflict, all instructions that are fetched into the pipeline after that instruction are set with a refetch flag; the instruction with the refetch flag is like an exception flagged, i.e., it cannot produce any execution effect by itself, and at the same time, it will block the execution of the instructions in the pipeline that are after it. When an instruction with a retry flag reaches the pipeline stage, it clears the pipeline as if it had been reported as an exception. The instruction with the refetch flag will clear the pipeline when it reaches the write-back stage, just as an exception would. Except that it is not a real exception, so it does not modify any CSRs, it does not raise the privilege level of the processor, and the nextPC of the pre-IF stage update is the PC of the instruction that is starting to refetch the instruction that refers to the exception, not the entry address of any exception.

9.3.2 Implementation of TLB-Related Instructions

Let's start with the TLBSRCH instruction. This instruction requires a lookup of the TLB, which means that its execution needs to utilize the lookup logic in the TLB module. There are only two sets of lookup logic in the TLB module, one set is used to fetch the instruction, and the other set is used to access the stored instruction. If the execution of TLBSRCH instruction can reuse one set of lookup logic, it can avoid adding a lot of new lookup logic, and at the same time, we would like to make sure that the reuse does not block other instructions from accessing the TLB module, so it seems to be the most appropriate to reuse the TLB lookup port of the access instruction, and to initiate the lookup request at the EX stage. However, there are two problems with this design: (1) the lookup contents of the TLBSRCH instruction are from CSR.ASID and CSR.TLBEHI, but they can be modified by the CSRWR, CSRX- CHG, or TLBRD instructions at the WB stage. If a CSR instruction or TLBRD instruction that modifies CSR.ASID or CSR.TLBEHI happens to be at the MEM stage when the TLBSRCH instruction is at the EX stage, there will be a problem in using the values of ASID and TLBEHI directly from the CSR module. (2) The TLB to be searched by the TLBSRCH instruction may be updated by the TLBWR, TLBFILL, and INVTLB instructions. As we will see later, not all of these updates take place at the EX stage, and thus problems may occur if they are not handled. Only problem 1 will be discussed here; problem 2 will be solved by the refetching mechanism described later when analyzing the TLBWR, TLBFILL, and INVTLB instructions. For the write-after-read-related conflicts described in the problem, either blocking or forwarding is used. We believe that the execution frequency of TLBSRCH instruction is very low, and the probability of the conflict mentioned above is even lower, so the input-output ratio of designing a set of forward logic to deal with this kind of conflict is too low, and we choose to use the blocking method.

Turning to the TLBWR and TLBFILL instructions. Since the TLB module is designed with a dedicated set of write interfaces for TLB instructions, the timing of TLBWR and TLBFILL instructions writing to the TLB is directly related to when the source operand of the instruction is read. Consider that the control status registers ASID, TLBEHI, TLBELO0, TLBELO1, and TLBIDX are updated by the CSRWR, CSRXCHG, or TLBRD instruction in WB stage, it is appropriate to have the TLBWR and TLBFILL instructions write TLB at the WB stage, since the CSR values read at that point are correct. However, the most complicated aspect of implementing the TLBWR and TLBFILL instructions is reflected in other aspects: since all instruction fetch and memory access instructions may look up the TLB[2] for physical-virtual address translation, and the TLBWR and TLBFILL instructions update the contents of the TLB, which forms a read-after-write dependency around the TLB. Since the TLBWR and TLBFILL write operations occur at the WB stage, this write-after-read correlation will cause a conflict. How can such conflicts be resolved? Some readers may think of the idea of blocking the execution of subsequent instructions once they encounter the TLBWR and TLBFILL instructions, but this idea cannot solve the problem completely, for the same reason that the CSR instruction modifies the MMU-related control status register as analyzed in the previous subsection, and so it can only be dealt with by marking a retry flag for the subsequent instructions.

Next, look at the TLBRD instruction. Since the TLB module is designed with a separate set of readout interfaces, there is no restriction on when the TLBRD instruction reads the TLB. We will focus on the impact of the CSRs involved in the execution of the TLBR instruction. First, the TLBRD instruction needs to read the Index field of CSR.TLBIDX as the read address, which will be updated by the CSRWR, CSRXCHG, or TLBSRCH instruction at the WB stage. Second, the TLBRD instruction needs to update ASID, TLBEHI, TLBELO0, TLBELO1, and TLBIDX, which will be read by the CSR instruction at the WB stage. From these two analyses, we can see that the TLBRD instruction reads TLB and updates the related CSRs at the WB stage, which is the most suitable. However, there is another correlation that will lead to a problem: since TLBRD instruction will update the ASID field of CSR.ASID, but all the fetch instructions and access instructions may read the ASID field of CSR.ASID to look for the TLB, which means that the TLBRD instruction has to solve the problem of CSR conflict just like the TLBWR and TLBFILL instructions. This means that the TLBRD instruction has to solve

---

[2] A find operation implies a read operation.

the CSR conflict problem just like the TLBWR and TLBFILL instructions. The solution is the same as the TLBWR and TLBFILL instructions, which is to mark the subsequent instruction with a refetch flag.

Finally, let's look at the INVTLB instruction. Let us first analyze the handling of conflicts related to privileged resources. On the one hand, from the consumer's point of view, the source operands of IN-VTLB instruction come from general-purpose registers or immediate numbers, and it needs to (partially) reuse the existing lookup logic in the TLB module, so from these aspects, it is more appropriate for it to initiate the TLB lookup request at the EX stage. As for the read-after-write conflict between the read operation of the IN-VTLB instruction to look up the TLB and the write operation of the TLBWR and TLBFILL instructions to update the TLB at the WB stage, it has been unified and solved by the refetching mechanism of the TLBWR and TLBFILL instructions. On the other hand, from the producer's point of view, the INVTLB instruction will update the content of TLB, and this update will not be earlier than the EX stage, so it needs to solve the conflict related to the read-after-write of TLB with the fetch operation of the subsequent instruction and the store operation of the store access instruction by marking the fetch flag to the subsequent instruction, just like the TLBWR and TLBFILL instructions. Find invalid operation has already been realized in the previous design of TLB module, so it is only necessary to pass the relevant information into TLB module.

9.4   Implementation of Virtual-Physical Address Translation and MMU-Related Exceptions with MMUs

We have already integrated the TLB module into the CPU and implemented the MMU-related CSRs and instructions. Next, we will finish the finalization of the MMU functionality in the CPU, which includes the use of MMU for physical-virtual address translation and the implementation of MMU-related exceptions.

The book emphasizes the physical-virtual address translation between the fetch and access parts in Chap. 5, which introduces simple CPU design, so please review where the physical-virtual address translation logic is located in the context of your own design. In the current design, the fetch request is issued at the pre-IF stage, and the physical-virtual address translation of the access is done at this stage, so it needs to be realized by combinational logic. Examining the direct address translation, direct mapping window address translation, and TLB address translation logics, we can see that they can all be implemented using combinational logic. Then, the implementation of the virtual-physical address translation at the pointing place is to send the requested virtual address, nextPC, to the direct address translation, the direct mapping window address translation, and the TLB address translation at the same time, and perform the virtual-physical address translation at the same time, and then decide whether to choose the translation result of the direct address translation logic or the TLB module's address translation result based on the address translation mode currently in place. Then, according to the current address translation mode, decide whether to select the translation result of the direct address translation logic, or else decide whether to select the translation result of the address translation logic of the direct mapping window or the address translation result of the TLB module based on the information of whether the direct mapping window is hit or not. The virtual and physical address translation of the access part is similar to the instruction fetching, except that the translation operation takes place at the EX stage, and the virtual address to be translated is the virtual address of the access calculated at the EX stage. After completing the above connection and selection logic, the function of physical-virtual address translation using MMU in CPU is realized.

Next, we add the implementation of MMU-related exceptions. These exceptions are related to the result of TLB lookup in page-mapped address translation mode, and the required result information has already been set up with corresponding output interfaces in the implementation of the TLB module. Therefore, what we need to do in this stage is to utilize the output information of the TLB module in the fetch-instruction and store sections, and at the same time implement the judgment logic of these exceptions according to the exception judgment conditions given in Section 5.4.4 of the instruction manual, taking into account of the type of the access (fetch-instruction, load, or store?), and then get the judgment results of the MMU-related exceptions in the fetch-instruction and store sections. The rest of the design is the same as the general implementation of exceptions introduced in Chap. 7, which is to pass the exception judgment results generated in the instruction fetch and memory access sections along the pipeline step by step to the write back stage, and then update the related CSR registers in the write back stage, trigger the exception, clear the pipeline, and jump to the entry point of the exception.

There is one more detail that needs to be discussed here. If an MMU-related exception is detected during the physical-virtual address translation, can an access request be made to the bus? The answer is no. The answer is no, because the resulting physical address is either meaningless or illegal. Unless you can ensure that all objects in the computer system associated with the access address react in a deterministic and controlled manner to the meaningless or illegal address, it is unacceptable to put such an address on the bus and have the system behave in a way that exceeds the software people's expectations. Usually, we design from a conservative point of view, i.e., all meaningless and illegal addresses must not be sent to the bus.

After completing the above design, some readers may find that the latency of the final generated access addresses at the pre-IF and EXE stages has been greatly extended. This problem can be alleviated to a certain extent after the implementation of the time cache, and further timing optimization can also be done to address this problem. This chapter is mainly for beginners, trying to complete a functionally correct implementation first, and the timing optimization problem will be an advanced content for readers to explore further in the subsequent practice.

9.5 Tasks and Practices

After completing this chapter, readers are expected to complete the following three practical tasks:

1. Design the TLB module. See Sect. 9.5.1.
2. Integrate the TLB module into the CPU and add TLB-related instructions and CSR registers. See Sect. 9.5.2.
3. Improve the TLB MMU functionality in the CPU and add TLB-related exception support. See Sect. 9.5.3.

9.5.1 Practical Task 17: TLB Module Design

The requirements for this practical task are as follows:

1. Design the TLB module.
2. The designed TLBs are verified by simulation and onboard verification using the TLB module-level verification environment.

Please refer to Sect. 2.3.1 to obtain the experimental development environment for this practical task. **The specific experimental environment is different from the previous one;** it is a separate verification environment for TLB module, which is located in the directory of `mycpu_env/module_verify/tlb_verify/`. The specific directory structure and functions of each part are as follows:

```
|--tlb_verify/           TLB Module-Level Validation
 ↪  Environment
 |  |--rtl/              Source code of TLB module design and
 ↪  verification top module
 |  |  |--tlb_top.v      TLB top module
 |  |--testbench/        Simulation environment
 |  |  |--testbench.v    Simulation top module
 |  |--run_vivado/       Vivado project running directory
 |  |  |--constraints/   Vivado project design constraints
 |  |  |--tlb_prj/       Vivado project files directory
```

Once the lab environment is ready, please refer to the following steps to complete this practical task:

1. Complete the design and RTL writing of the TLB module as tlb.v. The module name needs to be named "tlb," and the input/output ports are described in Sect. 9.2 of this chapter. Place the tlb.v file in the mycpu_env/myCPU/ directory.
2. Go to the mycpu_env/module_verify/tlb_verify/run_vivado/tlb_prj/ directory to start the project for verifying tlb. If a project has not been created in this directory, refer to the steps described in Appendix D.2 to create a project using

the create_project.tcl file in this directory. If necessary, refer to Appendix D.4 for IP core upgrade.

3. Run the simulation in the project where the tlb module is verified (click run all directly after entering the simulation interface), and carry out the function verification and debugging until the simulation test is passed.
4. Generate a bit stream file after synthesizing the implementation in the project where the tlb module is verified, and verify it on the board. (Skip this step if you do not have a hardware lab platform.)

9.5.1.1   Simulation Verification Result Judgment

During the simulation, there will be 16 write, 16, read and 26 check operations, and PASS will be printed after all operations are completed, as shown below:

```
[   2705 ns] OK!!!write

. . . . . . . . . . .

=============================================================
Test end!
----PASS!!!
```

If an error is found in the simulation, debug it. At this point, you need to observe the access to the TLB interface to understand the effect of the request, and then check if the readout data from the TLB is as expected.

9.5.1.2   Upper Board Validation Result Judgment

The effect of a correct upper board run is shown in Fig. 9.1.

When the first stage is run on the board, you should see the digital tube change as follows:

1. Firstly, for write operation (W), the rightmost digital pipe will accumulate from 0x00 to 0x0f, and then the rightmost monochrome LED will light up to indicate that the write operation is completed.
2. After that, the read operation and the lookup operation are performed at the same time, and the corresponding digital tube will start to accumulate:

   - For a read operation (R), 16 reads are performed, and the digit on the right-hand side of the sub will accumulate from 0x00 to 0x0f.
   - For lookup operation 0 (S0), 13 lookups are performed (lookup even request), and the digit pipe on the left-hand side of the sub will be incremented from 0x00 to 0x18 in step 2, i.e., 0, 2, 4, ..., 0x18.
   - For lookup operation #1 (S1), 13 lookups are performed (checking an odd number of requests), and the leftmost digit tube is incremented from 0x01 to 0x19 in step 2, i.e., 1, 3, 5, ..., 0x19.

Fig. 9.1 TLB Module verify Fpga result

3. When the totalization in step 2 is complete, all three of the LEDs on the right side of the LED will light up, indicating that the test is complete. The correct digital display is 0x19180f0f. If the digital display stops at any other value, it indicates that the board has failed.

9.5.2 Practical Task 18: Adding TLB-Related Instructions and CSR Registers

This practical task requires the following to be accomplished in addition to Practical Task 16 and Practical Task 17:

1. Integrate the TLB module completed in Practice Task 17 into the CPU completed in Practice Task 16.
2. Add TLBSRCH, TLBRD, TLBWR, TLBFILL, INVTLB instructions to the CPU.
3. Add TLBIDX, TLBEHI, TLBELO0, TLBELO1, ASID, TLBRENTRY CSRs to CPU Registers.
4. Complete the functional verification of the exp18 corresponding func in a SoC verification environment utilizing the AXI bus, requiring successful simulation and board verification.

Please refer to the method described in Sect. 2.3.1 to obtain the experimental development environment required for this practical task. The specific experimental environment is located at `mycpu_env/`, and continue to use the `soc_axi/` subdirectory.

Once the lab environment is ready, please refer to the following steps to complete this practical task:

1. Update CPU code at `mycpu_env/myCPU/`.
2. Modify the func configuration file, `mycpu_env/func/include/test_config.h`, select the configuration of `exp18`, and compile. (If you obtained the experimental development environment from the package `exp18.zip`, please skip this step.)
3. Open the gettrace project, `mycpu_env/gettrace/gettrace.xpr` (the IP core in this Vivado project was created using Vivado2019.2; if you open it with a higher version of Vivado, refer to Appendix D.4 for the IP core upgrade). Run the simulation of the gettrace project (after entering the simulation interface, click `run all` and wait for the simulation to finish), and generate a new reference trace file `golden_trace.txt` (`mycpu_env/gettrace/golden_trace.txt`). The `golden_trace.txt` will not be complete until the simulation has finished running. (If you obtained the experimental development environment from the package `exp18.zip`, please skip this step.)
4. Start the project in `mycpu_env/soc_verify/soc_axi/run_vivado/` to verify myCPU. If you have not created a project in this directory, please refer to the steps described in Appendix D.2 to create a project using the `create_project.tcl` file in this directory. If necessary, please refer to Appendix D.4 to upgrade the IP core. If there is a project in this directory that has been created by a previous practice task, you can update the file list of CPU implementations in the project by referring to the steps described in Appendix D.3 after opening the project.
5. Refer to Chap. 4 Sect. 4.4.5.2 to re-customize `inst_ram` in the project. (If you obtained the experimental development environment from the package `exp18.zip`, please skip this step.)
6. Run the simulation in the project (click `run all` directly after entering the simulation interface), and carry out the function verification until the simulation test is passed.
7. Generate a bit stream file after Synthesis and Implementation in the project, and verify it on FPGA. (Please skip this step if you don't have a hardware experiment platform.)

9.5.3 Practical Task 19: Adding TLB-Related Exception Support

This practical task requires the following work based on the CPU implemented in Practical Task 18:

1. Add TLB-related exceptions for CPU: TLB refill exception, load/store/fetch instruction operation page invalid exception, page modification exception, and page privilege level noncompliance exception.
2. Add DMW CSR register to CPU.
3. Add the function of virtual-physical address mapping for CPU.
4. Complete the functional verification of the exp19 func in a SoC verification environment utilizing the AXI bus, requiring successful simulation and board verification.

Please refer to the method described in Sect. 2.3.1 to obtain the experimental development environment required for this practical task. The specific experimental environment is located at `mycpu_env/`, and continue to use the `soc_axi/` subdirectory.

Once the lab environment is ready, please refer to the following steps to complete this practical task:

1. Update CPU code at `mycpu_env/myCPU/`.
2. Modify the func configuration file, `mycpu_env/func/include/test_config.h`, select the configuration of `exp19`, and compile. (If you obtained the experimental development environment from the package `exp19.zip`, please skip this step.)
3. Open the gettrace project, `mycpu_env/gettrace/gettrace.xpr` (the IP core in this Vivado project was created using Vivado2019.2; if you open it with a higher version of Vivado, refer to Appendix D.4 for the IP core upgrade). Run the simulation of the gettrace project (after entering the simulation interface, click `run all` and wait for the simulation to finish), and generate a new reference trace file `golden_trace.txt` (`mycpu_env/gettrace/golden_trace.txt`). The `golden_trace.txt` will not be complete until the simulation has finished running. (If you obtained the experimental development environment from the package `exp19.zip`, please skip this step.)
4. Start the project in `mycpu_env/soc_verify/soc_axi/run_vivado/` to verify myCPU. If you have not created a project in this directory, please refer to the steps described in Appendix D.2 to create a project using the `create_project.tcl` file in this directory. If necessary, please refer to Appendix D.4 to upgrade the IP core. If there is a project in this directory that has been created by a previous practice task, you can update the file list of CPU implementations in the project by referring to the steps described in Appendix D.3 after opening the project.

5. Refer to Chap. 4 Sect. 4.4.5.2 to re-customize `inst_ram` in the project. (If you obtained the experimental development environment from the package `exp19.zip`, please skip this step.)
6. Run the simulation in the project (click `run all` directly after entering the simulation interface), and carry out the function verification until the simulation test is passed.
7. Generate a bit stream file after Synthesis and Implementation in the project, and verify it on FPGA. (Please skip this step if you don't have a hardware experiment platform.)

Chapter 10
Cache Design

The observant reader will notice that since we added the AXI bus interface to the CPU and removed the instruction RAM and data RAM, it has become much less efficient, taking more execution cycles to run the same program. So, is removing instruction RAM and data RAM a retrograde step in design? No. The use of instruction RAM and data RAM requires software developers to have a clear understanding of the capacity and starting address of physical memory, which makes software development more difficult. Currently, this hardware architecture is only widely used in low-end embedded applications that are extremely sensitive to cost, power, or execution latency determinism. These application areas are also characterized by small software sizes and relatively deterministic program behavior; otherwise, the absence of virtualized storage management would be a "disaster" for application development. However, despite the shortcomings of instruction RAM and data RAM, there are performance issues that need to be addressed. Our solution is to add a cache.

In this chapter, we will move on to the final design phase, adding Cache to the CPU, which is a challenging task because there are so many design optimization techniques around Cache, resulting in a wide range of Cache design complexity. In this chapter, we will keep the design complexity of the Cache at an entry level, with a focus on performance. We will also give a clear set of parameters for the details of the Cache implementation specification. However, the reader can rest assured that the parameters we have chosen are representative, and most of them, if they need to be adjusted at all, will only be the difference between 1 and 2, rather than a leap from 0 to 1. In terms of implementation steps, we have divided the program into four phases:

- Phase 1 Design the Cache module.
- Phase 2 Integrate the Cache module into the CPU as an ICache (Instruction Cache), complete the matching and adjustment with the CPU's indexing, and complete the design adjustment of the bus interface module.

© The Author(s), under exclusive license to Springer Nature Singapore Pte Ltd. 2025
W. Wang, J. Xing, *CPU Design and Practice*,
https://doi.org/10.1007/978-981-96-6573-0_10

- Phase 3 integrates the Cache module into the CPU as a DCache (Data Cache), completes the coordination and adjustment with the CPU access memory, and completes the design adjustment of the bus interface module.
- Phase 4 Implement support for the Cache instruction.

Before you begin, make sure that you have carefully studied Section 9.5.4 of *Fundamentals of Computer Architecture (3rd Edition)* or other literature on the basic concepts of Cache.

Learning Goals for This Chapter
- Understand the organization and working mechanism of Cache.
- Understand the Cache-related control status registers and instructions in the LoongArch architecture.
- Learn how to add Cache support to a pipelined CPU.

Practical Tasks of This Chapter
There are four practical tasks in this chapter (see Sect. 10.4 of this chapter). These tasks can be completed as part of your study of this chapter and correspond to each other as follows:

- The content of Sect. 10.1 corresponds to Practice Task 20 (Sect. 10.4.1).
- The content of Sect. 10.2 corresponds to Practice Task 21 (Sect. 10.4.2) and Practice Task 22 (Sect. 10.4.3).
- The content of Sect. 10.3 corresponds to Practice Task 23 (Sect. 10.4.4).

10.1   Design of the Cache Module

10.1.1   Cache Design Specifications

Let's start by identifying the main design specifications associated with the Cache module, so that the ensuing discussion doesn't become too macro to get down to the nitty-gritty. These design specifications include the following:

1. The CPU integrates an instruction Cache and a data Cache.
2. Instruction Cache and Data Cache both have a capacity of 8 KB and are connected in two groups, and the size of the Cache line is 16 bytes.
3. Instruction Cache and Data Cache are synchronized with Tag and Data.
4. Both Instruction Cache and Data Cache adopt the access form of "Virtual Index Real Tag" (VIPT for short).
5. Instruction Cache and Data Cache both use pseudo-random replacement algorithm.
6. The Data Cache utilizes a write-back write-allocation strategy.

7. Both the Instruction Cache and the Data Cache use a blocking design, i.e., once a Cache Miss occurs, subsequent accesses are blocked until the data is filled back into the Cache.
8. Cache does not use "keyword first" techniques.

We explain the original intent of developing the above design specifications.

- An Instruction Cache and a Data Cache are designed to keep the pipeline running at full capacity.
- Instruction Cache and Data Cache have the same specifications in all aspects to ensure that even if the Cache module is not written as a parameterizable configuration, it is still possible to instantiate two copies of the defined Cache module to be used for implementing Instruction Cache and Data Cache, respectively, to reduce the workload of code development and debugging.
- The design specification of a two-way association is used because direct mapping is too simple and requires substantial adjustments if it is later adapted to multiple-way association, whereas two-way association is the least complex and representative of multiple-way association structures.
- Defining the capacity of each Cache as 4 KB is intended to circumvent the Cache aliasing problem[1] while using VIPT access.
- The Cache line size of 16 bytes was set to keep the number of components in the Cache Data section at a moderate size, so the 64-byte size commonly applied in commercial processors today is not used here.
- The synchronized Tag and Data access to the Cache is designed to reduce the number of cycles in the event of a Cache hit, since a Tag and Data serial access can take as little as three cycles to read a number. However, with existing CPUs requiring only two cycles to access both instruction RAM and data RAM, the three-cycle access latency requires a significant design change to the CPU pipeline.
- The use of VIPT for the Cache allows the TLB lookups to be performed in parallel with the Cache accesses, thus increasing the CPU frequency.
- The pseudo-random replacement algorithm is used for Cache because it is the simplest and most practical replacement algorithm for Cache. The LRU algorithm has better average performance, but it involves the maintenance of LRU information, which increases the complexity of the design.
- The data cache uses write-back allocation because the processing flow of a write operation when a cache miss occurs is almost the same as that of a read operation when a cache miss occurs, thus simplifying the design of the control logic.

---

[1]The Cache alias problem is that multiple virtual addresses correspond to the same physical address, but each of these virtual addresses may have a copy of the data in the Cache, which results in multiple backups of the same physical address in the Cache. If you are interested in this issue, you can find out more about it on your own.

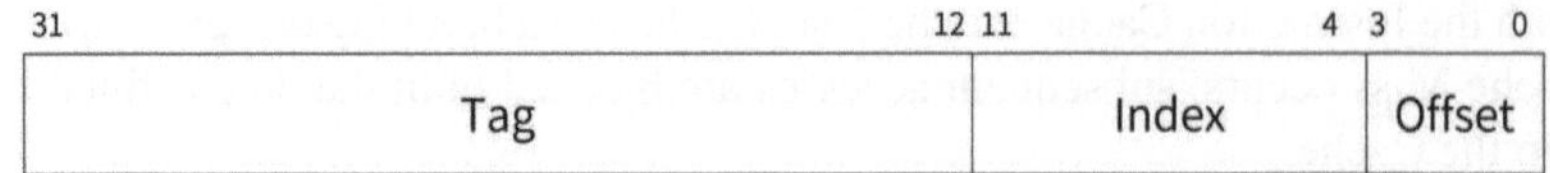

Fig. 10.1 Cache access Addresss division

- Cache uses a blocking design, mainly because we currently implement a static sequential execution pipeline; designing the Cache to be non-blocking also does not result in an overall performance improvement.
- The Cache does not use "keyword first" technology, which reduces the complexity of interacting with the AXI bus.

Based on the above design specifications, we can calculate the Cache capacity as follows:

$$\text{Cache_size} = \text{way_number} \times \text{way_size} = 2_\text{ways} \times 4\,\text{KB} = 8\,\text{KB}$$

The capacity calculated above is the size of the data that can be cached, not the actual RAM used to implement the Cache. The size of the RAM required for the actual implementation should also take into account the TAG, Dirty, etc. fields of the Cache.

Based on the above design specifications, we can calculate the number of bits in the address-related Tag, Index, and Offset.

- Offset: Cache line offset. The width is log2 (the size of the Cache line), i.e., 4 bits.
- Index: Index of the Cache group. The width is (log2(road size)-5), which is 8 bits.
- Tag: Tag field of the Cache line. The width is (physical address width - log2 (road size)), which is 20 bits.

Therefore, the Cache is accessed using [11:4] of the virtual address [31:0] as the Index index, and the upper 20 bits of the physical address ([31:12]) as the TAG for comparison. The address division is shown in Fig. 10.1.

10.1.2   Data Path Design for Cache Module

10.1.2.1   Read and Write Operations to Access the Cache

Before designing the datapath for the Cache module, let's review the execution of read and write operations to access the Cache.

Let's start with a read operation.

The First Cycle   The [11:4] bits of the virtual address in the request are sent to the Cache as the index value, and the two cache lines corresponding to the same index

in the two Caches are read out. At the same time, the virtual address of the read
operation is sent to the MMU logic for real-virtual address conversion. At this time,
the physical address comes from the result of the combinational logic operation of
the virtual address, and it is necessary to register the physical address with a flip-flop
(reg-type variable) for use in the second cycle.

Second Cycle Get the Tag information of the two Cache lines read out by Cache
RAM (we require Cache RAM to be synchronous RAM with single-cycle return),
and compare it with the [31:12] of the latched physical address for equality. If the
Tag comparison of a Cache line is equal and the valid bit V of that Cache line
is equal to 1, then the access hit is on that Cache line. At the same time of Tag
comparison, the Data information of the two cache lines can be selected according
to the [3:2] bits of the latched dummy address to get the 32-bit data where the access
is located.[2] Finally, the 32-bit data of the accessed row is returned according to the
Tag comparison result. If there is no hit Cache line, it is necessary to initiate access
request through the bus interface, and when the access result is returned to the Cache
module, retrieve the 32-bit data of the access from the returned result and return it.

Let's look at write operations.

The first steps of a write operation are basically the same as a read operation, the
only difference being that the write operation can start without reading the Cache's
Data information. It only needs to read the Tag and V information in the two cache
lines to determine whether the Cache is hit or not. If the Cache is hit, it generates
the Index, route number, offset, and write-enable (which bytes of 32-bit data are to
be written) and transfers the write data to the Write Buffer, which in the next cycle
sends a write request to the Cache to write the data cached in the Write Buffer to the
corresponding position in the hit Cache line, and sets the dirty bit D of this Cache
line to 1. The reason for introducing a Write Buffer between the Write Hit Cache
and the Write Cache is to avoid introducing a path from the RAM outputs to the
RAM inputs due to timing considerations: the Cache hit information comes from
comparing the Tag read from the Cache RAM, and the Write Hit operation needs to
generate a Write Cache based on the Tag comparison result. Cache hit information
comes from the comparison result of the Tag read from the Cache RAM, and the
write operation of the hit needs to be generated according to the comparison result
of the Tag to write which path in the Cache. If a Cache hit store is written directly, it
will introduce a path from the Tag read out of Cache RAM to the Data write enable
of Cache RAM. If the cache is missing, since it is writing back to the write-allocated
cache, as in the case of a cache miss during a read operation, the cache request is sent
out through the bus, the result of which is returned to the Cache module, and then
the data to be written from the store and the data to be reloaded from the memory
are combined and written to the Cache together.

---

[2] According to our current implementation of the instruction, all Cache read operations must access
no more than a 32-bit data range aligned to a 4-byte boundary at the start address.

Both read and write operations involve the handling of Cache misses. For the sake of brevity, the above description only briefly describes the handling of this problem, which is actually a multistep process.

The first step is to record the Cache's missing address and the type of operation (and write data if it is a write operation).

In the second step, an access to the missing cache line is initiated outward through the AXI bus interface module. The address of this access is the start address of the missing Cache line, and the size is the size of a Cache line.

In the third step, while waiting for the read request data to be returned (or at the same time as the second step), according to the substitution algorithm, select one of the two cache lines corresponding to the index of the Cache Miss address, and read out the whole cache line. If the V=1 and D=1 of the cache line means that it is a cache line with valid dirty data, then the data of this cache line should be written out through the AXI bus interface module; otherwise, no additional operation is needed, which means that the data of this cache line is simply discarded. This step also documents which path was selected.

In the fourth step, after the missing requested data is returned from the bus, the Cache line information to be filled into the Cache is generated, where V bit of Cache of the line is set to 1, and the Tag information comes from the previously saved Cache Miss address. If this Cache Miss request is a write operation, then D in the Cache line is set to 1, and the Data information is the new data formed after the value to be written by the store operation partially overwrites the data returned from the bus; otherwise, D is set to 0, and the Data information is only from the data returned from the bus.

In the fifth step, fill this Cache line with the information you recorded in step 3.

10.1.2.2   Organization and Management of Cache Tables

From the execution process of accessing the Cache introduced earlier, we can know that the main body of the data path is the Cache, and from the perspective of functional logic, we can understand each Cache as a two-dimensional table, and in this regard, you can refer to Figure 9.25c in the *Fundamentals of Computer Architecture (3rd edition)*. Although almost all the textbooks and materials on the principle of composition and architecture adopt this way of drawing, this way of drawing is still a little far from the concrete implementation. This gap is the first obstacle for beginners when designing and implementing a Cache, so let's break this "windowpaper" below.

Let's split the original table into several tables according to the information in the cache lines. For example, for the Cache specification we are trying to implement, there are 2 Tag tables with 256 items × 20 bits, 2 V tables with 256 items × 1 bit, 2 D tables with 256 items × 1 bit, and two Data tables with 256 × 128 bits. The reason why all the tables are two is that each table corresponds to one way of the Cache, and the item 0 of all the tables of the 0th way of the Cache constitutes the cache line of the 0th way of the Cache with index=0, and the item 1 of all the tables corresponds to the cache line of the Cache with index=1, ..., and so on. After the decomposition of all Cache module operations, the only operations implemented on these tables are reads and writes. Next, we analyze how many reads and writes each table should support, and the sources of the read and write requests.

The accesses to the Cache module are categorized into four types, Look Up, Hit Write, Replace, and Refill, depending on the stage of the Cache execution where the read and write operations are performed, and are defined below:

- Look Up: determine whether it is in the Cache or not, and select the content of Data section according to the hit information3.
- Hit Write: A hit write operation enters the Write Buffer and subsequently writes the data to the corresponding location in the hit cache line.
- Replace: An operation initiated to read a cache line in order to make room for data in a Refill.
- Refill: fills the empty Replace position with the data returned from memory (and the data to be written by store miss).

We analyze the access behavior of the four accesses to various parts of the Cache and get the results shown in Table 10.1.

From Table 10.1, we observe that for both Tag and V, all Cache accesses are identical for both, so a natural idea is to horizontally splice the Tag and V tables into a single table, which we call the {Tag, V} table, with a size of 256 items × 21 bits, where [20:1] corresponds to the Tag information and [0] corresponds to the V information for each item.

Analyzing further, we know that Replace and Refill do not happen at the same time, which means that for all tables, Replace reads and Refill writes do not happen at the same time. Since we are designing a blocking Cache, we don't receive new access requests while Replace and Refill are in progress, so naturally there will be no Cache hit store, which means that for all tables, Replace and Refill reads and writes won't occur at the same time as Look Up and Hit Write reads and writes. Since Hit Write does not access the {Tag, V} table, for the {Tag, V} table, it receives at most one read request or write request at the same time, and since Look Up does not access the D table, for the D table, it receives at most one read request or write request at the same time.

Table 10.1 Various cache-ops access different cache parts

...1	Look up	Hit Write	Replace	Refill
Tag	read all ways	–	read victim way	update victim way
V	read all ways	–	read victim way	update victim way
Data	read part of all ways	update part of hit way	read all part of victim way	update all part of victim way
D	–	update hit way	read victim way	update victim way

The situation with Data tables is slightly more complicated. This is because a Look Up from a Read operation and a Hit Write from a Write operation can occur at the same time. A straightforward solution is to have the Data table support both a read request and a write request. This approach is the simplest in terms of design and the best in terms of performance, but the underlying circuitry to support a Hit Read and a Hit Write is not well implemented in terms of area and latency. Another straightforward solution is to block the Look Up of a read operation whenever a Hit Write occurs, so that the data table receives at most one read request or one write request at a time. This approach goes to the other extreme: sacrificing significant performance for low overhead in terms of circuit area and latency. On second thought, we can see that both Look Up and Hit Write accesses to the Data table are "localized" to no more than a word aligned to the 4-byte boundary of the start address, as far as the currently implemented instructions are concerned. If the words updated by Hit Write and read by Look Up don't conflict, they can actually be done at the same time. If we split the Data table horizontally into four equal parts, each sub-table will still receive at most one read request or one write request at the same time when Look Up and Hit Write do not conflict. We call the split sub-table the Bank table, and its size is 256 items × 32 bits. Of course, if a Look Up and a Hit Write occur at the same time in the same Bank table, we can only solve the problem by blocking the Look Up request. However, the probability of this situation is much lower than the probability of both Look Up and Hit Write occurring at the same time, so the performance loss is not as big as the second method mentioned above. In order to support write operations such as SB, SH, etc., the write granularity of the Bank table should be as fine as bytes.

Through the above analysis process, we finally organize the Cache logically into a collection of 12 tables, as shown in Fig. 10.2.

So far, we have designed the **logical** organization of the Cache. This means that we have to further define the relationship between these logical tables and the underlying circuit implementation. Since they are tables that store information, the circuitry must be implemented as memory devices, usually in the form of a Regfile or RAM. A common design guideline is to use RAM for large capacity tables (e.g., Bank tables) and Regfile for small capacity tables (e.g., D tables). In addition

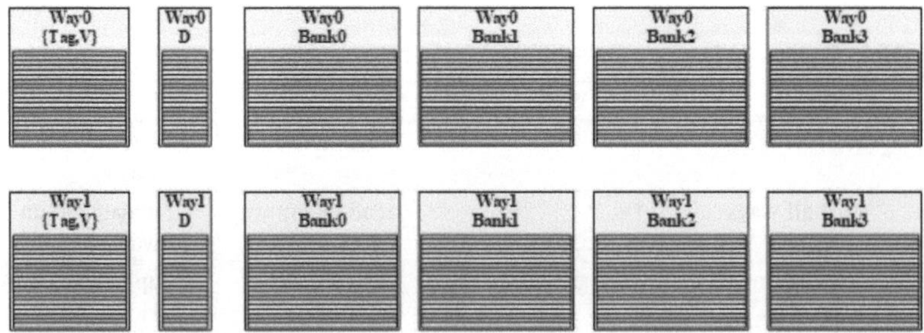

Fig. 10.2 Cache logical structure

to determining the shape of the circuitry for the underlying implementation, we need to determine the mapping between the logical tables and the Regfile or RAM. The simplest way to do this is to use a one-to-one mapping. For example, Way0's Bank0 table has a specification of 256 items × 32 bits, and supports at most one read or one write, with write granularity down to the byte. Then, we instantiate a RAM with a depth of 256 and a width of 32 bits, with a single port that supports byte-write enablement; of course, we further recommend Block RAM rather than Distributed RAM, as this solution is more effective in terms of area and timing. It should be noted that for a Cache, the mapping between logical tables and Regfiles or RAM is not one-by-one mapping. For example, two D-tables can be combined and mapped to a 256×2 Regfile, and Bank tables with the same serial numbers of Way0 and Way1 can be combined and mapped to a 256×64 RAM. For the first implementation, we suggest that readers use the simplest one-to-one mapping relationship, and then try other feasible mappings if they have the capacity to do so.

Finally, it is important to note that the practical tasks in this chapter require you to customize each of the specifications of the Cache RAM. Based on the above analysis, we determined that the RAM specifications to be customized are:

- TAGV RAM: RAM 256 × 21 (depth × width) is selected, and a total of 2 blocks are instantiated.
- DATA Bank RAM: RAM 256 × 32 (depth × width) is selected, and a total of 8 blocks are instantiated.

You can refer to Sect. 3.1 to customize the synchronous RAM with the above specifications, but please note that the DATA Bank RAM needs to be enabled for byte writing. Meanwhile, for all customized synchronous RAMs, be careful not to check "Primitives Output Register" and "Core Output Register"; otherwise, the RAM will no longer be single-cycle return, as shown in Fig. 10.3.

10.1.2.3   Cache Module Functional Boundaries

In addition to the datapaths that must be implemented in the Cache table, the datapaths that need to be implemented within the Cache module depend on which

Fig. 10.3 Attention for Cache RAM

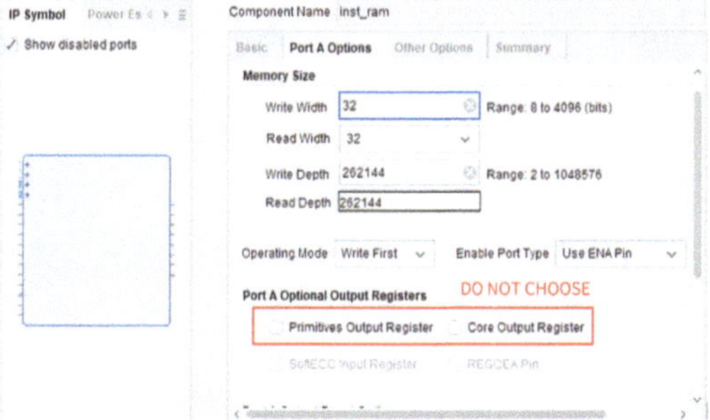

of the remaining functions of the entire read and write access to the Cache are implemented within the Cache module and which are implemented in other modules. Therefore, it is necessary to define the functional boundaries first.

As mentioned earlier, we prefer that the functional boundaries between the Cache and the CPU pipeline be consistent with the functional boundaries between the existing "SRAM-AXI-like" adapter bridges and the CPU pipeline. Simply put, the CPU pipeline sends a request to the Cache module, and the Cache module returns data or a successful write response to the CPU pipeline. Obviously, after this division, there is basically no need to change the CPU pipeline. In addition, because the current Cache access method is VIPT, the TLB module in the CPU needs to send the translated physical address to the Cache module, which will store the physical address for a period of time and then use it for Cache Tag comparison.

For example, we can define the interaction of the Cache module with the CPU pipeline according to Table 10.2.

Next, we need to consider how the functions accessed by the Cache module through the AXI bus interface should be divided. The most extreme way of partitioning is to put all the functions into the Cache module. You could think of this as replacing the existing "SRAM-like-AXI" adapter bridge with a new Cache module. However, since the name is Cache module and it contains a lot of logic for AXI protocol processing, this is obviously not an appropriate way to divide the modules. Even if the name is changed to, say, `cache_mem_module`, the module has too much internal functionality. Therefore, we propose to keep an interface conversion module from the internal access bus to the AXI bus. This converter module has several ports inside the CPU and only one AXI bus interface outside the CPU. The arbitration between the Cache module and the AXI bus interface module

Table 10.2　Interface between Cache module and CPU pipeline

Name	Bit width	Orientation	Meaning
Valid	1	IN	Indicates that the request is valid
op	1	IN	1: WRITE; 0: READ
Index	8	IN	Index field of address (addr[11:4])
Tag	20	IN	The tag formed by paddr after real-virtual address conversion is the same beat signal as index because it comes from combinational logic operation
Offset	4	IN	Offset field of the address (addr[3:0])
wstrb	4	IN	Write byte enable signal
wdata	32	IN	Write data
addr_ok	1	OUT	Address transmission for this request OK, read: address received; write: address and data received
data_ok	1	OUT	The data transfer of this request is OK, read: data return; write: data write complete
rdata	32	OUT	Read results for Cache

and the processing of the AXI protocol are all placed in this module, so that the division of functions between the Cache module and the AXI bus interface module remains simple. The Cache module sends a request to the AXI bus interface, and the AXI bus interface module returns the data or a response.

Based on the above division, it is easy to design the interaction of address, operation type, length, and other information in the request sent by the Cache module to the AXI bus interface module, which are very short and can be interacted within one cycle. What needs to be considered is how to interact with the read or write data. Since the cache line is 16 bytes long, we would like to use Burst access mode on the AXI bus for read and write accesses to minimize the interaction overhead on the request channel. The question is: do we need to define a similar Burst transfer mode for the data interaction between the Cache module and the AXI bus interface module? Or do the two interact with the 16 bytes in a single cycle? The design here depends on the starting point of our design. We feel that for the learning goals of this book, the first priority is to ensure functionality, followed by performance and, if possible, some power consumption optimizations. Therefore, our design suggestions are the following: for read operations, the AXI bus interface module returns up to 32 bits of data to the Cache module per cycle, and the Cache module fills the returned data into the Bank RAM of the Cache or returns it directly to the CPU pipeline; for write operations, the Cache module directly passes the data of a cache line to the AXI bus interface module in one cycle; for write operations, the Cache module directly passes the data of a cache line to the AXI bus interface module in one cycle. For write operations, the Cache module passes the data of a Cache line directly to the AXI Bus Interface Module in one cycle, and the AXI Bus Interface Module sets up a 16-byte internal write cache to save these numbers, and then sends them out slowly in Burst mode.

Thus, we can define the interface between the Cache module and the AXI bus interface module as per Table 10.3.

The reason why byte, half word, and word accesses are also considered in the signals defined above is to support Uncache accesses. This will be explained later in Sect. 10.2.

After the above interfaces have been defined, the existing SRAM-AXI-like bus adapter bridge module has to be adapted accordingly. Note that there are two sets of read interfaces and one set of write interfaces, the first being `rd_*` and `ret_*` for the command cache, the second being `rd_*` and `ret_*` for the data cache, and the third being `wr_*` for the data cache. Although there is an additional set of interfaces, the datapath within the bridge does not need to be adjusted significantly.

10.1.2.4 Data Paths in the Cache Module Other Than the Cache Table

Once we have delineated the functional boundaries between the Cache module and the outside world, we can finalize the design of the remaining data paths within the Cache module. In the previous subsection, we summarized the accesses to the Cache module into four types, Look Up, Hit Write, Replace, and Refill, and since

Table 10.3 Interface between Cache module and AXI bus

Name	Bit width	Orientation	Meaning
rd_req	1	OUT	Read request valid signal. Valid high
rd_type	3	OUT	Read request type. 3'b000 - byte, 3'b001 - half word, 3'b010 –word, 3'b100 –Cache line
rd_addr	32	OUT	Read request start address
rd_rdy	1	IN	Handshake signal for whether a read request can be received. Active high
ret_valid	1	IN	After returning the data valid signal. Valid high
ret_last	2	IN	The return data is the last return data corresponding to a read request
ret_data	32	IN	Read the returned data
wr_req	1	OUT	Write request valid signal. Valid high
wr_type	3	OUT	Write request type. 3'b000 - Byte, 3'b001 - Half Word, 3'b010 –word, 3'b100 –Cache line
wr_addr	32	OUT	Write request start address
wr_wstrb	4	OUT	Byte mask for write operations. Only meaningful if the write request type is 3'b000, 3'b001, 3'b010
wr_data	128	OUT	Write data
wr_rdy	1	IN	Handshake signal for whether a write request can be received. Active high. This requires that wr_rdy be set before wr_req, and that wr_req see wr_rdy before it can be set

we are designing a blocking Cache, Look Up and Replace and Refill can reuse some of the datapaths. We are designing a blocking Cache so Look Up and Repalce and Refill can multiplex some datapaths, the core parts of which are Request Buffer, Tag Compare, Data Select, Miss Buffer, and LSFR. Hit Write is a separate access from Look Up and Repalce and Refill, the core part of which is the Write Buffer.

Request Buffer is responsible to latch the information of op, index, tag, offset, wstrb, wdata, etc. as defined in Table 10.2. The output of the Request Buffer is in the same cycle as the Tag and Data information read from the RAM, since the RAM read access will span two cycles. In our blocking Cache, the Request Buffer maintains the information needed for Tag comparison and Miss processing.

The Tag Compare datapath takes the tags read from each Cache and the tags hosted in the Request Buffer(notation `reg_tag`) for equal comparison to generate the result of whether or not the hit (this does not take into account the Uncache case, if it is Uncache, must not hit). The Verilog code is shown below:

```
assign way0_hit = way0_v && (way0_tag == reg_tag);
assign way1_hit = way1_v && (way1_tag == reg_tag);
assign cache_hit = way0_hit || way1_hit;
```

The Data Select datapath selects the data information read from the two caches and obtains the results required for various access operations. The read load operation corresponding to a hit first selects one word from the data read from each Cache using address [3:2], and then selects the load result from two words based on the result of the Cache hit (Miss is not taken into account here; if it is, the final result of the load will come from the return of the AXI interface, and so it should be a triple selection logic). For the Replace operation, you only need to select the read data according to the path information decided by the replacement algorithm. The Verilog code is shown below:

```verilog
assign way0_load_word = way0_data[pa[3:2]*32 +: 32];
assign way1_load_word = way1_data[pa[3:2]*32 +: 32];

assign load_res = {32{way0_hit}} & way0_load_word
                | {32{way1_hit}} & way1_load_word;
     //if consider Miss, this should be a 3-to-1 Mux

assign replace_data = replace_way ? way1_data : way0_data;
```

The Miss Buffer is used to record information about the path in which the missing cache line is ready to be replaced, and how many rows have been returned from the AXI bus. Information such as the address required for Miss processing and whether it is a Store instruction is still maintained in the Request Buffer.

LFSR is Linear Feedback Shift Register, we use pseudo-random substitution algorithm, and LFSR will be used as a pseudo-random number source.

The Write Buffer is activated on a Hit Wire (when a Store operation finds a hit on the Cache during a Look Up), and it hosts the way, bank, index, byte write enable within the bank, and write data that the Store wants to write, and then writes to the Cache with the hosted values.

With the above five core components designed, let's go back to the input generation logic for the Cache tables. Since each table is implemented as a single-port Regfile or RAM, the access addresses, write data, and write byte enables for each table may come from multiple sources, and are therefore selected by a multiplexer before being connected to the input ports of the Regfile or RAM. Table 10.4 briefly summarizes the input sources for these ports. How the information is generated from these sources can be deduced from the procedure for accessing the Cache described in Sect. 10.1. The derivation is not complicated and is left to the reader.

```
## Warning: One or more parsing issues, see `problems()`
## for details
```

Table 10.4 Cache RAM address data generation

...1	...2	Look Up	Hit Write	Replace	Refill
{Tag, V}		address	Module Input Ports	–	Request Buffer & LFSR, Request Buffer & Miss Buffer
	write data	–	–	–	Request Buffer
D	address	–	Write Buffer	Request Buffer & LFSR	Request Buffer & Miss Buffer
	write data	–	Write Buffer	–	Request Buffer
Data	address	Module Input Ports	Write Buffer	Request Buffer & LFSR	Request Buffer & Miss Buffer
	Byte Write Enable	–	Write Buffer	–	Miss Buffer
	write data	–	Write Buffer	–	Module Input Ports

10.1.3   Design of Control Logic Inside the Cache Module

10.1.3.1   State Machine Design of the Cache Module Itself

Since the operation may result in a Cache Miss, followed by a Read request to the AXI and a Replace and Refill to the Cache RAM, we need to introduce a state machine to control this sequence of operations. Since we are implementing a blocking Cache that does not receive new requests when the Cache is Missed, the Look Up and Replace and Refill processes can be shared in a single state machine (called the main state machine). In addition, Hit Write is a separate access from Look Up and Replace and Refill, and is maintained in a separate state machine called the Write Buffer state machine.

The main state machine consists of five states; see Fig. 10.4a:

- IDLE: The Cache module is not currently in operation.
- LOOKUP: The Cache module is currently executing an operation and getting the result of its query.
- MISS: The Cache module is currently processing a missing operation Cache and is waiting for the `wr_rdy` signal from the AXI bus.
- REPLACE: The Cache line to be replaced has been read from the Cache and is waiting for an `rd_rdy` signal from the AXI bus.
- REFILL: Cache Missing Access Request has been issued and is ready/in the process of writing the missing cache line data to the Cache.

The Write Buffer state machine consists of a total of two states; see Fig. 10.4b.

- IDLE: Write Buffer There is currently no data to be written.

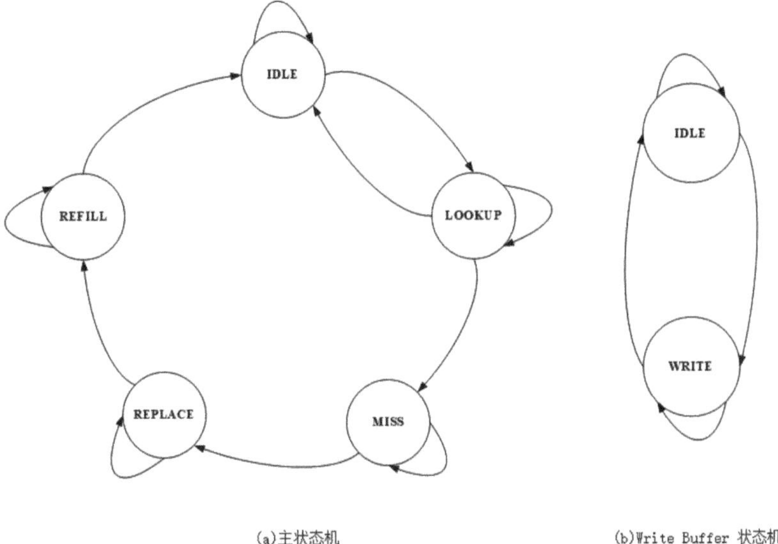

Fig. 10.4 Cache module state transition diagram

- WRITE: Write the data to be written to the Cache. When the main state machine is in LOOKUP state and the Store operation is found to hit the Cache, it triggers the Write Buffer state machine to enter the WRITE state, and at the same time, the Write Buffer registers the Index, Route, offset, write enable (which bytes of 32-bit data to write), and write data to be written by the Store.

The transition conditions between states in the main state machine are described below:

- IDLE →IDLE: For this cycle, the pipeline has no new Cache access requests, or there is a request, but it cannot be received by the Cache because the request conflicts with a Hit Write.
- IDLE →LOOKUP: In this cycle, the Cache receives a new Cache access request from the pipeline (necessarily has no conflicts with Hit Write).
- LOOKUP →IDLE: The currently processed operation is a Cache hit, and there is no new Cache access request in this pipeline, or there is a request, but it cannot be received by the Cache due to a conflict between the request and the Hit Write.
- LOOKUP →LOOKUP: the currently processed operation is a Cache hit, and the Cache receives a new Cache access request from the pipeline (there must be no conflict with Hit Write).
- LOOKUP →MISS: The currently processed operation is missing from the Cache.
- MISS →MISS: AXI bus interface module returns `wr_rdy` as 0 (note that `wr_rdy` should precede `wr_req`).

- MISS →REPLACE: The AXI bus interface module returns a `wr_rdy` of 1 (indicating that the AXI bus internal 16-byte write cache is empty to receive a `wr_req`). When `wr_rdy` is 1, a replacement read request is made to the Cache and it goes to the REPLACE state.
- REPLACE →REPLACE: The AXI bus interface module returns `rd_rdy` as 0. On the first cycle of REPLACE, it gets the data of the replaced Cache line and initiates a `wr_req` to the AXI bus interface. Since `wr_rdy` is 1, `wr_req` must be received. At the same time, a read request for the missing Cache is initiated to the AXI bus.
- REPLACE →REFILL: The `rd_rdy` returned by the AXI bus interface module is 1, indicating that the read request for the missing cache initiated on the AXI bus will be received.
- REFILL →REFILL: The last 32-bit data (`ret_valid=1&&ret_last=1`) of the missing Cache line has not been returned.
- REFILL →IDLE: missing the last 32-bit data of the Cache line (`ret_valid=1&&ret_last=1`) from the AXI bus interface module returns.

The transition conditions between states in the Write Buffer state machine are described below:

- IDLE → IDLE: For this cycle, the Write Buffer has no data to be written and the main state machine has no new Hit Write.
- IDLE →WRITE: In this cycle, the Write Buffer has no data to be written, and the main state machine finds a new Hit Write. (The primary state machine is in the LOOKUP state and a Store operation is found to hit the Cache.)
- WRITE →WRITE: In this cycle, the Write Buffer has data to be written and the main state machine finds a new Hit Write.
- WRITE →IDLE: In this cycle, the Write Buffer has data to be written and there is no new Hit Write in the main state machine.

In the state transition process of the main state machine, it is mentioned several times that there is "conflict/no conflict with Hit Write," and the conflict here is divided into two cases:

(1) The main state machine is in the LOOPUP state and finds that the Store operation hits the Cache, at this time, a new Load class Cache access request is sent from the pipeline, and the Load request is related to the Store request address in the LOOKUP state with a write-after-read.
(2) The Write Buffer state machine is in the WRITE state, that is, it is writing a pending data to the Cache, when a new Load class Cache access request is sent from the pipeline, and the Load request overlaps with the address of the pending write request in the Write Buffer. "Address Overlap" means that [3:2] of the Load request address is equal to [3:2] of the Store request address.

Both of the above cases can be considered as "Conflict with Hit Write." However, the first case can be solved by "Write Buffer to LOOKUP" without blocking the main state machine transition. For simplicity, the blocking method is recommended.

However, the second case can only be solved by blocking, either by blocking the transition of the main state machine or by blocking the transition of the Write Buffer state machine. Obviously, the implementation method given above is to block the transition of the main state machine. The reader should notice that the solution we gave for the "Hit Write conflict" sacrifices a little bit of performance.

It is also important to note that **during the "LOOKUP →LOOKUP" transition of the main state machine, care should be taken to avoid introducing a path from the RAM outputs to the RAM inputs**, i.e., when the main state machine finds a hit Cache access and receives a new Cache access request, it is important to avoid using the hit information (Tag comparison from RAM readout) to control the read enable of the new RAM. In other words, the master state machine finds a hit Cache access and receives a new Cache access request, and then avoids using the hit information (from the Tag comparison of the RAM reads) to generate the new RAM read-enable signal. Our solution is that regardless of whether a request for LOOPUP status hits the Cache or not, the control "Hit Write Conflict" and the generation of a new RAM enable should be considered as a hit. Obviously, even if it turns out not to be a hit, it will not cause an error.

Finally, as can be seen from the "MISS →REPLACE" transition in the main state machine, in the MISS state we are making sure that the AXI bus interface can receive the write of the replaced Cache line while at the same time initiating a read request to the Cache RAM to replace the Cache line. In the next cycle (REPLACE state), the data of the replaced Cache line is obtained and sent to the AXI bus interface module (which must be able to receive it at this time). At the same time, a read request for the missing Cache line can be made to the AXI bus. The reason for this setting is that we always unconditionally write the data returned by the bus interface module directly to the Cache, so this unconditional write is only safe if we make sure that the dirty data in the written location can be written back to the memory. This is actually sacrificing a little bit of performance in order to minimize the complexity of the handshake between the Cache module and the AXI bus interface module on the read return path.

Also, as a reminder to readers, for ICache, we can set `wr_rdy` constant to 1 (when the MISS state will only last one cycle), since ICache will not actually issue a `wr_req`.

10.1.4   Chip Select and Write Enable for Cache Table

The logic for generating slice select and write enable for all Cache tables is not difficult, but requires care. It is recommended that you use a table such as Table 10.5 to analyze it.

```
## Warning: One or more parsing issues, see `problems()`
## for details
```

Table 10.5 Cache RAM cs we generation

		Look Up	Hit Write	Replace	Refill
{Tag, V}	bank selection	2 ways	–	Replace way	
	write enable	2 ways	–	–	Replace way
D	bank selection	–	the way recorded by Write Buffer	Replace way	Replace way
	write enable	–	the way recorded by Write Buffer	–	Replace way
Data	bank selection	2 ways, requesting Bank	the way recorded by Write Buffer,the bank that request locate	Replace way, all banks	Replace way, all banks
	write enable	–	the way recorded by Write Buffer,the bank that request locate	–	Replace way, all banks

10.1.4.1   Request/Miss Buffer Write Enable for Each Field

The write enable of the field in the Request Buffer that records request information from the pipeline direction is the concatenation of IDLE →LOOKUP and LOOKUP →LOOKUP sets of state transition occurrence conditions of the Cache Module state machine.

The write enable of the field in the Miss Buffer that records the information about the path that the missing cache line is intended to replace (the path number generated by the LFSR for the replacement) is the condition for the MISS →REPLACE state transition of the Cache module state machine to occur.

The Miss Buffer records the write enable that has returned several data from the bus, on the one hand from the Cache module state machine RE- PLACE →REFILL state transition occurrence condition (for clearing 0) and on the other hand from the `ret_valid` input in the bus direction.

10.1.4.2   Control-Related Signals Output from the Module Interface

We will only analyze the conditions when the control-related signals output from the module interface are set to 1:

1. `addr_ok` signal in the direction of the pipeline:

   - The Cache main state machine is in IDLE.
   - Alternatively, the main Cache state machine is in LOOKUP and will undergo a "LOOKUP →LOOKUP" transition, which is categorized as follows: LOOKUP finds that the Cache is hit, and the new Cache request sent by the pipeline is a write operation; LOOKUP finds that the Cache is hit, and the new Cache request is a read operation and there is no "Hit Write conflict."

LOOKUP finds that the Cache is hit and the new Cache request is a write operation; LOOKUP finds that the Cache is hit and the new Cache request is a read operation and there is no Hit Write conflict.

2. `data_ok` signal in the direction of the pipeline:

   - The current state of the Cache is LOOKUP and the Cache is hit.
   - Alternatively, the Cache's current state is LOOKUP and it is handling a write operation.
   - Alternatively, the current state of the Cache is REFILL with `ret_valid=1`, and the number of return words recorded in the Miss Buffer is equal to [3:2] of the Cache's missing address.

3. `rd_req` signal in the direction of the AXI interface:

   - When the Cache module state machine is in the REPLACE state, the combinatorial logic sets `rd_req` to 1. In the non-RE- PLACE state, `rd_req` is naturally 0.

4. `wr_req` signal in the direction of the AXI interface:

   - Set a trigger to clear 0 during a reset. The Cache module state machine MISS →REPLACE state transition occurs with a condition that sets it to 1. Subsequently, a `wr_rdy` of 1 clears it from 1 to 0.

10.1.5 *Hardware Initialization Issues for Cache*

In the LoongArch lite instruction set, the Cache can be initialized by software. After a processor reset, the DATF and DMTM fields of CSR.CRMD are both 0. At this time, fetches and accesses are strongly out-of-order, and software can set the Tag portion of the Cache to 0 using the CACOP instruction.

In our practical task, the implementation of the CACHE instruction is placed in the last stage of the Cache experiment for the sake of implementation workload, which leads to a problem: how to ensure that the Cache has been initialized when verifying on the board while the CACHE instruction is not implemented. So in our experiment scenario, we have to consider the hardware initialization of Cache.

Cache initialization must at least set the state of Tag, V, and D of each item in the Cache to a defined invalid value. Since the Tag and V information are stored in RAM, the solution to this problem is to design a small hardware circuit to write all zeros on each line of the RAM that holds the Cache Tag and V information. There is also a lazy way to simplify the implementation of the Cache hardware initialization by using the FPGA hardware platform in the experiment. You can choose to initialize the RAM to all zeros when generating the RAM for the Cache, by checking the "Fill Remaining Memory Locations" box under the "Other Options" tab in the RAM IP Generation dialog box. Specifically, under the "Other Options" tab of the

Fig. 10.5 xilinx RAM IP
initlized all zero

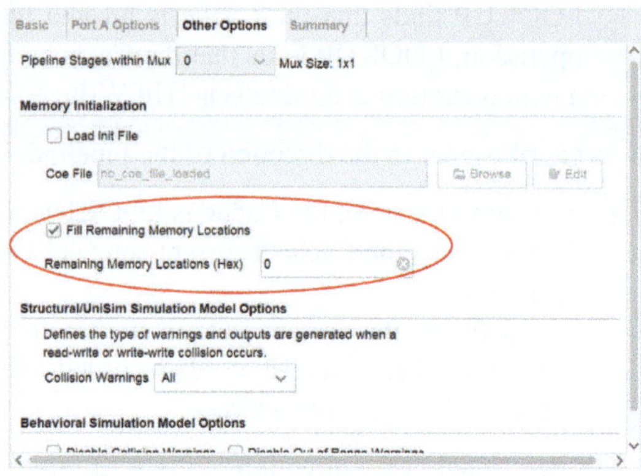

RAM IP Generation dialog box, check the "Fill Remaining Memory Locations" box
and set the initial value to 0, as shown in Fig. 10.5.

As for the D-table realized by Regfile, it can be reset directly by the reset signal.

10.2   Integrating CACHE into the CPU

The integration of the Cache module into the CPU requires a solution for its
interaction with the CPU pipeline on the one hand, and with the bus interface on
the other hand; the interaction boundary between the Cache module and the AXI
bus interface module has already been fully discussed in the previous section. In
the proposed interface division, the adjustment of the AXI bus interface module is
relatively simple, so it is not the focus of the analysis here. We will focus on the
CPU pipeline side. According to the principle of "from easy to hard," we will first
consider the case of Cache hit, then the case of Cache miss, and finally consider
how to harmonize the Uncache access and Cache access organically.

10.2.1   CPU Pipeline Adaptation for Cache Hit Scenarios

In the case of a Cache hit, in addition to being functionally correct, the most
prominent design requirement is that the execution efficiency of the pipeline is the
same as, or as close as possible to, that of the instruction RAM and the data RAM.
Originally, when fetching instructions or accessing RAM, only two clock cycles
were needed, the first cycle to send a request and the second cycle to get the data.
This means that we only need two clock cycles to read out the data in case of a
Cache hit. Considering that most of the information in the Cache is stored in the
Block RAM and the read timing behavior of the Block RAM, an intuitive design
idea is as follows: for the Look Up access to the Instruction Cache, the request is

sent from the pre-IF level, and the result is sent to the IF level; for the Look Up access to the Data Cache, the request is sent from the EX level, and the result is sent to the MF level; for the Look Up access to the Data Cache, the request is sent from the EX level, and the result is sent to the MF level. For Look Up access to Data Cache, the request is sent from EX level and the returned result is sent to MEM level.

For Cache-hit read requests, the Cache module receives and processes one request per cycle, so the waterline is fully operational. For a write request on a Cache hit, it completes the Look Up access and then enters the Write Buffer to write the Cache. In the design of the Cache module we have given, if there is a bank conflict with a read request from the current pipeline and a hit write from the Look Up or a write in the Write Buffer (the "Hit Write Conflict" mentioned earlier), the read request from the current pipeline needs to be blocked. Accordingly, the instruction corresponding to this read request is blocked in the pipeline. The control signal for this blocking is passed to the pipeline via addr_ok in the Cache module. Reviewing the design of the logic for generating the addr_ok output signal from the Cache module in Section 10.1.3, we can see that we need to take into account the type of read/write request passed to the pipeline, as well as the address of the request. Therefore, when integrating the Cache module, it is important to make sure that the read/write type and address signals sent to the Cache module from the pre-IF and EX levels do not have any combinatorial logic introduced into the addr_ok signals from the Cache module, as this could lead to combinatorial loops. As long as this error does not occur, the addr_ok signal from the Cache module will perform the pipeline control task just fine. If the EX level happens to have an instruction that is blocked due to a Cache Bank conflict, then when it finds that addr_ok is 0, it indicates that the request was not received, and therefore it will not proceed to the next level of the pipeline. This control logic for deciding whether to proceed to the next level based on addr_ok is already implemented, and we don't need to make any adjustments.

10.2.2 CPU Pipeline Adaptation for Cache Missing Cases

In the case of a missing Cache, it takes several cycles to process. Since we are implementing a simple blocking Cache, the Cache will not receive new requests during this process. This means that instructions requesting the Cache need to be blocked in the pipeline in the meantime. This is controlled by the addr_ok signal. Reviewing the logic design of the addr_ok output signal of the Cache module in the previous section, we can see that if the result of the Cache Tag Compare in this cycle is Miss, then the addr_ok of this cycle will become 0 and then the status of the Cache will be MISS, REPLACE, and REFILL in turn, during which addr_ok is still 0; until the missing cache lines are all filled into the Cache, the Cache state will return to IDLE, at which time addr_ok will change to 1. Obviously, the current design of the `addr_ok` signal ensures that when the Cache is processing a Miss, the subsequent requests to access the Cache will be blocked.

For read operations, if the Cache is missing, the corresponding instruction has to wait in the pipeline for the result to be returned, which is guaranteed by the `data_ok` output signal of the Cache module. This is guaranteed by the `data_ok` output signal of the Cache module. The principle is the same as the control of the pipeline by the `data_ok` signal when designing the bus interface, so I won't explain it here.

For write operations, if the Cache is missing, there is no need for the corresponding store instruction to wait at the MEM level of the pipeline. This is why, in the Cache module `data_ok` output signal generation logic given in Section 10.1.3; once the Cache module is processing a write operation in the LOOKUP state, `data_ok` can be set to 1 regardless of whether or not it is a hit, in order to release the store instruction at the MEM level, so that subsequent non-visit instructions can continue to move forward in the pipeline. The purpose is to release the store instruction at the MEM level so that subsequent non-store-accessing instructions can continue to flow in the pipeline.

10.2.3 Handling of Non-cached Accesses

LoongArch lite supports two types of store accesses: Coherent Cache (CC) and Strongly ordered Uncached (SUC). The most common mistake that many beginners make when implementing Cache in a CPU is to forget to handle non-cached memory accesses and put all memory accesses into Cache. For a practical CPU, non-cached memory accesses must not be missing. For example, the status and control registers of most peripherals do not have cacheable memory access. For example, if you want to create a blinking effect by alternately writing 0s and 1s to the confreg that controls an LED, then accessing the confreg with cacheable accesses will cause problems: the value in the Cache will be alternately written 0 and 1, while the register that actually controls the LED will remain unchanged.

10.2.3.1 Determination of Storage Access Type

In LoongArch instruction system, the storage access type is configured by the system software. In different address translation modes, the sources of configuration information are different: in direct address translation mode, the memory access type of fetch instruction is determined by the DATF domain of CSR.CRMD, and the memory access type of load/store instruction access is determined by the DATM domain of CSR.CRMD; in direct mapping address translation mode, the memory access type of fetch instruction or access is determined by the MAT configuration information (from the MAT domain of CSR.DMW0/1) in the direct mapping window of hit; in page-mapped address translation mode, the memory access type of page-mapped address is determined by the MAT configuration information (from the MAT domain of CSR. In direct mapping address translation mode, the type of memory access for fetch or store is determined by the MAT configuration information in the hit direct mapping window (from the MAT domain of CSR.DMW0/1); in page table mapping address translation mode, the type of memory access for fetch or store is determined by the MAT domain configuration information in the page table entry used for real-virtual address translation.

10.2.3.2 Handling Non-cached Accesses in the Cache Module

How can we handle non-cached types of storage accesses while implementing Cache? There are two things to keep in mind:

(1) All access requests to the Cache module should be able to distinguish between cacheable and non-cacheable, so it is necessary to add a 1-bit signal to the interface of the Cache module to indicate the type of storage access being requested.
(2) The implementation of non-cached access in Cache module should reuse the processing flow and datapath of Cache Miss as much as possible.

For example, after a non-cached load instruction enters the Cache module with a non-cached flag, the Cache module will not be able to access the non-cached access. The block also checks the Cache internally and then treats it as a Cache Miss without looking at the result of the Cache Tag comparison. The subsequent processing is done. Since a Cache Miss sends a store request off the bus, a non-cache naturally utilizes this process to initiate a bus request and wait for the data to be returned, except that it doesn't really need to replace a Cache line. In other words, the state machine can perform MISS $\rightarrow$ REPLACE $\rightarrow$ REFILL state transitions, but it does not send reads to the Cache, so naturally it does not generate external replacement writes. How to treat these local control signals differently? The answer is based on the type of memory access recorded in the Request Buffer.

The non-cached store instruction is also processed with a similar idea, i.e., the store instruction must be recorded as a Cache Miss, and then walks around empty, not initiating bus reads, Cache reads, or Cache writes, but just using the datapath that replaces the writes to write out the data.

In order to handle non-cached accesses, some modifications to the Cache module are required. The reason we didn't do this in one step in the first phase of the design was to avoid confusing beginners with cacheable and non-cacheable accesses.

Another area that is easily overlooked by beginners is the need to maintain a strict ordering of strongly ordered non-cached Load/Store operations. If there is a non-cached write request within the AXI interface module that has not yet received its write response, then all subsequent non-cached reads or writes (whether address-dependent or not) must be blocked until the bvalid of the non-cached write request is returned. This is to ensure correct access to I/O peripherals using non-cached access.

10.3 Cache Maintenance Instructions

Although the Cache is a software-transparent structure used in the microarchitecture domain to optimize performance, the LoongArch Instruction System Specification defines the CACOP instruction, which is used primarily for Cache initialization and maintaining Cache consistency. The CACOP instruction is defined in the LoongArch Instruction System Specification for Cache initialization and maintenance of Cache consistency.

We put the implementation of CACOP instruction in the last stage to realize, which comes from our recommended way of implementing CACOP instruction: reuse the datapath of normal access to complete the function of CACHE instruction. Therefore, the support of the normal access function of Cache is the basis for the realization of CACOP instruction. If you do not do it all by yourself, the inexperienced beginner will easily lose the whole thing.

By analyzing the definition of the CACHE instruction to be implemented in the experiment, we can summarize the following features:

1. All CACOP instructions involve modification of the Cache. The so-called Invalid operation essentially involves writing a 0 to the V (valid) bit of the corresponding cache line.
2. Some CACOP instructions perform Hit judgment on the Cache.
3. Some CACOP instructions require reading a Cache line and writing it back to memory.

The functions corresponding to each of the above features can be accomplished using the implemented datapaths:

(1) The modification of V in the cache line can be accomplished by reusing the datapath accessed by Refill.
(2) The Hit judgment of the Cache can be accomplished by reusing the Tag reading and comparing parts accessed by Look Up.
(3) The datapath accessed by Replace can be accomplished by reading the cache line and writing it back to memory.

The above three sentences have broken the "window paper" of the CACOP instruction implementation. Following this idea, the rest of the design refinement work is to correctly generate the corresponding control signals, and add a multiplexer in some positions of the datapath to add new input sources. This is not a difficult process to accomplish, and the reader is encouraged to do it on their own. To solve this problem, we can refer to the control mechanism of clearing the pipeline and re-fetching the instructions used in the previous implementation of the TLBWR command.

10.4 Tasks and Practices

After completing this chapter, readers are expected to complete the following four practical tasks:

1. To design the Cache module. See Sect. 10.4.1.
2. Integrate ICache in the CPU. See Sect. 10.4.2.
3. Integration of the DCache in the CPU. See Sect. 10.4.3.
4. Add the CACOP instruction to the CPU. See Sect. 10.4.4.

10.4.1 Practical Task 20: Cache Module Design

The requirements for this practical task are as follows:

1. Designing the Cache Module.
2. The designed Cache is verified through simulation and onboard verification using the Cache module-level verification environment.

Please refer to Sect. 2.3.1 to obtain the experimental development environment for this practical task. **The specific experimental environment is different from the previous one; it is a separate verification environment for the Cache module,** which is located in the `mycpu_env/module_verify/cache_verify/` directory. The specific directory structure and the functions of each part are summarized as follows:

```
|--cache_verify/          Cache Module-Level Validation
↪  Environment
|   |--rtl/               Source code of Cache module design and
↪  verification top module
|   |   |--cache_top.v    Cache top module
|   |--testbench/         Simulation environment
|   |   |--testbench.v    Simulation top module
|   |--run_vivado/        Vivado project running directory
|   |   |--constraints/   Vivado project design constraints
|   |   |--cache_prj/     Vivado project files directory
```

Once the lab environment is ready, please refer to the following steps to complete this practical task:

1. Complete the design and RTL writing of the Cache module, notated as cache.v. The module name needs to be named "cache," and the input/output ports, except for the clock input clk and the low-level active reset input resetn, are defined in Tables 10.2 and 10.3 in Sect. 10.1 of this chapter. The design specifications for the Cache module are two groups of 4 KB each, LRU or pseudo-random

replacement algorithm, hardware initialization recommended. Place the cache.v file in the `mycpu_env/myCPU/` directory.

2. Go to the `mycpu_env/module_verify/cache_verify/run_vivado/` `cache_prj/` directory to start the project to verify the cache. If you have not created a project in this directory, please refer to the steps described in Appendix D.2 to create a project using the `create_project.tcl` file in this directory. If necessary, please refer to Appendix D.4 to upgrade the IP core.

3. Run the simulation in the project where the Cache module is verified (click run all directly after entering the simulation interface), and carry out functional verification and debugging until the simulation test is passed.

4. Generate a bit stream file after synthesizing the implementation in the project that verifies the Cache module, and verify it on the board. (If there is no hardware experiment platform, please skip this step.)

10.4.1.1 Simulation Verification Result Judgment

Module-level validation starts at index=0, and for each index, four randomized tag and data pairs are generated. A write request is generated to write these four pairs into the cache, and then a read request is generated to read them. If no error occurs, the index is incremented and the same test is performed again until the test is completed for index==ff.

For write cache requests. The result that the validation environment expects is that the write request is issued with a Cache miss, the Cache module issues an rd request, and the validation environment returns an all 1's value (0xFFFFFFFF). The write request may trigger a replace operation, where the validating environment compares `wr_addr` and `wr_data` to the tag/data combination described above, and aborts the test if the replace value is wrong.

After all the writes have been performed, there is a read, and the validation environment does the same test. When the cache returns the result of the read operation, the validation environment will check whether the read result is the same as the result of the previous write.

In the simulation, four cache lines are generated for each index, and a PASS is printed after all operations are completed, as shown below:

```
[   2705 ns] index 00 finishd
... ... ... ...
============================================================
Test end!
----PASS!!!
```

If you find an error in the simulation, debug it and the console will print out the cause of the error. The verification environment will only check for data errors on replace and data errors on Cache read.

Fig. 10.6 Cache onboard validation of the correct effect graphic

10.4.1.2   Onboard Verification Result Judgment

The correct running effect on the board is shown in Fig. 10.6. The left two digits of the digital pipe on the board display the index value of the current test, and the test stops when the index is 0xff.

10.4.2   Practical Task 21: Integrating ICache in the CPU

This practical task requires the following tasks to be completed in addition to the completion of Practical Task 19 and Practical Task 20:

1. Integrate the Cache module completed in Practice Task 20 as an ICache into the CPU completed in Practical Task 19.
2. Modify the AXI translation bridge in the CPU to support Burst transfers.
3. Complete the functional verification of the exp21 func in a SoC verification environment using the AXI bus, requiring successful simulation and board verification.

Please refer to the method described in Sect. 2.3.1 to obtain the experimental development environment required for this practical task. The specific experimental environment is located at `mycpu_env/`, and continue to use the `soc_axi/` subdirectory.

Once the lab environment is ready, please refer to the following steps to complete this practical task:

1. Update CPU code at `mycpu_env/myCPU/`.
2. Modify the func configuration file, `mycpu_env/func/include/test_config.h`, select the configuration of `exp21`, and compile. (If you obtained the experimental development environment from the package `exp21.zip`, please skip this step.)

3. Open the gettrace project, `mycpu_env/gettrace/gettrace.xpr` (the IP core in this Vivado project was created using Vivado2019.2; if you open it with a higher version of Vivado, refer to Appendix D.4 for the IP core upgrade). Run the simulation of the gettrace project (after entering the simulation interface, click `run all` and wait for the simulation to finish), and generate a new reference trace file `golden_trace.txt` (`mycpu_env/gettrace/golden_trace.txt`). The `golden_trace.txt` will not be complete until the simulation has finished running. (If you obtained the experimental development environment from the package `exp21.zip`, please skip this step.)

4. Start the project in `mycpu_env/soc_verify/soc_axi/run_vivado/` to verify myCPU. If you have not created a project in this directory, please refer to the steps described in Appendix D.2 to create a project using the `create_project.tcl` file in this directory. If necessary, please refer to Appendix D.4 to upgrade the IP core. If there is a project in this directory that has been created by a previous practice task, you can update the file list of CPU implementations in the project by referring to the steps described in Appendix D.3 after opening the project.

5. Refer to Chap. 4 Sect. 4.4.5.2 to re-customize `inst_ram` in the project. (If you obtained the experimental development environment from the package `exp21.zip`, please skip this step.)

6. Run the simulation in the project (click `run all` directly after entering the simulation interface), and carry out the function verification until the simulation test is passed.

7. Generate a bit stream file after Synthesis and Implementation in the project, and verify it on FPGA. (Please skip this step if you don't have a hardware experiment platform.)

10.4.3   *Practical Task 22: Integrating DCache in the CPU*

This practical task requires the following work based on the CPU implemented in Practical Task 21:

1. Integrate the Cache module completed in practice task 20 as a DCache into the CPU completed in Practical Task 21.

2. Complete the functional verification of the exp22 corresponding func in a SoC verification environment using the AXI bus, requiring successful simulation and board verification.

Please refer to the method described in Sect. 2.3.1 to obtain the experimental development environment required for this practical task. The specific experimental environment is located at `mycpu_env/`, and continue to use the `soc_axi/` subdirectory.

Once the lab environment is ready, please refer to the following steps to complete this practical task:

1. Update CPU code at `mycpu_env/myCPU/`.
2. Modify the func configuration file, `mycpu_env/func/include/test_config.h`, select the configuration of `exp22`, and compile. (If you obtained the experimental development environment from the package `exp22.zip`, please skip this step.)
3. Open the gettrace project, `mycpu_env/gettrace/gettrace.xpr` (the IP core in this Vivado project was created using Vivado2019.2; if you open it with a higher version of Vivado, refer to Appendix D.4 for the IP core upgrade). Run the simulation of the gettrace project (After entering the simulation interface, click `run all` and wait for the simulation to finish), and generate a new reference trace file `golden_trace.txt` (`mycpu_env/gettrace/golden_trace.txt`). The `golden_trace.txt` will not be complete until the simulation has finished running. (If you obtained the experimental development environment from the package `exp22.zip`, please skip this step.)
4. Start the project in `mycpu_env/soc_verify/soc_axi/run_vivado/` to verify myCPU. If you have not created a project in this directory, please refer to the steps described in Appendix D.2 to create a project using the `create_project.tcl` file in this directory. If necessary, please refer to Appendix D.4 to upgrade the IP core. If there is a project in this directory that has been created by a previous practice task, you can update the file list of CPU implementations in the project by referring to the steps described in Appendix D.3 after opening the project.
5. Refer to Chap. 4 Sect. 4.4.5.2 to re-customize `inst_ram` in the project. (If you obtained the experimental development environment from the package `exp22.zip`, please skip this step.)
6. Run the simulation in the project (click `run all` directly after entering the simulation interface), and carry out the function verification until the simulation test is passed.
7. Generate a bit stream file after Synthesis and Implementation in the project, and verify it on FPGA. (Please skip this step if you don't have a hardware experiment platform.)

10.4.4   Practical Task 23: Adding a CACOP Instruction to the CPU

This practical task requires the following work based on the CPU implemented in Practical Task 22:

1. Add the CACOP instruction implementation to the CPU completed in Practice Task 22.

2. Complete the functional verification of the exp23 func in a SoC verification environment using the AXI bus, requiring successful simulation and board verification.

Please refer to the method described in Sect. 2.3.1 to obtain the experimental development environment required for this practical task. The specific experimental environment is located at mycpu_env/, and continue to use the soc_axi/ subdirectory.

Once the lab environment is ready, please refer to the following steps to complete this practical task:

1. Update CPU code at mycpu_env/myCPU/.
2. Modify the func configuration file, mycpu_env/func/include/test_config.h, select the configuration of exp23, and compile. (If you obtained the experimental development environment from the package exp23.zip, please skip this step.)
3. Open the gettrace project, mycpu_env/gettrace/gettrace.xpr (the IP core in this Vivado project was created using Vivado2019.2; if you open it with a higher version of Vivado, refer to Appendix D.4 for the IP core upgrade). Run the simulation of the gettrace project (After entering the simulation interface, click run all and wait for the simulation to finish), and generate a new reference trace file golden_trace.txt (mycpu_env/gettrace/golden_trace.txt). The golden_trace.txt will not be complete until the simulation has finished running. (If you obtained the experimental development environment from the package exp23.zip, please skip this step.)
4. Start the project in mycpu_env/soc_verify/soc_axi/run_vivado/ to verify myCPU. If you have not created a project in this directory, please refer to the steps described in Appendix D.2 to create a project using the create_project.tcl file in this directory. If necessary, please refer to Appendix D.4 to upgrade the IP core. If there is a project in this directory that has been created by a previous practice task, you can update the file list of CPU implementations in the project by referring to the steps described in Appendix D.3 after opening the project.
5. Refer to Chap. 4 Sect. 4.4.5.2 to re-customize inst_ram in the project. (If you obtained the experimental development environment from the package exp23.zip, please skip this step.)
6. Run the simulation in the project (click run all directly after entering the simulation interface), and carry out the function verification until the simulation test is passed.
7. Generate a bit stream file after Synthesis and Implementation in the project, and verify it on FPGA. (Please skip this step if you don't have a hardware experiment platform.)

Chapter 11
Advanced Experimental Environments

Through the basic experiments earlier in this book, you should have designed a processor core with basic functionality to run a simple system. Next, we can further improve and optimize this processor core. For example, we can try to run the Linux operating system on the core, optimize the circuit structure to increase the frequency of the processor on FPGAs, and implement more complex microstructures, such as superscalar, chaotic execution, branch prediction, etc., to further improve the execution efficiency of the core. Starting from this chapter, we will give some hints and suggestions to the readers around this work. In this chapter, we will introduce an advanced experimental environment to accompany this work, and in the next chapter, we will introduce some design-specific aspects.

We provide a "one-stop" experimental development environment, chiplab (Fig. 11.1), for advanced experiments. The code for this project is hosted on the code cloud (https://gitee.com/loongson-edu/). The next step is to introduce the basic components of chiplab to the readers.

11.1 Organization and Composition of the chiplab Development Environment

In the advanced experiments, we continue the verification concept used in the basic experiments, i.e., integrating a processor core into a SoC chip design and then verifying it in a system environment. Therefore, the chiplab contains the IP cores and top-level design required for the SoC chip, the top-level design of the SoC chip system verification system, the test programs required for software simulation and FPGA onboard verification, and the execution scripts for verification-related EDA tools. The entire development environment currently consists of the following seven subdirectories:

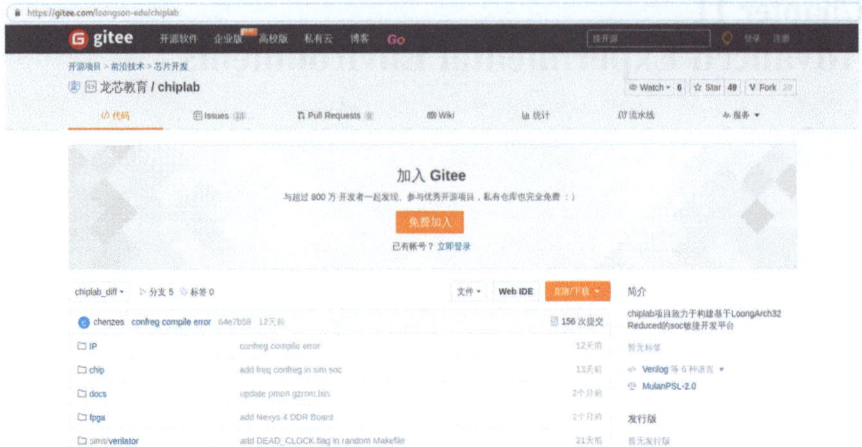

Fig. 11.1 Chiplab webpage

1. IP subdirectory: stores the source code of IP cores required for building SoCs. Typical IP cores include processor cores, on-chip Internet, memory controller, flash controller, network controller, and IP cores provided by some FPGA vendors, etc. The myCPU subdirectory is designated for storing the code of the processor core, where users need to put the RTL code of their own processor core design before starting the verification. In order to allow users to try out the whole experimental environment before their processor cores are completed, a basic version of the single-issue static five-stage flow processor core reference design, OpenLA500, is provided in the myCPU subdirectory in advance. In addition to the environment trial, the top-level interface definition of OpenLA500 is also provided as an example to be followed by the processor core of the user's design.
2. `chip` subdirectory: It stores the source code of the SoC chip top-level design for verification. Currently, four sets of top-level designs are provided, among which the sim subdirectory is for SoCs used for simulation and verification only, and the remaining subdirectories, `Baixin`, `loongson`, and `nexys4ddr`, provide reference SoCs on three kinds of FPGA development boards: Loongson's "Baixin Program FPGA Development Board," "Loongson CPU Design and Architecture Teaching Experiment System," and "Nexys4DDR," respectively. The reference SoC for simulation verification is relatively simple, only integrating non-integrable GPIO, UART, and SRAM interface function simulation modules, but including the AXI rand delay module to introduce random delays, which is useful for generating more combinations of events faster to accelerate the verification in the simulation verification. The reference SoC design for FPGA development boards is more complete, with all the integrated IP synthesized on the FPGA. Typical storage and IO devices include SPI flash, DDR3 memory interfaces, network ports, GPIOs (for controlling digital tubes, LEDs, and on/off lights), and UARTs. The processor core, together with these peripherals, can realize a

functional embedded computing system capable of running the Linux operating system and a number of other embedded real-time operating systems.

3. `software` subdirectory: stores the test cases used in the validation process. It currently contains the following subdirectories:

   - `func`: simple function test program. The func program here is the same as the func test principle used in the basic experiments, with two main differences: first, the test program is adapted to the address space division of the SoC for chiplab simulation and verification, and second, the function test points in the `func_advance` subdirectory have been added. The latter contains test points mainly for some function points required by the Linux kernel boot process. Since these function points cannot be covered by the existing func test in the basic experiment and the random instruction test environment mentioned in Sect. 11.3.2, and the cost of debugging through kernel simulation is relatively high, a targeted test program is developed. In other words, the `func_advance` subdirectory contains tests for the edge functions of the instruction set. This section will be continuously enriched, and readers of this book are welcome to submit more targeted tests to the chiplab project based on their own practical experience.
   - `dhrystone`, `coremark`: Versions ported from performance test applets such as Dhrystone, Coremark, etc. that run in bare metal environments.
   - `my_program`: a sample hello world program developed in bare metal environment. Users can port some simple C test programs to the bare metal environment based on this environment.
   - `random_boot`: boot code dedicated to random instruction testing.
   - `linux`: "Linux kernel + BusyBox" for software emulation, with emulation support to perform interactive operations in the simple shell launched. This directory holds only a pre-compiled `vmlinx`, and the Linux kernel's source code is available as a separate project at https://gitee.com/loongson-edu/la32r-Linux. Users who need to modify the kernel should download and obtain it themselves.

4. toolchains subdirectory: store some tools needed for the verification process. Including GCC toolchain, NEMU-based LA32R instruction function simulator, newlib embedded lightweight C library, etc. Initially, this directory is empty. Initially, this directory is empty; users need to download and install them according to the instructions in the README.md file in this subdirectory.

5. sims subdirectory: the working directory for software simulation verification, storing the running scripts of testbench and EDA simulation tools for software simulation verification. At present, the only supported EDA simulation tool is the open-source Verilator, and the running scripts of other open-source or commercial EDA simulation tools will be released in the future as appropriate. The contents of the simulation catalog will be further described in Sect. 11.3.

6. fpga subdirectory: the working directory for FPGA onboard verification, mainly storing FPGA development project files. Each subdirectory corresponds to a

different FPGA verification platform, and its details will be further introduced in Sect. 11.4.

7. docs subdirectory: stores the source code for the online documentation of the chiplab platform.

11.2 Recommended Use of the Chiplab Development Environment

The recommended usage given here is geared toward beginners.

In the preliminary preparation stage, users should complete all the basic functions of the processor core according to the basic experimental guide in this book and its experimental environment. The design and development of the chiplab development environment can be done before starting to complete advanced experiments with the chiplab development environment. Here, it is strongly recommended that beginners conduct a comprehensive review and organization of the designed processor core, and carry out a round of code refactoring if necessary. The reason for this recommendation is that the basic experimental part of this book artificially divides the design and development of a processor core into several phases in order to slow down the learning curve of beginners. However, the processor core is essentially an organic whole, a small system, and its local design should be put into the system for overall consideration, so as to finally get a more "suitable" overall design. During the basic experiments, the reader's knowledge and experience with processor core design is not yet sufficient to support a "proper" overall design, and it is worthwhile to review, reflect, and optimize at the point where all basic experiments have been completed and advanced experiments are about to begin.

The following steps are suggested for chiplab-based advanced experiments:

Step 1: Prepare the chiplab local development environment, including installing the GCC toolchain, LA32R-NEMU, and newlib according to `toolchains/README.md`, installing the EDA tools verilator[1] and gtkwave, and setting up the `CHIPLAB_HOME` system variable for subsequent scripts. The verilator version should be higher than 4.108; otherwise, chiplab may not work properly.

Step 2: Replace the code in the `IP/myCPU` directory with the processor core of your design. However, if you intend to use all the verification environment and tool scripts directly, make sure that the processor core top-level module names and interface definitions are strictly consistent with those in `IP/myCPU/mycpu_top.v`. The main top-level interfaces to the processor core are the clock (aclk), reset (aresetn), external interrupt input (intrpt),

---

[1]The online instructions at chiplab give a direct installation using apt, but in practice, it is recommended to follow the instructions at https://verilator.org/guide/ latest/install.html to compile and install a higher version of verilator to get a faster simulation.

and a set of AXI3 main interfaces. These three types of interfaces have been covered in the basic experiments earlier in this book, so we will not explain the principles here, but mainly explain the content related to configurability. The AXI data bit width is adjustable, and the configuration file is `chip/config-generator.mak`. In this configuration file, one (and at most one) of the two options, AXI64 or AXI128, is set to y to indicate the configuration In this configuration file, one (or more) of the AXI64 or AXI128 options is set to y to configure the AXI data bit width to be 64 or 128 bits, and both are set to n to configure the AXI data bit width to be the default of 32 bits:

```
...
AXI64=n
AXI128=n
...
```

Step 3: The processor core is fully functionally verified through software simulation. The roughly recommended steps are the following: first, pass all func tests, second, pass random instruction tests of a certain size (at least 10 million instructions is recommended), and finally, run Linux kernel boot simulation tests. During this time, performance tests such as dhrystone, coremark, etc. can be run to see if there are any significant performance design flaws.

Step 4: After passing the above software simulation, we can proceed to the FPGA onboard verification. Specifically, use the reference project in the `fpga` directory, add your own design, pass the software simulation of FPGA to make sure that there is no simple wiring error, and then go through the steps of comprehensive realization and onboard verification. Taking Linux system as an example, the board verification starts with running PMON, then load the kernel image under PMON and start the operating system, and then run other applications after entering the system.

Steps 3 and 4 above contain work that is mainly validation, which will be further developed in the next section.

11.3 Functional Verification of Software Simulation

The configuration and compilation of the test program and the configuration and compilation of the RTL design are arranged in the sims directory for software simulation and verification. Currently, there is only a runtime environment for the Verilator simulation tool, which is located in the `sims/verilator` directory. The run environment is divided into two parts, `run_prog` and `run_random`, the former is used to verify the fixed test program and the latter is used to verify the random instruction test program.

11.3.1 Fixed Test Program Validation

The fixed test programs currently supported under run_prog are:

- func: simple functional test program.
- dhrystone: Dhrystone performance test program that runs in bare metal environments.
- coremark: Coremark performance testing program that runs in bare metal environments
- my_program: user-defined functionality and performance test programs that can be run in a bare metal environment.
- linux: "Linux kernel + BusyBox" for software emulation.

The next step is to introduce the content with step-by-step instructions.

Go to the working directory sims/verilator/run_prog. First run configure.sh to configure the simulation run. You can find out all the options and instructions by running the following command:

```
$ ./configure.sh --help
```

The most basic of these options is --run software, which is used to select simulation test cases. For example, choosing to run the set of functional test points corresponding to lab15 in func, other options default, then run the following command to generate the Makefile:

```
$ ./configure.sh --run func/func_lab15
```

Once the configuration is complete, it will automatically start rtl compilation, test case compilation, and testbench compilation. If there are no errors in the compilation process, the simulation will start automatically:

```
$ make
```

The terminal prints a variety of information as shown in Fig. 11.2, of which the key is the commit information of each instruction, including the instruction PC, the modified register number, the updated value of the modified register, and the runtime. In addition, it also includes simulation data, which can be used to analyze the performance.

At the end of the run, two folders will be created in the current directory, log and obj. The following files will be created in the log directory:

- simu_trace.txt: log of command commit messages.

```
[0001256548ns] mycpu : pc = 1c07bb24,  reg = 13, val = ffffffff
[0001256550ns] mycpu : pc = 1c07bb28,  reg = 14, val = ffffffff
[0001256600ns] mycpu : pc = 1c07bb34,  reg = 26, val = 0000004f
[0001256624ns] mycpu : pc = 1c07bb38,  reg = 12, val = 00000008
[0001256646ns] mycpu : pc = 1c07bb3c,  reg = 13, val = 0000001f
[0001256662ns] mycpu : pc = 1c07bb40,  reg = 12, val = 00000030
[0001256704ns] mycpu : pc = 1c07bb44,  reg = 13, val = 4f000000
[0001256720ns] mycpu : pc = 1c07bb48,  reg = 12, val = 4f00004f
[0001256750ns] mycpu : pc = 1c07bb50,  reg = 00, val = 1c07bb54
[0001256782ns] mycpu : pc = 1c00f444,  reg = 01, val = 1c00f448
[0001256816ns] mycpu : pc = 1c00f4b0,  reg = 00, val = 1c00f4b4
[0001256832ns] mycpu : pc = 1c00f448,  reg = 23, val = 00000000
[0001256850ns] mycpu : pc = 1c00f44c,  reg = 23, val = 0000004f
[0001256906ns] mycpu : pc = 1c00f488,  reg = 13, val = 00000000
[0001256922ns] mycpu : pc = 1c00f48c,  reg = 13, val = 00000001
[0001256936ns] mycpu : pc = 1c00f490,  reg = 04, val = bfaff000
[0001256950ns] mycpu : pc = 1c00f494,  reg = 04, val = bfaff040
[0001256964ns] mycpu : pc = 1c00f498,  reg = 05, val = bfaff000
[0001256984ns] mycpu : pc = 1c00f49c,  reg = 05, val = bfaff030
[0001257040ns] mycpu : pc = 1c00f4a8,  reg = 04, val = 00000000
[0001257058ns] mycpu : pc = 1c00f4ac,  reg = 01, val = 1c00f4b0
[0001257100ns] mycpu : pc = 1c000100,  reg = 12, val = 4f000050
[0001257118ns] mycpu : pc = 1c000104,  reg = 14, val = bfb00000
[0001257134ns] mycpu : pc = 1c000108,  reg = 14, val = bfafff10
This is syscall 0x11, end
[src/cpu/cpu-exec.c,321,cpu_exec] nemu: HIT GOOD TRAP at pc = 0x1c000130
[src/cpu/cpu-exec.c,61,monitor_statistic] host time spent = 9,513,220 us
[src/cpu/cpu-exec.c,63,monitor_statistic] total guest instructions = 172,565
[src/cpu/cpu-exec.c,64,monitor_statistic] simulation frequency = 18,139 instr/s
==================================================================
test end!!
END by Syscall
total clock is 628598


==================================================================
total clock            is 628598
total instruction      is 172525
instruction per cycle  is 0.274460
simulation time        is 48.527410 s
==================================================================
```

Fig. 11.2 func run log

- `mem_trace.txt`: log of access information, including ld/st and fetch instructions.
- `uart_output.txt`: analog serial port output log.
- `uart_output.txt.real`: real serial output log.

The difference between real and analog serial ports is that the former interacts with the outside world through a real UART controller, whereas analog serial ports listen to a specified MMIO address in testbench to output the bytes to be printed one by one. `func` and bare metal test programs in the chiplab environment use analog serial ports, whereas the Linux kernel uses the real serial port.

The `obj` directory generates the compilation results of the test cases, the most critical of which is the `test.S` file, which is a decompilation of the compilation results and can be used for debugging.

The above demonstrates the operation status in the correct case. In an error situation, such as an incorrect multiplication implementation, the message shown in Fig. 11.3 will be presented.

```
[0000734960ns] mycpu : pc = 1c04e6e4,   reg = 12, val = 45b90738
[0000734962ns] mycpu : pc = 1c04e6e8,   reg = 13, val = d70d6000
[0000734964ns] mycpu : pc = 1c04e6ec,   reg = 13, val = d70d64f0
[0000734978ns] mycpu : pc = 1c04e6f0,   reg = 15, val = dd996c80

============== DUT Regs  ==============
r0(r  0): 0x00000000 ra(r  1): 0x1c00f1c8 tp(r  2): 0x00000000 sp(r  3): 0x00000000
a0(r  4): 0x1c02d3e8 a1(r  5): 0x1c02d404 a2(r  6): 0x1c02d404 a3(r  7): 0x00000000
a4(r  8): 0x00000000 a5(r  9): 0x00000000 a6(r10): 0x00000000 a7(r11): 0x00000000
t0(r12): 0x45b90738 t1(r13): 0xd70d64f0 t2(r14): 0x00001000 t3(r15): 0xdd996c80
t4(r16): 0x00000000 t5(r17): 0x18e08d00 t6(r18): 0x00000000 t7(r19): 0x00000000
t8(r20): 0x00000000  x(r21): 0x00000000 fp(r22): 0x00000000 s0(r23): 0x00000020
s1(r24): 0xbfaff050 s2(r25): 0x00000000 s3(r26): 0x0000001f s4(r27): 0x00000000
s5(r28): 0x87151984 s6(r29): 0x381fd770 s7(r30): 0x1c00f160 s8(r31): 0x00000000
pc: 0x1c04e6f0
CRMD: 0x00000028,    PRMD: 0x00000000,    EUEN: 0x00000000
ECFG: 0x00000000,   ESTAT: 0x00000000,     ERA: 0x00000000
BADV: 0x00000000,  EENTRY: 0x00000000, LLBCTL: 0x00000000
cpu.ll_bit: 0
INDEX: 0x00000000, TLBEHI: 0x00000000, TLBELO0: 0x00000000, TLBELO1: 0x00000000
ASID: 0x000a0000, TLBRENTRY: 0x00000000, DMW0: 0x00000000, DMW1: 0x00000000
***********************************************************************

============== REF Regs  ==============
r0(r  0): 0x00000000 ra(r  1): 0x1c00f1c8 tp(r  2): 0x00000000 sp(r  3): 0x00000000
a0(r  4): 0x1c02d3e8 a1(r  5): 0x1c02d404 a2(r  6): 0x1c02d404 a3(r  7): 0x00000000
a4(r  8): 0x00000000 a5(r  9): 0x00000000 a6(r10): 0x00000000 a7(r11): 0x00000000
t0(r12): 0x45b90738 t1(r13): 0xd70d64f0 t2(r14): 0x00001000 t3(r15): 0x0a20a480
t4(r16): 0x00000000 t5(r17): 0x18e08d00 t6(r18): 0x00000000 t7(r19): 0x00000000
t8(r20): 0x00000000  x(r21): 0x00000000 fp(r22): 0x00000000 s0(r23): 0x00000020
s1(r24): 0xbfaff050 s2(r25): 0x00000000 s3(r26): 0x0000001f s4(r27): 0x00000000
s5(r28): 0x87151984 s6(r29): 0x381fd770 s7(r30): 0x1c00f160 s8(r31): 0x00000000
pc: 0x1c04e6f4
Current MMU state is: MMU_DIRECT
CRMD: 0x00000028,    PRMD: 0x00000000,    EUEN: 0x00000000
ECFG: 0x00000000,   ESTAT: 0x00000000,     ERA: 0x00000000
BADV: 0x00000000,  EENTRY: 0x00000000, LLBCTL: 0x00000000
cpu.ll_bit: 0
INDEX: 0x00000000, TLBEHI: 0x00000000, TLBELO0: 0x00000000, TLBELO1: 0x00000000
ASID: 0x000a0000, TLBRENTRY: 0x00000000, DMW0: 0x00000000, DMW1: 0x00000000
***********************************************************************
i = 15
    t3 different at pc = 0x001c04e6f0, right= 0x000000000a20a480, wrong = 0x00000000dd996c80
total clock is 367483

======================================================================
```

Fig. 11.3 func compare error

The comparison in the above runtime is accomplished through the debugging assistance mechanism of differential testing (difftest). To put it simply, the LA32R-NEMU instruction simulator is run while simulating and verifying the processor core design, and the same inputs are given to both sides, and the results of both sides are compared in real time to see if they are the same, including logic registers, CSR registers, etc. If they are not the same, then it will indicate that there is an error, and then output the specific comparison information, and then stop the simulation. In order to use the differential test debugging assistant mechanism, it is necessary to adapt the interface, which has more details and is discussed in Sect. 11.3.3.

Continue to the error message shown in Fig. 11.3. The DUT is the verified RTL design and the REF is the LA32R-NEMU. The figure shows that there is a difference between the two at PC=0x1c04e6f0 and register t3 (r15). The debugger can use this as a basis to check the disassembly file and debug the processor.

When debugging complex bugs, it is not enough to rely on the above logging information alone, and it is often necessary to look at the simulation waveforms to see more comprehensive information about the processor's operation. The configuration for controlling the generation of waveform files is in the `Makefile_run` file in the current directory. It is important to note that this configuration file only affects the runtime phase of the simulation, so there is no need to recompile the RTL, testbench, etc. The Makefile_run file has three main configuration parameters related to waveform file generation—DUMP_WAVEFORM, DUMP_DELAY, and DUMP_WAVEFORM, DUMP_DELAY, and TIME_LIMIT.

- DUMP_WAVEFORM is set to 1 to enable waveform generation. However, generating waveforms for the whole simulation process will result in a very large waveform file, and it will consume a lot of time to open the waveform file. In fact, only the waveform information near the error point is enough to help debugging. For this reason, Makefile_run provides an option to generate waveforms at specific time intervals.
- DUMP_DELAY sets the start time of waveform generation. The time is obtained from the commit message of the command, for example, for the bug mentioned above, the log shows PC=0x1c04e6f0 which corresponds to 734,978 ns; it can be advanced by a certain amount of time, for example, set it to 730,000 ns.
- TIME_LIMIT configures when the simulation run ends. For the bug described above, the simulation ends when the processor runs to expose the problem, so TIME_LIMIT can be set or not. However, if the simulation does not end immediately after the processor runs to expose the problem, the TIME_LIMIT setting is necessary.

After Makefile_run is configured, make it again to take effect. At the end of the run, the simu_trace.fst wave file will be generated under log directory, which can be opened with the gtkwave:

```
$ gtkwave simu_trace.fst
```

For more complex test programs, such as the Linux kernel, the software simulation time is longer and can be effectively reduced by adjusting the configuration parameters of the simulation. In the case of the basic single-issue, five-stage pipelined processor core design provided by default in chiplab, the simulation time can be reduced by adjusting the simulation configuration parameters. With real-time comparison turned on, the Linux kernel boot emulation process can take up to 10 hours. Therefore, we need to carefully configure the parameters of the emulation to avoid wasting time. For example, if the processor kernel is already in a stable state and you want it to finish the boot process quickly and enter the command line, you can choose the following configuration:

- The -disable-trace-comp option, which disables real-time comparison, can save nearly half of the simulation time.
- The -output-uart-info option prints the serial output on the terminal and also allows input interaction through the terminal.
- disable-read-miss Option to disable alerting for accessing uninitialized address voids to avoid log swiping.

- The -disable-simu-trace option can even be used to disable the printing of command commits if there is no need to retain any debugging information at all.

The commands run with the above configuration are as follows:

```
$ ./configure.sh --run linux --disable-trace-comp
↪  --output-uart-info
                          --disable-read-miss --disable-simu-trace
$ make
```

The simulation run output information is shown in Fig. 11.4. The output on the serial port is essentially the same as the output when booting on the FPGA. The kernel boot process is reduced to about 3–4 hours with this configuration.

```
[    0.132000] UDP-Lite hash table entries: 256 (order: 0, 4096 bytes, linear)
[    0.136000] NET: Registered PF_UNIX/PF_LOCAL protocol family
[    0.148000] workingset: timestamp_bits=14 max_order=15 bucket_order=1
[    0.204000] IPMI message handler: version 39.2
[    0.204000] ipmi device interface
[    0.204000] ipmi_si: IPMI System Interface driver
[    0.204000] ipmi_si: Unable to find any System Interface(s)
[    0.244000] Serial: 8250/16550 driver, 16 ports, IRQ sharing enabled
[    0.276000] printk: console [ttyS0] disabled
[    0.276000] 1fe001e0.serial: ttyS0 at MMIO 0x1fe001e0 (irq = 18, base_baud = 2062500) is a 16550A
[    0.276000] printk: console [ttyS0] enabled
[    0.276000] printk: console [ttyS0] enabled
[    0.276000] printk: bootconsole [early0] disabled
[    0.276000] printk: bootconsole [early0] disabled
[    0.284000] ls1a-nand driver initializing
[    0.292000] dormouse! now start ls1a_nand_probe
[    0.292000] ls1a_nand : mtd struct base address is a102b800
[    0.292000] info->data_buff===================0xa115e000
[    0.300000] nand: No NAND device found
[    0.300000] ls1a-nand 1fe78000.nand: failed to scan nand
[    0.308000] ERROR dormouse: dont go to fail_free_mtd
[    0.308000] ITC MAC 10/100M Fast Ethernet Adapter driver 1.0 init
[    0.324000] libphy: Fixed MDIO Bus: probed
[    0.324000] mousedev: PS/2 mouse device common for all mice
[    0.332000] IR MCE Keyboard/mouse protocol handler initialized
[    0.332000] hid: raw HID events driver (C) Jiri Kosina
[    0.348000] NET: Registered PF_INET6 protocol family
[    0.356000] Segment Routing with IPv6
[    0.364000] sit: IPv6, IPv4 and MPLS over IPv4 tunneling driver
[    1.016000] random: fast init done
[    2.644000] Freeing unused kernel image (initmem) memory: 4352K
[    2.644000] This architecture does not have kernel memory protection.
[    2.644000] Run /init as init process
[    2.648000]   with arguments:
[    2.648000]     /init
[    2.648000]   with environment:
[    2.648000]     HOME=/
[    2.648000]     TERM=linux
can't run '/etc/init.d/rcS': No such file or directory

Please press Enter to activate this console.

/ # ls
ls
a.sh         dev          init         linuxrc      results      usr
bin          emb          lib          media        sbin         var
chroot.sh    etc          liblp32      mnt          sys
chroot1.sh   gen.sh       liblp64      proc         tmp
/ #
```

Fig. 11.4 Linux run log

11.3.2 *Random Command Test Program Validation*

General-purpose processors are required to run all types of applications without error, which means that they must strive to execute in all combinations of instruction sequences. The fixed test program verification approach is limited by both the form of expression of the test source program (to be meaningful) and the compilation process of the compiler, which makes it impossible to generate various combinations of instruction sequences quickly. To solve this problem, random generation can be used to generate a large number of legal and random instruction sequences for testing. Such a test environment is provided in the chiplab development platform, which is run in the `sims/verilator/run_random/` directory.

In order to simplify the operation process, chiplab provides the generated random command sequences, which can be downloaded by users according to the download link provided in the chiplab online documentation. There are several random command sequences stored on the server (`random_res_$(num).tar.bz2`), where `$(num)` indicates how many random command sequences are stored under the zip file. Each random instruction sequence has about 300,000 instructions, and will occupy a certain amount of storage space after decompression. Users can choose a random instruction sequence zip package of a suitable size according to the debugging status of the processor. After downloading the instruction sequence zip package, you need to copy the `RES_cluster_*` and `RES_jump_*` folders in the zip package (they indicate different generation tendencies; the jump category tends to repeat the same type of instructions, while the cluster category is a mixture of multiple types of instructions) to the `software/random_res/` directory, and then start the simulation and verification process under `run_random`. The simulation verification process under `run_random` can automatically recognize and parse these random command sequences. Note that there is no `random_res` subdirectory in the `software` directory by default, so you need to create it by yourself.

The `run_random` verification environment is similar to `run_prog`, but with `run_random` there are few configuration options, so you can adjust the configuration directly in the config-random.mak file. If you are using the default configuration, you can run `make` to start the random instruction sequence verification process.

The output message on the screen during the run to complete a set of random instruction sequences is shown in Fig. 11.5.

It can be seen that the randomized instruction sequence runs with basically no information printed. Since the default is for large-scale testing, continuous output

```
Run test RES_cluster_0000
mkdir -p logs
mkdir -p ../../log
../../output --simu-bus-delay --simu-bus-delay-random-seed 5570123 --dump-delay 0 --dump-waveform 0 --time-limit 0 --save-bp-time 0 --restore-bp-time 0 --rand-path
./ --end-pc=9c005000 --ram ram.dat > logs/run.log
Verilator Simulation Start.

Terminated at 7987102 ns.
Test exit.
Reached test end PC.
mkdir -p ../../log/RES_cluster_0000/
cp logs/* ../../log/RES_cluster_0000/
```

Fig. 11.5 Specific log messages verified for a set of random instruction sequences

to the endpoint will affect the speed of verification. The results are recorded in the generated log directory, and the pass/fail information for each group of the overall random command sequence is summarized in `log/${time}/pass.log` or `log/${time}/fail.log`. For example, if a random sequence of commands with the number `RES_cluster_0000` passes, you will see a line in the pass.log file that summarizes the logging information as follows:

```
log/RES_cluster_0000/run.log:Random_PASS
```

Additional run log information for each group of tests is recorded in the `log/RES_*/run.log` file, where RES_* corresponds to the directory name of the random instruction sequence group. For the `RES_cluster_0000` test mentioned in the above example, its complete runtime information is recorded in the `log/RES_cluster_0000/run.log` file. The specific log information for each test group is shown in Fig. 11.6. It can be seen that in order to improve the running speed, even the specific information does not record the execution of each command, but only records the initialization information and the information of TLB table entry refilling.

```
rand64 c++ version tlb refill start
Looking for this address: 1a4b4d0
Found 1 entry
=================================================================
tlb index = 000000000c000002
tlb_hi    = 0000000001a4a000
tlb_lo0   = 0000000000000000
tlb_lo1   = 0000000000141211
=================================================================
rand64 c++ version tlb refill start
Looking for this address: 59e2960
Found 1 entry
=================================================================
tlb index = 000000000c000003
tlb_hi    = 00000000059e2000
tlb_lo0   = 000000000013c711
tlb_lo1   = 0000000000000000
=================================================================
rand64 c++ version tlb refill start
Looking for this address: 1d806a0
Found 1 entry
=================================================================
tlb index = 000000000c000004
tlb_hi    = 0000000001d80000
tlb_lo0   = 0000000000142511
tlb_lo1   = 0000000000000000
=================================================================
test end!!
END by Syscall
Random_PASS
total clock is 3993544
```

Fig. 11.6 Chiplab random concrete log

```
log/RES_cluster_0000/run.log:      t2 different at pc = 0x0000000810, right= 0x00000000c8da00a0, wrong = 0x000000009fae5520
```

Fig. 11.7 Summary log messages for random command test errors

```
============== DUT Regs ==============
r0(r  0): 0x00000000 ra(r  1): 0x654000e2 tp(r  2): 0x06f6a8ac sp(r  3): 0x0161e34c
a0(r  4): 0x07853bdc a1(r  5): 0x0502a5e8 a2(r  6): 0x037e04ac a3(r  7): 0x00000000
a4(r  8): 0x079222f4 a5(r  9): 0x04cb6da3 a6(r10): 0x026abab8 a7(r11): 0x04cb6ef4
t0(r12): 0x04c1b9e8 t1(r13): 0x077f4f4c t2(r14): 0x9fae5520 t3(r15): 0x0303d530
t4(r16): 0x074470c0 t5(r17): 0x0621d848 t6(r18): 0x057082f4 t7(r19): 0x0511bd54
t8(r20): 0x06cd8b04  x(r21): 0x018351e4 fp(r22): 0x07e97914 s0(r23): 0x03b71d90
s1(r24): 0x00000010 s2(r25): 0x1d2d180c s3(r26): 0x01da76b0 s4(r27): 0x0678caf0
s5(r28): 0xfb3e4607 s6(r29): 0x03213650 s7(r30): 0x07ab3fe8 s8(r31): 0x09a455c0
pc: 0x00000810
CRMD: 0x00000030,    PRMD: 0x00000000,    EUEN: 0x00000000
ECFG: 0x00000000,   ESTAT: 0x00000000,    ERA: 0x00000000
BADV: 0x09a4b6e0, EENTRY: 0x9c004000, LLBCTL: 0x00000001
cpu.ll_bit: 1
INDEX: 0x0c000001, TLBEHI: 0x09a4a000, TLBELO0: 0x0011a113, TLBELO1: 0x00000513
ASID: 0x000a000f, TLBRENTRY: 0x1c001000, DMW0: 0x80000009, DMW1: 0xa0000019
***************************************************************************
####### INIT HERE ########
TLB_ENTRY = 32
PC: 0x0 [NEMU]: EXCEOTION TLBR
PC: 0x4 [NEMU]: EXCEOTION TLBR
r0(r  0): 0x00000000 ra(r  1): 0x654000e2 tp(r  2): 0x06f6a8ac sp(r  3): 0x0161e34c
a0(r  4): 0x07853bdc a1(r  5): 0x0502a5e8 a2(r  6): 0x037e04ac a3(r  7): 0x00000000
a4(r  8): 0x079222f4 a5(r  9): 0x04cb6da3 a6(r10): 0x026abab8 a7(r11): 0x04cb6ef4
t0(r12): 0x04c1b9e8 t1(r13): 0x077f4f4c t2(r14): 0xc8da00a0 t3(r15): 0x0303d530
t4(r16): 0x074470c0 t5(r17): 0x0621d848 t6(r18): 0x057082f4 t7(r19): 0x0511bd54
t8(r20): 0x06cd8b04  x(r21): 0x018351e4 fp(r22): 0x07e97914 s0(r23): 0x03b71d90
s1(r24): 0x00000010 s2(r25): 0x1d2d180c s3(r26): 0x01da76b0 s4(r27): 0x0678caf0
s5(r28): 0xfb3e4607 s6(r29): 0x03213650 s7(r30): 0x07ab3fe8 s8(r31): 0x09a455c0
pc: 0x00000814
Current MMU state is: MMU_TRANSLATE
CRMD: 0x00000030,    PRMD: 0x00000000,    EUEN: 0x00000000
ECFG: 0x00000000,   ESTAT: 0x003f0000,    ERA: 0x00000000
BADV: 0x09a4b6e0, EENTRY: 0x9c004000, LLBCTL: 0x00000000
cpu.ll_bit: 1
INDEX: 0x0c000001, TLBEHI: 0x09a4a000, TLBELO0: 0x0011a113, TLBELO1: 0x00000513
ASID: 0x000a000f, TLBRENTRY: 0x1c001000, DMW0: 0x80000009, DMW1: 0xa0000019
***************************************************************************
============== REF Regs ==============
i = 14
    t2 different at pc = 0x0000000810, right= 0x00000000c8da00a0, wrong = 0x000000009fae5520
total clock is 909
===========================================================
```

Fig. 11.8 Chiplab random error log concrete

Here's what the log message looks like when a random instruction sequence
is verified to be wrong. If the multiplication implementation of a processor
core has an error and it is detected during the test of the instruction sequence
RES_cluster_0000, then the test execution will result in the summary error log
message fail.log as shown in Fig. 11.7.

After seeing the error of RES_cluster_0000 in the fail.log, you can further
check log\RES_cluster_0000\run.log to get more information about the error,
and the specific log information is shown in Fig. 11.8. It can be seen that the
log information is basically the same as that of the fixed program test error. In
this example, from the output log information, it can be seen that the instruction
PC=0x810 has run wrongly, and the t2 (r14) register has been modified incorrectly.

When Debugging, we often need to know what the specific instruction that
went wrong or the context near the location of the error; in the case of a fixed
program, we usually check the disassembly file(test.S) of the test program,

```
[0]ll.w $25,$31,0x1848          00 00 00 00 00 00 00 00
[1]mod.wu $28,$ 2,$11           04 00 00 00 00 00 00 00
[2]slt $ 7,$ 1,$10              08 00 00 00 00 00 00 00
[3]jirl $24,$ 7,0x0202          0c 00 00 00 00 00 00 00
[4]nor $28,$12,$24              08 08 00 00 00 00 00 00
[5]addi.w $ 9, $11, 0xeaf       0c 08 00 00 00 00 00 00
[6]mul.w $14,$10,$25            10 08 00 00 00 00 00 00
[7]or $ 1,$24,$ 7               14 08 00 00 00 00 00 00
[8]sltui $29, $ 3, 0xa99        18 08 00 00 00 00 00 00
[9]andi $28, $13, 0xbbb         1c 08 00 00 00 00 00 00
[10]div.wu $26,$10,$15          20 08 00 00 00 00 00 00
```

Fig. 11.9 Random comment pc result

but in the case of random instruction sequences, we look at the res files that accompany each random instruction sequence. These res files record the sequence of instructions, the correct operation of the program, which can be useful for debugging purposes. Each random instruction sequence contains a set of res files, which are stored in the `random/random/RES_#####` directory. Take the previous multiplication error as an example; if you want to know what instruction is at the address PC=0x810, you can check the `comment.res` and `pc.res` files in the `random/random/RES_cluster_0000` directory, as shown in Fig. 11.9; you can see that there is a multiplication instruction at the PC address in the error report.

11.3.3   Debugging Aids Based on Differential Testing

The chiplab development platform implements a set of debugging assistance mechanisms based on dynamic differential testing by borrowing the EasyDiff design[2] from the Xiangshan team of the Institute of Computing Research, Chinese Academy of Sciences (ICCR). Differential testing is a common testing methodology in the software engineering field, the core idea of which is that two different implementations of the same specification should have the same behavior if given the same valid inputs. In processor development, the "unified specification" here refers to the instruction set architecture manual; the two implementations that follow the same specification are the test object (DUT, Design Under Test) that needs validation for correctness and the reference implementation (REF, REFerence) that has been verified for correctness; valid input refers to the instruction stream that complies with the instruction set specification. In the process of differential testing, the DUT and REF execute the same instruction stream; if the DUT implementation is correct, they should produce the same execution effect after executing each instruction. If the execution effect is different during the instruction execution, it means that there is an implementation error in the DUT. In this way, it is possible to locate bugs in the RTL code during the processor development. This idea of bug location has already been adopted in the trace comparison mechanism in the basic

---

[2] Yu, Zihao. EasyDiff-an efficient and practical framework for processor validation [EB/OL]. 2019. https://crvf2019.github.io/pdf/14.pdf.

experiments of this book, which can greatly improve the efficiency of processor design bug location, as readers have already fully experienced. However, since the behavior of the test program is simple and can be determined statically, the REF executes in advance and records the execution result of each instruction, which can be understood as a kind of static differential test. However, static differential testing is not suitable for debugging complex applications, such as the Linux kernel, because the execution trajectory of the program is affected by nondeterministic events in the DUT design and execution process, so it is necessary to implement differential testing as a dynamic one.

11.3.3.1 Fundamentals of the Dynamic Differential Testing Framework

In chiplab's dynamic differential test framework, the DUT is the RTL implementation of the CPU designed by the developer, and the REF is the LA32R-NEMU instruction set simulator, which is implemented on the basis of NEMU, a lightweight open-source instruction set simulator led by Nanjing University, and its execution effect is equivalent to that of a single-cycle CPU, as well as providing the APIs necessary for dynamic differential testing. The LA32R-NEMU instruction set simulator is used in the dynamic differential test framework in the form of a dynamic link library, whose valid input is the .bin file of the running program. The current dynamic test framework in chiplab can be used for software emulation of all fixed program tests and random instruction tests.

The running logic of the whole framework is shown in the following pseudocode:

```
while(!Simulation_Finished){
    DUT.step(1);
    DUT_state = DUT.getstate();
    REF.step(1);
    REF_state = REF.getstate();
    if (DUT_state != REF_state){
        Abort();
    }
}
```

The basic process is that whenever the DUT submits an instruction, the REF also executes an instruction (since it is executed by the simulator, it can be regarded as an instantaneous completion), and then compares the architecture state of the DUT and the REF. If there is any inconsistency, then an error will be thrown; otherwise, the simulation will continue. The default "architecture state" includes 32 general-purpose registers and the PC, and the user can also customize the value of some CSR registers for comparison, as well as customize the value of the physical address of the store instruction for comparing the access to the physical address and the value of the memory written to the store instruction.

For a DUT with superscalar design, if it submits multiple instructions in a clock cycle, the REF will execute the same number of instructions consecutively before comparing the architecture states.

The core comparison logic code for the dynamic difference test framework is located at `$CHIPLAB_HOME/sims/verilator/testbench/difftest.cpp`

Handling of Exceptions and Interrupts

All exceptions (floating point related not yet implemented) can be recognized and triggered by LA32R-NEMU itself. When using this framework, it is important to note that the DUT needs to be consistent with LA32R-NEMU on whether or not the instruction that generates the exception is committed; otherwise, the instruction streams of the DUT and LA32R-NEMU will not be synchronized when entering the exception handling. The current example in chiplab treats syscall and break as uncommitted like other normal instructions with exception flags.

The LA32R-NEMU also recognizes software interrupts on its own. However, since the behavior of LA32R-NEMU is equivalent to a single-cycle processor, the software interrupt exception flag must be attached to the next instruction that makes the soft interrupt signal high. This also means that the DUT, when facing a software interrupt, also needs to attach the interrupt exception flag to the next instruction that causes the soft interrupt signal to go high[3] (there is no such requirement in the instruction manual), or else the instruction flow of the DUT and the LA32R-NEMU cannot be synchronized.

For hardware interrupt and clock interrupt, LA32R- NEMU can only get the interrupt signal from the DUT. When the DUT submits an instruction with a clock interrupt or hardware interrupt flag, the dynamic differential test framework calls the API provided by the LA32R-NEMU to set the corresponding interrupt bit in the CSR register inside the LA32R-NEMU to ensure that the DUT and the LA32R-NEMU can trigger the hardware interrupt and clock interrupt at the same time and have the same instruction flow. NEMU can trigger hardware interrupts and clock interrupts at the same time and have the same instruction flow.

MMIO Access Processing

The LA32R-NEMU, as an instruction set emulator, is not intended to emulate the behavior of peripherals.[4] Therefore, it is necessary to solve the problem of how to continue to keep the instruction flow synchronized with that of the LA32R-NEMU when the DUT accesses a peripheral. Given that the Linux kernel provided in chiplab for emulation only considers the address space from 0 to 128 MB as the memory region, accesses to address ranges above 128 MB are treated as MMIO accesses. The DUT provides the physical address of the load instruction, which is

---

[3]One possible implementation suggestion is to make the instruction that modifies the three CSRs, CRMD, ECFG, and ESTAT, "clear the pipeline and refetch its next instruction" on writeback/commit. Please review Sect. 9.3.1 for details on how to handle this.

[4]As in the QEMU simulator.

judged by the dynamic differential test framework, and calls the API provided by the LA32R-NEMU to synchronize the DUT's accesses with the instruction stream of the LA32R-NEMU if it falls in the MMIO region. The DUT provides the physical address of the load instruction, which is judged by the dynamic differential test framework. If it falls in the MMIO region, the API provided by the LA32R-NEMU will be called to synchronize the access result of the DUT to the LA32R-NEMU. However, the store instruction whose physical address falls in the MMIO region will not be compared even if the comparison between the address of the store instruction and the value of the write value is enabled. In other words, the current dynamic differential test framework cannot check the correctness of peripheral access, and users should not believe that all functional errors can be quickly located based on the dynamic differential test framework.

TLBFILL Command Handling
In the LA32R processor, which table entry the TLBFILL instruction selects to fill in the TLB when executing is related to the specific implementation of the processor microstructure. Therefore, when executing the TLBFILL instruction, it is also necessary to synchronize the table entries selected by the DUT to the LA32R-NEMU in order to ensure the consistency of the TLB information and the subsequent access behaviors of the two. In addition, the number of TLB table entries configured in LA32R- NEMU should be consistent with that of the DUT.

Timer, Timer Read Command
As an instruction set simulator, it is difficult for LA32R-NEMU to simulate the clock running in the DUT, so for the instructions that need to read timers and timers (such as the rdcnt instruction and the CSR instruction that reads TVAL), the results of these instructions in the DUT are synchronized to LA32R-NEMU.

11.3.3.2 Adaptation of the Dynamic Differential Testing Framework

From the above introduction of the basic working principle of the dynamic differential test framework, we understand that in order to carry out comparison and synchronization, the DUT needs to pass some internal information to the dynamic differential test framework at runtime, which is realized through the DPIC interface. For the definition of the signals of the DPIC interface, please refer to the DIFFTEST User's Guide[5] in the chiplab online manual. However, the correct implementation of these signals in the DPIC interface to enable the DTF to function properly is tied to the specific design details of the processor under test, and a specific and universal design specification has not yet been concluded. However, a generalized core design guideline is that **at the moment when an instruction is committed according to the relevant signals of the DPIC interface, the effect of the instruction on the**

---

[5]https://chiplab.readthedocs.io/zh/latest/Simulation/difftest.html

processor state can also be observed precisely through other related interfaces of the DPIC, which means that it is seen neither too early nor too late. For example, in the case of a single-issue, five-stage static pipelined processor, the instruction initiates a write request to the general-purpose register stack at the same time as the WB stage commit, so the effect of the instruction modifying the general-purpose register stack will not be seen until the next clock cycle. Therefore, the commit signal through the DPIC interface should be delayed by one beat after the WB-level instruction commit signal, so that when the dynamic differential test framework sees the DifftestInstrCommit.valid=1 of the DPIC interface and starts checking, the DifftestGRegState through the DPIC interface will be able to obtain the updated register values after the DifftestGRegState is updated.

The above is just an introduction to the main functions of software simulation verification in chiplab, for a more comprehensive and detailed introduction, please refer to the relevant chapters in the online documentation of chiplab, and readers can read by themselves according to their actual needs.

11.4 FPGA Onboard Functional Verification

11.4.1 FPGA Integrated Implementation

The processor core design verified by the previous functional simulations can be further verified on FPGA boards. To this end, chiplab development environment based on the Loongson architecture teaching experiment box and the hundred core program FPGA boards and so on gives the reference design of FPGA integrated realization and its engineering environment. Taking the implementation on the Loongson test box as an example, the FPGA board is verified with Vivado software to open the `$CHIPLAB_HOME/fpga/loongson/system_run/system_run.xpr`, after adding your own processor core design code to the corresponding program in the file, and simulating to make sure there is no simple wiring error, you can realize the synthesis and test it on the board.

The above process basically does not require the user to modify the design outside the core; however, the input clock frequency of the processor core in the reference project is silently considered 33 MHz; if you feel that this frequency is not appropriate, the user needs to adjust the output clock frequency of the `clk_pll_33` xilinx IP in the FPGA reference design by themselves, and modify the clock frequency to their own expectations as shown in Fig. 11.10.

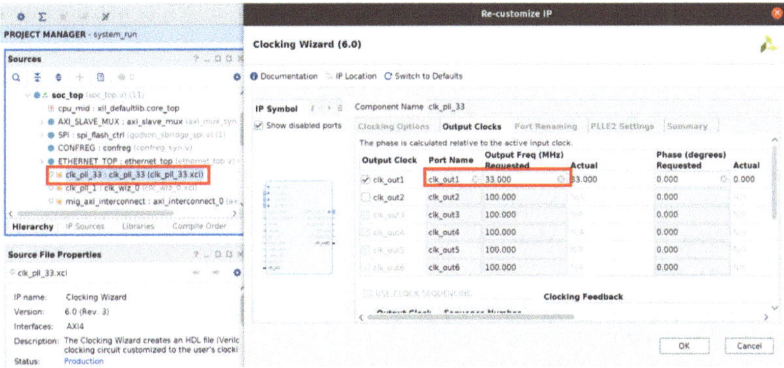

Fig. 11.10 FPGA change pll freq

11.4.2 Running Linux OS on FPGA

To run the Linux operating system on the FPGA, you need to complete the following steps in sequence:

1. Burn the PMON file (gzrom.bin) onto the pluggable SPI Flash chip.
2. Download the bit stream file.
3. Run PMON.
4. Set up a tftp server to download the kernel (vmlinux).
5. Boot the kernel.

The descriptions are expanded in turn below.

11.4.2.1 Programming Flash Chip with PMON

The easiest and most efficient way to program the Flash chip with PMON is to use a Flash burner. If you have a Flash burner, then the contents of this subsection can be skipped.

This subsection introduces a method to program the Flash chips using a Loongson experiment box. This method realizes a simple SoC on FPGA, which can realize online programming of Flash chip through serial port. During the programming process, there is no need to unplug the Flash chip, and the speed reaches 6 KB/sec.

The following tools are required for the burn-in process:

- FPGA Development Boards
- FPGA Power Cord
- FPGA Download Cable
- Flash Chip
- Serial cable
- Vivado software

- For serial port software, you can use SecureCRT for windows, or use the minicom for linux.

The specific procedure for burning is as follows:

1. The Flash chip is correctly placed on the FPGA development board.
2. The FPGA development board is connected to the computer with a download cable and a serial port cable.
3. Open Open Hardware Manager in Vivado Tools on your computer to open the serial port software.
4. Power up the FPGA board and download programmer_by_uart.bit to the FPGA as you would a normal bit stream file.
5. Serial software, baud rate selected as 230400.
6. When the serial port is properly connected, follow the prompts and enter x at the keypad to start the xmodem transfer.
7. The serial software uses xmodem mode to transfer binary files.
8. Wait for the transmission to be completed.

There are differences in the operation process of different serial port software; the following will introduce the use of minicom, SecureCRT serial port tools.

Steps to Burn Flash with minicom
Enter the command to start minicom in the terminal:

```
$ minicom -s
```

Select Serial port setup to complete the Serial device and Bps/Par/Bits settings (Fig. 11.11).

Select Filenames and paths to complete the setting of Upload directory (Fig. 11.12).

In the serial communication interface, input x on the keyboard to indicate that you are ready to accept the file. ctrl-a + s, select xmodem, select the file to be transferred in space, and enter to start the transfer; the following interface appears to indicate that the transfer is complete (Fig. 11.13).

```
+-----------------------------------------------------------------------+
|   A -      Serial Device       : /dev/ttyUSB1                          |
|   B - Lockfile Location        : /var/lock                            |
|   C -     Callin Program       :                                      |
|   D -   Callout Program        :                                      |
|   E -     Bps/Par/Bits         : 230400 5N1                            |
|   F - Hardware Flow Control    : No                                   |
|   G - Software Flow Control    : No                                   |
|                                                                       |
|       Change which setting?                                           |
+-----------------------------------------------------------------------+
```

Fig. 11.11 minicom select Serial port setup

```
A - Download directory :
B - Upload directory    : /home/fpga/pmon
C - Script directory    :
D - Script program      : runscript
E - Kermit program      :
F - Logging options

    Change which setting? █
```

Fig. 11.12 minicom select Filenames and paths

```
+-----------[xmodem upload - Press CTRL-C to quit]-----------+
|Sending gzrom.bin, 2144 blocks: Give your local XMODEM receiv|
|e command now.                                              |
|Bytes Sent: 274560     BPS:6504                             |
|                                                            |
|Transfer complete                                           |
|                                                            |
| READY: press any key to continue...█                       |
+------------------------------------------------------------+
```

Fig. 11.13 minicom transmit finish

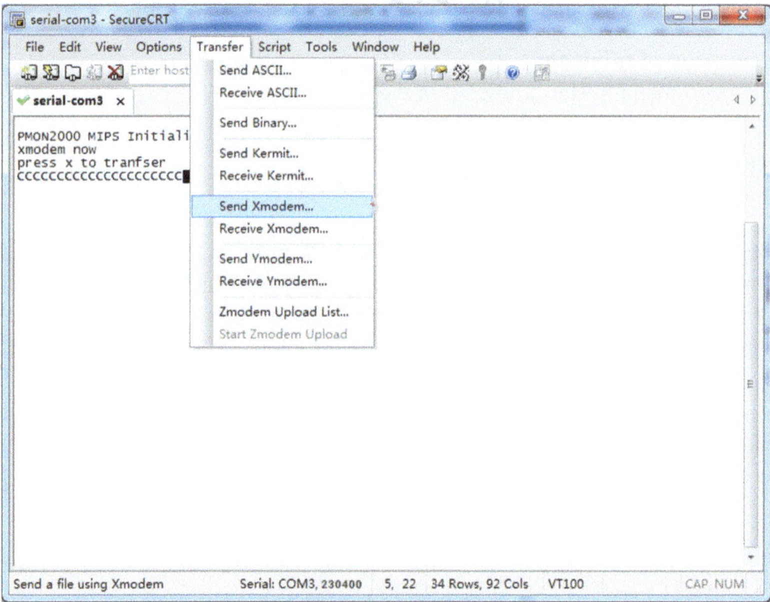

Fig. 11.14 SecureCRT Steps for Burning Flash

Steps for SecureCRT to Burn Flash

The steps to burn Flash with SecureCRT are shown in Fig. 11.14.

11.4.2.2   Download Bit Stream Files

Connect the download cable between the development board and the host computer, power up the development board, and use the "Open Hardware Manager" in the Vivado tool to download the bit file obtained from the synthesized SoC to the development board.

11.4.2.3   Running PMON

To run PMON on FPGA, you need to use the serial port for interaction. Before running PMON on the FPGA, we need to connect the serial cable between the development board and the host computer. Usually, we need to use a USB-to-serial connector on the host computer side to connect one end of the serial cable and connect the other end of the serial cable to the serial port on the FPGA development board. Open the serial communication software and set the baud rate to 115200. For the configuration of the serial communication software, the following is a brief introduction to the two commonly used software under Linux and Windows systems.

Configuration of minicom

Enter the command to start minicom in the terminal:

```
$ minicom -s
```

Select `Serial port setup` to enter the configuration interface, complete the serial port baud rate setting in the `E - Bps/Par/Bits` line, and select No in the `F - Hardware Flow Control` and `G - Software Flow Control` lines. Press Enter to return to the interface after the configuration is completed, and select `Save setup as dfl` to save the default setting. Press Enter to return and select Save setup as dfl to save the settings as default. After setup, if you start up again, you don't need the `-s` option to configure the serial port, but you need super user privilege to access the hardware device:

```
$ sudo minicom
```

SecureCRT Configuration

The SecureCRT software can be installed for free on Windows systems. Before configuring the software, make sure that the serial cables between the board and the host computer are connected. When you start the software for the first time, you will see the following interface (Fig. 11.15):

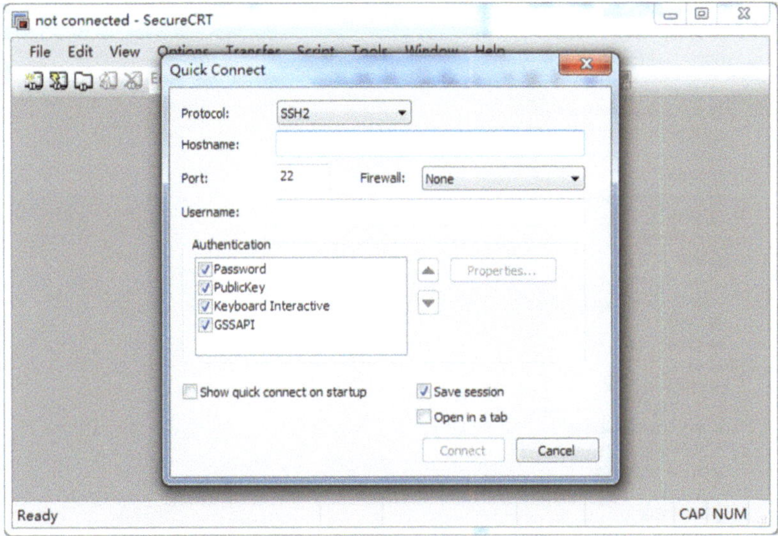

Fig. 11.15 SecureCRT boot configuration interface

Fig. 11.16 SecureCRT
configuration serial port
interface

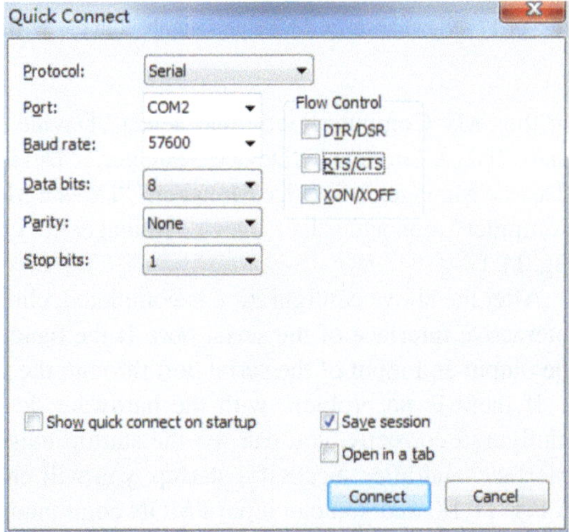

Change the drop-down selection for Protocol in the first line of the window to
`Serial`, and the configuration window interface changes to the following (Fig.
11.16):

`Baud rate` is the baud rate, according to the baud rate set in the initialization
code of the serial controller on the development board (the default baud rate in
this experimental environment is 115200). `Flow Control` on the right side of the
window are all unselected. `Port` selection should be based on the connection of the
serial port displayed on the Windows system to select the port; you can right-click

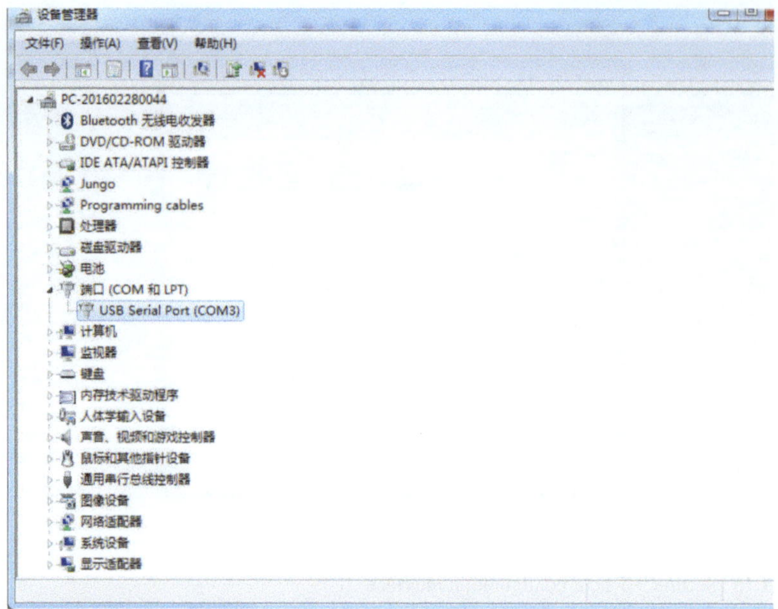

Fig. 11.17 Viewing serial device port numbers in the Windows system device manager

on the "My Computer" icon and select "Device Manager" to view the following chart: "My Computer," "Device Manager," "Device Manager," "Device Manager," "Device Manager," "Device Manager," "Device Manager." You can right-click "My Computer" icon and select "Device Manager" to check it, as shown in the following Fig. 11.17.

After the above configuration is completed, click the `connect` button to enter the interactive interface of the serial port. If the baud rate is set correctly, you can see the output and input of the serial port through the interactive interface.

If there is no problem with the hardware design and the above serial port is configured correctly, you can see the startup message of PMON in the interactive interface, and after successful startup, you will enter the PMON prompt, as shown in Fig. 11.18, and you can input PMON commands at this time.

11.4.2.4   Loading the Kernel Over the Network and Booting Under PMON

If the SoC design downloaded on the FPGA has a network interface, the core can be loaded over the network under PMON.

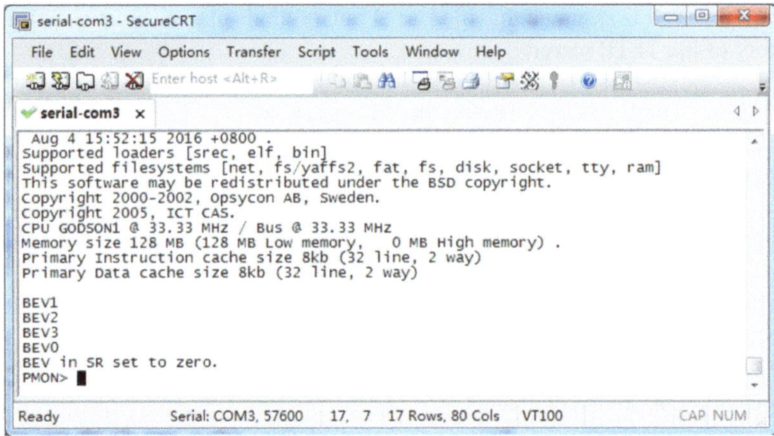

Fig. 11.18 PMON cmd line

However, before we can configure the network for download in PMON, we need to set up a TFTP service on another computer, the specific method of setting up the TFTP server depends on the operating system used on the TFTP server's computer, so please refer to the relevant information by yourself. This is done and will not be repeated in this book. The Linux kernel binaries are then uploaded to the TFTP server you have set up. The vmlinux files compiled directly are large because they contain symbol tables and other information, so you can use the strip command to streamline them:

```
$ loongarch32r-linux-gnusf-strip vmlinux
```

After the above preparations for the TFTP server side are completed, we load the kernel from the PMON command line running on the FPGA. We load the kernel from the PMON command line running on the FPGA. The first step is to configure the network. First check the IP address of the network where the TFTP server is located (assuming 10.90.50.43), and then set the IP address in PMON:

```
PMON> ifconfig dmfe0 10.90.50.44
```

After configuring the IP address, you can use the ping command to check whether the network is successfully accessed. ping command under PMON will keep sending ping packets, which can be canceled by using Ctrl + C:

```
PMON> ping 10.90.50.43
```

After confirming the network connection, the kernel binary file can be downloaded from the TFTP server and written to the memory on the FPGA board via the load command. It is assumed that the kernel binary file is placed directly in the root directory of the TFTP server:

```
PMON> load tftp://10.90.50.43/vmlinux
```

After successful loading, you can boot the kernel:

```
PMON> g console=ttyS0,115200 rdinit=sbin/init
```

In the above command, 115200 is the baud rate of the serial port; if it is set incorrectly, the serial port will display garbled code.

After running the Linux kernel successfully, the / # prompt will appear and you can use common Linux commands.

11.4.2.5   Load the Kernel and Boot from NAND Flash Under PMON

The above method of loading the kernel through the network is suitable for the scenario that the content of the operating system kernel changes frequently during the debugging period, but if the content of the operating system has been stabilized, it will be a bit cumbersome to load the kernel from the network every time. On the FPGA development board of Longchip Teaching Lab Box, 128 MB NAND Flash is integrated, which can be used as a hard disk in the system to store the binary files of the OS kernel. At the same time, the corresponding startup parameters are set in PMON; then, after each subsequent system reset, the system first loads and runs PMON from SPI Flash to complete the initialization of the processor core and peripherals, and then automatically loads the operating system kernel stored in NAND Flash into the memory, and then automatically starts the kernel at last. The whole boot process is basically a simplified version of the common computer boot process.

The following section describes how to write the operating system image to the NAND Flash chip of the FPGA development board and configure PMON:

Step 1:   Start PMON to the command line.
Step 2:   Execute the command to erase the NAND Flash chip under PMON.

```
PMON> mtd_erase /dev/mtd0r
PMON> mtd_erase /dev/mtd1r
```

Step 3:   The lab box connects to the network cable and downloads the kernel image from the TFTP server.

```
PMON> ifconfig dmfe0 XX.XX.XX.XX
PMON> devcp tftp://XX.XX.XX.XX/vmlinux /dev/mtd0
```

The XX.XX.XX.XX in the above hit is the IP address of the TFTP server. If you get stuck during the transfer, press `Ctrl + C` to cancel the transfer, and then execute the devcp command again. If the transfer still fails after canceling several times, please reset the board and try again. If the devcp command reports an error, reset the board and try again.

Step 4: Set the partition space size. Warning may appear during this process, but you can ignore it:

```
PMON> set mtdparts nand-flash:50M@0(kernel)ro,-(rootfs)
```

Step 5: Set the boot partition and parameters:

```
PMON> set al /dev/mtd0
PMON> set append "console=ttyS0,115200 rdinit=/sbin/init
  ↪  initcall_debug=1 loglevel=20"
```

After the above loading and configuration is complete, the system will automatically load the kernel from NAND Flash when FPGA reset and PMON booting done, without the need to network and enter additional boot commands.

11.5 Summary of the Chapter

This chapter introduces the advanced experimental environment around the chiplab open-source development platform. The environment provides more abundant test cases, faster software simulation and verification environment, and more convenient dynamic differential test framework. Readers can utilize these environments to discover design errors as early as possible, and lay a good foundation for successfully running Linux system in FPGA onboard verification.

Chapter 12
Advanced Design

While the previous chapter introduced the reader to the experimental environment used for advanced design, this chapter will return to the design itself and look at some processor core microarchitecture design optimization techniques, including common methods for increasing the frequency, implementation of superscalar pipelining, implementation of dynamic scheduling mechanisms, hardware transfer prediction and access optimization techniques, and implementation of multicore processors. These advanced design points are not in any particular order of implementation, so you have the flexibility to try as many of them as you like.

In the following introduction, we will continue the original writing intention of this book to emphasize the practical aspects. We will focus on classic and mature technologies in the following discussion. However, due to space constraints, we will not fully discuss the principles of each technology in this book. There are many excellent references in this area, and simply repeating their contents would not add value, so we will give some recommended learning materials here. First of all, we recommend textbooks, which are more suitable for beginners than technical reports, theses, or overviews because of the systematic nature of their contents. Three books are recommended: *Computer Architecture: A Quantitative Research Approach* by John L. Hennessy and David A. Patterson; *Computer Architecture*, a graduate textbook written by Mr. Hu Weiwu's Loongson team; and *Superscalar Processor Design* edited by Mr. Yao Yongbin. In these three books, *"Quantization"* and *"Architecture"* are typical teaching materials, which are more suitable to be used to establish a basic conceptual system, and *"Quantization"* involves a lot of knowledge points, which are directly related to the knowledge points taught in this chapter. The *"Quantization"* covers a lot of knowledge points, which are directly related to the advanced design in the first three chapters of this chapter, while the *"Architecture"* focuses on the CPU microstructure design, which is directly related to the subsequent contents of this chapter, including Chapters 6 to 12. The *"Superscalar"* book is characterized by a full analysis of the design details, which is suitable for the stage where the basic concepts of the technology are clear but

© The Author(s), under exclusive license to Springer Nature Singapore Pte Ltd. 2025
W. Wang, J. Xing, *CPU Design and Practice*,
https://doi.org/10.1007/978-981-96-6573-0_12

has no clue how to form a concrete design plan. If, after reading the textbook, you feel that it is still not specific enough, you can further consult the papers or patents cited in the textbook for each technical point. If after reading the textbook you feel that the principles are clear but you are still not sure how to implement them, then we recommend that you observe some good open-source processor core designs to get inspired. Resources in this area have become more and more abundant in recent years, such as the LA32R open-source processor core design project collected on the home page of the chiplab project and the designs made public by the winning teams of the "Loongson Cup" National Computer System Ability Cultivation Competition for College Students in previous years; also, open-source processor cores of other instruction architectures can also be used for reference. In addition, various open-source processor cores of other instruction architectures can also be used for reference.

Based on the knowledge presented in the excellent references mentioned above, this chapter then focuses on some specific design recommendations for each of the advanced design techniques.

12.1   Common Ways to Boost the Frequency

Increasing the frequency is a very direct way to improve processor performance. In the design explanation of the basic practice stage in the previous part of this book, some methods of increasing the frequency were introduced sporadically. Here, we summarize them and add some new content.

12.1.1   Balancing Latency of All Levels of the Pipeline

The processor pipeline design described in this book is implemented using synchronous circuits. Typically, the entire processor pipeline uses the same clock, so the frequency is determined by the pipeline with the longest latency. Once the number of pipeline stages and the physical implementation process have been determined, we need to fine-tune the distribution of logic among the pipeline stages based on the physically synthesized latency feedback, in order to achieve roughly the same latency for each stage as much as possible.

However, this adjustment may not be ideal. For example, if a path contains RAM read logic, the most you can do is to reduce the latency of that pipeline stage to the latency of the RAM read plus the setup time of the flip-flop, and if it's still much longer than the rest of the pipeline stage, then it's out of your reach.

12.1.2 Optimize Logic for High-Probability Events

After the optimization of balancing pipeline latency has been done to the extent possible, it is no longer a "sure thing" to increase the frequency. If we continue to keep the number of pipeline stages the same, then we need to reduce the complexity of the circuit logic by keeping only the performance-optimized processing logic for high-likelihood events for specific application scenarios.

For example, pass-forwarding is a common performance optimization technique. In order to achieve the most in pipeline execution efficiency, the result of any instruction, once computed in the pipeline, should be forwarded as early as possible to any place where it can be utilized. In addition to alignment delay, the logical delay on the network depends on two things: first, how many preemptions a single preemptive originator has to go to and how many preemptive receivers it has to go to (the more endpoints there are, the higher the load and the higher the latency) and, second, how many preemptive receivers have to select the desired preemptive value from among the preemptive data (the more sources there are and the more input ports there are to choose from, the higher the latency). When we find that a critical path has a forward network involved, we can analyze whether there are forward paths with low probability of occurring on this path in the context of the specific design, and if there are, we can experimentally check whether the overall gain after adjustment is positive. If the overall gain is positive, then the adjustment is effective.

As another example, if the delay of the multiplication circuit becomes a major component of the critical path and we analyze the input data of the multiplication in the application and find that the absolute value of the two operands of the multiplication is within 216 in a high proportion, then the size of the Wallace tree in the multiplier can then be scaled down so that the multiplier can execute in full flow if the absolute value of both operands is less than 216; otherwise, it blocks one more beat and completes the computation by iterating two rounds.

12.1.3 Trading Area and Power Consumption for Latency

In applications where performance is the top priority, frequency optimization can be achieved by trading off area and power for delay. A quintessential example in processor design is the use of a multi-entry FIFO instead of a single-entry buffer to eliminate the critical path caused by the `allowin` signal that results from pipeline backpressure. After adopting a multi-entry FIFO, we decide whether the content of the previous stage can be entered based solely on whether there is empty slot in the FIFO for the current cycle. In this way, the `allowin` signal from the output of this stage to the previous stage will not introduce the delay impact of the `allowin` signals from subsequent pipeline stages.

Another technique of trading area for latency is often used in conjunction with pipeline delay balance optimization. Suppose that a signal (usually many bits long) has to go to several physically distant locations at this level and is a critical path due to high fanout loads and long alignment delays; however, it happens that the signal has a very generous latency at the previous level; in such case, we can make multiple copies of the latch that holds the signal at this level and move some of the fanout and alignment delays to the previous level.

To give another example, in a pipeline design related to Cache access, if the first pipeline sends a request, the second Cache reads it and judges whether it is a hit or not, and if it is not a hit, it blocks the request at the second level. If the design is such that the Cache operation is only allowed to send a request to the first stage if it can enter the second stage pipeline, then there will be an excessively long path of "RAM readout $\rightarrow$ tag comparing to determine if it is a hit $\rightarrow$ allowin from the second stage to the first stage $\rightarrow$ RAM slice enable." We have to break this path, i.e., the instruction sends a request signal to the Cache in the first stage without checking whether it can enter the second stage in the next beat. Of course, this is not without cost. On one hand, it will waste power consumption, and on the other hand, since the command input from the RAM may have been modified, the operation blocked in the second stage cannot use the output data from the RAM directly in the next beat, and in order to store the content read out from the RAM in a timely manner, it is necessary to additionally use the flip-flop to save the content.

12.1.4   Further Slice and Dice Pipeline

If the application scenario of your processor is more generalized, which means that the probability distribution of various events is more balanced, then the abovementioned methods of optimizing the probabilistic event processing logic will probably not be able to achieve satisfactory performance optimization results. If you want to further increase the frequency, you have to further slice the pipeline to realize it.

However, the performance impact of pipelining is not easy to predict. Although it will increase the frequency, the execution efficiency of the pipeline will also be affected. For example, increasing the number of pipeline stages in the fetch phase causes an increase in control-related pipeline blocking cycles, and increasing the number of pipeline stages in the access phase causes an increase in load-to-use latency, which delays the execution of subsequent instructions with which there is data. Overcoming these efficiency losses due to the increase in the number of pipeline stages requires the introduction of techniques such as branch prediction and dynamic scheduling, which in turn may introduce more complex logic and lead to the emergence of new critical paths.

As to how to slice and dice, it needs to be analyzed on a design-by-design basis, and it is difficult to give a general recommendation here. However, in terms of the number of levels of the main flow waterline, the static scheduling is usually in the range of 6–8 levels, and the dynamic scheduling is usually in the range of 9–12 levels.

12.1.5 Implementation Example of Frequency Enhancement Technology

The open-source LA32R processor core "LiuYun"[1] is a static single-launch, seven-stage streaming processor core, and we will analyze some of the frequency enhancement techniques it employs.

Compared to the classic five-stage pipeline design, "Streaming Cloud" split the original Fe pipeline level into two levels, Fe1 and Fe2, and expanded the EX and MEM stages into three stages, Ex1, Ex2, and Ex3. The adjustments to the number of stages in these two pipeline sections are mainly aimed at addressing the issue of long Cache access latencies. In addition, considering that the design of "Streaming Cloud" processor core is positioned as a high-efficiency soft core on FPGA, the microstructure design makes full use of the timing characteristics of devices on FPGA. Unlike the traditional ASIC circuit implementation, the access latency of the block RAM on the FPGA is much smaller than that of the LUT. Taking advantage of this feature, Streaming adopts a pipelined function slicing method that is different from the traditional ASIC circuit implementation. For example, the I-Cache access request is deferred to the Fe1 level, so that the I-Cache RAM request comes from the flip-flop in the Fe1 flow level instead of the combinational logic for generating the nextPC in the pre-IF level, and on the other hand, the logic for comparing the tags and selecting the hit-path data after the readout of the I-Cache is placed in the Fe2 level to be completed in a single shot. Taking advantage of the timing characteristics of the RAM on the FPGA, Streaming Cloud even changes the accesses to the Tag and Data parts of the D-Cache to serial to optimize power consumption.

In the classic static five-stage pipeline, besides the Cache access, the TLB access is also a key point that affects the frequency. In order to improve the system performance, we hope to increase the TLB capacity, but this will lead to an increase in the TLB lookup access delay, which in turn affects the frequency. In order to solve this problem, Streaming Cloud introduces a two-level TLB design, i.e., a separate L1 TLB for fetch and access, and a shared L2 TLB. The L1 TLB is accessed by every instruction, while the L2 TLB is accessed only when the L1 TLB search fails, so the access latency of the former is expected to be as short as possible, while the access latency of the latter is slightly longer with little impact on performance. Based on this consideration, the L1 TLBs on the critical path are designed with a small capacity to ensure that their access latency is low, while the L2 TLBs are designed with a larger capacity and their accesses are accomplished through multiple cycles.

The "flow cloud" cuts the pipeline stage into seven stages, which improves the frequency but affects the efficiency of the pipeline (IPC). This negative effect is mainly due to the increased overhead of transfer instruction processing: firstly, the change of fetch finger from one level to two levels means that the branch-taken bubble is further increased; secondly, from the execution of the transfer instruction

---

[1] https://gitee.com/UCAS-Muradil/LiuYun

at Ex1 level to generate the misprediction cancellation signal to the update of the PC at Fe1 level, there are four levels of pipelining in between, which increases the misprediction overhead of the transfer instruction; and finally, the load-to-use delay increases from two to three beats due to the serial access of the Cache, which also increases the number of blocking cycles caused by the RAW correlation that cannot be resolved by forward passing.

The first two of the abovementioned problems of pipeline efficiency degradation triggered by pipeline splitting can be mitigated to a certain extent by enhancing the transfer prediction. For this purpose, StreamCloud adopts a BTB-based transfer prediction design. The design of transfer prediction is described later in this chapter.

12.2   Implementation of Superscalar Pipelines

Another way to increase the performance of the processor is to increase the width of the pipeline, often referred to as a superscalar pipeline if it can execute more than one command per cycle. The concern here is the continued execution of the pipeline, so it is not enough to just widen the execution pipeline in the processor but to widen it at all stages, from fetch to write (commit). Incidentally, we often refer to a superscalar pipeline as a few-launch pipeline, which, despite the use of the word "launch" in the name, does not imply that the width of the execution phase alone is sufficient to handle at most that many instructions (operations) per cycle. The number of firings refers to the width of the narrowest position in the pipeline.

Superscalar pipelined processors can be either statically or dynamically scheduled. In this section, we will start with the simpler superscalar pipeline with static scheduling. However, before we get into the specifics of superscalar, we emphasize the general architectural perspective of pipelines as front end and back end. Intuitively, we can simply think of the front end of the pipeline as being responsible for fetching and providing instructions and the back end of the pipeline as being responsible for executing instructions. Why do we emphasize such a division? It is because the so-called static and dynamic scheduling is for the execution of instructions and the front end of the pipeline in general has nothing to do with the use of static and dynamic scheduling at the back end. If a beginner wants to realize a superscalar out-of-order pipelined processor but feels that the amount of work is too large to control, then it is worthwhile to start with a superscalar sequential pipelined processor and then consider adjusting the back end to a dynamic scheduling mechanism after the design is stabilized. The front-end part of the improvement process is relatively small, and the only change is basically to match the adjustments made to the back end.

A typical superscalar sequential pipeline is divided into the phases of fetch, decode, launch, execute, and write back/submit, where fetch and decode constitute the front end and the rest constitute the back end. A typical superscalar out-of-order pipeline is divided into the phases of fetch, decode, rename and distribute, wake up and launch, execute, write back, and submit, with fetch and decode forming the front end and the rest forming the back end. Beginners may wonder why there is an extra "launch" stage in a superscalar sequential pipeline, whereas the classic static five-stage pipeline has only a decoding stage. The decoding and launching phases we mentioned here are both completed in the decoding stage in the five-stage static pipeline. Is this division a useless move just for the sake of consistency with out-of-order pipeline in context of the front end and back end? In fact, in the next analysis, we will find that in the superscalar pipeline design there are more combinations of instructions in the back end than in the single-launch pipeline, which means that the logic of control and judgment will become complex, and if we still want to complete the decoding, make relevant judgments, decide which instructions can be launched, and select the forward value in one cycle, it is very difficult to reduce the frequency. Therefore, it would be more reasonable to cut it into two pipeline stages.

12.3   Super Scalar Pipeline Front-End Design Essentials

In order to provide a theoretical peak IPC greater than 1, the front end of the superscalar pipeline needs to fetch more than one instruction per cycle. The baseline we are discussing has a separate instruction Cache, so this means that we need to consider fetching a set of instructions from the instruction Cache every cycle. This book is intended for beginners, and the set of instructions here is only considered for the PC-continuous case. Even with this simplification, the designer still has to consider these questions: How many consecutive instructions are readout per cycle? Will the set of instructions it fetches each week be allowed to span two Cache lines, and how should the RAM in the instruction Cache be sized and organized to ensure that it provides the required fetch bandwidth? Another area that is easy for the beginner to overlook is that if the PC is located in an address range that is strongly non-Cache-accessible, then strictly speaking, it can only fetch one instruction at a time from the processor core's external interface bus, not several consecutive instructions at a time.

In addition to the design considerations of the instruction Cache, the maintenance of the fetch-indicating PC should also be kept in mind. There are still three sources of PC updates: sequential fetches, branch-predicted targets, and exception entries. The front end of superscalar mainly affects the source of sequential fetches. Due to problems such as crossing Cache line boundaries and landing in non-Cache areas, the PC of a sequential fetch is not always simply added to the maximum width of the fetch finger.

Another front-end design concern is whether a set of instructions fetched from the instruction Cache can all be sent to the back end of the pipeline. This involves a problem related to transfer prediction, and it is recommended that you understand the basic mechanism of transfer prediction before reading the description here. When there is a transfer instruction that is predicted to be a jump in a group of instructions fetched in a cycle, then only that transfer instruction and the instructions before it can be sent to the back end of the pipeline.

12.3.1   Static Scheduling Superscalar Pipeline Back-End Design Points

The static scheduling mechanism is already familiar to everyone, so the design of a static scheduling back end for a superscalar pipeline needs to focus on the following points:

1. Not all execution pipelines in an N-emission superscalar pipeline need to be designed with N lines. For example, for a dual-issue pipeline, it is reasonable to have only one execution pipeline for store access, fixed-point multiply-divide, or floating-point instructions.
2. Structure-related checks at the time of launch need to take into account that commands with only a single actuating component cannot be launched more than once in a single beat.
3. The data correlation check at launch considers whether there is a RAW data correlation between multiple instructions on the same beat. An intuitive way to handle this is to block the correlated instructions in the launch phase until they are ready to launch.
4. In addition to considering that instructions cannot cross over previous instructions in the execution pipeline in which they are placed, instructions must also consider that they cannot cross over previous instructions in the order of the program in other execution pipelines; otherwise, it is not a static pipeline; and additional mechanisms need to be introduced to avoid conflicts caused by this and to ensure that exceptions are made precisely.

Finally, as a side note, for superscalar pipelines with static scheduling, double launch is basically the "sweet spot" of the structural design, and triple issue can be considered if there is a more advanced process technology or a higher performance requirement. If a larger pipeline width is used, the static scheduling mechanism itself may be limited to obtain an effective output/input ratio.

If the above discussion is still a bit abstract, interested readers are encouraged to look at the Cortex-A53 processor core from Arm and the U74 processor core from SiFive for a better intuitive understanding. If you would like to look at a specific design to gain a deeper understanding, consider looking at the LA32R static triple-launch open-source processor core "Sa".[2]

12.4   Implementation of the Dynamic Scheduling Mechanism

Dynamic scheduling mechanisms can further exploit the instruction-level parallelism that exists in a program and improve the execution efficiency of the pipeline.

---

[2]https://gitee.com/MJ_Wang/spinal-loong-arch-core

Almost all high-performance general-purpose processors today are using dynamic scheduling. Many architecture enthusiasts would like to design a processor with a superscalar out-of-order pipeline. A real problem is how to control the complexity of the design. Almost every enthusiast who has attempted this challenge knows the "classic" superscalar out-of-order processor, Alpha21264, and even knows the details of its architecture. However, please do not assume it shall be easy to imitate since it's an "old" processor from the 1990s. For example, its completely out-of-order launch-execute and speculative write-back memory access parts will be a nightmare for beginner to debug; the renaming mechanism based on CAM-type mapping tables looks elegant, but it turns out that the frequency degradation is extremely high during the FPGA synthesis stage after the simulation has been basically stable, while unfortunately nothing can be done to solve it by then. If your goal is to design a CPU that runs, rather than just staying in the C simulator and RTL functional simulation phase, then some basic advice for beginners is:

1. The design should first establish an overall understanding of the topic, and the most effective way for beginners is to learn from references. As mentioned above, Alpha21264 is slightly complicated for beginners. Lonngson 1[3] is a good entry-level reference design, and it is well connected with the Tomasulo algorithm introduced in the book *"Quantization."* If the reader is able to break through the detailed form of the Tomasulo algorithm introduced in Quantization and develops an understanding of the essence of renaming, then it is worthwhile to considering the MIPS R10000 processor[4] and the Loongson 2.[5] The basic structure of these two processors is close to the modern superscalar out-of-order pipeline processors, and their design is not too complex.

2. At the beginning, we should not rush to the design of out-of-order launch of access instructions in one step, so that we can focus on rename, wake up, launch, and submit, which are the newly introduced aspects of the dynamic scheduling mechanism, and focus on building out a back-end framework for dynamic scheduling.

3. If you are experiencing difficulties in practice due to the interweaving of superscalar and dynamic scheduling, you might as well start with a backend that has a renaming, issuing, writing back, and committing width of just 1. After the implementation and debugging, consider increasing the launch width moderately by using a distributed launch queue with one execution pipeline corresponding to one launch queue/retention battle, and then consider increasing the widths of rename and submit moderately. In this process, design one transfer instruction

---

[3]Recommended reference paper: Architectural design of the Lonngson 1 processor. Journal of Computer Science. 2003,26(4):385–396.

[4]Recommended reference paper: The MIPS R10000 Superscalar Microprocessor. IEEE Micro. 1996, 16(2):28–41.

[5]Recommended reference paper: Design and performance analysis of the Lonngson 2 processor. Computer Research and Development. Computer Research and Development. 2006,43(6):959–966; for renaming, we recommend reading Chapter 7 in the book Computer Architecture.

to be launched and executed per cycle and design only one access execution pipeline.

4. The implementation of a dynamic scheduling mechanism results in centralized structures such as rename tables, launch queues/reserve stations, ROBs, etc., which may be read or written to at the same time by multiple instructions from multiple locations (usually different pipeline stages). Readers may have concerns about how to implement such a centralized structure, unless they already utilized the centralized structure such as scoreboard to manage the instructions after they are launched during the implementation of the superscalar sequential pipelines. This is because most people are used to breakdown functionality according to the pipeline stages. Our suggestion is that since the structure is centralized it should be maintained in a single module and interacts with different pipeline stages.

The above suggestions hopefully can help beginners to avoid some detours in scheduling and top-level design. Below, we will share some experiences on design implementation details. These experiences are specific and detailed, so it may be more valuable to the readers with practical experience.

12.4.1   Key Points for Dynamic Scheduling Mechanism Design

12.4.1.1   Register Renaming

Register renaming essentially follows the process:

- Assign a physical storage to each destination (logical) register (rename registers).
- Until the logical register is renamed again, the operations on the logical register (listen-ready, read, write) are directed to the renamed register.
- Upon the instruction is committed, the processor (logic) state is updated according to the content of renamed register.

There are several ways to implement register renaming. According to how the allocated physical storage is organized, it can be divided into two categories: logical register file + rename register file and unified physical register file. In the first category, according to the specific location of the rename register stack, it can be divided into renaming to reservation station and renaming to ROB, and in the second category, according to the organization of the Register Allocation Table (RAT), it can be divided into RAM-type RAT and CAM-type RAT.

The main operations of the register renaming mechanism based on a unified physical register file during the renaming stage are:

- Use the logical register number of the source operand to look up RAT and find and record the corresponding physical register number for each source operand.
- Use the logical register number of the destination operand to look up RAT and find and record the physical register number, which is used to release the physical register back to the free state in the subsequent stages.

- Search the free physical register table, allocate a new physical register for each valid destination register, and update the RAT with this new mapping relationship.
- The dependency among multiple instructions undergoing register renaming in the same cycle must also be correctly handled, meaning that the RAT information seen by the subsequent instruction must consider all updates to the RAT by all instructions in the same cycle.

In addition to lookup and update operations during the renaming stage, RAT also undergoes status updates during instruction write-back and commit and rollback operations for mispredicted branches or exceptions. Here, I would like to highlight the overall state rollback.

The update of the renaming mapping relationship occurs during the renaming stage, and instructions at this stage may be in a speculative execution state. If an instruction is canceled later in its execution, the renaming mapping relationship it modified must be restored to its state before the modification. Therefore, when an instruction undergoes renaming, the renaming mapping relationship seen before its update must be saved as a checkpoint for subsequent restoration.

For the implementation of "logical register file + renaming register file," if the misprediction of branches is also canceled at commit time, then the rollback of instructions only occurs at commit time. At this point, the latest values of all logical registers are only in the logical register file, and the so-called rollback requires almost no action.

For the implementation of a unified physical register file, it is much more complex, as the RAT needs to be rolled back. The core issue here is how to organize and maintain the RAT's checkpoints. For RAM-type RATs, each checkpoint is the entire RAT, which consumes a lot of resources, limiting the number of checkpoints. When there is not enough checkpoint resource, it will stall the pipeline. Designs to address the high-resource consumption of checkpoints include canceling branches only at commit time and using replay to roll back mapping relationships one by one. For CAM-type RATs, each checkpoint only needs to record which physical registers correspond to the latest mapping (a bit vector the same length as the number of physical register file entries), which consumes less resources and allows for more checkpoints. However, CAM-type RATs are not perfect either, as the size of the RAT table is related to the number of physical registers. When the number of physical register file entries is large, the timing for lookup and update becomes more critical.

12.4.1.2 Issue Queue

The content discussed in this section mainly targets issue queue that reads registers after issue, but most of the content is also applicable to the issue queue that reads registers before issue. Surrounding the issue queue, there are several main operations, dispatch, wake up, and select, as well as the closely related regread operation after issue.

Dispatch Operation: The dispatch operation primarily involves selecting several empty items from the issue queue and writing the renamed instruction information into them. The issues that designers need to consider include:

- Does the peak capacity of one-cycle write-in need to be equal to the renaming width?
- How to implement the circuit that finds multiple empty items, especially when using a non-compressed queue structure?

Wake-Up Operation: The wake-up operation essentially maintains the ready state of each source operand in every item of the issue queue. In addition to the instructions already in the queue that need to be maintained by listening to the instruction write-back information, do not forget that the instructions that are entering the queue should also see the information about the results being written back in this cycle in a timely manner.

Select Operation: The select operation involves choosing several items for dispatch from all instructions whose source operands are ready. The main structural design issues include:

- Is it random selection or selection of the earliest entry?
- How to determine the earliest entry?
- Is the queue structure compressed or non-compressed?
- If it is a non-compressed queue, how to maintain age information?
- For queues with a dispatch width greater than 1, how to select multiple instructions?

The design choices for regread will also impact the design of the dispatch queue, and the issues to consider include:

- Is the number of read ports of the physical register file equal to or less than the maximum demand?
- When there is a read-write conflict in the physical register file in the same cycle, can the new value being written be read out?

In addition to the above function-related design issues, let's talk about several timing-related issues. The timing path for selecting several items based on age during the select operation and then dispatching them is already relatively long. Also, because the physical register file typically requires an entire cycle to read due to the large number of items and read ports, regread and select are usually completed in two pipeline stages. This also means that the execution operations can start at the earliest in the next stage of regread. Instructions from wake up to the start of execution need to go through several cycles, so notifying the issue queue for wake up after the instruction produces results will increase the execution delay between related instructions, so it is necessary to notify the issue queue earlier. In order for single-cycle instructions with data dependency to execute back-to-back, it is necessary to complete select and wake up within one cycle, which is one of the classic key paths of superscalar out-of-order processors. These issues introduce two design philosophies: centralized dispatch queue and distributed dispatch queue.

The former has high queue resource utilization, but timing convergence is difficult, while the latter has relatively easy timing convergence but the balance of resources between queues is a challenge.

12.4.1.3 Execution Stage

Superscalar processors require multiple functional units to execute multiple instructions within a single cycle. Due to the presence of long-latency operations, the execution bandwidth of a processor is typically higher than the renaming bandwidth to compensate for the wasted execution bandwidth caused by waiting for source operands to become ready. The style of functional units is related to the style of renaming registers and issue queues. For instance, if general-purpose registers and floating-point registers are renamed using different physical register files, then fixed-point and floating-point computation units are suitable to be placed in separate functional units. Conversely, if a unified physical register file renames both general-purpose and floating-point registers simultaneously, then fixed-point and floating-point computation units can be integrated into the same functional unit. When the number of execution pipelines is not very large, each functional unit typically has an exclusive register file write port. However, there may be computational units with different execution latencies within the same functional unit, which may compete for the register file write port, necessitating the design of an arbitration mechanism.

Similar to static pipelines, the execution stage of a superscalar out-of-order processor also requires a "forwarding" network for results. Since registers have been renamed, it is only necessary to compare whether the physical register numbers are the same when taking values from the forwarding network, regardless of the location of the result source. The forwarding network can theoretically be a fully connected structure, but the area overhead is too large, so its size needs to be controlled. Based on the trade-off between area, timing investment, and performance output, some paths are deleted in the fully connected network.

12.4.1.4 Commit Stage

A reminder for beginners: The commit phase is far from just retiring instructions from the Reorder Buffer (ROB). Even the act of retiring from the ROB involves finding a number of contiguous instructions from the ROB head that are ready to commit; do not exceed the maximum number of instructions that can be committed per cycle, all in write-back state; and are not marked as exceptions and then performing the commit operations in sequence. Alternatively, if the ROB head is an instruction marked with an exception, then only that instruction is committed. However, there are usually further restrictions, such as the maximum number of branch instructions that can be committed per cycle or the maximum number of memory access instructions, which require precise control of the ROB head movement.

At commit stage, register renaming operations mainly include:

- Committed instructions need to release the physical registers corresponding to their recorded old pdest and record them into the phy reg free list.
- Committed instructions need to adjust the correspondence between their own new pdest and logic registers to be architecturally visible.
- If a committed instruction is marked with an exception, then the above three operations are not performed. Instead, the renaming mapping relationship table is restored to the nearest architectural state, and all physical registers allocated to instructions in the ROB are released and recorded into the phy reg free list.

The commit stage is also related to store memory operations. Committed store instructions notify the store queue or store buffer that they can begin the memory write operation for that store instruction.

12.4.2   RTL Implementation of Common Circuit Structures in Dynamic Scheduling

To implement the dynamic scheduling design from the previous section, it is necessary to realize structures such as the renaming table and reservation stations in the circuit, which can be a significant challenge for many beginners. The difficulty arises from the need to convert the data structures and operational processes described in natural language in the design scheme into datapaths and state machines in the circuit.

Let's start with the renaming table. Suppose it has 64 entries, each with fields such as state, valid, and name. In the circuit, each field of each entry corresponds to individual flip-flops. However, it is not recommended to try to understand it as a regfile or FIFO, because the read and write logic of this table is more complex than that of a regfile or FIFO and simplifying it may be very difficult to design the circuit. The only way is to carefully consider each write enable and the data written to each flip-flop. When reading a certain field of an entry from the table, the focus is on generating the read address index value or the decoded read address vector and then explicitly constructing the multiplexer circuit for the readout.

As for the renaming phase, selecting two idle entries from the renaming table: Many beginners want to use a for loop to implement this selection process, but this is not the way of thinking in circuit design. The way of thinking in circuit design is to generate a 64-bit bit vector by determining whether the state of each entry is equal to empty and then find the first 1 from the 0th bit and the first 1 from the 63rd bit of this bit vector. The subscript of these two leading_one_bit positions corresponds to the index values of the idle entries.

As for the renaming phase, selecting two idle entries from the renaming table: Many beginners want to use a for loop to implement this selection process, but this is not the way of thinking in circuit design. The way of thinking in circuit design is to generate a 64-bit bit vector by determining whether the state of each entry is equal to empty and then find the first 1 from the 0th bit and the first 1 from the 63rd bit of this bit vector. The subscript of these two leading_one_bit locations corresponds to the index values of the idle entries.

Let's talk about the action of listening to the result bus in the reservation station to determine whether the source operands are ready. In fact, from the circuit point of view, each source operand in the reservation station corresponds to two fields, prdy and psrc[5:0], which correspond to flip-flops in the circuit. To maintain prdy, you need to look at two signals on the result bus: res_valid and res_pdst[5:0]. When the `res_valid=1 && (res_pdest==psrc)` is met, set prdy to 1. Each prdy uses its own corresponding psrc.

Finally, let's look at how to implement the selection of an instruction with all source operands ready from the reservation station. We logically AND the valid and prdy bits in each entry of the reservation station to form a 1-bit result, which indicates that this entry has an instruction and all source operands are ready. Assuming the reservation station has 16 entries, we get a 16-bit-long bit vector. Thus, finding the position of an instruction with all source operands ready in the reservation station becomes finding the subscript of the first 1 in this 16-bit bit vector. The specific circuit can refer to the circuit for selecting idle entries in the renaming process.

12.5   Hardware Branch Prediction Technology

When we use techniques such as deepening the pipeline and superscalar technology to improve processor performance, branch instructions once again become one of the main factors limiting performance gains due to control hazards they cause. To address this issue, hardware branch prediction technology has been developed. Hardware branch prediction technology is extensively discussed in many textbooks, focusing mostly on the construction of predictors and prediction algorithms. Therefore, we do not intend to elaborate on this aspect here but rather focus on introducing some design adjustments that need to be considered after the pipeline introduces hardware branch prediction technology.

12.5.1 Hardware Branch Prediction Pipeline Design Framework

The term "framework" is used here because the content we discuss is not targeted at a specific hardware prediction algorithm. In other words, once you have designed this framework within the pipeline, you can flexibly adjust the type and implementation size of the prediction algorithm according to specific requirements for performance, area, and power consumption, without the need for significant adjustments to the main structure of the pipeline.

Hardware branch prediction design in the pipeline includes the following four aspects:

1. During the fetch or decode stage, use information such as PC, branch history, and instruction type to query various branch predictors to obtain the direction and target of the branch prediction and update the fetch PC in a timely manner using the predicted direction and target.
2. Pass the predicted direction and target information, along with the branch instruction, down the pipeline. If some predictors are designed to update their content using the prediction results on the speculative execution path, it is also necessary to carry information for restoring the predictor content in case of a prediction error.
3. In the execution stage, calculate the actual direction and target of the branch instruction and compare it with the predicted direction and target of the instruction. If they are consistent, the front end of the pipeline continues to fetch instructions normally; if not, cancel all instructions following the branch instruction in the pipeline, and then refetch instructions according to the actual direction and target.
4. For predictors that are maintained only with the actual execution information of the branch instruction, pass the execution results of the branch instruction to the predictor regardless of whether the prediction is correct or not. For predictors that can be updated in a timely manner with prediction results, when a branch prediction is incorrect, pass the information carried for restoring the predictor content to the predictor.

We assume that beginners will directly adopt existing research results of branch predictors or make only minor adjustments. For point 1 and point 4 mentioned above, a paper introducing the design of branch predictors will definitely elaborate on it, and the paper should not be difficult to understand.

As for point 2, the operation of passing prediction information and other information down the pipeline, from a design perspective, as long as you clearly define what information needs to be passed, the rest of the process is no more difficult than passing the PC or instruction code.

Let's discuss the instruction cancellation operation on the mispredicted path in point 3. If it is a statically scheduled pipeline, it is not difficult to implement. Because the execution and prediction correctness determination of the branch instruction have a delay comparable to the delay of addition and subtraction operations, so they can be completed at the first stage of the execution stage. For a single-issue static pipeline, the instructions following the branch instruction have not yet started to execute, so there is no need to worry about them modifying the machine state, and they can be directly invalidated. For a multi-issue static pipeline, it is only necessary to process the other instructions at the same level as the branch instruction. Instructions that are in sequence before the branch instruction do not need to be processed, only the instructions that are in sequence after it need to be canceled.

If it is a dynamically scheduled pipeline, the instruction cancellation operation on the mispredicted path in point 3 will take more efforts. Because instructions are executed out of order at this time, it is impossible to judge the front and back relationship of an instruction in the program order through the physical location relationship of the instruction in the pipeline Cache. Therefore, an additional mechanism is needed to identify this program order relationship in order to decide whether to cancel. The simplest implementation method is to wait until the branch instruction is committed to decide whether to cancel. At this time, the branch instruction is the oldest instruction in the pipeline, and all other instructions in the pipeline are behind it in program order, so the branch misprediction cancellation can directly clear the entire pipeline. The biggest disadvantage of this method is that the cost required by branch misprediction is too large. So we think of another approach, using the sequence relationship maintained by the ROB for judgment. Each instruction in the out-of-order execution state carries its index number in the ROB. By comparing this index number with the ROB index number of the mispredicted branch instruction, the program order relationship between the two can be judged. When the ROB is a shift queue, the two index numbers can be directly compared; when the ROB is a pointer queue, considering the two index numbers together with the ROB head pointer can also obtain the result. However, we feel that there are too many entries in the ROB, and the number of bits in the index number is relatively large, which leads to a high cost of comparison. Considering that the instruction stream is not all branch instructions under normal circumstances and when performing branch misprediction cancellation, we are only concerned with the sequence relationship of the instruction relative to the branch. So further, we introduce the design of the branch queue (BRQ). This queue, like the ROB, is also an ordered queue. When the branch instruction enters the ROB, it also enters the BRQ, and when the branch instruction exits from the ROB, it exits from the BRQ synchronously. All instructions that enter the out-of-order execution phase will check which branch instruction corresponds to the basic block they are in and then carry the BRQ index number of that branch instruction. In this way, when performing branch misprediction cancellation operations, it is only necessary to compare the BRQ index number carried by the instruction with the BRQ index number of the mispredicted branch instruction.

In fact, the role of BRQ is not limited to this. Do you still remember the prediction information that was passed down from the fetch and decode stages and the content of the branch predictor that was rolled back? In a dynamically scheduled pipeline, you will find that there needs to be a place to store them, because they may not be able to be issued immediately after renaming. When there is a BRQ, this information is naturally placed in the BRQ.

In fact, in a dynamically scheduled pipeline, if the implementation method of "physical register file + renaming mapping table" is adopted, then the state maintenance of the RAT when a branch misprediction occurs is also a design point that needs to be focused on. The specific design needs to be determined in combination with whether the RAT uses CAM-type or RAM-type.

12.5.2 A Lightweight Branch Predictor Design Specification

The design of the branch predictor is the focal point of addition of branch prediction mechanisms to the entire pipeline. Here, a design specification for a branch predictor is provided for entry-level general processors, serving as a reference for beginners.

The entire branch predictor module adopts a combined prediction strategy, which specifically includes four predictors:

1. Branch Target Buffer (BTB): Directly obtains the branch's jump target based on PC information, used to eliminate the taken branch fetch bubble caused by a large number of fetch and decode pipeline stages. It typically uses a CAM structure with 4~16 entries, usually storing taken branch instructions and direct jump instructions.
2. Branch History Table (BHT): Used to predict the jump direction of conditional branch instructions. It employs 2-bit saturating counters and has a global history length of about 32 bits. The specific algorithm can use tagless lightweight BHTs such as the Gshare predictor or the Bi-Mode predictor. The number of entries does not exceed 4K.
3. Return Address Stack (RAS): Used to predict indirect jump instructions (in the LoongArch architecture, for example, jirl $r0, $r1, 0). The number of entries is between 6 and 8.
4. Indirect Jump Target Cache (IJTC): Used to predict indirect jump instructions other than indirect return jump instructions. It can adopt a structure similar to the Gshare predictor, except that the table queried after XORing the PC and global history does not store a two-bit saturating counter but rather the predicted target of the indirect jump. The number of entries does not exceed 256.

Among the four predictors mentioned, the access latency of the BTB should be controlled within one cycle; otherwise, it cannot completely eliminate the taken branch fetch bubble. The access latency of BHT, RAS, and IJTC can be slightly longer. Generally speaking, their access latency is the same as the latency of fetching instruction codes from the front end. Since the BHT, RAS, and IJTC predictors are aimed at different types of branch instructions, only after the instruction is fetched (and it is known whether it is a branch instruction and what specific type of branch instruction it is) can the corresponding prediction result be selected. Moreover, since the BHT only predicts the jump direction of conditional branches, if it predicts a jump, the jump target actually needs to be calculated through the PC plus the offset in the instruction code. Therefore, considering these two characteristics, there is not much benefit in having too fast access for BHT, RAS, and IJTC.

Among the four predictors, the BTB can be considered the first level of prediction, while BHT, RAS, and IJTC can be considered the second level of prediction. If the prediction result of the BTB is inconsistent with the result of the second level, the BTB's prediction will be canceled, and the instruction fetch will be reinitiated using the second level's prediction result.

12.6 Memory Access Optimization Techniques

The structural design of general-purpose processors emphasizes balance. If we adopt performance optimization techniques, such as deep pipelining, superscalar, dynamic scheduling, and branch prediction, but do not focus on optimizing memory access, then although significant performance gains can be achieved when there is a Cache hit within the core, the performance improvement benefits will quickly decline for real-world application loads. Therefore, we mention some memory access optimization techniques here.

12.6.1 Store Buffer

In the previous discussions on Cache design, we have already touched upon the store buffer. However, to control the complexity of the Cache design, we only implemented a single-store buffer that holds store operations when there is a Cache hit, and the priority of the store buffer writing to the Cache is higher than that of subsequent load operations. In fact, all these limitations can be broken. You can expand the store buffer to multiple entries, and store operations can enter the store buffer regardless of whether they hit in the Cache or not. Assuming that the store buffer stores write data with a width of 8 bytes, different store operations falling within the same 8-byte range can be combined in the store buffer. If there is a Cache bank conflict between the writes in the store buffer and subsequent load operations, the write from the store buffer can be delayed to give priority to the load operation to avoid pipeline stalls. To some extent, you can regard the store buffer as a special L0-level Cache. All load instructions must not only check the L1 Cache but also synchronously query the store buffer. If there is a hit in the store buffer, the value must be fetched from it.

All the aforementioned enhancements to the functionality of the store buffer are primarily designed to allow store operations that cause a Level 1 (L1) Cache miss to leave the main pipeline as soon as possible to prevent blockage of the main pipeline. However, keen readers should have noticed that relying solely on the store buffer cannot achieve this, because the Cache is still blocking; when it is handling a miss, subsequent memory access operations are still blocked.

12.6.2 Non-blocking Cache

The difference between a non-blocking Cache and a blocking Cache lies in whether it blocks subsequent memory access operations when a Cache miss occurs. The large-capacity store buffer design mentioned earlier can only truly exert its effectiveness with the support of a non-blocking Cache.

The design philosophy of a non-blocking Cache is simple: when a Cache miss is detected, store the Cache miss request in another place for slow processing, and quickly clear the main path to the Cache to accept new memory access operations. The core structure that holds these Cache miss requests is commonly referred to in the industry as Miss Status Handling Registers (MSHR).

The specific implementation details of MSHR can actually be determined by the structural designer, but regardless of the changes the most basic elements include:

1. State: Whether this MSHR is valid, whether the request to access the next level of storage has been sent, which bus transaction it corresponds to, whether the data from the next level of storage has been returned, how much has been returned, and whether the returned data should be filled into the Cache. These states all need to be maintained.
2. Address: One MSHR usually corresponds to a Cache block. The address of this Cache block must be recorded. Generally, this address is a physical address.
3. Data: Generally speaking, since so much effort has been made to avoid blocking the memory access path, the data returned from the lower level of storage is temporarily stored in the data field of the MSHR. This makes it possible to fill the Cache at the appropriate time to avoid blocking subsequent memory access operations as much as possible. Moreover, if the MSHR can store data, store operations that miss the Cache can leave the store buffer in advance, writing the value into the MSHR, as long as it is marked to ensure that the old value returned from the next level of storage is not overwritten.

Some designs also record information related to the corresponding memory access instruction in the MSHR (such as the destination register number, operation type, block offset address, etc.). However, this information does not necessarily have to be stored in the MSHR. The advantage of recording it in the MSHR is that when the data is returned the result of the instruction can be written back directly based on this information, but this means there is an additional source of write-back. Moreover, the number of miss instructions corresponding to one MSHR varies, and the resource usage is not very flexible.

The most common mistake beginners make when implementing a non-blocking Cache is sending two memory access requests to the next level of storage for the same Cache block, which leads to chaos soon after. In summary, during the design phase, it is crucial to pay attention to the situation where instructions with Cache misses request a new entry in the MSHR. It must be proven that when this signal is valid, the corresponding Cache block is indeed not within the processor core. Please note the wording here: "not within the processor core," not simply "not in the Cache." All data that is waiting in various Caches, queues, and has not yet been written to the Cache but has been determined to be written to the Cache, as well as all data that has been replaced from the Cache and is on the way but has not yet been seen by the next level of storage, and all data whose status has changed during the period from when you generate this miss signal to when you use this miss signal to generate the write enable for writing into the MSHR all need to be checked.

After you have implemented a non-blocking Cache with great effort, you will suddenly discover a problem: it seems that only store misses do not block subsequent memory access instructions, and if it is a load miss, it still blocks the main pipeline. After thinking about it, you find that there is no other way but to transform the entire pipeline into dynamic scheduling. After you have changed the pipeline to dynamic scheduling, you start to think about making the issuance of memory access operations out of order as well. As the saying goes, "insatiable as humans are, having obtained one thing, they immediately desire another."

12.6.3   Out-of-Order Memory Access Execution

Out-of-order memory access execution does not necessarily mean that memory access instructions must be issued out of order.

If your dynamic scheduling window is not large, with only a few dozen entries, allowing memory access instructions to be issued in order, while permitting later-issued hitting loads to write back before earlier-issued missing loads, can already provide a certain performance improvement.

If you want to be more aggressive, you can strictly issue store operations in order and restrict load operations from being issued before their preceding store operations, with the rest being issued out of order. This can further enhance performance without a significant increase in implementation complexity.

The most aggressive approach is to impose no restrictions on the issuance of memory access operations; as long as the operands are ready, they can be issued, which is complete out-of-order issuance. At this point, there are two main issues that designers need to consider how to address:

1. Since issuance is out of order, the order in which stores enter the store queue after going through the memory access pipeline does not reflect the program order of the stores. Similarly, for a load instruction to find the most recent store to the same address in program order from the store queue, it cannot be directly obtained from the physical location relationship. Therefore, it is necessary to maintain the order relationship between all memory access instructions.

2. For two instructions with store-load data dependency, if the load instruction is issued and executed before the store instruction, how to ensure that the load definitely retrieves the correct value? This is divided into two situations: when the store instruction enters the store queue and the load instruction has not yet written back in the load queue and when the load instruction has already written back. Both situations must be handled correctly.

12.6.4   Multi-level Cache

The write buffer, non-blocking Cache, and out-of-order memory access technologies mentioned earlier all focus on scheduling, overlapping the Cache miss latency of previous instructions with the execution of subsequent instructions to improve pipeline efficiency. The multi-level Cache strategy discussed here is aimed directly at reducing the latency of Cache misses. If you are only experimenting on the FPGA platform introduced in this book, you can skip this section. This is because the implementation frequency of a normally structured processor core on this FPGA platform is almost never higher than 200 MHz, while the FPGA's own DDR3 controller hardcore can reach the rate of DDR3-800. The frequencies are inverted, so the benefit of implementing a multi-level Cache is not as great as simply increasing the capacity of the L1 Cache until the access path to the L1 Cache becomes the timing-critical path.

If you want to implement a multi-level Cache as a practice, it is not too difficult after mastering the implementation of a DCache. Here are some points to note during the design phase:

1. It is best to use the same Cache block size between different levels of Caches to avoid unnecessary increases in design complexity.
2. Define the data width for transferring data between the various levels of Caches and between the last level of Cache and memory.
3. Define the protocol for interaction between the various levels of Caches and between the last level of Cache and memory, whether it is a custom bus or a standard bus protocol.
4. The larger the Cache capacity or the more ways there are, the more pipeline stages can be appropriately added to the path going to the Cache RAM and the path for the return from the Cache RAM.
5. Don't forget that the newly added Cache also needs to support Cache instruction operations.

12.6.5   Cache Prefetching

Cache prefetching is the process of loading data that will be used into the Cache or a dedicated prefetch buffer in advance, thereby reducing the Cache miss rate or the latency of Cache misses. Cache prefetching includes both hardware prefetching and software prefetching.

Cache hardware prefetching is automatically performed by hardware. Typically, hardware records the addresses of past Cache misses and analyzes whether there is any regularity (such as sequential row-by-row increments). Once a stream of memory access with a certain address change pattern is detected, subsequent memory access requests are generated and sent out according to this pattern. The simplest hardware prefetcher is a stream buffer. This prefetcher recognizes access streams with continuous increasing or decreasing addresses. Once recognized, it issues memory requests across several Cache blocks in the direction of the stream from the current miss address. The prefetched data is filled into a dedicated stream buffer to avoid polluting the Cache. Subsequent Cache miss requests will first check the stream buffer; if a hit occurs, it returns data directly from the stream buffer without issuing a memory request, and this Cache miss request in the stream buffer will continue to trigger new prefetch memory requests.

Cache software prefetching is done by inserting prefetch instructions into the program through the compiler or manually to load data into the Cache in advance. The prefetch instruction in the LoongArch architecture is preld. When implemented, the preld instruction still checks the Cache first and only issues a request when there is a Cache miss. Most importantly, after preld issues a Cache miss request, it does not wait for the result to return; it writes back and exits the pipeline immediately; otherwise, the preld instruction would block the pipeline and fail to achieve the effect of prefetching. Since preld instructions do not generate any address or TLB-related exceptions, when their addresses are indeed incorrect, although there is no need to mark them as exceptions, do not issue Cache miss requests, as the physical address obtained at this time may be risky.

12.7   **Implementation of Multicore Processors**

When considering transforming your design to support multiple cores, you first need to determine whether you need to run an operating system like Linux on this multicore CPU. Since we often see multicore forms in computer or mobile phone chips, we might think that multicores can only look like this. In fact, in some embedded application scenarios, due to the fixed task division and interaction behavior on the multicore, there may not even be a need to run any operating system, which means the hardware design adjustments required to support multicores can be much simpler. However, here, we introduce the design target as a symmetric multiprocessor (SMP) that supports the operation of a Linux system. The modifications involved naturally also apply to simpler application scenarios.

12.7.1 Multicore Interconnection Architecture

We will only consider one type of interconnection structure here, where several processor cores are connected together through a bus or crossbar switch to access shared Cache or memory, and all processor cores have the same access latency to the shared Cache or memory. In promotional materials for some commercial processors, you may often see the term "cluster," which refers to the number of clusters in a multicore chip and how many cores are within each cluster. The internal organization of each "cluster" usually adopts the interconnection structure we are discussing here. It is common to have two to four processor cores connected by this interconnection structure, generally not exceeding six.

Although the interconnection structure used here is already quite simple in terms of structural design difficulty and complexity, it still poses challenges for most beginners. From an engineering development perspective, if you are implementing your design on the Xilinx platform, it is recommended to directly use the AXI Crossbar IP in Vivado; if you plan to implement a design that goes beyond the FPGA platform, you can try to find some open-source bus interconnect IP. If you want to develop one from scratch, here are some tips:

1. From multiple masters (processor cores) to a single slave (shared memory or Cache), the core of the datapath is a multiplexer. When there are multiple requests at the same time, an arbitrator is needed to select one.
2. The results returned from the slave must be uniquely routed to the corresponding master based on the source of the request. If the higher bits of the ID are used to distinguish different masters, then the higher bits of the ID can be used to quickly complete routing upon return.
3. If the processor core's bus interface will issue burst transfer transactions that require multiple cycles, using transactions as the unit in arbitration and routing processes can help avoid some design risks.
4. Do not design it as pure combinational logic, as the timing is likely to be very poor.

12.7.2 Multicore Identification

In a multicore system, each processor core must have its own unique identifier. This identifier must be readable by the system software running on the core. Under the LoongArch architecture, software reads the CoreID field of CSR.CPUID to obtain this information. For an SMP system, the processor core module you design will be instantiated multiple times, so the value of the CoreID field in CSR.CPUID is obtained through either a parameter or a configuration pin at the top level of the processor core. In the entire chip top-level code, the instantiated processor cores are numbered sequentially starting from 0.

12.7.3 Inter-Core Interrupts

Inter-core interrupts are an essential inter-core communication mechanism. For the processor core that receives the interrupt, there is no fundamental difference between inter-core interrupts and other externally input interrupts, so hardware modification is not difficult. For the processor core that initiates the interrupt, the interrupt signal does not necessarily have to be directly issued from its own output. The status bits of these inter-core interrupts can be implemented in a unified on-chip interrupt controller (in previous experiments, the interrupt controller was implemented in confreg). This implementation method is recommended because the on-chip interrupt controller naturally has pathways to each processor core, and each processor core definitely has access to the interrupt controller.

When implementing the inter-core interrupt function, the difficulty in RTL code development in hardware is not significant; the main work lies in the consistent cooperation between software and hardware. If you do not want to modify the low-level code related to inter-core interrupts in the operating system, you must find the system specification corresponding to the kernel code you use and strictly implement it according to the specification, including the format and address of the registers, interrupt numbers, etc. It should be added that the LoongArch architecture does not specify the specific implementation of this part in the instruction set specification, so you need to refer to the user manual of the processor chip corresponding to the kernel code based on which you are porting. If you are using your own hardware design, please modify the code related to inter-core interrupts in the kernel accordingly.

12.7.4 Storage Consistency in Multicore Systems

In a single-core processor, since there is only one core accessing memory, it is naturally assumed that as long as a load operation always retrieves the value written by the "most recent" store operation to the same memory location and the store operation uniquely determines the value retrieved by "subsequent" load operations on the same memory location, then the execution is correct. However, in a shared memory multicore processor, multiple processor cores can simultaneously read and write to the same memory unit, and the latency of their access to that memory unit may not be consistent. Moreover, the same memory unit may have multiple copies within the processor, leading to changes in the content of the same memory unit being recognized at different times by different processor cores. The concepts of "most recent" and "subsequent" from the single-core processor scenario no longer exist. Therefore, in a multicore processor scenario, stricter restrictions on the order of memory access operations are needed to ensure correct execution. As a result, people have proposed storage consistency models to define the standards for correct execution in multicore scenarios.

The common storage consistency models currently are not unique, and their differences are reflected in the strength of the restrictions imposed on the order of memory access events. The weaker the restrictions imposed by the storage consistency model on the number of memory access events, the more it is conducive to improving performance, but the more difficult it is to program. The design recommendations we will provide later will be based on the release consistency (RC) model. The RC model is a weak storage consistency model. Under this model, memory access operations are distinguished as synchronous operations and ordinary memory access operations. Programmers must use hardware-recognizable synchronous operations to protect write accesses to shared memory units to ensure that write accesses to shared memory units by multiple processor cores are mutually exclusive. Synchronous operations are further divided into acquire operations and release operations. Acquire is used to obtain exclusive access rights to certain shared memory units, while release is used to relinquish such access rights. The RC model imposes the following restrictions on the order of memory access events:

1. The execution of synchronous operations meets the sequentially consistent condition.
2. Before any ordinary memory access operation is allowed to be executed, all acquire operations that precede this memory access operation in the same processor core have been completed.
3. Before any release is allowed to be executed, all ordinary memory access operations that precede this release in the same processor core have been completed.

For a more systematic exposition and argumentation of the concept of storage consistency, interested readers can refer to Chapter 12 of *"Computer Architecture"* (Second Edition). Next, we will focus on the considerations that need to be made in hardware design based on the RC model.

12.7.4.1   Synchronous Operation

In the definition of the RC model, two types of synchronization operations are involved: acquire and release. In the LoongArch 32-bit simplified version, there are no native atomic memory access instructions with acquire and release operations. Software programmers need to implement the synchronization operations defined in the model in conjunction with the dbar instruction. Therefore, to support multicore, it is necessary to add the implementation of the dbar instruction to the processor core.

Here, we only discuss the synchronization operation of the dbar instruction when hint=0, that is, all program orders of memory access operations that comply with the hint field before the dbar instruction must be completed before the execution of the dbar instruction, and all program orders of memory access operations that comply with the hint field after the dbar instruction can only start execution after the dbar instruction has been executed. The memory access operations considered here include not only various load and store instructions but also cacop and preld instructions.

If the memory access instructions of the processor core you designed are single-issue and sequentially executed and without any non-blocking Cache, write buffer, or other optimized designs, then you can implement the dbar instruction as an NOP. If it's not this simple case, a feasible and simple implementation method is as follows: the dbar instruction can only start executing after all program orders of memory access operations before it in the pipeline are completed; at the same time, the dbar instruction should block the issuance of all program orders of memory access operations after it until the dbar instruction leaves the pipeline. It should be noted that "completion" here refers to "global completion." For consistent cacheable memory access types of load and store operations, in the case of implementing a directory-based write-invalidation ESI Cache coherence protocol (which will be introduced later), the "global completion" of a load operation means that the load operation has retrieved the data and written it back, and the "global completion" of a store operation means that the processor core holds the exclusive Cache block to be accessed by the store operation and the value of the store has been updated to that Cache block. For strong order non-cacheable load and store operations, the "global completion" of a load operation means that the load operation has retrieved the data and written it back, and the "global completion" of a store operation means that the store operation has been written to the destination. Two reminders for beginners: (1) If you have implemented performance optimization structures such as write buffers, even though the store operation has exited the pipeline and it is still in the write buffer and has not completed the storage action, then this store operation is not "globally complete." (2) When using AXI as the processor core bus interface, ensure that an uncached store operation is written to the destination, which means you need to see the response of this write transaction returned from the b channel.

12.7.5 Cache Coherence Protocol

12.7.5.1 Directory-Based Cache Coherence Protocol

In the second part of the practices earlier in this book, we implemented Cache in the processor to enhance memory access performance. Since Cache is a backup of memory, when the storage consistency of a multicore processor is determined, the implementation of its Cache must also meet the consistency requirements proposed by the storage consistency. This set of implementation mechanisms that meet the consistency requirements is what we often refer to as the Cache coherence protocol. There are various specific implementations of Cache coherence protocols, and here we only introduce the directory-based write-invalidate ESI Cache coherence protocol. Moreover, we only consider the design where the private Cache within the core uses a write-back write-allocate strategy, all Cache blocks are of equal size, and the shared storage (which can be shared Cache or shared memory) maintains a strict inclusive relationship with the private Cache within the core.

Private Cache Block States

In this protocol, each Cache block in the private Cache has three states: invalid (INV), shared (SHD), and exclusive (EXC). If the Cache block state is INV, the processor's load and store operations on this Cache block do not hit; if the Cache block state is SHD, it indicates that there may be other processor cores holding a valid backup of this memory block; if the Cache block state is EXC, it indicates that this is the only valid backup of the memory block.

Shared Storage Block States

At the shared storage, a directory entry is maintained for each memory block (the size is the same as the Cache block size). Each directory entry has an n-bit vector, where n is the number of processor cores in the system. Bit i of the bit vector is 1, indicating that the Cache block is backed up in the private Cache of processor core Pi. In addition, each directory entry also maintains a dirty bit. When the dirty bit is 1, it indicates that a processor has exclusively written to this Cache block, and the block is in a DIRTY state; otherwise, the block is in a CLEAN state.

Load Operations

When processor Pi issues a load operation "load x," different operations are taken based on the different states of x in its private Cache and shared storage:

If the Tag comparison of x hits in Pi's private Cache and the Cache block is in SHD or EXC state, then the load operation "load x" hits in the Cache.

If the Tag comparison of x does not hit in Pi's private Cache or the Tag comparison hits but the Cache block is in the INV state, then Pi first replaces a Cache block from its private Cache and then sends a read request read(x) to the shared storage. After receiving the read(x) request, the shared storage looks up the directory entry corresponding to the memory block where x is located:

(1) If the content of the directory entry shows that the memory block where x is located is CLEAN, then the shared storage sends a read response rdack(x) to the requesting processor core Pi to provide a valid backup of the memory block where x is located and sets bit i of the bit vector in the directory entry to 1.

(2) If the content of the directory entry shows that the memory block where x is located is DIRTY and the current exclusive valid backup is held by processor core Pj, then the shared storage sends a write-back request wb(x) to Pj. After receiving the wb(x) request, Pj changes the backup in its private Cache from the EXC state to the SHD state and sends a write-back response wback(x) to

the shared storage to provide a valid backup of the memory block where x is located. After receiving the wback(x) from Pj, the shared storage sends a read response rdack(x) to the requesting processor core Pi to provide a valid backup of the memory block where x is located, clears the dirty bit in the directory entry, and sets bit i of the bit vector to 1.

(3) If the directory entry does not yet have the memory block where x is located, then this level of shared storage needs to first pick a replacement item from the directory.

(a) If the state of the selected directory entry is DIRTY and bit j of the bit vector is 1, then the shared storage sends an invalidate and write-back request invwb(x) to processor core Pj. After receiving the invwb(x) request, Pj changes the backup in its private Cache from the EXC state to the INV state and sends an invalidate and write-back response invwback(x) to the shared storage to provide a valid backup of the memory block where x is located.

(b) If the selected directory entry is in the CLEAN state and the bit vector is not all zeros, then the shared storage needs to send an invalidate request inv(x) to all processor cores holding a shared backup of the memory block, excluding Pi, based on the information in the directory entry's bit vector. The processor core holding the shared backup of x, upon receiving the inv(x) request, changes the backup of x in its private Cache from the SHD state to the INV state and sends an invalidate acknowledgment invack(x) back to the shared storage.

After receiving the invwback(x) acknowledgment (for case a) or all invack(x) acknowledgments (for case b), the shared storage initiates a read request to this level of memory (if the shared storage is memory itself) or the next level of memory (if the shared storage is a shared Cache). It then waits for the read response from the shared storage. Once the read response is returned, a new directory entry is created at the position of the replaced directory entry. The write-back bit is set to 0, and bit i of the bit vector is set to 1. Concurrently, a read response rdack(x) is generated and returned to the requesting processor core Pi.

After receiving the read response rdack(x), processor core Pi fills the previously replaced Cache block's location with the new data and sets the state of the new Cache to SHD (shared).

Store Operations

When processor Pi issues a store operation "store x," different operations are taken based on the different states of x in its private Cache and shared storage:

1. If the Tag comparison for x hits in Pi's private Cache and the Cache block is in the EXC state, then the store operation "store x" hits in the Cache.
2. If the Tag comparison for x hits in Pi's private Cache and the Cache block is in the SHD state, then processor core Pi sends a write request write(x) to the shared storage. After receiving the write(x) request, the shared storage looks up the directory entry corresponding to the memory block where x is located.

(1) If the bit vector in the directory entry has only the i-th bit set to 1 and all other bits are 0, this means that no other processor core holds the memory block, so the shared storage sends a write acknowledgment wtack(x) to the requesting processor core Pi, indicating that Pi is allowed to exclusively access the memory block where x is located, and sets the dirty bit in the directory entry to 1.

(2) If the bit vector in the directory entry has more than just the i-th bit set to 1, this means that other processor cores hold a shared backup of the memory block, so the shared storage needs to send an invalidate request inv(x) to all processor cores holding a shared backup of the memory block, based on the information in the directory entry's bit vector. The processor core holding the shared backup of x, after receiving the inv(x) request, changes the backup of x in its private Cache from the SHD state to the INV state and sends an invalidate acknowledgment invack(x) to the shared storage. After the shared storage receives all invack(x), it sends a write acknowledgment wtack(x) to the requesting processor core Pi, indicating that Pi is allowed to exclusively access the memory block where x is located, sets the dirty bit in the directory entry to 1, and sets the i-th bit of the bit vector to 1, clearing all other bits.

After processor core Pi receives the write acknowledgment wtack(x), it changes the state of the Cache block from SHD to EXC.

3. If the Tag comparison for x does not hit in Pi's private Cache or the Tag comparison hits but the Cache block is in the INV state, then Pi first replaces a Cache block from its private Cache and then sends a read request write(x) to the shared storage. After receiving the write(x) request, the shared storage looks up the directory entry corresponding to the memory block where x is located.

(1) If the state in the directory entry is CLEAN and the bit vector is not all zeros, this means that other processor cores hold a shared backup of the memory block, so the shared storage needs to send an invalidate request inv(x) to all processor cores holding a shared backup of the memory block, based on the information in the directory entry's bit vector. The processor core holding the shared backup of x, after receiving the inv(x) request, changes the backup of x in its private Cache from the SHD state to the INV state and sends an invalidate acknowledgment invack(x) to the shared storage. After the shared storage receives all invack(x), it sends a write acknowledgment wtack(x) to the requesting processor core Pi, providing a valid backup of the memory block where x is located, sets the dirty bit in the directory entry to 1, and sets the i-th bit of the bit vector to 1, clearing all other bits.

(2) If the state in the directory entry is DIRTY and the j-th bit of the bit vector is 1, then the shared storage sends an invalidate and write-back request invwb(x) to processor core Pj. After receiving the invwb(x) request, processor core Pj changes the backup in its private Cache from the EXC state to the INV state and sends an invalidate and write-back acknowledgment invwback(x) to the shared storage, providing a valid backup of the memory block where x is located. After receiving the invwback(x), the shared storage sends a write acknowledgment

wtack(x) to the requesting processor core Pi, providing a valid backup of the memory block where x is located, sets the dirty bit in the directory entry to 1, and sets the i-th bit of the bit vector to 1, clearing all other bits.

(3) If the directory entry does not yet have the memory block where x is located, then this level of shared storage needs to first pick a replacement item from the directory.

(a) If the state of the selected directory entry is DIRTY and the j-th bit of the bit vector is 1, then the shared storage sends an invalidate and write-back request invwb(x) to processor core Pj. After receiving the invwb(x) request, processor core Pj changes the backup in its private Cache from the EXC state to the INV state and sends an invalidate and write-back acknowledgment invwback(x) to the shared storage, providing a valid backup of the memory block where x is located.

(b) If the state of the selected directory entry is CLEAN and the bit vector is not all zeros, then the shared storage needs to send an invalidate request inv(x) to all processor cores holding a shared backup of the memory block, excluding Pi, based on the information in the directory entry's bit vector. The processor core holding the shared backup of x, after receiving the inv(x) request, changes the backup of x in its private Cache from the SHD state to the INV state and sends an invalidate acknowledgment invack(x) to the shared storage.

After the shared storage receives the invwback(x) acknowledgment (for case a) or all invack(x) acknowledgments (for case b), it sends a read request to this level of storage (if the shared storage is memory) or the next level of storage (if the shared storage is an LLC). After waiting for the shared storage to return the read data, it creates a new directory entry at the position of the replaced directory entry, sets the dirty bit to 1, sets the i-th bit of the bit vector to 1, and generates a write acknowledgment wtack(x), which is then returned to the requesting processor core Pi.

After receiving the write acknowledgment wtack(x), processor core Pi fills it into the location previously occupied by the replaced Cache block and sets the state of the new Cache to EXC.

Replacement Operations

If a processor core needs to replace a Cache block, whether the Cache block is in the SHD state or the EXC state, the processor core must send a replacement request rep(x) to the shared storage. When the replaced Cache block is in the EXC state and indeed contains dirty data, the data of the replaced Cache block must also be written back to the shared storage. After receiving the rep(x) request, the shared storage clears the corresponding bit in the bit vector according to the source of the request, and if the bit vector has become all zeros, the dirty bit must also be cleared.

12.7.5.2   Maintaining Consistency Between Instruction Cache and Data Cache Within a Core

In the directory-based Cache coherence protocol described above, the bit vector in the directory entry corresponds to only one bit for each processor core. This means that if the instruction Cache and data Cache within a processor core each hold a valid copy of a memory block, the shared directory cannot distinguish between them. In other words, under this Cache coherence protocol, it is not possible for the hardware to maintain consistency between the instruction Cache and data Cache within the same core. When self-modifying code occurs, software still needs to maintain consistency between the instruction Cache and data Cache within the same core using Cache instructions or SYNCI instructions. Note that it is only necessary for software to maintain consistency between the instruction Cache and data Cache within the same core; if consistency between data Cache A and instruction Cache B of different cores needs to be maintained, it is still accomplished by hardware. Since the need for such consistency maintenance already exists in single-core scenarios, no additional adjustments are required in the software. In applications where self-modifying code does not occur frequently, we recommend this division of labor between hardware and software, where hardware accelerates frequent or unpredictable transactions and infrequent and predictable transactions are handled by software to reduce hardware implementation cost.

12.7.5.3   Transmission of Cache Coherence Maintenance Transactions

The introduction to the Cache coherence protocol mentioned above should be easy to understand, and many textbooks also provide detailed explanations. However, when you consider the specific implementation, the first design issue you encounter is how are requests and responses such as read, write, rep, rdack, wtack, inv, invack, wb, wback, invwb, and invwback, which are used to maintain Cache coherence, transmitted between the processor core and shared storage. Since even without implementing the Cache coherence protocol functions there will be data transmission paths between the processor core and shared storage, a more natural design consideration is to reuse existing data transmission paths as much as possible to complete the transmission of these coherence transactions. For example, read and write requests are requests sent by the processor to shared storage, and rdack and wtack are responses returned from shared storage to the processor. If the original connection between the processor core and shared storage uses an AXI bus, you will find that this process is very similar to the execution process of a read transaction on the ar and r channels. When we consider appropriately modifying the AXI bus to support the transmission of read and write requests and rdack and wtack responses, we can add some signals on the ar channel to distinguish between read and write requests, and at the same time, add some signals on the r channel to distinguish between rdack and wtack responses. Similarly, we can add some signals on the aw+w channels to represent rep requests. However, the inv, wb, and invwb requests are different from the original AXI bus transactions because, according to the AXI concept, shared storage is the master and the processor core is the slave at this time. One implementation method is to forcibly add a set of AXI ar and r channels where shared storage is the master and the processor core is the slave. The inv, wb, and invwb requests are transmitted through the newly added ar channels, and the invack, wback, and invwback responses are transmitted through the newly added r channels. This approach not only is resource-intensive but also introduces other design issues, which we will mention later. Therefore, we consider a more aggressive modification of the r channel to transmit inv, wb, and invwb requests and slightly modify the aw+w channels to transmit invack, wback, and invwback responses. The aforementioned design approach requires adding some signals based on the original AXI signals, all of which can be implemented using the newly added USER field in the AXI4 protocol.

However, when we reuse the existing AXI bus channels between the processor core and shared storage to transmit Cache coherence maintenance transactions, we need to be cautious about some common pitfalls in the design:

Firstly, we need to always be mindful of the separation of read and write channels in the AXI bus protocol. For example, suppose processor core Pi initially holds an EXC block for x and then replaces the EXC block containing x by issuing a replacement operation, sending it out through the write channel. Subsequently, a "store x" operation that finds a Cache miss issues a write(x) request through the read channel. Due to the separation of read and write channels, it is possible that the replaced request is blocked on the write channel, while the later write(x) request arrives at the shared storage first. The shared storage then follows the aforementioned processing procedure, returning a write response and setting the dirty bit and the i-th bit of the bit vector in the directory entry to 1. Only after this, the initially sent replacement request rep(x) from the processor core arrives at the shared storage, causing the shared storage to clear the dirty bit and the i-th bit of the bit vector in the directory entry. In this case, a situation arises where the shared storage believes that there is no valid backup in the processor core Pi, but in fact processor core Pi holds a valid backup. The value updated by "store x" in the processor core Pi could be incorrectly discarded, leading to program execution errors. To solve such problems, one approach is to handle it at the shared storage. When encountering a situation where the directory entry state does not match the request, it is assumed that there must be a reversal of order in the coherence request response path. The request processing is paused until the earlier request response arrives and is then processed. Although this approach is feasible, it is not ideal. Not to mention that the enumeration of directory entry state and request mismatches and the timing of resuming blocked requests are not so easy to implement logically, this design of blocking one request and waiting for another request, if not well considered, may lead to deadlock in some extreme conditions. Our design suggestion is to compare the addresses of every read or write request issued from the read channel with the rep requests that have been issued on the write channel but have not yet been confirmed to be received by the shared storage. If there is a conflict, block the issuance of the read or write request until the conflict is resolved. It can be seen that this comparison logic is almost the same as the logic for handling write-after-read dependency when designing the AXI bus interface before, which means we can largely reuse existing logic to solve such problems.

Secondly, whether we are adding a new set of shared storage to the processor core's ar channel or reusing the existing r channel to pass invack, wback, and invwback requests, we must consider the out-of-order issue between them and the rdack and wtack responses. For example, processor core Pi sends a read(x) request to the shared storage, and after processing, the shared storage returns an rdack(x) to it. However, due to other requests, the shared storage then sends an inv(x) request to Pj. If the rdack(x) response and the inv(x) request take different channels or even though they both take the r channel, because their rids are different, the interconnect network can reverse their transmission order, ultimately causing the processor core to see the inv(x) before receiving the rdack(x). If no processing is done, the shared storage will eventually think that there is no backup at processor core Pi, but in fact there is a backup at processor core Pi. As mentioned earlier, this is a very dangerous state and is very likely to cause subsequent program errors. If the rdack(x) response and the inv(x) request take different channels, this problem seems quite difficult to solve because the shared storage cannot know when the first sent rdack(x) is truly received by the processor core. Forcibly handling it on the processor core side by blocking the inv(x) request, once not considered comprehensively, can lead to deadlock. If the rdack(x) response and the inv(x) request both take the r channel, the problem will be much easier to handle. We just need to make it clear that there is only one physical path from the shared storage to a certain processor core's r channel and there are no Caches on the road that can produce out-of-order; then the problem will naturally not occur. Fortunately, in most cases, this requirement is guaranteed in implementation.

12.7.5.4   Design Adjustments for Cache Coherence Support Within the Core

To implement a Cache coherence protocol, in addition to modifying the interconnect between the processor core and the shared storage, the internal design of the processor core also needs to be adjusted accordingly. Here are six design suggestions:

1. Modify the bus interface module to enable it to generate coherence transactions based on the added signals input from the instruction pipeline and to distinguish between received ordinary transactions and coherence transactions, translating them into corresponding internal signals output to the instruction pipeline.
2. The state field of the core's data Cache should be adjusted from invalid and valid to invalid, shared, and exclusive. Accordingly, the conditions for determining whether the load and store operations hit the data Cache also need to be adjusted. The state field and hit determination logic of the core's instruction Cache do not need to change, but the meaning of its state field is translated from invalid and valid to invalid and shared. Both the miss of the instruction Cache and the load

miss of the data Cache should send read requests to the bus interface module, and the store miss of the data Cache should send write requests to the bus interface module.

3. When handling the misses of the instruction Cache and data Cache, even if the replaced Cache block is not dirty, a rep request should be sent to the shared directory through the bus interface module, while the data part of the Cache block can be omitted to save bus bandwidth.

4. Adjust the implementation of the Cache instruction. All index invalidate Cache instructions should not directly set the state of the specified Cache block to invalid but should first read out the content and send a rep request to the shared directory according to the state of the read Cache block and then perform the invalid operation after the request is sent. All hit invalidate Cache instructions, during the first execution of the lookup operation, if there is a hit, need to send a rep request to the shared directory according to the state of the hit Cache block and then perform the invalid operation after the request is sent. For hit invalidate write-back Cache instructions, even if the hit Cache block is not dirty, a rep request should be sent to the shared directory, and the invalid operation should be performed after the request is sent.

5. Reuse the implementation path and state machine of the hit class Cache instructions adjusted in the fourth point to handle coherence transactions from outside the core. It is necessary to add selection to the entire processing process, with the address and other information input during the execution of Cache instructions coming from the internal pipeline and the address and other information input during the execution of external coherence transactions coming from the content input after parsing by the bus interface module. However, the implemented Cache instructions do not have a hit write-back operation for DCache, so to execute the wb request from outside the core, the execution logic of DCache hit invalidate write back can be implemented by omitting the last invalidate step. In addition, it should be noted that if the Cache coherence protocol described earlier is implemented, since the directory does not distinguish between the instruction Cache and data Cache within the same core, when an inv request is received from outside the core, both the data Cache should perform D_Hit_Inv operation, and the instruction Cache should perform I_Hit_Inv operation.

6. If the inv, wb, and invwb coherence requests are transmitted through the r channel of the AXI bus, it is essential to reserve enough physical resources in the bus interface to ensure that at least one coherence request can be received at any time to avoid deadlock.

12.7.5.5   Design of Directory at Shared Storage

The design of the directory at the shared storage is very similar to the design of the Tag part in the Cache, so I will not introduce its specific implementation here. A suggestion for beginners is the access efficiency of the directory does not need to be as aggressive as that of the data Cache. When implementing for the first time, you can handle only one transaction at a time, and it can take multiple cycles to complete the processing of a transaction.

If the directory is implemented in the on-chip shared Cache and the shared Cache and the core's private Cache have a strict inclusive relationship, it is recommended to directly add a rewrite bit and a directory bit vector in the Tag of the shared Cache.

If the directory is implemented in the shared memory, you can implement it as a shared Cache that maintains a strict inclusive relationship with the core's Cache and has no data part. The difference is that the original read and write operations on the data part of this Cache are all converted into read and write commands sent to the memory controller.

If the shared Cache and the core's private Cache have an exclusive relationship, a feasible implementation is that the Tag part of the shared Cache has a strict inclusive relationship with the core's private Cache, while the data part of the shared Cache maintains an exclusive relationship with the core's private Cache. An extra bit of information is added to the Tag to indicate whether the data of this Cache block is local to the LLC or in the private Cache of some core.

12.7.6 *Atomicity of ll.w-sc.w Instruction Pair in Memory Access*

Multicore processors require synchronization mechanisms to coordinate access to shared variables by multiple processor cores. The LoongArch 32-bit simplified architecture defines the ll.w and sc.w instructions for implementing synchronization operations, including lock operations and barrier operations. In the earlier content of this book, we discussed how to implement the ll.w and sc.w instructions in a single-core scenario. The focus of the implementation is to maintain the LLbit properly. After the ll.w instruction is executed, the LLbit is set to 1, and the address accessed by the ll.w instruction is recorded. The ertn instruction will clear the LLbit to 0. When the sc.w instruction is executed, it needs to check whether the LLbit is 1. If the LLbit is 1, the sc.w can write the value into memory and return 1; if the LLbit is 0, the sc.w does not write to memory and directly returns 0.

When implementing multicore support, the processing of the ll.w and sc.w instructions does not need to be changed. It is only necessary to add a consideration for the condition under which the LLbit is cleared to 0, that is, between the execution of ll.w and the execution of sc.w; if there is another core's consistent cacheable store operation that accesses an address falling within the same "Cache coherence maintenance unit" as the address of ll.w and sc.w, then the LLbit should also be cleared to 0. The size of this "Cache coherence maintenance basic unit" is determined by the designer, and it is usually set to the Cache block where the accessed address is located.

The starting point of this design is that we only consider the case where the addresses accessed by the ll.w-sc.w instruction pair are of the coherent cacheable access type. It is unreasonable for SMP processors running the Linux operating system to consider the case where the addresses accessed by the ll.w-sc.w instruction pair are of the strongly ordered non-cacheable access type, so you can ignore this situation when implementing the hardware. However, in some embedded application scenarios, it is reasonable for the software to do so, and we will discuss this situation at the end of this section.

When considering single-core operation, the LLbit is implemented within the processor core. So, when considering multicore support, since the maintenance of the LLbit needs to consider the access of other cores, does it mean that the LLbit should be implemented outside the core? This is not necessary. The LLbit is still implemented within the core, and the new condition for clearing to 0 can be generated through information input from outside the core. When the ll.w-sc.w instruction pair accesses addresses that fall in the Cached space, since the hardware will maintain Cache coherence among multiple cores, the store operations of other cores on the Cache block where the address is located will definitely be passed to this core through Cache coherence maintenance messages, so using this message, the required LLbit clear signal can be generated.

In the specific implementation of the above mechanism, there is a detail that needs attention: if the Cache coherence maintenance message is caused by the exclusive Cache block request of the store operation of local core, then the LLbit should not be cleared to 0. Otherwise, even if the atomicity of the ll.w-sc.w execution is not broken, the sc.w still cannot successfully write to memory, and only when it loops back to the second execution can it be written in. This obviously reduces the execution efficiency, not only because an extra loop is executed but also because the additional time taken by the extra loop allows other processor cores' store operations to access this Cache block, further reducing the probability of successful sc.w execution.

Finally, let's consider another situation: when after the execution of ll.w and before the execution of sc.w a Cache replacement is caused by another ordinary memory access operation executed by this core, which actively replaces the Cache block accessed by ll.w-sc.w (we are accustomed to calling the replacement caused by receiving Cache coherence maintenance messages from outside the core as passive replacement), then other cores will not send coherence maintenance requests to this core when they perform store operations. If this core does not consider the handling of this situation and still keeps the LLbit as 1, then the sc.w will write to memory when executed, violating the atomicity of the entire RMW process. The MIPS architecture documentation considers that "portable" software should avoid this situation. So, in theory, you can do nothing about it, and if there is an error, it is considered to be the software's fault. However, from the author's past experience, it is better to put more effort into hardware design than to spend a long time locating a non-"portable" bug in the software. Therefore, when encountering this situation, please also clear the LLbit to 0.

12.7.6.1 Accessing Non-Cached Access Types with ll.w/sc.w Instructions

As previously mentioned, there are situations where the ll.w-sc.w instruction pair accesses addresses of non-Cached memory types. In some cost-sensitive embedded application scenarios, the task division on multicores is fixed, and the communication patterns between tasks are also very fixed (e.g., they are only producer-consumer patterns). In such cases, the Cache coherence between multicores can be handled by software to reduce circuit cost (and perhaps each core originally has no Cache but only TCM). However, synchronization mechanisms between cores are still needed. A typical situation is that the communication between cores is not all conducted through hardware FIFO circuits, but through message queues implemented in software on shared on-chip RAM. At least the updates of these queues' read and write pointers need to be synchronized. Since there is no Cache or there is a Cache but no hardware to maintain Cache coherence between multicores, locks and semaphores that implement synchronization mechanisms are naturally not placed in the Cache; they are usually placed in a block of storage shared by these cores (usually on-chip RAM). Since it is not in the Cache, it is naturally accessed using non-cached memory types, which leads to the situation where ll.w/sc.w accesses non-cached memory-type addresses.

If you are implementing such a multicore system, how should the memory access atomicity required by the ll.w/sc.w instruction sequence be maintained? Here, we combine the exclusive access mechanism provided in the AXI bus protocol to give a design suggestion: Design point one, the arlock signal of the bus read request issued by the non-Cached ll.w instruction is set to 0b01. If the rresp signal returned by the read request is 0b01, the local_LLbit within the core is set to 1; otherwise, it is set to 0. Design point two, if the non-cached sc.w instruction sees local_LLbit=0, it directly returns 0 and does not issue any bus write request. If it sees local_LLbit=1, it issues an external bus write request with awlock=0b01, but at this point the sc.w instruction cannot write back and exit the pipeline. It must wait for the bresp returned by the write request. If bresp=0b01, the sc.w instruction writes back 1; otherwise, it clears the local_LLbit and writes back 0. This mechanism requires the AXI slave accessed by ll.w and sc.w instructions to support exclusive access.

12.8 Summary of This Chapter

In this chapter, we have discussed a variety of microarchitectural design optimization techniques such as clock frequency enhancement, superscalar pipelines, dynamic scheduling, branch prediction, memory access optimization, and multicore processors at a brisk pace. It is impossible to cover all these topics in just a few pages. The hope is to inspire more readers to actively practice the aforementioned optimization techniques.

Appendix A
Loongson Lab Box

The core of Loongson Lab Box is an embedded system development board based on FPGA chip (hereinafter referred to as the "development board"), and other devices in the box include one power adapter supporting the development board, one set of JTAG download cable and adapter, and one serial port cable. The following is a brief introduction to the development of the board's hardware design program and clock design program. If you want to know more about the board, please refer to the provided schematic.

A.1 Hardware Design Scheme for the Development Board

Figure A.1 gives a schematic of the logic structure of the development board. The design scheme of the main parts of the development board is shown in the list in Fig. A.2.

A.2 Development Board Schematic

When completing experiments with the development board, i.e., when implementing a circuit using the Vivado tools, you need to bind the top-level input/output interface signals of the designed circuit to the I/O pins of the FPGA chip on the development board, which is specified by the constraint file (*.xdc) in the Vivado project.

Therefore, when using the Vivado tools for circuit implementation, you need to write constraint files, and then you need to look up the schematic of the development board to determine the pin numbers. We have compiled a pin list of common

Fig. A.1 Logic structure and physical diagram of the development board

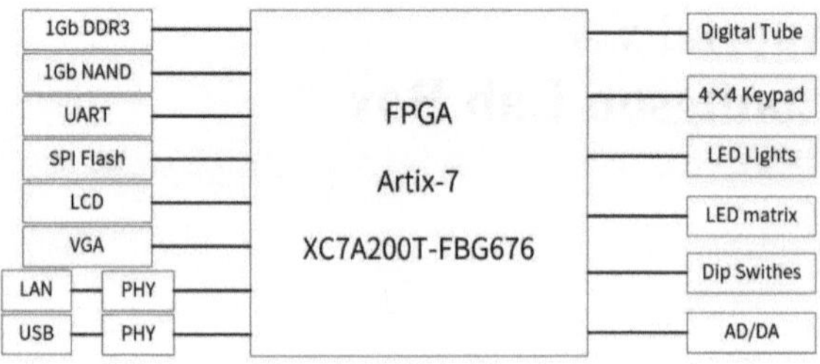

Functional Module	Design scheme overview
FPGA	Using Artix-7 XC7A200T-FBG676
DDR3	Using FPGA implement a DDR3 controller, with onboard K4B1G1646G-BCK0 DDR3 chip
SRAM	Using FPGA implement a SRAM controller, with onboard IDT71V124SATY SRAM chips
NAND	Using FPGA implement a NAND controller, with onboard K9F1G08U0C-PCB0 Flash chip
SPI Flash 1	Using FPGA implement a SPI controller (support boot), with onboard Flash chip socket
SPI Flash 2	Onboard non-removable Flash chip for FPGA programming
VGA	Using FPGA implement a digital display module, with onboard MM74HC573SJ for 332 digital-to-analog conversion, emulating the R, G, B signals of VGA
LCD	Using FPGA implement a LCD display controller, with onboard TFT-LCD screen
USB	Using FPGA implement a USB controller, with onboard USB PHY (USB3500) and a USB interface
LAN	Using FPGA implement a MAC controller, with onboard Ethernet PHY (DM9161AEP) and a RJ45 interface
PS2	Using FPGA implement a PS2 controller, with onboard PS2 interface
UART	Using FPGA implement a UART controller, with onboard UART interface
GPIO	16 single-color LED lights; 2 dual-color LED lights; 8x8 LED matrix (capable of character display function); 8 common-cathode seven-segment displays (for digital display); other gpios.

Fig. A.2 Design scheme of the main part of the development board

I/O devices on the development board, such as LEDs, digital tubes, etc. See "Pin Correspondence.xlsx" in the resources of this book.

For example, let's say that the circuit implementation uses a 4×4 matrix keypad, and now we need to determine the interface to the matrix keypad. We can obtain the I/O numbers of the FPGA chips that correspond to the pins of the matrix keypad directly from the "Pin Correspondence.xlsx" file, or we can look at the schematic to obtain the corresponding numbers. 4×4 matrix keypad schematic is shown in Fig. A.3.

As you can see, the 4×4 keyboard matrix only uses eight pins: FPGA_KEY_COL_1 to FPGA_KEY_COL_4 and FPGA_KEY_ROW_1 to FPGA_KEY_ROW_4. The column FPGA_KEY_COL* is connected to ground through a high resistor, and the row FPGA_KEY_ROW* is connected to high level through a relatively low resistor. When a switch is closed, the corresponding column FPGA_KEY_COL* and row FPGA_KEY_ROW* have the same level.

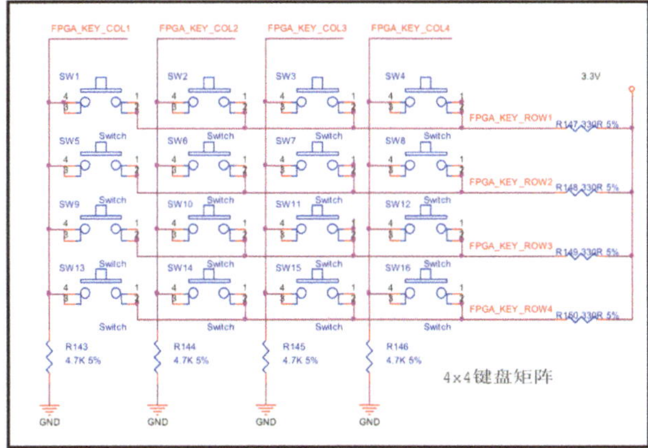

Fig. A.3 4×4 matrix keypad schematic

If only the keys of the same row need to be used, since the column FPGA_KEY_ROW* is connected to high level by default, the corresponding row FPGA_KEY_COL* will receive a high level when there is a key press, i.e., it will get a "1," and it will get a "0" when there is no key press. Note that it is better to add an anti-dither function when detecting key presses.

When multiple rows of keys are used, a scan is required to confirm the key positions. The scanning method is to input a low level "0" from column FPGA_KEY_COL* once and then detect the level value at row FPGA_KEY_ROW*. If all four rows are high "1," it means the key is not in that column; if one row is low "0," it means the key is in that column and in that row.

If the circuit is implemented using the keys in the upper left corner of the keypad, look for the line FPGA_KEY_COL_1 in the schematic and see that it is connected to the I/O pin numbered V8 on the FPGA chip.

Similarly, look for FPGA_KEY_COL_2~FPGA_KEY_COL_4 and FPGA_KEY _ROW_1~FPGA_KEY_ROW_4 the I/O pin number of the corresponding FPGA chip.

Appendix B
Vivado Installation

This appendix is illustrated based on Vivado 2019.2 and is equally applicable to the installation of other versions of Vivado.

You will need to prepare the following environment before studying this section:

(1) A computer with Windows or Linux operating system
(2) Connected networks

If you already have a local installer for the corresponding version of Vivado, you can start directly from Sect. B.3.

If you already have a local installation of Vivado, you can update to the latest version.

If you do not have Vivado installed on your local computer, you will need to download the Vivado installation package, which can be found on the download page 1 of the Xilinx website.[1]

The installation of Vivado supports local installation and online installation, and we recommend using the online installation method.

B.1 About Vivado

Vivado is an EDA tool developed by Xilinx. The following is an example of installing the WebPACK version of Vivado 2019.2 on Windows, which is a license-free version of Vivado with limited device support. It supports Artix-7 devices, which is sufficient for the hands-on tasks in this book. At least 20GB of hard disk space is required to install the software:

- Windows 7.1: 64 bit(Vivado 2019.2 is the last version to support Windows 7.)

---

[1] https://china.xilinx.com/support/download.html

© The Author(s), under exclusive license to Springer Nature Singapore Pte Ltd. 2025
W. Wang, J. Xing, *CPU Design and Practice*,
https://doi.org/10.1007/978-981-96-6573-0

Fig. B.1 Vivado design suite download screen

- Windows 10.0 1809/1903 Update: 64-bit
- Red Hat Enterprise Workstation/Server 7.4–7.6: 64 bit
- SUSE Linux Enterprise 12.4: 64 bit
- CentOS 7.4–7.6: 64 bit
- Ubuntu Linux 16.04.5/16.04.6/18.04.1/18.04.2 LTS: 64 bit
- Amazon Linux 2 LTS: 64 bit

B.2   Vivado Installation File Download

Download the required version of Vivado at https://china.xilinx.com/support/download.html. Once on the page, click on "Vivado Archives" on the left, and then select 2019.2 version[2] as shown in Fig. B.1. You can choose to download and install the Web Installer first and then download and install it through the installer, thus reducing the download time and download package size, or you can directly download the installer file to install it, which is over 20 GB in size.

The Vivado Design Suite provides online installation packages for Windows and Linux systems, as well as local installation packages for all systems, which can be downloaded by selecting the appropriate version as shown in Fig. B.2.

To download, you need to log in to Xilinx; if you already have a Xilinx account, you can log in directly by filling in your account number and password; if you don't have an account, you can create a new account for free by clicking on "Create Account," as shown in Fig. B.3.

---

[2]It is not to say that a higher version of Vivado is not an option, just that the 2019.2 version of Vivado is sufficient for the hands-on tasks in this book and that a higher version will require longer installation time and disk space, at the reader's discretion.

Fig. B.2 Vivado 2019.2
download link screen

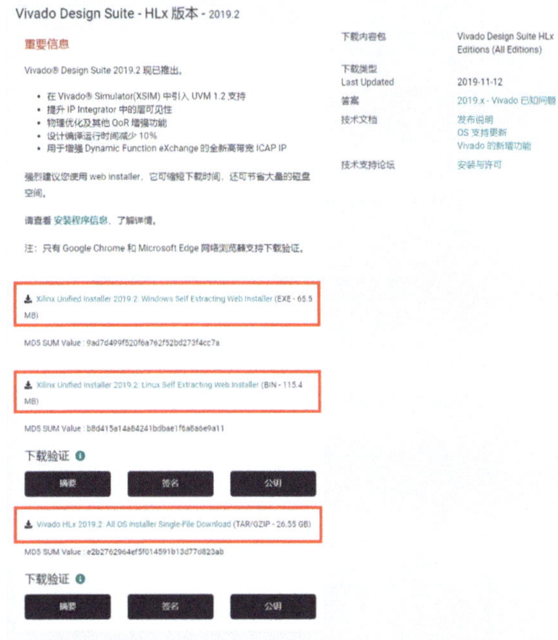

Fig. B.3 Xilinx login screen

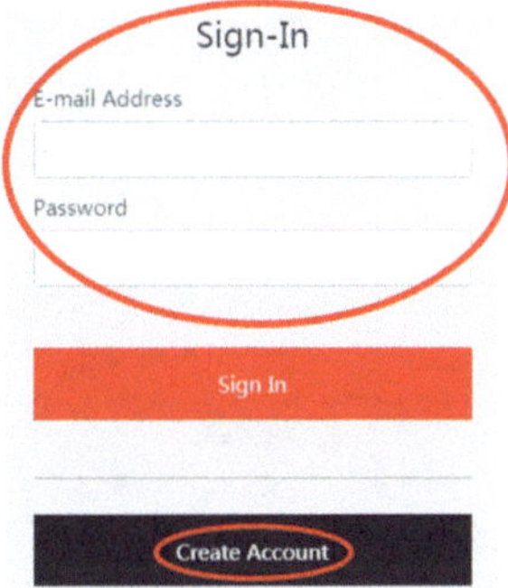

B.3   Vivado Local Installation

After downloading, extract the Vivado installation package, Xilinx_Vivado_2019.2_
1106_2127.tar.gz, to a path that *does not contain Chinese characters or spaces*, and
note that this path is not the path where the Vivado software will be installed but
only a temporary storage path for the installation files. Note that this path is not the
installation path of the Vivado software but only the temporary storage path of the
installation files, as shown in Fig. B.4.

Double-click xsetup.exe in the installation package to open the installation
wizard. At this point, the software may prompt if you want to allow the application

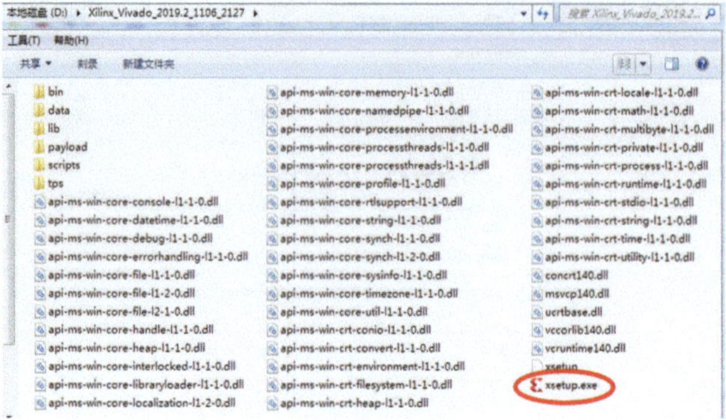

Fig. B.4 Unzipped Vivado installation package

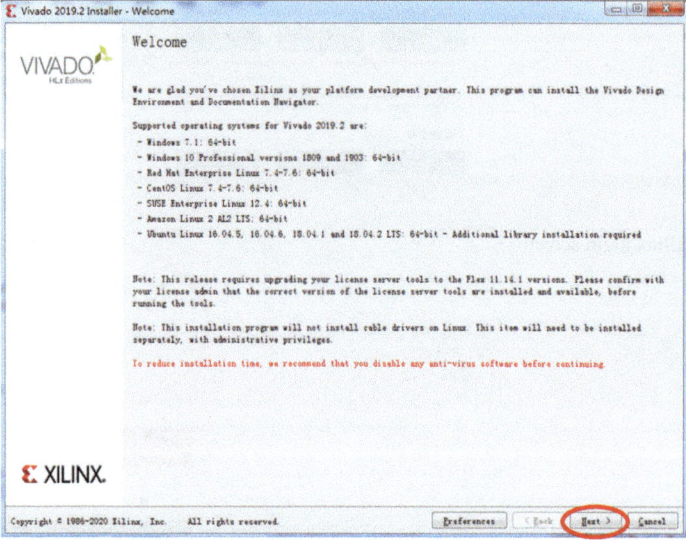

Fig. B.5 Vivado installation welcome screen

to make changes to the device select "Yes." Then the welcome screen will appear; click "Next" as shown in Fig. B.5.

In the screen shown in Fig. B.6, check all the "I Agree" options and click "Next."

Next, select the Vivado installation version; here, check the Vivado HL Web-PACK version (the free version of Vivado); and click "Next." Click "Next" as shown in Fig. B.7.

Select design tools and supported devices. By default, "Design Vivado Suite" and "DocNav" are selected for "Design Tools"; Select "7 Series" for "Device," because the FPGA equipped on the development board in the experiment box is Artix-7 of

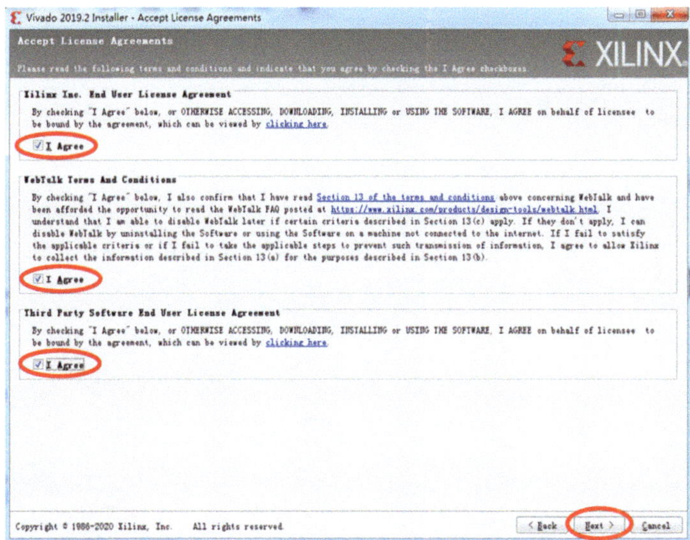

Fig. B.6 Xilinx license

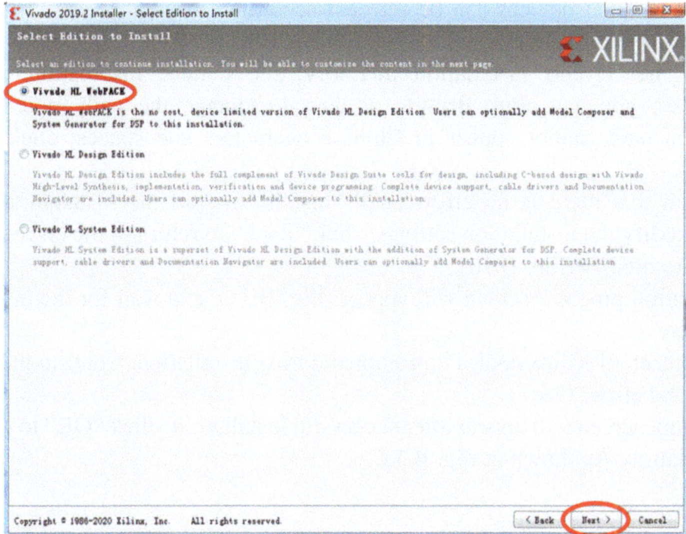

Fig. B.7 Selecting the installed version

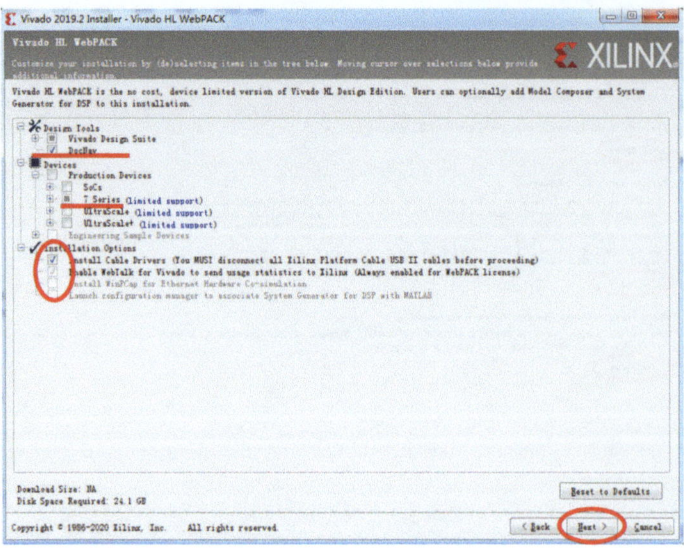

Fig. B.8 Selecting design tools and devices and other installation options

7 series, and other devices can be selected according to your needs; "Installation Options" follows the default; click "Next." (Fig. B.8).

Select the Vivado installation directory; the default installation is under "C:\Xilinx"; you can click Browse or directly change the path; note that the installation path cannot appear in Chinese characters and spaces; click "Next." (Fig. B.9).

Confirm that there is no error; click "Install" to start the installation; if you want to modify the installation settings, click "Back" to return to the corresponding interface to modify (Fig. B.10).

Installation progress screen will appear (Fig. B.11), and wait for the installation to complete.

Disconnect all Xilinx cables if prompted during installation. Confirm the disconnections and click "OK."

A prompt screen will appear after successful installation; click "OK" to complete the installation. As shown in Fig. B.12.

B.4   Vivado Online Installation

Obtain the corresponding Vivado online installation package for Windows.

Ensure that your computer is connected to the Internet and has access to the Xilinx website. Double-click on the online installer and the following welcome screen will appear; click "Next."

The following screen appears and requires you to enter your Xilinx account. Select "Download and Install Now." Click "Next." If you select "Download Full

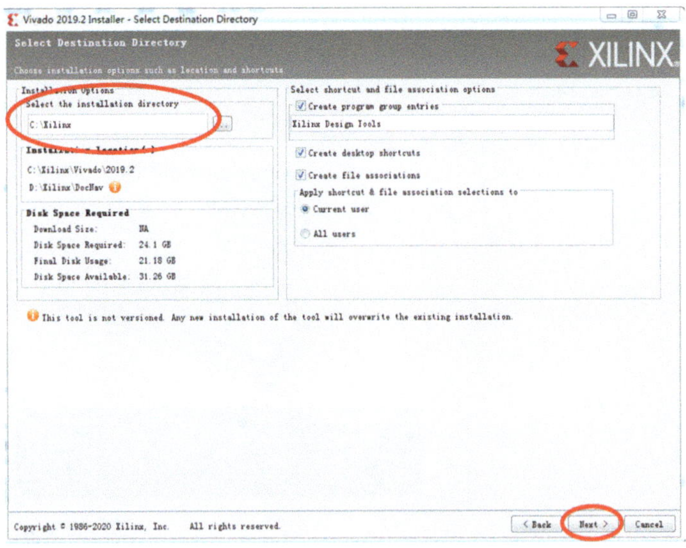

Fig. B.9 Selecting the installation directory

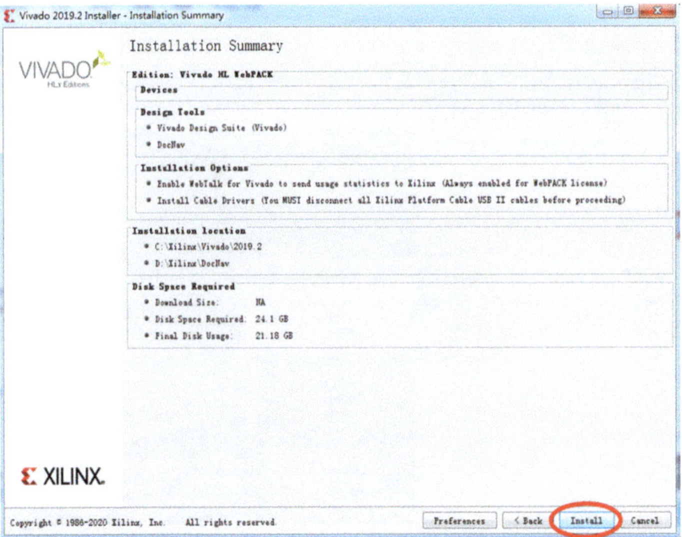

Fig. B.10 Installation summary screen

Image," a standalone installation package will be downloaded and can be installed locally.

Follow-up steps are the same as in the second half of Sect. B.3. Please use the same procedure (Figs. B.10, B.11, B.12, B.13 and B.14).

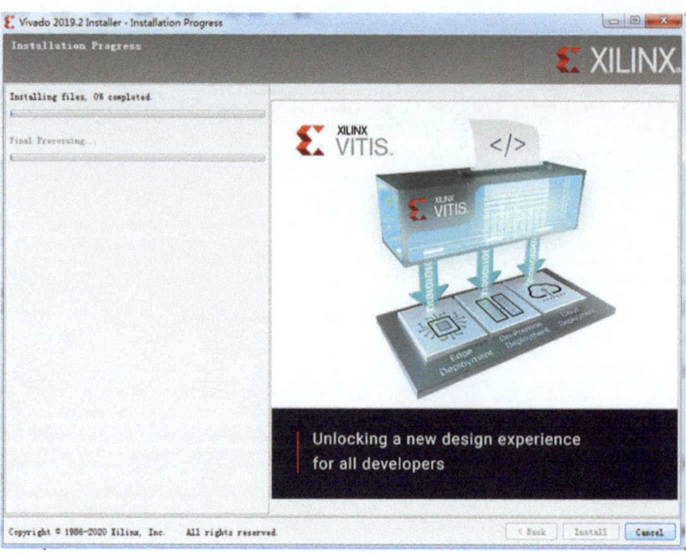

Fig. B.11 Installation progress screen

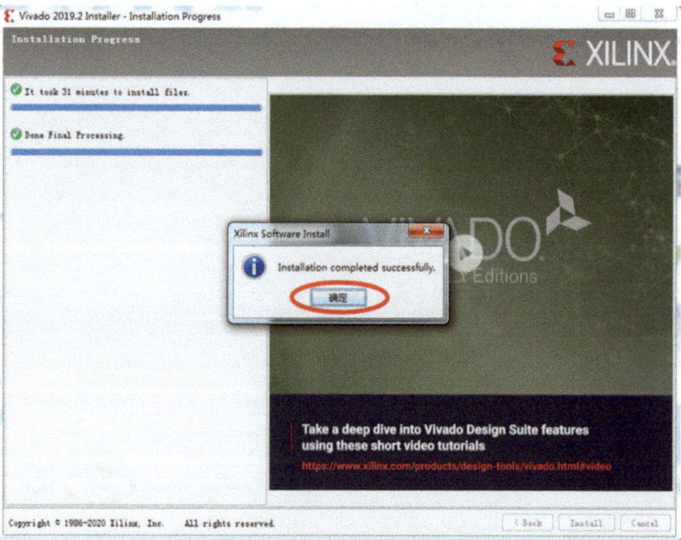

Fig. B.12 Installation success screen

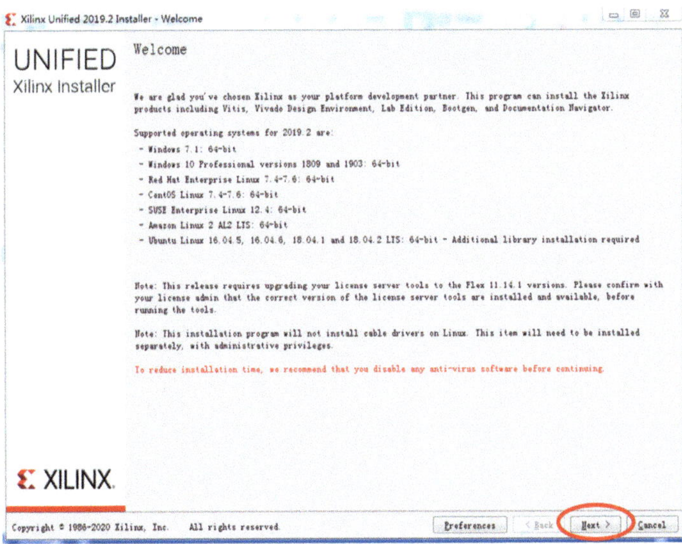

Fig. B.13 Online installation welcome screen

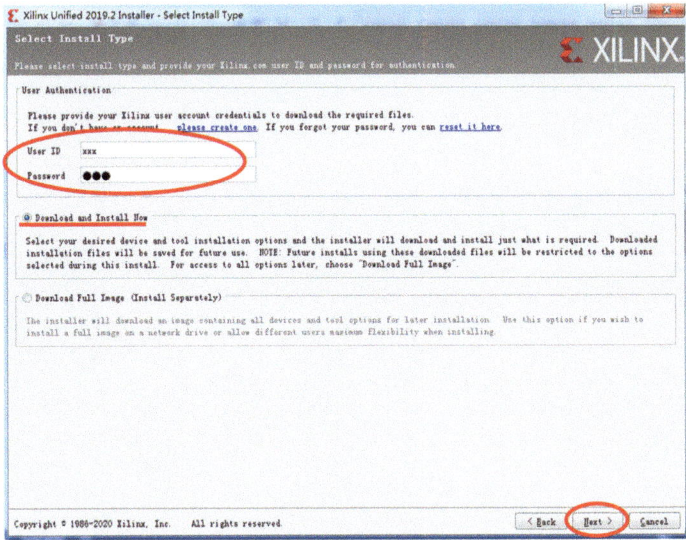

Fig. B.14 Online installation entering Xilinx accounts

Appendix C
Getting Started with Vivado

Here is an example of a circuit design for controlling an LED light via a dip switch, which describes the FPGA design implementation flow based on Vivado. Although this example is based on Vivado 2019.2, the content presented here is fully applicable to all versions of Vivado since Vivado 2017.1. For subsequent releases, readers are encouraged to try out the tool on a case-by-case basis, but we believe that the basic flow and functionality presented here will be retained.

C.1 Creating a Project

Open Vivado 2019.2 by double-clicking the desktop shortcut or "Xilinx Design Tools → Vivado 2019.2" in the start menu, and under "Quick Start" on the interface, select "Create Project" as shown in Fig. C.1.

At this point, the New Project Wizard can be created; click "Next" as shown in Fig. C.2.

In the interface shown in Fig. C.3, enter the project name, select the storage path for the project, and check the box "Create project subdirectory" option to create a separate directory for the project under the specified storage path. After the setting is completed, click "Next." (Note: **Chinese characters and spaces are not allowed** in the project name and storage path, and it is recommended that the project name be composed of letters, numbers, and underscores.)

In the interface shown in Fig. C.4, select "RTL Project," and check "Do not specify sources at this time" (this option is checked to skip adding the design source files during the process of creating a new project; if you want to add the source files during the process of creating a new project, then do not check this option). (This option is checked to skip adding source files during the process of creating a new project; if you want to add source files during the process of creating a new project, then do not check this option). Click "Next."

© The Author(s), under exclusive license to Springer Nature Singapore Pte Ltd. 2025
W. Wang, J. Xing, *CPU Design and Practice*,
https://doi.org/10.1007/978-981-96-6573-0

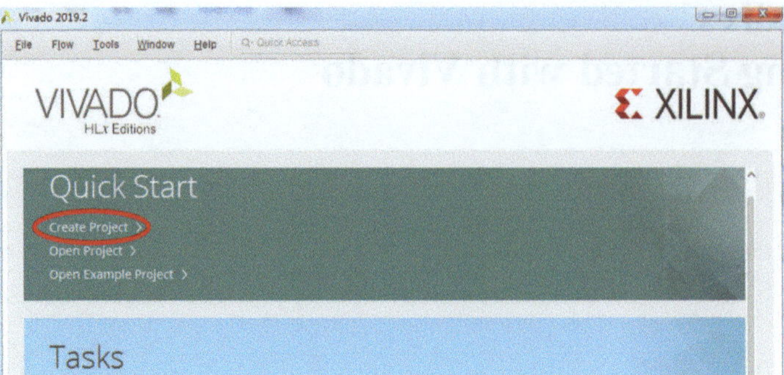

Fig. C.1 Vivado startup screen

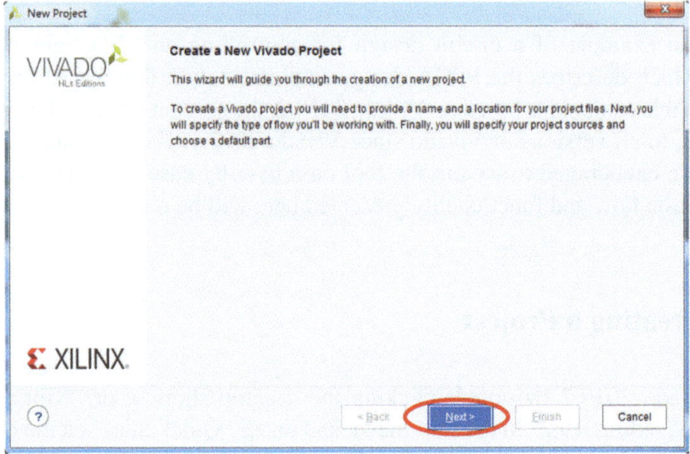

Fig. C.2 New project wizard

Select the corresponding FPGA target device in the screen shown in Fig. C.5. The recommended FPGA models for the local experiment box and the remote experiment platform are the same. Select "Artix 7" in "Family," "fbg676" in "Package," and "xxg676" in the filtered model number. Select "Artix 7" in "Family," "fbg676" in "Package," and "xc7a200tfbg676-1" in the filtered models. Click "Next" after selecting the above.

Confirm that the setting information of the project is correct in the screen shown in Fig. C.6. If it is correct, click "Finish"; if not correct, then click "Previous" to return to the appropriate step to make changes.

The interface after completing the project new creation is shown in Fig. C.7.

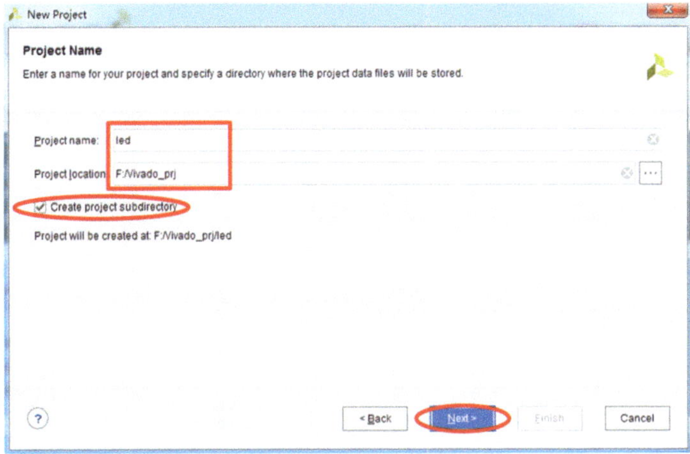

Fig. C.3 Setting the project name and location

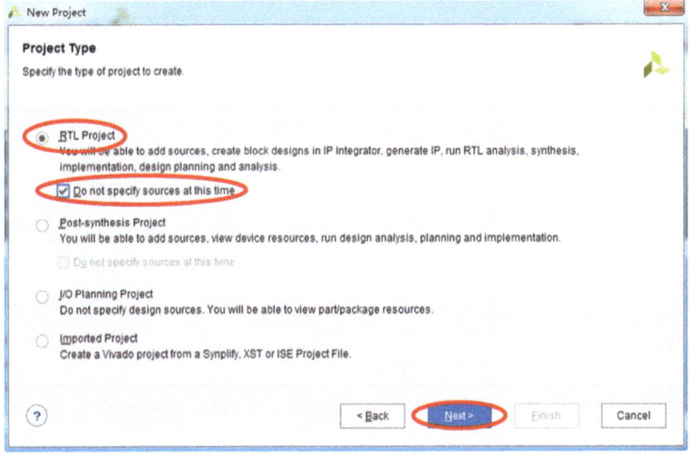

Fig. C.4 Setting the project type

C.2 Adding Design Files

Let's take Verilog as an example to illustrate how to add a design file to an RTL design. Verilog code is a file with ".v" extension, so you can write the code in other file editors before adding it to the newly created project, or you can create a new file in the project and then edit it.

First add the source file. Click "Add sources" under "PROJECT MANAGER" in the "Flow Navigator" window, or click the "Add Sources" button in the "Sources" window (see Fig. C.8), or use the shortcut key "Alt + A" to add the source file.

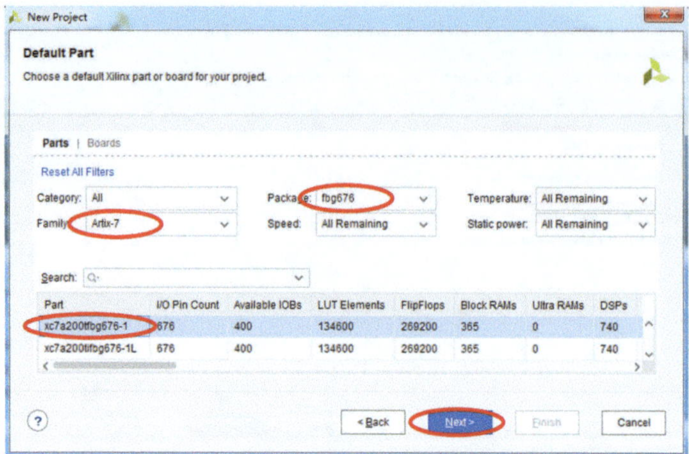

Fig. C.5 Selecting the target device

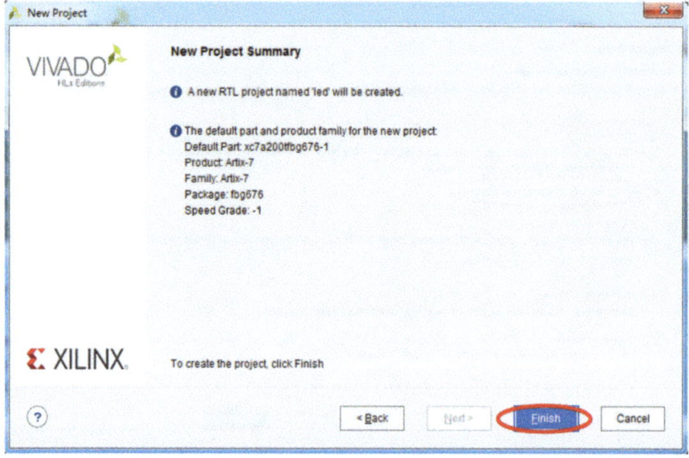

Fig. C.6 Project information

Then add the design files. Select "Add or create design sources" to add or create new Verilog/VHDL source files, and then click "Next," as shown in Fig. C.9.

Next, add or create a new design file. If you want to add an existing design file or a folder containing an existing design file, you can select "Add Files" or "Add Directories" as shown in Fig. C.10 and then select the existing design file in the file browser window to complete the addition. Then select the existing design file in the file browser window to complete the addition.

To create a new design file, select "Create File" as shown in Fig. C.11. The next section describes how to create a new design file.

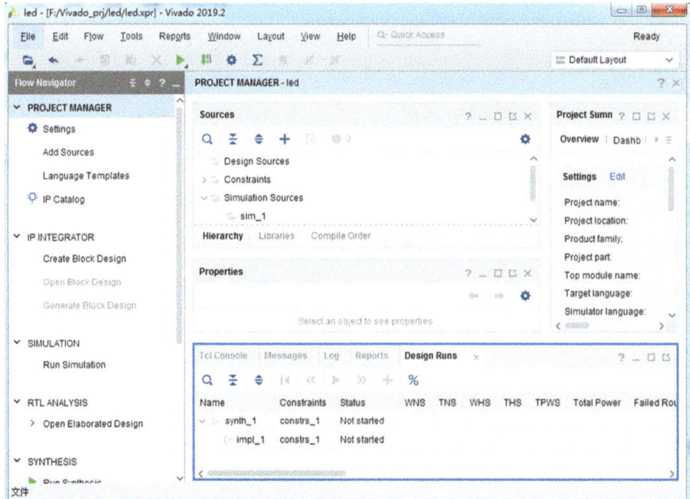

Fig. C.7 Creating project completion screen

Fig. C.8 Adding source files

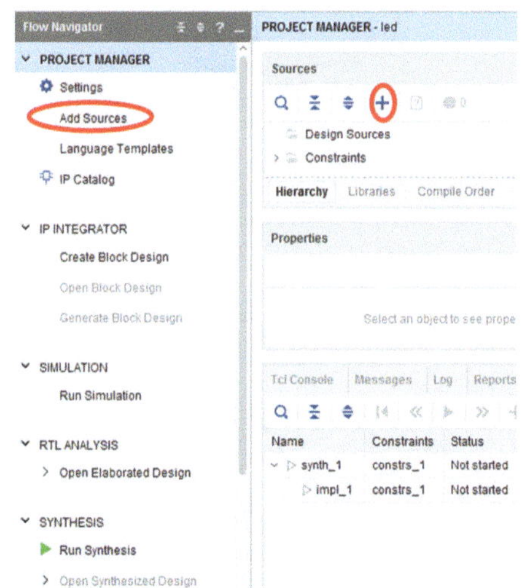

Set the type, name, and location of the newly created file in the screen shown in Fig. C.12. Note: Chinese characters and spaces are not allowed in the file name and location path.

Continue to add other design files or modify the added design files. Click "Finish" when finished, as shown in Fig. C.13.

The next step is to make module port settings. In the "Module Definitions" section, enter the following in the "I/O Port Definitions" section for the module, and set the port orientation. If the port is a bus type, check the "Bus" option, and set the port direction by "MSB" and "LSB" parameters to determine the bus width.

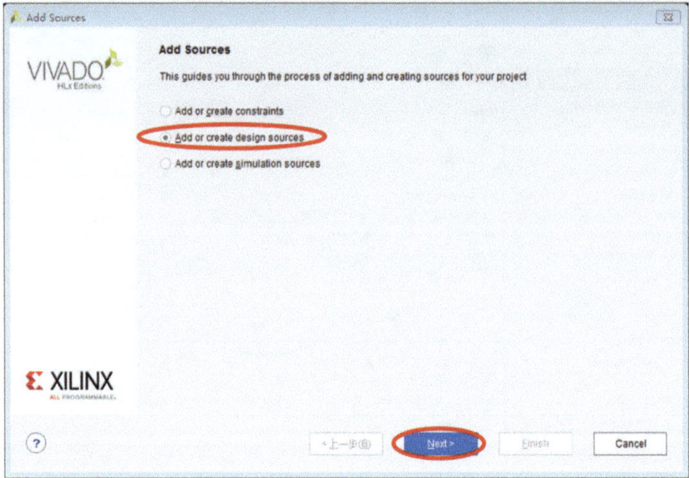

Fig. C.9 Adding design files

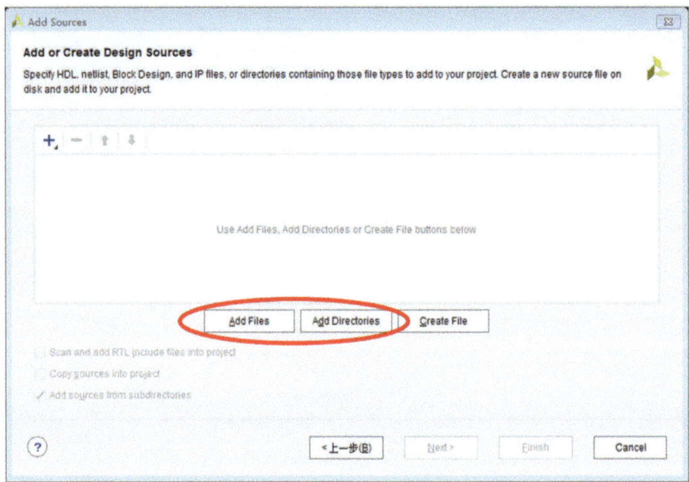

Fig. C.10 Adding an existing design file

Click "OK" when finished, as shown in Fig. C.14. If the port settings have already been completed when editing the source file, this step can be skipped by clicking "OK."

Double-click "Sources" in the interface shown in Fig. C.15, open the file "led.v" under "Design Sources," and input the corresponding design code. If the default file location is <Local to Project> (see Fig. C.12), the design file is located in "\led.srcs\sources_1\new" in the project directory. The completed design file is shown in Fig. C.15.

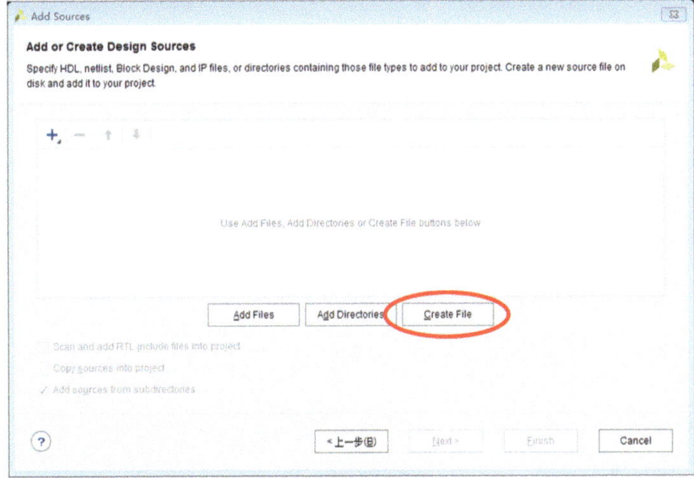

Fig. C.11 New design file

Fig. C.12 Settings of the new design file

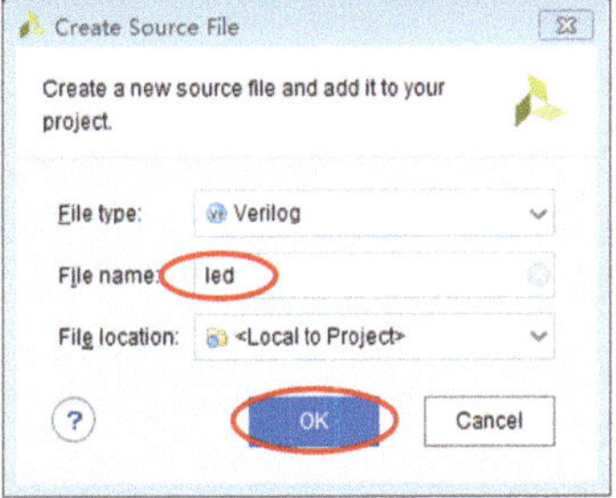

C.3   Functional Simulation

The simulator Vivado Simulator is integrated in Vivado and can be used to perform functional simulation.

First add the test excitation file. Right-click on "Simulation Sources" in "Source" and select "Add source" as shown in Fig. C.16.

In the "Add Sources" screen, select "Add or create simulation sources" and click "Next." Click "Next" as shown in Fig. C.17.

If you are adding an existing incentive test file, select "Add Files" as shown in Fig. C.18.

If you are creating a new excitation test file in Vivado, select "Create File" as shown in Fig. C.19. The next section describes how to create a new excitation test file.

Enter the name of the incentive test file in the screen shown in Fig. C.20.

File Setup: After completing the new test file, click "Finish" as shown in Fig. C.21.

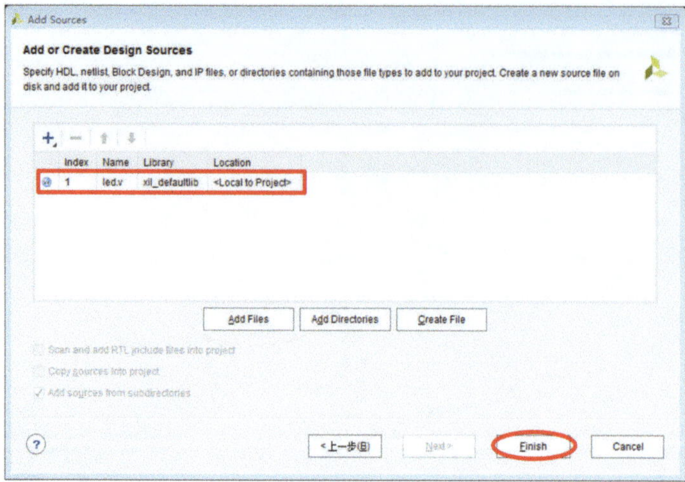

Fig. C.13 Completing design file additions

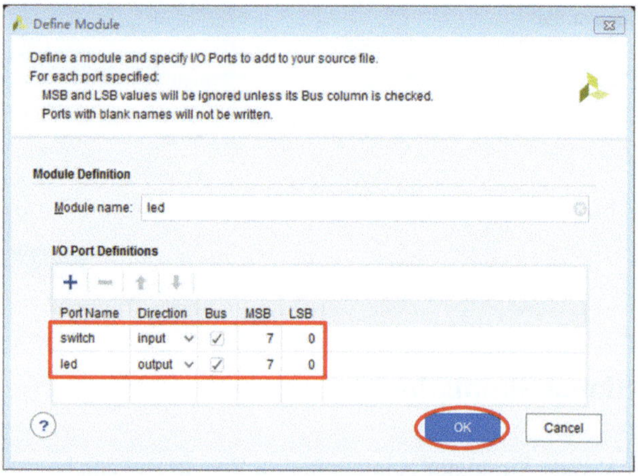

Fig. C.14 Module port settings

The next step is to define the module port for the test incentive file. Since the test stimulus file does not need to have an external interface, it is not necessary to define a module port for the test stimulus file; just click "OK" to complete the creation of a blank excitation test file as shown in Fig. C.22.

As shown in Fig. C.23, double-click under the "Sources" window to open a blank excitation test file. The test file led_tb.v is located in the folder "\led.srcs\sim_1\new" in the project directory.

Optionally, the code for the test stimulus file can be written in Vivado's editor. The completed test stimulus file code for this example is shown in Fig. C.24.

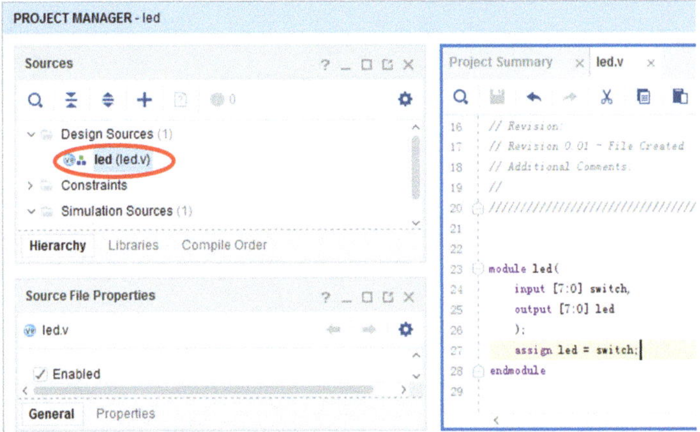

Fig. C.15 Editing the design file

Fig. C.16 Adding a test stimulus file

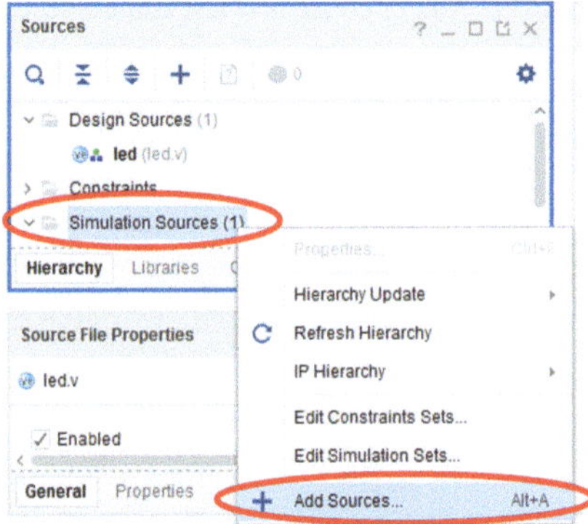

After the excitation test file has been added or created, the simulation can be performed. Click the "Run Simulation" option under "SIMULATION" in the "Flow Navigator" window on the left (as shown in Fig. C.25), and select "Run Behavioral" to enter the simulation interface (shown in Fig. C.26).

You can locate the signal you want to view through the directory structure in the "Scope" column on the left side of Fig. C.26, right-click on the signal name corresponding to "Objects," and select "Add To Wave Window" to add the signal into the waveform diagram (as shown in Fig. C.27). The emulator displays the I/O signals by default. Since there is no internal signal in this example, there is no need to add other observation signals.

You can control the simulation time of the waveform by selecting the options in the toolbar. As shown in Fig. C.28, the tools in the toolbar are Reset Waveform (i.e., go back to simulation time 0), Run Simulation, Run Simulation for Specific Duration, Simulation Duration Setting, Simulation Duration Units, Single-Step Running, Pause, and Restart (to recompile the design and simulation files and

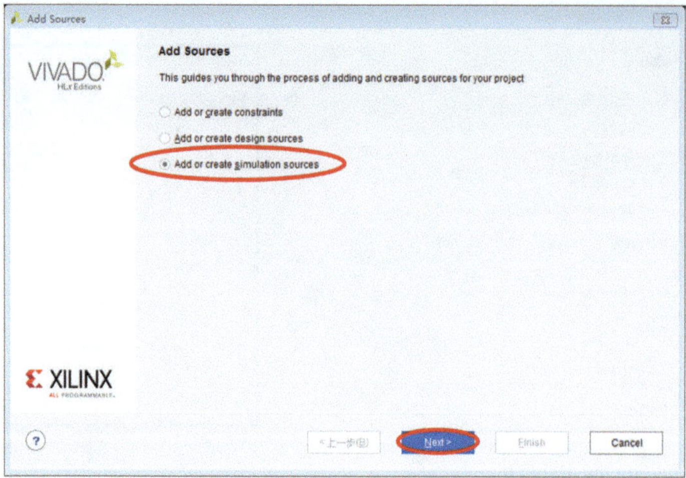

Fig. C.17 Add or create new test stimulus file

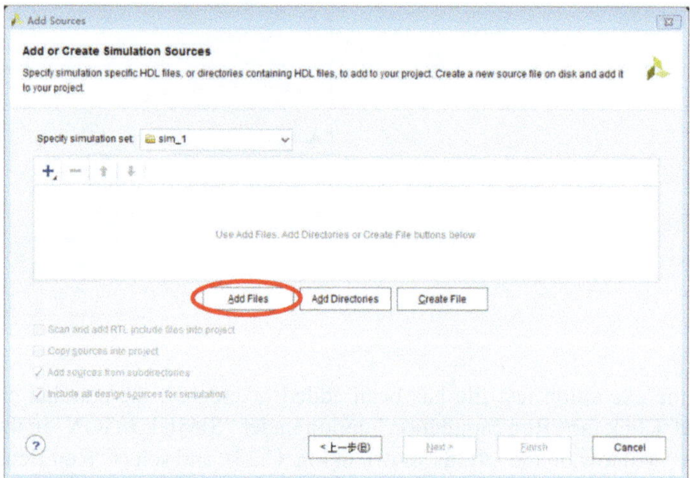

Fig. C.18 Adding an existing test stimulus file

restart the simulation waveform interface). We can observe whether the simulation waveform meets the expected function.

On the upper side of the waveform display window are the waveform control tools, from left to right: Find, Save Waveform Configuration, Zoom In, Zoom Out, Zoom to Full, Go to Cursor, Go to Moment 0, Go to Last Moment, Previous Jump, Next Jump, Add Marker, Previous Marker, Next Marker, and Exchange Cursor (see Fig. C.29).

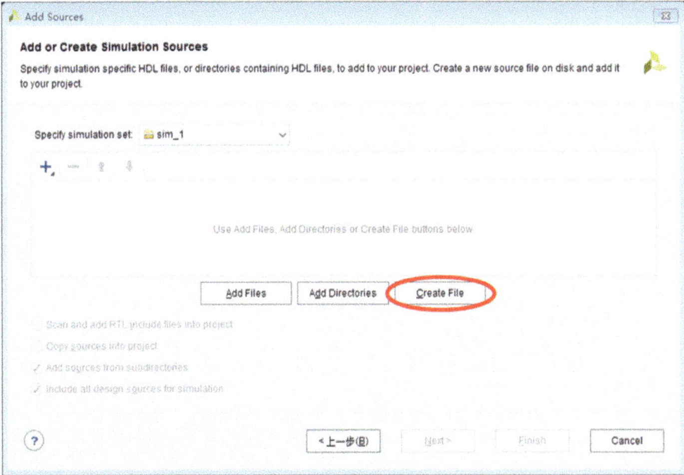

Fig. C.19 New test incentive file

Fig. C.20 New test set

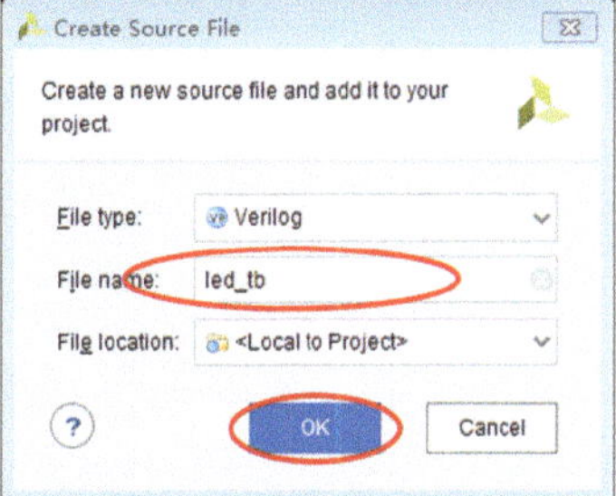

The number of display binary of the signal value can be changed by right-clicking and selecting the signal. The signal is changed to a binary display as shown in Fig. C.30.

View the waveforms to check the correctness of the design function, as shown in Fig. C.31.

C.4   Adding a Constraint File

There are two ways to add a constraint file: one is to utilize the I/O planning feature in Vivado, and the other is to create a direct XDC constraint file, manually input the constraint command, and then add it to the project. Here mainly introduces the second method.

First click "Add Sources," select "Add or create constraints," and click "Next," as Fig. C.32 shows.

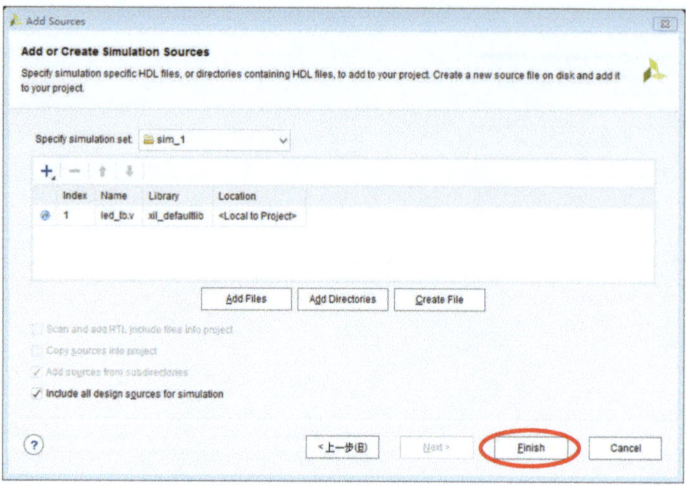

Fig. C.21 Completion of creating new test stimulus file

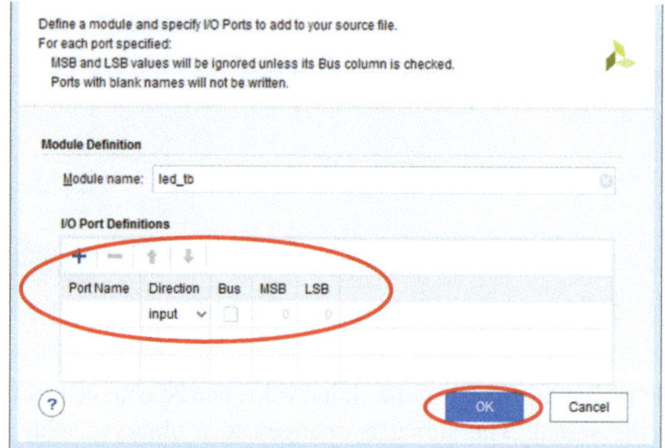

Fig. C.22 New test incentive top-level file without port configuration

Then add or create constraint file. If you use the method of adding an already edited constraint file, then click "Add Files" as shown in Fig. C.33.

If the method of creating a new constraint file is used, then click "Create Files" as shown in Fig. C.34.

If you are using the Create New Constraint File method, you will need to set up the newly created XDC file next, enter the XDC file name, and click "OK." The default file is located in "\led.srcs\constrs_1\new" in the project directory. See Fig. C.35.

After adding a constraint file either by adding or creating, click "Finish" in the interface as shown in Fig. C.36.

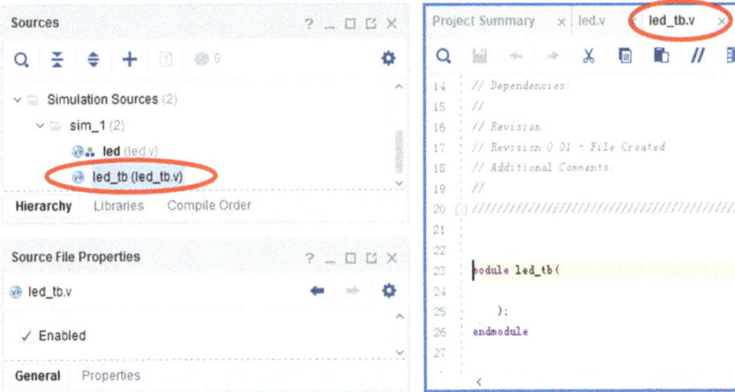

Fig. C.23 Blank new test stimulus file

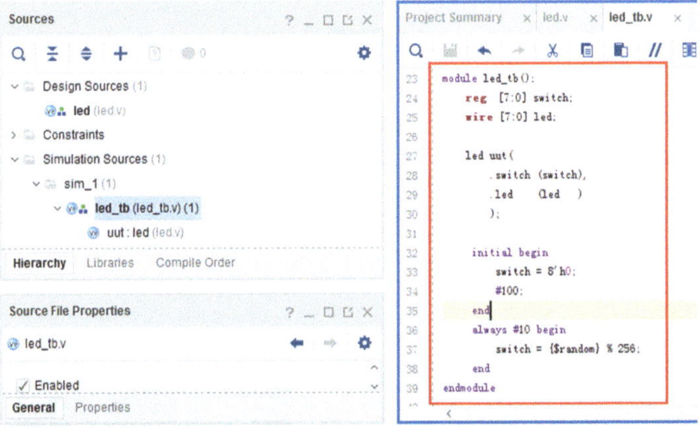

Fig. C.24 New test incentive file for completed code writing

If you have just used the method of creating a new constraint file, then you can open the newly created XDC file "led_xdc.xdc" by double-clicking under "Constraints" in the "Sources" window, as shown in Fig. C.37.

Populate the led_xdc.xdc file with the constraint code shown below, which is mainly FPGA pin constraint information and level standards:

```
set_property PACKAGE_PIN H8 [get_ports {led[7]}]
set_property PACKAGE_PIN G8 [get_ports {led[6]}]
set_property PACKAGE_PIN F7 [get_ports {led[5]}]
set_property PACKAGE_PIN A4 [get_ports {led[4]}]
set_property PACKAGE_PIN A5 [get_ports {led[3]}]
set_property PACKAGE_PIN A3 [get_ports {led[2]}]
set_property PACKAGE_PIN D5 [get_ports {led[1]}]
set_property PACKAGE_PIN H7 [get_ports {led[0]}]
set_property PACKAGE_PIN Y6 [get_ports {switch[7]}]
```

Fig. C.25 Running behavioral-level simulation

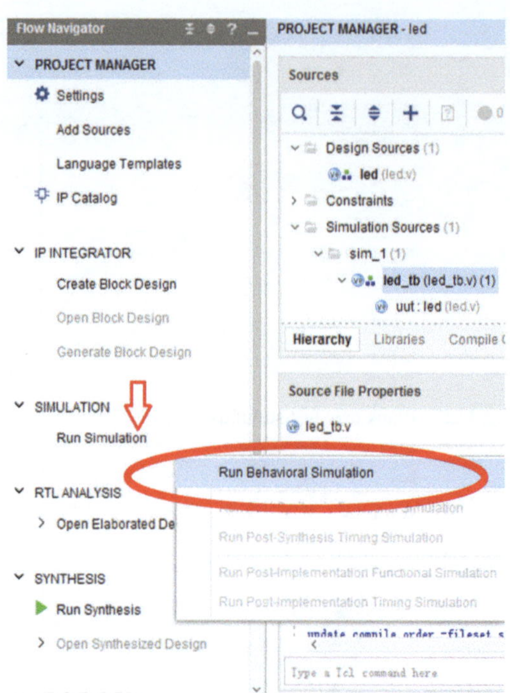

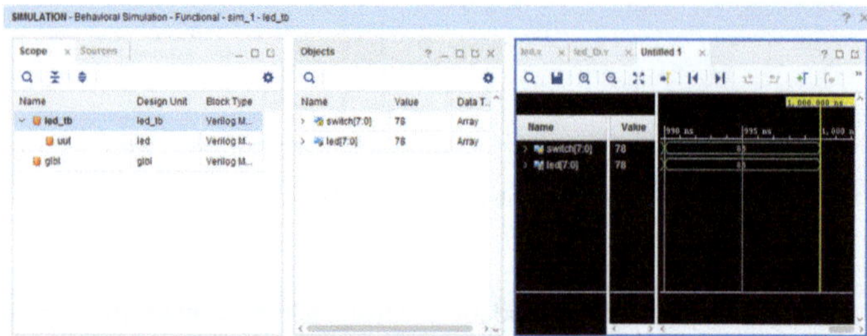

Fig. C.26 Behavioral-level simulation interface

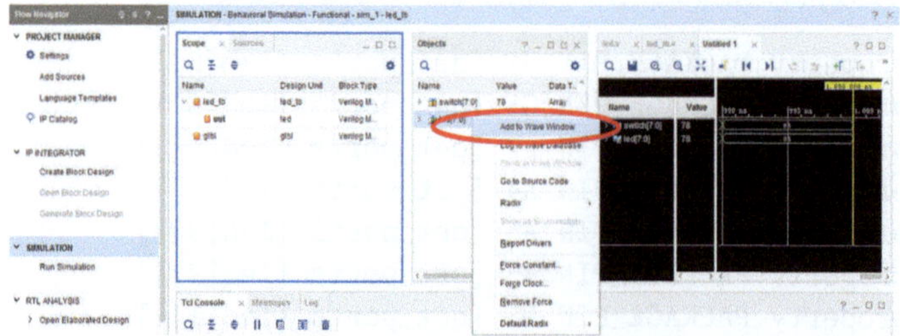

Fig. C.27 Adding internal signals to the waveform diagram

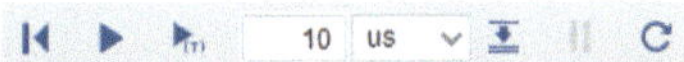

Fig. C.28 Emulation control toolbar

Fig. C.29 Waveform chart control toolbar

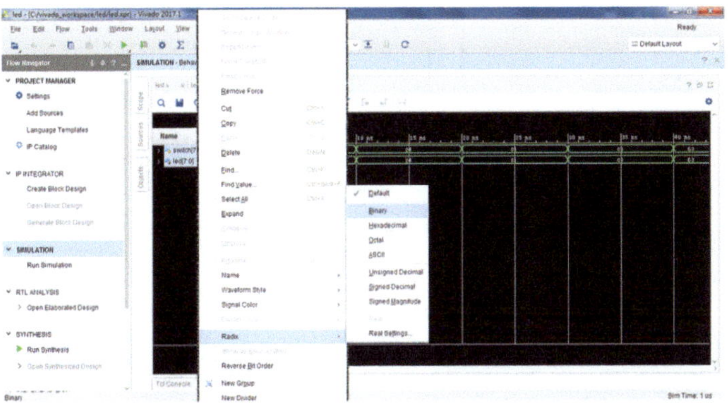

Fig. C.30 Simulation waveform window

Fig. C.31 Simulation waveform results

```
set_property PACKAGE_PIN AA7 [get_ports {switch[6]}]
set_property PACKAGE_PIN W6 [get_ports {switch[5]}]
set_property PACKAGE_PIN AB6 [get_ports {switch[4]}]
set_property PACKAGE_PIN AC23 [get_ports {switch[3]}]
set_property PACKAGE_PIN AC22 [get_ports {switch[2]}]
set_property PACKAGE_PIN AD24 [get_ports {switch[1]}]
set_property PACKAGE_PIN AC21 [get_ports {switch[0]}]
set_property IOSTANDARD LVCMOS33 [get_ports {led[7]}]
set_property IOSTANDARD LVCMOS33 [get_ports {led[6]}]
set_property IOSTANDARD LVCMOS33 [get_ports {led[5]}]
set_property IOSTANDARD LVCMOS33 [get_ports {led[4]}]
set_property IOSTANDARD LVCMOS33 [get_ports {led[3]}]
set_property IOSTANDARD LVCMOS33 [get_ports {led[2]}]
set_property IOSTANDARD LVCMOS33 [get_ports {led[1]}]
set_property IOSTANDARD LVCMOS33 [get_ports {led[0]}]
set_property IOSTANDARD LVCMOS33 [get_ports {switch[7]}]
set_property IOSTANDARD LVCMOS33 [get_ports {switch[6]}]
```

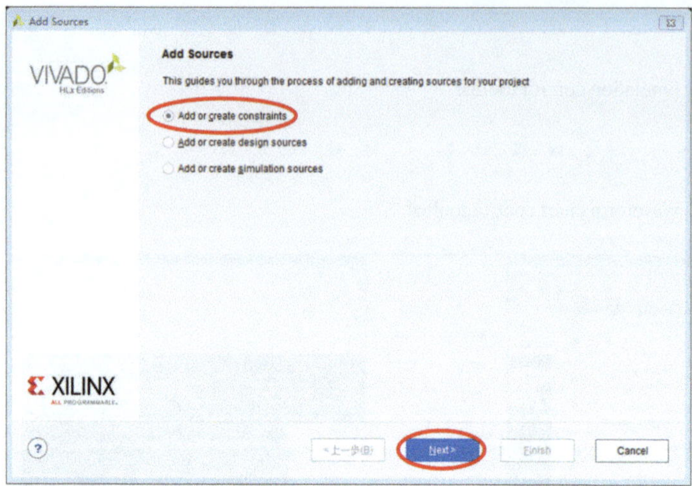

Fig. C.32 Adding constraints

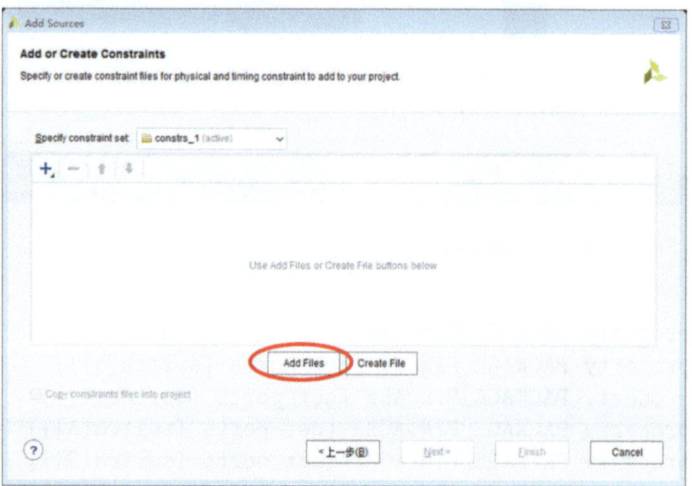

Fig. C.33 Adding a constraint file

```
set_property IOSTANDARD LVCMOS33 [get_ports {switch[5]}]
set_property IOSTANDARD LVCMOS33 [get_ports {switch[4]}]
set_property IOSTANDARD LVCMOS33 [get_ports {switch[3]}]
set_property IOSTANDARD LVCMOS33 [get_ports {switch[2]}]
set_property IOSTANDARD LVCMOS33 [get_ports {switch[1]}]
set_property IOSTANDARD LVCMOS33 [get_ports {switch[0]}]
```

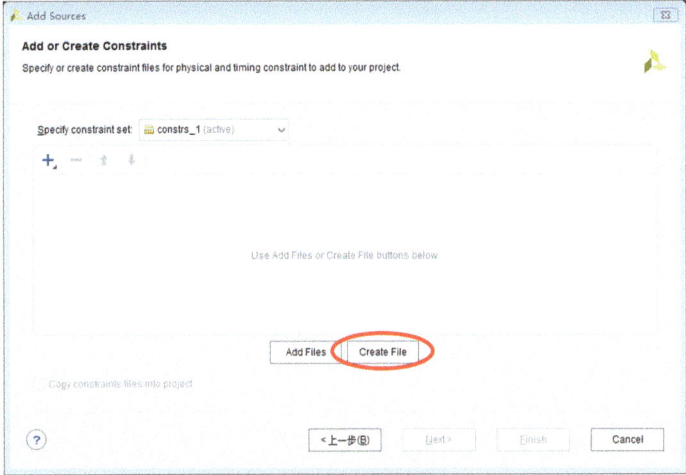

Fig. C.34 New constraint file

Fig. C.35 Settings for the
new constraint file

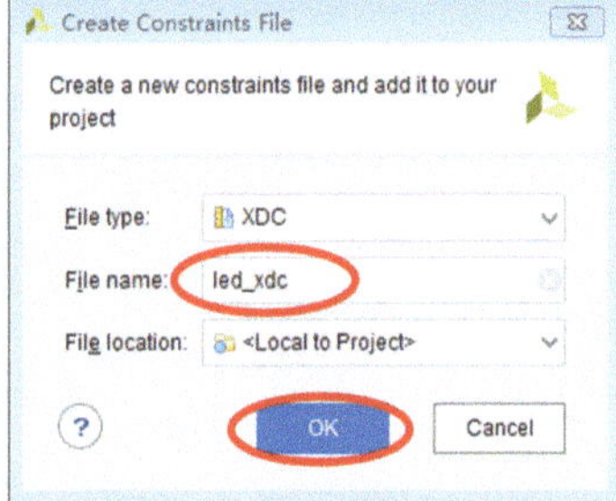

C.5   Synthesis, Implementation, and Generation of Bitstream File

In "Flow Navigator," click "Generate Bitstream" under "PROGRAM AND DEBUG." The project will automatically complete the synthesis, layout and wiring, and bitstream file generation as shown in Fig. C.38. Once finished, you can click "Open Implemented Design" to view the result of the project.

If the prompt shown in Fig. C.39 appears, it means that the synthesis has expired, and you need to rerun the synthesis and implementation. At this point, click "Yes," and click "OK" on the "Launch Runs" pop-up window.

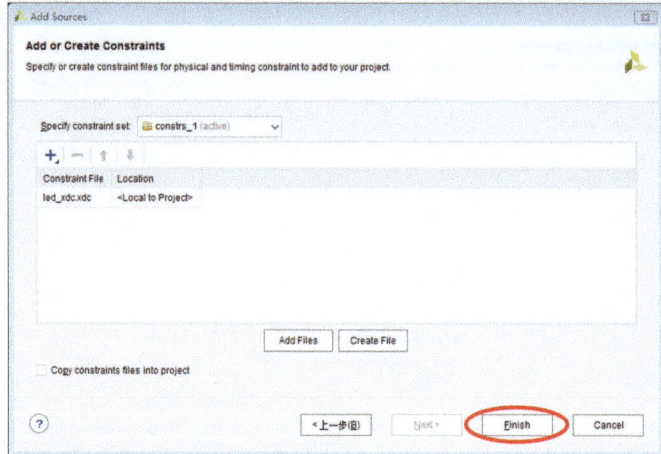

Fig. C.36 Completing adding constraints

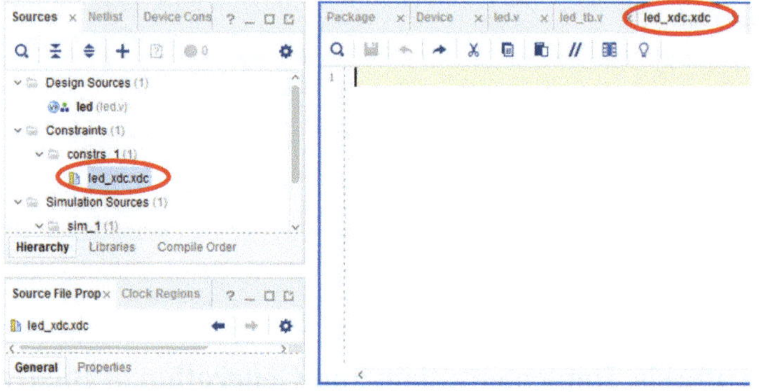

Fig. C.37 Opening a blank XDC file

Fig. C.38 Generating a
bitstream file

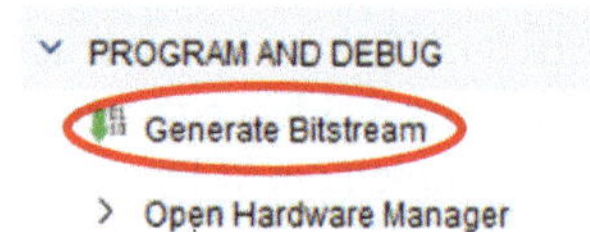

Fig. C.39 Prompt to rerun
synthesis and implementation

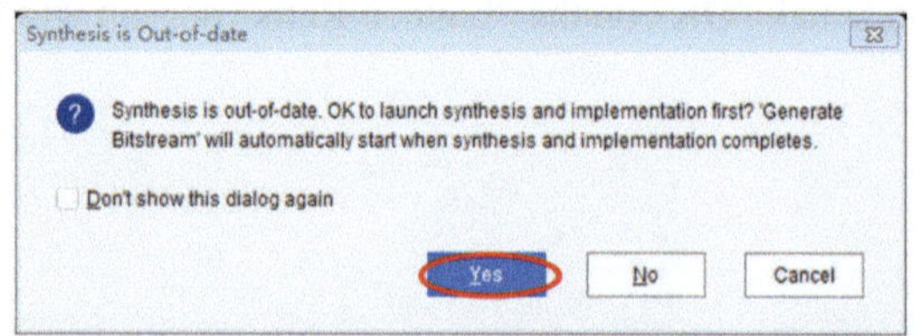

C.6   Local FPGA Burn Configuration

If you choose the local FPGA experiment platform, you can enter the stage of burning and configuring FPGA after the bitstream file is generated. The specific operation is select "Open Hardware Manager" in the window where the bitstream file generation is completed, and click OK to enter the hardware management interface, as shown in Fig. C.40. Connect the power cable of the FPGA development board and the download cable with the computer, and turn on the FPGA power.

At the "Hardware Manager" window prompt, click "Open New Target" in the "Open target" drop-down menu (or expand "Open Hardware Manager" in "PRO-GRAM AND DEBUG" under "Flow Navigator," and click "Open Target →Open New Target"), or you can select "AutoConnect" to connect the device automatically, as shown in Fig. C.41.

In the "Open Hardware Target" wizard, click "Next" to enter the Server Selection Wizard, as shown in Fig. C.42.

Select to connect to "Local server," and click "Next" as shown in Fig. C.43.

Select the target hardware in the screen shown in Fig. C.44, and click "Next."

Click "Finish" to open the target hardware, as shown in Fig. C.45.

Next, program the target hardware. Right-click the target device "xc7a200t_0" in the "Hardware" window, and select "Program Device...," or click "PROGRAM

Fig. C.40 Open hardware program and debug management

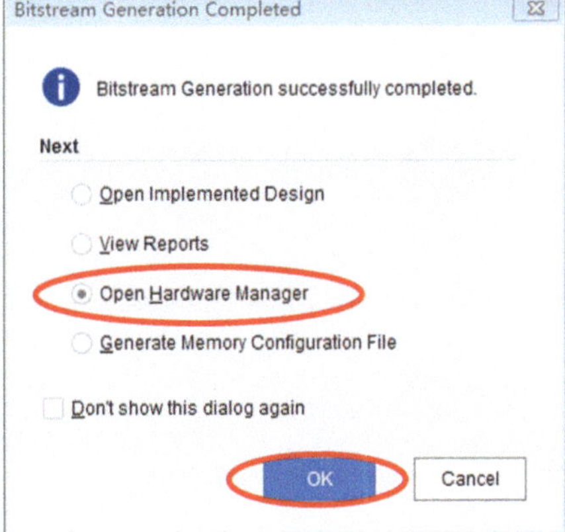

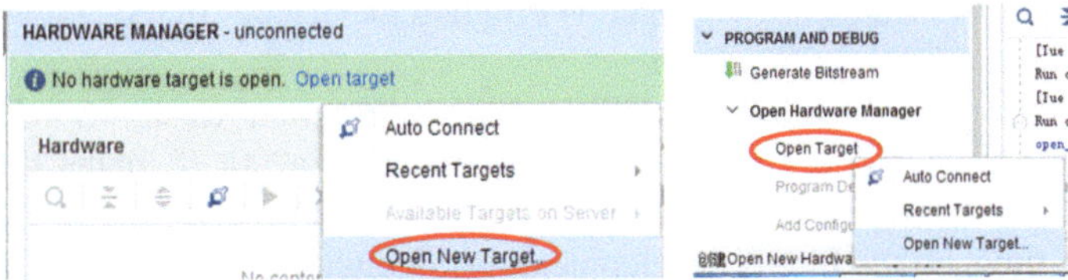

Fig. C.41 Opening a new target

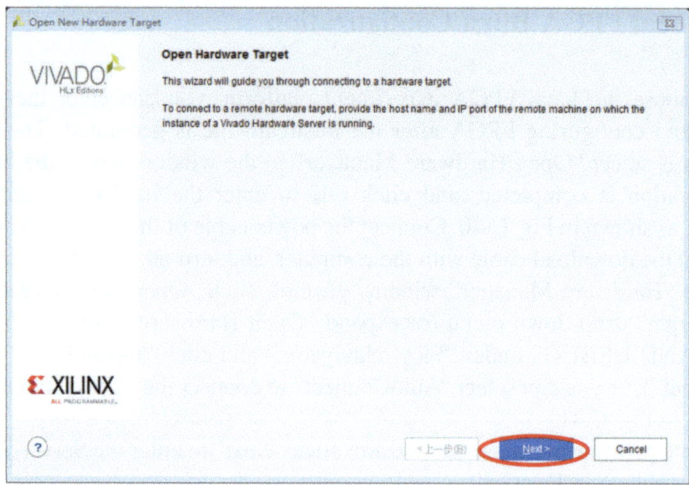

Fig. C.42 Open hardware target wizard

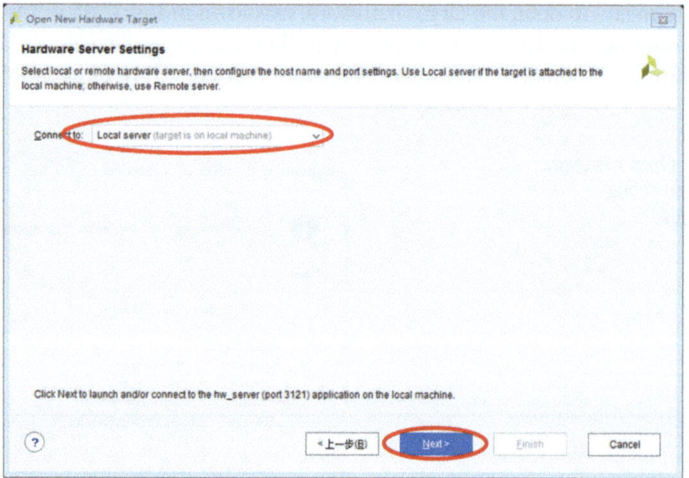

Fig. C.43 Connecting to local server

AND DEBUG →Hardware Manager →Program Device…" in the "Flow Navigator" window as shown in Fig. C.46.

Select the downloaded bitstream file, and click "Program" as shown in Fig. C.47.

After the download is completed, the status of "xc7a200t_0" under the "Hardware" window changes to "Programmed," as shown in Fig. C.48.

At this time, on the FPGA development board, eight dip switches SW18~SW25 correspond to control eight LED lamps LED1~LED8. The lighting of the design is complete. The result of the run is shown in Fig. C.49.

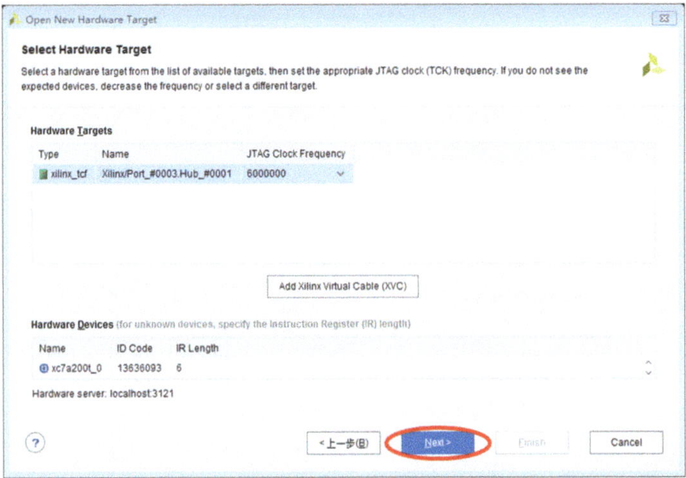

Fig. C.44 Selecting target hardware

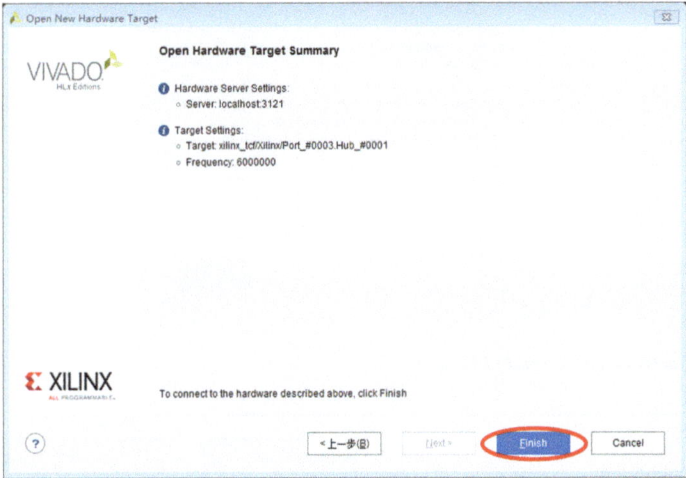

Fig. C.45 Turning on target hardware

C.7   Remote FPGA Burn Configuration

If a remote FPGA lab platform is used, only the last step of the burn-in configuration is different from that of the local FPGA lab platform, and the previous steps are exactly the same.

First, locate the bitstream file generated by Vivado. For the examples in this section, this is usually the led.bit file in the led\led.runs\impl_1\ directory. When

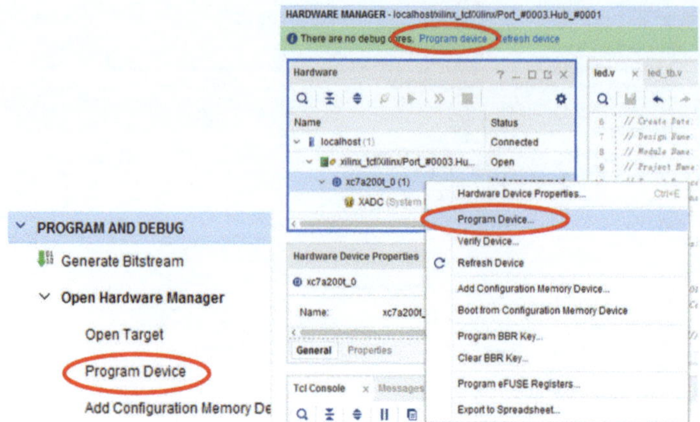

Fig. C.46 Programming the target device

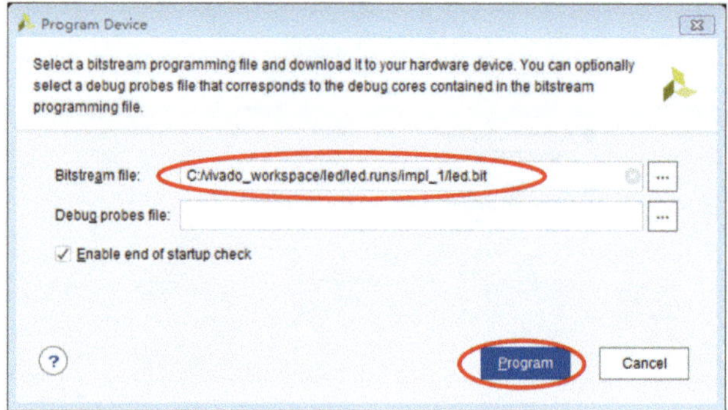

Fig. C.47 Selecting a bitstream file

Fig. C.48 Completing
FPGA programming

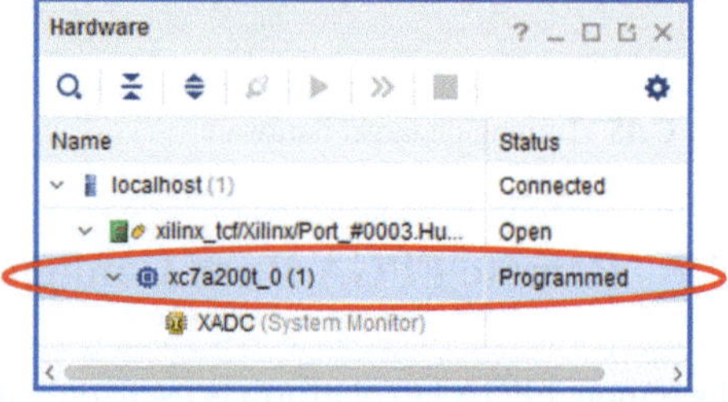

Fig. C.49 FPGA run results

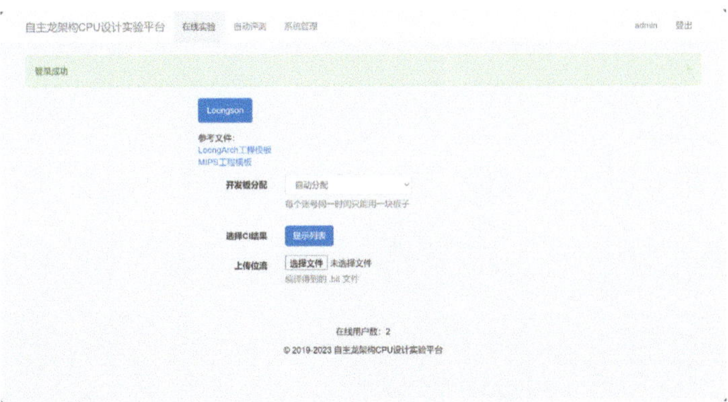

Fig. C.50 Remote FPGA lab platform bitstream file upload interface

the project name is changed, replace led in the above path and file name with the name of the new project.

Then, open the login page of the "Remote Experiment Platform for Computer System Competency Development" in the browser. After entering the platform, select the bitstream file in the interface as shown in Fig. C.50, and then click "Upload and Start."

After uploading the bitstream file, you will enter the remote FPGA development board interface as shown in Fig. C.51. Follow the instructions on the page to perform the corresponding operations.

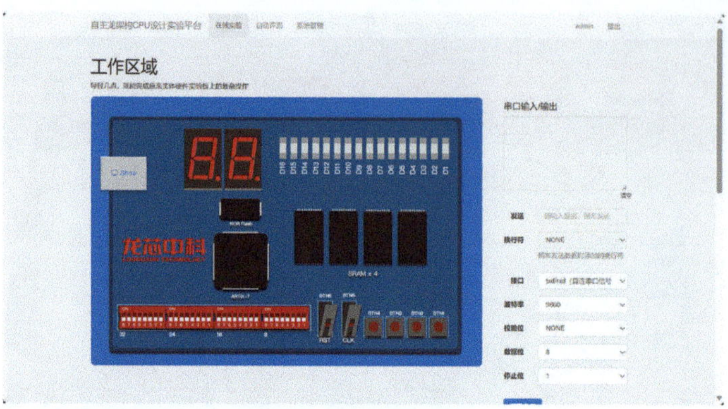

Fig. C.51 Remote FPGA experiment platform development board interface

Appendix D
Advanced Vivado Usage

D.1 Customized RAM IP Cores

Commonly used IP units such as RAM, AXI conversion bridges, Ethernet controllers, etc. are integrated into Vivado.

D.1.1 Custom Synchronized RAM IP Cores

The way to customize a single-cycle return synchronous RAM IP in Vivado is as follows:

(1) After opening or creating a new Vivado project, click "IP Catalog" in "PROJECT MANAGER," as shown in Fig. D.1.
(2) Double-click on "Memories and Storage" in the list on the right, Elements →RAMs & ROMs & BRAM" in the Block Memory Generator, as shown in Fig. D.2.
(3) Set the RAM parameters in the IP customization screen that opens.

1. In the "Basic" tab of RAM interface, rename the IP to block_ram, set the memory type to single-port RAM, and do not check "Byte Write Enable," as shown in Fig. D.3.
2. In the "Port A Options" tab, set RAM depth to 65,536 and width to 32, enable port to "Always Enabled," and do not check "Primitives Output Register." Otherwise, just keep the default settings and click "OK" as shown in Fig. D.4.

© The Author(s), under exclusive license to Springer Nature Singapore Pte Ltd. 2025   411
W. Wang, J. Xing, *CPU Design and Practice*,
https://doi.org/10.1007/978-981-96-6573-0

Fig. D.1 Click on "IP Catalog" in "PROJECT MANAGER"

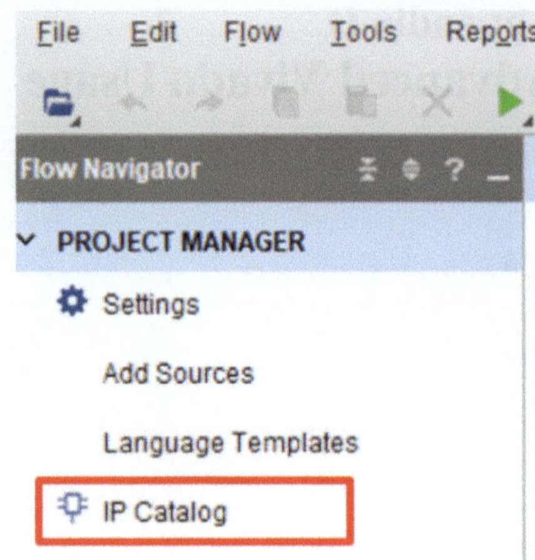

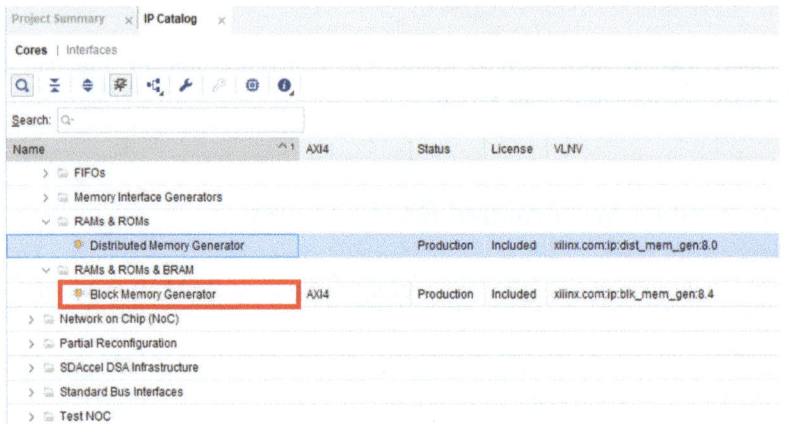

Fig. D.2 Select "Block Memory Generator" in the "IP Catalog"

D.1.2 Customized Asynchronous RAM IP Cores

Similar to customizing a synchronous RAMIP core, customizing an asynchronous RAMIP is done as follows:

(1) After opening or creating a new Vivado project, click "IP Catalog" in "PROJECT MANAGER."
(2) Double-click on "Memories and Storage Elements →RAMs & ROMs" in the list on the right, and select "Distributed Memory Generator," as shown in Fig. D.5.
(3) Set the RAM parameters in the IP customization interface. In the "memory config" interface, rename the IP to distributed_ram; set the memory type to

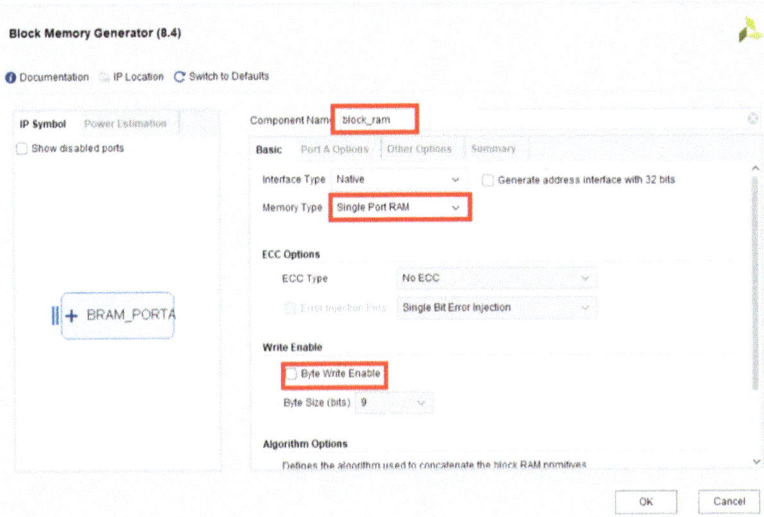

Fig. D.3 Setting basic parameters for synchronization RAM

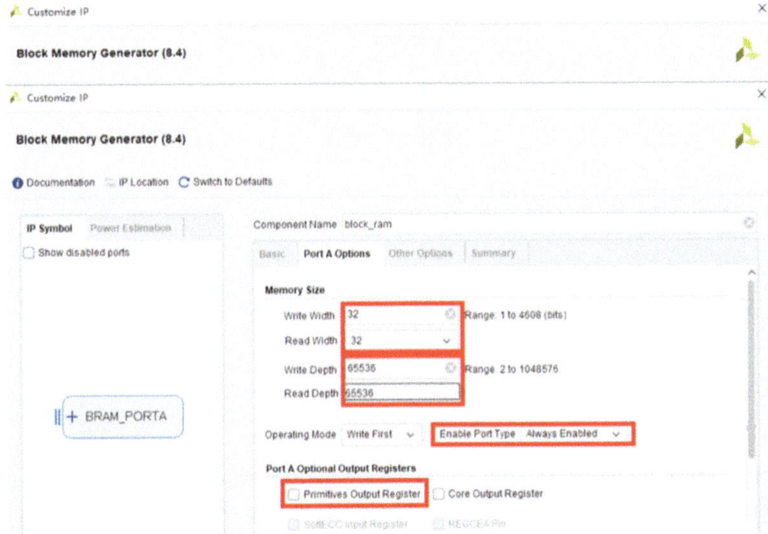

Fig. D.4 Setting Port A Options parameters for synchronization RAMs

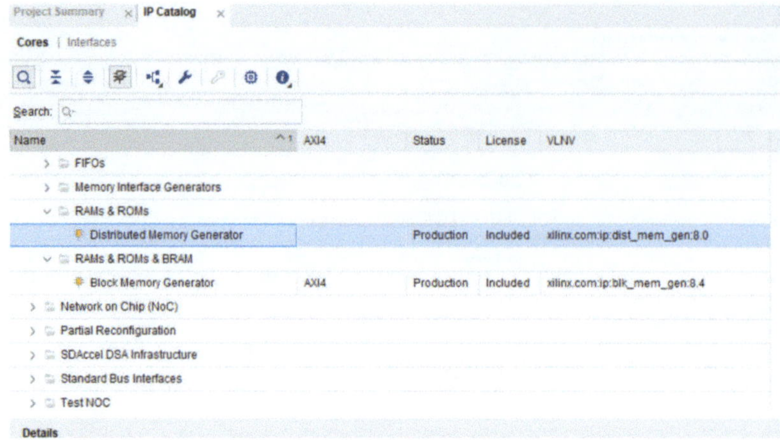

Fig. D.5 Select "Distributed Memory Generator" in the "IP Catalog"

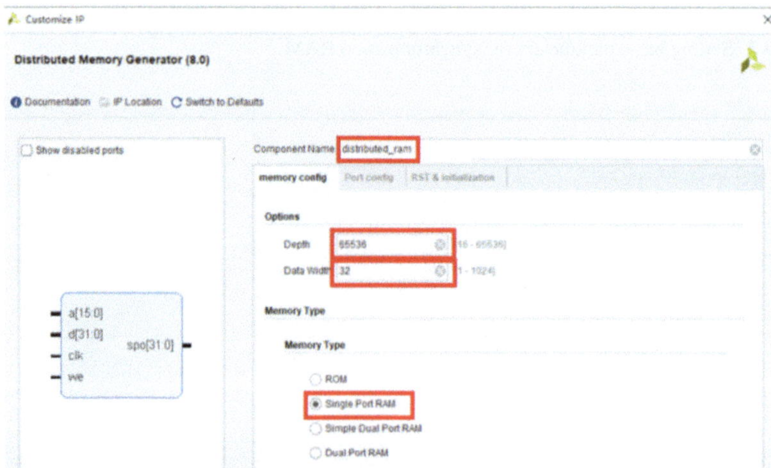

Fig. D.6 Setting parameters for asynchronization RAM

single-port RAM, the depth to 65,536, and the width to 32; leave the other settings as default; and click "OK" as shown in Fig. D.6.

D.1.3   Viewing Timing Results and Resource Utilization

After synthesizing and implementing Vivado, we can view the timing results and resource utilization (make sure you have completed the synthesis implementation), as shown in Fig. D.7.

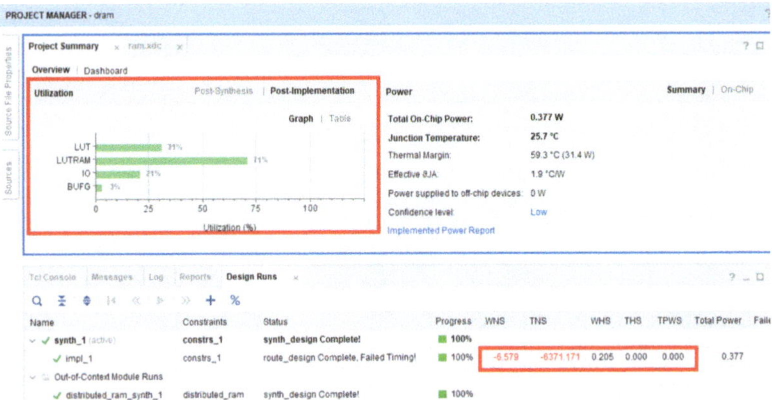

Fig. D.7 Viewing timing results and resource utilization

(1) View the timing results (WNS and TNS columns) in Vivado's "Design Runs" screen. wns indicates the default value for the longest path, and tns indicates the total default value for all the defaulted paths. wns and tns in negative red indicate a default. wns is the default value for the longest path, and tns is the total default value for all the defaulted paths. wns is the default value for the longest path, and tns is the total default value for all the defaulted paths.

(2) Check the resource utilization in the "Project Summary" interface of Vivado; LUT is the main resource, that is, the resource of the lookup table (the implementation principle of FPGA is mainly the lookup table); RAM is the resource of the synchronous RAM integrated internally; IO is the resource of the FPGA I/O interface; BUFG is the resource of the BUF integrated internally in FPGA.

In addition to the above, we can also open the implementation design in the left navigation bar under Implementation, generating timing reports (report timing summary) or resource reports (report utilization).

D.2   Creating a Vivado Project with tcl

It is recommended that you use tcl to create Vivado projects in the lab environments that accompany this book. The tcl scripts used to create Vivado projects are stored in the run_vivado directory of each lab environment. The following is a step-by-step procedure for creating a Vivado project using tcl:

Step 1:   After starting Vivado, click on the "Tcl Console" tab at the bottom as shown in Fig. D.8.

Step 2:   As shown in Fig. D.9, enter the command in the open Tcl Console, cd to where create_project.tcl is used (as shown in Fig. D.10).

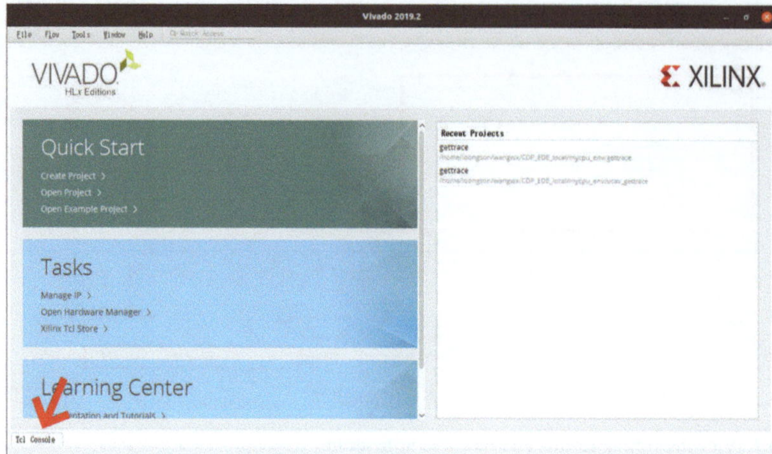

Fig. D.8 Opening the Tcl Console

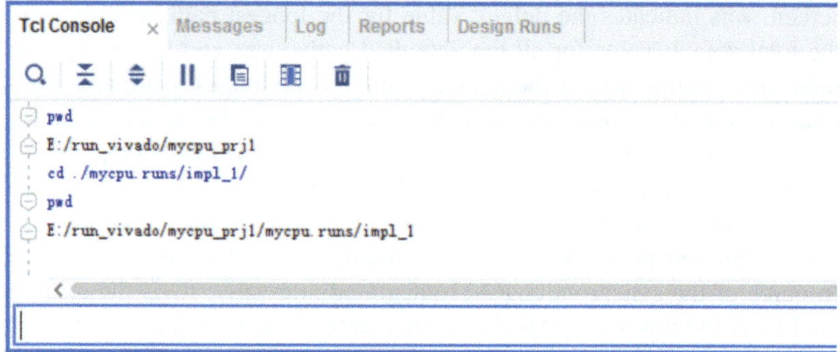

Fig. D.9 Location of input commands in the Tcl Console

Step 3:   As shown in Fig. D.11, proceed to the Tcl Console, and enter the
           command "source ./create_project.tcl." Vivado will then create the project
           based on the contents of create_project.tcl.

D.3   Adding Design Files to a Vivado Project with tcl

If you use our recommended method of obtaining the experimental development
environment, you will have multiple hands-on tasks that will use the same Vivado
project in the same directory. Since new design files may be added in new hands-on
tasks, you will need to update the list of source files in the project. In addition to the
graphical interface described in Appendix C.2, if the designer can ensure that there

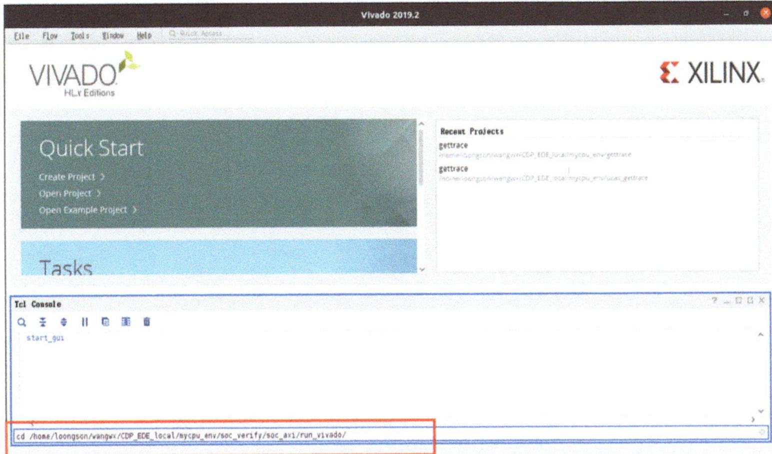

Fig. D.10 Enter where create_project.tcl is located

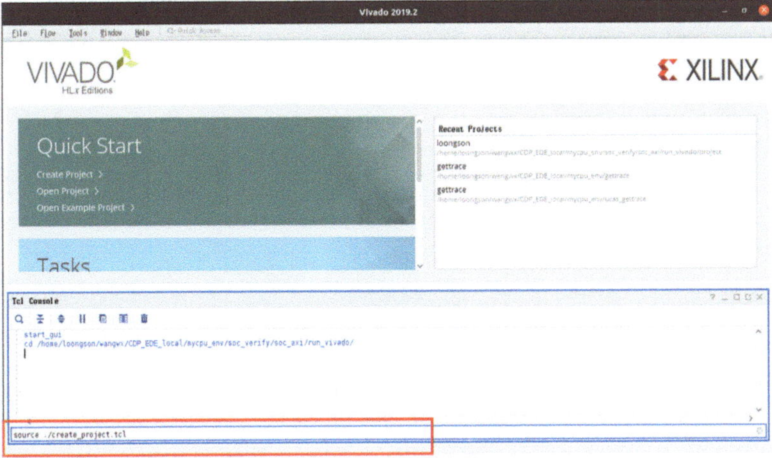

Fig. D.11 Source create_project.tcl creating a Vivado project

are no useless files in the myCPU directory, then the following is a faster way to add design files:

Step 1:   Locate the Tcl Console command entry location in the opened project as shown in Fig. D.12.

Step 2:   In Tcl Console, enter the command "add_files -scan_for_includes … /… /… /myCPU/" as shown in Fig. D.13.

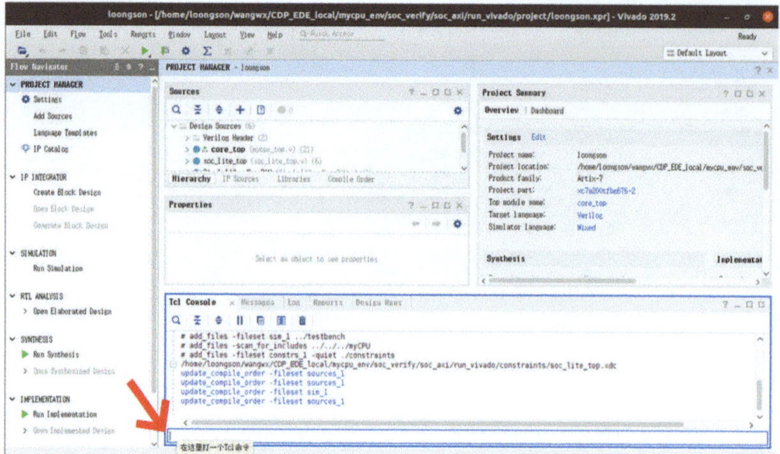

Fig. D.12 Location of input commands in the Tcl Console in an opened Vivado project

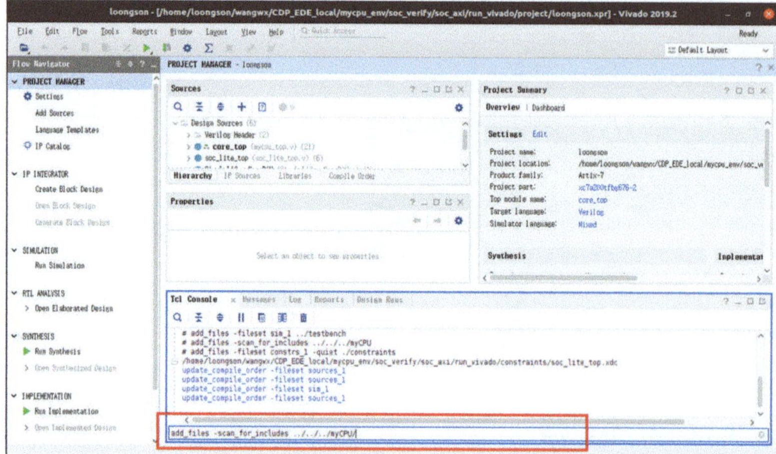

Fig. D.13 Adding design files in the myCPU directory by entering commands in the Tcl console

D.4   Upgrade Project and IP Cores

The experimental development environment for CPU design that accompanies this book was created in Vivado 2019.2. If you use a higher version of Vivado to open it, you need to upgrade your project and IP core. Note: Vivado does not support forward compatibility, which means that a lower version of Vivado cannot use the projects and IP cores created by a higher version of Vivado; if you encounter this situation, please upgrade the version of Vivado. A higher version of Vivado opens a lower version of the project and upgrades the project and IP cores as follows:

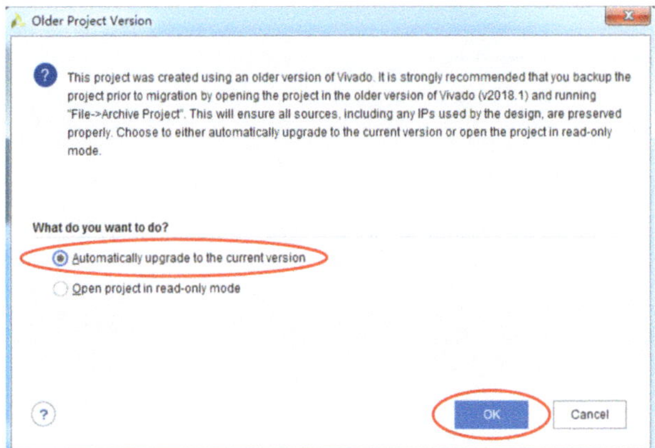

Fig. D.14 Low-version project upgrade

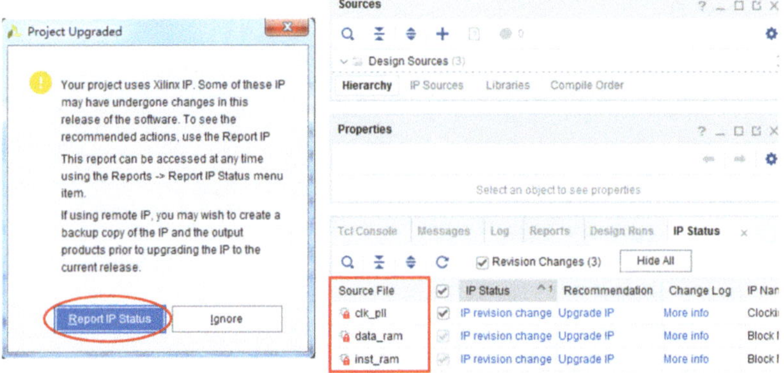

Fig. D.15 Showing IP core locked up

(1) Higher version of Vivado opens a project created by a lower version of Vivado. It will pop up as in Fig. D.14 interface. Select the first option "Automatically Upgrade…"and click "OK" to upgrade.

(2) If your project contains custom-built Vivado IPs, you will be prompted with a reminder on the left side of Fig. D.15; select "Report IP Status," and then the IP core status will be displayed, as shown on the right side of Fig. D.15: three Ips, displaying a red lock mark, which indicates that the IP core is currently locked and cannot be modified.

(3) The locked IP cores need to be upgraded sequentially before they can be modified in this version of Vivado. In the Sources window, find the IP to be upgraded in the window, right-click, and then click "Upgrade IP…" as in Fig. D.16.

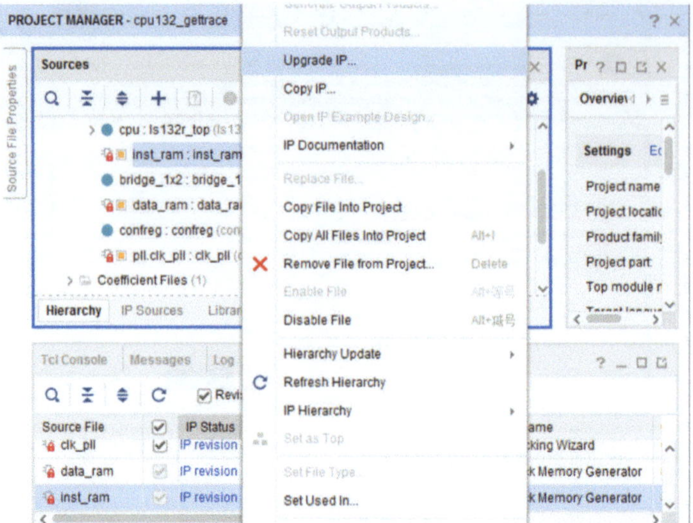

Fig. D.16 Right-click on the IP core and select "Upgrade IP…"

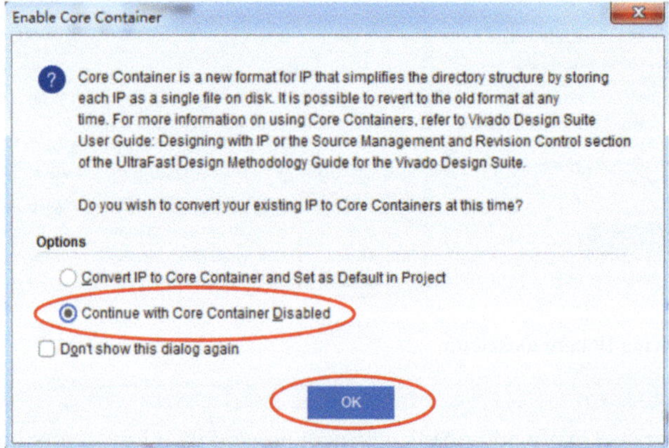

Fig. D.17 Upgrading the IP core

(4) After that, the interface as shown in Fig. D.17 will pop up, select the second option "Continue with Core…," and click "OK."

(5) In the Generate Output Product pop-up window (as shown in Fig. D.18), click Generate (select global or OOC mode as needed) to complete the upgrade.

Fig. D.18 Completes IP core upgrade

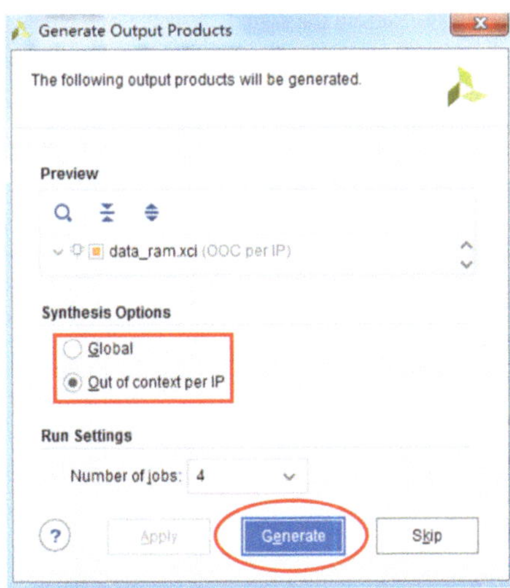

D.5   Online Debugging with Chipscope

In the process of developing with FPGAs, it is common to encounter the phenomenon of "passing simulation but failing on board." Due to the weak debugging techniques on board, it is difficult to locate the error. In this case, you can use the Chipscope integrated in Vivado for online debugging. Online debugging is the process of detecting the set signals while running on the FPGA and then displaying them to the debugging host computer via the USB programming cable.

This appendix gives the basic method of using in-circuit debugging: set up the signals to be detected in RTL, synthesize and create a debug, realize and produce a bitstream file, download the bitstream and debug file, and observe on the board.

D.5.1   Grabbing the Signal to Be Detected

In the RTL source code, add (*mark_debug = "true"*) before the declaration of the signal you want to probe on the FPGA.

For example, if we want to observe the debug signal, PC registers, and digital pipe registers on the FPGA board, we need to make the settings according to Fig. D.19 in the source code. Once the settings are complete, you can run the synthesis.

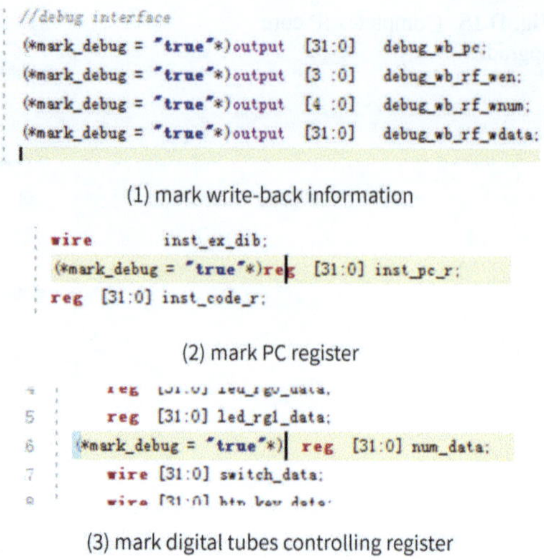

Fig. D.19 Setting the signal
to be detected in RTL

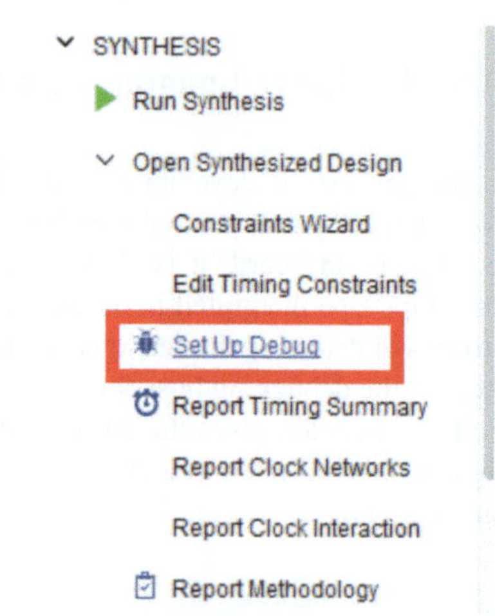

Fig. D.20 After synthesizing
and selecting "Set Up Debug"

D.5.2   Synthesize and Create Debug

Debug needs to be created after synthesis is complete.

Click "synthesis → Open Synthesized Desgin → Set Up Debug" on the left side
of Vivado project, as shown in Fig. D.20.

The screen shown in Fig. D.21 will then appear, click Next.

The debug information of the capture will then be listed; click Next, as shown in
Fig. D.22.

Select the depth of the capture and the type of trigger control; click Next
(for more advanced debugging, you can check "Advanced trigger"), as shown in
Fig. D.23.

Fig. D.21 ""Set Up Debug"
prompt screen

Fig. D.22 Showing all
captured signals

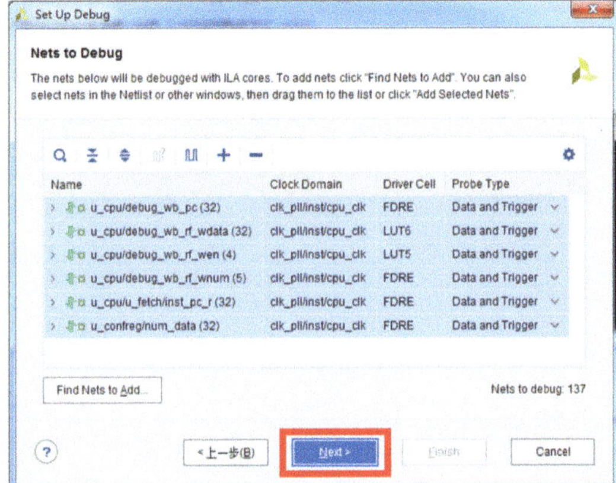

Fig. D.23 Parameterization
of the gripping signal

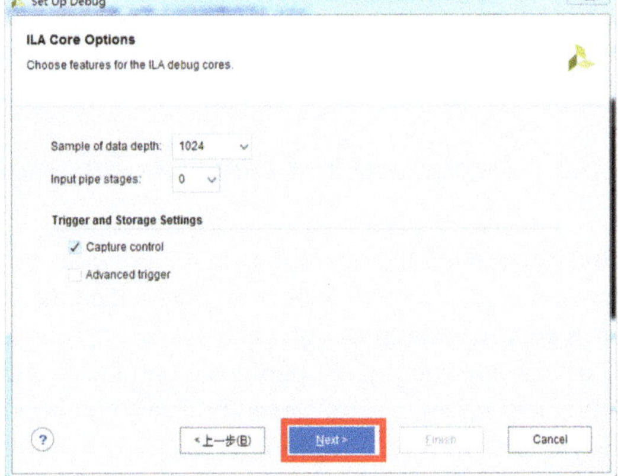

Fig. D.24 Completing the "Set Up Debug"

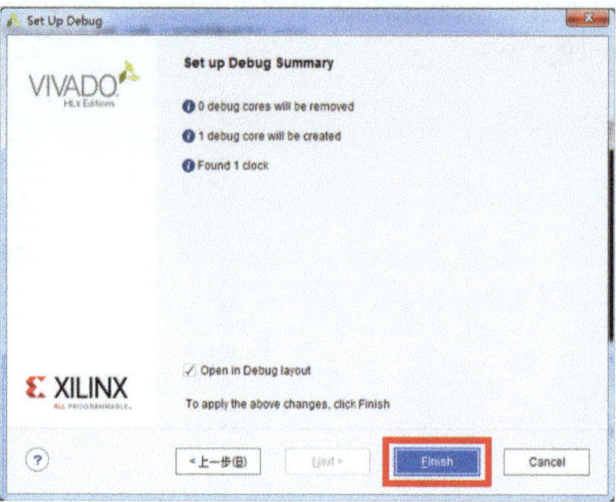

Fig. D.25 Selecting "Generate Bitstream"

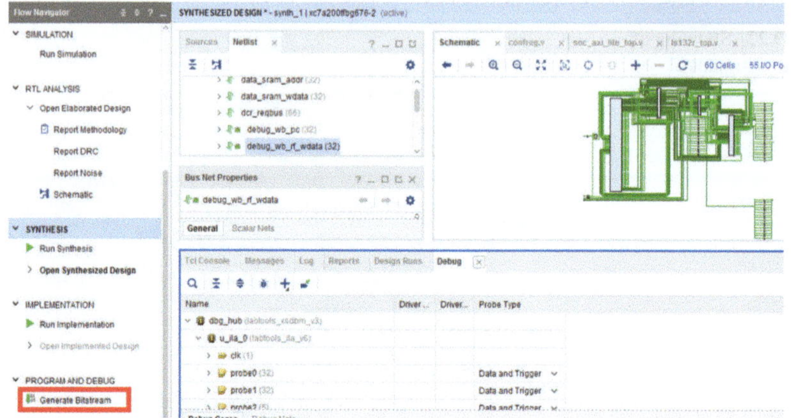

Finally, click Finish, as shown in Fig. D.24.

D.5.3 Implement and Generate Bitstream Files

After completing the operations in the previous section, a screen similar to the one shown in Fig. D.25 will appear, so click Generate Bitstream directly, and click Save when popping screen as Fig. D.26.

If there are subsequent pop-ups, continue to click OK or Yes. At this point, you will enter the process of generating the bit file, and you can close the synthesis design screen in the Vivado interface at this point. If you see the error shown in Fig. D.27, it is because the path is too deep and the reference name is too long, just lower the path depth of the project directory:

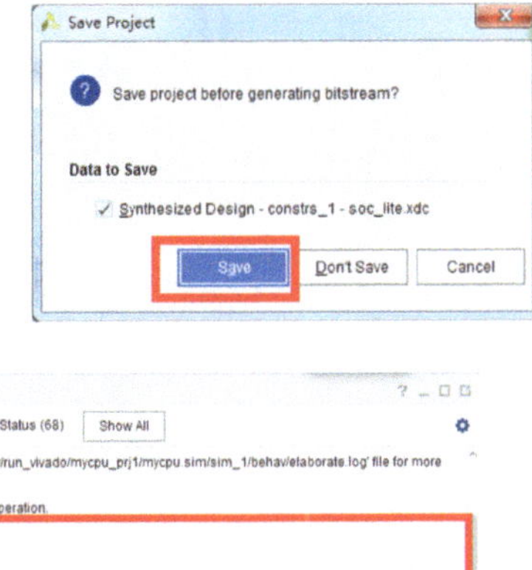

Fig. D.26 Saving constraint file

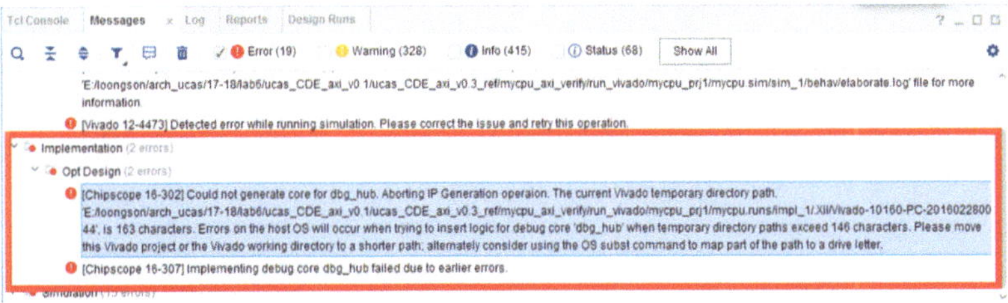

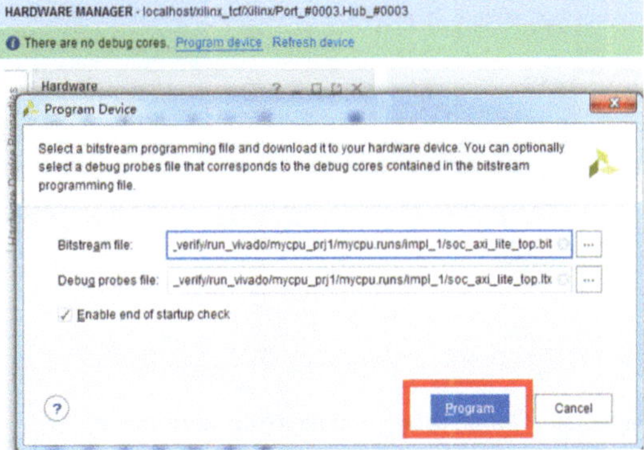

Fig. D.27 Suggesting that the project path is too long

Fig. D.28 Downloading bitstream files and ltx files

D.5.4   Downloading Bitstream Files and Debug Files

After completing the operations in the previous section, the bitstream file and the ltx file for debugging will be generated. Open Open Hardware Manager, connect the FPGA development board, and select Program Device, as shown in Fig. D.28; the bitstream file and the ltx file for debugging will be loaded automatically. Select Program and wait for the download to complete.

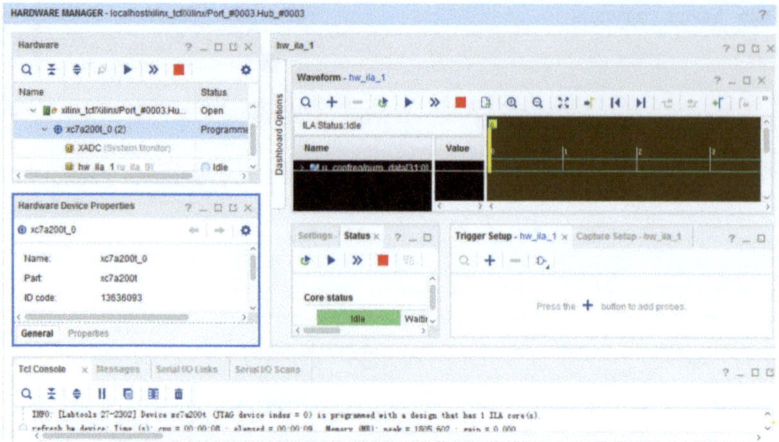

Fig. D.29 Online debugging interface

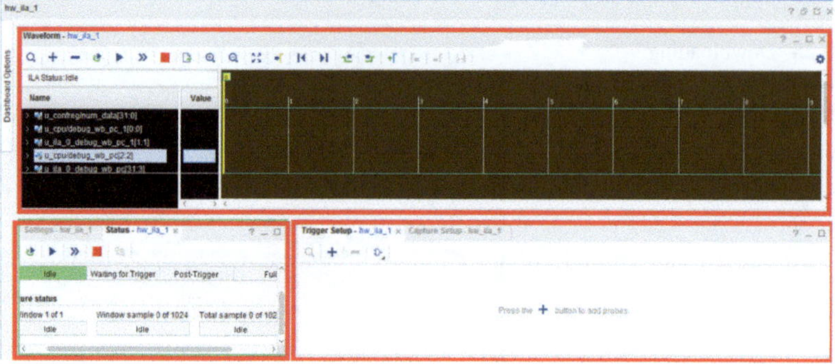

Fig. D.30 Online debugging interface partitioning

D.5.5 Benchmarking

After the download is complete, the Vivado interface is shown in Fig. D.29, and
online debugging is done in the hw_ila_1 interface.

The hw_ila_1 interface is mainly divided into three partitions, as shown in
Fig. D.30.

First of all, we need to set the trigger condition in the lower right area. The
so-called trigger condition is to set the condition to get the waveform when the
condition is satisfied, for example, first set the trigger condition that the digital pipe
register reaches 0x0500_0005. In Fig. D.31, first click the "+"; then double-click the
num_data.

After that, the interface shown in Fig. D.32 will appear to set the trigger
condition.

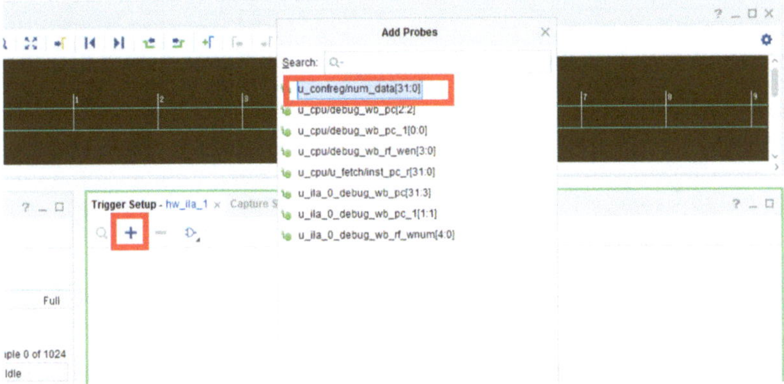

Fig. D.31 Getting the signal to be triggered

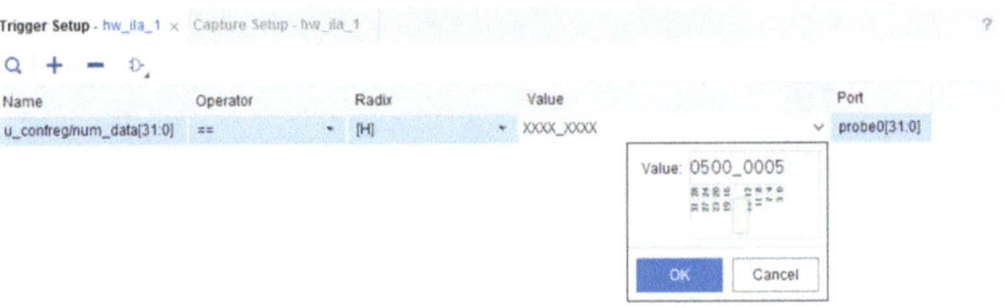

Fig. D.32 Setting trigger conditions

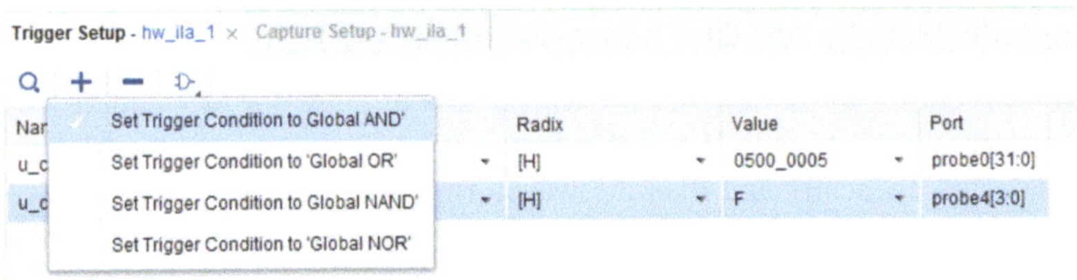

Fig. D.33 Setting multiple trigger conditions

You can set more than one trigger condition, for example, add another division condition that the write-back enable is 0xf; you can set more than one trigger condition relationship between them, e.g., whether any one condition is satisfied, both conditions are satisfied, etc., as shown in Fig. D.33.

In the lower left window, select settings to set Capture options; the most frequently used one is Trigger position in window, which is used to set the position in the waveform window at the moment when the trigger condition is satisfied. For example, Fig. D.34 sets it to 500, which means that when the trigger condition is met, the position of the 500th clk in the waveform window will fulfill the condition. Refresh rate sets the refresh frequency of the waveform window.

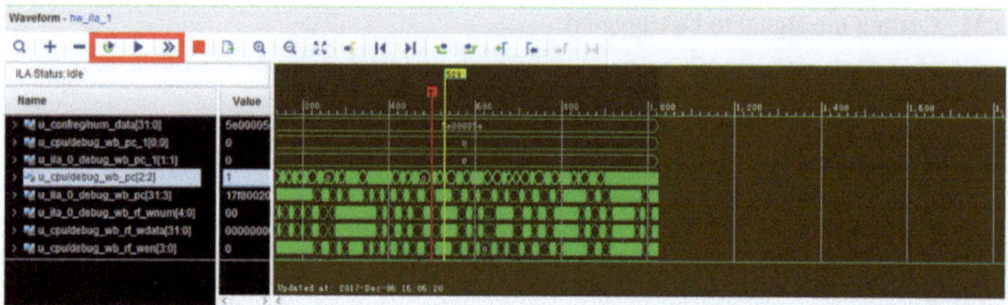

Fig. D.34 Setting the grab mode

Fig. D.35 Three trigger keys

Trigger condition is established; waveform capture can be started; there are three key trigger buttons, i.e., the three presses circled in Fig. D.35:

- The first one from the left, set the trigger mode; there are two options: single trigger and cyclic trigger. When this button is pressed, it means the trigger will be detected cyclically and then the waveform window will be updated as long as the trigger conditions are met. When set to single trigger, it means the trigger will not be detected again after the trigger is completed once. For example, if the trigger condition is PC=0x1c000690, then the PC will be executed several times. If you set the trigger condition to single trigger, then press the reset button on the FPGA board; the waveform window will only show the condition of the first trigger. If the setting is cyclic trigger, then the waveform window will keep refreshing the captured trigger condition with refresh rate.
- Second from the left, wait for the trigger condition to be satisfied. Clicking on this button is waiting for the division condition to be met, showing the waveform.
- Third from the left, trigger immediately. Clicking this button means that a waveform is immediately captured and displayed in the window regardless of the trigger condition.

Figure D.35 shows the waveform obtained by clicking the third button, because it is triggered immediately, so the num_data is not 0x0500_0005, and there is a red line labeled "T," which is the trigger moment. Since the trigger moment is located

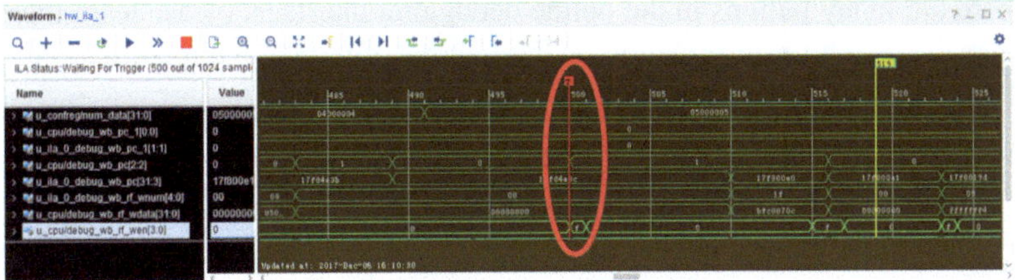

Fig. D.36 Waveform when the trigger condition is satisfied

at the 500 clk position of the waveform window, the red color is exactly at the 500 clk position.

As you can also see from Fig. D.35, num_data is 0x5c00_005c, indicating that one test has been completed. When you click the second trigger button and wait for the trigger, you will find that there is no response from the waveform window. This is because the trigger condition has not been met, so press the reset button on the FPGA board. The result is shown in Fig. D.36. The circled condition is the trigger condition: num_data==32'h5c00_005c && rf_wen==4'hf.

The rest of the debugging process is similar to the simulation debugging. However, when debugging in-circuit, you cannot add signals that have not been debug marked in the RTL before. During online debugging, you may need to keep changing the trigger conditions and pressing the reset button.

D.5.6   Attentions

When adding signals to be captured, be careful not to mark too many signals with debug mark. Capturing waveforms during online debugging consumes circuit resources and memory cells, so the size of waveforms that can be captured is limited. You should only add debug marks to the necessary debug signals.

The depth of waveform capture should not be too deep. If the depth is set too deep, then there will not be enough storage resources, resulting in failure in the final generation of the bitstream and debug file.

The number of signals to be captured and the depth of capture are contradictory variables. If the depth of capture is low, then the number of signals captured can be relatively high.

Compared with simulation debugging, online debugging has higher requirements for debugging ideas and skills; please organize your thoughts and summarize your skills. Special emphasis is given in on the following points:

- There are many combinations of trigger condition settings, so please consider them carefully and design them well according to your needs.
- Often, it is only necessary to use the single trigger mode, but cyclic triggering can sometimes be useful and should be utilized when necessary.

- There are many buttons in the online debugging interface, please learn them by yourself, search for information on the Internet, go to the Xilinx official website to search for official documentation, etc.

Finally, when you encounter the problem of "simulation passes, board fails," please focus on other problems first, and then use the online debugging method. According to our past experience, many of the small-scale CPU designs in this book are caused by one of the following problems: "simulation passes, board fails":

1. Multiple drivers.
2. The input/output ports of the module are connected to the wrong signal direction.
3. Clock reset signal is connected incorrectly.
4. Code irregularities, indiscriminate use of blocking assignments, the arbitrary use of always statement.
5. There is "X" for control signal during emulation. When emulating, there is "X" to tune "X" and "Z" to tune "Z."
6. Timing violation.
7. Signals on the control path in the module are not reset.

D.6 Method of Curing a Design on a Lab Box

This section gives the methodology for curing an FPGA design based on a lab box.

After curing, the development board on the lab box will automatically load the design onto the FPGA chip every time it is powered on. Therefore, there is no need to re-download the bitstream file after power-up, which greatly facilitates software development and debugging of hardware-based designs.

The process of curing is to convert a bitstream file to an mcs file and download the mcs file to an SPI flash on the development board in the lab box.

D.6.1 Generate mcs File

First, you need to make sure that the bitstream file for the FPGA design has been generated. However, the bitstream file is used to download directly to the FPGA, which cannot be downloaded to the Flash chip and need to be converted to mcs files.

In the Vivado tool, generating an mcs file requires entering commands into the tcl console, as shown in Fig. D.37.

The commands entered in blue are shown in Fig. D.37, and "pwd" is used to view the directory. Afterward, use the "cd" command to enter the directory where the bitstream file is located.

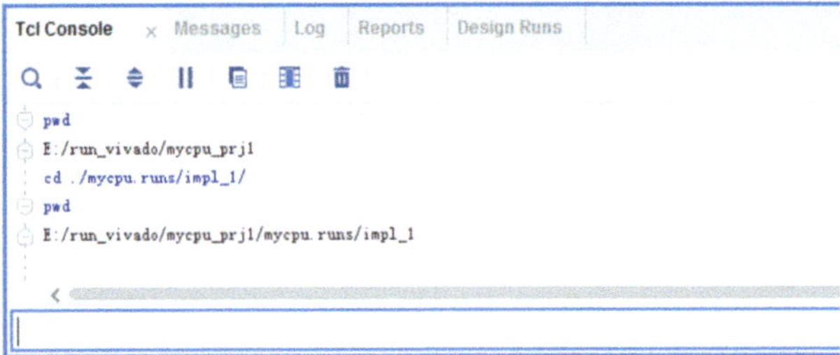

Fig. D.37 Entering commands into the "tcl console"

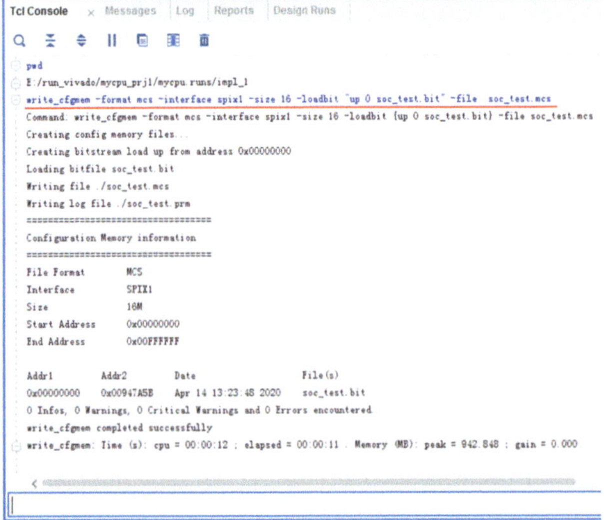

Fig. D.38 Inputting command to generate mcs file

Assuming that the generated bitstream file is soc, _test.bit, input the command string "write, _cfgmem -format mcs -interface spix1 -size 16 -loadbit "up 0 soc, _test.bit " -file soc, _test.mcs" to generate the mcs file, as shown in Fig. D.38.

In the command, soc_test.bit is the bit file of the FPGA design to be converted, and soc_test.mcs is the name of the generated mcs file, which can be customized. The soc_test.mcs is the name of the generated mcs file, which can be customized. In addition, the soc_test.prm file will be generated at the same time as the soc_test.mcs file.

The effect of the above command is to switch the directory to the directory of the bitstream file by typing the command "cd" and then use the command "write_cfgmem" to convert the bitstream file to an mcs file. These two steps can be done using the command "write_cfgmem -format mcs -interface spix1 -size 16 -loadbit"up 0 E:/run_vivado/mycpu_prj1/mycpu.runs/impl_1/soc_test.bit" -file E:/run_vivado/mycpu_prj1/mycpu.runs/impl_1/soc_test.mcs." Finish in one pass.

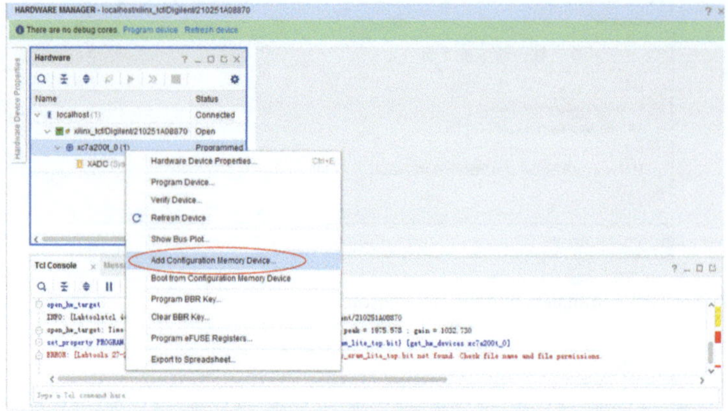

Fig. D.39 Selecting "Add Configuration Memory Device" in download screen

This command specifies the directory of the bitstream file and the directory where the generated mcs file is saved. The directory and file name of the bitstream file must be correct, but the directory and file name of the mcs file can be customized.

D.6.2   Download mcs File

Once the mcs file has been generated, it needs to be downloaded to the SPI flash on the development board in the lab box. As with the bitstream file, open the "Open Hardware Target" in the Vivado tool, and connect the device. Left-click on the xc7a200t and right-click on "Add Configuration Memory Device," as shown in Fig. D.39.

The screen shown in Fig. D.40 appears. Enter s25fl128s in the search field, and two optional chip models appear: s25fl128sxxxxxx0-spi-x1_x2_x4 and s25fl128sxxxxxx1-spi-x1_x2_x4. The selected model needs to be the same as the fixed Flash chip on the board (0 or 1 at the end of the Flash model number). Alternatively, you can select one of the two models first and then come back and select the other model if subsequent programming of the Flash fails. After selecting the Flash model, click OK.

The window shown in Fig. D.41 pops up asking if you want to program Flash now click OK.

After the interface of programming Flash shown in Fig. D.42 appears, select the previously generated mcs file in the "Configuration file" column, and select the previously generated prm file in the "PRM file" column. Click OK.

Wait for the download of mcs to the Flash chip to be completed. The Flash chip will be erased first and then programmed, and when it is completed, it will prompt "Flash programming completed successfully," as shown in Fig. D.43.

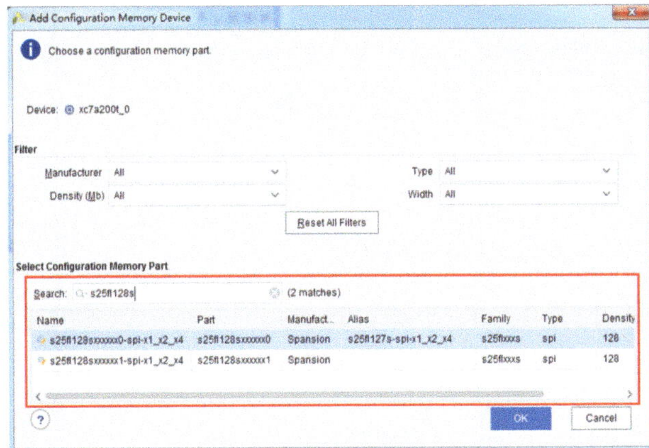

Fig. D.40 Setting memory device configuration

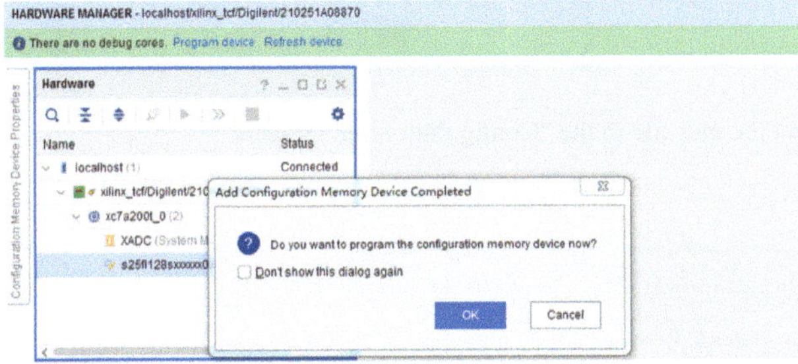

Fig. D.41 Asking if Flash is programmed

At this point, the burn-in is complete; you need to disconnect the download cable and power down and repower up the board, wait for some time (about 30 seconds), and the design that has been cured to the board will be automatically loaded onto the FPGA chip and start to run.

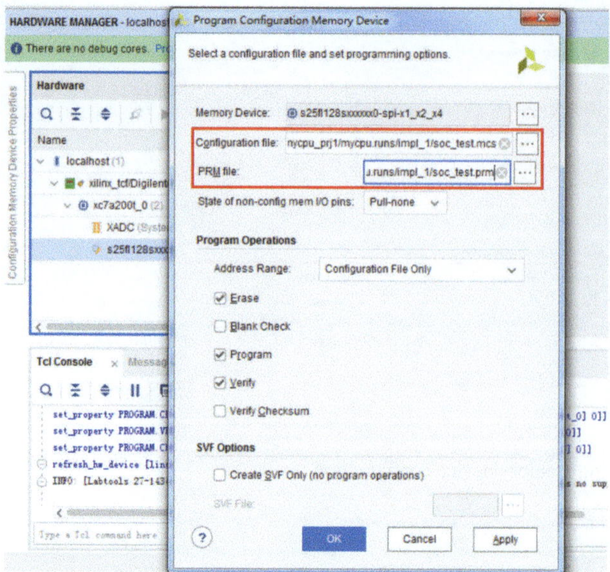

Fig. D.42 Select the mcs file in the "Configuration file" screen

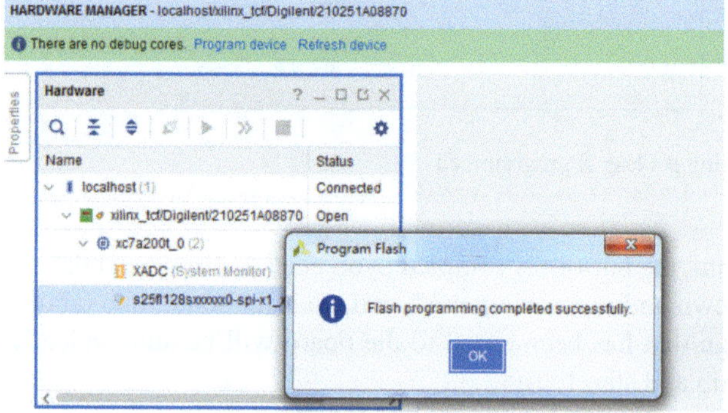

Fig. D.43 Flash programmed successfully